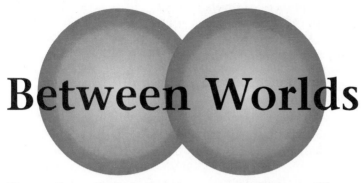

Between Worlds

A Reader, Rhetoric, and Handbook

Fourth Edition

Susan Bachmann

El Camino College

Melinda Barth

El Camino College

PEARSON
Longman

New York San Francisco Boston
London Toronto Sydney Tokyo Singapore Madrid
Mexico City Munich Paris Cape Town Hong Kong Montreal

Senior Vice President/Publisher: Joe Opiela
Acquisitions Editor: Lynn M. Huddon
Developmental Editor: Margaret Manos
Executive Marketing Manager: Ann Stypuloski
Senior Supplements Editor: Donna Campion
Production Manager: Charles Annis
Project Coordination, Text Design, and Electronic Page Makeup: Pre-Press Company, Inc.
Cover Design Manager: Wendy Fredericks
Cover Designer: Maria Ilardi
Cover Art: © Dale Chihuly, *Niijma Floats*, 2001, Garfield Park Conservatory, Chicago
Photo: Terry Rishel
Manufacturing Buyer: Lucy Hebard
Printer and Binder: Hamilton Printing Co.
Cover Printer: Phoenix Color Corp.

Library of Congress Cataloging-in-Publication Data
Between worlds : a reader, rhetoric, and handbook / [compiled by] Susan Bachmann, Melinda Barth.— 4th ed.
        p. cm.
    Includes biographical references (p.) and index.
      ISBN 0-321-10670-9 (alk. paper)
    1. College readers. 2. English language-—Rhetoric—Handbooks, manuals, etc. 3. English language—Grammar—Handbooks, manuals, etc. 4. Report writing—Handbooks, manuals, etc. I. Bachmann, Susan. II. Barth, Melinda.

PE1417 .B43 2004
808'.0427—dc21

                                                            2002043851

Please visit our website at http://www.ablongman.com

ISBN 0-321-10670-9

1 2 3 4 5 6 7 8 9 10—HT—06 05 04 03

Again, and again, to the men in our lives:
Ron, Dylan, and Evan Barth
and
Walter, Ryan, and Adam Gajewski

Contents

STUDENT EXAMPLE:

Mirror Image *by Georgina I. Montoya* 496

Frida Kahlo was an extraordinary woman who overcame unimaginable physical and emotional pain and who developed into one of the most charismatic and important artists of our time.

Chapter 11   Writing the Research Paper 506

PART III   THE HANDBOOK   563

Chapter 12   Understanding How Sentences Work   566

Editing Symbols chart appears opposite page 642.

THEMATIC CONTENTS

RHETORICAL CONTENTS

Poems for Analysis

Short Stories for Analysis

One-Act Play for Analysis

Preface

The fourth edition of *Between Worlds* remains a reader, rhetoric, and handbook that offers students and instructors essential materials to support their writing courses. The reader features thematically arranged selections with writing prompts to help students respond to each reading individually or in relation to other texts. A concise rhetoric and handbook follow the reader. They are designed to guide students through every aspect of the writing process and through some of the most common writing assignments, including the research paper. Although each part of this textbook can be used independently, both instructor and student will find the cross-referencing of material between the reader and the rhetoric an advantage for teaching and learning.

Since the publication of the first edition, we have received overwhelming support for combining three texts within one cover, for our selection of provocative readings, and for the cross-referencing of these readings with meaningful assignments and accessible rhetorical instruction. The fourth edition retains our successes and includes some exciting changes and additions.

New Readings and More Varied Topics   New selections revitalize each of the existing chapters to reflect the conflicting realms—the "between worlds"—in which most of us live. Like us, the individuals in these readings are caught *between* balancing the burdens of work and school, *between* satisfying family obligations and meeting personal needs, and *between* defining self while relating with others. New paired readings show divergent views about love and dating, the individual in society, the role of computers in the classrooms, the nature of families, and the use of Native American team names. Additional new readings complement the existing themes of family pressures and expectations, gender and culture identification, self-images and perceptions, and value choices. Recognizing the value of wit in creating memorable writing (and keeping readers awake!), we have added more humorous selections. In response to instructors' recommendations, we have also added many more provocative argument essays.

New Voices and Favorite Voices   This edition continues to include writers favored by students and instructors: John Updike, Ellen Goodman, Anne Tyler, Joyce Carol Oates, Sharon Olds, Brent Staples, Marge Piercy, Martin Luther King, Jr., Seamus Heaney, Anne Lamott, Howard Rosenberg, Susan Douglas, and Luis Valdez. Esteemed writers new to this edition include Barbara Ehrenreich, S. I. Hayakawa, Anna Quindlen, Joan Didion, George Orwell, Carol Tavris, Jonathan Alter, Clifford Stoll, David and Arlie Hochschild, Meghan Daum, Susan Jacoby, Jack Balkin, Jill Tweedie, Eugene August, Mike McGrady, Don Sabo, John Balzar, Judith Ortiz Cofer, Carmen Vazquez, Jenny Jones, Todd Gitlin, Don Tapscott, and Andrew Vachss.

New Reading Questions and Writing Assignments   The "Thinking About the Text" questions have been revised to focus less on content and more on audience and purpose—to encourage students to examine the writer's strategies and to experiment with their own. The "Writing from the Text" sections provide students with varied writing prompts for each reading. In "Connecting with Other Texts," both the new and retained readings are linked thematically within each chapter and throughout the book. These assignments direct students to examine multiple perspectives critically and then use diverse materials to support their points.

New Genres   Diverse forms, styles, and techniques are reflected in the readings in this edition. In addition to the standard academic essay exemplified in both short, focused pieces and longer, more complex forms, the readings include editorials and commentaries, expository essays, provocative arguments, descriptive narratives, a play, five short stories, eight poems, and two biographies.

New Additions to Part II   Throughout this edition we continue to focus on understanding the writer's purpose or aim. Several model essays are new and illustrate popular methods for developing essays: narrative, definition, and biographical analysis. In addition, the process analysis essay—how to create your own Web page—has been updated to reflect improvements in the Web-authoring software, making the process easier for all readers.

Because we recognize that writing is a discovery process, we continue to emphasize relevant techniques: numerous prewriting strategies; practical advice for considering audience; ideas about arrangement, outlining, drafting, and revision; and tips for constructing and revising the thesis. Throughout Part II we show that writing is not a step-by-step process; it involves concurrent and recursive activities. Additional practice exercises are included to help students develop skills and to connect the rhetoric more closely to the reader.

New Chapter on Analysis   Recognizing the vital role of critical thinking in college writing, we have created a new chapter, Analysis. Within this chapter, we not only examine and illustrate three types of analysis—process, problem, and subject—but we have added a new assignment, a biographical analysis. Instructors seeking an alternative to the multiple-source research paper will find that the analysis of a person in a full-length biography produces a rewarding paper. Students enjoy selecting a subject relevant to their lives—sometimes their career aspirations, race, or ethnicity—and instructors will value the results of this project. Our new chapter features a student analysis of the life of Frida Kahlo—an icon of the art world. Biographical selections, in the Rhetoric and in the Reader, are bound to capture student interest and invigorate student writing.

New Materials on Research Chapter 11 includes updated MLA and APA guidelines and documentation forms. Because so much of the research process is now online, we continue to offer a section on using and abusing electronic sources as well as on documenting them. In addition, we have retained and updated the glossary of computer-related terms to help novices shuttle between the world of books and cyberspace.

New Handbook Entries Part III, a handbook designed to empower students but not overwhelm them, focuses on the most common errors—the "terrible ten"—that persist in student writing. To help students interpret their instructors' comments, a list of marginal symbols is included in the text (pp. 564–565) and, for quicker access, on the inside back cover. We have a new section to help writers correct errors in pronoun case, and we have added new entries and examples to the ever-expanding list of troublesome words that many writers confuse or misuse.

An updated **Instructor's Manual** is also available to adopters of this new edition. The *Instructor's Manual* includes answers to "Thinking About the Text" questions, subthemes found in each chapter, cross-referencing of readings between chapters, and examples of outside readings.

Applause

This textbook could never have been written without the help of many people who have been particularly supportive and generous with their time as we worked on this book. Superb librarians and computer specialists assisted us in countless ways. We remain grateful to Judy Harris, Ed Martinez, Claudia Striepe, and Moon Ichinaga from the El Camino College library, and computer expert Walter Gajewski from California State University at Long Beach. All of these knowledgeable individuals gave us enough information on computers to keep us from looking foolish in front of our students. Over the years, colleagues at El Camino College have readily and generously shared strategies and writing ideas that inspired many aspects of this book. At El Camino we are especially indebted to Marilyn Anderson, Mimi Ansite, Elaine Bender, Sara Blake, Debra Breckheimer, Dana Crotwell, Karen Forney, Julia Hackner, Zahid Hossain, Barbara Jaffe, Debra Mochidome, Kareema Nasouf, Sharon Osburg, and Steve Waterworth. Students Shannon Paaske and Marianela Enriquez worked energetically to help us meet our deadline, and we are pleased that some of our other students—Rebekah Hall-Naganuma, Chris Thomas, Jennifer Tabaldo, Marin Kheng, and Georgina Montoya—also are published writers with the printing of this text. Our students merit hearty applause.

Special thanks must go to Ken Clark at Chihuly Studios for his gracious search through the archives for yet another dazzling photo for our cover. We want, also, to thank a number of fine reviewers who brought insights from their teaching to improve our efforts in creating this text. We wish to thank these supportive critics: Craig Bartholomaus, Penn Valley Community College; Beth P. Hafner, Clinton Community College; Phoenix Lundstrom, Kapiʻolani Community College; Susan Quarrell, CUNY—Lehman College; Amanda Fields Rivers, Randolph Community College; and James Wilson, La-Guardia Community College

We are grateful to our editor at Longman, Lynn Huddon, who kept the book on schedule, and Margaret Manos, our sensitive and supportive development editor, who helped us prune and strengthen our wordings. We also are indebted to Robin Gordon and Elsa van Bergen at Pre-Press Company for their diligent reading and perceptive editing of our text.

Finally, we want to try to thank the men in our families who have, for a decade, lived *Between Worlds* with us. As the book has grown and changed its shape, our families, too, have metamorphosed, and one now has expanded to include two women, Tia and Delaiah, both English teachers. The children we once banished so we could write—Dylan, Evan, Ryan, and Adam—are now adults and offer cogent comments as they use our book in their writing and their own teaching. Walter and Ron still rescue us from computer chaos and do not seem to mind that we are only slightly less inept with computers than we were at the start. Other family members and friends continue to send us relevant articles, to offer their help, and to understand when we turn down invitations and do not answer Emails or phone calls. They all believe this project is worth their being temporarily "displaced," and we applaud their willingness to live "between worlds" with us.

Susan Bachmann

Melinda Barth

Part I
The Reader

The readings in this book have been chosen to reflect the interests of college students like you, who are juggling school and work as well as social lives and family expectations. The selections in Part I have been arranged into five chapter themes:

Ch. 1. *Between Generations:* Many of the authors in this chapter are caught between generations and, like you, may be trying to understand themselves in relation to parents and grandparents.

Ch. 2. *Between Genders:* Just as you may be examining the roles that define your gender, many of the authors in this chapter argue for a reexamination of the roles that limit the lives of people of both sexes.

Ch. 3. *Between Cultures:* Whether you are a newcomer to the United States, a second- or third-generation American, or a native whose roots go back for generations, you may find that the writers in this chapter describe experiences that you have had living between cultures.

Ch. 4. *Between Perceptions:* The perception that you have of yourself is inevitably colored by the images that others have of you. Yet your desire to be perceived as an individual, rather than a stereotype, is also the experience of many college students and of the authors who write about being between perceptions.

Ch. 5. *Between Values:* The selections in this chapter will prompt you to think about your values—something you may be doing more seriously since you started college. Examining the ideas of the authors included here will help you to assess your own convictions.

These chapters describe the multiple worlds in which all of us live and the tensions that pull us between the realms of generations, genders, cultures, perceptions, and values. We chose these readings to stimulate your thinking and to enable you to write meaningful essays—the goal of any composition course.

Each chapter contains essays, short stories, and poems, all arranged to illustrate parallels or contrasts with each other. After each reading you will find three sets of exercises. The first, called "Thinking about the Text," consists of questions designed as a review prior to class and for small-group discussions during class. These questions are followed by "Writing from the Text," writing assignments drawn from the readings and from your own experience. These topics may be assigned by your instructor, or they may be used for practice writing in a journal. You will find help for writing these assignments in Part II, the rhetoric portion of this book. The last set of exercises, "Connecting with Other Texts," will ask you to compare two or more readings in this book. Some assignments encourage you to find additional material in the library, which is useful if your instructor assigns a paper that requires research. You will find information on how to write research papers of various lengths in Part II.

Getting the Most from Your Reading

How often have you spent time reading something only to discover that you have no idea what you've just read? Worse still, have you ever found yourself supposedly reading but, instead, daydreaming about your last date, a great play-off game, or a conversation with friends? The hours that you waste in unproductive reading can be saved. Here's how.

Active Reading

Active reading is a strategy that helps you remain focused on the material before you and retain what you have read. Useful in all of your courses, active reading enables you to perceive the author's thesis and key points, supporting details, and meaningful lines, as well as to discover your own thoughts about the material.

Active reading involves reading with a pen in your hand. Although highlighters are popular with many students, it is impossible to use them to write summary notes in the margin and too difficult to switch between highlighter and pen. If you are using your own book, you can make marks directly on your copy as you are reading. If you are using a library book, you will need to photocopy the pages you intend to read actively. With either method, you should do the following as you read:

- *Underline* the thesis (if it is explicitly stated), key points, and supporting details.

- *Mark* meaningful or quotable language.
- *Place checkmarks and asterisks* next to important lines.
- *Jot* brief summary or commentary notes in the margins. Infer the thesis and write it in the margin if it is not explicitly stated.
- *Circle* unfamiliar words and references to look up later.
- *Ask* questions as you read.
- *Seek* answers to those questions.
- *Question* the writer's assumptions and assertions as well as your own.

Reading actively allows you to enter into a conversation with your authors, to examine and challenge their ideas. Active reading will also help you find important lines more easily so that you don't have to reread the entire work each time that you refer to it during class discussions or in your essays. You will also have the key points underlined so that you can quickly review them for a quiz. If your instructor asks you to keep a journal of your responses to readings, you can use the meaningful lines you have marked or the marginal notes to begin your journal entry. Don't underline or highlight *everything,* however, or you will defeat your purpose of finding just the important points.

Let's now look at an active reading of Ellen Goodman's "Thanksgiving." What comments or questions can you add?

Thanksgiving
Ellen Goodman

A journalist who has worked for *Newsweek,* CBS, NBC, and a number of metropolitan newspapers, Ellen Goodman (b. 1941) has written a widely syndicated column from her home paper, the *Boston Globe,* since 1967. Goodman won the Pulitzer Prize in 1980 for distinguished commentary. She is coauthor with Patricia O'Brien of *I Know Just What You Mean: The Power of Friendship in Women's Lives* (2000) and the author of *Value Judgments,* a collection of newspaper columns (1993). Her subject matter is diverse, and her responses are entertaining. As Diane McWhorter of the *Washington Journalism Review* has said, Goodman "attacks controversies from abortion to housework to Alexander Solzhenitsyn with the combined grace and grit of a paratrooper." Goodman's own comment about her work is that she writes about "more important questions than the average columnist." She asserts that it is "much more important to look at the underlying values by which this country exists . . . the vast social changes in the way men and women lead their lives and deal with each other, [and] about children" than to write about the "trivia," like politics, that other columnists write about. The essay included here, on the importance of family in our lives, is characteristic of Goodman's concerns. The piece was first published in the *Boston Globe* in 1980.

*Thanksgiving:
"a ritual of
belonging"*

1   Soon they will be together again, all the people who travel between their own lives and each other's. The package tour of the season will lure them this week to the family table. By Thursday, feast day, family day, Thanksgiving day, Americans who value individualism like no other people will collect around a million tables in a <u>ritual of belonging.</u>

2   They will assemble their families the way they assemble dinner: <u>each one bearing a personality as different as cranberry sauce and pumpkin pie.</u> For one dinner they will cook for each other, fuss for each other, feed each other and argue with each other. They will nod at their <u>common heritage,</u> the craziness and caring of other generations. They will measure their <u>common legacy . . . the children.</u>

*common
heritage
& legacy*

*2 principles:
families &
individuals*

3   All these complex cells, these men and women, old and young, with different dreams and disappointments will give homage again to the group they are a part of and apart from: their family. <u>Families and individuals. The "we" and the "I."</u> As good Americans we all travel between these two ideals. We take value trips from the great American notion of individualism to the great American vision of family. We wear out our tires driving back and forth, using speed to shorten the distance between these two principles.

*focus—
a paradox:
We are raised
in families
to be
individuals.
Thesis?*

4   There has always been some pavement between a person and a family. From the first moment we recognize that we are separate we begin to wrestle with aloneness and togetherness. Here and now these conflicts are especially acute. We are, after all, <u>raised in families . . . to be individuals.</u> This <u>double message</u> follows us through life. We are taught about the <u>freedom of the "I"</u> and the <u>safety of the "we."</u> The loneliness of the "I" and the intrusiveness of the "we." The selfishness of the "I" and the burdens of the "we."

5   We are taught what André Malraux said: <u>"Without a family, man, alone in the world, trembles with the cold."</u> And taught what he said another day: "The denial of the supreme importance of the mind's development accounts for many revolts against the family." In theory, the world rewards "the supreme importance" of the individual, the ego. We think alone, inside our heads. We write music and literature with an enlarged sense of self. We are graded and paid, hired and fired, on our own merit. The (rank) individualism is both exciting and cruel. Here is where the fittest survive.

*good
quote for
journal*

*individuals are
rewarded for
excellence*

meaning?

Is this true?

6   The family, on the other hand, at its best, works very differently. <u>We don't have to achieve to be accepted by our families.</u> We just have to be. Our membership is not based on credentials but on birth. As Malraux put it, "A friend loves you for your intelligence, a

mistress for your charm, but your family's love is unreasoning: You were born into it and of its flesh and blood."

7   The family is formed not for the survival of the fittest but for the weakest. It is not an economic unit but an emotional one. This is not the place where people ruthlessly compete with each other but where they work for each other. Its business is taking care, and when it works, it is not callous but kind.

Ideal: Family is supportive, not competitive

8   There are fewer heroes, fewer stars in family life. While the world may glorify the self, the family asks us, at one time or another, to submerge it. While the <u>world may abandon</u> us, the <u>family promises,</u> at one time or another, <u>to protect us.</u> So we commute daily, weekly, yearly <u>between one world and another.</u> Between a life as a family member that can be nurturing or smothering. Between life as an individual that can free us or flatten us. We (vacillate) between two separate sets of demands and possibilities.

world abandons vs. family protects

Between Worlds meaning?

9   The people who will gather around this table Thursday live in both of these worlds, <u>a part of and apart from each other.</u> With any luck the territory they travel from one to another can be a fertile one, rich with care and space. It can be a place where the "I" and the "we" interact. On this day at least, they will bring to each other something both special and something to be shared: these <u>separate selves.</u>

a part of / apart from

Thanksgiving = separate selves sharing

Discussion of Active Reading

As we read Ellen Goodman's essay, we were on the lookout for key phrases, important concepts, unfamiliar words, and the thesis or focus of the essay. As soon as we found memorable phrases like defining Thanksgiving as "a ritual of belonging" or the simile comparing personalities of family members "as different as cranberry sauce and pumpkin pie," we underlined these and noted them with an asterisk in the margin.

We circled two words that we thought students might not be familiar with, and we wrote "meaning ?" in the margin as a reminder to look them up in the dictionary. When we spotted what we thought was Goodman's focus or thesis, we identified it in the margin. We continued to underline key phrases or meaningful lines and noted a brief response to each in the margin. You will find another example of active reading on page 340.

Active Reading as Prewriting

Because active reading is a natural warm-up for writing, we encourage you, as we do our students, to keep a journal of meaningful lines from readings. It helps to copy each quotation at the top of a journal page as a prompt for your response. You can respond with your personal feelings about the ideas in the quoted line. These ideas might remind you of an experience from your childhood or comments made by a family member or friend.

Sometimes you may react vehemently to the author's tone or idea in the quoted line and write responses you wouldn't feel comfortable giving in class discussion. The journal responses to these quoted lines can become a part of future writing assignments or can just help you sort out your own ideas in an uncensored place.

PRACTICING ACTIVE READING

1. Select any reading in the first chapter, "Between Generations," or use the first reading assigned by your instructor to practice active reading. Follow the steps described above to interact with the text.

2. Actively read Robert L. Heilbroner's essay "Don't Let Stereotypes Warp Your Judgments" (p. 469), underlining meaningful lines and making summary notes in the margin. Look for his thesis and infer it if it is not explicitly stated.

3. Select a line from "Thanksgiving" that you find meaningful and copy it at the top of a page. Then write an uncensored response that expresses your feelings or your analysis of that quotation. If you keep your journal on a computer, you will be amazed by how much you have to express.

Chapter 1

Between Generations

In the essay that we used to demonstrate active reading (p. 4), author Ellen Goodman quotes Andre Malraux's belief that "without a family" the individual "alone in the world, trembles with the cold." The family often nurtures its members and tolerates differences and failings that friends and lovers cannot accept. Hadley Moore finds this love and acceptance so strong that she longs to move closer to her family. If you have, or have had, a strong bond with a grandparent, you will value Eric Marcus's essay and appreciate the friendship and understanding he gains when his grandmother accepts his sexual orientation. The narrator in Seamus Heaney's poem respects his father and grandfather but comes to accept how he differs from them.

The differences between generations can be both instructive and poignant, as you will see in the short stories by John Updike and Anne Tyler, the essays by Caroline Hwang and S. I. Hayakawa, and the poem by Stephen Perry. But as you may realize from your own experiences and observations, people also tremble with fear or anxiety even within the family unit. John Leonard illustrates in his essay that family members sometimes are forced to turn from one another, and, as Barbara Ehrenreich shows, the family can also be a place where love becomes an obsession and can turn into something murderous. The writers in this chapter show the family as a source of both nurturing and anxiety.

Your awareness of gaps between generations, as well as a deeper sense of family connection, may inspire your own writing. The essays, short stories, and poems in this chapter attest to the will of the human spirit to mitigate family tension, to smile at some of the chaos, and to survive and thrive from one generation to the next.

My Deep, Dark Secret
Hadley Moore

With a B.A. in psychology from Kalamazoo College in Michigan, Hadley Moore (b. 1977) has taken graduate courses at the University of Utah in psychology, but she is planning to pursue a career in journalism. She works as a writing tutor at Salt Lake Community College and is still hoping to move closer to her family in the Midwest. This essay appeared in the "My Turn" column of *Newsweek* on January 14, 2002.

1   When I was applying to colleges as a high-school senior, I wanted nothing more than to go somewhere far, far from home. I believed, as so many young people do, that my success and maturity would be measured largely by how far away from my family I went to attend college and, eventually, get a job. As it turned out, my parents balked at paying for me to fly home for four years of Thanksgiving, Christmas and summer vacations, so I had to look for schools within a few hours' driving distance. I applied to two schools that were in state and two in bordering states. Not very exotic.

2   In the end, I chose the school that was just an hour away because it offered me the most scholarship money. I can remember the mother of one of my friends saying with disdain in her voice, "So, you decided to stick around here, huh?" My response—my rationalization to myself and others—was that I wouldn't have to come home, or even call, any more than if I were at a school thousands of miles away.

3   But I did call and visit often. I justified this by telling myself I would move away after college, when I would no longer be financially dependent on my parents. I also took every opportunity I had to travel as an undergraduate. I studied for six months in France and for three months in New York City, in a program for fine-arts students. I knew that my parents were telling their friends and neighbors about the far-flung adventures I was having, and it made me feel that I had somehow compensated for choosing a school so close to home.

4   When it came time for graduate school, I applied all over the country. My first choice—which happened to be several states away—offered me a spot, and I accepted immediately. In all the excitement of planning and packing, I overlooked the fact that this would be the first time I would leave my family without knowing that it was only temporary, that I would soon return. I was totally unprepared for the grief I felt.

5   The night before I left, my parents tried to comfort me. They assured me we would all see each other again soon, that this was something I had to do and that they would enjoy visiting me in my new city, but I was inconsolable. I cried during most of the three-day drive to my new school and

every day after that for two weeks. It was devastating to realize that for the next few years I would see my mother and father only on special occasions and major holidays.

6   Since then I have seen my family three times, for two Christmas visits and my wedding last summer. Unfortunately, it has never gotten any easier for me to say goodbye when the time comes. My husband (who grew up near my hometown) and I plan to move again in a year and a half. One of our top priorities will be to get closer to our families.

7   I am 24 years old, a full-fledged adult. And I miss my mom and dad and my brother. Not long ago, that statement would have felt confessional. I had internalized the not-so-subtle message that once you reach your magical 18th birthday, you should be completely self-reliant. I had bought into the idea that while you should certainly continue to love your parents, and even ask their advice once in a while, you shouldn't be sad if you don't get to see them on a regular basis. I saw a sitcom recently in which the young husband complained to his wife about her parents, wondering why they couldn't be like "normal" parents and live far away. This character had perfectly captured the essence of it: parents who live near their grown children are smothering, and children who stay near their parents are clingy, codependent, unsuccessful.

8   That perception may finally be changing. Before September 11, I felt unique in my strong attachment to my family. Since then, however, many of my friends say they wish they could gather together everyone they love so they could keep them safe, and so they wouldn't have to face alone whatever new dangers may come.

9   But it's more than fear, I think, that makes us want to be with our loved ones. It's a cliché to say that adversity and trauma force us to seriously re-examine our lives. But since the attacks, I've heard my peers say they feel a renewed appreciation for their families. I have spoken to so many young people who visited or called their relatives on September 11—even if they were not in physical danger—to say I love you, are you OK, I am so grateful for you. It's too early to know whether our gratitude and our desire for more contact with our families will last, or if, as the fear and shock continue to abate, those feelings will fade, too. But for now, at least, it seems as though my family and I, in our closeness, are not so unusual.

THINKING ABOUT THE TEXT

1. Despite the author's "secret," what does she try to establish immediately about her sense of independence? What did she once feel was a measure of "success and maturity"?

2. How did the author rationalize choosing a nearby college? To what extent did this rationalization prove true? How did she feel about going to graduate school? What did she discover?

3. Do you agree with the writer that once young people reach eighteen, there is a "not-so-subtle message" or expectation about self-reliance that most internalize? Explain the pressures to conform to this expectation.

4. Even though the writer refers to her time in graduate school and to her marriage, how does she manage to keep this essay focused? Are any details irrelevant?

5. In what way did the tragedy of September 11 affect the writer's relationship with her family? What impact has it had on her friends' relationships with their families?

WRITING FROM THE TEXT

1. Write an analysis of how your own life has changed as a result of September 11. Try to stay focused, as Moore does, on a key thesis about these changes and only include relevant details. Clarify which changes seem temporary and which seem long-lasting.

2. Describe a "deep, dark secret" that you and your family have only recently shared with others. Let the reader see the pressure you felt to keep it from others, the reactions of others, and the consequences of sharing it.

3. Brainstorm for a number of "messages" or expectations that you have internalized over the years and evaluate their power and influence over you. Then analyze one, in particular, that you have or have not been able to counter or oppose, illustrate your efforts and the extent of your success.

CONNECTING WITH OTHER TEXTS

1. After reading "Ignorance Is Not Bliss" (p. 14), compare and contrast Marcus's and Moore's "secrets" as well as the causes and effects of the "internalized messages" in both essays. See the section on how to write a cause-and-effect essay (pp. 434–438) for help in structuring this assignment.

2. Read Carolyn Hwang's "The Good Daughter" (p. 20). Compare the pressures and expectations—or lack thereof—on Moore and Hwang and write an essay analyzing the underlying reason for these differences. How significant is the role of gender in these essays? Do you think "good sons" might share the same expectations that both women feel? Support your thesis with specific statements from both essays and from your own experiences.

Are Families Dangerous?

Barbara Ehrenreich

Long known as a journalist and social critic, Barbara Ehrenreich (b. 1941) has written extensively as an advocate for women and for the poor. In addition to her frequent articles in the popular press—the *New York Times Magazine*, *Ms.*, *Esquire*, *Vogue*, *The Atlantic Monthly*, and *Mother Jones*—Ehrenreich is also known for *Witches, Midwives, and Nurses: A History of Women Healers* (1972), *The Sexual Politics of Sickness* (1973), *The Hearts of Men: American Dreams and the Flight from Commitment* (1983), *The Worst Years of Our Lives: Irreverent Notes from a Decade of Greed* (1990), and *Nickel and Dimed: On (Not) Getting By in America* (2001). First published in *Time* in 1994, the essay that follows reflects Ehrenreich's concern for an institution—here the American family—and the social consequences of ignoring some of its problems.

1   A disturbing subtext runs through our recent media fixations. Parents abuse sons—allegedly at least, in the Menendez case—who in turn rise up and kill them. A husband torments a wife, who retaliates with a kitchen knife. Love turns into obsession, between the Simpsons anyway, and then perhaps into murderous rage: the family, in other words, becomes personal hell.

2   This accounts for at least part of our fascination with the Bobbitts and the Simpsons and the rest of them. We live in a culture that fetishes the family as the ideal unit of human community, the perfect container for our lusts and loves. Politicians of both parties are aggressively "pro-family;" even abortion-rights bumper stickers proudly link "pro-family" and "pro-choice." Only with the occasional celebrity crime do we allow ourselves to think the nearly unthinkable: that the family may not be the ideal and perfect living arrangement after all—that it can be a nest of pathology and a cradle of gruesome violence.

3   It's a scary thought, because the family is at the same time our "haven in a heartless world." Theoretically, and sometimes actually, the family nurtures warm, loving feelings, uncontaminated by greed or power hunger. Within the family, and often only within the family, individuals are loved "for themselves," whether or not they are infirm, incontinent, infantile or eccentric. The strong (adults and especially males) lie down peaceably with the small and weak.

4   But consider the matter of wife battery. We managed to dodge it in the Bobbitt case and downplay it as a force in Tonya Harding's life. Thanks to O. J., though, we're caught up now in a mass consciousness-raising session, grimly absorbing the fact that in some areas domestic violence sends as many women to emergency rooms as any other form of illness, injury or assault.

5   Still, we shrink from the obvious inference: for a woman, home is, statistically speaking, the most dangerous place to be. Her worst enemies and potential killers are not strangers but lovers, husbands and those who claimed to love her once. Similarly, for every child like Polly Klaas who is killed by a deranged criminal on parole, dozens are abused and murdered by their own relatives. Home is all too often where the small and weak fear to lie down and shut their eyes.

6   At some deep, queasy, Freudian level, we all know this. Even in the ostensibly "functional," nonviolent family, where no one is killed or maimed, feelings are routinely bruised and often twisted out of shape. There is the slap or put-down that violates a child's shaky sense of self, the cold, distracted stare that drives a spouse to tears, the little digs and rivalries. At best, the family teaches the finest things human beings can learn from one another—generosity and love. But it is also, all too often, where we learn nasty things like hate and rage and shame.

7   Americans act out their ambivalence about the family without ever owning up to it. Millions adhere to creeds that are militantly "pro-family." But at the same time millions flock to therapy groups that offer to heal the "inner child" from damage inflicted by family life. Legions of women band together to revive the self-esteem they lost in supposedly loving relationships and to learn to love a little less. We are all, it is often said, "in recovery." And from what? Our families, in most cases.

8   There is a long and honorable tradition of "anti-family" thought. The French philosopher Charles Fourier taught that the family was a barrier to human progress; early feminists saw a degrading parallel between marriage and prostitution. More recently, the renowned British anthropologist Edmund Leach stated that "far from being the basis of the good society, the family, with its narrow privacy and tawdry secrets, is the source of all discontents."

9   Communes proved harder to sustain than plain old couples, and the conservatism of the '80s crushed the last vestiges of life-style experimentation. Today even gays and lesbians are eager to get married and take up family life. Feminists have learned to couch their concerns as "family issues," and public figures would sooner advocate free cocaine on demand than criticize the family. Hence our unseemly interest in O. J. and Erik, Lyle and Lorena: they allow us, however gingerly, to break the silence on the hellish side of family life.

10   But the discussion needs to become a lot more open and forthright. We may be stuck with the family—at least until someone invents a sustainable alternative—but the family, with its deep, impacted tensions and longings, can hardly be expected to be the moral foundation of everything else. In fact, many families could use a lot more outside interference in the form of counseling and policing, and some are so dangerously dysfunctional that they ought

to be encouraged to disband right away. Even healthy families need outside sources of moral guidance to keep the internal tensions from imploding— and this means, at the very least, a public philosophy of gender equality and concern for child welfare. When, instead, the larger culture aggrandizes wife beaters, degrades women or nods approvingly at child slappers, the family gets a little more dangerous for everyone, and so, inevitably, does the larger world.

Thinking about the Text

1. Ehrenreich suggests that beyond their notoriety, we are fascinated with the "subtext" revealed in recent highly publicized criminal and civil trials. What is the collective view or "subtext" that underlies the Menendez brothers' murder of their parents, Lorena Bobbitt's attack on her husband, and O. J. Simpson's relationship with his former wife?

2. How are the theoretical and popular concepts of family life in marked contrast to what these trials reveal about families?

3. What is the "obvious inference" that Ehrenreich wants her readers to draw? Which of her specific statistics and examples support the inference?

4. Ehrenreich acknowledges the virtues family life can teach. What are they? But she also refers to the nonphysical, yet violent abuses inflicted on people in a family. What are they?

5. After acknowledging that "anti-family" ideas are not new, what specific suggestions does Ehrenreich make for working on the problems that exist in families?

Writing from the Text

1. Write an analysis of family life that demonstrates how "the finest things human beings can learn from one another" are evident in the specific examples you use to illustrate your position.

2. In an analysis of family life, show how even in functional and nonviolent families, "feelings are routinely bruised and often twisted out of shape," and how "nasty things like hate and rage and shame" are learned. Use specific examples from families that you know to support your position. Is there a solution to the problems of these families that you can propose in your conclusion?

3. Take one or two examples from families that you know well and write an essay illustrating how outside help—moral guidance, education, or counseling—helped these particular families survive.

CONNECTING WITH OTHER TEXTS

1. Read "The Good Daughter" (p. 20) and consider Ehrenreich's idea that even in functional, nonviolent families "feelings are bruised" and the "slap or put-down" threatens self-esteem. Write an analysis of Carolyn Hwang's life that suggests Ehrenreich may be right.

2. How do the families described in "Our Son Mark" (p. 24) and "Ignorance Is Not Bliss" (below) illustrate that a family can teach "the finest things human beings can learn from one another—generosity and love"? Use the theoretical goodness noted by Ehrenreich to analyze how Hayakawa's and Marcus's families exemplify those specific virtues.

3. Using "Thanksgiving" (p. 3), "The Good Daughter" (p. 20), and "Are Families Dangerous," (p. 11) argue that even nonviolent families can bruise egos and create unhealthy individuals within the family unit.

 Ignorance Is Not Bliss

Eric Marcus

A graduate of Vassar and Columbia, Eric Marcus (b. 1958) is a journalist who has published articles and book reviews on a variety of subjects. A contributing editor of *The Hip Pocket Guide to New York*, Marcus has also written *Making History: The Struggle for Gay and Lesbian Equal Rights, 1945–1990; An Oral History*; and *Is It a Choice? Answers to 300 of the Most Frequently Asked Questions About Gays and Lesbians*. Marcus lives in New York, where he volunteers as a peer counselor at Identity House and works as an associate producer for *Good Morning America*. The essay included here originally appeared in *Newsweek* in 1993.

1   Sam Nunn didn't need to hold Senate hearings to come up with his "don't ask, don't tell" solution for handling gays in the military. If he'd asked me, I could have told him this was exactly the policy some of my relatives suggested years ago when I informed them that I planned to tell my grandmother that I was gay. They said, "She's old, it'll kill her. You'll destroy her image of you. If she doesn't ask, why tell?"

2   "Don't ask, don't tell" made a lot of sense to these relatives because it sounded like an easy solution. For them, it was. If I didn't say anything to my grandmother, they wouldn't have to deal with her upset over the truth about her grandson. But for me, "not telling" was an exhausting nightmare, because it meant withholding everything that could possibly give me away and living in fear of being found out. At the same time, I didn't want to cause

Grandma pain by telling her I was gay, so I was easily persuaded to continue the charade.

3   If I hadn't been close to my grandmother, or saw her once a year, hiding the truth would have been relatively easy. But we'd had a special relationship since she cared for me as a child when my mother was ill, and we visited often, so lying to her was especially difficult.

4   I started hiding the truth from everyone in 1965, when I had my first crush. That was in second grade and his name was Hugh. No one told me, but I knew I shouldn't tell anyone about it, not even Hugh. I don't know how I knew that liking another boy was something to hide, but I did, so I kept it a secret.

5   I fell in love for the first time when I was 17. It was a wondrous experience, but I didn't dare tell anyone, especially my family, because telling them about Bob would have given me away. I couldn't explain to them that for the first time in my life I felt like a normal human being.

6   By the time I was an adult, I'd stopped lying to my immediate family, with the exception of my grandmother, and told them that I was gay. I was a second-rate liar so I was lucky that Grandma was the only person in my life around whom I had to be something I wasn't. I can't imagine what it's like for gays and lesbians in the military to hide the truth from the men and women with whom they serve. The fear of exposure must be extraordinary, especially because exposure would mean the end of their careers. For me, the only risk was losing Grandma's love.

7   Hiding the truth from her grew ever more challenging in the years that followed. I couldn't tell her about the man I then shared my life with. I couldn't talk about my friends who had AIDS because she would have wondered why I knew so many ill men. I couldn't tell her that I volunteered for a gay peer-counseling center. I couldn't talk to her about the political issues that most interested me because she would have wondered why I had such passionate feelings about gay rights. Eventually I couldn't even tell her about all of my work, because some of my writing was on gay issues. In the end, all we had left to talk about was the weather.

8   If being gay were only what I did behind closed doors, there would have been plenty of my life left over to share with my grandmother. But my life as a gay man isn't something that takes place only in the privacy of my bedroom. It affects who my friends are, whom I choose to share my life with, the work I do, the organizations I belong to, the magazines I read, where I vacation and what I talk about. I know it's the same for heterosexuals because their sexual orientation affects everything, from a choice of senior-prom date and the finger on which they wear their wedding band to the birth announcements they send and every emotion they feel.

9   So the reality of the "don't ask, don't tell" solution for dealing with my grandmother and for dealing with gays in the military means having to lie about or hide almost every aspect of your life. It's not nearly as simple as just not saying, "I'm gay."

10   After years of "protecting" my grandmother I decided it was time to stop lying. In the worst case, I figured she might reject me, although that seemed unlikely. But whatever the outcome, I could not pretend anymore. Some might think that was selfish on my part, but I'd had enough of the "don't tell" policy, which had forced me into a life of deceit. I also hoped that by telling her the truth, we could build a relationship based on honesty, a possibility that was worth the risk.

11   The actual telling was far less terrifying than all the anticipation. While my grandmother cried plenty, my family was wrong, because the truth didn't kill her. In the five years since, Grandma and I have talked a lot about the realities of my life and the lives of my gay and lesbian friends. She's read many articles and a few books, including mine. She's surprised us by how quickly she's set aside her myths and misconceptions.

12   Grandma and I are far closer than we ever were. Last fall we even spent a week together in Paris for her birthday. And these days, we have plenty to talk about, including the gays in the military issue.

13   A few months ago, Grandma traveled with me to Lafayette College, Pennsylvania, where I was invited to give a speech on the history of the gay civil-rights movement. After my talk, several students took us to dinner. As I conversed with the young women across the table from me, I overheard my grandmother talking to the student sitting next to her. She told him he was right to tell his parents he was gay, that with time and his help they would adjust. She said, "Don't underestimate their ability to change."

14   I wish Sam Nunn had called my grandmother to testify before his Senate committee. He and the other senators, as well as Defense Secretary Les Aspin and the president, could do far worse than listen to her advice.

THINKING ABOUT THE TEXT

1. What are the expressed reasons why Eric Marcus didn't tell his grandmother he is gay? What do you imagine his unexpressed concerns might be?

2. What parts of his life could Marcus not talk about with his grandmother? Why was this secret a problem for him?

3. Why does Marcus believe that the policy of "don't ask, don't tell" is not a solution for gays in the military?

4. How does Marcus illustrate his grandmother's understanding and acceptance of his sexual identity?

WRITING FROM THE TEXT

1. Write an essay telling about a time that you feared family members' responses to some revelation about you—something you had done, a choice you made, or one of your beliefs or values. Describe the responses of others when you revealed this truth.

2. On the basis of your own or a friend's experience in telling some important truth, argue for or against revealing the truth to others.

3. Write an analysis of your own or a friend's sexual orientation to support Marcus's view that one's sexual identity influences one's choice of friends and leisure activities.

CONNECTING WITH OTHER TEXTS

1. In "My Deep, Dark Secret" (p. 8), Hadley Moore is embarrassed to admit that she wants her family close-by. Marcus is comfortable with his sexual orientation, but has been admonished to keep it a secret from his grandmother. Write an essay that compares the roles of families in these two authors' experience. Structure your paper as a comparison study (pp. 439–445) or problem analysis (pp. 467–473), whichever seems better to you.

2. Although Eric Marcus and ultimately his grandmother encourage young people to be open about their homosexuality, in "Appearances" (p. 228) Carmen Vasquez shows some dire consequences of being perceived as gay. Write an essay supporting or refuting Eric Marcus's stance with information from both essays.

◖◗ Blue Spruce ◖◗
Stephen Perry

While teaching creative writing—at Long Beach City College, University of California at Irvine, and the UCLA Extension Writers' Program—Stephen Perry (b. 1950) has published more than sixty-five poems in anthologies and in journals such as the *New Yorker*, *Yale Review*, *Virginia Quarterly Review*, *Kenyon Review*, *Antioch Review*, and *Salmagundi*. Perry has also served as poetry consultant to the Disney Corporation—the only such consultant in the company's history. He is currently seeking a publisher for his collection of poems, *Homecoming*. Perry shares a "co-dependent website" with his author wife, Susan Perry, and invites readers to visit and interact with them at <www.bunnyape.com>.

Referring to "Blue Spruce," Perry reveals, "When I read this poem at poetry readings, I usually tell people that everything in the poem is true, except for the title. There were no blue spruces (that I know of) in the little town in Missouri where I set the poem. I just like the double pun on 'blue' and 'spruce.'" The poem was published in the *New Yorker* in 1991.

My grandfather worked in a barbershop
smelling of lotions he'd slap on your face,
hair and talc. The black razor strop

hung like the penis of an ox. He'd draw
5   the sharp blade in quick strokes over
the smooth-rough hide, and then carefully

over your face. The tiny hairs would gather
on the blade, a congregation singing
under blue spruce in winter,

10   a bandstand in the center of town
bright with instruments, altso sax, tenor
sax, tuba or sousaphone—the bright

oompah-pahs shaving the town somehow,
a bright cloth shaking the air
15   into flakes of silvering hair

floating down past the houses, the horses
pulling carriages past the town fountain,
which had frozen into a coiffure

of curly glass. My grandfather had an affair
20   with the girl who did their nails
bright pink, bright red, never blue,

perhaps as the horses clip-clopped on ice
outside his shop, his kisses
smelling of lather and new skin—

25   when she grew too big and round
with his child, with his oompah love,
with his bandstand love, with his brassy love,

and the town dropped its grace notes
of gossip and whispered hiss,
30   he bundled her out of town

with the savings which should have gone
to my mom. But how could you hate him?
My mother did, my father did,

and my grandmother, who bore his neglect.
35   When she was covered in sheets
at her last death,

he flirted with the nurses, bright
as winter birds in spruces
above a bandstand—

40   I'll always remember him in snow, a deep lather
of laughter, the picture
where he took me from my mother

and raised me high, a baby, into the bell
of his sousaphone, as if I were a note
45   he'd play into light—

THINKING ABOUT THE TEXT

1. List all the images that Perry uses to characterize the grandfather, then describe the resulting "portrait."

2. Discuss the narrator's perception of his grandfather and compare and contrast it with the views of family members and the townspeople.

3. Look up both "blue" and "spruce" in the dictionary. Which definitions relate to this poem? Discuss possible meanings of the title.

4. Cluster (see p. 337) all the references to music or anything musical in the poem. Why might the poet have chosen to connect the grandfather with music and, specifically, with the sousaphone? How do these references add to your understanding of his character?

5. How does the winter setting contribute to the poem? What is the significance of the reference to "light" at the end and of the repetitions of the word "bright" throughout?

WRITING FROM THE TEXT

1. Referring to the images you listed in exercise 1 of "Thinking about the Text," write a character analysis of the grandfather from his grandson's perspective.

2. Working from the clustering you did for exercise 4, write an analysis of the poet's use of music to help characterize the grandfather and the town.

3. With supporting details from this poem, write an essay analyzing the poet's depiction of life in a small town and its effect on the individual. Does the poet seem at all critical of the small town or of the grandfather?

CONNECTING WITH OTHER TEXTS

1. Using details from this poem and from at least one other reading—"The Only Child" (p. 31), "Ignorance Is Not Bliss" (p. 14), "Your Place Is Empty" (p. 45), and "Black Men and Public Space" (p. 237)—write a paper analyzing the pressures of "fitting into" a particular society and the individual's varying responses to such pressures.

2. Consider the images used to describe the grandfathers in "Blue Spruce" and in "Digging" (p. 42). With these images in mind, write a paper contrasting these two portraits.

3. Visit Perry's Website at <www.bunnyape.com> and read some of his other poems. Write an essay focusing on a recurring image or theme in Perry's writing as exhibited in "Blue Spruce" and any of his other works.

The Good Daughter
Caroline Hwang

Caroline Hwang (b. 1969) earned a B.A. in English from the University of Pennsylvania and has worked as an editor at *American Health, Mademoiselle, Glamour,* and *Redbook.* Constantly juggling her varied projects as both a writer and an editor, Hwang observes, "I've often heard it said that the difference between being an editor and writer is that the editor has power and the writer gets the glory. I don't know that the difference is so clear-cut, but I can say that being on both sides has helped my writing and editing."

1   The moment I walked into the dry-cleaning store, I knew the woman behind the counter was from Korea, like my parents. To show her that we

shared a heritage, and possibly get a fellow countryman's discount, I tilted my head forward, in shy imitation of a traditional bow.

2 "Name?" she asked, not noticing my attempted obeisance.

3 "Hwang," I answered.

4 "Hwang? Are you Chinese?"

5 Her question caught me off-guard. I was used to hearing such queries from non-Asians who think Asians all look alike, but never from one of my own people. Of course, the only Koreans I knew were my parents and their friends, people who've never asked me where I came from, since they knew better than I.

6 I ransacked my mind for the Korean words that would tell her who I was. It's always struck me as funny (in a mirthless sort of way) that I can more readily say "I am Korean" in Spanish, German and even Latin than I can in the language of my ancestry. In the end, I told her in English.

7 The dry-cleaning woman squinted as though trying to see past the glare of my strangeness, repeating my surname under her breath. "Oh, *Fxuang*," she said, doubling over with laughter. "You don't know how to speak your name."

8 I flinched. Perhaps I was particularly sensitive at the time, having just dropped out of graduate school. I had torn up my map for the future, the one that said not only where I was going but who I was. My sense of identity was already disintegrating.

9 When I got home, I called my parents to ask why they had never bothered to correct me. "Big deal," my mother said, sounding more flippant than I knew she intended. (Like many people who learn English in a classroom, she uses idioms that don't always fit the occasion.) "So what if you can't pronounce your name? You are American," she said.

10 Though I didn't challenge her explanation, it left me unsatisfied. The fact is, my cultural identity is hardly that clear-cut.

11 My parents immigrated to this country 30 years ago, two years before I was born. They told me often, while I was growing up, that, if I wanted to, I could be president someday, that here my grasp would be as long as my reach.

12 To ensure that I reaped all the advantages of this country, my parents saw to it that I became fully assimilated. So, like any American of my generation, I whiled away my youth strolling malls and talking on the phone, rhapsodizing over Andrew McCarthy's blue eyes or analyzing the meaning of a certain upper-classman's offer of a ride to the Homecoming football game.

13 To my parents, I am all American, and the sacrifices they made in leaving Korea—including my mispronounced name—pale in comparison to the opportunities those sacrifices gave me. They do not see that I straddle

two cultures, nor that I feel displaced in the only country I know. I identify with Americans, but Americans do not identify with me. I've never known what it's like to belong to a community—neither one at large, nor of an extended family. I know more about Europe than the continent my ancestors unmistakably come from. I sometimes wonder, as I did that day in the dry cleaner's, if I would be a happier person had my parents stayed in Korea.

14   I first began to consider this thought around the time I decided to go to graduate school. It has been a compromise: my parents wanted me to go to law school; I wanted to skip the starched-collar track and be a writer—the hungrier the better. But after 20-some years of following their wishes and meeting all of their expectations, I couldn't bring myself to disobey or disappoint. A writing career is riskier than law, I remember thinking. If I'm a failure and my life is a washout, then what does that make my parents' lives?

15   I know that many of my friends had to choose between pleasing their parents and being true to themselves. But for the children of immigrants, the choice seems more complicated, a happy outcome impossible. By making the biggest move of their lives for me, my parents indentured me to the largest debt imaginable—I owe them the fulfillment of their hopes for me.

16   It tore me up inside to suppress my dream, but I went to school for a Ph.D. in English literature, thinking I had found the perfect compromise. I would be able to write at least about books while pursuing a graduate degree. Predictably, it didn't work out. How could I labor for five years in a program I had no passion for? When I finally left school, my parents were disappointed, but since it wasn't what they wanted me to do, they weren't devastated. I, on the other hand, felt I was staring at the bottom of the abyss. I had seen the flaw in my life of halfwayness, in my planned life of compromises.

17   I hadn't thought about my love life, but I had a vague plan to make concessions there, too. Though they raised me as an American, my parents expect me to marry someone Korean and give them grandchildren who look like them. This didn't seem like such a huge request when I was 14, but now I don't know what I'm going to do. I've never been in love with someone I dated, or dated someone I loved. (Since I can't bring myself even to entertain the thought of marrying the non-Korean men I'm attracted to, I've been dating only those I know I can stay clearheaded about.) And as I near that age when the question of marriage stalks every relationship, I can't help but wonder if my parents' expectations are responsible for the lack of passion in my life.

18   My parents didn't want their daughter to be Korean, but they don't want her fully American, either. Children of immigrants are living paradoxes.

We are the first generation and the last. We are in this country for its opportunities, yet filial duty binds us. When my parents boarded the plane, they knew they were embarking on a rough trip. I don't think they imagined the rocks in the path of their daughter who can't even pronounce her own name.

THINKING ABOUT THE TEXT

1. What might be Hwang's strategy for opening her essay with a brief narration of her encounter with the Korean dry-cleaning woman? What multiple issues does she introduce with this personal anecdote?

2. Explain how the dry cleaner's comment "You don't know how to speak your name" functions not simply as an observation but as a symbol throughout the essay.

3. What details does Hwang use to support the claim that "I straddle two cultures" and "I feel displaced in the only country I know"?

4. Using your own words along with phrases from the essay, identify Hwang's *aim* or purpose in this essay as well as her key *claim* or thesis.

WRITING FROM THE TEXT

1. Including details from this essay and your own experiences and observations, write an evaluative response essay agreeing or disagreeing with Hwang's claim that "Children of immigrants are living paradoxes." Use examples from the essay to define "living paradoxes" and to support your key claim.

2. Incorporate specific details from Hwang's essay to write an analysis of the causes and effects of her parents' expectations.

CONNECTING WITH OTHER TEXTS

1. Focusing on "The Good Daughter" and "Your Place Is Empty" (p. 45), write an essay analyzing the special pressures and demands on the children of immigrants.

2. Create a thesis about effective or ineffective parenting to write an essay incorporating support from any three of the following: "The Good Daughter," "Ace in the Hole" (p. 34), "Your Place Is Empty" (p. 45), "Where Are You Going, Where Have You Been?" (p. 126), "Living in Two Worlds" (p. 144), and "Peaches" (p. 147). Include direct quotations and analyze them fully.

Our Son Mark

S. I. *Hayakawa*

Influential linguist, scholar, senator, university administrator, and writer, Samuel Ichiye Hayakawa (1906–1992) has had a major impact not only on the world of politics but also on the realm of semantics—the meaning of words and how they affect our lives. Born in Canada, Hayakawa earned an M.A. from McGill University and a Ph.D. from the University of Wisconsin at Madison, where he began his teaching career. He served as president of San Francisco State College during the tumultuous antiwar movement but resigned in 1973 to run for the United States Senate. His books include *Language in Thought and Action* (1941), *Symbol, Status, and Personality* (1963), and *Through the Communication Barrier: On Speaking, Listening, and Understanding* (1979). He wrote many articles on social and personal issues, including the following essay, which was written for *McCall's* magazine and published in *Through the Communication Barrier* (1979).

1   It was a terrible blow for us to discover that we had brought a retarded child into the world. My wife and I had had no previous acquaintance with the problems of retardation—not even with the words to discuss it. Only such words as imbecile, idiot, and moron came to mind. And the prevailing opinion was that such a child must be "put away," to live out his life in an institution.

2   Mark was born with Down's syndrome, popularly known as mongolism. The prognosis for his ever reaching anything approaching normality was hopeless. Medical authorities advised us that he would show some mental development, but the progress would be painfully slow and he would never reach an adolescent's mental age. We could do nothing about it, they said. They sympathetically but firmly advised us to find a private institution that would take him. To get him into a public institution, they said, would require a waiting period of five years. To keep him at home for this length of time, they warned, would have a disastrous effect on our family.

3   That was twenty-seven years ago. In that time, Mark has never been "put away." He has lived at home. The only institution he sees regularly is the workshop he attends, a special workshop for retarded adults. He is as much a part of the family as his mother, his older brother, his younger sister, his father, or our longtime housekeeper and friend, Daisy Rosebourgh.

4   Mark has contributed to our stability and serenity. His retardation has brought us grief, but we did not go on dwelling on what might have been, and we have been rewarded by finding much good in things the way they are. From the beginning, we have enjoyed Mark for his delightful self. He has never seemed like a burden. He was an "easy" baby, quiet, friendly, and passive; but he needed a baby's care for a long time. It was easy to be patient

with him, although I must say that some of his stages, such as his love of making chaos, as we called it, by pulling all the books he could reach off the shelves, lasted much longer than normal children's.

5   Mark seems more capable of accepting things as they are than his immediate relatives; his mental limitation has given him a capacity for contentment, a focus on the present moment, which is often enviable. His world may be circumscribed, but it is a happy and bright one. His enjoyment of simple experiences—swimming, food, birthday candles, sports-car rides, and cuddly cats—has that directness and intensity so many philosophers recommended to all of us.

6   Mark's contentment has been a happy contribution to our family, and the challenge of communicating with him, of doing things we can all enjoy, has drawn the family together. And seeing Mark's communicative process develop in slow motion has taught me much about the process in all children.

7   Fortunately, Mark was born at a time when a whole generation of parents of retarded children had begun to question the accepted dogmas about retardation. Whatever they were told by their physicians about their children, parents began to ask: "Is that so? Let's see." For what is meant by "retarded child"? There are different kinds of retardation. Retarded child No. 1 is not retarded child No. 2, or 3, or 4. Down's syndrome is one condition, while brain damage is something else. There are different degrees of retardation, just as there are different kinds of brain damage. No two retarded children are exactly alike in all respects. Institutional care *does* turn out to be the best answer for some kinds of retarded children or some family situations. The point is that one observes and reacts to the *specific* case and circumstances rather than to the generalization.

8   This sort of attitude has helped public understanding of the nature and problems of retardation to become much deeper and more widespread. It's hard to believe now that it was "definitely known" twenty years ago that institutionalization was the "only way." We were told that a retarded child could not be kept at home because "it would not be fair to the other children." The family would not be able to stand the stress. "Everybody" believed these things and repeated them, to comfort and guide the parents of the retarded.

9   We did not, of course, lightly disregard the well-meant advice of university neurologists and their social-worker teams, for they had had much experience and we were new at this shattering experience. But our general semantics, or our parental feelings, made us aware that their reaction to Mark was to a generalization, while to us he was an individual. They might have a valid generalization about statistical stresses on statistical families, but they knew virtually nothing about our particular family and its evaluative processes.

10   Mark was eight months old before we were told he was retarded. Of course we had known that he was slower than the average child in smiling, in sitting up, in responding to others around him. Having had one child who was extraordinarily ahead of such schedules, we simply thought that Mark was at the other end of the average range.

11   In the course of his baby checkups, at home and while traveling, we had seen three different pediatricians. None of them gave us the slightest indication that all was not well. Perhaps, they were made uncertain by the fact that Mark, with his part Japanese parentage, had a right to have "mongolian" features. Or perhaps this news is as hard for a pediatrician to tell as it is for parents to hear, and they kept putting off the job of telling us. Finally, Mark's doctor did suggest a neurologist, indicating what his fears were, and made an appointment.

12   It was Marge who bore the brunt of the first diagnosis and accompanying advice, given at the university hospital at a time when I had to be out of town. Stunned and crushed, she was told: "Your husband is a professional man. You can't keep a child like this at home."

13   "But he lives on love," she protested.

14   "Don't your other children live on love, too?" the social worker asked.

15   Grief stricken as she was, my wife was still able to recognize a non sequitur. One does not lessen the love for one's children by dividing it among several.

16   "What can I read to find out more about his condition and how to take care of him?" Marge asked.

17   "You can't get help from a book," answered the social worker. "You must put him away."

18   Today this sounds like dialogue from the Dark Ages. And it *was* the Dark Ages. Today professional advice runs generally in the opposite direction: "Keep your retarded child at home if it's at all possible."

19   It was parents who led the way: They organized into parents' groups; they pointed out the need for preschools, schools, diagnostic centers, work-training centers, and sheltered workshops to serve children who were being cared for at home; they worked to get these services, which are now being provided in increasing numbers. But the needs are a long way from being fully met.

20   Yet even now the cost in money—not to mention the cost in human terms—is much less if the child is kept at home than if he is sent to the institutions in which children are put away. And many of the retarded are living useful and independent lives, which would never have been thought possible for them.

21   But for us at that time, as for other parents who were unknowingly pioneering new ways for the retarded, it was a matter of going along from day to day, learning, observing, and saying, "Let's see."

22   There was one more frightening hurdle for our family to get over. On that traumatic day Marge got the diagnosis, the doctor told her that it was too risky for us to have any more children, that there was a fifty percent chance of our having another mongoloid child. In those days, nothing was known of the cause of mongolism. There were many theories. Now, at least, it is known to be caused by presence of an extra chromosome, a fault of cell division. But the question "Why does it happen?" had not yet been answered.

23   Today, genetic counseling is available to guide parents as to the probabilities of recurrence on a scientific basis. We were flying blind. With the help of a doctor friend, we plunged into medical books and discovered that the doctor who gave us the advice was flying as blind as we were. No evidence could be found for the fifty percent odds. Although there did seem to be some danger of recurrence, we estimated that the probabilities were with us. We took the risk and won.

24   Our daughter, Wynne, is now twenty-five. She started as Mark's baby sister, passed him in every way, and really helped bring him up. The fact that she had a retarded brother must have contributed at least something to the fact that she is at once delightfully playful and mature, observant, and understanding. She has a fine relationship with her two brothers.

25   Both Wynne and Alan, Mark's older brother, have participated, with patience and delight, in Mark's development. They have shown remarkable ingenuity in instructing and amusing him. On one occasion, when Mark was not drinking his milk, Alan called him to his place at the table and said, "I'm a service station. What kind of car are you?" Mark, quickly entering into the make-believe, said, "Pord."

26   Alan: "Shall I fill her up?"

27   Mark: "Yes."

28   Alan: "Ethyl or regular?"

29   Mark: "Reg'lar"

30   Alan (bringing the glass to Mark's mouth): "Here you are."

31   When Mark finished his glass of milk, Alan asked him, "Do you want your windshield cleaned?" Then, taking a napkin, he rubbed it briskly across Mark's face, while Mark grinned with delight. This routine became a regular game for many weeks.

32   Alan and Wynne interpret and explain Mark to their friends, but never once have I heard them apologize for him or deprecate him. It is almost as if they judge the quality of other people by how they react to Mark. They think he is "great," and expect their friends to think so too.

33   Their affection and understanding were shown when Wynne flew to Oregon with Mark to visit Alan and his wife, Cynthea, who went to college there.

Wynne described the whole reunion as "tremendous" and especially enjoyed Mark's delight in the trip.

34   "He was great on the plane," she recalls. "He didn't cause any trouble except that he rang the bell for the stewardess a couple of times when he didn't need anything. He was so great that I was going to send him back on the plane alone. He would have enjoyed that." But she didn't, finally, because she didn't trust others to be able to understand his speech or to know how to treat him without her there to give them clues.

35   Mark looks reasonably normal. He is small for his age (about five feet tall) and childlike. Anyone who is aware of these matters would recognize in him some of the characteristic symptomatic features, but they are not extreme. His almost incomprehensible speech, which few besides his family and teachers can understand, is his most obvious sign of retardation.

36   Mark fortunately does not notice any stares of curiosity he may attract. To imagine how one looks in the eyes of others takes a level of awareness that appears to be beyond him. Hence he is extremely direct and totally without self-consciousness.

37   I have seen him come into our living room, walk up to a woman he has never seen before, and kiss her in response to a genuinely friendly greeting. Since few of us are accustomed to such directness of expression—especially the expression of affection—the people to whom this has happened are deeply moved.

38   Like other children, Mark responds to the evaluation of others. In our family, he is accepted just as he is. Because others have always treated him as an individual, a valued individual, he feels good about himself, and, consequently, he is good to live with. In every situation between parent and child or between children, evaluations are involved—and these interact on each other. Certainly, having Mark at home has helped us be more aware and be more flexible in our evaluations.

39   This kind of sensitivity must have carried over into relations between the two normal children, because I cannot remember a single real fight or a really nasty incident between Alan and Wynne. It's as if their readiness to try to understand Mark extended into a general method of dealing with people. And I think Marge and I found the same thing happening to us, so that we became more understanding with Alan and Wynne than we might otherwise have been. If we had time and patience for Mark, why not for the children who were quick and able? We knew we could do serious damage to Mark by expecting too much of him and being disappointed. But how easy it is to expect too much of bright children and how quickly they feel your disappointment! Seeing Mark's slow, slow progress certainly gave us real appreciation of the marvelous perception and quick learning processes of the other two, so

that all we had to do was open our eyes and our ears, and listen and enjoy them.

40   I don't want to sound as if we were never impatient or obtuse as parents. We were, of course. But parents need to be accepted as they are, too. And I think our children—bless their hearts—were reasonably able to do so.

41   With Mark, it was easy to feel surprise and delight at any of his accomplishments. He cannot read and will never be able to. But he can pick out on request almost any record from his huge collection—Fleetwood Mac, or the Rolling Stones, or Christmas carols—because he knows so well what each record looks like. Once we were discussing the forthcoming marriage of some friends of ours, and Mark disappeared into his playroom to bring out, a few minutes later, a record with the song "A House, a Car and a Wedding Ring."

42   His love for music enables him to figure out how to operate almost any record changer or hi-fi set. He never tries to force a piece of machinery because he cannot figure out how it works, as brighter people often do. And in a strange hotel room, with a TV set of unknown make, it is Mark—not Marge or I—who figures out how to turn it on and get a clear picture. As Alan once remarked: "Mark may be retarded, but he's not stupid!"

43   Of course, it has not all been easy—but when has easiness been the test of the value of anything? To us, the difficult problems that must be faced in the future only emphasize the value of Mark as a person.

44   What does that future hold for Mark?

45   He will never be able to be independent; he will always have to live in a protected environment. His below-50 IQ reflects the fact that he cannot cope with unfamiliar situations.

46   Like most parents of the retarded, we are concentrating on providing financial security for Mark in the future, and fortunately we expect to be able to achieve this. Alan and his wife and Wynne have all offered to be guardians for Mark. It is wonderful to know they feel this way. But we hope that Mark can find a happy place in one of the new residence homes for the retarded.

47   The residence home is something new and promising and it fills an enormous need. It is somewhat like a club, or a family, with a house-mother or manager. The residents share the work around the house, go out to work if they can, share in recreation and companionship. Away from their families, who may be overprotective and not aware of how much the retarded can do for themselves (are we not guilty of this, too!), they are able to live more fully as adults.

48   An indication that there is still much need for public education about the retarded here in California is that there has been difficulty in renting decent houses for this kind of home. Prospective neighbors have objected. In some

ways the Dark Ages are still with us; there are still fear and hostility where the retarded are concerned.

49   Is Mark able to work? Perhaps. He thrives on routine and enjoys things others despise, like clearing the table and loading the dishwasher. To Mark, it's fun. It has been hard to develop in him the idea of work, which to so many of us is "doing what you don't want to do because you have to." We don't know yet if he could work in a restaurant loading a dishwasher. In school, he learned jobs like sorting and stacking scrap wood and operating a delightful machine that swoops the string around and ties up a bundle of wood to be sold in the supermarket. That's fun, too.

50   He is now in a sheltered workshop where he can get the kind—the one kind—of pleasure he doesn't have much chance for. That's the pleasure of contributing something productive and useful to the outside world. He does various kinds of assembling jobs, packaging, sorting, and simple machine operations. He enjoys getting a paycheck and cashing it at the bank. He cannot count, but he takes pride in reaching for the check in a restaurant and pulling out his wallet. And when we thank him for dinner, he glows with pleasure.

51   It's a strange thing to say, and I am a little startled to find myself saying it, but often I feel that I wouldn't have had Mark any different.

THINKING ABOUT THE TEXT

1. In what ways was the era when Mark was born like "the Dark Ages" for the mentally retarded? What were some of the misconceptions and ignorance that the Hayakawas encountered?

2. According to Hayakawa, what are some reasons to care for mentally retarded children at home rather than in an institution, if it is at all possible?

3. In what ways did Mark contribute to and enrich his siblings' and parents' daily lives? How did Mark bring out some fine qualities in others?

4. What are the advantages that "residence homes" can offer mentally retarded adults? What are the indications that more education is still needed about the mentally retarded?

5. Throughout his essay, Hayakawa suggests that there were certainly trying moments rearing Mark. List some indications of these frustrations. Does it weaken or strengthen Hayakawa's essay to include them? Explain.

WRITING FROM THE TEXT

1. Using details from Hayakawa's essay, write an essay to convince the parents of a child with Down's syndrome of the benefits (for the child and family) of keeping the child at home rather than in an institution.

2. Write an essay fully defining "mental retardation" as Hayakawa portrays it and include examples from his experiences with Mark to support your claims. See pp. 426–433 for multiple ways of developing this assignment so your explanation goes far beyond any dictionary definition.

3. Based on specific details and inferences from this essay, contrast the attitudes and advice about mental retardation in the era when Mark was born with current attitudes and practices today.

Connecting with Other Texts

1. Both Matthew Soyster (p. 213) and S. I. Hayakawa acknowledge the difficulties of living with disabilities, yet neither author's work seems dominated by a sense of doom. Write an essay analyzing how both authors remain positive yet realistic; include examples from each to support your thesis.

2. Read "From Access to Acceptance: Enabling America's Largest Minority" (p. 522), and use details from it and from Hayakawa's essay to argue that more access and acceptance are needed not only for the physically disabled but for the mentally disabled, too.

 The Only Child

John Leonard

After studying at Harvard University and Berkeley, where he received his B.A. in 1962, John Leonard (b. 1939) worked as a book reviewer, a producer of dramas and literature programs, a publicity writer, a staff writer for the *New York Times*, and a cultural critic for *Variety, Nation,* and *CBS This Morning.* He is the author of *Smoke and Mirrors: Violence, Television, and Other American Cultures* (1997) and *When the Kissing Had to Stop* (1999), a collection of previously published pieces. Leonard intends his writing to ask moral questions: How do you want your children to grow up? What do you think is decent and fair? Who are your friends, and why? The work included here, from *Private Lives in the Imperial City* (1976), probes family tensions and concerns.

1   He is big. He always has been, over six feet, with that slump of the shoulders and tuck in the neck big men in the country often affect, as if to apologize for being above the democratic norm in size. (In high school and at college he played varsity basketball. In high school he was senior class president.) And he looks healthy enough, blue-eyed behind his beard, like a trapper or a mountain man, acquainted with silences. He also grins a lot.

2   Odd, then, to have noticed earlier—at the house, when he took off his shabby coat to play Ping-Pong—that the white arms were unmuscled. The coat may have been a comment. This, after all, is southern California, where every man is an artist, an advertiser of himself; where every surface is painted and every object potted; where even the statues seem to wear socks. The entire population ambles, in polyesters, toward a Taco Bell. To wear a brown shabby cloth coat in southern California is to admit something.

3   So he hasn't been getting much exercise. Nor would the children have elected him president of any class. At the house they avoided him. Or, since he was too big to be avoided entirely, they treated his presence as a kind of odor to pass through hurriedly, to be safe on the other side. They behaved like cats. Of course, he ignored them. But I think they were up to more than just protecting themselves from his lack of curiosity. Children are expert readers of grins.

4   His grin is intermittent. The dimples twitch on and off; between them, teeth are bared; above them, the blue eyes disappear in a wince. This grin isn't connected to any humor the children know about. It may be a tic. It could also be a function of some metronome made on Mars. It registers inappropriate intervals. We aren't listening to the same music.

5   This is the man who introduced me to the mysteries of mathematical science, the man I could never beat at chess, the man who wrote haiku and played with computers. Now there is static in his head, as though the mind had drifted off its signal during sleep. He has an attention span of about thirty seconds.

6   I am to take him back to where he lives, in the car I have rented in order to pretend to be a Californian. We are headed for a rooming house in one of the beach cities along a coast of off-ramps and oil wells. It is a rooming house that thinks of itself as Spanish. The ruined-hacienda look requires a patio, a palm tree and several miles of corrugated tile. He does not expect me to come up to his room, but I insist. I have brought along a six-pack of beer.

7   The room is a slum, and it stinks. It is wall-to-wall beer cans, hundreds of them, under a film of ash. He lights cigarettes and leaves them burning on the windowsill or the edge of the dresser or the lip of the sink, while he thinks of something else—Gupta sculpture, maybe, or the Sephiroth Tree of the Kabbalah. The sink is filthy, and so is the toilet. Holes have been burnt in the sheet on the bed, where he sits. He likes to crush the beer cans after he has emptied them, then toss them aside.

8   He tells me that he is making a statement, that this room is a statement, that the landlord will understand the meaning of his statement. In a week or so, according to the pattern, they will evict him, and someone will find him another room, which he will turn into another statement, with the help of

the welfare checks he receives on account of his disability, which is the static in his head.

9   There are no books, no newspapers or magazines, no pictures on the wall. There is a television set, which he watches all day long while drinking beer and smoking cigarettes. I am sufficiently familiar with the literature on schizophrenia to realize that this room is a statement he is making about himself. I am also sufficiently familiar with his history to understand that, along with his contempt for himself, there is an abiding arrogance. He refuses medication. They can't make him take it, any more than they can keep him in a hospital. He has harmed no one. One night, in one of these rooms, he will set himself on fire.

10   He talks. Or blurts: scraps from Oriental philosophers—Lao-tzu, I think— puns, incantations, obscenities, names from the past. There are conspiracies; I am part of one of them. He grins, winces, slumps, is suddenly tired, wants me to get out almost as much as I want to get out, seems to have lapsed in a permanent parenthesis. Anyway, I have a busy schedule.

11   Well, speed kills slowly, and he fiddled too much with the oxygen flow to his brain. He wanted ecstasy and revelation, the way we grew up wanting a bicycle, a car, a girlfriend. These belonged to us by right, as middle-class Americans. So, then, did salvation belong to us by right. I would like to thank Timothy Leary and all the other sports of the 1960s who helped make this bad trip possible. I wish R. D. Laing would explain to me, once again and slowly, how madness is a proof of grace. "The greatest magician," said Novalis, "would be the one who would cast over himself a spell so complete that he would take his own phantasmagorias as autonomous appearances."

12   One goes back to the rented car and pretending to be a Californian as, perhaps, one had been pretending to be a brother. It is odd, at my age, suddenly to have become an only child.

THINKING ABOUT THE TEXT

1. Discuss how each "telling detail" about Leonard's brother provides a glimpse of his early promise. Then explain how these same details now underscore his sad transformation.

2. Why does Leonard's brother feel his lifestyle and room are "making a statement"? What type of "statement" does the author feel his brother is making?

3. In this autobiographical essay, Leonard, a New Yorker, can only "pretend to be a Californian." Find details that illustrate what California represents for him.

4. Who or what does Leonard seem to blame for his brother's experimentation with drugs? Why? What is Leonard's implied thesis?

5. Discuss all possible meanings of the title. Why does Leonard wait until the end to focus on it?

WRITING FROM THE TEXT

1. Write an essay contrasting Leonard's recollection of his brother before taking drugs with his perception of him now.

2. If drug addiction or mental illness has plagued any members of your own family, write an essay that illustrates an important insight you have learned from this experience.

3. Find a photograph that shows you with one of your relatives—a sibling, a parent, a cousin, or grandfather. Write an analysis of your relationship with that relative based on the dynamics that you perceive in the photograph.

CONNECTING WITH OTHER TEXTS

1. Read "Living in Two Worlds" (p. 144) and write an essay that shows how both Marcus Mabry and John Leonard live between worlds because of their families.

2. Using "The Only Child," (p. 31) "Thanksgiving" (p. 3), "Ignorance Is Not Bliss" (p. 14), or "Your Place Is Empty" (p. 45), write an essay describing and analyzing the positive and negative aspects of family members reuniting and discovering how they have changed.

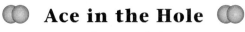

Ace in the Hole

John Updike

John Updike (b. 1932) graduated from Harvard University, where he edited the humor magazine, *The Harvard Lampoon.* While studying art on a fellowship at Oxford University, he sold a poem to the *New Yorker,* thus beginning a long-time affiliation with that magazine. Over the years, he has worked as a staff writer and contributed poetry, essays, short stories, and reviews. Updike is best known for his fiction, including the novels *The Witches of Eastwick* (1984), which was made into a film; *Rabbit at Rest,* which won the Pulitzer Prize in 1991; *Toward the End of Time* (1997); and *Gertrude and Claudius* (2000), an imaginative prequel to Shakespeare's *Hamlet.* "Ace in the Hole" first appeared in the *New Yorker* in 1955 and subsequently in his first collection of short stories, *The Same Door* (1959). The story seems to have sparked Updike's second novel, *Rabbit, Run* (1960), also about an ex-basketball player in a troubled marriage.

1   No sooner did his car touch the boulevard heading home than Ace flicked on the radio. He needed the radio, especially today. In the seconds before the tubes warmed up, he said aloud, doing it just to hear a human voice, "Jesus. She'll pop her lid." His voice, though familiar, irked him; it sounded thin and scratchy, as if the bones in his head were picking up static. In a deeper register Ace added, "She'll murder me." Then the radio came on, warm and strong, so he stopped worrying. The Five Kings were doing "Blueberry Hill"; to hear them made Ace feel so sure inside that from the pack pinched between the car roof and the sun shield he plucked a cigarette, hung it on his lower lip, snapped a match across the rusty place on the dash, held the flame in the instinctive spot near the tip of his nose, dragged, and blew out the match, all in time to the music. He rolled down the window and snapped the match so it spun end-over-end into the gutter. "Two points," he said, and cocked the cigarette toward the roof of the car, sucked powerfully, and exhaled two plumes through his nostrils. He was beginning to feel like himself, Ace Anderson, for the first time that whole day, a bad day. He beat time on the accelerator. The car jerked crazily. "On Blueberry Hill," he sang, "my heart stood still. The wind in the wil-low tree"—he braked for a red light—"played love's suh-*weet* melodee—"

2   "Go, Dad, bust your lungs!" a kid's voice blared. The kid was riding in a '52 Pontiac that had pulled up beside Ace at the light. The profile of the driver, another kid, was dark over his shoulder.

3   Ace looked over at him and smiled slowly, just letting one side of his mouth lift a little. "Shove it," he said, good-naturedly, across the little gap of years that separated them. He knew how they felt, young and mean and shy.

4   But the kid, who looked Greek, lifted his thick upper lip and spat out the window. The spit gleamed on the asphalt like a half-dollar.

5   "Now isn't that pretty?" Ace said, keeping one eye on the light. "You miserable wop. You are *mise*rable." While the kid was trying to think of some smart comeback, the light changed. Ace dug out so hard he smelled burned rubber. In his rear-view mirror he saw the Pontiac lurch forward a few yards, then stop dead, right in the middle of the intersection.

6   The idea of them stalling their fat tin Pontiac kept him in a good humor all the way home. He decided to stop at his mother's place and pick up the baby, instead of waiting for Evey to do it. His mother must have seen him drive up. She came out on the porch holding a plastic spoon and smelling of cake.

7   "You're out early," she told him.

8   "Friedman fired me," Ace told her.

9   "Good for you," his mother said. "I always said he never treated you right." She brought a cigarette out of her apron pocket and tucked it deep into one corner of her mouth, the way she did when something pleased her.

10   Ace lighted it for her. "Friedman was O.K. personally," he said. "He just wanted too much for his money. I didn't mind working Saturdays, but until eleven, twelve Friday nights was too much. Everybody has a right to some leisure."

11   "Well, I don't dare think what Evey will say, but I, for one, thank dear God you had the brains to get out of it. I always said that job had no future to it—no future of any kind, Freddy."

12   "I guess," Ace admitted. "But I wanted to keep at it, for the family's sake."

13   "Now, I know I shouldn't be saying this, but any time Evey—this is just between us—any time Evey thinks she can do better, there's room for you *and* Bonnie right in your father's house." She pinched her lips together. He could almost hear the old lady think, *There, I've said it.*

14   "Look Mom, Evey tries awfully hard, and anyway you know she can't work that way. Not that *that*—I mean, she's a realist, too . . ." He let the rest of the thought fade as he watched a kid across the street dribbling a basketball around a telephone pole that had a backboard and net nailed on it.

15   "Evey's a wonderful girl of her own kind. But I've always said, and your father agrees, Roman Catholics ought to marry among themselves. Now I know I've said it before, but when they get out in the greater world—"

16   "*No,* Mom."

17   She frowned, smoothed herself, and said, "Your name was in the paper today."

18   Ace chose to let that go by. He kept watching the kid with the basketball. If was funny how, though the whole point was to get the ball up into the air, kids grabbed it by the sides and squeezed. Kids just didn't think.

19   "Did you hear?" his mother asked.

20   "Sure, but so what?" Ace said. His mother's lower lip was coming at him, so he changed the subject. "I guess I'll take Bonnie."

21   His mother went into the house and brought back his daughter, wrapped in a blue blanket. The baby looked dopey. "She fussed all day," his mother complained. "I said to your father, 'Bonnie is a dear little girl, but without a doubt she's her mother's daughter.' You were the best-natured boy."

22   "Well I *had* everything," Ace said with an impatience that made his mother blink. He nicely dropped his cigarette into a brown flowerpot on the edge of the porch and took his daughter into his arms. She was getting heavier, solid. When he reached the end of the cement walk, his mother was still on the porch, waving to him. He was so close he could see the fat around her elbow jiggle, and he only lived a half block up the street, yet here she was, waving to him as if he was going to Japan.

23   At the door of his car, it seemed stupid to him to drive the measly half block home. His old coach, Bob Behn, used to say never to ride where you

could walk. Cars were the death of legs. Ace left the ignition keys in his pocket and ran along the pavement with Bonnie laughing and bouncing at his chest. He slammed the door of his landlady's house open and shut, pounded up the two flights of stairs, and was panting so hard when he reached the door of his apartment that it took him a couple of seconds to fit the key into the lock.

24   The run must have tuned Bonnie up. As soon as he lowered her into the crib, she began to shout and wave her arms. He didn't want to play with her. He tossed some blocks and a rattle into the crib and walked into the bathroom, where he turned on the hot water and began to comb his hair. Holding the comb under the faucet before every stroke, he combed his hair forward. It was so long, one strand curled under his nose and touched his lips. He whipped the whole mass back with a single pull. He tucked in the tufts around his ears, and ran the comb straight back on both sides of his head. With his fingers he felt for the little ridge at the back where the two sides met. It was there, as it should have been. Finally, he mussed the hair in front enough for one little lock to droop over his forehead, like Alan Ladd. It made the temple seem lower than it was. Every day, his hair-line looked higher. He had observed all around him how blond men went bald first. He remembered reading somewhere, though, that baldness shows virility.

25   On his way to the kitchen he flipped the left-hand knob of the television. Bonnie was always quieter with the set on. Ace didn't see how she could understand much of it, but it seemed to mean something to her. He found a can of beer in the refrigerator behind some brownish lettuce and those hot dogs Evey never got around to cooking. She'd be home any time. The clock said 5:12. She'd pop her lid.

26   Ace didn't see what he could do but try and reason with her. "Evey," he'd say, "you ought to thank God I got out of it. It had no future to it at all." He hoped she wouldn't get too mad, because when she was mad he wondered if he should have married her, and doubting that made him feel crowded. It was bad enough, his mother always crowding him. He punched the two triangles in the top of the beer can, the little triangle first, and then the big one, the one he drank from. He hoped Evey wouldn't say anything that couldn't be forgotten. What women didn't seem to realize was that there were things you knew but shouldn't say.

27   He felt sorry he had called the kid in the car a wop.

28   Ace balanced the beer on a corner where two rails of the crib met and looked under the chairs for the morning paper. He had trouble finding his name, because it was at the bottom of a column on an inside sports page, in a small article about the county basketball statistics:

"Dusty" Tremwick, Grosvenor Park's sure-fingered center, copped the individual scoring honors with a season's grand (and we do mean grand) total of 376 points. This is within eighteen points of the all-time record of 394 racked up in the 1949–1950 season by Olinger High's Fred Anderson.

29   Ace angrily sailed the paper into an armchair. Now it was Fred Anderson; it used to be Ace. He hated being called Fred, especially in print, but then the sportswriters were all office boys anyway, Behn used to say.

30   "Do not just ask for shoe polish," a man on television said, "but ask for *Emu Shoe Gloss,* the *only* polish that absolutely *guarantees* to make your shoes look shinier than new." Ace turned the sound off, so that the man moved his mouth like a fish blowing bubbles. Right away, Bonnie howled, so Ace turned it up loud enough to drown her out and went into the kitchen, without knowing what he wanted there. He wasn't hungry; his stomach was tight. It used to be like that when he walked to the gymnasium alone in the dark before a game and could see the people from town, kids and parents, crowding in at the lighted doors. But once he was inside, the locker room would be bright and hot, and the other guys would be there, laughing it up and towel-slapping, and the tight feeling would leave. Now there were whole days when it didn't leave.

31   A key scratched at the door lock. Ace decided to stay in the kitchen. Let *her* find *him.* Her heels clicked on the floor for a step or two; then the television set went off. Bonnie began to cry. "Shut up, honey," Evey said. There was a silence.

32   "I'm home," Ace called.

33   "No kidding. I thought Bonnie got the beer by herself."

34   Ace laughed. She was in a sarcastic mood, thinking she was Lauren Bacall. That was all right, just so she kept funny. Still smiling, Ace eased into the living room and got hit with, "What are *you* smirking about? Another question: What's the idea running up the street with Bonnie like she was a football?"

35   "You saw that?"

36   "Your mother told me."

37   "You saw her?"

38   "Of course I saw her. I dropped by to pick up Bonnie. What the hell do you think?—I read her tiny mind?"

39   "Take it easy," Ace said, wondering if Mom had told her about Friedman.

40   "Take it easy? Don't coach *me.* Another question: Why's the car out in front of her place? You give the car to her?"

41   "Look, I parked it there to pick up Bonnie, and I thought I'd leave it there."

42   "Why?"

43   "Whaddeya mean, why? I just did. I just thought I'd walk. It's not that far, you know."

44   "No, I don't know. If you'd been on your feet all day a block would look like one hell of a long way."

45   "Okay. I'm sorry."

46   She hung up her coat and stepped out of her shoes and walked around the room picking up things. She stuck the newspaper in the wastebasket.

47   Ace said, "My name was in the paper today."

48   "They spell it right?" She shoved the paper deep into the basket with her foot. There was no doubt; she knew about Friedman.

49   "They called me Fred."

50   "Isn't that your name? What *is* your name anyway? Hero J. Great?"

51   There wasn't any answer, so Ace didn't try any. He sat down on the sofa, lighted a cigarette, and waited.

52   Evey picked up Bonnie. "Poor thing stinks. What does your mother do, scrub out the toilet with her?"

53   "Can't you take it easy? I know you're tired."

54   "You should. I'm always tired."

55   Evey and Bonnie went into the bathroom; when they came out, Bonnie was clean and Evey was calm. Evey sat down in an easy chair beside Ace and rested her stocking feet on his knees. "Hit me," she said, twiddling her fingers for the cigarette.

56   The baby crawled up to her chair and tried to stand, to see what he gave her. Leaning over close to Bonnie's nose, Evey grinned, smoke leaking through her teeth, and said, "Only for grownups, honey."

57   "Eve," Ace began, "there was no future in that job. Working all Saturday, and then Friday nights on top of it."

58   "I know. Your mother told *me* all that, too. All I want from you is what happened."

59   She was going to take it like a sport, then. He tried to remember how it *did* happen. "It wasn't my fault," he said. "Friedman told me to back this '51 Chevy into the line that faces Church Street. He just bought it from an old guy this morning who said it only had thirteen thousand on it. So in I jump and start her up. There was a knock in the engine like a machine gun. I almost told Friedman he'd bought a squirrel, but you know I cut that smart stuff out ever since Palotta laid me off."

60   "You told me that story. What happens in this one?"

61   "Look Eve, I *am* telling ya. Do you want me to go out to a movie or something?"

62   "Suit yourself."

63   "So I jump in the Chevy and snap it back in line, and there was a kind of scrape and thump. I get out and look and Friedman's running over, his arms going like *this*"—Ace whirled his own arms and laughed—"and here was the whole back fender of a '49 Merc mashed in. Just looked like somebody took a planer and shaved off the bulge, you know, there at the back." He tried to show her with his hands. "The Chevy, though, didn't have a dent. It even gained some paint. But *Friedman,* to *hear* him—Boy, they can rave when their pocketbook's hit. He said"—Ace laughed again—"never mind."

64   Evey said, "You're proud of yourself."

65   "No, listen. I'm not happy about it. But there wasn't a thing I could *do*. It wasn't my driving at all. I looked over on the other side, and there was just two or three inches between the Chevy and a Buick. *Nobody* could have gotten into that hole. Even if it had hair on it." He thought this was pretty good.

66   She didn't. "You could have looked."

67   "There just wasn't the *space*. Friedman said stick it in; I stuck it in."

68   "But you could have looked and moved the other cars to make more room."

69   "I guess that would have been the smart thing."

70   "I guess, too. Now what?"

71   "What do you mean?"

72   "I mean now what? Are you going to give up? Go back to the Army? Your mother? Be a basketball pro? What?"

73   "You know I'm not tall enough. Anybody under six-six they don't want."

74   "Is that so? Six-six? Well, please listen to this, Mr. Six-Foot-Five-and-a-Half: I'm fed up. I'm ready as Christ to let you run." She stabbed her cigarette into an ashtray on the arm of the chair so hard the ashtray jumped to the floor. Evey flushed and shut up.

75   What Ace hated most in their arguments was these silences after Evey had said something so ugly she wanted to take it back. "Better ask the priest first," he murmured.

76   She sat right up. "If there's one thing I don't want to hear about from you it's priests. You let the priests to me. You don't know a damn thing about it. Not a damn thing."

77   "Hey, look at Bonnie," he said, trying to make a fresh start with his tone.

78   Evey didn't hear him. "If you think," she went on, "if for one rotten moment you think, Mr. Fred, that the be-all and end-all of my life is you and your hot-shot stunts—"

79   "Look, Mother," Ace pleaded, pointing at Bonnie. The baby had picked up the ashtray and put it on her head for a hat and was waiting for praise.

80   Evey glanced down sharply at the child. "Cute," she said. "Cute as her daddy."

81   The ashtray slid from Bonnie's head and she patted where it had been and looked around puzzled.

82   "Yeah, but watch," Ace said. "Watch her hands. They're really terrific hands."

83   "You're nuts," Evey said.

84   "No, honest. Bonnie's great. She's a natural. Get the rattle for her. Never mind, I'll get it." In two steps, Ace was at Bonnie's crib, picking the rattle out of the mess of blocks and plastic rings and beanbags. He extended the rattle toward his daughter, shaking it delicately. Made wary by this burst of attention, Bonnie reached with both hands; like two separate animals they approached from opposite sides and touched the smooth rattle simultaneously. A smile bubbled up on her face. Ace tugged weakly. She held on, and then tugged back. "She's a natural," Ace said, "and it won't do her any good because she's a girl. Baby, we got to have a boy."

85   "I'm not your baby," Evey said, closing her eyes.

86   Saying "Baby" over and over again, Ace backed up to the radio and, without turning around, switched on the volume knob. In the moment before the tubes warmed up, Evey had time to say, "Wise up, Freddy. What shall we do?"

87   The radio came in on something slow: dinner music. Ace picked Bonnie up and set her in the crib. "Shall we dance?" he asked his wife, bowing.

88   "I want to talk."

89   "Baby. It's the cocktail hour."

90   "This is getting us no place," she said, rising from her chair, though.

91   "Fred Junior. I can see him now," he said, seeing nothing.

92   "We will have no Juniors."

93   In her crib, Bonnie whimpered at the sight of her mother being seized. Ace fitted his hand into the natural place on Evey's back and she shuffled stiffly into his lead. When, with a sudden injection of saxophones, the tempo quickened, he spun her out carefully, keeping the beat with his shoulders. Her hair brushed his lips as she minced in, then swung away, to the end of his arm; he could feel her toes dig into the carpet. He flipped his own hair back from his eyes. The music ate through his skin and mixed with the nerves and small veins; he seemed to be great again, and all the other kids were around them, in a ring, clapping time.

Thinking about the Text

1. Sometimes short stories have obvious conflicts, such as good versus evil. Other times, as seems evident in "Ace in the Hole," the conflicts are more subtle. Make a list of all of the conflicts that you perceive in this short story and be prepared to share them during class discussion.

2. What do you imagine are the histories of the characters in the story? Specifically, who was Fred Anderson in high school? What do you understand about his parents? What might be his history with Evey? Use details from the story to support your views.

3. Why does Fred want to be called "Ace"? What details from the story help you understand why he prefers his high school nickname?

4. What are Ace's values? What are his concerns? What is "crowding him"? Which of his traits do you admire? Which do you dislike?

5. How many ways can you interpret the meaning of Updike's title?

WRITING FROM THE TEXT

1. Make a list of Ace's behavior and thinking patterns. Then write a character analysis of Ace that uses specific details from the text to support your perceptions of him. You may want to review the process and tips for writing a character analysis on pages 484–505.

2. Write an analysis of Ace and Evey's family life that reflects your judgment of the life they are creating for Bonnie.

3. We might be tempted to see Ace as a cocky and insensitive young man. Write an analysis of his thinking that shows that he is sensitive and concerned.

CONNECTING WITH OTHER TEXTS

1. Read or reread "Proper Care and Maintenance" (p. 186), and compare and contrast the parenting techniques and family relationships of Ace and Darnell.

2. Read "Pigskin, Patriarchy, and Pain" (p. 101) and write an analysis of how Don Sabo might perceive Ace's self image because of his high school athleticism.

3. After reading "The Second Shift" (p. 84) and "Let 'em Eat Leftovers" (p. 91), write an essay examining how Ace's behavior and attitude are weakening his marriage.

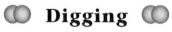 Digging

Seamus Heaney

A native of Northern Ireland, Seamus Heaney (b. 1939) is at home in Dublin as well as at Harvard University, where he teaches. Heaney is recognized as one of Ireland's finest living poets, and since his Nobel Prize for Literature in 1995, he is one of Ireland's most famous poets. His recent collections include *The Spirit Level* (1996), *Opened Ground: Selected Poems, 1966–1996* (1998), and *Electric Light* (2001). Critic Blake Morrison describes Heaney as a rare poet, one "rated highly by critics and academics yet popular with the common reader." At boarding school, where he was sent when he was eleven, Heaney read poets like Robert Frost who created poetry from their local environments. Heaney learned to value his childhood experience which he says he once "considered archaic and irrelevant to 'the modern world.'" Do you see any of Heaney's initial ambivalence about his past reflected in this early poem from *Death of a Naturalist*?

Between my finger and my thumb
The squat pen rests; snug as a gun.

Under my window, a clean rasping sound
When the spade sinks into gravelly ground:
5   My father, digging. I look down

Till his straining rump among the flowerbeds
Bends low, comes up twenty years away
Stooping in rhythm through potato drills
Where he was digging.

10   The coarse boot nestled on the lug, the shaft
Against the inside knee was levered firmly.
He rooted out tall tops, buried the bright edge deep
To scatter new potatoes that we picked
Loving their cool hardness in our hands.

15   By God, the old man could handle a spade.
Just like his old man.

My grandfather cut more turf in a day
Than any other man on Toner's bog.
Once I carried him milk in a bottle
20   Corked sloppily with paper. He straightened up
To drink it, then fell to right away
Nicking and slicing neatly, heaving sods
Over his shoulder, going down and down
For the good turf. Digging.

25   The cold smell of potato mould, the squelch and slap
Of soggy peat, the curt cuts of an edge
Through living roots awaken in my head.
But I've no spade to follow men like them.

Between my finger and my thumb
30   The squat pen rests.
I'll dig with it.

THINKING ABOUT THE TEXT

1. The speaker in the poem seems to have a pen in his hand when he is interrupted by a sound under his window. What thoughts are triggered by that sound?

2. How are the activities of the three men in this poem—the narrator and his father and grandfather—comparable? Use the text of the poem and your own thoughts to list as many comparisons as you can.

3. The narrator expresses his pride in the manual skills of his father and his grandfather, but he decides to follow a career that uses a different tool. Which lines in the poem show the speaker's perception of the work of his forefathers? Which lines reflect his own decision and the reasons for it?

4. In what specific ways does the title of the poem link all three generations?

WRITING FROM THE TEXT

1. Using the poem as a reference, copy all of the definitions of the words "dig" and "digging." Then write an analysis of the poem that shows how knowing these definitions contributes to an understanding of the poem.

2. Write an essay that illustrates how the negative images in the poem help the narrator decide not to follow his father's and grandfather's choice of work. (See p. 475 for a definition and discussion of image.)

3. Write an essay that shows a specific moment in your life when you realized that you would not follow the paths of your family members. (See p. 417 for a discussion of "showing" in a narrative.)

CONNECTING WITH OTHER TEXTS

1. In Seamus Heaney's poem, the narrator-son has an epiphany—a moment of realization—and decides to depart from family tradition. In Eric Marcus's "Ignorance Is Not Bliss" (p. 14), the author also departs from his family's expectations by telling his grandmother of his sexual identity. Using details from both works, write an essay that focuses on the importance and difficulty of revealing a choice that deviates from family expectations.

2. In "Proper Care and Maintenance" (p. 186), Darnell has an epiphany that helps him determine how to get a job. Compare or contrast his moment of sudden insight with the epiphany of the narrator in "Digging." (See pp. 439–441 for information on how to write a comparison-contrast paper.)

Your Place Is Empty
Anne Tyler

Known to many as the author of *The Accidental Tourist*, Anne Tyler (b. 1941) is a critically acclaimed writer of many other novels and of short fiction. She is the author of *A Patchwork Planet* (1988), *Breathing Lessons* (1988), for which she won the Pulitzer Prize, and *Back When We Were Grownups* (2001). She grew up in a number of Quaker communities in the Midwest and the South. It was this "setting-apart situation" and her attempt "to fit into the outside world" that helped mold Tyler into a writer. "I don't talk well," she writes. "For me, writing something down was the only road out." A theme that runs through Tyler's work, and that you may recognize in the following story, is that people cannot fully communicate with one another. This story first appeared in the *New Yorker* in 1976.

1   Early in October, Hassan Ardavi invited his mother to come from Iran for a visit. His mother accepted immediately. It wasn't clear how long the visit was to last. Hassan's wife thought three months would be a good length of time. Hassan himself had planned on six months, and said so in his letter of invitation. But his mother felt that after such a long trip six months would be too short, and she was counting on staying a year. Hassan's little girl, who wasn't yet two, had no idea of time at all. She was told that her grandmother was coming but she soon forgot about it.

2   Hassan's wife was named Elizabeth, not an easy word for Iranians to pronounce. She would have been recognized as American the world over—a blond, pretty girl with long bones and an ungraceful way of walking. One of her strong points was an ability to pick up foreign languages, and before her mother-in-law's arrival she bought a textbook and taught herself Persian. "*Salaam aleikum*," she told the mirror every morning. Her daughter watched, startled, from her place on the potty-chair. Elizabeth ran through possible situations in her mind and looked up the words for them. "Would you like more tea? Do you take sugar?" At suppertime she spoke Persian to her husband, who looked amused at the new tone she gave his language, with her flat, factual American voice. He wrote his mother and told her Elizabeth had a surprise for her.

3   Their house was a three-story brick Colonial, but only the first two stories were in use. Now they cleared the third of its trunks and china barrels and *National Geographics*, and they moved in a few pieces of furniture. Elizabeth sewed flowered curtains for the window. She was unusually careful with them; to a foreign mother-in-law, fine seams might matter. Also, Hassan bought a pocket compass, which he placed in the top dresser drawer. "For her prayers," he said. "She'll want to face Mecca. She prays three times a day."

4   "But which direction is Mecca from here?" Elizabeth asked.

5   Hassan only shrugged. He had never said the prayers himself, not even as a child. His earliest memory was of tickling the soles of his mother's feet while she prayed steadfastly on; everyone knew it was forbidden to pause once you'd started.

6   Mrs. Ardavi felt nervous about the descent from the plane. She inched down the staircase sideways, one hand tight on the railing, the other clutching her shawl. It was night, and cold. The air seemed curiously opaque. She arrived on solid ground and stood collecting herself—a small, stocky woman in black, with a kerchief over her smooth gray hair. She held her back very straight, as if she had just had her feelings hurt. In picturing this moment she had always thought Hassan would be waiting beside the plane, but there was no sign of him. Blue lights dotted the darkness behind her, an angular terminal loomed ahead, and an official was herding the passengers toward a plate-glass door. She followed, entangled in a web of meaningless sounds such as those you might hear in a fever dream.

7   Immigration. Baggage Claims. Customs. To all she spread her hands and beamed and shrugged, showing she spoke no English. Meanwhile her fellow-passengers waved to a blur of faces beyond a glass wall. It seemed they all knew people here; she was the only one who didn't. She had issued from the plane like a newborn baby, speechless and friendless. And the customs official didn't seem pleased with her. She had brought too many gifts. She had stuffed her bags with them, discarding all but the most necessary pieces of her clothing so that she would have more room. There were silver tea sets and gold jewelry for her daughter-in-law, and for her granddaughter a doll dressed in the complicated costume of a nomad tribe, an embroidered sheepskin vest, and two religious medals on chains—one a disc inscribed with the name of Allah, the other a tiny gold Koran, with a very effective prayer for long life folded up within it. The customs official sifted gold through his fingers like sand and frowned at the Koran. "Have I done something wrong?" she asked. But of course he didn't understand her. Though you'd think, really, that if he would just *listen* hard enough, just meet her eyes once . . . it was a very simple language, there was no reason why it shouldn't come through to him.

8   For Hassan, she'd brought food. She had gathered all his favorite foods and put them in a drawstring bag embroidered with peacocks. When the official opened the bag he said something under his breath and called another man over. Together they unwrapped tiny newspaper packets and sniffed at various herbs. "Sumac," she told them. "Powder of lemons. *Shambahleh.*" They gazed at her blankly. They untied a small cloth sack and rummaged through the *kashk* she had brought for soup. It rolled beneath their fingers and across the counter—hard white balls of yogurt curd, stuck with bits of sheep hair and manure. Some peasant had labored for hours to make that *kashk.* Mrs. Ardavi picked up one piece and replaced it firmly in the sack. Maybe the official understood her meaning: she was running out of patience. He threw up his hands. He slid her belongings down the counter. She was free to go.

9   Free to go where?

10   Dazed and stumbling, a pyramid of knobby parcels and bags, scraps of velvet and brocade and tapestry, she made her way to the glass wall. A door opened out of nowhere and a stranger blocked her path. "Khanom Jun," he said. It was a name that only her children would use, but she passed him blindly and he had to touch her arm before she would look up.

11   He had put on weight. She didn't know him. The last time she'd seen him he was a thin, stoop-shouldered medical student disappearing into an Air France jet without a backward glance. "Khanom Jun, it's me," this stranger said, but she went on searching his face with cloudy eyes. No doubt he was a bearer of bad news. Was that it? A recurrent dream had warned her that she would never see her son again—that he would die on his way to the airport, or had already been dead for months but no one wanted to break the news; some second or third cousin in America had continued signing Hassan's name to his cheerful, anonymous letters. Now here was this man with graying hair and a thick mustache, his clothes American but his face Iranian, his eyes sadly familiar, as if they belonged to someone else. "Don't you believe me?" he said. He kissed her on both cheeks. It was his smell she recognized first—a pleasantly bitter, herblike smell that brought her the image of Hassan as a child, reaching thin arms around her neck. "It's you, Hassan," she said, and then she started crying against his gray tweed shoulder.

12   They were quiet during the long drive home. Once she reached over to touch his face, having wanted to do so for miles. None of the out-of-focus snapshots he'd sent had prepared her for the way he had aged. "How long has it been?" she asked. "Twelve years?" But both of them knew to the day how long it had been. All those letters of hers: "My dear Hassan, ten years now and still your place is empty." "Eleven years and still . . ."

13   Hassan squinted through the windshield at the oncoming headlights. His mother started fretting over her kerchief, which she knew she ought not to have worn. She'd been told so by her youngest sister, who had been to America twice. "It marks you," her sister had said. But that square of silk was the last, shrunken reminder of the veil she used to hide beneath, before the previous Shah had banished such things. At her age, how could she expose herself? And then her teeth; her teeth were a problem too. Her youngest sister had said, "You ought to get dentures made, I'm sure there aren't three whole teeth in your head." But Mrs. Ardavi was scared of dentists. Now she covered her mouth with one hand and looked sideways at Hassan, though so far he hadn't seemed to notice. He was busy maneuvering his car into the right-hand lane.

14   This silence was the last thing she had expected. For weeks she'd been saving up stray bits of gossip, weaving together the family stories she would tell him. There were three hundred people in her family—most of them related to each other in three or four different ways, all leading intricate and scandalous lives she had planned to discuss in detail, but instead she stared sadly out the window. You'd think Hassan would ask. You'd think they could have a better conversation than this, after such a long time. Disappointment made her cross, and now she stubbornly refused to speak even when she saw something she wanted to comment on, some imposing building or unfamiliar brand of car sliding past her into the darkness.

15   By the time they arrived it was nearly midnight. None of the houses were lit but Hassan's—worn brick, older than she would have expected. "Here we are," said Hassan. The competence with which he parked the car, fitting it neatly into a small space by the curb, put him firmly on the other side of the fence, the American side. She would have to face her daughter-in-law alone. As they climbed the front steps she whispered, "How do you say it again?"

16   "Say what?" Hassan asked.

17   "Her name. Lizabet?"

18   "Elizabeth. Like Elizabeth Taylor. *You* know."

19   "Yes, yes, of course," said his mother. Then she lifted her chin, holding tight to the straps of her purse.

20   Elizabeth was wearing bluejeans and a pair of fluffy slippers. Her hair was blond as corn silk, cut short and straight, and her face had the grave, sleepy look of a child's. As soon as she had opened the door she said, *"Salaam aleikum."* Mrs. Ardavi, overcome with relief at the Persian greeting, threw her arms around her and kissed both cheeks. Then they led her into the living room, which looked comfortable but a little too plain. The furniture was straight-edged, the rugs uninteresting, though the curtains had a nice figured pattern that caught her eye. In one corner sat a shiny red kiddie car complete

with license plates. "Is that the child's?" she asked. "Hilary's?" She hesitated over the name. "Could I see her?"

21   *"Now?"* said Hassan.

22   But Elizabeth told him, "That's all right." (Women understood these things.) She beckoned to her mother-in-law. They climbed the stairs together, up to the second floor, into a little room that smelled of milk and rubber and talcum powder, smells she would know anywhere. Even in the half-light from the hallway, she could tell that Hilary was beautiful. She had black, tumbling hair, long black lashes, and skin of a tone they called wheat-colored, lighter than Hassan's. "There," said Elizabeth. "Thank you," said Mrs. Ardavi. Her voice was formal, but this was her first grandchild and it took her a moment to recover herself. Then they stepped back into the hallway. "I brought her some medals," she whispered. "I hope you don't mind."

23   "Medals?" said Elizabeth. She repeated the word anxiously, mispronouncing it.

24   "Only an Allah and a Koran, both very tiny. You'll hardly know they're there. I'm not used to seeing a child without a medal. It worries me."

25   Automatically her fingers traced a chain around her neck, ending in the hollow of her collarbone. Elizabeth nodded, looking relieved. *"Oh* yes. Medals," she said.

26   "Is that all right?"

27   "Yes, of course."

28   Mrs. Ardavi took heart. "Hassan laughs," she said. "He doesn't believe in these things. But when he left I put a prayer in his suitcase pocket, and you see he's been protected. Now if Hilary wore a medal, I could sleep nights."

29   "Of course," Elizabeth said again.

30   When they re-entered the living room, Mrs. Ardavi was smiling, and she kissed Hassan on the top of his head before she sat down.

31   American days were tightly scheduled, divided not into morning and afternoon but into 9:00, 9:30, and so forth, each half hour possessing its own set activity. It was marvellous. Mrs. Ardavi wrote her sisters: "They're more organized here. My daughter-in-law never wastes a minute." How terrible, her sisters wrote back. They were all in Teheran, drinking cup after cup of tea and idly guessing who might come and visit. "No, you misunderstand," Mrs. Ardavi protested. "I like it this way. I'm fitting in wonderfully." And to her youngest sister she wrote, "You'd think I was American. No one guesses otherwise." This wasn't true, of course, but she hoped it would be true in the future.

32   Hassan was a doctor. He worked long hours, from six in the morning until six at night. While she was still washing for her morning prayers she could hear him tiptoe down the stairs and out the front door. His car would start

up, a distant rumble far below her, and from her bathroom window she could watch it swing out from beneath a tatter of red leaves and round the corner and disappear. Then she would sigh and return to her sink. Before prayers she had to wash her face, her hands, and the soles of her feet. She had to draw her wet fingers down the part in her hair. After that she returned to her room, where she swathed herself tightly in her long black veil and knelt on a beaded velvet prayer mat. East was where the window was, curtained by chintz and misted over. On the east wall she hung a lithograph of the Caliph Ali and a color snapshot of her third son, Babak, whose marriage she had arranged just a few months before this visit. If Babak hadn't married, she never could have come. He was the youngest, spoiled by being the only son at home. It had taken her three years to find a wife for him. (One was too modern, one too lazy, one so perfect she had been suspicious.) But finally the proper girl had turned up, modest and well-mannered and sufficiently wide of hip, and Mrs. Ardavi and the bridal couple had settled in a fine new house on the outskirts of Teheran. Now every time she prayed, she added a word of thanks that at last she had a home for her old age. After that, she unwound her veil and laid it carefully in a drawer. From another drawer she took thick cotton stockings and elastic garters; she stuffed her swollen feet into open-toed vinyl sandals. Unless she was going out, she wore a housecoat. It amazed her how wasteful Americans were with their clothing.

33   Downstairs, Elizabeth would have started her tea and buttered a piece of toast for her. Elizabeth and Hilary ate bacon and eggs, but bacon of course was unclean and Mrs. Ardavi never accepted any. Nor had it even been offered to her, except once, jokingly, by Hassan. The distinctive, smoky smell rose to meet her as she descended the stairs. "What does it taste like?" she always asked. She was dying to know. But Elizabeth's vocabulary didn't cover the taste of bacon; she only said it was salty and then laughed and gave up. They had learned very early to travel a well-worn conversational path, avoiding the dead ends caused by unfamiliar words. "Did you sleep well?" Elizabeth always asked in her funny, childish accent, and Mrs. Ardavi answered, "So-so." Then they would turn and watch Hilary, who sat on a booster seat eating scrambled eggs, a thin chain of Persian gold crossing the back of her neck. Conversation was easier, or even unnecessary, as long as Hilary was there.

34   In the mornings Elizabeth cleaned house. Mrs. Ardavi used that time for letter writing. She had dozens of letters to write, to all her aunts and uncles and her thirteen sisters. (Her father had had three wives, and a surprising number of children even for that day and age.) Then there was Babak. His wife was in her second month of pregnancy, so Mrs. Ardavi wrote long ac-

counts of the American child-rearing methods. "There are some things I don't agree with," she wrote. "They let Hilary play outdoors by herself, with not even a servant to keep an eye on her." Then she would trail off and gaze thoughtfully at Hilary, who sat on the floor watching a television program called "Captain Kangaroo."

35   Mrs. Ardavi's own childhood had been murky and grim. From the age of nine she was wrapped in a veil, one corner of it clenched in her teeth to hide her face whenever she appeared on the streets. Her father, a respected man high up in public life, used to chase servant girls through the halls and trap them, giggling, in vacant bedrooms. At the age of ten she was forced to watch her mother bleed to death in childbirth, and when she screamed the midwife had struck her across the face and held her down till she had properly kissed her mother goodbye. There seemed no connection at all between her and this little overalled American. At times, when Hilary had one of her temper tantrums, Mrs. Ardavi waited in horror for Elizabeth to slap her and then, when no slap came, felt a mixture of relief and anger. "In Iran—" she would begin, and if Hassan was there he always said, "But this is not Iran, remember?"

36   After lunch Hilary took a nap, and Mrs. Ardavi went upstairs to say her noontime prayers and take a nap as well. Then she might do a little laundry in her bathtub. Laundry was a problem here. Although she liked Elizabeth, the fact was that the girl was a Christian, and therefore unclean; it would never do to have a Christian wash a Moslem's clothes. The automatic dryer was also unclean, having contained, at some point, a Christian's underwear. So she had to ask Hassan to buy her a drying rack. It came unassembled. Elizabeth put it together for her, stick by stick, and then Mrs. Ardavi held it under her shower and rinsed it off, hoping that would be enough to remove any taint. The Koran didn't cover this sort of situation.

37   When Hilary was up from her nap they walked her to the park—Elizabeth in her eternal bluejeans and Mrs. Ardavi in her kerchief and shawl, taking short painful steps in small shoes that bulged over her bunions. They still hadn't seen to her teeth, although by now Hassan had noticed them. She was hoping he might forget about the dentist, but then she saw him remembering every time she laughed and revealed her five brown teeth set wide apart.

38   At the park she laughed a great deal. It was her only way of communicating with the other women. They sat on the benches ringing the playground, and while Elizabeth translated their questions Mrs. Ardavi laughed and nodded at them over and over. "They want to know if you like it here," Elizabeth said. Mrs. Ardavi answered at length, but Elizabeth's translation was very short. Then gradually the other women forgot her, and conversation rattled

on while she sat silent and watched each speaker's lips. The few recognizable words—"telephone," "television," "radio"—gave her the impression that American conversations were largely technical, even among women. Their gestures were wide and slow, disproving her youngest sister's statement that in America everyone was in a hurry. On the contrary, these women were dreamlike, moving singly or in twos across wide flat spaces beneath white November skies when they departed.

39   Later, at home, Mrs. Ardavi would say, "The red-haired girl, is she pregnant? She looked it, I thought. Is the fat girl happy in her marriage?" She asked with some urgency, plucking Elizabeth's sleeve when she was slow to answer. People's private lives fascinated her. On Saturday trips to the supermarket she liked to single out some interesting stranger. "What's the matter with that *jerky*-moving man? That girl, is she one of your dark-skinned people?" Elizabeth answered too softly, and never seemed to follow Mrs. Ardavi's pointing finger.

40   Supper was difficult; Mrs. Ardavi didn't like American food. Even when Elizabeth made something Iranian, it had an American taste to it—the vegetables still faintly crisp, the onions transparent rather than nicely blackened. "Vegetables not thoroughly cooked retain a certain acidity," Mrs. Ardavi said, laying down her fork. "This is a cause of constipation and stomach aches. At night I often have heartburn. It's been three full days since I moved my bowels." Elizabeth merely bent over her plate, offering no symptoms of her own in return. Hassan said, "At the table, Khanom? At the table?"

41   Eventually she decided to cook supper herself. Over Elizabeth's protests she began at three every afternoon, filling the house with the smell of dillweed and arranging pots on counters and cabinets and finally, when there was no more space, on the floor. She squatted on the floor with her skirt tucked between her knees and stirred great bowls of minced greens while behind her, on the gas range, four different pots of food bubbled and steamed. The kitchen was becoming more homelike, she thought. A bowl of yogurt brewed beside the stove, a kettle of rice soaked in the sink, and the top of the dishwasher was curlicued with the yellow dye from saffron. In one corner sat the pudding pan, black on the bottom from the times she had cooked down sugar to make a sweet for her intestines. "Now, this is your rest period," she always told Elizabeth. "Come to the table in three hours and be surprised." But Elizabeth only hovered around the kitchen, disturbing the serene, steam-filled air with clatter and slams as she put away pots, or pacing between stove and sink, her arms folded across her chest. At supper she ate little; Mrs. Ardavi wondered how Americans got so tall on such small suppers. Hassan,

on the other hand, had second and third helpings. "I must be gaining five pounds a week," he said. "None of my clothes fit."

42   "That's good to hear," said his mother. And Elizabeth added something but in English, which Hassan answered in English also. Often now they broke into English for paragraphs at a time—Elizabeth speaking softly, looking at her plate, and Hassan answering at length and sometimes reaching across the table to cover her hand.

43   At night, after her evening prayers, Mrs. Ardavi watched television on the living-room couch. She brought her veil downstairs and wrapped it around her to keep the drafts away. Her shoes lay on the rug beneath her, and scattered down the length of the couch were her knitting bag, her sack of burned sugar, her magnifying glass, and *My First Golden Dictionary.* Elizabeth read novels in an easy chair, and Hassan watched TV so that he could translate the difficult parts of the plot. Not that Mrs. Ardavi had much trouble. American plots were easy to guess at, particularly the Westerns. And when the program was boring—a documentary or a special news feature—she could pass the time by talking to Hassan. "Your cousin Farah wrote," she said. "Do you remember her? A homely girl, too dark. She's getting a divorce and in my opinion it's fortunate; he's from a lower class. Do you remember Farah?"

44   Hassan only grunted, his eyes on the screen. He was interested in American politics. So was she, for that matter. She had wept for President Kennedy, and carried Jackie's picture in her purse. But these news programs were long and dry, and if Hassan wouldn't talk she was forced to turn at last to her *Golden Dictionary.*

45   In her childhood, she had been taught by expensive foreign tutors. Her mind was her great gift, the compensation for a large, plain face and a stocky figure. But now what she had learned seemed lost, forgotten utterly or fogged by years, so that Hassan gave a snort whenever she told him some fact that she had dredged up from her memory. It seemed that everything she studied now had to penetrate through a great thick layer before it reached her mind. "Tonk you," she practiced. "Tonk you. Tonk you." "Thank you," Hassan corrected her. He pointed out useful words in her dictionary—grocery-store words, household words—but she grew impatient with their woodenness. What she wanted was the language to display her personality, her famous courtesy, and her magical intuition about the inside lives of other people. Nightly she learned "salt," "bread," "spoon," but with an inner sense of dullness, and every morning when she woke her English was once again confined to "thank you" and "NBC."

46   Elizabeth, meanwhile, read on, finishing one book and reaching for the next without even glancing up. Hassan chewed a thumbnail and watched a senator. He shouldn't be disturbed, of course, but time after time his mother

felt the silence and the whispery turning of pages stretching her nerves until she had to speak. "Hassan?"

47 "Hmm."

48 "My chest seems tight. I'm sure a cold is coming on. Don't you have a tonic?"

49 "No," said Hassan.

50 He dispensed medicines all day; he listened to complaints. Common sense told her to stop, but she persisted, encouraged by some demon that wouldn't let her tongue lie still. "Don't you have some syrup? What about that liquid you gave me for constipation? Would that help?"

51 "No, it wouldn't," said Hassan.

52 He drove her on, somehow. The less he gave, the more she had to ask. "Well, aspirin? Vitamins?" Until Hassan said, "Will you just let me *watch?*" Then she could lapse into silence again, or even gather up the clutter of her belongings and bid the two of them good night.

53 She slept badly. Often she lay awake for hours, fingering the edge of the sheet and staring at the ceiling. Memories crowded in on her, old grievances and fears, injustices that had never been righted. For the first time in years she thought of her husband, a gentle, weak man given to surprising outbursts of temper. She hadn't loved him when she married him, and at his death from a liver ailment six years later her main feeling had been resentment. Was it fair to be widowed so young, while other women were supported and protected? She had moved from her husband's home back to the old family estate, where five of her sisters still lived. There she had stayed till Babak's wedding, drinking tea all day with her sisters and pulling the strings by which the rest of the family was attached. Marriages were arranged, funerals attended, childbirth discussed in fine detail; servants' disputes were settled, and feuds patched up and then restarted. Her husband's face had quickly faded, leaving only a vacant spot in her mind. But now she could see him so clearly—a wasted figure on his deathbed, beard untrimmed, turban coming loose, eyes imploring her for something more than an absent-minded pat on the cheek as she passed through his room on her way to check the children.

54 She saw the thin faces of her three small boys as they sat on the rug eating rice. Hassan was the stubborn, mischievous one, with perpetual scabs on his knees. Babak was the cuddly one. Ali was the oldest, who had caused so much worry—weak, like his father, demanding, but capable of turning suddenly charming. Four years ago he had died of a brain hemorrhage, slumping over a dinner table in faraway Shiraz, where he'd gone to be free of his wife, who was also his double first cousin. Ever since he was born he had disturbed his mother's sleep, first because she worried over what he would

amount to and now, after his death, because she lay awake listing all she had done wrong with him. She had been too lenient. No, too harsh. There was no telling. Mistakes she had made floated on the ceiling like ghosts— allowances she'd made when she knew she shouldn't have, protections he had not deserved, blows which perhaps he had not deserved either.

55   She would have liked to talk to Hassan about it, but any time she tried he changed the subject. Maybe he was angry about the way he had heard of Ali's death. It was customary to break such news gradually. She had started a series of tactful letters, beginning by saying that Ali was seriously ill when in truth he was already buried. Something in the letter had given her away— perhaps her plans for a rest cure by the seaside, which she never would have considered if she'd had an ailing son at home. Hassan had telephoned over- seas, taking three nights to reach her. "Tell me what's wrong," he said. "I know there's something." When her tears kept her from answering, he asked, "Is he dead?" His voice sounded angry, but that might have been due to a poor connection. And when he hung up, cutting her off before she could say all she wanted, she thought, I should have told him straight out. I had for- gotten that about him. Now when she spoke of Ali he listened politely, with his face frozen. She would have told him anything, all about the death and burial and that witch of a wife throwing herself, too late, into the grave; but Hassan never asked.

56   Death was moving in on her. Oh, not on her personally (the women in her family lived a century or longer, burying the men one by one) but on everybody around her, all the cousins and uncles and brothers-in-law. No sooner had she laid away her mourning clothes than it was time to bring them out again. Recently she had begun to feel she would outlive her two other sons as well, and she fought off sleep because of the dreams it brought—Babak lying stiff and cold in his grave, Hassan crumpled over in some dark American alley. Terrifying images would zoom at her out of the night. In the end she had to wrap herself in her veil and sleep instead on the Persian rug, which had the dusty smell of home and was, anyway, more com- fortable than her unsteady foreign mattress.

57   At Christmas time, Hassan and Elizabeth gave Mrs. Ardavi a brightly col- ored American dress with short sleeves. She wore it to an Iranian party, even leaving off her kerchief in a sudden fit of daring. Everyone commented on how nice she looked. "Really you fit right in," a girl told her. "May I write to my mother about you? She was over here for a year and a half and never once stepped out of the house without her kerchief." Mrs. Ardavi beamed. It was true she would never have associated with these people at home—children of civil servants and bank clerks, newly rich now they'd finished medical school. The wives called their husbands "Doctor" even in direct address. But still it felt

good to be speaking so much Persian; her tongue nearly ran away with her. "I see you're expecting a baby," she said to one of the wives. "Is it your first? I could tell by your eyes. Now don't be nervous. I had three myself; my mother had seven and never felt a pain in her life. She would squat down to serve my father's breakfast and 'Eh?' she would say. 'Aga Jun, it's the baby!' and there it would be on the floor between her feet, waiting for her to cut the cord and finish pouring the tea." She neglected to mention how her mother had died. All her natural tact came back to her, her gift with words and her knowledge of how to hold an audience. She bubbled and sparkled like a girl, and her face fell when it was time to go home.

58   After the party, she spent two or three days noticing more keenly than ever the loss of her language, and talking more feverishly when Hassan came home in the evening. This business of being a foreigner was something changeable. Boundaries kept shifting, and sometimes it was she who was the foreigner but other times Elizabeth, or even Hassan. (Wasn't it true, she often wondered, that there was a greater distance between men and women than between Americans and Iranians, or even *Eskimos* and Iranians?) Hassan was the foreigner when she and Elizabeth conspired to hide a miniature Koran in his glove compartment; he would have laughed at them. "You see," she told Elizabeth, "I know there's nothing to it, but it makes me feel better. When my sons were born I took them all to the bath attendant to have their blood let. People say it brings long life. I know that's superstition, but whenever afterward I saw those ridges down their backs I felt safe. Don't you understand?" And Elizabeth said, "Of course." She smuggled the Koran into the car herself, and hid it beneath the Texaco maps. Hassan saw nothing.

59   Hilary was a foreigner forever. She dodged her grandmother's yearning hands, and when the grownups spoke Persian she fretted and misbehaved and pulled on Elizabeth's sleeve. Mrs. Ardavi had to remind herself constantly not to kiss the child too much, not to reach out for a hug, not to offer her lap. In this country people kept more separate. They kept so separate that at times she felt hurt. They tried to be so subtle, so undemonstrative. She would never understand this place.

60   In January they took her to a dentist, who made clucking noises when he looked in her mouth. "What does he say?" she asked. "Tell me the worst." But Hassan was talking in a low voice to Elizabeth, and he waved her aside. They seemed to be having a misunderstanding of some sort. "What does he *say*, Hassan?"

61   "Just a minute."

62   She craned around in the high-backed chair, fighting off the dentist's little mirror. "I have to know," she told Hassan.

63   "He says your teeth are terrible. They have to be extracted and the gums surgically smoothed. He wants to know if you'll be here for another few months; he can't schedule you till later."

64   A cold lump of fear swelled in her stomach. Unfortunately she *would* be here; it had only been three months so far and she was planning to stay a year. So she had to watch numbly while her life was signed away, whole strings of appointments made, and little white cards filled out. And Hassan didn't even look sympathetic. He was still involved in whatever this argument was with Elizabeth. The two of them failed to notice how her hands were shaking.

65   It snowed all of January, the worst snow they had had in years. When she came downstairs in the mornings she found the kitchen icy cold, crisscrossed by drafts. "The sort of cold enters your bones," she told Elizabeth. "I'm sure to fall sick." Elizabeth only nodded. Some mornings now her face was pale and puffy, as if she had a secret worry, but Mrs. Ardavi had learned that it was better not to ask about it.

66   Early in February there was a sudden warm spell. Snow melted and all the trees dripped in the sunshine. "We're going for a walk," Elizabeth said, and Mrs. Ardavi said, "I'll come too." In spite of the warmth, she toiled upstairs for her woolen shawl. She didn't like to take chances. And she worried over Hilary's bare ears. "Won't she catch cold?" she asked. "I think we should cover her head."

67   "She'll be all right," said Elizabeth, and then shut her face in a certain stubborn way she had.

68   In the park, Elizabeth and Hilary made snowballs from the last of the snow and threw them at each other, narrowly missing Mrs. Ardavi, who stood watching with her arms folded and her hands tucked in her sleeves.

69   The next morning, something was wrong with Hilary. She sat at the breakfast table and cried steadily, refusing all food. "Now, now," her grandmother said, "won't you tell old Ka Jun what's wrong?" But when she came close Hilary screamed louder. By noon she was worse. Elizabeth called Hassan, and he came home immediately and laid a hand on Hilary's forehead and said she should go to the pediatrician. He drove them there himself. "It's her ears, I'm sure of it," Mrs. Ardavi said in the waiting room. For some reason Hassan grew angry. "Do you always know better than the experts?" he asked her. "What are we coming to the doctor for? We could have talked to you and saved the trip." His mother lowered her eyes and examined her purse straps. She understood that he was anxious, but all the same her feelings were hurt and when they rose to go into the office she stayed behind.

70   Later Hassan came back and sat down again. "There's an infection in her middle ear," he told her. "The doctor's going to give her a shot of penicillin." His mother nodded, careful not to annoy him by reminding him she had thought as much. Then Hilary started crying. She must be getting her shot now. Mrs. Ardavi herself was terrified of needles, and she sat gripping her purse until her fingers turned white, staring around the waiting room, which seemed pathetically cheerful, with its worn wooden toys and nursery-school paintings. Her own ear ached in sympathy. She thought of a time when she had boxed Ali's ears too hard and he had wept all that day and gone to sleep sucking his thumb.

71   While Hassan was there she was careful not to say anything, but the following morning at breakfast she said, "Elizabeth dear, do you remember that walk we took day before yesterday?"

72   "Yes," said Elizabeth. She was squeezing oranges for Hilary, who'd grown cheerful again and was eating a huge breakfast.

73   "Remember I said Hilary should wear a hat? Now you see you should have been more careful. Because of you she fell sick; she could have died. Do you see that now?"

74   "No," said Elizabeth.

75   Was her Persian that scanty? Lately it seemed to have shrunk and hardened, like a stale piece of bread. Mrs. Ardavi sighed and tried again. "Without a hat, you see—" she began. But Elizabeth had set down her orange, picked up Hilary, and walked out of the room. Mrs. Ardavi stared after her, wondering if she'd said something wrong.

76   For the rest of the day, Elizabeth was busy in her room. She was cleaning out bureaus and closets. A couple of times Mrs. Ardavi advanced as far as the doorway, where she stood awkwardly watching. Hilary sat on the floor playing with a discarded perfume bottle. Everything, it seemed, was about to be thrown away—buttonless blouses and stretched-out sweaters, stockings and combs and empty lipstick tubes. "Could I be of any help?" Mrs. Ardavi asked, but Elizabeth said, "Oh, no. Thank you very much." Her voice was cheerful. Yet when Hassan came home he went upstairs and stayed a long time, and the door remained shut behind him.

77   Supper that night was an especially fine stew, Hassan's favorite ever since childhood, but he didn't say a word about it. He hardly spoke at all, in fact. Then later, when Elizabeth was upstairs putting Hilary to bed, he said, "Khanom Jun, I want to talk to you."

78   "Yes, Hassan," she said, laying aside her knitting. She was frightened by his seriousness, the black weight of his mustache, and her own father's deep black eyes. But what had she done? She knotted her hands and looked up at him, swallowing.

79   "I understand you've been interfering," he said.

80   "I, Hassan?"

81   "Elizabeth isn't the kind you can do that with. And she's raising the child just fine on her own."

82   "Well, of course she is," said his mother. "Did I ever say otherwise?"

83   "Show it, then. Don't offer criticisms."

84   "Very well," she said. She picked up her knitting and began counting stitches, as if she'd forgotten the conversation entirely. But that evening she was unusually quiet, and at nine o'clock she excused herself to go to bed. "So early?" Hassan asked.

85   "I'm tired," she told him, and left with her back very straight.

86   Her room surrounded her like a nest. She had built up layers of herself on every surface—tapestries and bits of lace and lengths of paisley. The bureau was covered with gilt-framed pictures of the saints, and snapshots of her sisters at family gatherings. On the windowsill were little plants in orange and aqua plastic pots—her favorite American colors. Her bedside table held bottles of medicine, ivory prayer beads, and a tiny brick of holy earth. The rest of the house was bare and shiny, impersonal; this room was as comforting as her shawl.

87   Still, she didn't sleep well. Ghosts rose up again, tugging at her thoughts. Why did things turn out so badly for her? Her father had preferred her brothers, a fact that crushed her even after all these years. Her husband had had three children by her and then complained that she was cold. And what comfort were children? If she had stayed in Iran any longer Babak would have asked her to move; she'd seen it coming. There'd been some disrespect creeping into his bride's behavior, some unwillingness to take advice, which Babak had overlooked even when his mother pointed it out to him. And Hassan was worse—always so stubborn, much too independent. She had offered him anything if he would just stay in Iran but he had said no; he was set on leaving her. And he had flatly refused to take along his cousin Shora as his wife, though everyone pointed out how lonely he would be. He was so anxious to break away, to get *going,* to come to this hardhearted country and take up with a Christian girl. Oh, she should have laughed when he left, and saved her tears for someone more deserving. She never should have come here, she never should have asked anything of him again. When finally she went to sleep it seemed that her eyes remained open, burning large and dry beneath her lids.

88   In the morning she had a toothache. She could hardly walk for the pain. It was only Friday (the first of her dental appointments was for Monday), but the dentist made time for her during the afternoon and pulled the tooth. Elizabeth said it wouldn't hurt, but it did. Elizabeth treated it as something insignificant, merely a small break in her schedule, which required the hiring

of a babysitter. She wouldn't even call Hassan home from work. "What could he do?" she asked.

89   So when Hassan returned that evening it was all a surprise to him—the sight of his mother with a bloody cotton cylinder hanging out over her lower lip like a long tooth. "What *happened* to you?" he asked. To make it worse, Hilary was screaming and had been all afternoon. Mrs. Ardavi put her hands over her ears, wincing. "Will you make that child hush?" Hassan told Elizabeth. "I think we should get my mother to bed." He guided her toward the stairs, and she allowed herself to lean on him. "It's mainly my heart," she said. "You know how scared I am of dentists." When he had folded back her bedspread and helped her to lie down she closed her eyes gratefully, resting one arm across her forehead. Even the comfort of hot tea was denied her; she had to stay on cold foods for twelve hours. Hassan fixed her a glass of ice water. He was very considerate, she thought. He seemed as shaken at the sight of her as Hilary had been. All during the evening he kept coming to check on her, and twice in the night she heard him climbing the stairs to listen at her door. When she moaned he called, "Are you awake?"

90   "Of course," she said.

91   "Can I get you anything?"

92   "No, no."

93   In the morning she descended the stairs with slow, groping feet, keeping a tight hold on the railing. "It was a very hard night," she said. "At four my gum started throbbing. Is that normal? I think these American pain pills are constipating. Maybe a little prune juice would restore my regularity."

94   "I'll get it," Hassan said. "You sit down. Did you take the milk of magnesia?"

95   "Oh, yes, but I'm afraid it wasn't enough," she said.

96   Elizabeth handed Hassan a platter of bacon, not looking at him.

97   After breakfast, while Hassan and his mother were still sitting over their tea, Elizabeth started cleaning the kitchen. She made quite a bit of noise. She sorted the silverware and then went through a tangle of utensils, discarding bent spatulas and rusty tongs. "May I help?" asked Mrs. Ardavi. Elizabeth shook her head. She seemed to have these fits of throwing things away. Now she was standing on the counter to take everything from the upper cabinets—crackers, cereals, half-empty bottles of spices. On the very top shelf was a flowered tin confectioner's box with Persian lettering on it, forgotten since the day Mrs. Ardavi had brought it. "My!" said Mrs. Ardavi. "Won't Hilary be surprised!" Elizabeth pried the lid off. Out flew a cloud of insects, grayish-brown with V-shaped wings. They brushed past Elizabeth's face and fluttered through her hair and swarmed toward the ceiling, where they dimmed the light fixture. Elizabeth flung the box as far from her as possible and climbed down from the

counter. "Goodness!" said Mrs. Ardavi. "Why, *we* have those at home!" Hassan lowered his teacup. Mixed nuts and dried currants rolled every which way on the floor; more insects swung toward the ceiling. Elizabeth sat on the nearest chair and buried her head in her hands. "Elizabeth?" said Hassan.

98 But she wouldn't look at him. In the end she simply rose and went upstairs, shutting the bedroom door with a gentle, definite click, which they heard all the way down in the kitchen because they were listening so hard.

99 "Excuse me," Hassan said to his mother.

100 She nodded and stared into her tea.

101 After he was gone she went to find Hilary, and she set her on her knee, babbling various folk rhymes to her while straining her ears toward the silence overhead. But Hilary squirmed off her lap and went to play with a truck. Then Hassan came downstairs again. He didn't say a word about Elizabeth.

102 On the following day, when Mrs. Ardavi's tooth was better, she and Hassan had a little talk upstairs in her room. They were very polite with each other. Hassan asked his mother how long they could hope for her to stay. His mother said she hadn't really thought about it. Hassan said that in America it was the custom to have house guests for three months only. After that they moved to a separate apartment nearby, which he'd be glad to provide for her as soon as he could find one, maybe next week. "Ah, an apartment," said his mother, looking impressed. But she had never lived alone a day in her life, and so after a suitable pause she said that she would hate to put him to so much expense. "Especially," she said, "when I'm going in such a short time anyway, since I'm homesick for my sisters."

103 "Well, then," said Hassan.

104 At supper that night, Hassan announced that his mother was missing her sisters and would like to leave. Elizabeth lowered her glass. "Leave?" she said.

105 Mrs. Ardavi said, "And Babak's wife, of course, will be asking for me when the baby arrives."

106 "Well . . . but what about the dentist? You were supposed to start your appointments on Monday."

107 "It's not important," Mrs. Ardavi said.

108 "But we set up all those—"

109 "There are plenty of dentists she can see at home," Hassan told Elizabeth. "We have dentists in Iran, for God's sake. Do you imagine we're barbarians?"

110 "No," Elizabeth said.

111 On the evening of the third of March, Hassan drove his mother to the airport. He was worrying about the road, which was slippery after a snowfall. He couldn't find much to say to his mother. And once they had arrived, he deliberately kept the conversation to trivia—the verifying of tickets, checking

of departure times, weighing of baggage. Her baggage was fourteen pounds overweight. It didn't make sense; all she had were her clothes and a few small gifts for her sisters. "Why is it so heavy?" Hassan asked. "What have you got in there?" But his mother only said, "I don't know," and straightened her shawl, looking elsewhere. Hassan bent to open a tooled-leather suitcase. Inside he found three empty urn-shaped wine bottles, the permanent-press sheets from her bed, and a sample box of detergent that had come in yesterday's mail. "Listen," said Hassan, "do you know how much I'd have to pay to fly these things over? What's the matter with you?"

112   "I wanted to show my sisters," his mother said.

113   "Well, forget it. Now, what else have you got?"

114   But something about her—the vague, childlike eyes set upon some faraway object—made him give in. He opened no more bags. He even regretted his sharpness, and when her flight was announced he hugged her closely and kissed the top of her head. "Go with God," he said.

115   "Goodbye, Hassan."

116   She set off down the corridor by herself, straggling behind a line of businessmen. They all wore hats. His mother wore her scarf, and of all the travelers she alone, securely kerchiefed and shawled, setting her small shoes resolutely on the gleaming tiles, seemed undeniably a foreigner.

THINKING ABOUT THE TEXT

1. Discuss Mrs. Ardavi's effort to adjust to American culture. Where do you see her making a genuine effort, and where do you see her clinging to her own customs?

2. At first Elizabeth tries hard to make her mother-in-law feel at home. Discuss her efforts; then specify the signs that Elizabeth is feeling stressed by Mrs. Ardavi's prolonged stay.

3. Mrs. Ardavi recognizes that "boundaries kept shifting and sometimes it was she who was the foreigner but other times Elizabeth, or even Hassan." Point out scenes where each seems the foreigner and explain why.

4. Discuss scenes where Mrs. Ardavi is "interfering." Explain each from her perspective, and then from Hassan's or Elizabeth's.

5. In what ways does the title relate to the story?

WRITING FROM THE TEXT

1. Write an essay comparing Mrs. Ardavi's beliefs and behaviors with Elizabeth's. What are the barriers between them, and which are hardest to re-

solve? What is Hassan's role in their relationship? Focus on an assertion or thesis you can prove about the key differences or bonds between them.

2. Rather than portraying Mrs. Ardavi as a stereotypical mother-in-law, Tyler helps us understand her as a complex and rich individual, caught between worlds. Consider Mrs. Ardavi's upbringing and past as well as her current predicament in a new culture and write an analysis of her character. (See the character analysis section, pp. 484–505.)

3. Write an essay focusing on an experience where you felt "undeniably a foreigner." As Tyler suggests, this alienation may happen in your own environment or your own home, as it does to Hassan and Elizabeth. Include examples that illustrate the alienation you felt.

Connecting with Other Texts

1. Using this story and any two other readings in this book, write an essay analyzing the pressure and demands of parenting. Suggested readings include "The Good Daughter" (p. 20), "Our Son Mark" (p. 24), "The Second Shift" (p. 84), "Let 'em Eat Leftovers" (p. 91), "Peaches" (p. 147), "Proper Care and Maintenance" (p. 186), and "Coke" (p. 287).

2. Intercultural marriages bring an added complexity to family relationships. Research a specific Islamic custom or belief that relates to this story (arranged marriages, the belief that Christians are unclean, the wearing of medals, carrying the Koran, etc.) and explain its origin and significance.

Chapter 2

Between Genders

If women and men were completely satisfied with their lives, the readings in this chapter would probably have a distinctly different tone. Essays would show that gender conflicts were issues of the past, poems would celebrate gender equality, and memoirs would attest to universal self-acceptance.

But as the selections in this chapter reveal, women and men still live with gender-related tensions. The women's movements of the last four decades have helped to identify and address these tensions, and the men's movement at the end of the twentieth century has raised questions that also disturb the status quo. While some individuals embrace this disturbance, others fear it, and many feel caught in between. You and your friends may be in the process of exploring or resolving some of the same gender issues that the writers in this chapter discuss.

All of the writers show how stereotypes circumscribe the actions and thinking of women and men. Jill Tweedie questions whether our notion of love is bound by stereotypical role-playing, a concern that Adair Lara reiterates when she humorously recounts anecdotes that reveal how both women and men can be cunning about their cash. Eugene R. August exposes language bias against males, Marge Piercy illustrates social conditioning that is biased against women, and Anna Quindlen argues that the bias against women can hurt men if women are not also required to register for the draft.

Susan Jacoby, Ellen Goodman, and Joyce Carol Oates explore, in analytical essays and a short story, a problem affecting both genders—violence against women. Don Sabo exposes his disillusionment with the violence of high school football, while, in another essay, Meghan Daum reveals her disillusionment with Internet romance. The difficulties of sustaining relationships and sharing household responsibilities are examined by Arlie Hochschild and more humorously by Mike McGrady. Each of these essays explores how social conditioning and role-playing may threaten genuine intimacy. Reading some of these essays, you may find ideas that will help you understand your feelings and expectations.

In your own life, you likely have found that gender issues are everywhere, showing up in such diverse places as popular music lyrics and newspaper and magazine articles. In this chapter, our writers reexamine gender roles, expose myths, and pose solutions that may help both sexes move beyond where we are today.

 The Future of Love

Jill Tweedie

A journalist writing for the British publication *The Guardian*, Jill Tweedie (b. 1936) is also the author of *It's Only Me, Letters from a Fainthearted Feminist, More from Martha,* and *Jewels,* her first novel. The essay that follows appears in her book *In the Name of Love* (1979).

1   Love, it seems, is as much a part of the unique equipment of homo sapiens as language or laughter and far more celebrated. If all the words that have been written about it since mankind first put stick to clay were laid end to end, they would rocket past Venus and vanish into deep space. Histories of love, philosophies of love, psychologies of love, guidebooks to love, love letters, love hymns, love stories, love poems, love songs have covered tablets and papyrus, parchment and paper and walls, filled theatres across time and lands from Epidaurus to Radio City, and been declaimed by gods and goddesses of love from Sappho to Warren Beatty. Love has been, is now, and ever shall be our scourge and balm, our wound and salve, source of our finest and most bestial actions, the emotion that passeth all understanding. It is a heavenly body out of our orbit, beyond man-made laws, ethics, or control, a magical splendour that descends upon us like the gift of tongues and possesses us whether we will or no. Love transforms us into something strange and rare, it ignites our lives and, dying, takes all meaning away.

> The mind has a thousand eyes
> And the heart but one
> Yet the light of a whole life dies
> When love is done.

We die of love and die without it, our hearts beat for it and break for it. Love built the Taj Mahal, wrote the Song of Solomon and cooks a billion meals every day, across the world. Love is the only thing that matters at all, after all.

2   Or so they say. And in my opinion what they say, give or take an epigram or two, is rubbish. Take off the rose-coloured glasses and what does a close examination of the facts reveal to the naked eye? That love, true love, is the rarest of all the emotions and one that has been conspicuous only by its absence ever since mankind dropped from the trees. If we condense the earth's history into one calendar year, homo sapiens appeared in the late evening of December 31st and love, his much-vaunted race-long companion, is still merely a glimmer on the midnight horizon of the coming New Year. Love, in other words, inhabits the future, a kind of reverse star whose light reaches us before it is born instead of after it has died. Certainly, intimations of love's coming have touched an individual here and there through time and its prophets have started new religions, composed great symphonies, made beautiful sculpture, and painted exquisite canvases. But for the wide river of humanity, the ordinary mass of men and women who have peopled our planet and reproduced our race, love was not necessary, not possible, and not there.

3   Why, then, the stories, the poems, and the songs, the jubilations and the suicides? How can you argue that love does not exist when human beings deliberately end their own existence for love? Surely nothing is as indisputable as that love and mankind go hand in hand. I love, therefore I am. But is it love they feel? I think not. The word is a vast umbrella that covers a multitude of virtues and sins and because we are perfectly familiar with all of love's precursors and understudies, we imagine that we have pinned down love itself when we have merely trapped its shadow. Co-operation, for instance, midwife to that most ancient of drives, survival. You scratch my back and I'll scratch yours. Sex, a powerhouse so overwhelming in its assault upon us that, trying to domesticate it, we have given it the prettier name of love. We know about affection and friendship. We feel liking, duty, deference, greed, lust, ambition, attraction, protectiveness, ingratiation, and the desire to conform. We are gripped by infatuation, obsession, adoration, vanity, addiction, jealousy, fear, and the dread of being alone. Very deeply we know about need. I need you. He needs me. Needs must.

4   But love is somewhere else and all those other drives and needs and feelings are like the gases that swirl about in space, inwardly spiralling through the centuries to centre at last on a small hard core, gases that are only hot air in themselves but essential for the eventual formation of a new world, a world of real love. We may arrive at it one day, given time, but we are not there yet. . . .

5   The interesting thing is that the slow emergence of true love does not predicate some higher version of morality. No sudden conversions, no lights upon the road to Damascus are in any way necessary. A new generation with new standards of loving will not come about as a result of some mystical mutation or spiritual growth, though these may well follow. The facts are more practical. As equality becomes commonplace between men and women, they themselves will perforce change from stereotypes, however successful or unsuccessful, into ordinary human beings, each one rather different from the next. Standard sexual roles—the breadwinner, the housewife and mother— already blurred, will eventually disappear and with them will go the suppression or exaggeration of parts of the individual character made necessary by those roles. And as these masks, stylised as the masks of Japanese Kabuki, slip to reveal the human face behind, romantic love, so heavily dependent upon an artificial facade and predictable masculine or feminine behaviour, will die from starvation. Already it is showing the first signs of incipient malnutrition. When, added to that, children are raised in equality and mothers, secure in their own identity, no longer pass their fears and inferiorities on to their daughters or too great an admiration on to their sons; when both parents are equally concerned with the upbringing of children and therefore ensure that those children cannot divide their emotions between the sexes and discard one whole area, we will have bred a race of human beings differentiated by their own personalities rather than their genitalia. The old war-cry of sexists—*vive la différence*—actually implied exactly the opposite; the rigid division of an infinite variety of people into just two categories, male and female. *Vive la similarité.* Variety will replace conformity and variety, apart from being an evolutionary must, forces each potential lover to take stock of an individual rather than search for the stereotyped ideal of a whole sex.

6   Nor is this change dependent solely on a conscious wish for change. Evolution has always had a voracious appetite for variety; it is literally the spice of life, offering as it does a wide menu for natural selection. And it is becoming clear to many of us that the old stereotypes of male and female are increasingly a positive threat to the well-being of the race and the earth. Women, confined to a domestic and biological cage, produce unwanted children to crowd an already overpopulated world, while their own abilities wither on the hearth. Men, driven by out-dated standards of virility, continue to denude the planet and threaten each other with uncontemplatable war. Love between such men and such women serves only their own artificial needs and seals them off in their *folie à deux* from the rest of the world instead of involving them more deeply, as real love would do. Our planetary problems are rapidly becoming too serious to permit the net-curtain mentality

of the average self-satisfied couple as they peep out at trouble and hastily withdraw, safe in the certainty that God himself blesses their cosy two-some and demands nothing more than its continuation, properly seeded with kiddies.

7   That is not to say that monogamy is on its way out, only that monogamy as we know it today—sacrosanct, heterosexual, reproductive, lifelong, and almost always a retreat from life, no longer adequately fulfills either the individuals concerned or society. All research done recently, whether anthropological, paediatric, psychiatric, criminal, or social, arrives at the same conclusion: human beings develop most fully and happily if they can feel loved as children by one or two constantly present adults and, as adults themselves, reproduce the same closeness with one other adult. But there is nothing to prove that years of monogamy with the *same* adult are necessarily beneficial. Lifelong monogamy may be nice for the Church and useful for the tax-collector but it has many drawbacks for the individual, who is a learning as well as an imprinted being. As we change and learn, from youth to old age, we must give ourselves room for that change. Like snakes, we need occasionally to shed our old skins and often we cannot do that if we are tied by bonds of guilt to an outgrown love. None of us grows at the same speed or in the same way and the chances of a parallel development with one other human being are not great. But nor does this imply a lack of love or some pervasive shame. Each of us may give another person love and help in inner growth for a while. But in a changing world, with changing people, why should we expect that love to last forever or denigrate it if it does not? Why should love, once a mansion, be made into a cage through false expectations of what love is?

8   Lifelong monogamy has other drawbacks, even when it works, perhaps *especially* when it works. In a cold and problematic world it is all too easy to withdraw into the cosiness of a familiar love, leaving those problems for others to solve. We have a genetic need for other people; monogamous love, in attempting to assuage that need with one other person, may not only sour into neuroses or a mutual flattery that reduces both partners, making them fear the outside world, but may also isolate us from our fellows and allow us to care less about their fate. When my husband is away from home, I turn in need to my friends, even to strangers. I become vulnerable once again to their larger opinion of me. I see myself as others, more coldly, see me. On his return my instinct is to warm myself at his me-centred love, to soothe my slightly bruised ego. Luckily for me, he does not need to build me up for his own ego and so he is not all *that* warm, just warm enough. He leaves place in me for others, because he himself has place for others.

9   All this—changing women, the danger of stereotypes, and intractable monogamy, the needs of our race and our planet in the future—implies one imperative. We must leave adolescence behind and grow up. It is absolutely vital, if we are to continue to exist in some comfort upon our earth, that we take a giant step into true adulthood, learn to filter the emotions through our reasoning capacities and learn that survival itself rests on knowing who we are, respecting others' space, and endeavouring justly to balance our own and others' needs.

10   And this is where love truly comes into its own as an evolutionary tool. Parental love teaches children one vital fact: that they are loved and lovable and therefore can themselves love. But the love between adults differs in one absolute from parental love: it is conditional, or should be. We find out who we are by feeling our outlines against other people, by finding out who we are not. In loving but honest eyes we see prisms of our own vague face; slowly we put the prisms together and distinguish certain unchanging features, form certain principles. Inside, a centre begins to form and once it is firmly established, roots well grown, blossoms flourishing, we can turn from it towards others with a real sense of where we differ and where we are the same. And once we know that, once we respect ourselves, it becomes impossible to accept another who violates our beliefs and ourselves. A weak ego, a weak hold on reality, opens the doors to any passing stranger who flatters us enough and makes us feel real. A strong ego, a firm knowledge of who we are, demands conditions of that stranger, demands a similarity of belief and behaviour and can discard what it does not respect, even at the price of rejecting easy flattery.

11   And that is what true love is there to help us do. Properly informed, lovingly detached, centred respectfully in itself, it provides us with a real reflection of ourselves, to help us grow. Principles do not need to be suppressed for fear of displeasing, for fear of loss, because when the crunch comes, we can cope alone.

12   Love cannot thrive in inequality or extreme poverty. It requires enough leisure for introspection and enough introspection for empathy. It demands that the individual feel a certain control over his life because, in too great a storm, we tend to seek any refuge. It thrives on honesty and therefore must do away with great need, since need drives out honesty. It is rational, it knows its own roots, it is moral and controllable because it stems from the head and not the heart. Any resemblance it bears to love as we know it today is purely fictional.

13   And true love is still in embryo, fragile compared to other ties because it derives no strength from more ancient needs. Its roots are not in the past but

in the future. It is a beginning, a new survival mechanism slowly evolving to suit new circumstances.

Thinking about the Text

1. After opening her essay with what are apparently exuberant descriptions of and tributes to love, Tweedie offers her opinion that what is said about love is "rubbish." What does she mean?

2. Explain Tweedie's image that love is "a vast umbrella that covers a multitude of virtues and sins." What are the specific words under the umbrella that Tweedie argues are not love at all? Do you agree with her?

3. Tweedie insists that love is like a distant star, a world possible to attain only when "equality becomes commonplace between men and women" and when we defeat the stereotypes that delimit our existence. What does understanding and attaining love have to do with eliminating gender stereotypes?

4. Why is the author against monogamy even though studies show that human beings develop most fully in a monogamous setting? How does she argue her point? What does that point have to do with her beliefs about love?

5. What are the "adolescent" ideas that people must leave behind in order to know what love truly is? How does self-respect permit the individual to know real love?

6. What does the author mean when she writes that love cannot exist with inequality and extreme poverty? How do these closing points relate to the rest of her argument?

Writing from the Text

1. After summarizing Tweedie's argument in an opening paragraph, write an analysis of a couple who seem to you to have "left adolescence behind" and achieved an adult love. Use specific descriptions from Tweedie's essay and specific details from the couple's life to present your case.

2. Write an essay in which you agree or disagree with Tweedie's point that love between adults should be conditional, not unconditional as it is between parent and child. Are "honest eyes" necessary or unnecessary between adults for love to exist? Use specific illustrations to support your thesis.

3. Use the lyrics of a popular song about love, and words from greeting cards, aphorisms, and film, to illustrate Tweedie's view that most of what has been written about love is "rubbish."

CONNECTING WITH OTHER TEXTS

1. Read "The Second Shift" (p. 84) and use specific details from Hochschild's essay as well as Tweedie's to illustrate that something other than love is apparent in homes where the couple is bound by stereotypes and by what Tweedie might call an adolescent notion of love.

2. Read "Who's Cheap" (p. 94) and write an essay that shows how "romantic love, so heavily dependent upon an artificial facade and predictable masculine or feminine behavior" defeats the possibility of real love in Lara's dating descriptions.

3. Write an essay that shows how Tweedie's notion of parental, unconditional love is illustrated in the essays by Marcus (p. 14) and Hayakawa (p. 24).

Real Men Don't: Anti-Male Bias in English

Eugene R. August

A professor of English at the University of Dayton, Ohio, Eugene R. August (b. 1935) was awarded the Younger Humanist Fellowship from the National Endowment for the Humanities. He has published essays on the philosopher John Stuart Mill and is the editor of *Men's Studies: A Selected and Annotated Interdisciplinary Bibliography* (1985). The following essay was first published in *The University of Dayton Review* in 1986 and serves as a fine model of scholarly writing.

1   Despite numerous studies of sex bias in language during the past fifteen years, only rarely has anti-male bias been examined. In part, this neglect occurs because many of these studies have been based upon assumptions which are questionable at best and which at worst exhibit their own form of sex bias. Whether explicitly or implicitly, many of these studies reduce human history to a tale of male oppressors and female victims or rebels. In this view of things, all societies become *patriarchal societies,* a familiar term used to suggest that for centuries males have conspired to exploit and demean females. Accordingly, it is alleged in many of these studies that men control language and that they use it to define women and women's roles as inferior.

2   Despite the popularity of such a view, it has received scant support from leading social scientists, including one of the giants of modern anthropology, Margaret Mead. Anticipating current ideology, Mead in *Male and Female*

firmly rejected the notion of a "male conspiracy to keep women in their place," arguing instead that

> the historical trend that listed women among the abused minorities . . . lingers on to obscure the issue and gives apparent point to the contention that this is a man-made world in which women have always been abused and must always fight for their rights.
>
> It takes considerable effort on the part of both men and women to reorient ourselves to thinking—when we think basically—that this is a world not made by men alone, in which women are unwilling and helpless dupes and fools or else powerful schemers hiding their power under their ruffled petticoats, but a world made of mankind for human beings of both sexes. (298, 299–300)

The model described by Mead and other social scientists shows a world in which women and men have lived together throughout history in a symbiotic relationship, often mutually agreeing upon the definition of gender roles and the distribution of various powers and duties.

3   More importantly for the subject of bias in speech and writing, women—as well as men—have shaped language. As Walter J. Ong reminds us,

> Women talk and think as much as men do, and with few exceptions we all . . . learn to talk and think in the first instance largely from women, usually and predominantly our mothers. Our first tongue is called our "mother tongue" in English and in many other languages. . . . There are no father tongues. . . . (36)

Feminists like Dorothy Dinnerstein agree: "There seems no reason to doubt that the baby-tending sex contributed at least equally with the history-making one to the most fundamental of all human inventions: language" (22). Because gender roles and language are shaped by society in general—that is, by both men and women—anti-male bias in language is as possible as anti-female bias.

4   To say this, however, is emphatically not to blame women alone, or even primarily, for anti-male usage. If guilt must be assigned, it would have to be placed upon sexist people, both male and female, who use language to manipulate gender role behavior and to create negative social attitudes towards males. But often it is difficult to point a finger of blame: except where prejudiced gender stereotypes are deliberately fostered, most people evidently use sex-biased terminology without clearly understanding its import. In the long run, it is wiser to concentrate not on fixing blame, but on heightening public awareness of anti-male language and on discouraging its use. In particular,

teachers and writers need to become aware of and to question language which denigrates or stereotypes males.

5   In modern English, three kinds of anti-male usage are evident: first, gender-exclusive language which omits males from certain kinds of consideration; second, gender-restrictive language which attempts to restrict males to an accepted gender role, some aspects of which may be outmoded, burdensome, or destructive; and third, negative stereotypes of males which are insulting, dehumanizing, and potentially dangerous.

6   Although gender-exclusive language which excludes females has often been studied, few students of language have noted usage which excludes males. Those academics, for example, who have protested *alumnus* and *alumni* as gender-exclusive terms to describe a university's male and female graduates have failed to notice that, by the same logic, *alma mater* (nourishing mother) is an equally gender-exclusive term to describe the university itself. Those who have protested *man* and *mankind* as generic terms have not begun to question *mammal* as a term of biological classification, but by categorizing animals according to the female's ability to suckle the young through her mammary glands, *mammal* clearly omits the male of the species. Consequently, it is as suspect as generic *man*.

7   In general, gender-exclusive usage in English excludes males as parents and as victims. Until recently, the equating of *mother* with *parent* in the social sciences was notorious: a major sociological study published in 1958 with the title *The Changing American Parent* was based upon interviews with 582 mothers and no fathers (Roman and Haddad 87). Although no longer prevalent in the social sciences, the interchangeability of *mother* and *parent* is still common, except for *noncustodial parent* which is almost always a synonym for *father*. A recent ad for *Parents* magazine begins: "To be the best mother you can be, you want practical, reliable answers to the questions a mother must face." Despite the large number of men now seen pushing shopping carts, advertisers still insist that "Choosy mothers choose Jif" and "My Mom's a Butternut Mom." Frequently, children are regarded as belonging solely to the mother, as in phrases like *women and their children*. The idea of the mother as primary parent can be glimpsed in such expressions as *mother tongue, mother wit, mother lode, mother of invention,* and *mothering* as a synonym for *parenting*.

8   The male as victim is ignored in such familiar expressions as *innocent women and children*. In June 1985, when President Reagan rejected a bombing strike to counter terrorist activities, newspapers reported that the decision had been made to prevent "the deaths of many innocent women and children in strife-torn Lebanon" (Glass). Presumably strife-torn Lebanon contained no innocent men. Likewise, *rape victim* means females only, an

assumption made explicit in the opening sentences of this newspaper article on rape: "Crime knows no gender. Yet, there is one offense that only women are prey to: rape" (Mougey). The thousands of males raped annually, in addition to the sexual assaults regularly inflicted upon males in prison, are here entirely overlooked. (That these males have been victimized mostly by other males does not disqualify them as victims of sexual violence, as some people assume.) Similarly, the term *wife and child abuse* conceals the existence of an estimated 282,000 husbands who are battered annually (O'Reilly et al. 23). According to many expressions in English, males are not parents and they are never victimized.

9   Unlike gender-exclusive language, gender-restrictive language is usually applied to males only, often to keep them within the confines of a socially prescribed gender role. When considering gender-restrictive language, one must keep in mind that—as Ruth E. Hartley has pointed out—the masculine gender role is enforced earlier and more harshly than the feminine role is (235). In addition, because the boy is often raised primarily by females in the virtual absence of close adult males, his grasp of what is required of him to *be a man* is often unsure. Likewise, prescriptions for male behavior are usually given in the negative, leading to the "Real Men Don't" syndrome, a process which further confuses the boy. Such circumstances leave many males extremely vulnerable to language which questions their sense of masculinity.

10   Furthermore, during the past twenty years an increasing number of men and women have been arguing that aspects of our society's masculine gender role are emotionally constrictive, unnecessarily stressful, and potentially lethal. Rejecting "the myth of masculine privilege," psychologist Herb Goldberg reports in *The Hazards of Being Male* that "every critical statistic in the area of [early death], disease, suicide, crime, accidents, childhood emotional disorders, alcoholism, and drug addiction shows a disproportionately higher male rate" (5). But changes in the masculine role are so disturbing to so many people that the male who attempts to break out of familiar gender patterns often finds himself facing hostile opposition which can be readily and powerfully expressed in a formidable array of sex-biased terms.

11   To see how the process works, let us begin early in the male life cycle. A boy quickly learns that, while it is usually acceptable for girls to be *tomboys,* God forbid that he should be a *sissy*. In *Sexual Signatures: On Being a Man or a Woman* John Money and Patricia Tucker note:

> The current feminine stereotype in our culture is flexible enough to let a girl behave "boyishly" if she wants to without bringing her femininity into question, but any boy who exhibits "girlish" behavior is

promptly suspected of being queer. There isn't even a word corresponding to "tomboy" to describe such a boy. "Sissy" perhaps comes closest,
or "artistic" and "sensitive," but unlike "tomboy," such terms are burdened with unfavorable connotations. (72)

Lacking a favorable or even neutral term to describe the boy who is quiet,
gentle, and emotional, the English language has long had a rich vocabulary
to insult and ridicule such boys—*mama's boy, mollycoddle, milksop, muff, twit,*
softy, creampuff, pantywaist, weenie, Miss Nancy, and so on. Although sometimes used playfully, the current popular *wimp* can be used to insult males
from childhood right into adulthood.

12   Discussion of words like *sissy* as insults has been often one-sided: most
commentators are content to argue that the female, not the male, is being insulted by such usage. "The implicit sexism" in such terms, writes one com-
mentator, "disparages the woman, not the man" (Sorrels 87). Although the
female is being slurred indirectly by these terms, a moment's reflection will
show that the primary force of the insult is being directed against the male,
specifically the male who cannot differentiate himself from the feminine.
Ong argues in *Fighting for Life* that most societies place heavy pressure on
males to differentiate themselves from females because the prevailing environment of human society is feminine (70–71). In English-speaking societies,
terms like *sissy* and *weak sister,* which have been used by both females and
males, are usually perceived not as insults to females but as ridicule of males
who have allegedly failed to differentiate themselves from the feminine.

13   Being *all boy* carries penalties, however: for one thing, it means being less
lovable. As the nursery rhyme tells children, little girls are made of "sugar and
spice and all that's nice," while little boys are made of "frogs and snails and
puppy-dogs' tails." Or as an American version of the rhyme puts it:

> Girls are dandy,
> Made of candy—
> That's what little girls are made of.
> Boys are rotten,
> Made of cotton—
> That's what little boys are made of.
>   (Baring-Gould 176n116)

When not enjoined to *be all boy,* our young lad will be urged to *be a big boy,*
be a brave soldier, and (the ultimate appeal) *be a man.* These expressions
almost invariably mean that the boy is about to suffer something painful

or humiliating. The variant—*take it like a man*—provides the clue. As Paul Theroux defines it, *be a man* means: "Be stupid, be unfeeling, obedient and soldierly, and stop thinking."

14   Following our boy further into the life cycle, we discover that in school he will find himself in a cruel bind: girls his age will be biologically and socially more mature than he is, at least until around age eighteen. Until then, any ineptness in his social role will be castigated by a host of terms which are reserved almost entirely for males. "For all practical purposes," John Gordon remarks, "the word 'turkey' (or whatever the equivalent is now) can be translated as 'a boy spurned by influential girls'" (141). The equivalents of *turkey* are many: *jerk, nerd, clod, klutz, schmuck, dummy, goon, dork, square, dweeb, jackass, meathead, geek, zero, reject, goofball, drip,* and numerous others, including many obscene terms. Recently, a Michigan high school decided to do away with a scheduled "Nerd Day" after a fourteen-year-old male student, who apparently had been so harassed as a nerd by other students, committed suicide ("'Nerd' day"). In this case, the ability of language to devastate the emotionally vulnerable young male is powerfully and pathetically dramatized.

15   As our boy grows, he faces threats and taunts if he does not take risks or endure pain to prove his manhood. *Coward,* for example is a word applied almost exclusively to males in our society, as are its numerous variants— *chicken, chickenshit, yellow, yellow-bellied, lily-livered, weak-kneed, spineless, squirrelly, fraidy cat, gutless wonder, weakling, butterfly, jellyfish,* and so on. If our young man walks away from a stupid quarrel or prefers to settle differences more rationally than with a swift jab to the jaw, the English language is richly supplied with these and other expressions to call his masculinity into question.

16   Chief among the other expressions that question masculinity is a lengthy list of homophobic terms, such as *queer, pansy, fag, faggot, queen, queeny, pervert, bugger, deviant, fairy, tinkerbell, puss, priss, flamer, feller, sweet, precious, fruit, sodomite,* and numerous others, many obscene. For many people, *gay* is an all-purpose word of ridicule and condemnation. Once again, although homosexuals are being insulted by these terms, the primary target is more often the heterosexual male who fails or refuses to live up to someone else's idea of masculinity. In "Homophobia Among Men" Gregory Lehne explains, "Homophobia is used as a technique of social control . . . to enforce the norms of male sex-role behavior. . . . [H]omosexuality is not the real threat, the real threat is change in the male sex-role" (77).

17   Nowhere is this threat more apparent than in challenges to our society's male-only military obligation. When a young man and a young woman reach the age of eighteen, both may register to vote; only the young man is required by law to register for military service. For the next decade at least,

he must stand ready to be called into military service and even into combat duty in wars, "police actions," "peace-keeping missions," and "rescue missions," often initiated by legally dubious means. Should he resist this obligation, he may be called a *draft dodger, deserter, peacenik, traitor, shirker, slacker, malingerer,* and similar terms. Should he declare himself a conscientious objector, he may be labeled a *conchy* or any of the variants of *coward.*

18   In his relationships with women, he will find that the age of equality has not yet arrived. Usually, he will be expected to take the initiative, do the driving, pick up the tab, and in general show a deferential respect for women that is a left-over from the chivalric code. Should he behave in an *ungentlemanly* fashion, a host of words—which are applied almost always to males alone—can be used to tell him so: *louse, rat, creep, sleaze, scum, stain, worm, fink, heel, stinker, animal, savage, bounder, cad, wolf, gigolo, womanizer, Don Juan, pig, rotter, boor,* and so on.

19   In sexual matters he will usually be expected to take the initiative and to *perform.* If he does not, he will be labeled *impotent.* This word, writes Goldberg, "is clearly sexist because it implies a standard of acceptable masculine sexual performance that makes a man abnormal if he can't live up to it" (*New Male* 248). Metaphorically, *impotent* can be used to demean any male whose efforts in any area are deemed unacceptable. Even if our young man succeeds at his sexual performance, the sex manuals are ready to warn him that if he reaches orgasm before a specified time he is guilty of *premature ejaculation.*

20   When our young man marries, he will be required by law and social custom to support his wife and children. Should he not succeed as breadwinner or should he relax in his efforts, the language offers numerous terms to revile him: *loser, deadbeat, bum, freeloader, leech, parasite, goldbrick, sponge, mooch, ne'er-do-well, good for nothing,* and so on. If women in our society have been regarded as sex objects, men have been regarded as success objects, that is, judged by their ability to provide a standard of living. The title of a recent book—*How to Marry a Winner*—reveals immediately that the intended audience is female (Collier).

21   When he becomes a father, our young man will discover that he is a second-class parent, as the traditional interchangeability of *mother* and *parent* indicates. The law has been particularly obtuse in recognizing fathers as parents, as evidenced by the awarding of child custody to mothers in ninety percent of divorce cases. In 1975 a father's petition for custody of his four-year-old was denied because, as the family court judge said, "Fathers don't make good mothers" (qtd. in Levine 21). The judge apparently never considered whether *fathers* make good *parents.*

22   And so it goes throughout our young man's life: if he deviates from society's gender role norm, he will be penalized and he will hear about it.

23   The final form of anti-male bias to be considered is negative stereotyping. Sometimes this stereotyping is indirectly embedded in the language, sometimes it resides in people's assumptions about males and shapes their response to seemingly neutral words, and sometimes it is overtly created for political reasons. It is one thing to say that some aspects of the traditional masculine gender role are limiting and hurtful; it is quite another to gratuitously suspect males in general of being criminal and evil or to denounce them in wholesale fashion as oppressors, exploiters, and rapists. In *The New Male* Goldberg writes, "Men may very well be the last remaining subgroup in our society that can be blatantly, negatively and vilely stereotyped with little objection or resistance" (103). As our language demonstrates, such sexist stereotyping, whether unintentional or deliberate, is not only familiar but fashionable.

24   In English, crime and evil are usually attributed to the male. As an experiment I have compiled lists of nouns which I read to my composition students, asking them to check whether the words suggest "primarily females," "primarily males," or "could be either." Nearly all the words for lawbreakers suggest males rather than females to most students. These words include *murderer, swindler, crook, criminal, burglar, thief, gangster, mobster, hood, hitman, killer, pickpocket, mugger,* and *terrorist.* Accounting for this phenomenon is not always easy. *Hitman* may obviously suggest "primarily males," and the *-er* in *murderer* may do the same, especially if it reminds students of the word's feminine form, *murderess.* Likewise, students may be aware that most murders are committed by males. Other words—like *criminal* and *thief*—are more clearly gender-neutral in form, and it is less clear why they should be so closely linked with "primarily males." Although the dynamics of the association may be unclear, English usage somehow conveys a subtle suggestion that males are to be regarded as guilty in matters of law-breaking.

25   This hint of male guilt extends to a term like *suspect.* When the person's gender is unknown, the suspect is usually presumed to be a male. For example, even before a definite suspect had been identified, the perpetrator of the 1980–1981 Atlanta child murders was popularly known as *The Man.* When a male and female are suspected of the crime, the male is usually presumed the guilty party. In a recent murder case, when two suspects—Debra Brown and Alton Coleman—were apprehended, police discovered *Brown's* fingerprint in a victim's car and interpreted this as evidence of *Coleman's* guilt. As the Associated Press reported:

> Authorities say for the first time they have evidence linking Alton Coleman with the death of an Indianapolis man.
>   A fingerprint found in the car of Eugene Scott has been identified as that of Debra Brown, Coleman's traveling companion. . . ." ("Police")

Nowhere does the article suggest that Brown's fingerprint found in the victim's car linked Brown with the death: the male suspect was presumed the guilty party, while the female was only a "traveling companion." Even after Brown had been convicted of two murders, the Associated Press was still describing her as "the accused accomplice of convicted killer Alton Coleman" ("Indiana").

26   In some cases, this presumption of male guilt extends to crimes in which males are not the principal offenders. As noted earlier, a term like *wife and child abuse* ignores battered husbands, but it does more: it suggests that males alone abuse children. In reality most child abuse is committed by mothers (Straus, Gelles, Steinmetz 71). Despite this fact, a 1978 study of child abuse bears the title *Sins of the Fathers* (Inglis).

27   The term *rape* creates special problems. While the majority of rapes are committed by males and the number of female rape victims outdistances the number of male rape victims, it is widely assumed—as evidenced by the newspaper article cited above—that rape is a crime committed only by males in which only females are victims. Consequently, the word *rape* is often used as a brush to tar all males. In *Against Our Will* Susan Brownmiller writes: "From prehistoric times to the present, I believe, rape . . . is nothing more or less than a conscious process in intimidation by which *all men* keep *all women* in a state of fear" (15; italics in original). Making the point explicitly, Marilyn French states, "All men are rapists and that's all they are" (qtd. in Jennes 33). Given this kind of smear tactic, *rape* can be used metaphorically to indict males alone and to exonerate females, as in this sentence: "The rape of nature—and the ecological disaster it presages—is part and parcel of a dominating masculinity gone out of control" (Hoch 137). The statement neatly blames males alone even when the damage to the environment has been caused in part by females like Anne Gorsuch Burford and Rita Lavelle.

28   Not only crimes but vices of all sorts have been typically attributed to males. As Muriel R. Schulz points out, "The synonyms for *inebriate* . . . seem to be coded primarily 'male': for example, *boozer, drunkard, tippler, toper, swiller, tosspot, guzzler, barfly, drunk, lush, boozehound, souse, tank, stew, rummy,* and *bum*" (126). Likewise, someone may be *drunk as a lord* but never *drunk as a lady.*

29   Sex bias or sexism itself is widely held to be a male-only fault. When *sexism* is defined as "contempt for women"—as if there were no such thing as contempt for men—the definition of *sexism* is itself sexist (Bardwick 34).

30   Part of the reason for this masculinization of evil may be that in the Western world the source of evil has long been depicted in male terms. In the Bible, the Evil One is consistently referred to as *he,* whether the reference is to the serpent in the Garden of Eden, Satan as Adversary in Job, Lucifer and

Beelzebub in the gospels, Jesus' tempter in the desert, or the dragon in Revelations. *Beelzebub,* incidentally, is often translated as *lord of the flies,* a term designating the demon as masculine. So masculine is the word *devil* that the female prefix is needed, as in *she-devil,* to make a feminine noun of it. The masculinization of evil is so unconsciously accepted that writers often attest to it even while attempting to deny it, as in this passage:

> From the very beginning, the Judeo-Christian tradition has linked women and evil. When second-century theologians struggled to explain the Devil's origins, they surmised that Satan and his various devils had once been angels. (Gerzon 224)

If the Judeo-Christian tradition has linked women and evil so closely, why is the writer using the masculine pronoun *his* to refer to Satan, the source of evil according to that tradition? Critics of sex-bias in religious language seldom notice or mention its masculinization of evil: of those objecting to *God the Father* as sexist, no one—to my knowledge—has suggested that designating Satan as the *Father of Lies* is equally sexist. Few theologians talk about Satan and her legions.

31   The tendency to blame nearly everything on men has climaxed in recent times with the popularity of such terms as *patriarchy, patriarchal society,* and *male-dominated society.* More political than descriptive, these terms are rapidly becoming meaningless, used as all-purpose smear words to conjure up images of male oppressors and female victims. They are a linguistic sleight of hand which obscures the point that, as Mead has observed (299–300), societies are largely created by both sexes for both sexes. By using a swift reference to *patriarchal structures* or *patriarchal attitudes,* a writer can absolve females of all blame for society's flaws while fixing the onus solely on males. The give-away of this ploy can be detected when *patriarchy* and its related terms are never used in a positive or neutral context, but are always used to assign blame to males alone.

32   Wholesale denunciations of males as oppressors, exploiters, rapists, Nazis, and slave-drivers have become all too familiar during the past fifteen years. Too often the academic community, rather than opposing this sexism, has been encouraging it. All too many scholars and teachers have hopped on the male-bashing bandwagon to disseminate what John Gordon calls "the myth of the monstrous male." With increasing frequency, this academically fashionable sexism can also be heard echoing from our students. "A white upper-middle-class straight male should seriously consider another college," declares a mid-western college student in *The New York Times Selective Guide to Colleges.* "You [the white male] are the bane of the world. . . . Ten generations of social ills can and will be strapped upon your

shoulders" (qtd. in Fiske 12). It would be comforting to dismiss this student's compound of misinformation, sexism, racism, and self-righteousness as an extreme example, but similar yahooisms go unchallenged almost everywhere in modern academia.

33   Surely it is time for men and women of good will to reject and protest such bigotry. For teachers and writers, the first task is to recognize and condemn forms of anti-male bias in language, whether they are used to exclude males from equal consideration with females, to reinforce restrictive aspects of the masculine gender role, or to stereotype males callously. For whether males are told that *fathers don't make good mothers,* that *real men don't cry,* or that *all men are rapists,* the results are potentially dangerous: like any other group, males can be subtly shaped into what society keeps telling them they are. In *Why Men Are the Way They Are* Warren Farrell puts the matter succinctly: "The more we make men the enemy, the more they will have to behave like the enemy" (357).

Works Cited

Bardwick, Judith. *In Transition: How Feminism, Sexual Liberation, and the Search for Self-Fulfillment Have Altered Our Lives.* New York: Holt, 1979.

Baring-Gould, William S., and Ceil Baring-Gould. *The Annotated Mother Goose Nursery Rhymes Old and New, Arranged and Explained.* New York: Clarkson N. Potter, 1962.

Brownmiller, Susan. *Against Our Will: Men, Women and Rape.* New York: Simon, 1975.

Collier, Phyllis K. *How to Marry a Winner.* Englewood Cliffs, NJ: Prentice, 1982.

Dinnerstein, Dorothy. *The Mermaid and the Minotaur: Sexual Arrangements and Human Malaise.* NY: Harper, 1976.

Farrell, Warren. *Why Men Are the Way They Are: The Male-Female Dynamic.* New York: McGraw-Hill, 1986.

Fiske, Edward B. *The New York Times Selective Guide to Colleges.* New York: Times Books, 1982.

Gerzon, Mark. *A Choice of Heroes: The Changing Faces of American Manhood.* Boston: Houghton, 1982.

Glass, Andrew J. "President wants to unleash military power, but cannot." *Dayton Daily News* 18 June 1985: 1.

Goldberg, Herb. *The Hazards of Being Male: Surviving the Myth of Masculine Privilege.* 1976. New York: NAL, 1977.

—*The New Male: From Self-Destruction to Self-Care.* 1979. New York: NAL, 1980.

Gordon, John. *The Myth of the Monstrous Male, and Other Feminist Fables.* New York: Playboy P, 1982.

Hartley, Ruth E. "Sex-Role Pressures and the Socialization of the Male Child." *The Forty-Nine Percent Majority: The Male Sex Role.* Ed. Deborah S. David and Robert Brannon. Reading, MA: Addison-Wesley, 1976, 235-44.

Hoch, Paul, *White Hero, Black Beast: Racism, Sexism and the Mask of Masculinity.* London: Pluto P, 1979.

"Indiana jury finds Brown guilty of murder, molesting." *Dayton Daily News* 18 May 1986: 7A.

Inglis, Ruth. *Sins of the Fathers: A Study of the Physical and Emotional Abuse of Children.* New York: St. Martin's, 1978.

Jennes, Gail. "All Men Are Rapists." *People* 20 Feb. 1978: 33-4.

Lehne, Gregory. "Homophobia Among Men." *The Forty-Nine Percent Majority: The Male Sex Role.* Ed. Deborah S. David and Robert Brannon. Reading, MA: Addison-Wesley, 1976, 66-88.

Levine, James A. *Who Will Raise the Children? New Options for Fathers (and Mothers).* Philadelphia: Lippincott, 1976.

Mead, Margaret. *Male and Female: A Study of the Sexes in a Changing World.* New York: Morrow, 1949, 1967.

Money, John, and Patricia Tucker. *Sexual Signatures: On Being a Man or a Woman.* Boston: Little, 1975.

Mougey, Kate. "An act of confiscation: Rape." *Kettering Oakwood* [OH] *Times* 4 Feb. 1981: 1b.

"'Nerd' day gets a boot after suicide." *Dayton Daily News* 24 Jan. 1986: 38.

Ong, Walter J. *Fighting for Life: Contest, Sexuality, and Consciousness.* Ithaca, NY: Cornell UP, 1981.

O'Reilly, Jane, et al. "Wife-Beating: The Silent Crime." *Time* 5 Sept. 1983: 23-4, 26.

"Police: Print links Coleman, death." *Dayton Daily News* 31 Aug. 1984: 26.

Roman, Mel, and William Haddad. *The Disposable Parent: The Case for Joint Custody.* 1978. New York: Penguin, 1979.

Schulz, Muriel R. "Is the English Language Anybody's Enemy? *Speaking of Words: A Language Reader.* Ed. James MacKillop and Donna Woolfolk Cross. 3rd ed. New York: Holt, 1986, 125-27.

Sorrels, Bobbye D. *The Nonsexist Communicator: Solving the Problems of Gender and Awkwardness in Modern English.* Englewood Cliffs, NJ: Prentice, 1983.

Straus, Murray A., Richard J. Gelles, and Suzanne K. Steinmetz. *Behind Closed Doors: Violence in the American Family.* 1980. Garden City, NY: Doubleday, 1981.

Theroux, Paul. "The Male Myth." *New York Times Magazine* 27 Nov. 1983: 116.

THINKING ABOUT THE TEXT

1. What bias in language has been studied more often than anti-male bias? Why do you think this is the case?

2. The author asserts that fixing blame for the use of anti-male language is not as important as "heightening public awareness" of it and finally "discouraging its use" (72). According to the author, who particularly must be aware of this language problem?

3. August's essay is extraordinarily well organized. In which paragraph does he forecast the categories of anti-male usage that exist in English? What is the advantage for the reader of his organization system?

4. What are examples of "gender-exclusive language" that the author gives, and what are the ramifications of such exclusion for males and for society as a whole?

5. What are examples of "gender-restrictive language" in the essay and how do the language restrictions confine males to certain gender expectations? The author suggests that the language restrictions actually contribute to poor health in men. Do you agree with his reasoning?

6. The author illustrates that the term "tomboy" is not a pejorative in describing a girl's behavior, but no neutral or positive term exists to describe a boy's behavior if he acts like a girl. How do you explain this restriction?

7. The author traces, through adulthood, restrictive terms applied only to males. What social consequences does he perceive that start from restrictive language that is hostile to males?

8. The author gives many examples of negative stereotyping—anti-male bias that exists in the language, "resides in people's assumptions about males," or has been created for political reasons. Which words support the author's points about each of these types of anti-male bias in language? How does the press reporting of the arrest of Debra Brown and Alton Coleman vividly illustrate the author's point?

9. In addition to getting people "to recognize and condemn" the use of anti-male terms in the language, what additional social consequence might result if anti-male stereotyping in language is obliterated?

WRITING FROM THE TEXT

1. Describe a time when you observed the problems created by anti-male bias in language—perhaps the use of vocabulary that ridicules men and confines them to prescribed behavior. What was the situation, what were your feelings, and what insight do you have as a result of this situation? Review how to write a narrative (pp. 409–18) for guidance on how to shape your story.

2. The author observes that the English language "excludes males as parents and as victims," and he uses examples of language from advertising and the press to support both of his points. With current examples of language derived from these two areas, argue whether or not August's analysis is still relevant.

3. Support Eugene August's point that people can be "subtly shaped into what society keeps telling them they are." You might want to observe how language has given both genders permission (*tomboy*) and restrictions (*sissy*). Show in your essay how significant this problem is.

4. The author states that when the word *sexism* is defined as "contempt for women," the definition of the word is itself sexist because it sees sexism

as a fault only of men. Using examples of sexist language that you have observed, write an essay showing that sexist language stereotypes or denigrates both males and females.

Connecting with Other Texts

1. In "The Future of Love" (p. 65), Jill Tweedie writes that romantic love is "heavily dependent upon an artificial facade and predictable masculine or feminine behavior" (67). Is Tweedie's negativity about romantic love based in part on language biases described by Eugene August? Write an essay that argues your point, using material from both essays for support.

2. In "Let 'em Eat Leftovers" (p. 91), author Mike McGrady asserts that giving the housewife a superior title like "household engineer," "domestic scientist," or even "Maharanee of the Vacuum Cleaner" will not elevate her status. But Eugene August believes that biased language shapes people into "what society keeps telling them they are" (81). In an essay, argue that language does or does not condition people's behavior and feelings about themselves. Use plenty of specific examples to support your points. Your essay, like McGrady's, might be humorous.

3. Consider August's essay while you read Adair Lara's essay "Who's Cheap?" (p. 94). In an essay, show how August's perceptions illuminate the many gender biases evident in Lara's scenarios.

The Second Shift

Arlie Russell Hochschild

Author and professor of sociology at University of California, Berkeley, Arlie Russell Hochschild (b. 1940) has published works that have attracted mainstream audiences as well as earned her acclaim from professionals in her field. She is accredited with inventing what one critic has called "a truism about American life"—the concept of the "second shift" to describe the work that American women do at home after they leave their paying jobs. Her works include *The Unexpected Community: Portrait of an Old Age Subculture* (1978), *The Managed Heart: Commercialization of Human Feeling* (1983), and *The Time Bind: When Work Becomes Home and Home Becomes Work* (1997). Hochschild's findings and conclusions have provoked considerable controversy and media coverage. The following excerpt is from *The Second Shift: Working Parents and the Revolution at Home* (1989), which she wrote with Anne Machung.

1   Every American household bears the footprints of economic and cultural trends that originate far outside its walls. A rise in inflation eroding the earn-

ing power of the male wage, an expanding service sector opening for women, and the inroads made by women into many professions—all these changes do not simply go on around the American family. They occur *within* a marriage or living-together arrangement and transform it. Problems between couples, problems that seem "unique" or "marital," are often the individual ripples of powerful economic and cultural shock waves. Quarrels between husbands and wives in households across the nation result mainly from a friction between faster-changing women and slower-changing men.

2   The exodus of women from the home to the workplace has not been accompanied by a new view of marriage and work that would make this transition smooth. Most workplaces have remained inflexible in the face of the changing needs of workers with families, and most men have yet to really adapt to the changes in women. I call the strain caused by the disparity between the change in women and absence of change elsewhere the "stalled revolution."

3   If women begin to do less at home because they have less time, if men do little more, and if the work of raising children and tending a home requires roughly the same effort, then the questions of who does what at home and of what "needs doing" become a source of deep tension in a marriage.

4   Over the past 30 years in the United States, more and more women have begun to work outside the home, and more have divorced. While some commentators conclude that women's work *causes* divorce, my research into changes in the American family suggests something else. Since all the wives in the families I studied (over an eight-year period) worked outside the home, the fact that they worked did not account for why some marriages were happy and others were not. What *did* contribute to happiness was the husband's willingness to do the work at home. Whether they were traditional or more egalitarian in their relationship, couples were happier when the men did a sizable share of housework and child care.

5   In one study of 600 couples filing for divorce, researcher George Levinger found that the second most common reason women cited for wanting to divorce—after "mental cruelty"—was their husbands' "neglect of home or children." Women mentioned this reason more often than financial problems, physical abuse, drinking, or infidelity.

6   A happy marriage is supported by a couple's being economically secure, by their enjoying a supportive community, and by their having compatible needs and values. But these days it may also depend on a shared appreciation of the work it takes to nurture others. As the role of the homemaker is being abandoned by many women, the homemaker's work has been continually devalued and passed on to low-paid housekeepers, baby-sitters, or day-care workers. Long devalued by men, the contribution of cooking, cleaning,

and care-giving is now being devalued as mere drudgery by many women, too.

7   In the era of the stalled revolution, one way to make housework and child care more valued is for men to share in that work. Many working mothers are already doing all they can at home. Now it's time for the men to make the move.

8   If more mothers of young children are working at full-time jobs outside the home, and if most couples can't afford household help, who's doing the work at home? Adding together the time it takes to do a paid job and to do housework and child care and using estimates from major studies on time use done in the 1960s and 1970s, I found that women worked roughly 15 more hours each week than men. Over a year, they worked an extra month of 24-hours a days. Over a dozen years, it was an extra year of 24-hour days. Most women without children spend much more time than men on housework. Women with children devote more time to both housework and child care. Just as there is a wage gap between men and women in the workplace, there is a "leisure gap" between them at home. Most women work one shift at the office or factory and a "second shift" at home.

9   In my research, I interviewed and observed 52 couples over an eight-year period as they cooked dinner, shopped, bathed their children, and in general struggled to find enough time to make their complex lives work. The women I interviewed seemed to be far more deeply torn between the demands of work and family than were their husbands. They talked more about the abiding conflict between work and family. They felt the second shift was *their* issue, and most of their husbands agreed. When I telephoned one husband to arrange an interview with him, explaining that I wanted to ask him how he managed work and family life, he replied genially, "Oh, this will *really* interest my *wife*."

10   Men who shared the load at home seemed just as pressed for time as their wives, and as torn between the demands of career and small children. But of the men I surveyed, the majority did not share the load at home. Some refused outright. Others refused more passively, often offering a loving shoulder to lean on, or an understanding ear, as their working wife faced the conflict they both saw as hers. At first it seemed to me that the problem of the second shift *was* hers. But I came to realize that those husbands who helped very little at home were often just as deeply affected as their wives—through the resentment their wives felt toward them and through their own need to steel themselves against that resentment.

11   A clear example of this phenomenon is Evan Holt, a warehouse furniture salesman who did very little housework and played with his four-year-old

son, Joey, only at his convenience. His wife, Nancy, did the second shift, but she resented it keenly and half-consciously expressed her frustration and rage by losing interest in sex and becoming overly absorbed in Joey.

12   Even when husbands happily shared the work, their wives *felt* more responsible for home and children. More women than men kept track of doctor's appointments and arranged for kids' playmates to come over. More mothers than fathers worried about a child's Halloween costume or a birthday present for a school friend. They were more likely to think about their children while at work and to check in by phone with the baby-sitter.

13   Partly because of this, more women felt torn between two kinds of urgency, between the need to soothe a child's fear of being left at day-care and the need to show the boss she's "serious" at work. Twenty percent of the men in my study shared housework equally. Seventy percent did a substantial amount (less than half of it, but more than a third), and 10 percent did less than a third. But even when couples more equitably share the work at home, women do two thirds of the daily jobs at home, such as cooking and cleaning up—jobs that fix them into a rigid routine. Most women cook dinner, for instance, while men change the oil in the family car. But, as one mother pointed out, dinner needs to be prepared every evening around six o'clock, whereas the car oil needs to be changed every six months, with no particular deadline. Women do more child care than men, and men repair more household appliances. A child needs to be tended to daily, whereas the repair of household appliances can often wait, said the men, "until I have time." Men thus have more control over when they make their contributions than women do. They may be very busy with family chores, but, like the executive who tells his secretary to "hold my calls," the man has more control over his time.

14   Another reason why women may feel under more strain than men is that women more often do two things at once—for example, write checks and return phone calls, vacuum and keep an eye on a three-year-old, fold laundry and think out the shopping list. Men more often will either cook dinner *or* watch the kids. Women more often do both at the same time.

15   Beyond doing more at home, women also devote, proportionately, more of their time at home to housework than men and proportionately less of it to child care. Of all the time men spend working at home, a growing amount of it goes to child care. Since most parents prefer to tend to their children than to clean house, men do more of what they'd rather do. More men than women take their children on "fun" outings to the park, the zoo, the movies. Women spend more time on maintenance, such as feeding and bathing children—enjoyable activities, to be sure, but often less leisurely or "special"

than going to the zoo. Men also do fewer of the most undesirable household chores, such as scrubbing the toilet.

16   As a result, women tend to talk more intensely about being overtired, sick, and emotionally, drained. Many women interviewed were fixated on the topic of sleep. They talked about how much they could "get by on" six and a half, seven, seven and a half, less, more. They talked about who they knew who needed more or less. Some apologized for how much sleep they needed—"I'm afraid I need eight hours of sleep"—as if eight was "too much." They talked about how to avoid fully waking up when a child called them at night, and how to get back to sleep. These women talked about sleep the way a hungry person talks about food.

17   If, all in all, the two-job family is suffering from a speedup of work and family life, working mothers are its primary victims. It is ironic, then, that often it falls to women to be the time-and-motion experts of family life. As I observed families inside their homes, I noticed it was often the mother who rushed children, saying, "Hurry up! It's time to go." "Finish your cereal now," "You can do that later," or "Let's go!" When a bath needed to be crammed into a slot between 7:45 and 8:00, it was often the mother who called out "Let's see who can take their bath the quickest." Often a younger child would rush out, scurrying to be first in bed, while the older and wiser one stalled, resistant, sometimes resentful: "Mother is always rushing us." Sadly, women are more often the lightning rods for family tensions aroused by this speedup of work and family life. They are the villains in a process in which they are also the primary victims. More than the longer hours and the lack of sleep, this is the saddest cost to women of this extra month of work each year.

18   Raising children in a nuclear family is still the overwhelming preference of most people. Yet in the face of new problems for this family mode we have not created an adequate support system so that the nuclear family can do its job well in the era of the two-career couple. Corporations have done little to accommodate the needs of working parents, and the government has done little to prod them.

19   We really need, as sociologist Frank Furstenberg has suggested, a Marshall Plan for the family. After World War II we saw that it was in our best interests to aid the war-torn nations of Europe. Now—it seems obvious in an era of growing concern over drugs, crime, and family instability—is in our best interests to aid the overworked two-job families right here at home. We should look to other nations for a model of what could be done. In Sweden, for example, upon the birth of a child every working couple is entitled to 12 months of paid parental leave—nine months at 90 percent of the worker's

salary, plus an additional three months at about three hundred dollars a month. The mother and father are free to divide this year off between them as they wish. Working parents of a child under eight have the opportunity to work no more than six hours a day, at six hours' pay. Parental insurance offers parents money for work time lost while visiting a child's school or caring for a sick child. That's a true pro-family policy.

20   A pro-family policy in the United States could give tax breaks to companies that encourage job sharing, part-time work, flex time, and family leave for new parents. By implementing comparable worth policies we could increase pay scales for "women's" jobs. Another key element of a pro-family policy would be instituting fewer-hour, more flexible options—called "family phases"—for all regular jobs filled by parents of young children.

21   Day-care centers could be made more warm and creative through generous public and private funding. If the best form of day-care comes from the attention of elderly neighbors, students, and grandparents, these people could be paid to care for children through social programs.

22   In these ways, the American government would create a safer environment for the two-job family. If the government encouraged corporations to consider the long-ranged interests of workers and their families, they would save on long-range costs caused by absenteeism, turnover, juvenile delinquency, mental illness, and welfare support for single mothers.

23   These are real pro-family reforms. If they seem utopian today, we should remember that in the past the eight-hour day, the abolition of child labor, and the vote for women seemed utopian, too. Among top-rated employers listed in the *100 Best Companies to Work for in America* are many offering country-club memberships, first-class air travel, and million-dollar fitness centers. But only a handful offer job sharing, flex time, or part-time work. Not one provides on-site day-care, and only three offer child-care deductions: Control Data, Polaroid, and Honeywell. In his book *Megatrends,* John Naisbitt reports that 83 percent of corporate executives believed that more men feel the need to share the responsibilities of parenting; yet only 9 percent of corporations offer paternity leave.

24   Public strategies are linked to private ones. Economic and cultural trends bear on family relations in ways it would be useful for all of us to understand. The happiest two-job marriages I saw during my research were ones in which men and women shared the housework and parenting. What couples called good communication often meant that they were good at saying thanks to one another for small aspects of taking care of the family. Making it to the school play, helping a child read, cooking dinner in good spirit, remembering the grocery list, taking responsibility for cleaning up the bedrooms—these were the silver and gold of the marital exchange. Until now, couples committed to an equal sharing of housework and child care have been rare. But, if we

as a culture come to see the urgent need of meeting the new problems posed by the second shift, and if society and government begin to shape new policies that allow working parents more flexibility, then we will be making some progress toward happier times at home and work. And as the young learn by example, many more women and men will be able to enjoy the pleasure that arises when family life is family life, and not a second shift.

THINKING ABOUT THE TEXT

1. What does Hochschild mean by the "stalled revolution"? Does this accurately represent the tension she describes? Support your answer.

2. In Levinger's study of 600 divorcing couples, what was the second most common reason women gave, after "mental cruelty," for wanting a divorce? What are the more critical implications of this reason, considering the two-career family?

3. What does Hochschild reveal are the most important findings in her study of 52 couples over an eight-year period?

4. What does Hochschild mean when she writes that women "are the villains in a process in which they are also the primary victims" (88)?

5. Make a list of the pro-family reforms that Hochschild proposes and evaluate each.

WRITING FROM THE TEXT

1. Write an analysis of the difficulties plaguing many two-career families, according to Hochschild's eight-year study of 52 couples. Explain the complexities fully and offer any possible solutions.

2. Write a proposal for alleviating the tension between work and family responsibilities. You may include and expand on Hochschild's pro-family reforms and devise your own.

3. Using your own family experience as a starting point, write an evaluative response essay critiquing Hochschild's thesis, findings, and solutions. Make sure that your thesis articulates your position regarding her main points.

CONNECTING WITH OTHER TEXTS

1. Focusing on the short stories by Updike (p. 34), Tyler (p. 45), Oates (p. 126), or Straight (p. 186), write an essay evaluating the extent of the story's treatment of the "stalled revolution," "second shift," and other phenomena and tensions that Hochschild examines. Include quotations from the story and from Hochschild's essay in your analysis.

2. Using criteria from "The Second Shift," write an essay comparing and contrasting the parenting styles and abilities of Ace (p. 34) and McGrady (below).

Let 'em Eat Leftovers
Mike McGrady

Freelance writer Mike McGrady (b. 1933) earned a B.A. from Yale University and did additional study at Harvard University. He served for two years in the army, and then a decade later won the Overseas Press Club Award for best interpretive reporting for *A Dove in Vietnam* (1968). After sixteen years of marriage, McGrady and his wife reversed roles for a year, and he stayed home to care for the children and the house. He relates his experiences in *The Kitchen Sink Papers: My Life as a Househusband* (1975). He also published *The Husband's Cookbook* (1979). In addition to his news columns and books for adults, McGrady has written and coauthored books for teens. His work often reflects a delightful sense of humor, as you can see in the next essay, which first appeared in a 1976 issue of *Newsweek.*

1   Last year my wife and I traded roles. Every morning she went off to an office and earned the money that paid the bills. I cooked and cleaned, picked up after three kids, went head-to-head with bargain-hunting shoppers, pleaded for a raise in allowance and lived the generally hellish life that half the human race accepts as its lot.

2   The year is over now but the memories won't go away. What is guaranteed to stir them up is any of those Total Woman or Fascinating Womanhood people singing the praises of the happy housewife—that mythical woman who manages a spotless house, runs herd over half a dozen kids, whips up short-order culinary masterpieces, smells good and still finds time to read Great Books and study Japanese line engraving.

3   I never qualified. Never even came close. In fact, I never quite mastered that most basic task, the cleaning of the house. Any job that requires six hours to do and can be undone in six minutes by one small child carrying a plate of crackers and a Monopoly set—this is not a job that will long capture my interest. After a year of such futility, I have arrived at a rule of thumb—if the debris accumulates to a point where small animals can be seen to be living there, it should be cleaned up, preferably by someone hired for the occasion.

4   Housekeeping was just one facet of the nightmare. I think back to a long night spent matching up four dozen bachelor socks, all of them wool, most of them gray. Running an all-hours taxi service for subteens. Growing older in orthodontists' waiting rooms. Pasting trading stamps into little

booklets. Oh, the nightmare had as many aspects as there were hours in the day.

5   At the heart of my difficulty was this simple fact: for the past two decades I had been paid for my work. I had come to feel my time was valuable. Suddenly my sole payment was a weekly allowance given to me with considerable fanfare by my breadwinning wife. I began to see that as a trap, a many-strings-attached offering that barely survived a single session in the supermarket and never got me through a neighborhood poker game.

6   The pay was bad and the hours were long but what bothered me most was my own ineptitude, my inability to apply myself to the business of managing a home. No longer do I feel guilty about my failure as a homemaker. I would no more applaud the marvelously efficient and content housewife than I would applaud the marvelously efficient and content elevator operator. The image strikes me as useful on several levels but the point is this: it is always someone else who goes up, someone else who gets off.

7   Some people seem to feel that the housewife's lot would be bettered if she were given a new title, one that takes into account the full range and complexity of her role, something along the lines of "household engineer" or, perhaps, "domestic scientist." Wonderful. You come and take care of my house and my kids and you can be the Empress of the Domestic Arts, the Maharanee of the Vacuum Cleaner.

8   A more intriguing suggestion is that husbands pay their wives salaries for housework. I suggested this to my wife and she said I don't make enough money to pay her to do that job again. Neither, according to her, does J. Paul Getty. I am coming to the feeling that this is a job that should not be done by any one person for love or for money.

9   This is not to put down the whole experience. By the end of the year, I had succeeded in organizing my time so that there were a few hours for the occasional book, the random round of golf. Then, too, it was a pleasure to be more than a weekend visitor in my kids' lives. While my wife and I are now willing to de-emphasize housekeeping, neither of us would cut back on what some people call parenting and what I look at as the one solid reward in this belated and male motherhood of mine.

10   Of course, I had it easy—relatively easy anyway. This was my little experiment, not my destiny. There is a considerable difference between a year in prison and a life sentence.

11   It will be argued: well, *someone* has to do these things. Not necessarily. In the first place, some two can do most of these things. Secondly, I can think of no area in modern life that could more easily sustain a policy of benign

neglect than the home. I'm arguing here in favor of letting the dust gather where it may; in favor of making greater use of slow cookers and nearby fish-and-chips stands; of abolishing, as far as possible, the position of unpaid servant in the family.

12   Many men surely will find this line of thought threatening. That's just as it should be. Few plantation owners were enthusiastic about the Emancipation Proclamation. What is more surprising is that these thoughts will prove equally threatening to many women. OK. Those females who demand the right to remain in service should not necessarily be discouraged—we all know how hard it is to find decent household help these days.

13   I suspect the real reason for many women's reluctance to break bonds is fear of the world that exists outside the home. They sense the enormous complexity of their husbands' lives, the tremendous skills required to head up a team of salesmen or to write cigarette commercials or to manufacture lawn fertilizer. The mind that feels these fears may be beyond the reach of change. It is another sort of mind, the mind that finds itself in constant rebellion against the limitations of housewifery, that concerns me more here.

14   To this mind, this person, we should say: go ahead. There is a world out there, a whole planet of possibilities. The real danger is that you won't do it. If Gutenburg had been a housewife, I might be writing these words with a quill pen. And if Edison had been a housewife, you might be reading them by candlelight.

15   No escape is simple and a certain amount of toughness will be required. How do you do it? You might start by learning how to sweep things under the rug. You might have to stop pampering the rest of the family—let 'em eat leftovers. And be prepared for the opposition that will surely develop. Even the most loving family hates to lose that trusted servant, that faithful family retainer, that little old homemaker, you. No one enjoys it when the most marvelous appliance of them all breaks down. But if it will be any comfort to you, the life you save will surely be your own.

THINKING ABOUT THE TEXT

1. List the expected achievements of the "happy housewife" according to proponents of the "Total Woman" or "Fascinating Womanhood."

2. Describe specifically how McGrady's experiences contradict the stereotype of the perfect housewife and prove it to be "mythical."

3. What does McGrady claim is the most frustrating aspect of housecleaning? What did he establish as a rule of thumb for cleaning?

4. What does McGrady feel about changing the title "housewife" or about paying housewives an actual salary? What is one solid reward of staying at home?

5. How does McGrady counter the argument that "someone has to do" the cleaning and other menial chores? What does he feel are the real reasons that some women continue to do this job?

6. When Marie Antoinette was informed that the French citizens were starving and had no bread, she allegedly responded, "Let them eat cake." Beginning with his title, which alludes to the queen's callous retort, McGrady's essay is filled with humor, verbal irony, and sarcasm. List specific examples and analyze their effect.

WRITING FROM THE TEXT

1. Write an essay analyzing the difficulties in your own household of getting the menial work done equitably. Describe any creative experiments—failures and successes—and feel free to use humor, as McGrady did.

2. If you have ever tried to be the "happy housewife" or have lived in a house with one, write an essay describing that experience and the consequences.

CONNECTING WITH OTHER TEXTS

1. Using details from McGrady's essay, write an analysis of his behavior and attitude as it relates to Arlie Hochschild's findings in "The Second Shift" (p. 84). How would she evaluate him in terms of the "stalled revolution"?

2. Several of our authors use humor to advance serious assertions. Consider the works on family life by McGrady, Updike (p. 34), and Douglas (p. 284) to analyze how their use of humor helps readers better understand and support their more serious points.

Who's Cheap?

Adair Lara

A columnist for the *San Francisco Chronicle*, Adair Lara (b. 1952) is also a teacher of writing and the author of *Welcome to Earth, Mom: Tales of a Single Mother* (1992), *Slowing Down in a Speeded-Up World*, (1994), and *The Best of Adair Lara* (1999). The essay included here originally appeared in the *San Francisco Chronicle*.

1   It was our second date, and we had driven one hundred miles up the coast in my car to go abalone-diving. When I stopped to fill the tank at the only gas station in sight, Craig scowled and said, "You shouldn't get gas here. It's a rip-off."

2   But he didn't offer to help pay. And that night, after dinner in a restaurant, he leaned over and whispered intimately, "You get the next one." Though he was sensitive and smart, and looked unnervingly good, Craig was as cheap as a two-dollar watch.

3   This is not an ethical dilemma, you're all shouting. *Lose the guy,* and fast.

4   Lose the guy? Is this fair? My friend Jill is always heading for the john when the check comes, but I don't hear anybody telling me to lose *her.* And she's far from the only cheap woman I know. A lot of us make decent money these days, yet I haven't seen women knocking over tables in fights for the lunch tab. In fact, many women with 20/20 vision seem to have trouble distinguishing the check from the salt, pepper and other tabletop items. But if a guy forgets to chip in for gas or gloats too long over the deal he got on his Nikes, he's had it.

5   Why is this double standard so enduring? One reason is that, while neither sex has a monopoly on imperfection, there *are* such things as flaws that are much more distasteful in one sex than in the other. Women seem especially unpleasant when they get drunk, swear or even insist on pursuing an argument they'll never win. And men seem beneath contempt when they're cheap.

6   These judgments are a holdover from the days when women stayed home and men earned the money. Though that old order has passed, we still associate men with paying for things. And besides, there's just something appealing about generosity. Buying something for someone is, in a sense, taking care of her. The gesture says, "I like you, I want to give you something." If it comes from a man to whom we are about to entrust our hearts, this is a comforting message. We miss it when it's not forthcoming.

7   Then why *not* dump on cheap men?

8   Some men are just skinflints and that's it. My friend Skye broke up with her boyfriend because when they went to the movies he doled out M&Ms to her one at a time. Craig, my date back at the gas station, liked to talk about how he'd bought his car—which in California, where I live, is like buying shoes—as a special present to himself.

9   This kind of cheapness is ingrained; you'll never change it. That guy who parks two miles away to avoid the parking lot fee was once a little boy who saved his birthday money without being told to. Now he's a man who studies the menu and sputters, "Ten dollars for *pasta?*" His stinginess will always grate on you, since he is likely to dole out his feelings as parsimoniously as his dollars.

10   On the other hand, I know a wonderful man, crippled with debts from a former marriage, who had to break up with a woman because she never paid her share, and he was simply running out of money. Though she earned a lot more than he did, she couldn't expand her definition of masculinity to include "sometimes needs to go Dutch treat."

11   To men, such women seem grasping. One friend of mine, who spends a lot of money on concerts and theater and sailing but not on restaurants he considers overpriced, has evolved a strategy for women who are annoyed at the bohemian places he favors. If his date complains, he offers to donate to the charity of her choice the cost of an evening at her favorite spot. "Some women have bad values," he says, "And if the idea of spending money on a good cause, but not on her, makes her livid, I know she's one of them."

12   I had a bracing encounter with my own values when I told my friend Danny the humorous (I thought) story of a recent date who asked if I wanted a drink after a concert, then led me to the nearest water fountain.

13   Danny gave one of his wry looks. "Let's get this straight," he said, laughing. "As a woman, you are so genetically precious that you deserve attention just because you grace the planet. So, of course, he should buy you drinks. He should also drive the car, open the door, ask you to dance, coax you to bed. And then when you feel properly pampered, you can let out that little whine about how he doesn't treat you as an equal."

14   On second thought, I guess I'd rather buy my own drink.

15   So here's the deal. Before dumping a guy for ordering the sundowner dinner or the house white, better first make sure that you aren't burdening the relationship with outdated ideas of how the sexes should behave. Speaking for myself, I know that if a man looks up from the check and says, "Your share is eleven dollars," part of me remembers that, according to my mother, *my* share was to look charming in my flowered blouse.

16   Wanting the man to pay dies hard. What many of us do now is *offer* to split the check, then let our purses continue to dangle from the chair as we give him time to realize that the only proper response is to whip out his own wallet.

17   Is this a game worth playing? It's up to you, but consider that offering to help pay implies that the check is his responsibility. And this attitude can work both ways. My sister gets angry when her husband offers to help clean the house. "Like it's *my* house!" she snorts.

18   Like it's *his* check.

THINKING ABOUT THE TEXT

1. Authors may use humor to engage an audience—even when their intention is to argue a serious point. Is Lara's main purpose in this essay mostly to entertain or to persuade her audience?

2. Does Lara have a claim? If so, what is it? Does she have support?

3. What does Lara mean when she writes that some flaws seem "much more distasteful in one sex than in the other"? *Are* women more unpleasant than men when they "get drunk, swear or even insist on pursuing an argument they'll never win" or are these the author's sexist generalizations? (If they are generalizations, what is her goal in using them?)

4. Is there any truth to Lara's belief that a man who is stingy is also likely to "dole out his feelings as parsimoniously as his dollars"? Are women who are "cheap" also likely to withhold affection?

5. In what way is the point of Lara's essay embedded in Danny's response to Lara's anecdote about the after-concert drink? Why does Lara manipulate her essay so that its central wisdom appears in Danny's words? What is the author's strategy?

6. What are the conventional and sexist ideas that are challenged in this essay?

WRITING FROM THE TEXT

1. Lara cites a number of specific ways that people save money—avoiding commercial parking lots, eating the "sundowner" or "early bird" dinner, and drinking the house wine. Make a list of all of the ways that you save money. How many of your habits would be regarded by a date or friends as "cheap"? Develop your list into supporting examples for a thesis of your own.

2. Describe the habits of your dates and friends when it comes to ignoring a bill or saving money. The focus of your essay can be to laud or deplore your friends' habits.

3. Using Lara's essay for support, write an essay arguing that the double standard Lara describes hurts both men and women.

4. Write an essay arguing that the traditional roles—that women "look charming" and men pay for the date—should persist in the new century. You may employ humor and satire in your essay if you wish.

CONNECTING WITH OTHER TEXTS

1. In "The Future of Love" (p. 65), Jill Tweedie argues that adolescent notions about love threaten real relationships. Use Tweedie's specific points and your own observations to analyze the scenarios described in Lara's essay.

2. In an essay show how anti-male bias is operating in Lara's essay. Read "Real Men Don't: Anti-Male Bias in English" (p. 71) for specific points to use in your analysis.

3. In "A Work of Artifice" (p. 106), Marge Piercy suggests that men deliberately keep women in an "attractive pot." Lara suggests that "cheap men" may actually be freeing women. Link the poem and essay to support your own view on this subject.

 # Uncle Sam and Aunt Samantha

Anna Quindlen

Novelist and nationally syndicated newspaper columnist Anna Quindlen (b. 1953) landed a job as a news reporter before graduating with a B.A. from Barnard College in 1974. Three years later, she was offered a position at the *New York Times*, which remains her base as author of a syndicated biweekly column, "Public & Private." She is a regular columnist for *Newsweek*. Critics have praised her unaffected writing style, depth of insight, and ability to turn "the mundane into the meaningful." Awarded the 1992 Pulitzer Prize for commentary, Quindlen has published her columns in *Living Out Loud* (1988) and *Thinking Out Loud: On the Personal, the Political, the Public and the Private* (1994). In 2000 Quindlen published *A Short Guide to a Happy Life*. Her novels include the best-selling *Object Lessons* (1991), *One True Thing* (1995) which she adapted for a film starring Renee Zellweger and Meryl Streep (1998), and *Black and Blue* (1998). The following essay appeared in *Newsweek*, November 5, 2001.

1   One out of every five new recruits in the United States military is female.

2   The Marines gave the Combat Action Ribbon for service in the Persian Gulf to 23 women.

3   Two female soldiers were killed in the bombing of the USS Cole.

4   The Selective Services registers for the draft all male citizens between the ages of 18 and 25.

5   What's wrong with this picture?

6   As Americans read and realize that the lives of most women in this country are as different from those of Afghan women as a Cunard cruise is from maximum-security lockdown, there has nonetheless been little attention paid to one persistent gender inequity in U.S. public policy. An astonishing anachronism, really: while women are represented today in virtually all fields, including the armed forces, only men are required to register for the military draft that would be used in the event of a national-security crisis.

7   Since the nation is as close to such a crisis as it has been in more than 60 years, it's a good moment to consider how the draft wound up in this particular time warp. It's not the time warp of the Taliban, certainly, stuck in the worst part of the 13th century, forbidding women to attend school or hold

jobs or even reveal their arms, forcing them into sex and marriage. Our own time warp is several decades old. The last time the draft was considered seriously was 20 years ago, when registration with the Selective Service was restored by Jimmy Carter after the Soviet invasion of, yep, Afghanistan. The president, as well as the Army chief of staff, asked at the time for the registration of women as well as men.

8   Amid a welter of arguments—women interfere with esprit de corps, women don't have the physical strength, women prisoners could be sexually assaulted, women soldiers would distract male soldiers from their mission— Congress shot down the notion of gender-blind registration. So did the Supreme Court, ruling that since women were forbidden to serve in combat positions and the purpose of the draft was to create a combat-ready force, it made sense not to register them.

9   But that was then, and this is now. Women have indeed served in combat positions, in the Balkans and the Middle East. More than 40,000 managed to serve in the Persian Gulf without destroying unit cohesion or failing because of upper-body strength. Some are even now taking out targets in Afghanistan from fighter jets, and apparently without any male soldier's falling prey to some predicted excess of chivalry or lust.

10   Talk about cognitive dissonance. All these military personnel, male and female alike, have come of age at a time when a significant level of parity was taken for granted. Yet they are supposed to accept that only males will be required to defend their country in a time of national emergency. This is insulting to men. And it is insulting to women. Caroline Forell, an expert on women's legal rights and a professor at the University of Oregon School of Law, puts it bluntly: "Failing to require this of women makes us lesser citizens."

11   Neither the left nor the right has been particularly inclined to consider this issue judiciously. Many feminists came from the antiwar movement and have let their distaste for the military in general and the draft in particular mute their response. In 1980 NOW released a resolution that buried support for the registration of women beneath opposition to the draft, despite the fact that the draft had be redesigned to eliminate the vexing inequalities of Vietnam, when the sons of the working class served and the sons of the Ivy League did not. Conservatives, meanwhile, used an equal-opportunity draft as the linchpin of opposition to the Equal Rights Amendment, along with the terrifying specter of unisex bathrooms. (I have seen the urinal, and it is benign.) The legislative director of the right-wing group Concerned Women for America once defended the existing regulations by saying that most women "don't want to be included in the draft." All those young men who went to Canada during Vietnam and those who today register with fear and trembling in the

face of the Trade Center devastation might be amazed to discover that lack of desire is an affirmative defense.

12   Parents face a series of unique new challenges in this more egalitarian world, not the least of which would be sending a daughter off to war. But parents all over this country are doing that right now, with daughters who enlisted; some have even expressed surprise that young women, in this day and age, are not required to register alongside their brothers and friends. While all involved in this debate over the years have invoked the assumed opposition of the people, even 10 years ago more than half of all Americans polled believed women should be made eligible for the draft. Besides, this is not about comfort but about fairness. My son has to register with the Selective Service this year, and if his sister does not when she turns 18, it makes a mockery not only of the standards of this household but of the standards of this nation.

13   It is possible in Afghanistan for women to be treated like little more than fecund pack animals precisely because gender fear and ignorance and hatred have been codified and permitted to hold sway. In this country, largely because of the concerted efforts of those allied with the women's movement over a century of struggle, much of that bigotry has been beaten back, even buried. Yet in improbable places the creaky old ways surface, the ways suggesting that we women were made of finer stuff. The finer stuff was usually porcelain, decorative and on the shelf, suitable for meals and show. Happily, the finer stuff has been transmuted into the right stuff. But with rights come responsibilities, as teachers like to tell their students. This is a responsibility that should fall equally upon all, male and female alike. If the empirical evidence is considered rationally, if the decision is divested of outmoded stereotypes, that's the only possible conclusion to be reached.

THINKING ABOUT THE TEXT

1. What "inequity" does Quindlen expect readers to draw from her opening sentences? Why is this practice such "an astonishing anachronism"?

2. Twenty years ago when President Jimmy Carter and his Army chief of staff proposed gender-blind registration for the draft, what were the reasons that Congress and the Supreme Court refused? Why does Quindlen believe these reasons are not relevant today?

3. Why has neither the political left nor right "been inclined to consider this issue [of a gender-blind draft] judiciously"?

4. How does Quindlen anticipate and counter the objection that many parents cannot handle sending their daughters off to war? Why does she use her own children as examples in this debate?

5. Note Quindlen's various references to Afghanistan throughout her essay. Assess the reasons for and effectiveness of each.

WRITING FROM THE TEXT

1. Write an argument favoring or opposing Quindlen's position. Include direct quotations from her essay and well-reasoned support for your claims.

2. Focusing on Quindlen's essay, write an evaluative response of her thesis and key supporting points and reasons. Include select quotations and analyze them fully.

CONNECTING WITH OTHER TEXTS

1. Considering the key points in "Patriotism Demands Questioning Authority" (p. 266), write an essay arguing that Quindlen is or is not ultimately "patriotic," even though she is criticizing the current government policy concerning the draft.

2. Using points from Quindlen's essay and from "Diversity Offers Everyone a Stake" (p. 156), argue that diversity is or is not a definite benefit to a gender-blind draft. Analyze direct quotations from both essays as you support your thesis.

 Pigskin, Patriarchy, and Pain

Don Sabo

A professor of social science at D'Youville College in Buffalo, New York, Don Sabo (b. 1947) has lectured and written on men's issues. Sabo is a fitness enthusiast and a former NCAA Division I defensive football captain. He is the coauthor of *Jock: Sports and Male Identity, Humanism in Sociology, Sport, Men, and the Gender Order: Critical Feminist Perspectives,* and 1994's *Sex, Violence and Power in Sports,* where the following essay first appeared.

1   I am sitting down to write as I've done thousands of times over the last decade. But today there's something very different. I'm not in pain.

2   A half year ago I underwent back surgery. My physician removed two disks from the lumbar region of my spine and fused three vertebrae using bone scrapings from my right hip. The surgery is called a "spinal fusion." For seventy-two hours I was completely immobilized. On the fifth day, I took a few faltering first steps with one of those aluminum walkers that are usually associated with the elderly in nursing homes. I progressed rapidly and left the hospital after nine days completely free of pain for the first time in years.

3   How did I, a well-intending and reasonably gentle boy from western Pennsylvania, ever get into so much pain? At a simple level, I ended up in pain because I played a sport that brutalizes men's (and now sometimes women's) bodies. *Why* I played football and bit the bullet of pain, however, is more complicated. Like a young child who learns to dance or sing for a piece of candy, I played for rewards and payoffs. Winning at sport meant winning friends and carving a place for myself within the male pecking order. Success at the "game" would make me less like myself and more like the older boys and my hero, Dick Butkus. Pictures of his hulking and snarling form filled my head and hung over my bed, beckoning me forward like a mythic Siren. If I could be like Butkus, I told myself, people would adore me as much as I adored him. I might even adore myself. As an adolescent I hoped sport would get me attention from the girls. Later, I became more practical-minded and I worried more about my future. What kind of work would I do for a living? Football became my ticket to a college scholarship which, in western Pennsylvania during the early 'sixties, meant a career instead of getting stuck in the steelmills.

4   My bout with pain and spinal "pathology" began with a decision I made in 1955 when I was 8 years old. I "went out" for football. At the time, I felt uncomfortable inside my body—too fat, too short, too weak. Freckles and glasses, too! I wanted to change my image, and I felt that changing my body was one place to begin. My parents bought me a set of weights, and one of the older boys in the neighborhood was solicited to demonstrate their use. I can still remember the ease with which he lifted the barbell, the veins popping through his bulging biceps in the summer sun, and the sated look of strength and accomplishment on his face. This was to be the image of my future.

5   That fall I made a dinner-table announcement that I was going out for football. What followed was a rather inauspicious beginning. First, the initiation rites. Pricking the flesh with thorns until blood was drawn and having hot peppers rubbed in my eyes. Getting punched in the gut again and again. Being forced to wear a jockstrap around my nose and not knowing what was funny. Then came what was to be an endless series of proving myself: calisthenics until my arms ached; hitting hard and fast and knocking the other guy down; getting hit in the groin and not crying. I learned that pain and injury are "part of the game."

6   I "played" through grade school, co-captained my high school team, and went on to become an inside linebacker and defensive captain at the NCAA Division I level. I learned to be an animal. Coaches took notice of animals. Animals made first team. Being an animal meant being fanati-

cally aggressive and ruthlessly competitive. If I saw an arm in front of me, I trampled it. Whenever blood was spilled, I nodded approval. Broken bones (not mine of course) were secretly seen as little victories within the bigger struggle. The coaches taught me to "punish the other man," but little did I suspect that I was devastating my own body at the same time. There were broken noses, ribs, fingers, toes and teeth, torn muscles and ligaments, bruises, bad knees, and busted lips, and the gradual pulverizing of my spinal column that, by the time my jock career was long over at age 30, had resulted in seven years of near-constant pain. It was a long road to the surgeon's office.

7   Now surgically freed from its grip, my understanding of pain has changed. Pain had gnawed away at my insides. Pain turned my awareness inward. I blamed myself for my predicament; I thought that I was solely responsible for every twinge and sleepless night. But this view was an illusion. My pain, each individual's pain, is really an expression of a linkage to an outer world of people, events, and forces. The origins of our pain are rooted *outside,* not inside, our skins.

8   Sport is just one of the many areas in our culture where pain is more important than pleasure. Boys are taught that to endure pain is courageous, to survive pain is manly. The principle that pain is "good" and pleasure is "bad" is crudely evident in the "no pain, no gain" philosophy of so many coaches and athletes. The "pain principle" weaves its way into the lives and psyches of male athletes in two fundamental ways. It stifles men's awareness of their bodies and limits our emotional expression. We learn to ignore personal hurts and injuries because they interfere with the "efficiency" and "goals" of the "team." We become adept at taking the feelings that boil up inside us—feelings of insecurity and stress from striving so hard for success—and channeling them in a bundle of rage which is directed at opponents and enemies. This posture toward oneself and the world is not limited to "jocks." It is evident in the lives of many nonathletic men who, as tough guys, deny their authentic physical or emotional needs and develop health problems as a result.

9   Today, I no longer perceive myself as an *individual* ripped off by athletic injury. Rather, I see myself as just *one more man among many men* who got swallowed up by a social system predicated on male domination. Patriarchy has two structural aspects. First, it is a hierarchical system in which men dominate women in crude and debased, slick and subtle ways. Feminists have made great progress exposing and analyzing this dimension of the edifice of sexism. But it is also a system of *intermale dominance,* in which a minority of men dominates the masses of men. This intermale dominance

hierarchy exploits the majority of those it beckons to climb its heights. Patriarchy's mythos of heroism and its morality of power-worship implant visions of ecstasy and masculine excellence in the minds of the boys who ultimately will defend its inequities and ridicule its victims. It is inside this institutional framework that I have begun to explore the essence and scope of "the pain principle."

10   Patriarchy is a form of social hierarchy. Hierarchy breeds inequity and inequity breeds pain. To remain stable, the hierarchy must either justify the pain or explain it away. In a patriarchy, women and the masses of men are fed the cultural message that pain is inevitable and that pain enhances one's character and moral worth. This principle is expressed in Judeo-Christian beliefs. The Judeo-Christian god inflicts or permits pain, yet "the Father" is still revered and loved. Likewise, a chief disciplinarian in the patriarchal family, the father has the right to inflict pain. The "pain principle" also echoes throughout traditional Western sexual morality; it is better to experience the pain of *not* having sexual pleasure than it is to have sexual pleasure.

11   Most men learned to heed these cultural messages and take their "cues for survival" from the patriarchy. The Willie Lomans of the economy pander to the profit and the American Dream. Soldiers, young and old, salute their neo-Hun generals. Right-wing Christians genuflect before the idols of righteousness, affluence, and conformity. And male athletes adopt the visions and values that coaches are offering: to take orders, to take pain, to "take out" opponents, to take the game seriously, to take women, and to take their place on the team. And if they can't "take it," then the rewards of athletic camaraderie, prestige, scholarship, pro contracts, and community recognitions are not forthcoming.

12   Becoming a football player fosters conformity to male-chauvinistic values and self-abusing lifestyles. It contributes to the legitimacy of a social structure based on patriarchal power. Male competition for prestige and status in sport and elsewhere leads to identification with the relatively few males who control resources and are able to bestow rewards and inflict punishment. Male supremacists are not born, they are made, and traditional athletic socialization is a fundamental contribution to this complex social-psychological and political process. Through sport, many males, indeed, learn to "take it"—that is, to internalize patriarchal values which, in turn, become part of their gender identity and conception of women and society.

13   My high school coach once evoked the pain principle during a pre-game peptalk. For what seemed like an eternity, he paced frenetically and silently before us with fists clenched and head bowed. He suddenly stopped and faced

us with a smile. It was as though he had approached a podium to begin a long-awaited lecture. "Boys," he began, "people who say that football is a 'contact sport' are dead wrong. Dancing is a contact sport. Football is a game of pain and violence! Now get the hell out of here and kick some ass." We practically ran through the wall of the locker room, surging in unison to fight the coach's war. I see now that the coach was right but for all the wrong reasons. I should have taken him at his word and never played the game!

THINKING ABOUT THE TEXT

1. Why did the author decide, as a child, to play football? What were the specific rewards he gained by engaging in the sport? Can you relate Sabo's decision to one you have made in your own life?

2. What were the initiation rites that preceded his involvement with the football team? What do you imagine is the purpose of these rites?

3. Sabo relates that he became "an animal" inflicting pain on others and also incurring his own body injuries and pain. Why do boys (and increasingly girls) accept the pain of the game?

4. Sabo concludes that men suffer more than physical injury playing football. They suffer because they stifle their awareness of their bodies and they limit their emotional expression by directing their feelings, instead, to the team and its goals. School counselors often recommend that children play team sports to learn cooperation and willingness to apply themselves to a group goal. How might Sabo respond to this advice?

5. Today, Sabo sees himself as "one more man among many men who got swallowed up by a social system predicated on male domination" (103). What is the hierarchical system the author perceives and how does playing football support this system?

6. What is Sabo's strategy in examining the verb "to take"? In how many ways does he use the verb? What is the strategy of his title?

7. What does the author conclude are the serious social and psychological results of participation in football?

WRITING FROM THE TEXT

1. Sabo writes that "male supremacists are not born, they are made, and traditional athletic socialization is a fundamental contribution to this complex social-psychological and political process" (104). Show your agreement or disagreement with this assertion in an essay that uses specific examples from your involvement with or observations of team sports.

2. Write an essay that reveals how your ability "to take it" in some athletic activity helped you achieve a goal in your life outside of athletics.

3. Describe a time when you engaged in a socially approved activity because you wanted the rewards of friendship or public adoration. Review the strategies on how to write a narrative (pp. 409–418) after you have done some freewriting on the topic.

4. Write an essay that analyzes activities other than football that foster "conformity to male-chauvinistic values and self-abusing lifestyles." You might try using humor or irony in your essay.

CONNECTING WITH OTHER TEXTS

1. Read "Common Decency" (p. 119) and write an analysis of how the messages that males learn playing football may interfere with Jacoby's notion of decency.

2. Read "The Future of Love" (p. 65) to connect Tweedie's ideas about gender stereotyping with Sabo's perception of what boys learn playing football. Write an analysis of the problem and consequences of conforming to gender stereotypes.

3. In an analytic essay, show how Ace Anderson's problem ("Ace in the Hole," p. 34) is mostly the result of having been admired as a high school athlete. In your essay, show how Sabo's ideas are played out in Ace's life.

A Work of Artifice
Marge Piercy

Educated at the University of Michigan and Northwestern University, Marge Piercy (b. 1936) has served as a visiting lecturer, writer in residence, and professor at many universities in the United States. She has won numerous prizes, awards, and honors for her novels, short stories, plays, and essays. Her recent work includes the novel *Three Women* (1999), *The Art of Blessing the Day: Poems with a Jewish Theme* (1999), and *Early Grrl: The Early Poems of Marge Piercy* (1999). Since 1997 Piercy has been the editor of Leapfrog Press, and in 2000 she was resident poet at the Center for the Book in Fort Lauderdale, Florida. Of her work Piercy says, "I have been particularly although not exclusively concerned with the choices open to—or perceived to be open to—women of various eras, races, and classes. I am one of the few contemporary American novelists consciously and constantly preoccupied with social class and the economic underpinnings of decision and consequence." The poem included here is from *Circles on the Water* (1982), one of Piercy's many collections of poetry.

The bonsai tree
in the attractive pot
could have grown eighty feet tall
on the side of a mountain
5   till split by lightning.
But a gardener
carefully pruned it.
It is nine inches high.
Every day as he
10   whittles back the branches
the gardener croons,
It is your nature
to be small and cozy
domestic and weak;
15   how lucky, little tree,
to have a pot to grow in.
With living creatures
one must begin very early
to dwarf their growth:
20   the bound feet,
the crippled brain,
the hair in curlers,
the hands you
love to touch.

THINKING ABOUT THE TEXT

1. According to the poem, how is a bonsai tree created and maintained?

2. What are the comparisons between the creation and care of a bonsai and the creation and care of a woman? Do you object to the art of bonsai? How do you feel about what happens to women?

3. Look up the word *artifice* in a dictionary and copy all of the definitions listed for the word. In what ways is each meaning of the word useful to Piercy in conveying the point of her poem? What *is* her point?

WRITING FROM THE TEXT

1. Write an essay in which you explain how Marge Piercy's title contains the perfect word choice for conveying the theme of the poem. You will want to examine the multiple definitions of the word *artifice* as part of your analysis. (See poetry analysis, p. 475.)

2. Write an essay analyzing the ways that women are "crooned" to and the resultant "cozy" and "weak" ways that they are kept. Show your attitude or stance toward this situation in your essay.

CONNECTING WITH OTHER TEXTS

1. Look up information about the art of bonsai in an encyclopedia or gardening text in your school or city library. Write an essay about the goals of this art form, and summarize the process of maintaining a bonsai plant.

2. In an essay explain how the history of keeping women "small and cozy / domestic and weak" has been opposed in recent years. Use specific examples of the presence of women in professional, business, or academic worlds to argue that "the crippled brain" is a metaphor of the past.

3. Write an essay comparing Piercy's perception about what happens to women in "A Work of Artifice" with the insights about women in Kim Edwards' essay "In Rooms of Women" (p. 161).

4. Research the Chinese custom of footbinding and summarize the methods, purpose, and effects of this procedure. Incorporate your findings into an analysis of Piercy's description of the subtle and insidious ways that women's growth is stunted.

On the Fringes of the Physical World
Meghan Daum

A graduate of Vassar College with a B.A. in English, Meghan Daum (b. 1970) earned an M.F.A. in writing from Columbia University. Her work has appeared in such popular magazines as *The New Yorker, Harper's, G.Q., Harper's Bazaar,* and *Vogue.* Daum has been a columnist at *Self* magazine and has contributed commentaries and stories to public radio programs such as Morning Edition, This American Life, and The Savvy Traveler. A novel, *The Quality of Life Report,* was published in 2003. On writing, Meghan Daum has this advice: "Whether the form is fiction or nonfiction, I have always believed that the subject is only as interesting as the larger themes that fuel it. The reason I am such a fan of the essay form is that it allows room for a variety of literary approaches—personal narrative, reportage, satire, to name just a few—and the form encourages both the writer and the reader to explore intellectual and even controversial ideas in a way that is also engaging and entertaining." The following essay was first published in *The New Yorker* and is part of a collection of Daum's essays entitled *My Misspent Youth* (2001).

1   It started in cold weather; fall was drifting away into an intolerable chill. I was on the tail end of twenty-six, living in New York City, and trying to support myself as a writer. One morning I logged on to my America Online account to find a message under the heading "is this the real meghan daum?" It came from someone with the screen name PFSlider. The body of the message consisted of five sentences, written entirely in lowercase letters, of perfectly turned flattery, something about PFSlider's admiration of some newspaper and magazine articles I had published over the last year and a half, something else about his resulting infatuation with me, and something about his being a sportswriter in California.

2   I was charmed for a moment or so, engaged for the thirty seconds that it took me to read the message and fashion a reply. Though it felt strange to be in the position of confirming that I was indeed "the real meghan daum," I managed to say, "Yes, it's me. Thank you for writing." I clicked the "Send Now" icon and shot my words into the void, where I forgot about PFSlider until the next day when I received another message, this one entitled "eureka." "wow, it is you," he wrote, still in lowercase. He chronicled the various conditions under which he'd read my few and far between articles: a boardwalk in Laguna Beach, the spring training pressroom for the baseball team he covered for a Los Angeles newspaper. He confessed to having a "crazy crush" on me. He referred to me as "princess daum." He said he wanted to propose marriage or at least have lunch with me during one of his two annual trips to New York. He managed to do all of this without sounding like a schmuck. As I read the note, I smiled the kind of smile one tries to suppress, the kind of smile that arises during a sappy movie one never even admits to seeing. The letter was outrageous and endearingly pathetic, possibly the practical joke of a friend trying to rouse me out of a temporary writer's block. But the kindness pouring forth from my computer screen was unprecedented and bizarrely exhilarating. I logged off and thought about it for a few hours before writing back to express how flattered and touched—this was probably the first time I had ever used the word "touched" in earnest—I was by his message.

3   I had received e-mail messages from strangers before, most of them kind and friendly and courteous—all of those qualities that generally get checked with the coats at the cocktail parties that comprise what the information age has now forced us to call the "three-dimensional world." I am always warmed by an unsolicited gesture of admiration or encouragement, amazed that anyone would bother, shocked that communication from a stranger could be fueled by anything other than an attempt to get a job or make what the professional world has come to call "a connection."

4   I am not what most people would call a "computer person." I have utterly no interest in chat rooms, news groups, or most Web sites. I derive a palpable thrill from sticking an actual letter in the U.S. mail. But e-mail, though at that time I generally only sent and received a few messages a week, proves a useful forum for my particular communication anxieties. I have a constant, low-grade fear of the telephone. I often call people with the intention of getting their answering machines. There is something about the live voice that has become startling, unnervingly organic, as volatile as incendiary talk radio. PFSlider and I tossed a few innocuous, smart-assed notes back and forth over the week following his first message. His name was Pete. He was twenty-nine and single. I revealed very little about myself, relying instead on the ironic commentary and forced witticisms that are the conceit of most e-mail messages. But I quickly developed an oblique affection for PFSlider. I was excited when there was a message from him, mildly depressed when there wasn't. After a few weeks, he gave me his phone number. I did not give him mine but he looked me up anyway and called me one Friday night. I was home. I picked up the phone. His voice was jarring yet not unpleasant. He held up more than his end of the conversation for an hour, and when he asked permission to call me again, I accepted as though we were in a previous century.

5   Pete, as I was forced to call him on the phone—I could never wrap my mind around his actual name, privately referring to him as PFSlider, "e-mail guy," or even "baseball boy"—began calling me two or three times a week. He asked if he could meet me in person and I said that would be okay. Christmas was a few weeks away and he would be returning east to see his family. From there, he would take the short flight to New York and have lunch with me. "It is my off-season mission to meet you," he said. "There will probably be a snowstorm," I said. "I'll take a team of sled dogs," he answered. We talked about our work and our families, about baseball and Bill Clinton and Howard Stern and sex, about his hatred for Los Angeles and how much he wanted a new job. Other times we would find each other logged on to America Online at the same time and type back and forth for hours. For me, this was far superior to the phone. Through typos and misspellings, he flirted maniacally. "I have an absurd crush on you," he said. "If I like you in person you must promise to marry me." I was coy and conceited, telling him to get a life, baiting him into complimenting me further, teasing him in a way I would never have dared in the real world or even on the phone. I would stay up until 3 A.M. typing with him, smiling at the screen, getting so giddy that I couldn't fall asleep. I was having difficulty recalling what I used to do at night. My phone was tied up for hours at a time. No one in the real world could reach me, and I didn't really care.

6   In off moments, I heard echoes of things I'd said just weeks earlier: "The Internet is destroying the world. Human communication will be rendered obsolete. We will all develop carpal tunnel syndrome and die." But curiously, the Internet, at least in the limited form in which I was using it, was having the opposite effect. My interaction with PFSlider was more human than much of what I experienced in the daylight realm of live beings. I was certainly putting more energy into the relationship than I had put into any before, giving him attention that was by definition undivided, relishing the safety of the distance by opting to be truthful rather than doling out the white lies that have become the staple of real life. The outside world— the place where I walked around on the concrete, avoiding people I didn't want to deal with, peppering the ground with half-truths, and applying my motto of "let the machine take it" to almost any scenario—was sliding into the periphery of my mind. I was a better person with PFSlider. I was someone I could live with.

7   This borrowed identity is, of course, the primary convention of Internet relationships. The false comfort of the cyberspace persona has been identified as one of the maladies of our time, another avenue for the remoteness that so famously plagues contemporary life. But the better person that I was to PFSlider was not a result of being a different person to him. It was simply that I was a desired person, the object of a blind man's gaze. I may not have known my suitor, but for the first time in my life, I knew the deal. I knew when I'd hear from him and how I'd hear from him. I knew he wanted me because he said he wanted me, because the distance and facelessness and lack of gravity of it all allowed him to be sweeter to me than most real-life people had ever managed. For the first time in my life, I was involved in a ritualized courtship. Never before had I realized how much that kind of structure was missing from my everyday life.

8   And so PFSlider became my everyday life. All the tangible stuff—the trees outside, my friends, the weather—fell away. I could physically feel my brain. My body did not exist. I had no skin, no hair, no bones; all desire had converted itself into a cerebral current that reached nothing but my frontal lobe. Lust was something not felt but thought. My brain was devouring all of my other organs and gaining speed with each swallow. There was no outdoors, the sky and wind were irrelevant. There was only the computer screen and the phone, my chair and maybe a glass of water. Pete started calling every day, sometimes twice, even three times. Most mornings I would wake up to find a message from PFSlider, composed in Pacific time while I slept in the wee hours. "I had a date last night," he wrote, "and I am not ashamed to say it was doomed from the start because I couldn't stop thinking about you."

Then, a few days later, "If you stood before me now, I would plant the warmest kiss on your cheek that I could muster."

9   I fired back a message slapping his hand. "We must be careful where we tread," I said. This was true but not sincere. I wanted it, all of it. I wanted the deepest bow down before me. I wanted my ego not merely massaged but kneaded. I wanted unfettered affection, soul mating, true romance. In the weeks that had elapsed since I picked up "is this the real meghan daum?" the real me underwent some kind of meltdown, a systemic rejection of all the savvy and independence I had worn for years like a grown-up Girl Scout badge. Since graduating from college, I had spent three years in a serious relationship and two years in a state of neither looking for a boyfriend nor particularly avoiding one. I had had the requisite number of false starts and five-night stands, dates that I wasn't sure were dates, emphatically casual affairs that buckled under their own inertia even before dawn broke through the iron-guarded windows of stale, one-room city apartments. Even though I was heading into my late twenties, I was still a child, ignorant of dance steps or health insurance, a prisoner of credit-card debt and student loans and the nagging feeling that I didn't want anyone to find me until I had pulled myself into some semblance of an adult. I was a true believer in the urban dream—in years of struggle succumbing to brilliant success, in getting a break, in making it. Like most of my friends, I was selfish by design. To want was more virtuous than to need. I wanted someone to love me but I certainly didn't need it. I didn't want to be alone, but as long as I was, I had no choice but to wear my solitude as though it were haute couture. The worst sin imaginable was not cruelty or bitchiness or even professional failure but vulnerability. To admit to loneliness was to slap the face of progress. It was to betray the times in which we lived.

10   But PFSlider derailed me. He gave me all of what I'd never realized I wanted. He called not only when he said he would, but unexpectedly, just to say hello. His guard was not merely down but nonexistent. He let his phone bill grow to towering proportions. He thought about me all the time and admitted it. He talked about me with his friends and admitted it. He arranged his holiday schedule around our impending date. He managed to charm me with sports analogies. He courted and wooed and romanced me. He didn't hesitate. He was unblinking and unapologetic, all nerviness and balls to the wall. He wasn't cheap. He went out of his way. I'd never seen anything like it.

11   Of all the troubling details of this story, the one that bothers me the most is the way I slurped up his attention like some kind of dying animal. My addiction to PFSlider's messages indicated a monstrous narcissism. But it also revealed a subtler desire that I didn't fully understand at the time. My need to experience an old-fashioned kind of courtship was stronger than I had

ever imagined. The epistolary quality of our relationship put our communication closer to the eighteenth century than the uncertain millennium. For the first time in my life, I was not involved in a protracted "hang out" that would lead to a quasi-romance. I was involved in a well-defined structure, a neat little space in which we were both safe to express the panic and intrigue of our mutual affection. Our interaction was refreshingly orderly, noble in its vigor, dignified despite its shamelessness. It was far removed from the randomness of real-life relationships. We had an intimacy that seemed custom-made for our strange, lonely times. It seemed custom-made for me.

12   The day of our date was frigid and sunny. Pete was sitting at the bar of the restaurant when I arrived. We shook hands. For a split second he leaned toward me with his chin as if to kiss me. He was shorter than I had imagined, though he was not short. He registered to me as neither handsome nor unhandsome. He had very nice hands. He wore a very nice shirt. We were seated at a very nice table. I scanned the restaurant for people I knew, saw no one and couldn't decide how I felt about that.

13   He talked and I heard nothing he said. He talked and talked and talked. I stared at his profile and tried to figure out if I liked him. He seemed to be saying nothing in particular, though it went on forever. Later we went to the Museum of Natural History and watched a science film about the physics of storms. We walked around looking for the dinosaurs and he talked so much that I wanted to cry. Outside, walking along Central Park West at dusk, through the leaves, past the horse-drawn carriages and yellow cabs and splendid lights of Manhattan at Christmas, he grabbed my hand to kiss me and I didn't let him. I felt as if my brain had been stuffed with cotton. Then, for some reason, I invited him back to my apartment, gave him a few beers, and finally let him kiss me on the lumpy futon in my bedroom. The radiator clanked. The phone rang and the machine picked up. A car alarm blared outside. A key turned in the door as one of my roommates came home. I had no sensation at all, only the dull déjà vu of being back in some college dorm room, making out in a generic fashion on an Indian throw rug while Cat Stevens' *Greatest Hits* played on the portable stereo. I wanted Pete out of my apartment. I wanted to hand him his coat, close the door behind him, and fight the ensuing emptiness by turning on the computer and taking comfort in PFSlider.

14   When Pete finally did leave, I sulked. The ax had fallen. He'd talked way too much. He was hyper. He hadn't let me talk, although I hadn't tried very hard. I berated myself from every angle, for not kissing him on Central Park West, for letting him kiss me at all, for not liking him, for wanting to like him more than I had wanted anything in such a long time. I was horrified by the realization that I had invested so heavily in a made-up character, a character in whose creation I'd had a greater hand than even Pete himself. How

could I, a person so self-congratulatingly reasonable, have gotten sucked into a scenario that was more akin to a television talk show than the relatively full and sophisticated life I was so convinced I led? How could I have received a fan letter and allowed it to go this far? Then a huge bouquet of FTD flowers arrived from him. No one had ever sent me flowers before. I was sick with sadness. I hated either the world or myself, and probably both.

15   No one had ever forced me to forgive them before. But for some reason, I forgave Pete. I cut him more slack than I ever had anyone. I granted him an official pardon, excused his failure for not living up to PFSlider. Instead of blaming him, I blamed the Earth itself, the invasion of tangible things into the immaculate communication PFSlider and I had created. With its roommates and ringing phones and subzero temperatures, the physical world came barreling in with all the obstreperousness of a major weather system, and I ignored it. As human beings with actual flesh and hand gestures and Gap clothing, Pete and I were utterly incompatible, but I pretended otherwise. In the weeks that followed I pictured him and saw the image of a plane lifting off over an overcast city. PFSlider was otherworldly, more a concept than a person. His romance lay in the notion of flight, the physics of gravity defiance. So when he offered to send me a plane ticket to spend the weekend with him in Los Angeles, I took it as an extension of our blissful remoteness, a three-dimensional e-mail message lasting an entire weekend. I pretended it was a good idea.

16   The temperature on the runway at JFK was seven degrees Fahrenheit. We sat for three hours waiting for de-icing. Finally we took off over the frozen city, the DC-10 hurling itself against the wind. The ground below shrank into a drawing of itself. Laptop computers were plopped onto tray tables. The air recirculated and dried out my contact lenses. I watched movies without the sound and thought to myself that they were probably better that way. Something about the plastic interior of the fuselage and the plastic forks and the din of the air and the engines was soothing and strangely sexy, as fabricated and seductive as PFSlider. I thought about Pete and wondered if I could ever turn him into an actual human being, if I could ever even want to. I knew so many people in real life, people to whom I spoke face-to-face, people who made me laugh or made me frustrated or happy or bored. But I'd never given any of them as much as I'd given PFSlider. I'd never forgiven their spasms and their speeches, never tied up my phone for hours in order to talk to them. I'd never bestowed such senseless tenderness on anyone.

17   We descended into LAX. We hit the tarmac and the seat belt signs blinked off. I hadn't moved my body in eight hours, and now, I was walking through the tunnel to the gate, my clothes wrinkled, my hair matted, my hands shaking. When I saw Pete in the terminal, his face registered to me as blank and impossible to process as the first time I'd met him. He kissed me chastely. On

the way out to the parking lot, he told me that he was being seriously considered for a job in New York. He was flying back there next week. If he got the job he'd be moving within the month. I looked at him in astonishment. Something silent and invisible seemed to fall on us. Outside, the wind was warm and the Avis and Hertz buses ambled alongside the curb of Terminal 5. The palm trees shook and the air seemed as heavy and earthly as Pete's hand, which held mine for a few seconds before dropping it to get his car keys out of his pocket. The leaves on the trees were unmanageably real. He stood before me, all flesh and preoccupation. The physical world had invaded our space. For this I could not forgive him.

18   Everything now was for the touching. Everything was buildings and bushes, parking meters and screen doors and sofas. Gone was the computer; the erotic darkness of the telephone; the clean, single dimension of Pete's voice at 1 A.M. It was nighttime, yet the combination of sight and sound was blinding. We went to a restaurant and ate outside on the sidewalk. We were strained for conversation. I tried not to care. We drove to his apartment and stood under the ceiling light not really looking at each other. Something was happening that we needed to snap out of. Any moment now, I thought. Any moment and we'll be all right. These moments were crowded with elements, with carpet fibers and direct light and the smells of everything that has a smell. They left marks as they passed. It was all wrong. Gravity was all there was.

19   For three days, we crawled along the ground and tried to pull ourselves up. We talked about things that I can no longer remember. We read the *Los Angeles Times* over breakfast. We drove north past Santa Barbara to tour the wine country. I stomped around in my clunky shoes and black leather jacket, a killer of ants and earthworms and any hope in our abilities to speak and be understood. Not until studying myself in the bathroom mirror of a highway rest stop did I fully realize the preposterousness of my uniform. I felt like the shot in a human shot put, an object that could not be lifted, something that secretly weighed more than the world itself. We ate an expensive dinner. We checked into a hotel and watched television. Pete talked at me and through me and past me. I tried to listen. I tried to talk. But I bored myself and irritated him. Our conversation was a needle that could not be threaded. Still, we played nice. We tried to care and pretended to keep trying long after we had given up. In the car on the way home, he told me I was cynical, and I didn't have the presence of mind to ask him just how many cynics he had met who would travel three thousand miles to see someone they barely knew. Just for a chance. Just because the depths of my hope exceeded the thickness of my leather jacket and the thickness of my skin. And at that moment, I released myself into the sharp knowledge that communication had once again eliminated itself as a possibility.

20   Pete drove me to the airport at 7 A.M. so I could make my eight o'clock flight home. He kissed me goodbye, another chaste peck I recognized from countless dinner parties and dud dates from real life. He said he'd call me in a few days when he got to New York for his job interview, which we had discussed only in passing and with no reference to the fact that New York was where I happened to live. I returned home to the frozen January. A few days later, he came to New York and we didn't see each other. He called me from the plane back to Los Angeles to tell me, through the static, that he had gotten the job. He was moving to my city.

21   PFSlider was dead. Pete had killed him. I had killed him. I'd killed my own persona too, the girl on the phone and online, the character created by some writer who'd captured him one morning long ago as he read the newspaper. There would be no meeting him in distant hotel lobbies during the baseball season. There would be no more phone calls or e-mail messages. In a single moment, Pete had completed his journey out of our mating dance and officially stepped into the regular world, the world that gnawed at me daily, the world that fed those five-night stands, the world where romance could not be sustained because we simply did not know how to do it. Here, we were all chitchat and leather jackets, bold proclaimers of all that we did not need. But what struck me most about this affair was the unpredictable nature of our demise. Unlike most cyber romances, which seem to come fully equipped with the inevitable set of misrepresentations and false expectations, PFSlider and I had played it fairly straight. Neither of us had lied. We'd done the best we could. We were dead from natural causes rather than virtual ones.

22   Within a two-week period after I returned from Los Angeles, at least seven people confessed to me the vagaries of their own e-mail affairs. This topic arose, unprompted, over the course of normal conversation. Four of these people had gotten on planes and met their correspondents, traveling from New Haven to Baltimore, New York to Montana, Texas to Virginia, and New York to Johannesburg. These were normal people, writers and lawyers and scientists, whom I knew from the real world. They were all smart, attractive, and more than a little sheepish about admitting just how deep they had been sucked in. Very few had met in chat rooms. Instead, the messages had started after chance meetings at parties and on planes; some, like me, had received notes in response to things they'd written online or elsewhere. Two of these people had fallen in love, the others chalked it up to a strange, uniquely postmodern experience. They all did things they would never do in the real world: they sent flowers, they took chances, they forgave. I heard most of these stories in the close confines of smoky bars and crowded restau-

rants, and we would all shake our heads in bewilderment as we told our tales, our eyes focused on some distant point that could never be reigned in to the surface of the Earth. Mostly it was the courtship ritual that had drawn us in. We had finally wooed and been wooed, given an old-fashioned structure through which to attempt the process of romance. E-mail had become an electronic epistle, a yearned-for rule book. The black and white of the type, the welcome respite from the distractions of smells and weather and other people, had, in effect, allowed us to be vulnerable and passionate enough to actually care about something. It allowed us to do what was necessary to experience love. It was not the Internet that contributed to our remote, fragmented lives. The problem was life itself.

23   The story of PFSlider still makes me sad. Not so much because we no longer have anything to do with one another, but because it forces me to grapple with all three dimensions of daily life with greater awareness than I used to. After it became clear that our relationship would never transcend the screen and the phone, after the painful realization that our face-to-face knowledge of each other had in fact permanently contaminated the screen and the phone, I hit the pavement again, went through the motions of real life, said "hello" and "goodbye" to people in the regular way. In darker moments, I remain mortified by everything that happened with PFSlider. It terrifies me to admit to a firsthand understanding of the way the heart and the ego are entwined. Like diseased trees that have folded in on one another, our need to worship fuses with our need to be worshipped. Love eventually becomes only about how much mystique can be maintained. It upsets me even more to see how this entanglement is made so much more intense, so unhampered and intoxicating, by way of a remote access like e-mail. But I'm also thankful that I was forced to unpack the raw truth of my need and stare at it for a while. This was a dare I wouldn't have taken in three dimensions.

24   The last time I saw Pete he was in New York, thousands of miles away from what had been his home and a million miles away from PFSlider. In a final gesture of decency, in what I later realized was the most ordinary kind of closure, he took me out to dinner. We talked about nothing. He paid the bill. He drove me home in his rental car, the smell and sound of which was as arbitrary and impersonal as what we now were to each other. Then he disappeared forever. He became part of the muddy earth, as unmysterious as anything located next door. I stood on my stoop and felt that familiar rush of indifference. Pete had joined the angry and exhausted living. He drifted into my chaos, and joined me down in reality where, even if we met on the street, we'd never see each other again, our faces obscured by the branches and bodies and falling debris that make up the ether of the physical world.

THINKING ABOUT THE TEXT

1. What are the elements of the first e-mail message the author received from "PFSlider" that prompted her to send a short reply? What "touched" her in the second message?

2. Daum admits to not being a "computer person" and to not liking the telephone. Yet, in the course of a few weeks, she and PFSlider wrote a number of "smart-assed notes back and forth" and frequently spoke by phone. How do you explain this change in her habits?

3. Although the author once believed that "human communication will be rendered obsolete" by the Internet, she reports that her e-mailing with PFSlider "was more human than much of what [she] experienced in the daylight realm of live beings" (111). What does Daum mean by this? What was "more human" about her e-mail relationship than her real-life relationships? In what ways does this acknowledgment foretell the conclusion of her essay?

4. What is the "ritualized courtship" that Daum relished in her relationship with PFSlider? Cite specific examples of this courtship.

5. What does the author mean when she confesses that she was "still a child" when she became "derailed" by PFSlider? Why does she use the metaphoric word "derailed"? What self-awareness did the author come to when she analyzed the attraction she had to her e-mailing correspondent?

6. Analyze what happened when PFSlider and the author met. What is revealed by the author when she writes that she wanted Pete to leave her apartment so that she could turn on the computer and find comfort in PFSlider? What is the realization that the author has about her relationship with Pete as contrasted with PFSlider? Why do you think she accepted the invitation to spend a weekend with him in Los Angeles, a continent away from her home in New York City?

7. In describing their three days together, the author writes that "the physical world had invaded our space." Explain that statement and the author's metaphors that their "conversation was a needle that could not be threaded," and that "PFSlider was dead. Pete had killed him. I had killed him. I'd killed my own persona too." In what way is the author right when she describes these deaths as "from natural causes rather than virtual ones"?

8. What is significant about the author's revelation that seven of her friends—writers, lawyers, and scientists who are all smart and attractive—have engaged in e-mail affairs? What is Daum's strategy in ending her essay by moving away from her own experience? The author admits that the story of PFSlider still makes her sad, and she concludes with the idea that "love eventually becomes only about how much mystique can be

maintained." Analyze her statement and explain how that idea is central to the experience she has had.

WRITING FROM THE TEXT

1. Write a character analysis of Megan Daum. Analyze her as a person who has admitted certain preferences and who has revealed herself in candid and metaphoric language. Your analysis should be supported with specific details from the text. Review how to write a character analysis (pp. 484–93) for help with this assignment.

2. Describe a time when you enjoyed a "ritualized courtship" or perhaps longed for a relationship that might make you a "better person." Analyze what happened or describe what the ideal courtship—in the physical or virtual world—would be. Relate your analysis to Daum's experience if you can.

3. Work from Daum's assertion that the "borrowed identity is . . . the primary convention of Internet relationships" (111). Describe experiences you or your friends have had connecting with others on the Internet. Were those experiences "truthful" or more of the "white lies that have become the staple of real life"? What conclusions do you draw from your experiences and observations?

CONNECTING WITH OTHER TEXTS

1. In "The Future of Love" (p. 65), Jill Tweedie asserts that romantic love will disappear when ordinary human beings emerge from behind their stylized masks. How does that idea relate to Meghan Daum's experience? Connect Tweedie's ideas to Daum's to explore what love means to these authors.

2. In "Makes Learning Fun" (p. 304), Clifford Stoll observes that real learning takes work, discipline, commitment, and responsibility, and that these qualities are not available in an online education. Could the same claim be made that a virtual romance can't provide the qualities and tests of a conventional dating relationship? Connect Stoll's essay with Daum's and write an analysis of what is missing in a virtual romance.

 # Common Decency
Susan Jacoby

Personal heritage and multicultural backgrounds inform the writing of Susan Jacoby (b. 1945). After working as an education reporter for the *Washington Post* and as a columnist for the *New York Times*, Jacoby lived for a few years in the Soviet Union. She wrote several books about that experience, including *Moscow Conversations* (1972) and *Inside Soviet Schools* (1974), and she coauthored *Soul to Soul: A Black Russian American Family, 1865–1992* (1992). Her essays have been published in two collections, *The Possible She* (1979), and *Wild Justice: The Evolution of Revenge* (1983). Jacoby is also the author of *Half-Jew: A Daughter's Search for Her Family's Past* (2000). The following essay, first published in the *New York Times Magazine* (1991), demonstrates Jacoby's ability to move from personal experience to insightful analysis.

1   She was deeply in love with a man who was treating her badly. To assuage her wounded ego (and to prove to herself that she could get along nicely without him), she invited another man, an old boyfriend, to a dinner *à deux* in her apartment. They were on their way to the bedroom when, having realized that she wanted only the man who wasn't there, she changed her mind. Her ex-boyfriend was understandably angry. He left her apartment with a not-so-politely phrased request that she leave him out of any future plans.

2   And that is the end of the story—except for the fact that he was eventually kind enough to accept her apology for what was surely a classic case of "mixed signals."

3   I often recall this incident, in which I was the embarrassed female participant, as the controversy over "date rape" heats up across the nation. What seems clear to me is that those who place acquaintance rape in a different category from "stranger rape"—those who excuse friendly social rapists on grounds that they are too dumb to understand when "no" means no—are being even more insulting to men than to women.

4   These apologists for date rape—and some of them are women—are really saying that the average man cannot be trusted to exercise any impulse control. Men are nasty and men are brutes—and a woman must be constantly on her guard to avoid giving a man any excuse to give way to his baser instincts.

5   If this view were accurate, few women would manage to get through life without being raped, and few men would fail to commit rape. For the reality is that all of us, men as well as women, send and receive innumerable mixed signals in the course of our sexual lives—and that is as true in marital beds at age 50 as in the back seats of cars at age 15.

6   Most men somehow manage to decode these signals without using superior physical strength to force themselves on their partners. And most women manage to handle conflicting male signals without, say, picking up carving knives to demonstrate their displeasure at sexual rejection. This is called civilization.

7   Civilized is exactly what my old boyfriend was being when he didn't use my muddleheaded emotional distress as an excuse to rape me. But I don't

owe him excessive gratitude for his decent behavior—any more than he would have owed me special thanks for not stabbing him through the heart if our situations had been reversed. Most date rapes do not happen because a man honestly mistakes a woman's "no" for a "yes" or a "maybe." They occur because a minority of men—an ugly minority, to be sure—can't stand to take "no" for an answer.

8   This minority behavior—and a culture that excuses it on grounds that boys will be boys—is the target of the movement against date rape that has surfaced on many campuses during the past year.

9   It's not surprising that date rape is an issue of particular importance to college-age women. The campus concentration of large numbers of young people, in a unsupervised environment that encourages drinking and partying, tends to promote sexual aggression and discourage inhibition. Drunken young men who rape a woman at a party can always claim they didn't know what they were doing—and a great many people will blame the victim for having been there in the first place.

10   That is the line adopted by antifeminists like Camille Paglia, author of the controversial *Sexual Personae: Art and Decadence from Nefertiti to Emily Dickinson*. Paglia, whose views strongly resemble those expounded 20 years ago by Norman Mailer in *The Prisoner of Sex*, argues that feminists have deluded women by telling them they can go anywhere and do anything without fear of rape. Feminism, in this view, is both naïve and antisexual because it ignores the power of women to incite uncontrollable male passions.

11   Just to make sure there is no doubt about a woman's place, Paglia also links the male sexual aggression that leads to rape with the creative energy of art. "There is no female Mozart," she has declared, "because there is no female Jack the Ripper." According to this "logic," one might expect to discover the next generation of composers in fraternity houses and dorms that have been singled out as sites of brutal gang rapes.

12   This type of unsubtle analysis makes no distinction between sex as an expression of the will to power and sex as a source of pleasure. When domination is seen as an inevitable component of sex, the act of rape is defined not by a man's actions but by a woman's signals.

13   It is true, of course, that some women (especially the young) initially resist sex not out of real conviction but as part of the elaborate persuasion and seduction rituals accompanying what was once called courtship. And it is true that many men (again, especially the young) take pride in the ability to coax a woman a step further than she intended to go.

14   But these mating rituals do not justify or even explain date rape. Even the most callow youth is capable of understanding the difference between

resistance and genuine fear; between a halfhearted "no, we shouldn't" and tears or screams; between a woman who is physically free to leave a room and one who is physically restrained.

15   The immorality and absurdity of using mixed signals as an excuse for rape is cast in high relief when the assault involves one woman and a group of men. In cases of gang rape in a social setting (usually during or after a party), the defendants and their lawyers frequently claim that group sex took place but no force was involved. These upright young men, so the defense invariably contends, were confused because the girl had voluntarily gone to a party with them. Why, she may have even displayed sexual interest in *one* of them. How could they have been expected to understand that she didn't wish to have sex with the whole group?

16   The very existence of the term "date rape" attests to a slow change in women's consciousness that began with the feminist movement of the late 1960s. Implicit in this consciousness is the conviction that a woman has the right to say no at any point in the process leading to sexual intercourse—and that a man who fails to respect her wishes should incur serious legal and social consequences.

17   The other, equally important half of the equation is respect for men. If mixed signals are the real cause of sexual assault, it behooves every woman to regard every man as a potential rapist.

18   In such a benighted universe, it would be impossible for a woman (and, let us not forget, for a man) to engage in the tentative emotional and physical exploration that eventually produces a mature erotic life. She would have to make up her mind right from the start in order to prevent a rampaging male from misreading her intentions.

19   Fortunately for everyone, neither the character of men nor the general quality of relations between the sexes is that crude. By censuring the minority of men who use ordinary socializing as an excuse for a rape, feminists insist on sex as a source of pure pleasure rather than as a means of social control. Real men want an eager sexual partner—not a woman who is quaking with fear or even one who is ambivalent. Real men don't rape.

Thinking about the Text

1. Analyze Jacoby's strategy in opening with the third person—"She was deeply in love"—and then shifting to the first person—"I was the embarrassed female participant" (120). Why does she make this shift from "she" to "I" to refer to the same individual and how effective is it? Evaluate her use of this opening anecdote and her later references to it.

2. Opposing the distinction between "date rape" and "stranger rape," Jacoby adds that "those who excuse friendly social rapists on grounds that they are too dumb to understand when 'no' means no—are being even more insulting to men than to women" (120). Explain what she means by this statement. Discuss her tone when she mentions "friendly social rapists." Why does she feel that blaming rape on "mixed signals" is not a valid excuse?

3. Jacoby claims that apologists for date rape "are really saying that the average man cannot be trusted to exercise any impulse control" (120). Clearly, Jacoby disagrees with this view of men and feels that only "a minority of men—an ugly minority, to be sure—can't stand to take 'no' for an answer" (121). Do you agree with Jacoby or do you feel that women must be constantly on guard and that most men do have such "baser instincts"? Explain.

4. According to Jacoby, what is the position of "antifeminists like Camille Paglia" and what is so dangerous about seeing domination as an inevitable component of sex? How does Jacoby undercut Paglia's attempt to link male sexual aggression with the creative energy of art?

5. What is Jacoby's thesis? Explain how the title relates to her thesis and to her view of healthy, erotic relationships between men and women.

WRITING FROM THE TEXT

1. Write an evaluative response (p. 419) of this essay, making sure that your thesis clarifies whether you mostly support or oppose Jacoby's key points. Be careful to include and analyze important statements from the essay.

2. Jacoby argues that "date rape" and "stranger rape" shouldn't be put in two different categories. Write an essay clarifying your view of this issue while comparing and contrasting rape by strangers and rape by acquaintances. Use details from Jacoby's essay in your work.

CONNECTING WITH OTHER TEXTS

1. Although both Jacoby and Goodman (p. 124) define rape similarly and agree on several points, they have different approaches, focal points, and strategies. Write an essay comparing and contrasting the two articles and analyze key quotations from each.

2. Focusing on the character of Arnold Friend from "Where Are You Going, Where Have You Been?" (p. 127), write an essay supporting or countering Jacoby's contention that date rate and stranger rape shouldn't be put in different categories.

When a Woman Says No

Ellen Goodman

A widely syndicated columnist whose home paper is the *Boston Globe*, Ellen Goodman (b. 1941) has won a Pulitzer prize for her outstanding journalism. Goodman believes that she writes about issues more important than politics, like the "underlying values by which this country exists . . . the vast social changes in the way men and women lead their lives and deal with each other." The essay included here, first published in the *Boston Globe* in 1984, is indicative of Goodman's concerns.

Another essay by Goodman and additional biographical information appears on page 3.

1   There are a few times when, if you watch closely, you can actually see a change of public mind. This is one of those times.

2   For as long as I can remember, a conviction for rape depended as much on the character of the woman involved as on the action of the man. Most often the job of the defense lawyer was to prove that the woman had provoked or consented to the act, to prove that it was sex, not assault.

3   In the normal course of events the smallest blemish, misjudgment, misstep by the woman became proof that she had invited the man's attentions. Did she wear a tight sweater? Was she a "loose" woman? Was she in the wrong part of town at the wrong hour? A woman could waive her right to say no in an astonishing number of ways.

4   But in the past few weeks, in Massachusetts, three cases of multiple rape have come into court and three sets of convictions have come out of juries. These verdicts point to a sea change in attitudes. A simple definition seems to have seeped into the public consciousness. If she says no, it's rape.

5   The most famous of these cases is the New Bedford barroom rape. There, in two separate trials, juries cut through complicated testimony to decide the central issue within hours. Had the woman been drinking? Had she lied about that in testimony? Had she kissed one of the men? In the end none of these points were relevant. What mattered to the juries that found four of these six men guilty was that they had forced her. If she said no, it was rape.

6   The second of these cases involved a young woman soldier from Ft. Devens who accepted a ride with members of a rock band, the Grand Slamm. She was raped in the bus and left in a field hours later. Had she flirted with the band members? Had she told a friend that she intended to seduce one of the men? Had she boarded the bus willingly? The judge sentencing three of the men to jail said, "No longer will society accept the fact that a woman, even if she may initially act in a seductive or compromising manner, has waived her right to say no at any further time." If she said no, it was rape.

7   The third of these cases was in some ways the most notable. An Abington woman was driven from a bar to a parking lot where she was raped by four men, scratched with a knife, had her hair singed with a cigarette lighter and was left half-naked in the snow. The trial testimony showed that she previously had sex with three of the men, and with two of them in a group setting. Still, the jury was able to agree with the district attorney: "Sexual consent between a woman and a man on one occasion does not mean the man has access to her whenever it strikes his fancy." If she said no, it was rape.

8   Not every community, courtroom or jury today accepts this simple standard of justice. But ten years ago, five years ago, even three years ago these women might not have even dared press charges.

9   It was the change of climate that enabled, even encouraged, the women to come forward. It was the change of attitude that framed the arguments in the courtroom. It was the change of consciousness that infiltrated the jury chambers.

10   The question now is whether that change of consciousness has become part of our own day-to-day lives. In some ways rape is the brutal, repugnant extension of an ancient ritual of pursuit and capture. It isn't just rapists who refuse to take no for an answer. It isn't just rapists who believe that a woman says one thing and means another.

11   In the confusion of adolescence, in the chase of young adulthood, the sexes were often set up to persist and to resist. Many young men were taught that "no" means "try again." Many young women were allowed to excuse their sexuality only when they were "swept away," overwhelmed.

12   The confused messages, the yes-no-maybes, the overpowered heroines and overwhelming heroes, are still common to supermarket gothic novels and *Hustler* magazine. It isn't just X-rated movies that star a resistant woman who falls in love with her sexual aggressor. It isn't just pornographic cable-TV that features the woman who really "wanted it." In as spritely a sitcom as *Cheers,* Sam blithely locked a coyly ambivalent Diane into his apartment.

13   I know how many steps it is from that hint of sexual pressure to the brutality of rape. I know how far it is from lessons of sexual power plays to the violence of rape. But it's time that the verdict of those juries was fully transmitted to the culture from which violence emerges. If she says no, it means no.

THINKING ABOUT THE TEXT

1. In this essay, Goodman gives a brief history of social response to rape. In the past, how did lawyers defend alleged rapists? What seems to be the present attitude toward a charge of rape?

2. Goodman recounts three different rape trials. What is the logic of her arrangement of the three examples to support her thesis?

3. Beyond the assertion in the title of Goodman's essay, what is the important point she makes?

WRITING FROM THE TEXT

1. Describe a time when the "confused messages, the yes-no-maybes" resulted in an incomplete or erroneous understanding of a point you were trying to make.

2. Write a response to Goodman's allegation that "many young men were taught that 'no' means 'try again.'" Argue that she is correct or incorrect. Use specific examples to support your view.

CONNECTING WITH OTHER TEXTS

1. Use "Common Decency" (p. 119) and "When a Woman Says No" to write an analytical essay about preventing rape. What does Goodman mean about the "confused messages" in our culture? How does Jacoby also show confused messages? Propose a solution in your essay.

2. Read recent periodical accounts of rape trials. Is Goodman accurate in her essay that there is a "sea change" in public consciousness about rape?

3. Goodman notes that a few years ago, many women would not have dared to press rape charges. Today sexual harassment claims have become a media topic, and women are daring to charge that they are being or have been sexually harassed. Do research to learn the history of charges of sexual harassment. Focus your paper on the changes in public consciousness, and use specific examples from the reported cases to support your analysis.

4. Visit your campus Website or online catalog to see if your college has a statement on sexual misconduct. Does your campus discuss or define "no"? Incorporate your findings in an essay that evaluates your school's policy.

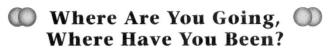

Where Are You Going, Where Have You Been?

Joyce Carol Oates

A novelist, poet, playwright, editor, and critic, Joyce Carol Oates (b. 1938) also teaches creative writing at Princeton University. Since her first collection of short stories appeared when she was 25, Oates has been averaging almost two books a year. Although she writes in a variety of genres and literary styles, Oates may be best known for her ability to write suspenseful tales and to create a sense of terror in an apparently ordinary situation, as the story included here illustrates. Oates has responded to critics' comments about the terror that permeates her work: "Uplifting endings and resolutely cheery world views are appropriate to television commercials but insulting elsewhere. It is not only wicked to pretend otherwise, it is futile." Some of Oates's book titles—*The Crosswicks Horror, Will You Always Love Me?* and *Zombie*—suggest the kinds of terror and anxieties embedded in her work. Recent books include *Middle Age: A Romance* (2001), *Beasts* (2002), and *I'll Take You There* (2002). The story included here, from *The Wheel of Love*, has been widely anthologized since its first publication in 1965.

For Bob Dylan

1   Her name was Connie. She was fifteen and she had a quick nervous giggling habit of craning her neck to glance into mirrors or checking other people's faces to make sure her own was all right. Her mother, who noticed everything and knew everything and who hadn't much reason any longer to look at her own face, always scolded Connie about it. "Stop gawking at yourself, who are you? You think you're so pretty?" she would say. Connie would raise her eyebrows at these familiar complaints and look right through her mother, into a shadowy vision of herself as she was right at that moment: she knew she was pretty and that was everything. Her mother had been pretty once too, if you could believe those old snapshots in the album, but now her looks were gone and that was why she was always after Connie.

2   "Why don't you keep your room clean like your sister? How've you got your hair fixed—what the hell stinks? Hair spray? You don't see your sister using that junk."

3   Her sister June was twenty-four and still lived at home. She was a secretary in the high school Connie attended, and if that wasn't bad enough—with her in the same building—she was so plain and chunky and steady that Connie had to hear her praised all the time by her mother and her mother's sisters. June did this, June did that, she saved money and helped clean the house and cooked and Connie couldn't do a thing, her mind was all filled with trashy daydreams. Their father was away at work most of the time and when he came home he wanted supper and he read the newspaper at supper and after supper he went to bed. He didn't bother talking much to them, but around his bent head Connie's mother kept picking at her until Connie wished her mother were dead and she herself were dead and it were all over. "She makes me want to throw up sometimes," she complained to her friends. She had a high, breathless, amused voice which made everything she said sound a little forced, whether it was sincere or not.

4   There was one good thing: June went places with girlfriends of hers, girls who were just as plain and steady as she, and so when Connie wanted to do that her mother had no objections. The father of Connie's best girlfriend drove the girls the three miles to town and left them off at a shopping plaza, so that they could walk through the stores or go to a movie, and when he came to pick them up again at eleven he never bothered to ask what they had done.

5   They must have been familiar sights, walking around that shopping plaza in their shorts and flat ballerina slippers that always scuffed the sidewalk, with charm bracelets jingling on their thin wrists: they would lean together to whisper and laugh secretly if someone passed by who amused or interested them. Connie had long dark blond hair that drew anyone's eye to it, and she wore part of it pulled up on her head and puffed out and the rest of it she let fall down her back. She wore a pullover jersey blouse that looked one way when she was at home and another way when she was away from home. Everything about her had two sides to it, one for home and one for anywhere that was not home: her walk that could be childlike and bobbing, or languid enough to make anyone think she was hearing music in her head, her mouth which was pale and smirking most of the time, but bright and pink on these evenings out, her laugh which was cynical and drawling at home—"Ha, ha, very funny"—but high-pitched and nervous anywhere else, like the jingling of the charms on her bracelet.

6   Sometimes they did go shopping or to a movie, but sometimes they went across the highway, ducking fast across the busy road, to a drive-in restaurant where older kids hung out. The restaurant was shaped like a big bottle, though squatter than a real bottle, and on its cap was a revolving figure of a grinning boy who held a hamburger aloft. One night in mid-summer they ran across, breathless with daring, and right away someone leaned out a car window and invited them over, but it was just a boy from high school they didn't like. It made them feel good to be able to ignore him. They went up through the maze of parked and cruising cars to the bright-lit, fly-infested restaurant, their faces pleased and expectant as if they were entering a sacred building that loomed out of the night to give them what haven and what blessing they yearned for. They sat at the counter and crossed their legs at the ankles, their thin shoulders rigid with excitement, and listened to the music that made everything so good: the music was always in the background like music at a church service, it was something to depend upon.

7   A boy named Eddie came in to talk with them. He sat backward on his stool, turning himself jerkily around in semicircles and then stopping and turning again, and after a while he asked Connie if she would like something to eat. She said she did and so she tapped her friend's arm on her way out—

her friend pulled her face up into a brave droll look—and Connie said she would meet her at eleven, across the way. "I just hate to leave her like that," Connie said earnestly, but the boy said that she wouldn't be alone for long. So they went out to his car and on the way Connie couldn't help but let her eyes wander over the windshields and faces all around her, her face gleaming with a joy that had nothing to do with Eddie or even this place; it might have been the music. She drew her shoulders up and sucked in her breath with the pure pleasure of being alive, and just at that moment she happened to glance at a face just a few feet from hers. It was a boy with shaggy black hair, in a convertible jalopy painted gold. He stared at her and then his lips widened into a grin. Connie slit her eyes at him and turned away, but she couldn't help glancing back and there he was still watching her. He wagged a finger and laughed and said, "Gonna get you, baby," and Connie turned away again without Eddie noticing anything.

8   She spent three hours with him, at the restaurant where they ate hamburgers and drank Cokes in wax cups that were always sweating, and then down an alley a mile or so away, and when he left her off at five to eleven only the movie house was still open at the plaza. Her girlfriend was there, talking with a boy. When Connie came up the two girls smiled at each other and Connie said, "How was the movie?" and the girl said, "*You* should know." They rode off with the girl's father, sleepy and pleased, and Connie couldn't help but look at the darkened shopping plaza with its big empty parking lot and its signs that were faded and ghostly now, and over at the drive-in restaurant where cars were still circling tirelessly. She couldn't hear the music at this distance.

9   Next morning June asked her how the movie was and Connie said, "So-so."

10   She and that girl and occasionally another girl went out several times a week that way, and the rest of the time Connie spent around the house—it was summer vacation—getting in her mother's way and thinking, dreaming, about the boys she met. But all the boys fell back and dissolved into a single face that was not even a face, but an idea, a feeling, mixed up with the urgent insistent pounding of the music and the humid night air of July. Connie's mother kept dragging her back to the daylight by finding things for her to do or saying, suddenly, "What's this about the Pettinger girl?"

11   And Connie would say nervously, "Oh, her. That dope." She always drew thick clear lines between herself and such girls, and her mother was simple and kindly enough to believe her. Her mother was so simple, Connie thought, that it was maybe cruel to fool her so much. Her mother went scuffling around the house in old bedroom slippers and complained over the telephone to one sister about the other, then the other called up and the two of

them complained about the third one. If June's name was mentioned her mother's tone was approving, and if Connie's name was mentioned it was disapproving. This did not really mean she disliked Connie and actually Connie thought that her mother preferred her to June because she was prettier, but the two of them kept up a pretense of exasperation, a sense that they were tugging and struggling over something of little value to either of them. Sometimes, over coffee, they were almost friends, but something would come up—some vexation that was like a fly buzzing suddenly around their heads—and their faces went hard with contempt.

12   One Sunday Connie got up at eleven—none of them bothered with church—and washed her hair so that it could dry all day long, in the sun. Her parents and sister were going to a barbecue at an aunt's house and Connie said no, she wasn't interested, rolling her eyes to let her mother know just what she thought of it. "Stay home alone then," her mother said sharply. Connie sat out back in a lawn chair and watched them drive away, her father quiet and bald, hunched around so that he could back the car out, her mother with a look that was still angry and not at all softened through the windshield, and in the back seat poor old June all dressed up as if she didn't know what a barbecue was, with all the running yelling kids and the flies. Connie sat with her eyes closed in the sun, dreaming and dazed with the warmth about her as if this were a kind of love, the caresses of love, and her mind slipped over onto thoughts of the boy she had been with the night before and how nice he had been, how sweet it always was, not the way someone like June would suppose but sweet, gentle, the way it was in movies and promised in songs; and when she opened her eyes she hardly knew where she was, the back yard ran off into weeds and a fence line of trees and behind it the sky was perfectly blue and still. The asbestos "ranch house" that was now three years old startled her—it looked small. She shook her head as if to get awake.

13   It was too hot. She went inside the house and turned on the radio to drown out the quiet. She sat on the edge of her bed, barefoot, and listened for an hour and a half to a program called *XYZ Sunday Jamboree,* record after record of hard, fast, shrieking songs she sang along with, interspersed by exclamations from "Bobby King": "An' look here you girls at Napoleon's—Son and Charley want you to pay real close attention to this song coming up!"

14   And Connie paid close attention herself, bathed in a glow of slow-pulsed joy that seemed to rise mysteriously out of the music itself and lay languidly about the airless little room, breathed in and breathed out with each gentle rise and fall of her chest.

15   After a while she heard a car coming up the drive. She sat up at once, startled, because it couldn't be her father so soon. The gravel kept crunching all the way in from the road—the driveway was long—and Connie ran to the

window. It was a car she didn't know. It was an open jalopy, painted a bright gold that caught the sunlight opaquely. Her heart began to pound and her fingers snatched at her hair, checking it, and she whispered "Christ, Christ," wondering how bad she looked. The car came to a stop at the side door and the horn sounded four short taps as if this were a signal Connie knew.

16   She went into the kitchen and approached the door slowly, then hung out the screen door, her bare toes curling down off the step. There were two boys in the car and now she recognized the driver: he had shaggy, shabby black hair that looked crazy as a wig and he was grinning at her.

17   "I ain't late, am I?" he said.

18   "Who the hell do you think you are?" Connie said.

19   "Toldja I'd be out, didn't I?"

20   "I don't even know who you are."

21   She spoke sullenly, careful to show no interest or pleasure, and he spoke in a fast bright monotone. Connie looked past him to the other boy, taking her time. He had fair brown hair, with a lock that fell onto his forehead. His sideburns gave him a fierce, embarrassed look, but so far he hadn't even bothered to glance at her. Both boys wore sunglasses. The driver's glasses were metallic and mirrored everything in miniature.

22   "You wanta come for a ride?" he said.

23   Connie smirked and let her hair fall loose over one shoulder.

24   "Don'tcha like my car? New paint job," he said. "Hey."

25   "What?"

26   "You're cute."

27   She pretended to fidget, chasing flies away from the door.

28   "Don'tcha believe me, or what?" he said.

29   "Look, I don't even know who you are," Connie said in disgust.

30   "Hey, Ellie's got a radio, see. Mine's broke down." He lifted his friend's arm and showed her the little transistor the boy was holding, and now Connie began to hear the music. It was the same program that was playing inside the house.

31   "Bobby King?" she said.

32   "I listen to him all the time. I think he's great."

33   "He's kind of great," Connie said reluctantly.

34   "Listen, that guy's *great*. He knows where the action is."

35   Connie blushed a little, because the glasses made it impossible for her to see just what this boy was looking at. She couldn't decide if she liked him or if he was just a jerk, and so she dawdled in the doorway and wouldn't come down or go back inside. She said, "What's all that stuff painted on your car?"

36   "Can'tcha read it?" He opened the door very carefully, as if he was afraid it might fall off. He slid out just as carefully, planting his feet firmly on the

ground, the tiny metallic world in his glasses slowing down like gelatine hardening and in the midst of it Connie's bright green blouse. "This here is my name, to begin with," he said. ARNOLD FRIEND was written in tarlike black letters on the side, with a drawing of a round grinning face that reminded Connie of a pumpkin, except it wore sunglasses. "I wanta introduce myself, I'm Arnold Friend and that's my real name and I'm gonna be your friend, honey, and inside the car's Ellie Oscar, he's kinda shy." Ellie brought his transistor radio up to his shoulder and balanced it there. "Now these numbers are a secret code, honey," Arnold Friend explained. He read off the numbers, 33, 19, 17 and raised his eyebrows at her to see what she thought of that, but she didn't think much of it. The left rear fender had been smashed and around it was written, on the gleaming gold background: DONE BY CRAZY WOMAN DRIVER. Connie had to laugh at that. Arnold Friend was pleased at her laughter and looked up at her. "Around the other side's a lot more—you wanta come and see them?"

37   "No."

38   "Why not?"

39   "Why should I?"

40   "Don'tcha wanta see what's on the car? Don'tcha wanta go for a ride?"

41   "I don't know."

42   "Why not?"

43   "I got things to do."

44   "Like what?"

45   "Things."

46   He laughed as if she had said something funny. He slapped his thighs. He was standing in a strange way, leaning back against the car as if he were balancing himself. He wasn't tall, only an inch or so taller than she would be if she came down to him. Connie liked the way he was dressed, which was the way all of them dressed: tight faded jeans stuffed into black, scuffed boots, a belt that pulled his waist in and showed how lean he was, and a white pullover shirt that was a little soiled and showed the hard small muscles of his arms and shoulders. He looked as if he probably did hard work, lifting and carrying things. Even his neck looked muscular. And his face was a familiar face, somehow: the jaw and chin and cheeks slightly darkened, because he hadn't shaved for a day or two, and the nose long and hawklike, sniffing as if she were a treat he was going to gobble up and it was all a joke.

47   "Connie, you ain't telling the truth. This is your day set aside for a ride with me and you know it," he said, still laughing. The way he straightened and recovered from his fit of laughing showed that it had been all fake.

48   "How do you know what my name is?" she said suspiciously.

49   "It's Connie."

50   "Maybe and maybe not."

51   "I know my Connie," he said, wagging his finger. Now she remembered him even better, back at the restaurant, and her cheeks warmed at the thought of how she sucked in her breath just at the moment she passed him—how she must have looked at him. And he had remembered her. "Ellie and I come out here especially for you," he said. "Ellie can sit in back. How about it?"

52   "Where?"

53   "Where what?"

54   "Where're we going?"

55   He looked at her. He took off the sunglasses and she saw how pale the skin around his eyes was, like holes that were not in shadow but instead in light. His eyes were like chips of broken glass that catch the light in an amiable way. He smiled. It was as if the idea of going for a ride somewhere, to some place, was a new idea to him.

56   "Just for a ride, Connie sweetheart."

57   "I never said my name was Connie," she said.

58   "But I know what it is. I know your name and all about you, lots of things," Arnold Friend said. He had not moved yet but stood still leaning back against the side of his jalopy. "I took a special interest in you, such a pretty girl, and found out all about you like I know your parents and sister are gone somewheres and I know where and how long they're going to be gone, and I know who you were with last night, and your best girlfriend's name is Betty. Right?"

59   He spoke in a simple lilting voice, exactly as if he were reciting the words to a song. His smile assured her that everything was fine. In the car Ellie turned up the volume on his radio and did not bother to look around at them.

60   "Ellie can sit in the back seat," Arnold Friend said. He indicated his friend with a casual jerk of his chin, as if Ellie did not count and she should not bother with him.

61   "How'd you find out all that stuff?" Connie said.

62   "Listen: Betty Schultz and Tony Fitch and Jimmy Pettinger and Nancy Pettinger," he said, in a chant. "Raymond Stanley and Bob Hutter—"

63   "Do you know all those kids?"

64   "I know everybody."

65   "Look, you're kidding. You're not from around here."

66   "Sure."

67   "But—how come we never saw you before?"

68   "Sure you saw me before," he said. He looked down at his boots, as if he were a little offended. "You just don't remember."

69   "I guess I'd remember you," Connie said.

70   "Yeah?" he looked up at this, beaming. He was pleased. He began to mark time with the music from Ellie's radio, tapping his fists lightly together. Connie looked away from his smile to the car, which was painted so bright it almost hurt her eyes to look at it. She looked at that name. ARNOLD FRIEND. And up at the front fender was an expression that was familiar—MAN THE FLY-ING SAUCERS. It was an expression kids had used the year before, but didn't use this year. She looked at it for a while as if the words meant something to her that she did not yet know.

71   "What're you thinking about? Huh?" Arnold Friend demanded. "Not worried about your hair blowing around in the car, are you?"

72   "No."

73   "Think I maybe can't drive good?"

74   "How do I know?"

75   "You're a hard girl to handle. How come?" he said. "Don't you know I'm your friend? Didn't you see me put my sign in the air when you walked by?"

76   "What sign?"

77   "My sign." And he drew an X in the air, leaning out toward her. They were maybe ten feet apart. After his hand fell back to his side the X was still in the air, almost visible. Connie let the screen door close and stood perfectly still in-side it, listening to the music from her radio and the boy's blend together. She stared at Arnold Friend. He stood there so stiffly relaxed, pretending to be re-laxed, with one hand idly on the door handle as if he were keeping himself up that way and had no intention of ever moving again. She recognized most things about him, the tight jeans that showed his thighs and buttocks and the greasy leather boots and the tight shirt, and even that slippery friendly smile of his, that sleepy dreamy smile that all the boys used to get across ideas they didn't want to put into words. She recognized all this and also the singsong way he talked, slightly mocking, kidding, but serious and a little melancholy, and she recognized the way he tapped one fist against the other in homage of the perpetual music behind him. But all these things did not come together.

78   She said suddenly, "Hey, how old are you?"

79   His smile faded. She could see then that he wasn't a kid, he was much older—thirty, maybe more. At this knowledge her heart began to pound faster.

80   "That's a crazy thing to ask. Can'tcha see I'm your own age?"

81   "Like hell you are."

82   "Or maybe a coupla years older, I'm eighteen."

83   "Eighteen?" she said doubtfully.

84   He grinned to reassure her and lines appeared at the corners of his mouth. His teeth were big and white. He grinned so broadly his eyes became

slits and she saw how thick the lashes were, thick and black as if painted with a black tarlike material. Then he seemed to become embarrassed, abruptly, and looked over his shoulder at Ellie. "*Him*, he's crazy," he said. "Ain't he a riot, he's a nut, a real character." Ellie was still listening to the music. His sunglasses told nothing about what he was thinking. He wore a bright orange shirt unbuttoned halfway to show his chest, which was a pale, bluish chest and not muscular like Arnold Friend's. His shirt collar was turned up all around and the very tips of the collar pointed out past his chin as if they were protecting him. He was pressing the transistor radio up against his ear and sat there in a kind of daze, right in the sun.

85   "He's kinda strange," Connie said.

86   "Hey, she says you're kinda strange! Kinda strange!" Arnold Friend cried. He pounded on the car to get Ellie's attention. Ellie turned for the first time and Connie saw with shock that he wasn't a kid either—he had a fair, hairless face, cheeks reddened slightly as if the veins grew too close to the surface of his skin, the face of a forty-year-old baby. Connie felt a wave of dizziness rise in her at this sight and she stared at him as if waiting for something to change the shock of the moment, make it all right again. Ellie's lips kept shaping words, mumbling along with the words blasting in his ear.

87   "Maybe you two better go away," Connie said faintly.

88   "What? How come?" Arnold Friend cried. "We come out here to take you for a ride. It's Sunday." He had the voice of the man on the radio now. It was the same voice, Connie thought. "Don'tcha know it's Sunday all day and honey, no matter who you were with last night today you're with Arnold Friend and don't you forget it!—Maybe you better step out here," he said, and this last was in a different voice. It was a little flatter, as if the heat was finally getting to him.

89   "No. I got things to do."

90   "Hey."

91   "You two better leave."

92   "We ain't leaving until you come with us."

93   "Like hell I am—"

94   "Connie, don't fool around with me. I mean, I mean, don't fool *around*," he said, shaking his head. He laughed incredulously. He placed his sunglasses on top of his head, carefully, as if he were indeed wearing a wig, and brought the stems down behind his ears. Connie stared at him, another wave of dizziness and fear rising in her so that for a moment he wasn't even in focus but was just a blur, standing there against his gold car, and she had the idea that he had driven up the driveway all right but had come from nowhere before that and belonged nowhere and that everything about him and even about the music that was so familiar to her was only half real.

95   "If my father comes and sees you—"

96   "He ain't coming. He's at a barbecue."

97   "How do you know that?"

98   "Aunt Tillie's. Right now they're—uh—they're drinking. Sitting around," he said vaguely, squinting as if he were staring all the way to town and over to Aunt Tillie's back yard. Then the vision seemed to get clear and he nodded energetically. "Yeah. Sitting around. There's your sister in a blue dress, huh? And high heels, the poor sad bitch—nothing like you, sweetheart! And your mother's helping some fat woman with the corn, they're cleaning the corn—husking the corn—"

99   "What fat woman?" Connie cried.

100   "How do I know what fat woman, I don't know every goddam fat woman in the world!" Arnold laughed.

101   "Oh, that's Mrs. Hornby . . . Who invited her?" Connie said. She felt a little light-headed. Her breath was coming quickly.

102   "She's too fat. I don't like them fat. I like them the way you are, honey," he said, smiling sleepily at her. They stared at each other for a while, through the screen door. He said softly, "Now what you're going to do is this: you're going to come out that door. You're going to sit up front with me and Ellie's going to sit in the back, the hell with Ellie, right? This isn't Ellie's date. You're my date. I'm your lover, honey."

103   "What? You're crazy—"

104   "Yes, I'm your lover. You don't know what that is, but you will," he said. "I know that too. I know all about you. But look: it's real nice and you couldn't ask for nobody better than me, or more polite. I always keep my word. I'll tell you how it is. I'm always nice at first, the first time. I'll hold you so tight you won't think you have to try to get away or pretend anything because you'll know you can't. And I'll come inside you where it's all secret and you'll give in to me and you'll love me—"

105   "Shut up! You're crazy!" Connie said. She backed away from the door. She put her hands against her ears as if she'd heard something terrible, something not meant for her. "People don't talk like that, you're crazy," she muttered. Her heart was almost too big now for her chest and its pumping made sweat break out all over her. She looked out to see Arnold Friend pause and then take a step toward the porch lurching. He almost fell. But, like a clever drunken man, he managed to catch his balance. He wobbled in his high boots and grabbed hold of one of the porch posts.

106   "Honey?" he said. "You still listening?"

107   "Get the hell out of here!"

108   "Be nice, honey. Listen."

109   "I'm going to call the police—"

110   He wobbled again and out of the side of his mouth came a fast spat curse, an aside not meant for her to hear. But even this "Christ!" sounded forced. Then he began to smile again. She watched this smile come, awkward as if he were smiling from inside a mask. His whole face was a mask, she thought wildly, tanned down onto his throat but then running out as if he had plastered makeup on his face but had forgotten about his throat.

111   "Honey—? Listen, here's how it is. I always tell the truth and I promise you this: I ain't coming in that house after you."

112   "You better not! I'm going to call the police if you—if you don't—"

113   "Honey," he said, talking right through her voice, "honey, I'm not coming in there but you are coming out here. You know why?"

114   She was panting. The kitchen looked like a place she had never seen before, some room she had run inside but which wasn't good enough, wasn't going to help her. The kitchen window had never had a curtain, after three years, and there were dishes in the sink for her to do—probably—and if you ran your hand across the table you'd probably feel something sticky there.

115   "You listening, honey? Hey?"

116   "—going to call the police—"

117   "Soon as you touch the phone I don't need to keep my promise and can come inside. You won't want that."

118   She rushed forward and tried to lock the door. Her fingers were shaking. "But why lock it," Arnold Friend said gently, talking right into her face. "It's just a screen door. It's just nothing." One of his boots was at a strange angle, as if his foot wasn't in it. It pointed out to the left, bent at the ankle. "I mean, anybody can break through a screen door and glass and wood and iron or anything else if he needs to, anybody at all and specially Arnold Friend. If the place got lit up with a fire honey you'd come runnin' out into my arms, right into my arms an' safe at home—like you knew I was your lover and'd stopped fooling around. I don't mind a nice shy girl but I don't like no fooling around." Part of those words were spoken with a slight rhythmic lilt, and Connie somehow recognized them—the echo of a song from last year, about a girl rushing into her boyfriend's arms and coming home again—

119   Connie stood barefoot on the linoleum floor, staring at him. "What do you want?" she whispered.

120   "I want you," he said.

121   "What?"

122   "Seen you that night and thought, that's the one, yes sir. I never needed to look anymore."

123   "But my father's coming back. He's coming to get me. I had to wash my hair first—" She spoke in a dry, rapid voice, hardly raising it for him to hear.

124   "No, your Daddy is not coming and yes, you had to wash your hair and you washed it for me. It's nice and shining and all for me. I thank you, sweetheart," he said, with a mock bow, but again he almost lost his balance. He had to bend and adjust his boots. Evidently his feet did not go all the way down; the boots must have been stuffed with something so that he would seem taller. Connie stared out at him and behind him Ellie in the car, who seemed to be looking off toward Connie's right into nothing. This Ellie said, pulling the words out of the air one after another as if he were just discovering them, "You want me to pull out the phone?"

125   "Shut your mouth and keep it shut," Arnold Friend said, his face red from bending over or maybe from embarrassment because Connie had seen his boots. "This ain't none of your business."

126   "What—what are you doing? What do you want?" Connie said. "If I call the police they'll get you, they'll arrest you—"

127   "Promise was not to come in unless you touch that phone, and I'll keep that promise," he said. He resumed his erect position and tried to force his shoulders back. He sounded like a hero in a movie, declaring something important. He spoke too loudly and it was as if he were speaking to someone behind Connie. "I ain't made plans for coming in that house where I don't belong but just for you to come out to me, the way you should. Don't you know who I am?"

128   "You're crazy," she whispered. She backed away from the door but did not want to go into another part of the house, as if this would give him permission to come through the door. "What do you . . . You're crazy, you . . ."

129   "Huh? What're you saying, honey?"

130   Her eyes darted everywhere in the kitchen. She could not remember what it was, this room.

131   "This is how it is, honey; you come out and we'll drive away, have a nice ride. But if you don't come out we're gonna wait till your people come home and then they're all going to get it."

132   "You want that telephone pulled out?" Ellie said. He held the radio away from his ear and grimaced, as if without the radio the air was too much for him.

133   "I toldja shut up, Ellie," Arnold Friend said, "you're deaf, get a hearing aid, right? Fix yourself up. This little girl's no trouble and's gonna be nice to me, so Ellie keep to yourself, this ain't your date—right? Don't hem in on me. Don't hog. Don't crush. Don't bird dog. Don't trail me," he said in a rapid meaningless voice, as if he were running through all the expressions he'd learned but was no longer sure which one of them was in style, then rushing on to new ones, making them up with his eyes closed, "Don't crawl under my fence, don't squeeze in my chipmunk hole, don't sniff my glue, suck my pop-

sicle, keep your own greasy fingers on yourself!" He shaded his eyes and peered in at Connie, who was backed against the kitchen table. "Don't mind him honey he's just a creep. He's a dope. Right? I'm the boy for you and like I said you come out here nice like a lady and give me your hand, and nobody else gets hurt, I mean, your nice old bald-headed daddy and your mummy and your sister in her high heels. Because listen: why bring them in this?"

134   "Leave me alone," Connie whispered.

135   "Hey, you know that old woman down the road, the one with the chickens and stuff—you know her?"

136   "She's dead!"

137   "Dead? What? You know her?" Arnold Friend said.

138   "She's dead—"

139   "Don't you like her?"

140   "She's dead—she's—she isn't there anymore—"

141   "But don't you like her, I mean, you got something against her? Some grudge or something?" Then his voice dipped as if he were conscious of a rudeness. He touched the sunglasses perched on top of his head as if to make sure they were still there. "Now you be a good girl."

142   "What are you going to do?"

143   "Just two things, or maybe three," Arnold Friend said. "But I promise it won't last long and you'll like me the way you get to like people you're close to. You will. It's all over for you here, so come on out. You don't want your people in any trouble, do you?"

144   She turned and bumped against a chair or something, hurting her leg, but she ran into the back room and picked up the telephone. Something roared in her ear, a tiny roaring, and she was so sick with fear that she could do nothing but listen to it—the telephone was clammy and very heavy and her fingers groped down to the dial but were too weak to touch it. She began to scream into the phone, into the roaring. She cried out, she cried for her mother, she felt her breath start jerking back and forth in her lungs as if it were something Arnold Friend were stabbing her with again and again with no tenderness. A noisy sorrowful wailing rose all about her and she was locked inside it the way she was locked inside this house.

145   After a while she could hear again. She was sitting on the floor with her wet back against the wall.

146   Arnold Friend was saying from the door, "That's a good girl. Put the phone back."

147   She kicked the phone away from her.

148   "No, honey. Pick it up. Put it back right."

149   She picked it up and put it back. The dial tone stopped.

150   "That's a good girl. Now you come outside."

151   She was hollow with what had been fear, but what was now just an emptiness. All that screaming had blasted it out of her. She sat, one leg cramped under her, and deep inside her brain was something like a pinpoint of light that kept going and would not let her relax. She thought, I'm not going to see my mother again. She thought, I'm not going to sleep in my bed again. Her bright green blouse was all wet.

152   Arnold Friend said, in a gentle-loud voice that was like a stage voice, "The place where you came from ain't there any more, and where you had in mind to go is canceled out. This place you are now—inside your daddy's house—is nothing but a cardboard box I can knock down any time. You know that and always did know it. You hear me?"

153   She thought, I have got to think. I have to know what to do.

154   "We'll go out in a nice field, out in the country here where it smells so nice and it's sunny," Arnold Friend said. "I'll have my arms tight around you so you won't need to try to get away and I'll show you what love is like, what it does. The hell with this house! It looks solid all right," he said. He ran a fingernail down the screen and the noise did not make Connie shiver, as it would have the day before. "Now put your hand on your heart, honey. Feel that? That feels solid too, but we know better, be nice to me, be sweet like you can because what else is there for a girl like you but to be sweet and pretty and give in?—and get away before her people come back?"

155   She felt her pounding heart. Her hand seemed to enclose it. She thought for the first time in her life that it was nothing that was hers, that belonged to her, but just a pounding, living thing inside this body that wasn't really hers either.

156   "You don't want them to get hurt," Arnold Friend went on. "Now get up, honey. Get up all by yourself."

157   She stood.

158   "Now turn this way. That's right. Come over here to me—Ellie, put that away, didn't I tell you? You dope. You miserable creepy dope," Arnold Friend said. His words were not angry but only part of an incantation. The incantation was kindly. "Now come out through the kitchen to me honey, and let's see a smile, try it, you're a brave sweet little girl and now they're eating corn and hot dogs cooked to bursting over an outdoor fire, and they don't know one thing about you and never did and honey you're better than them because not a one of them would have done this for you."

159   Connie felt the linoleum under her feet; it was cool. She brushed her hair back out of her eyes. Arnold Friend let go of the post tentatively and opened his arms for her, his elbows pointing in toward each other and his wrists limp, to show that this was an embarrassed embrace and a little mocking, he didn't want to make her self-conscious.

160   She put out her hand against the screen. She watched herself push the door slowly open as if she were safe back somewhere in the other doorway, watching this body and this head of long hair moving out into the sunlight where Arnold Friend waited.

161   "My sweet little blue-eyed girl," he said, in a half-sung sigh that had nothing to do with her brown eyes but was taken up just the same by the vast sunlit reaches of the land behind him and on all sides of him, so much land that Connie had never seen before and did not recognize except to know that she was going to it.

THINKING ABOUT THE TEXT

1. Identify Connie's character traits and illustrate each. How is she a rather typical 15-year-old, and how is she unique?

2. List the various ways that Arnold Friend initially appeals to Connie.

3. Identify the numerous intimidation tactics that Friend uses to manipulate Connie.

4. Study Ellie's role in this story. How does Oates use him to illuminate Arnold Friend's character, temperament, and motives?

5. Although the ending is ambiguous, Oates has revealed that this story was based on details from actual rapes and murders committed by Charles Schmid and his accomplice John Saunders in Tucson, Arizona, during the 1960s. How do various details in the story and, particularly, in the ending suggest that a crime was committed?

6. Without reducing this story to simple morals, discuss the insights (about subjects such as adolescence, parenting, role playing, manipulation, and intimidation) that we can draw from this story.

WRITING FROM THE TEXT

1. Write a character analysis (pp. 484–93) of Arnold Friend, demonstrating how he knows and preys upon the insecurities and fantasies of a 15-year-old girl. Include details from the story to support your thesis.

2. In an essay, argue that Connie does or does not *choose* to go with Arnold Friend at the end. Could she have resisted more than she did? Cite specific evidence from the story to support your thesis.

3. Considering Connie's character and lifestyle, is Oates suggesting that Connie is to be blamed for what happened to her, or does the blame fall on Arnold Friend for taking advantage of a vulnerable 15-year-old? Write an essay to support your argument.

CONNECTING WITH OTHER TEXTS

1. Read "When a Woman Says No" (p. 124) and write an essay applying Ellen Goodman's comments to Connie's experience.

2. Find and read the article in *Life* magazine (March 4, 1966) about the Charles Schmid case. Then write an essay comparing the actual details of his rapes and murders with this story.

3. Joyce Chopra's 1985 feature film *Smooth Talk,* based on Oates's story, is available on video, and Oates is reported to have been pleased with this adaptation. Note the differences between the video and the story versions, and write an essay analyzing the changes made in the film.

Chapter 3

Between Cultures

E very year, more than a million people from different countries come to
live in the United States. Your classrooms no doubt reflect this diversity—and your life after class probably does, too. You may find yourself enjoying sushi, falafel, or tacos, digesting cultural diversity as easily as
you munch a Big Mac. Or you may find yourself perplexed by cultural plural-
ism, unsure of its merits. The readings in this chapter illustrate the joys and
stress of living with cultural differences. As you will discover, assimilation and
rejection are issues not only for immigrants, but also for longtime residents of
the United States who experience the psychological, political, and economic
realities of living between cultures.

This chapter begins with an essay by someone like yourself, a college student, who describes the contrasts between his home and college environments. Marcus Mabry, an African American from New Jersey, writes of the
discomfort he experiences traveling "between the two worlds" of poverty at
home and affluence at Stanford University. In another selection, Kim Edwards describes the tensions of living in an Islamic society and feeling isolated from students and fellow faculty because of cultural and political
differences. These same tensions may be felt by Muslim women living in the
United States, as Laila Al-Marayati and Semeen Issa attest in their study of
bias against the burka. Even if you have not lived in a foreign country, you
sometimes may feel like you are living in a foreign environment. For example,
you may have grown up in the tranquil suburbs but now attend a busy city
university surrounded by street vendors and honking horns. You can thus find
yourself between cultures even in your own country.

Cultural characteristics are important because they define who we are, but they can also lead to misunderstanding and stereotyping. Yasmine Bahrani argues that we must avoid aggressively sorting people according to race or ethnicity, and Jack M. Balkin goes further to assert that diversity contributes to and ensures our democracy. Reginald McKnight, in his short story "Peaches," shows the problems of a couple facing individual and perhaps racial differences. The stereotypical images of Native Americans in popular culture is criticized by Ward Churchill in "Crimes Against Humanity," but John Balzar insists we need to "lighten up" about what we find offensive. After you have read these essays, you may find yourself thinking differently about Native Americans as well as the prevailing "Indian" images around you.

The stereotyping of African Americans is exposed in a poem by Sharon Olds and in a short story by Susan Straight. Finally, Luis Valdez treats with humor and satire the use and abuse of Latinos in his short play *Los Vendidos*. These writers remind us that not all Americans embrace people who seem different from themselves.

Despite these conflicts, most people would agree that the United States has been enriched by multiculturalism. Our art, music, literature, food, sports, dance, clothing—and so much more—all reflect the contributions of our diverse society. This chapter celebrates those contributions without ignoring the controversies.

Living in Two Worlds
Marcus Mabry

After completing his B.A. in English and French literature at Stanford University, Marcus Mabry (b. 1967) also earned a B.A. in international relations and an M.A. in English, all within the four years of his scholarship agreement. He has served as a correspondent for *Newsweek* at the State Department and in Paris, and is currently the Johannesburg bureau chief. In addition to freelance writing for *Emerge* and *Black Collegiate*, Mabry also conceived, wrote, produced, and narrated a documentary on African-American families for French television. His 1995 memoir, *White Bucks and Black-Eyed Peas: Coming of Age Black in White America*, examines Mabry's decision to live in the white world where he decides he is "more comfortable" because "it demanded less role-playing" of him. In "No Father, and No Answers," an essay appearing in *Newsweek* in 1992, Mabry addresses the concerns he has had in trying both to understand and to establish a relationship with the father he only recently met (who twenty years earlier left Mabry's unwed mother to raise her son without emotional or economic support). The selection included here also appeared in *Newsweek on Campus*.

1   A round, green cardboard sign hangs from a string proclaiming, "We built a proud new feeling," the slogan of a local supermarket. It is a souvenir

from one of my brother's last jobs. In addition to being a bagger, he's worked at a fast-food restaurant, a gas station, a garage and a textile factory. Now, in the icy clutches of the Northeastern winter, he is unemployed. He will soon be a father. He is 19 years old.

2   In mid-December I was at Stanford, among the palm trees and weighty chores of academe. And all I wanted to do was get out. I joined the rest of the undergrads in a chorus of excitement, singing the praises of Christmas break. No classes, no midterms, no finals . . . and no freshmen! (I'm a resident assistant.) Awesome! I was looking forward to escaping. I never gave a thought to what I was escaping to.

3   Once I got home to New Jersey, reality returned. My dreaded freshmen had been replaced by unemployed relatives; badgering professors had been replaced by hard-working single mothers, and cold classrooms by dilapidated bedrooms and kitchens. The room in which the "proud new feeling" sign hung contained the belongings of myself, my mom and my brother. But for these two weeks it was mine. They slept downstairs on couches.

4   Most students who travel between the universes of poverty and affluence during breaks experience similar conditions, as well as the guilt, the helplessness and, sometimes, the embarrassment associated with them. Our friends are willing to listen, but most of them are unable to imagine the pain of the impoverished lives that we see every six months. Each time I return home I feel further away from the realities of poverty in America and more ashamed that they are allowed to persist. What frightens me most is not that the American socioeconomic system permits poverty to continue, but that by participating in that system I share some of the blame.

5   Last year I lived in an on-campus apartment, with a (relatively) modern bathroom, kitchen and two bedrooms. Using summer earnings, I added some expensive prints, a potted palm and some other plants, making the place look like the more-than-humble abode of a New York City Yuppie. I gave dinner parties, even a *soirée française.*

6   For my roommate, a doctor's son, this kind of life was nothing extraordinary. But my mom was struggling to provide a life for herself and my brother. In addition to working 24-hour-a-day cases as a practical nurse, she was trying to ensure that my brother would graduate from high school and have a decent life. She knew that she had to compete for his attention with drugs and other potentially dangerous things that can look attractive to a young man when he sees no better future.

7   Living in my grandmother's house this Christmas break restored all the forgotten, and the never acknowledged, guilt. I had gone to boarding school on a full scholarship since the ninth grade, so being away from poverty was not new. But my own growing affluence has increased my distance. My friends

say that I should not feel guilty: what could I do substantially for my family at this age, they ask. Even though I know that education is the right thing to do, I can't help but feel, sometimes, that I have it too good. There is no reason that I deserve security and warmth, while my brother has to cope with potential unemployment and prejudice. I, too, encounter prejudice, but it is softened by my status as a student in an affluent and intellectual community.

8   More than my sense of guilt, my sense of helplessness increases each time I return home. As my success leads me further away for longer periods of time, poverty becomes harder to conceptualize and feels that much more oppressive when I visit with it. The first night of break, I lay in our bedroom, on a couch that let out into a bed that took up the whole room, except for a space heater. It was a little hard to sleep because the springs from the couch stuck through at inconvenient spots. But it would have been impossible to sleep anyway because of the groans coming from my grandmother's room next door. Only in her early sixties, she suffers from many chronic diseases and couldn't help but moan, then pray aloud, then moan, then pray aloud.

9   This wrenching of my heart was interrupted by the 3 A.M. entry of a relative who had been allowed to stay at the house despite rowdy behavior and threats toward the family in the past. As he came into the house, he slammed the door, and his heavy steps shook the second floor as he stomped into my grandmother's room to take his place, at the foot of her bed. There he slept, without blankets on a bare mattress. This was the first night. Later in the vacation, a Christmas turkey and a Christmas ham were stolen from my aunt's refrigerator on Christmas Eve. We think the thief was a relative. My mom and I decided not to exchange gifts that year because it just didn't seem festive.

10   A few days after New Year's I returned to California. The Northeast was soon hit by a blizzard. They were there, and I was here. That was the way it had to be, for now. I haven't forgotten; the ache of knowing their suffering is always there. It has to be kept deep down, or I can't find the logic in studying and partying while people, my people, are being killed by poverty. Ironically, success drives me away from those I most want to help by getting an education.

11   Somewhere in the midst of all that misery, my family has built, within me, "a proud feeling." As I travel between the two worlds it becomes harder to remember just how proud I should be—not just because of where I have come from and where I am going, but because of where they are. The fact that they survive in the world in which they live is something to be very proud of, indeed. It inspires within me a sense of tenacity and accomplishment that I hope every college graduate will someday possess.

Thinking about the Text

1. Describe Mabry's university world and his role in it. Then contrast it with details from his family's home.

2. Mabry describes living "between the universes of poverty and affluence." Detail the emotional toll this takes.

3. What happens during Christmas break to restore his sense of guilt?

4. How is the supermarket sign, hanging in the bedroom, both ironic and deeply symbolic of Mabry's life between worlds?

Writing from the Text

1. Using details from the story, compare and contrast Mabry's "worlds." What is ironic about the impact of success on his life?

2. For Mabry, attending college has secured him a spot in a new world vastly different from his past. Focus on your own between-worlds experience— college and home life, school and work worlds, high school and college relationships. Help the reader see each world as vividly as Mabry does; include your emotional responses, too.

3. Write about a time when you tried to escape one world and exchange it for another. How successful were you? What was your emotional toll?

Connecting with Other Texts

1. Analyze the between-worlds experiences described by Kim Edwards in "In Rooms of Women" (p. 161) and by Mabry. How do they compare? What conclusions can you draw about the "cultural tug of war"?

2. Write a research paper examining your college's admissions and recruiting policies, scholarship programs, dropout rate, and success record for minority students. You may want to focus your paper on what your research indicates has been the most serious obstacle or most successful accomplishment for affirmative action on your campus.

Peaches
Reginald McKnight

An assistant professor of English at the University of Pittsburgh, Reginald McKnight (b. 1956) received a B.A. from Colorado College and an M.A. from the University of Denver in 1987.

He has taught English and creative writing in Senegal as well as at the Metropolitan State University in Denver.

McKnight is the author of *Moustapha's Eclipse* (1988), *I Get on the Bus* (1990), *The Kind of Light That Shines on Texas: Stories* (1992), *White Boys* (1998), and *He Sleeps* (2001). He also is the editor of *African-American Wisdom* (1994) and *Wisdom of the African World* (1996). In addition, his work has been published in literary magazines such as *Leviathan, Prairie Schooner, Kenyon Review,* and the *Black American Literature Forum.* McKnight has said that his work generally "deals with the deracinated African-Americans who came of age after the civil rights struggle. These are people who are at the front lines of the current struggle for human rights." The following story is from *Moustapha's Eclipse.*

1   J.C. crosses the sun-faded carpet looking truculent and surly. He looks at me with his woman-get-out-my-seat-face. His tail points straight up to the ceiling. He lets out with his most irate meow, stomps back and forth in front of me in that stiff-legged strut that drives me crazy. He always does this when I sit in "his" chair. "Looks like everybody's mad at me today," I say, crossing my arms and legs at the same time. Momma doesn't say a word so I know what's up with her. Daddy drops the paper to his lap, and sits up in his chair. Its old, arthritic wood creaks. "Ain't nobody mad, Baby Sister," he says, removing his glasses. "Ain't nobody disappointed, hurt, upset—'cept that little pea-brain cat of yours. Mystery to me why you even sit in that chair after he done rubbed all his hair off in it."

2   "Have you heard from Marc lately, Rita?" asks Momma, not looking up from her puzzle.

3   "Good Lord Almighty have I heard from him. Tuesday I got four letters. Four separate letters. In four separate envelopes."

4   "What's all this 'Lord Almighty' business, girl," says Daddy. "I ain't sending you to no twenty-thousand-dollar-a-year college to hear you talk like a imitation me. You gonna be a scientist. Let me hear my money's worth."

5   "Your money?" Momma says, "You mean Uncle Sam's money."

6   "I'll take his money too if it help put Baby Sis through school. I ain't proud."

7   "You ain't rich neither," Momma says, snapping a puzzle piece into place.

8   J.C. leaps up into my lap. His purring irritates me so I get up and move to the other side of the room.

9   "We got a postcard from him a couple of days before you got here, Rita," my mother says, still not looking up from the table. "Didn't say much though."

10   "Why didn't you tell me when I got home, Momma?"

11   "Moody as you was? No ma'am. I got better things to do than listen to you bawl from sunup to sundown. Anyway, we already talked about your plans be-

fore you got here. Now if I'd been bringing up his name all the time you might have thought I was trying to push you into sending him that . . . the—"

12   "How 'bout 'Dear John,' Lucille."

13   "James!"

14   "Daddy—"

15   "Well, that's the truth. I'm calling a spade a spade. Just like he did."

16   "James! Now I am not going to have you—"

17   "All right now, I'm just playing. But I don't care how much ass that boy kiss. And I don't care how long he stay in Africa to sensitize hisself. Cain't no rich white boy call my child no nigger and—"

18   "Maybe not, but she grown, James. It's her life. Her decision. You and I got nothing to say whatsoever about what Rita decide. Now you promised me you'd leave the poor girl alone. Can't you see she upset as it is?" Momma snaps another piece into the puzzle, pushes her glasses up on her nose and looks up at Daddy. Daddy picks up the newspaper, crosses his legs, clears his throat. "You right," he grunts, then clears his throat again. "Yeah, you right. But if you ask me, you an apple, he an orange." I can tell from his eyes that he is staring at but not reading the paper. The room is as silent as the moon. Dust motes swim through the lamplight around Daddy's head. He looks hurt and I'd like to tell him he needn't be, because I myself am not hurting. I am numb. I don't know what to think or feel or do. I veer toward anger, then careen toward love, then roll toward regret and guilt. But as has been the case since the fight, I end up weightless and static like one of those motes around Daddy's head.

19   Daddy tosses the paper to the floor and in the silence it sounds like fire-crackers. J.C. springs up from the chair and scoots under the couch. The room again falls silent, the brief flurry of sound and action is swallowed up like stones tossed into the ocean.

20   After awhile Daddy's chair squeaks and cracks. He inhales deep and slow, then slips on his glasses. "I believe," he says, "I could use a little help outside picking some peaches for old Mrs. Li's sweet and sour sauce. She says she gonna make some extry for you to take back to school with you. Come on."

21   The fog has not yet lifted, but the air feels dryer than usual. Mr. Givens's dog yaps at us from behind the gray cedar fence. In the thirteen years my parents and I and my two sisters have lived here, I've never seen the old dog and I don't know its name. Each evening, when chastising the dog, when telling it to shut up, when calling it in, Mr. Givens calls it, "Git-yer-dumb-ass-outta-that-garden, Shut-the-hell-up-ya-stupid-mutt, and Giddin-here-ya-damn-dog." As far as I can tell the dog seldom obeys. In the evenings Mr. Givens can often be heard bellowing, "OK, then don't eat, ya stupid!"

22   When the dog has barked long enough, my father picks up the usual peach pit, zings it in the area of Mr. Givens's garden, and finally we hear:

"How many times I gotta tell ya to keep yer dumb ass outta that garden?" Silence. My father and I are alone in the backyard which is redolent with the smell of peaches, the sight of peaches. We feel peach pits beneath our feet.

23   "Grab that raggedy-looking box over next to the fence, Baby Sis," Daddy says. "Half them bushel baskets old Givens give me cain't hold air."

24   "This one?"

25   "Um hmm."

26   "Do we need a stepladder?"

27   "Well, they should be plenty of good ones on the ground. And if we shake us a branch or two we won't need a ladder." He kneels and begins sorting peaches, asks me a few questions about how school is going. I answer him in monosyllables, hoping the conversation won't drift toward anything that will upset us both. The afternoon air becomes cool all of a sudden. Goosebumps erupt on my arms and neck. "Daddy, I'll be right back," I say, "I need a jacket."

28   In my room I stand before the closet door, looking at my reflection in the full-length mirror. I look at myself, forgetting for several moments why I have come into the room. There I stand in baggy white pants and what Marcus calls my "favorite Dinty Moore shirt." He never told me he disliked the way I dress, but when I was clad in my flannels and baggies his eyes often glanced around—toward the bookshelf, "Hey, a new one by Mishima?" or my stereo, "Let's listen to some Marvin Gaye," or the Dali prints, "When did you say that one was painted?" He, like most men, wants to see women dress in anything tight enough to keep the blood static. He always told me he wasn't particularly a breast man, or a leg man—"I'm not an anything man," he'd say. "I'm an everything man. Legs, ass, brains, conscience." But he only seemed to tell me that kind of thing when I was wearing flannels and baggies.

29   "What does he see in me?" I think as I peruse the frizzy, uncombable black hair, the burdensome breasts, the face that he insisted no guy on campus could forget, the legs he insisted are not birdlike. "And look at my legs," he'd say, indicating with both hands, "They look like a couple of Venus number twos." He told me never to change a thing about myself. "I'm the one who needs to change," he'd say. And I'd tell him, in the beginning, he didn't need to change. That he was fine the way he was. But he would always sneer, "Simmons, you don't know the half of it." He kept saying things like that, becoming more strident, histrionic, and distant. "I'm no goddamned good," he'd say over and over. And soon enough, I began to feel as though his kisses were trying to smother something, that the walls of his apartment enfolded secret passages and chambers, that his conversation, numinous and trivial, full of New Age jargon, spoke around rather than of something. There was always something fleeting about him. Something just out the corner of my

eye, something just out of reach. I imagined that an invisible incubus paced between us when we were together, thumbing its invisible nose at us, flipping us the invisible finger. I felt its presence so acutely sometimes, that I could almost see it burst forth in hyperactive, muscled flesh. Sometimes it made me fear him. Sometimes I think it made me love him more.

30   The more I loved him, the less I understood him, the farther I slipped from him. And when he started punching walls, calling me at two in the morning to apologize for no reason at all, threatening to slash his wrists every time I told him I was busy, I sensed how ripe he was for procreation.

31   "You never have time anymore, Rita. What's the matter, you mad at me?"

32   "Why should I be mad at you? I'm mad at me. I've got to really get going on my thesis."

33   "I know, I understand. I just want to see you. Why are you hiding from me all of a sudden?"

34   I'd say nothing.

35   "What's wrong, Rita? I just want to see you for one hour."

36   "Marc, I just haven't got the time."

37   He never let up. He'd set his heels and push. And push.

38   "Is it something I said to you? Is it my beliefs? When we first met, you always said I was too rarefied for you. You said I strut around 'up there' acting fey while you're 'down here' accepting life for what it is. 'Fey,' you said. Jesus Christ, Rita, I got no problem with your science. Why can't you give me what's mine?"

39   "I know, Marc. I know. I should. I do. It's got nothing to do with your beliefs. Really. I'm just preoccupied. I've got two midterms tomorrow. I've got that lousy seminar. We can talk about this tomorrow, at dinner."

40   And push.

41   "It's because you think I got no soul or some crap like that, isn't it? I just can't give you what a black guy can give you, right? That's what you think, isn't it? Well if it is, Rita, then you're wrong. It's all an illusion. It's maya. If anything, I can give you more because my world is so different from yours."

42   "Marc, there's only this world—"

43   "Look, Rita, I've been through this before. I've had relationships with Black women and Hispanic women, and Asian women. You can tell me. I think I'd understand. You probably think I don't take you seriously. You think I'm just using you."

44   He'd ask me if it was his disapproving family, his derisive friends, his age, his intellect, or that he was an undergraduate English major and I was a semester away from a master's degree in chemistry. It often left us very little to talk about at dinner. He'd ask if his beard looked silly, or if he dressed poorly, or if my family really hadn't liked him but had simply been Oscarwinning

polite, or if he was too easily depressed, irascible, antisocial, untruthful, or was I sure-really-sure "it's not because I'm white?" I'd always say no.

45   I'd say no because it was easy to say no. Easier than unleashing untenable fears, easier, after awhile, than holding him close, feeling his diffuse heat. He'd push, and it was as if he'd started pushing too deeply inside himself, rummaging and scraping, uncovering things that I'm not sure were ever there. "What's wrong with me?" he'd demand. "Tell me. Just tell me something. Do you still love me? Do I offend you in some way?" I couldn't tell him. I knew I'd just have to wait, then I'd see, he'd know. I'd tried to tell him once or twice, but everything would lock up inside me when I'd try to explain. And then it finally just slid out from him, loud and ugly. The word. The beast-incubus word, the inevitable issue of the "yin-yan" relationship. His phrase, "yin-yan relationship." Had I drawn it from him, headfirst screaming, kicking into the world? Or did he plant it in me, water it with his tears, incubate it in the heat of my womblike reticence? I don't know.

46   All I could say that night was, "That, Marc. That's just what I was afraid of. Wasn't but a matter of time, was it?"

47   How would things have gone if I had just told him of my fears and talked it out with him? I never did because to do so would have implied that he had transcended nothing. I flat would have been calling him a liar, or blind. And he was neither. He had transcended something, somehow. Or what if I had just buried myself in his auburn beard, his ginseng breath, the bend and curve of his body, and listened to his nonsense about the Ghosts of Lemuria, the Light of Atlantis, the Race of Tan just for the sake of hearing his voice. His voice was so nice to listen to, a little raspy, a little flutelike. Sometimes it seemed he told his stories in song. Sweet nonsense. And when I actually heard him say the word I was so sure he would eventually say, I was shocked. Shocked both because it always shocks you when someone calls you nigger and because the word fell from his mouth so awkwardly—as if he had never heard it before, said it before, imagined saying it before.

48   So he bought a ticket to Liberia. I didn't know what to feel. He told me he wouldn't come back till he knew, till he really, really understood what blackness was. I didn't know what to say. He hugged me, kissed me longer than I could stand, said goodbye, promised he'd change, we'd get it straight, he'd return reborn, we'd marry and raise fat, tan, unrarefied babies. He got on the plane. He called me from Denver. He called me from New York. He called me from Dakar. He called me from Monrovia. I got his first letter in two weeks. By six weeks I'd received eight more. In three months over forty letters, bombarded by missives of love, the seed of self-discovery. They came daily, weekly. Tidings of hope, love, joy. Peace Profound. Images of beautiful babies, beautiful ocean, sleek, cat-black men, women in rich Day-glo rags. The

taste of this. The smell of that. The size, shape, volume of his ever-expanding, ever-pregnant African love. But I just didn't. His seed fell on unsettled dust, a haze of motes never coming to rest.

49   "It won't lie still," I say aloud, suddenly remembering why I've come up to my room. I grab something warm-looking and bluish, then run back outside.

50   I stand on the stoop and watch Daddy kneeling in the grass, peach in hand. He sniffs, squeezes, removes his glasses and inspects it, then tosses it aside. His face is grave, almost sullen. I cross the yard and kneel beside him, trying to imitate the way he inspects the peaches, but I'm not really sure what he's looking for.

51   I've always loved the way my father throws himself into the task at hand. Whether it be selecting peaches for Mrs. Li's sauce, adjusting a bicycle seat, or expounding to three enraptured daughters at the dinner table just what it is that makes a grocery clerk's job so much more dangerous than a San Francisco cop's, there is no one I know with the intensity, the undivided surrender to the action, the moment.

52   While we sort through hard, woody peaches and soft, muddy peaches, peaches bruised and scarred, peaches clear-complected, he tells me the secret of Mrs. Li's sauce: "She take a whisk broom to J.C.'s chair and use all them cat hairs and cookie crumbs y'all leave in it." And he hints at the secret secret to his peach cobbler, which he says he extracted, through torture, from a Japanese POW. "If I told you, you wouldn't eat it." He tells me it once rained peaches in San Francisco when I was "just a baby, and couldn't possibly remember." And that old Moses told God that no way on earth would he sign those "commandoes or commandants, or whatever you call em, till you take peaches off the list." He tells me he never would have looked twice at Momma had she never stuffed peaches under her sweater back in '47, that peaches, at one time, contained an explosive substance instead of sugar, and the last recorded use of the exploding peach was in the Boer War. "That was before your time," he is quick to add. He tells me about the Peach Bowl of 1968 (LSU won because they ate more peaches. "Well, why you think they call it Peach Bowl?").

53   "Paul Robeson couldn't sing note one 'less he had two, three quarts of peach wine in him," he says. And he tells me about the peachy-keen people he had ever known (me, Juanita, and Theresa May, "and sometimes that hard-head mother of yours"). He tells me how Big Daddy used to push his cart around the streets of Alabaster, Alabama, hollering, "Waaaatermelon? Strawberries and Peeeeachez! Cold, sweet Peeeeachez! Peaches and cream, peach ice cream, peacherinoes and peacherines, peach yogurt, peach popsicles, peach lipstick, peach pie, jam, and jelly. Cold, sweet peeeeachez!"

54   The box is full of what he assures me are the finest peaches that soil could possibly produce. I offer him a peach from the brimming box; he frowns and says, "Shooot, naw, Baby Sister, I cain't eat them things." We laugh for a long time, leaning away from each other, folding toward each other, like jazz dancers. And then I start to cry. I cry so hard I can scarcely breathe. Daddy holds me, saying nothing. He doesn't even try to shush me, just holds me till I stop. Then he reaches in the box, takes out a peach, examines it, sniffs it, throws it aside. He takes another one and does the same thing. Then another, and another, and another.

55   Finally, he turns the whole box over. Peaches tumble across the lawn. He inspects every last one. His long fingers caress each, every one. His nose and eye, inspecting, seed-deep, each, every one. And then he finds what he is looking for. It is very large, the color of a sunrise, flows into a sunset, flows into the color of Mrs. Li's blush. He rubs it on his sleeve, holds it out to me in the palm of his hand. I wipe my nose with a finger, regard the peach for a long, long time. Till Daddy's arm trembles a bit. "Naw," I say, "I can't eat 'em." He drops the fruit and it cracks on the green grass. He takes my hand, and we walk inside.

THINKING ABOUT THE TEXT

1. What is the effect of beginning and ending the story with Rita interacting with her family? Give details that characterize Rita and her parents, and that show their sensitivity toward each other.

2. Consider McKnight's strategy to have Rita escape to her room and to use the "mirror device." From her descriptions, speech, and behaviors, what do we learn about Rita when she is in her room and reflecting on her relationship with Marc?

3. To prepare for a character analysis, write a list of observations about Rita in one column and, in another column next to it, write the corresponding inferences that you have drawn from each observation. Then write another two columns of observations and inferences about Marc. (See pp. 484 for an example of listing for a character analysis.)

4. Rita claims that Marc's conversation "full of New Age jargon, spoke around rather than of something" (150). Look up some of the terms he uses—"incubus," "fey," "maya," "yin-yan," "Ghosts of Lemuria," "Light of Atlantis,"—and explain what Marc's language and his use of this particular vocabulary reveal about him.

5. Describe the different "worlds" that Rita and Marc inhabit. What has contributed to the gulf between them and how likely is it that they will marry and resolve their differences?

6. Referring to the title and closing scene, what are some possible meanings of "peaches" that relate to this story? Consider the father's litany of references to peaches and his search for one that "is very large, the color of a sunrise, flows into a sunset, flows into the color of Mrs. Li's blush" (154). Analyze this quotation in terms of the story and explore what the peach might symbolize.

7. What is ironic about the revelation that neither Rita nor her father can eat peaches? How might this revelation relate to the story and particularly to the central conflict between Rita and Marc? How does it contribute to the resolution of the story?

WRITING FROM THE TEXT

1. Using your lists for exercise 3 page 154, write a character analysis of either Rita or Marc. Focus on a strong assertion about your chosen character and include supporting details and direct quotations to illustrate your points. (See character analysis, pp. 484–93.)

2. Working from your responses to exercise 5 page 154, write an analysis of the factors contributing to the conflict between Rita and Marc. Assess which factors seem more difficult to resolve and whether a more lasting relationship between Marc and Rita seems likely. Support your assessment with specific details from the story.

3. Write an analysis of the multiple meanings of "peaches" in this story and show how this symbolism relates to the characters and central conflict. (See p. 473.)

4. If you have ever had someone call you an offensive name or if you have blurted out a racial or ethnic slur, write an essay explaining and dramatizing what prompted this name calling, what effect it had at the moment, how the incident ended, and what lasting effect it has had on you.

CONNECTING WITH OTHER TEXTS

1. Read "Living in Two Worlds" (p. 144) and examine Mabry's contrasting worlds—home and university—in terms of Rita's. Write an essay comparing their "between worlds" experiences and their ways of managing an attachment to family and a commitment to their own goals.

2. In "Why Does My Race Matter" (p. 158), the writer argues that one's race should not ultimately "matter," but Bahrani shares anecdotes that illustrate just how much race does matter to other people. Using details from her essay and from "Peaches," analyze Rita's experience and discuss what *she* discovers about biracial relationships through her experience with Marc.

3. In "On the Subway" (p. 184), Sharon Olds's narrator describes tension within herself because of a black man and notes: "I don't / know if I am in his power— / . . . or if he is in my power." Using images from the poem and the story, write an essay analyzing the relationship between Rita and Marc in terms of the power or control that both of them have.

 # Diversity Offers Everyone a Stake
Jack M. Balkin

Professor of Constitutional Law and the First Amendment at Yale University, Jack M. Balkin (b. 1956) is a prolific writer, prominent legal theorist, and constitutional scholar. With an undergraduate degree from Harvard College, Balkin earned a J.D. from Harvard Law School and a Ph.D. from Cambridge University. His publications include *Cultural Software: A Theory of Ideology* (1998), *Legal Canons* (coauthored with Sanford Levinson, 2000), *What Brown v. Board of Education Should Have Said: America's Top Legal Experts Rewrite America's Landmark Civil Rights Decision* (2001), and countless essays and online writings. Balkin asserts: "I get the greatest pleasure when I can explain things in a way that's clear and immediately accessible to my audience. Good writing shouldn't make you struggle to understand: it should illuminate, clarify, and bring you right to the heart of the matter." The essay that follows was published in the *Los Angeles Times*, May 17, 2002.

1   On the surface at least, the legal question in Tuesday's decision upholding the University of Michigan Law School's affirmative action policy was whether diversity is a constitutional justification for race-conscious affirmative action. A majority of the U.S. 6th Circuit Court of Appeals said it was.

2   But what really was at stake in the case was the meaning of diversity itself. After the 1978 Bakke decision—in which a white student sued UC Davis after he was rejected for medical school—diversity became the focal point of debate about affirmative action in higher education. The Bakke ruling banned racial set-asides but allowed universities to use race as one factor in admission decisions. Justice Lewis F. Powell's opinion in Bakke, which was cited in the Michigan case, however, obscured the fact that the concept of "diversity" was itself diverse.

3   One type of diversity is demographic diversity: ensuring that a broad cross section of American society has a fair shot at the opportunities that a university education can provide. To achieve this, universities must pay attention to which groups have had the least access to educational opportunity; that's why the University of Michigan's policy focused particularly on blacks and Latinos.

4   The second kind of diversity is diversity as community. It means trying to ensure that people from the different groups in American society learn to live with and work with one another. This vision of diversity tries to forge bonds of trust, loyalty and community among the people who will be running the nation in the next generation.

5   The third kind of diversity is diversity of perspective. Universities try to expose their students to other classmates with different histories, experiences and ways of living. One reason for this is to build trust, understanding and community. But another reason is educational: You can learn a lot from people who don't see things the same way you do.

6   Both proponents and opponents of diversity often run these different considerations together, as Powell himself did in Bakke, and that can sometimes be confusing. Demographic diversity isn't the same thing as diversity of perspective, but it helps produce it. Diversity of perspective isn't identical to the production of a community of trust, but it helps achieve it.

7   These three kinds of diversity are distinct but mutually reinforcing. All three assist the democratic mission of universities: by allowing a broad cross section of society to participate in institutions that create future opportunities and create future leaders, by giving people from different social groups a sense that they are part of the same community and by allowing lots of different ideas to compete. None of these forms of diversity require rigid quotas. But as the 6th Circuit correctly understood, they may require a critical mass of minorities so that minority students don't feel isolated and put upon, afraid to trust others or to express their views. That would undermine all three types of diversity.

8   Diversity is about more than ideological differences; it's about forging community and securing democracy. The dissenting judges in the 6th Circuit took a narrower view, identifying diversity with ideology—whether people think differently. They overlooked the university's democratic mission.

9   In the long run, the fate of our country will rest on the development of a multiethnic and multiracial coalition of people educated in our universities who are willing to strive together rather than against one another. To achieve that end, all people must feel that they have a stake in our country and a chance at shaping its future. If blacks and Latinos are excluded from the opportunity to have opportunities, we won't have cooperation and we won't have community. And we won't have democracy either.

THINKING ABOUT THE TEXT

1. Explain what Balkin identifies as the three types of diversity and why each is important in an educational setting.

2. How do the three types of diversity assist the democratic mission of the university? Are quotas needed or helpful? Explain.

3. According to Balkin, what was overlooked by the dissenting judges when they voted against the University of Michigan Law School's affirmative action policy and what does this threaten? Explain.

WRITING FROM THE TEXT

1. Expanding on Balkin's definition of diversity, write an essay showing how your college or university fails, fulfills, or surpasses his expectations for diversity and his belief in its benefits.

2. Write an evaluative response of Balkin's essay considering the clarity and development of his definition of diversity and his reasons for supporting the principle of affirmative action.

3. Using details from Balkin's essay about the ruling on affirmative action, imagine you are one of the judges—either supporting or dissenting—and write an argument defending your position.

CONNECTING WITH OTHER TEXTS

1. Write an essay supporting Balkin's argument with illustrations from your own experience and from Marcus Mabry's "Living in Two Worlds" (p. 144). Analyze the types of diversity that Mabry offers and how Mabry and others like him enrich Stanford and are served by it as well.

2. Using illustrations from "Black Men and Public Space" (p. 237), "Crimes Against Humanity" (p. 172), or "An Identity Reduced to a Burka" (p. 168), write an essay supporting Balkin's contention that diversity is often seen as threatening to many but is ultimately essential for a true democracy.

Why Does My Race Matter?
Yasmine Bahrani

Sent to a French kindergarten on Malta from her native Iraq, Yasmine Bahrani (b. 1962) later attended school in England and finally moved to the United States with her family where she earned a B.A. in English and an M.A. in journalism at Indiana University. Bahrani is an assistant news editor for Knight-Ridder News Agency in Washington, a frequent contributor to the *Washington Post*, and a freelance writer for the French periodical *Jeune Afrique* and the Arabic women's magazine *Sayidaty*. Originally published in the *Los Angeles Times* in 1998, the following essay reflects Bahrani's multicultural history.

1   When I lived in England, I was black. That's how the system there regards all former colonials like myself: We were generally black. But my blackness was only temporary. When I arrived in the United States, I continued to think of myself as black until my college friends in Indiana started laughing at me for it. They convinced me I wasn't black at all; I was white, they said. I believed them, but that didn't last long, either. A few years later, I discovered that my American employer had classified me as yet something else. To my surprise, I turned out to be one of his Asian employees.

2   By now, the primary benefit of racial classification is apparent to me: entertainment. The primary drawback is equally apparent: It has made my identity available for distortion by others who claim an interest in it.

3   In case you're wondering, I'm from Iraq, and my family tree includes Arabs, Persians, and Turks. A lot of blood has been mixed in Mesopotamia— almost as much as has been shed there—and I suppose that, "racially" speaking, I look like I might be from many places. Some Indians have guessed that I come from their subcontinent; some Iranians have taken me for one of them; so have some South Americans. My father used to smile at my freckles, no doubt exported by Europe, and teasingly called me his own "Crusader." But—so far at least—no Europeans have mistaken me for one of their own. Indeed, one otherwise pleasant German woman I once met challenged even the American identity (more specifically, the Hoosier identity) I sometimes choose to claim. She politely doubted that "real" Americans have black hair like mine.

4   Anyway, under such circumstances, it is very difficult for me to find a voice of my own in this country's ever-intensifying racial dialogue. I suspect the same is true for many other Americans whose racial identities are subject to as much quixotic shuffling as my own. For example, I take very seriously such matters as the future of affirmative action and the good it has done. But given my experience, I find it increasingly difficult to take seriously the premise of race from which such debates are proceeding.

5   There are many such debates going on. Take the government's decision that I, in the company of my fellow Americans, may choose from among an enriched list of racial categories in the 2000 census. This suggests a more democratic spirit than that shown by either Great Britain or my employers, all of whom categorized me without asking for my opinion on the matter. But my racialized experience has taught me that I am being offered a choice of social fictions—suspect social fictions—and I don't think the Census Bureau is doing me the favor it thinks it is.

6   The identities we accept are portentous because they will follow us around forever. For example, we have come to accept the term "Hispanic," which became a minority designation under the Nixon administration in

1973. "Latino," more popular in the Western states, will be offered as an alternative in the next census. Many who are labeled so today privately scorn the term, choosing instead to think of themselves as Mexicans, Bolivians, Dominicans, and so on. But because the government says they are Hispanic or Latino, so must they.

7   Of course, the move to create more "officially" recognized classifications is supported by a number of people who want to escape the racial cage they find themselves in, and I appreciate the irony. Many of these people consider themselves to be of mixed race and resent being forced to choose between their parents' identities. I have sympathy for this group. It is no more interested in an assigned identity than I am. But I don't see how an ever more refined listing of racial categories is the answer to such a problem, so much as a surrender to it. An end to official racial categories seems a much more appealing solution.

8   Now a whole national dialogue on race is underway. What I have come to want from such an exchange is what I used to think every American wanted: to be taken for who I am. I know that racism and other forms of prejudice have prevented this ideal from being realized, but it remains a respectable ideal nonetheless, and was, after all, best articulated by my sometime fellow black, the Rev. Martin Luther King Jr. For all that color blindness—and indeed blindness to ethnicity and even gender—has become perceived as utopian (if not actually reactionary), I'm sticking to it.

9   I should add that what I know about American ethnic hatred is not just intellectual. Among the myriad classifications I have been tagged with is a variation on the so-called n-word intended for Arabs. The epithet was hurled at me on at least two occasions back home in Indiana, along with, the first time, eggs, and the second time, a putrid tomato. All hit their target, the epithet included. Even so, I prefer to take my chances as an American among other Americans, and not to construct an alternate identity out of my ethnic origins as a shield against hurt. Don't misunderstand; I could not be more proud of those origins (despite troubles in my native land) and the magnificent history and language that accompany them. But I'm here now.

THINKING ABOUT THE TEXT

1. What is Yasmine Bahrani's history? What are the different ways she has been viewed in the various places that she has lived? How do these diverse responses contribute to her essay?

2. What is Bahrani's purpose in writing this essay? What is her claim?

3. What is Bahrani's tone in the first paragraph of her essay? What is her strategy in employing this tone? How does her tone reflect the stance she takes in her essay?

4. How does Yasmine Bahrani want to think of herself? How has her self-concept—a voice of her own—been threatened by others?

5. How does the government's decision to let people "choose from among an enriched list of racial categories in the 2000 census" actually create difficulties for many citizens? What are the examples Bahrani cites? What does Bahrani want instead of a choice in assigning herself a racial identity?

6. What are your responses to the ways Bahrani has been treated in Britain and in the United States?

WRITING FROM THE TEXT

1. Write an essay in which you analyze your own or a friend's experiences with racial categorizing and/or ethnic hatred.

2. Argue that Bahrani is correct, that race doesn't matter, and that the government census should not force people into racial categories.

3. Write an essay to convince your reader that too much of an individual's roots—language, traditions, foods, and history—will be lost if we cease to identify people by their racial origins.

CONNECTING WITH OTHER TEXTS

1. Analyze Bahrani's essay in light of "Diversity Offers Everyone a Stake" (p. 156). How does Balkin's view of diversity parallel Bahrani's? Draw specific ideas from both authors to support the points in your essay.

2. Both Brent Staples ("Black Men and Public Space," p. 237) and Yasmine Bahrani have been victims of racial hatred. Write an essay in which you examine these writers' experiences and their attitudes toward their experiences.

3. Bahrani mentions Martin Luther King, Jr., in her essay. Read King's essay "Three Ways of Meeting Oppression" (p. 280), and write an analysis of how Bahrani might respond to the people who have been unkind to her if she takes King's ideas and methods to heart.

In Rooms of Women
Kim Edwards

After earning her B.A. in English at Colgate, Kim Edwards (b. 1958) earned her M.F.A. from the Iowa Writers' Workshop and then her M.A. in linguistics. She has taught English in Malaysia, Japan, and Cambodia. She is a freelance writer of fiction and has had work published in the *Paris Review*. She won the Nelson Algren Award for fiction in 1990 and in

1997 published a short story collection, *Secrets of a Fire King.* The following piece, originally published as a longer essay in the *Michigan Quarterly,* evolved from her experiences
teaching in Malaysia and Japan.

1   When I lived on the east coast of Malaysia, I used to do aerobics over a
Chinese grocery store. I went there almost every afternoon, climbed up a tunnel of concrete stairs to a narrow room infused with the perfume of hair gel
and perspiration, cosmetics and worn shoes. In Malaysia, where more than
half the female population drifts through the tropical days beneath layers of
concealing polyester, this room was an unusual domain of women. We were
relaxed here, exposed in our leotards and shorts, our determination as strong
as the situation was ironic. For an hour each day we stretched and ran and
sweated, devoting ourselves entirely to the care of bodies which, in the outside world, we were encouraged to hide.

2   Malaysia is a multiracial country, with Islamic Malays comprising 55%
of the population. Chinese and Indians make up the rest, at 35% and 10%,
respectively. Though they have shared the Malay peninsula for generations,
these groups maintain distinct languages and cultural traditions. They live
together in uneasy proximity, with the biggest division occurring between the
Malays, who follow Islam, and the other two groups, who don't. At aerobics,
though, these population demographics were reversed; only one or two of the
women in that room were Malay. Their presence was an act of quiet daring.
Outside, they didn't wear the polyester robes and veils. Inside, they were bold
enough to appear among us in a leotard that revealed the contours of their
flesh.

3   From the windows of the aerobics room we could see other Malay women
as they shopped or chatted, their shiny skirts brushing their brown feet. They
wore long-sleeved tunics that hung loosely to the knees, designed to hide
every flux and curve of the body. On top of this most wore a *telicon,* a kind of
polyester scarf that fastens beneath the chin and flows down, elbow-length,
hiding the hair and curve of breasts simultaneously. Though this attire is
common now, in pictures from Malaysia that are more than 15 years old,
very few of the women cover their heads. Islam has been the predominant religion of the area for centuries, but traditionally it has been a gentle, even
tolerant force in Malaysia, tempered by the weather and the easy-going nature of the people. In more remote villages it is still possible to see a lifestyle
shaped by its quieter influence. The call to prayer comes five times a day, but
little children, both boys and girls, play naked under the fruit trees. Women
sit on porches, breast-feeding children. They bathe in the river together, wearing sarongs, and the most serious head-covering is a scarf draped gracefully
across the hair on formal occasions. There are separate spheres here, for men

and for women, but the focus is less on rules and their enforcement than it is on the harmonious flow of life from one day to another.

4   By the time I went to teach in Malaysia, however, much of the country had been profoundly influenced by the Iranian revolution. The gentle religion that had thrived in the country for centuries changed rapidly as televised images of the Middle East showed a different standard of dress and practice. This growing conservatism invaded every aspect of life, but it was most immediately visible in the dress mandated for girls and women. It began with pressure for them to discard Western clothes or sarongs in favor of the shapeless polyester dresses known as the *baju kurung.* By the time I reached Malaysia, the *baju kurung* and *telicon* were commonplace, and I watched the veils grow longer, heavier, and more somber during the two years I was there. For the more radical there was *purdah,* literally *curtain,* where a veil, usually black, hides the entire face, and dark gloves protect the fingers from view. When I first went to Malaysia, it was rare to glimpse a woman in *purdah.* By the time I left, I saw them almost every other day.

5   Yet at the same time that conservative Islam was strengthening in Malaysia, the government was sending a record number of Malay students overseas to study subjects essential to a developing country. Thus, the students were caught in two opposing forces, one that dictated a life focused solely on Islam, the other that demanded they learn technology from cultures outside of Islam. The place where these two forces met was in the preparatory schools that the students attended for two years before going overseas. Here, the stated administrative goal was to provide, as much as possible, an American style of education, in hopes of reducing culture shock and gaining transfer credit. Here too the religious teachers, alarmed by what they perceived to be a decadent influence, worked hard to ensure that the students understood the terrible evil of the West. Yet belief is an insubstantial thing, difficult to pin down or measure, especially in a population of nearly a thousand students. And so it was the rules they turned to. The equation was a simple one: Those who followed the rules were virtuous, and those who did not were damned.

6   It was in one of these schools that I taught. My college was located in the east coast of the peninsula, in the heart of the Islamic revival, and the religious teachers, or *ustaz,* were the most powerful men in the school. I'd had Malaysian students in the U.S., young women who appeared in class with tennis shoes poking out from beneath their polyester robes, and I'd been assured by the people who hired me that this dress code wouldn't affect my life; that, as a Westerner, I'd be outside the rules of Islam. Moreover, though I was an English teacher, it was also part of my job to *be* American, and to expose the students to other ways of living that they would encounter when they

went overseas. At the time of that interview I was teaching in a major university, with students from dozens of countries in my classes. The idea of being different didn't seem particularly intimidating. I packed my most discreet Western clothes, and expected that I'd exist with the local teachers in a state of mutual tolerance and respect.

7   What I didn't fully understand, before I left America, is what it means to be different in a society where anything but conformity is greeted with unease. In Malaysia, as in many Asian cultures, there is an emphasis on the group over the individual. This focus is made stronger by Islam, which demands a structured and visible compliance to group norms, and which viewed my particular differences—American, non-Islamic, uncovered woman—as both evil and a threat. In a community of covered women, my short-sleeved blouses and calf-length skirts seemed suddenly immodest. The religious teachers made sure I understood this on my first day there, when they veered off the path—literally walking through mud—to avoid me. They couldn't keep the government from hiring me, but they could isolate me. They treated me as an unclean person, and the most devout students and teachers soon followed their example.

8   What was hardest for me, though, was the difficulty I had making connections with other women. The veils that covered them were also a kind of barrier I could not seem to cross. I suppose my skin, my hair, the obvious isolation imposed on me by the *ustaz,* seemed as unnerving to them as their veils and long skirts sometimes seemed to me. Some of the women were kind, but distant. If we talked, the subject invariably came back to Islam. Others, those who were extremely devout, were visibly unfriendly. These were the women who wore thick socks with their sandals and dressed in the most somber shades of gray and brown and black. They covered even the heads of their infant daughters, and cast disapproving glances at my exposed forearms, my calves, my toes. In this atmosphere, it was more than a year before I made any women friends at school. There were never many, and I always understood that friendship with me carried risks for them. The *ustaz* and other teachers reprimanded them often for consorting with a Westerner. One of them told me this while we were at her village, sitting on the front steps eating mangos.

9   "But it isn't true," she said, thinking. "It isn't true what they say. You are not Islam. But you are good."

10   In another situation—if I'd been a Peace Corps volunteer—I might have given in, and sought a greater harmony with this community by wearing the *baju kurung.* It would have been the easiest choice—one by one, the few uncovered women at the college were folding under the pressure and donning

telicons—and I might have done it too, despite the fact that polyester beneath a tropical sun clings like plastic to the skin. I know this is true because I wore it once. I was in a village with my friend and I wanted to make a good impression. I remember it so clearly, the polyester slipping over my head, and the feeling of claustrophobia that accompanied it. At the school, though, wearing the *baju kurung* would have served no purpose except to mislead the students about what they could expect to find in America. Already the *ustaz* spewed a mixed and misleading propaganda: America was evil, all the people were greedy and had no morals. Though I tried to keep a low profile, and to show through my actions that different ways of dressing had very little to do with a person's character, it was clear that the *ustaz* saw my clothes, and the body they revealed, as clear manifestations of Western decadence. They did their best to isolate me, and this was more insidious than simple unfriendliness. In a society which puts its emphasis on the group, isolation is the cruelest punishment of all.

11   The longer I stayed in Malaysia, and the more friends I made, the more dangerous I became. It took my friend's comment, *you are not Islam, but you are good,* to make me realize this. Islam teaches that there is only one way. That way is strict, and tolerates no deviance. By wearing Western clothes, clothes that acknowledged waist and skin, the curve of female flesh, I was suggesting that this was not so, that there was, in fact, a choice. As long as I could be isolated, cast as a symbol of decadence and evil, the implications of my dress could be contained. But as I stayed longer, made friends, committed no evil acts, it became more difficult to cast me in the black-and-white terms that symbols require. I was not Islam, but neither was I evil. In essence, my presence was a kind of unspoken question, and it was seen by the devout as an act of absolute aggression. From time to time—often during moments of political tension in the Islamic world—the minimal tolerance I was granted waned. At these times I was thrust out of the middle ground with all its ambiguities and became suddenly, unwillingly, polemic.

12   There were several incidents in the two years I was there, but the one that stays most significantly in my mind occurred after the Ayatollah Khomeni called for the death of Salman Rushdie. Stirred up by the *ustaz,* the students made repeated denunciations—first against Rushdie himself, then the West in general, and finally against America and the three American teachers at the school. We watched this progression without reacting, but in the face of such anger, it was not enough to be silent. We were outside Islam, and our nonbelief, tolerated during calmer times, now evoked strong and emotional reactions. Even teachers who had seemed indifferent before soon joined in the general denunciation.

13   One day, in the worst of this, a Malay teacher who had never covered herself arrived at the college dressed in a *baju kurung* with a long black *telicon* falling over it. I remember the stir of pleasure she caused among those already covered. I remember that she passed me on the sidewalk and shot me a beatific smile. Lost, as she was, within a frame of black, I didn't recognize her at first. When I did, I understood her message immediately: *I belong, now, and I pity you, one among the damned.* She, like the more radical women in the town who donned *purdah* veils, was using her body, the negation of it, as a means of political expression. The denial of her body was a kind of aggression, and her aggression was sanctioned and supported—in this case, even demanded—by the community.

14   It is a terrible thing to hate your own body, yet in Malaysia I found that I was never far from this feeling. I was most aware of it every time I left the country, even briefly, and felt anxiety slipping from my shoulders like a heavy cloak. In Singapore I wore shorts without a stir; in Bangkok a sleeveless sundress was nothing to anyone but a sensible way of dealing with the heat. The first time it happened I was in Hong Kong, and I remember feeling light, joyously light, when the only people who followed me were the shopkeepers hoping for a sale. It is a big city, full of lovely, visible bodies. I was anonymous, and I had never felt so free.

15   In the end, of course, I left Malaysia for good. I took a job in Japan, where sometimes, at the end of a long week, I treated myself to a trip to the local hot spring. The first time I went was not long after I arrived. I remember that I felt oddly shy at the prospect of disrobing in a public area, and I realized at that moment how strongly my sense of what was appropriate had been shaped by two years in an Islamic country. Yet I made myself go. The room, at the top of an open stairway, was empty, lovely, built of pine. Moonlight flowed in through the windows and filled the wooden shelves. It was very cold. I undressed completely, as I knew was the custom, folding my clothes carefully. Wrapped in a towel, I stepped around the corner into the hot spring area.

16   At first I couldn't see much. Steam rose from the pool and caught the light, creating a kind of silver fog. Even with my closest friends in Malaysia, we had dressed and undressed discreetly, within sarongs, and the image of the body was never something that was shared. I still felt hesitant, standing on the smooth rocks with my towel clutched around me. Through the steam other women appeared, floating against the dark gray rocks, their bodies catching the light in a white and wavering contrast to the darkness below. They were all so different, women whose bodies plodded or strode or moved with grace, women whose breasts were rounded or sloped, pendulous or barely formed. I watched them all with appreciation, my body one among theirs, an individual collection of permutations and shapes, yet one of a set.

In that spring, a foreigner and further isolated by my stumbling Japanese, I nonetheless felt a sense of community. For two years I'd carried, unwillingly, a sense of the body as something to hide, and a message that the flesh was an aggression, a sin, an evocation of the darker forces in human nature. In a Japanese hot spring, all this was washed away.

THINKING ABOUT THE TEXT

1. What are the contrasting cultural experiences that Kim Edwards had teaching abroad? What insight resulted from her hot spring experience in Japan?

2. What history of the coverings for women does Edwards give in her essay? Why didn't Edwards wear the *baju kurung?* Do you agree with her reasoning?

3. What personal discomfort did Edwards feel about her decision? Why was her decision interpreted as political?

4. Why did Edwards leave her teaching position in Malaysia? How did her experience in Japan confirm that her decision was a good one for her?

WRITING FROM THE TEXT

1. Describe a time in your life when the way that you were dressed separated you from people with whom you wanted to be friends. Describe specifically the way that you were dressed and how you think people perceived you. *Why* did people respond to you as they did? Like Edwards, see if you can come to some awareness in the process of writing about this experience.

2. Write an analysis of the compromises you have made in dressing to please yourself and at the same time to satisfy some explicit or understood societal "dress code." You might contrast the expectations of others with your preferred style of dress.

CONNECTING WITH OTHER TEXTS

1. Women especially, although not exclusively, receive messages about their bodies and dress throughout their lives. Many of the selections in *Between Worlds* address or refer to this issue. Use the information presented in "A Work of Artifice" (p. 106) and "Bodily Harm" (p. 250) to write an analysis of one aspect of the issue of women in relation to their bodies.

2. Read Robert Heilbroner's essay "Don't Let Stereotypes Warp Your Judgments" (p. 469), and write an analysis of the problems that Edwards describes. Show in your essay that stereotyping is the source of the trouble.

3. Read "An Identity Reduced to a Burka" (below) and write an essay explaining how the authors' points illuminate the observations made by Kim Edwards.

 An Identity Reduced to a Burka

Semeen Issa and Laila Al-Marayati

Born in Tanzania in 1962, Semeen Issa is a teacher and also the president of the Muslim Women's League. She came to the United States in 1970 and graduated with both undergraduate and graduate degrees in education from the University of Southern California. Issa believes that "it is important in this country of great diversity that we take advantage of what others have to offer and that we stop judging people by how they look."

A practicing gynecologist as well as a writer, Laila Al-Marayati (b. 1962) is the author of articles on women's rights, women's sexuality, and female circumcision. She was born in the United States to a Palestinian father and a mother who is of French, German, and Native American heritage. The following article originally appeared in the *Los Angeles Times* on January 20, 2002 and was written because of the authors' growing frustration with the media's reductive perception of Muslim women.

1   A few years ago, someone from the Feminist Majority Foundation called the Muslim Women's League to ask if she could "borrow a burka" for a photo shoot the organization was doing to draw attention to the plight of women in Afghanistan under the Taliban. When we told her that we didn't have one, and that none of our Afghan friends did either, she expressed surprise, as if she'd assumed that all Muslim women keep *burkas* in their closets in case a militant Islamist comes to dinner. She didn't seem to understand that her assumption was the equivalent of assuming that every Latino has a Mexican sombrero in their closet.

2   We don't mean to make light of the suffering of our sisters in Afghanistan, but the *burka* was—and is—not their major focus of concern. Their priorities are more basic, like feeding their children, becoming literate and living free from violence. Nevertheless, recent articles in the Western media suggest the *burka* means everything to Muslim women, because they routinely express bewilderment at the fact that all Afghan women didn't cast off their *burkas* when the Taliban was defeated. The Western press' obsession with the dress of Muslim women is not surprising, however, since the press tends to view Muslims, in general, simplistically.

3   Headlines in the mainstream media have reduced Muslim female identity to an article of clothing—"the veil." One is hard-pressed to find an article, book or film about women in Islam that doesn't have "veil" in the title:

"Behind the Veil," "Beyond the Veil," "At the Drop of a Veil" and more. The use of the term borders on the absurd: Perhaps next will come "What Color is Your Veil?" or "Rebel Without a Veil" or "Whose Veil Is It, Anyway?"

4   The word "veil" does not even have a universal meaning. In some cultures, it refers to a face-covering known as a *niqab*; in others, to a simple head scarf, known as *hijab*. Other manifestations of "the veil" include all-encompassing outer garments like the ankle-length *abaya* from the Persian Gulf states, the *chador* in Iran or the *burka* in Afghanistan.

5   Like the differences in our clothing from one region to another, Muslim women are diverse. Stereotypical assumptions about Muslim women are as inaccurate as the assumption that all American women are personified by the bikini-clad cast of "Baywatch." Anyone who has spent time interacting with Muslims knows that, despite numerous obstacles, Muslim women are active, assertive and engaged in society. In Qatar, women make up the majority of graduate-school students. The Iranian parliament has more women members than the U.S. Senate. Throughout the world, many Muslim women are educated and professionally trained; they participate in public debates, are often catalysts for reform and champions for their own rights. At the same time, there is no denying that in many Muslim countries, dress has been used as a tool to wield power over women.

6   What doesn't penetrate Western consciousness, however, is that forced uncovering is also a tool of oppression. During the reign of Shah Mohammad Reza Pahlavi in Iran, wearing the veil was prohibited. As an expression of their opposition to his repressive regime, women who supported the 1979 Islamic Revolution marched in the street clothed in *chadors*. Many of them did not expect to have this "dress code" institutionalized by those who led the revolution and then took power in the new government.

7   In Turkey, the secular regime considers the head scarf a symbol of extremist elements that want to overthrow the government. Accordingly, women who wear any type of head-covering are banned from public office, government jobs and academia, including graduate school. Turkish women who believe the head-covering is a religious obligation are unfairly forced to give up public life or opportunities for higher education and career advancement.

8   Dress should not bar Muslim women from exercising their Islam-guaranteed rights, like the right to be educated, to earn a living, and to move about safely in society. Unfortunately, some governments impose a strict dress code along with other restrictions, like limiting education for women, to appear "authentically Islamic." Such laws, in fact, are inconsistent with Islam. Nevertheless, these associations lead to the general perception that "behind the veil" lurk other, more insidious examples of the repression of women, and that wearing the veil somehow causes the social ills that plague Muslim women around the world.

9   Many Muslim men and women alike are subjugated by despotic, dictatorial regimes. Their lot in life is worsened by extreme poverty and illiteracy, two conditions that are not caused by Islam but are sometimes exploited in the name of religion. Helping Muslim women overcome their misery is a major task. The reconstruction of Muslim Afghanistan will be a test case for the Afghan people and for the international community dedicated to making Afghan society work for everyone. To some, Islam is the root cause of the problems faced by women in Afghanistan. But what is truly at fault is a misguided, narrow interpretation of Islam designed to serve a rigid patriarchal system.

10   Traditional Muslim populations will be more receptive to change that is based on Islamic principles of justice, as expressed in the Koran, than they will be to change that abandons religion altogether or confines it to private life. Muslim scholars and leaders who emphasize Islamic principles that support women's rights to education, health care, marriage and divorce, equal pay for equal work and participation in public life could fill the vacuum now occupied by those who impose a vision of Islam that infringes on the rights of women.

11   Given the opportunity, Muslim women, like women everywhere, will become educated, pursue careers, strive to do what is best for their families and contribute positively according to their abilities. How they dress is irrelevant. It should be obvious that the critical element Muslim women need is freedom, especially the freedom to make choices that enable them to be independent agents of positive change. Choosing to dress modestly, including wearing a head scarf, should be as respected as choosing not to cover. Accusations that modestly dressed Muslim women are caving in to male-dominated understandings of Islam neglect the reality that most Muslim women who cover by choice do so out of subservience to God, not to any human being.

12   The worth of a woman—any woman—should not be determined by the length of her skirt, but by the dedication, knowledge and skills she brings to the task at hand.

THINKING ABOUT THE TEXT

1. What is the authors' strategy in opening their essay with a narrative? How does the anecdote embody the authors' point of view?

2. What do you infer is the authors' thesis? Despite the seriousness of their claim, the authors' tone is humorous throughout. What is their strategy in employing humor? What is their aim?

3. What did you learn about the "veil" in different Muslim countries? How do the differences in styles and purposes for covering relate to the authors' point about Muslim women?

4. The authors insist that enforced dress codes are not the major problem facing most Islamic women, and their religion is not the delimiting factor in their lives. What are the problems facing these women? How do the authors' points help non-Muslim readers perceive the situation of Muslim women?

Writing from the Text

1. Remember a time when a clothing code was imposed on you—for school, work, or for a social event within your peer group or family. Describe how you felt about the requirement, and whether you rebelled or conformed. Are identities reduced or enhanced by clothing regulations?

2. The authors observe that we tend to see Muslim women "simplistically" or stereotypically, in part because of our fixation on the *burka*. Write an essay that examines other nationalities and cultures that have been stereotyped by dress and analyze the consequences of such stereotyping.

3. Imagine yourself a traditional Muslim woman from an Afghan village who is transported to a city in the United States. You start to observe Western dress styles for women and now, in an essay, must show your approval or disapproval of American women's choices.

4. After this essay appeared in the *Los Angeles Times*, one letter to the editor pointed out that how women dress is not irrelevant, and that women who wear *burkas* would not become surgeons, for example, because veiling of any kind would not be possible in an operating room. Make a list of other activities or professions that you imagine could not reasonably be done by someone wearing a head covering. Write an essay that comes to some conclusion about whether how women dress is relevant.

Connecting with Other Texts

1. The authors write that "in many Muslim countries, dress has been used as a tool to wield power over women," and they note that "forced uncovering is also a tool of oppression." Write an essay that analyzes how clothing codes have wielded power over women and men in many cultures. You might consider styles of clothing in affluent nations, as well as compulsory garments or uniforms throughout the world.

2. Interview two Muslim women you know or can meet on your campus, one who wears a head covering of some kind and one who does not. In your prepared questions for the interview, you might consider asking why each has chosen "to veil or not to veil" and what experiences each has had as a result of her decision, including how she is perceived in the Muslim and non-Muslim cultures. In your comparative essay, come to some conclusion about the nature of "the veil."

3. Read "In Rooms of Women," (p. 161) and connect the experiences of Kim Edwards with the observations Al-Marayati and Issa make in their essay on the *burka*. Would Edwards and the Muslim authors agree or disagree with each other?

4. In an essay supported with research, examine what happens when a culture's traditional style of dress goes mainstream and becomes a fashion statement, like Guatemalan woven jackets, the Indian sari, soldiers' camouflage, or the Chinese padded jacket. Is it possible that the *burka* might be adapted in some form to clothe Western women?

 Crimes Against Humanity

Ward Churchill

Creek-Cherokee métis Ward Churchill (b. 1947) is the coordinator of the American Indian Movement (AIM) for the state of Colorado. A graduate in communications from Sangamon State University, Churchill is a prolific, self-taught writer. His many books on Native Americans include *From a Native Son: Selected Essays on Indigenism 1985–1995; Fantasies of the Master Race: Literature, Cinema, and the Colonization of American Indians; Struggle for the Land: Indigenous Resistance to Genocide, Ecocide, and Expropriation in Contemporary North America; A Little Matter of Genocide: Holocaust and Denial in the Americas 1492 to the Present;* and, most recently, with Vander Wall, *Agents of Repression: The FBI's Secret Wars Against the Black Panther Party and the American Indian Movement* (2002). He is the editor of *New Studies on the Left* and *Acts of Rebellion: The Ward Churchill Reader* (2002). Churchill has been a visiting scholar of the humanities at Alfred University, and he presently teaches at the Center for Studies of Ethnicity and Race in America at the University of Colorado, Boulder. Churchill is a frequent contributor to *Z Magazine*, where the essay included here was published in 1993.

1   During the past couple of seasons, there has been an increasing wave of controversy regarding the names of professional sports teams like the Atlanta "Braves," Cleveland "Indians," Washington "Redskins," and Kansas City "Chiefs." The issue extends to the names of college teams like Florida State University "Seminoles," University of Illinois "Fighting Illini," and so on, right on down to high school outfits like the Lamar (Colorado) "Savages." Also involved have been team adoption of "mascots," replete with feathers, buckskins, beads, spears and "warpaint" (some fans have opted to adorn themselves in the same fashion), and nifty little "pep" gestures like the "Indian Chant" and "Tomahawk Chop."

2   A substantial number of American Indians have protested that use of native names, images and symbols as sports team mascots and the like is, by definition, a virulently racist practice. Given the historical relationship between Indians and non-Indians during what has been called the "Conquest of America," American Indian Movement leader (and American Indian Anti-Defamation Council founder) Russell Means has compared the practice to contemporary Germans naming their soccer teams the "Jews," "Hebrews," and "Yids," while adorning their uniforms with grotesque caricatures of Jewish faces taken from the Nazis' anti-Semitic propaganda of the 1930s. Numerous demonstrations have occurred in conjunction with games—most notably during the November 15, 1992 match-up between the Chiefs and Redskins in Kansas City—by angry Indians and their supporters.

3   In response, a number of players—especially African-Americans and other minority athletes—have been trotted out by professional team owners like Ted Turner, as well as university and public school officials, to announce that they mean not to insult but to honor native people. They have been joined by the television networks and most major newspapers, all of which have editorialized that Indian discomfort with the situation is "no big deal," insisting that the whole thing is just "good, clean fun." The country needs more such fun, they've argued, and "a few disgruntled Native Americans" have no right to undermine the nation's enjoyment of its leisure time by complaining. This is especially the case, some have argued, "in hard times like these." It has even been contended that Indian outrage at being systematically degraded—rather than the degradation itself—creates "a serious barrier to the sort of intergroup communication so necessary in a multicultural society such as ours."

4   Okay, let's communicate. We are frankly dubious that those advancing such positions really believe their own rhetoric, but, just for the sake of argument, let's accept the premise that they are sincere. If what they say is true, then isn't it time we spread such "inoffensiveness" and "good cheer" around among *all* groups so that *everybody* can participate *equally* in fostering the round of national laughs they call for? Sure it is—the country can't have too much fun or "intergroup involvement"—so the more, the merrier. Simple consistency demands that anyone who thinks the Tomahawk Chop is a swell pastime must be just as hearty in his or her endorsement of the following ideas. The same logic used to defend the defamation of American Indians should help us all start yukking it up.

5   First, as a counterpart to the Redskins, we need an NFL team called "Niggers" to honor Afro-Americans. Half-time festivities for fans might include a simulated stewing of the opposing coach in a large pot while players and

cheerleaders dance around it, garbed in leopard skins and wearing fake bones in their noses. This concept obviously goes along with the kind of gaiety attending the Chop, but also with the actions of the Kansas City Chiefs, whose team members—prominently including black team members—lately appeared on a poster looking "fierce" and "savage" by way of wearing Indian regalia. Just a bit of harmless "morale boosting," says the Chiefs' front office. You bet.

6   So that the newly formed Niggers sports club won't end up too out of sync while expressing the "spirit" and "identity" of Afro-Americans in the above fashion, a baseball franchise—let's call this one the "Sambos"—should be formed. How about a basketball team called the "Spearchuckers"? A hockey team called the "Jungle Bunnies"? Maybe the "essence" of these teams could be depicted by images of tiny black faces adorned with huge pairs of lips. The players could appear on TV every week or so gnawing on chicken legs and spitting watermelon seeds at one another. Catchy, eh? Well, there's "nothing to be upset about," according to those who love wearing "war bonnets" to the Super Bowl or having "Chief Illiniwik" dance around the sports arenas of Urbana, Illinois.

7   And why stop there? There are plenty of other groups to include. Hispanics? They can be "represented" by the Galveston "Greasers" and San Diego "Spics," at least until the Wisconsin "Wetbacks" and Baltimore "Beaners" get off the ground. Asian Americans? How about the "Slopes," "Dinks," "Gooks," and "Zipperheads"? Owners of the latter teams might get their logo ideas from editorial page cartoons printed in the nation's newspapers during World War II: slant-eyes, buck teeth, big glasses, but nothing racially insulting or derogatory, according to the editors and artists involved at the time. Indeed, this Second World War–vintage stuff can be seen as just another barrel of laughs, at least by what current editors say are their "local standards" concerning American Indians.

8   Let's see. Who's been left out? Teams like the Kansas City "Kikes," Hanover "Honkies," San Leandro "Shylocks," Daytona "Dagos," and Pittsburgh "Polacks" will fill a certain social void among white folk. Have a religious belief? Let's all go for the gusto and gear up the Milwaukee "Mackerel Snappers" and Hollywood "Holy Rollers." The Fighting Irish of Notre Dame can be rechristened the "Drunken Irish" or "Papist Pigs." Issues of gender and sexual preference can be addressed through creation of teams like the St. Louis "Sluts," Boston "Bimbos," Detroit "Dykes," and the Fresno "Fags." How about the Gainesville "Gimps" and Richmond "Retards," so the physically and mentally impaired won't be excluded from our fun and games?

9   Now, don't go getting "overly sensitive" out there. None of this is demeaning or insulting, at least not when it's being done to Indians. Just ask the folks who are doing it, or their apologists like Andy Rooney in the national media.

They'll tell you—as in fact they *have* been telling you—that there's been no harm done, regardless of what their victims think, feel, or say. The situation is exactly the same as when those with precisely the same mentality used to insist that Step 'n' Fetchit was okay, or Rochester on the *Jack Benny Show,* or Amos and Andy, Charlie Chan, the Frito Bandito, or any of the other cutesy symbols making up the lexicon of American racism. Have we communicated yet?

10   Let's get just a little bit real here. The notion of "fun" embodied in rituals like the Tomahawk Chop must be understood for what it is. There's not a single non-Indian example used above which can be considered socially acceptable in even the most marginal sense. The reasons are obvious enough. So why is it different where American Indians are concerned? One can only conclude that, in contrast to the other groups at issue, Indians are (falsely) perceived as being too few, and therefore too weak, to defend themselves effectively against racist and otherwise offensive behavior.

11   Fortunately, there are some glimmers of hope. A few teams and their fans have gotten the message and have responded appropriately. Stanford University, which opted to drop the name "Indians" from Stanford, has experienced no resulting drop-off in attendance. Meanwhile, the local newspaper in Portland, Oregon recently decided its long-standing editorial policy prohibiting use of racial epithets should include derogatory team names. The Redskins, for instance, are now referred to as "the Washington team," and will continue to be described in this way until the franchise adopts an inoffensive moniker (newspaper sales in Portland have suffered no decline as a result).

12   Such examples are to be applauded and encouraged. They stand as figurative beacons in the night, proving beyond all doubt that it is quite possible to indulge in the pleasure of athletics without accepting blatant racism into the bargain.

13   On October 16, 1946, a man named Julius Streicher mounted the steps of a gallows. Moments later he was dead, the sentence of an international tribunal composed of representatives of the United States, France, Great Britain, and the Soviet Union having been imposed. Streicher's body was then cremated, and—so horrendous were his crimes thought to have been—his ashes dumped into an unspecified German river so that "no one should ever know a particular place to go for reasons of mourning his memory."

14   Julius Streicher had been convicted at Nuremberg, Germany, of what were termed "Crimes Against Humanity." The lead prosecutor in his case— Justice Robert Jackson of the United States Supreme Court—had not argued that the defendant had killed anyone, nor that he had personally committed any especially violent act. Nor was it contended that Streicher had held any particularly important position in the German government during the period in which the so-called Third Reich had exterminated some 6,000,000

Jews, as well as several million Gypsies, Poles, Slavs, homosexuals, and other *untermenschen* (subhumans).

15   The sole offense for which the accused was ordered put to death was in having served as publisher/editor of a Bavarian tabloid entitled *Der Sturmer* during the early-to-mid 1930s, years before the Nazi genocide actually began. In this capacity, he had penned a long series of virulently anti-Semitic editorials and "news" stories, usually accompanied by cartoons and other images graphically depicting Jews in extraordinarily derogatory fashion. This, the prosecution asserted, had done much to "dehumanize" the targets of his distortion in the mind of the German public. In turn, such dehumanization had made it possible—or at least easier—for average Germans to later indulge in the outright liquidation of Jewish "vermin." The tribunal agreed, holding that Streicher was therefore complicit in genocide and deserving of death by hanging.

16   During his remarks to the Nuremberg tribunal, Justice Jackson observed that, in implementing its sentences, the participating powers were morally and legally binding themselves to adhere forever after to the same standards of conduct that were being applied to Streicher and the other Nazi leaders. In the alternative, he said, the victorious allies would have committed "pure murder" at Nuremberg—no different in substance from that carried out by those they presumed to judge—rather than establishing the "permanent bench-mark for justice" which was intended.

17   Yet in the United States of Robert Jackson, the indigenous American Indian population had already been reduced, in a process which is ongoing to this day, from perhaps 12.5 million in the year 1500 to fewer than 250,000 by the beginning of the twentieth century. This was accomplished, according to official sources, "largely through the cruelty of [Euro-American] settlers," and an informal but clear governmental policy which had made it an articulated goal to "exterminate these red vermin," or at least whole segments of them.

18   Bounties had been placed on the scalps of Indians—any Indians—in places as diverse as Georgia, Kentucky, Texas, the Dakotas, Oregon, and California, and had been maintained until resident Indian populations were decimated or disappeared altogether. Entire peoples such as the Cherokee had been reduced to half their size through a policy of forced removal from their homelands east of the Mississippi River to what were then considered less preferable areas in the West.

19   Others, such as the Navajo, suffered the same fate while under military guard for years on end. The United States Army had also perpetrated a long series of wholesale massacres of Indians at places like Horseshoe Bend, Bear River, Sand Creek, the Washita River, the Marias River, Camp Robinson, and Wounded Knee.

20   Through it all, hundreds of popular novels—each competing with the next to make Indians appear more grotesque, menacing, and inhuman—were sold in the tens of millions of copies in the U.S. Plainly, the Euro-American public was being conditioned to see Indians in such a way as to allow their eradication to continue. And continue it did until the Manifest Destiny of the U.S.— a direct precursor to what Hitler would subsequently call *Lebensraumpolitik* (the politics of living space)—was consummated.

21   By 1900, the national project of "clearing" Native Americans from their land and replacing them with "superior" Anglo-American settlers was complete; the indigenous population had been reduced by as much as 98 percent while approximately 97.5 percent of their original territory had "passed" to the invaders. The survivors had been concentrated, out of sight and mind of the public, on scattered "reservations," all of them under the self-assigned "plenary" (full) power of the federal government. There was, of course, no Nuremberg-style tribunal passing judgment on those who had fostered such circumstances in North America. No U.S. official or private citizen was ever imprisoned—never mind hanged—for implementing or propagandizing what had been done. Nor had the process of genocide afflicting Indians been completed. Instead, it merely changed form.

22   Between the 1880s and the 1980s, nearly half of all Native American children were coercively transferred from their own families, communities, and cultures to those of the conquering society. This was done through compulsory attendance at remote boarding schools, often hundreds of miles from their homes, where native children were kept for years on end while being systematically "deculturated" (indoctrinated to think and act in the manner of Euro-Americans rather than as Indians). It was also accomplished through a pervasive foster home and adoption program—including "blind" adoptions, where children would be permanently denied information as to who they were/are and where they'd come from—placing native youths in non-Indian homes.

23   The express purpose of all this was to facilitate a U.S. governmental policy to bring about the "assimilation" (dissolution) of indigenous societies. In other words, Indian cultures as such were to be caused to disappear. Such policy objectives are directly contrary to the United Nations 1948 Convention on Punishment and Prevention of the Crime of Genocide, an element of international law arising from the Nuremberg proceedings. The forced "transfer of the children" of a targeted "racial, ethnical, or religious group" is explicitly prohibited as a genocidal activity under the Convention's second article.

24   Article II of the Genocide Convention also expressly prohibits involuntary sterilization as a means of "preventing births among" a targeted population.

Yet, in 1975, it was conceded by the U.S. government that its Indian Health Service (IHS), then a subpart of the Bureau of Indian Affairs (BIA), was even then conducting a secret program of involuntary sterilization that had affected approximately 40 percent of all Indian women. The program was allegedly discontinued, and the IHS was transferred to the Public Health Service, but no one was punished. In 1990, it came out that the IHS was inoculating Inuit children in Alaska with Hepatitis-B vaccine. The vaccine had already been banned by the World Health Organization as having a demonstrated correlation with the HIV-syndrome which is itself correlated to AIDS. As this is written, a "field test" of Hepatitis-A vaccine, also HIV-correlated, is being conducted on Indian reservations in the northern plains region.

25 The Genocide Convention makes it a "crime against humanity" to create conditions leading to the destruction of an identifiable human group, as such. Yet the BIA has utilized the government's plenary prerogatives to negotiate mineral leases "on behalf of" Indian peoples paying a fraction of standard royalty rates. The result has been "super profits" for a number of preferred U.S. corporations. Meanwhile, Indians, whose reservations ironically turned out to be in some of the most mineral-rich areas of North America, which makes us, the nominally wealthiest segment of the continent's population, live in dire poverty.

26 By the government's own data in the mid-1980s, Indians received the lowest annual and lifetime per capita incomes of any aggregate population group in the United States. Concomitantly, we suffer the highest rate of infant mortality, death by exposure and malnutrition, disease, and the like. Under such circumstances, alcoholism and other escapist forms of substance abuse are endemic in the Indian community, a situation which leads both to a general physical debilitation of the population and a catastrophic accident rate. Teen suicide among Indians is several times the national average.

27 The average life expectancy of a reservation-based Native American man is barely forty-five years; women can expect to live less than three years longer.

28 Such itemizations could be continued at great length, including matters like the radioactive contamination of large portions of contemporary Indian Country, the forced relocation of traditional Navajos, and so on. But the point should be made: Genocide, as defined in international law, is a continuing fact of day-to-day life (and death) for North America's native peoples. Yet there has been—and is—only the barest flicker of public concern about, or even consciousness of, this reality. Absent any serious expression of public outrage, no one is punished and the process continues.

29 A salient reason for public acquiescence before the ongoing holocaust in Native North America has been a continuation of the popular legacy, often

through more effective media. Since 1925, Hollywood has released more than 2,000 films, many of them rerun frequently on television, portraying Indians as strange, perverted, ridiculous, and often dangerous things of the past. Moreover, we are habitually presented to mass audiences one-dimensionally, devoid of recognizable human motivations and emotions; Indians thus serve as props, little more. We have thus been thoroughly and systematically dehumanized.

30   Nor is this the extent of it. Everywhere, we are used as logos, as mascots, as jokes: "Big Chief" writing tablets, "Red Man" chewing tobacco, "Winnebago" campers, "Navajo" and "Cherokee" and "Pontiac" and "Cadillac" pickups and automobiles. There are the Cleveland "Indians," the Kansas City "Chiefs," the Atlanta "Braves" and the Washington "Redskins" professional sports teams—not to mention those in thousands of colleges, high schools, and elementary schools across the country—each with their own degrading caricatures and parodies of Indians and/or things Indian. Pop fiction continues in the same vein, including an unending stream of New Age manuals purporting to expose the inner works of indigenous spirituality in everything from pseudo-philosophical to do-it-yourself styles. Blond yuppies from Beverly Hills amble about the country claiming to be reincarnated seventeenth-century Cheyenne Ushamans ready to perform previously secret ceremonies.

31   In effect, a concerted, sustained, and in some ways accelerating effort has gone into making Indians unreal. It is thus of obvious importance that the American public begin to think about the implications of such things the next time they witness a gaggle of face-painted and war-bonneted buffoons doing the "Tomahawk Chop" at a baseball or football game. It is necessary that they think about the implications of the grade-school teacher adorning their child in turkey feathers to commemorate Thanksgiving. Think about the significance of John Wayne or Charleton Heston killing a dozen "savages" with a single bullet the next time a western comes on TV. Think about why Land-o-Lakes finds it appropriate to market its butter with the stereotyped image of an "Indian princess" on the wrapper. Think about what it means when non-Indian academics profess—as they often do—to "know more about Indians than Indians do themselves." Think about the significance of charlatans like Carlos Castaneda and Jamake Highwater and Mary Summer Rain and Lynn Andrews churning out "Indian" bestsellers, one after the other, while Indians typically can't get into print.

32   Think about the real situation of American Indians. Think about Julius Streicher. Remember Justice Jackson's admonition. Understand that the treatment of Indians in American popular culture is not "cute" or "amusing" or just "good, clean fun."

33   Know that it causes real pain and real suffering to real people. Know that it threatens our very survival. And know that this is just as much a crime against humanity as anything the Nazis ever did. It is likely that the indigenous people of the United States will never demand that those guilty of such criminal activity be punished for their deeds. But the least we have the right to expect—indeed, to demand—is that such practices finally be brought to a halt.

THINKING ABOUT THE TEXT

1. What is the history of the controversy that Churchill describes?

2. What are the specific examples that Churchill proposes for other racial and ethnic groups to parallel the team names and halftime shows that refer to Native American culture? What is the effect on the reader of his examples? What is the author's intention?

3. What are the positive responses to the controversy that Churchill cites in his essay? Why does he include these two examples?

4. What is the history of the trial of Julius Streicher, and how do facts about the Nuremberg tribunal contribute to Churchill's argument?

5. What are the crimes against the American Indian that Churchill enumerates in his essay? Why does he believe that using American Indian culture for team names, logos, mascots, and advertising perpetuates the crimes against the Native American?

6. Do you perceive any flaws in Churchill's reasoning? Are you sympathetic to his point? Do you agree with his demand for change?

WRITING FROM THE TEXT

1. Write a response to Ward Churchill that agrees with his points or argues against them. Review the suggestions for writing argument (p. 446) in order to write a convincing paper.

2. Recall from your childhood the images of the American Indian that appeared in books, on television, and in films. Write a descriptive analysis of a few specific examples in order to show that Churchill is correct or incorrect in his position that popular images of the Native American are "degrading caricatures" that perpetuate the crimes against them.

CONNECTING WITH OTHER TEXTS

1. Respond to Ward Churchill's essay by writing a paper that argues that John Balzar (p. 181) is correct or incorrect in his perception of team names.

2. Write an essay arguing for the opposite of what Ward Churchill wants: the obliteration of ethnic characteristics, as argued by Yasmine Bahrani in "Why Does My Race Matter?" (p. 158).

3. In an analytical essay, compare the images of African-Americans that have disappeared from popular culture (like Little Black Sambo or Step 'n' Fetchit) with the images of Natives Americans that still permeate popular culture in the United States. What conclusion can you draw from an analysis of these images and their presence or absence in popular culture?

4. Write an analysis of recent film depictions of the Native American in order to argue that Hollywood has or has not moved beyond caricature in its depiction of this culture.

Lighten Up on Enlightenment
John Balzar

Employed by the *Los Angeles Times* for over twenty years, John Balzar (b. 1947) has served as their political writer, Seattle bureau chief, Africa bureau chief, and columnist. Previously, Balzar wrote for the *San Francisco Chronicle* and United Press International. Author of *Yukon Alone* (2000), a story of adventure on the Yukon-Alaska frontier, Balzar also has published in countless magazines and anthologies. This essay appeared in the *Los Angeles Times*, June 2, 2002.

1   Some years back, my bosses tried to reduce common sense to a decree. The subject was workplace harassment. Their thinking was progressive. Employees shouldn't have to endure come-ons and put-downs. Naturally, there was self-protection involved too. The Firm didn't want to be party to lawsuits.

2   After this policy memo was circulated, I assumed that vulnerable employees felt slightly more secure, having right officially on their side.

3   But I also detected a drop-off in what used to be known as compliments. As in, "That is a lovely outfit." Or, "Blue is definitely your color."

4   Here and there, a few people tried to make light of the trend. One editor and I began calling each other "honey" and "sweetie" by way of being witty. Generally, though, suspicions were heightened and distance was widened between those who did not know each other.

5   Maybe it was a more secure workplace, but it was also drearier.

6   The flaw was not the aim, it was the assumption. It boiled down to this: Harassment is anything that anyone says it is. That is, if you feel harassed, you are.

7   Which brings us to this matter of sports teams and their nicknames, in particular references to Indians such as Chiefs and Redskins.

8   Some earnest folks would impose the same standard to athletic mascots that business has tried to apply to workplace harassment: If someone or some segment of society is offended, then the nickname is offensive. You cannot argue the point without displaying insensitivity to someone's sensitivity. The charge becomes proof of a crime.

9   Actually, there are so many things out of whack with organized sports in our culture that team logos hardly bear concern. But the power we leverage out of language in the name of social fairness is a bigger matter—and has been intertwined with team names for some time now.

10   In the latest flare-up, the California state Assembly defeated a bill that would have banned Indian mascots from public schools. But we all know that we haven't heard the last of it. Once activists bear down on matters of symbolism, the stakes rise and people start to feel they cannot lose without losing big.

11   For the last 40 years of so, we have argued vigorously over the power of words in our culture, and the damage they inflict and the stereotypes they preserve. There is no question that oppression has been diminished and awareness heightened by those who police our language. Ours is a better society for the way we speak of each other now.

12   We are also a society wound very tight on these matters, too tight, actually. I don't think we'd find ourselves backsliding on social progress if we agreed that part of enlightenment is the ability to relax too. We are in danger of draining away not just bigotry and offensiveness in our language but things worth celebrating. Whether it is a simple workplace compliment or a ballpark cheer for our mixed ancestry, maybe we could dare to trust our good sense now.

13   So let's gripe about "Redskins."

14   Here's a word that in any context except football and apples is a pejorative, always has been. In the United States in the year 2002, surrendering the word would be a victory for our ideals.

15   On the other hand, "Chiefs" has far more going for it than against it. When I travel the West and interview Native American "chiefs," I'm looking up, not down.

16   To the extent that sports mascots are to suggest strength, unity, leadership, perhaps even integrity, I can think of few words more apt than "chief." Surely, it's a metaphor as worthy as "the 49ers," who were a rag-tag bunch of Gold Rush get-rich-quick schemers.

17   Yes, "chief" was once a commonplace term used by non-Indians to describe Indians. When I was in boot camp, all Indians were "chief." Yet we

shouldn't forget that everybody was typecast and slurred as something. And "chief" carried less stigma than any of the epithets I recall.

18   "Words," said the French writer Antoine de Saint-Exupery, "are the source of misunderstandings." Fortunately, they are also the source of understanding.

19   Native American culture is part of our shared national heritage. Even accounting for all the grudges of history and the contemporary gaps in justice, there are things we can honor and celebrate, and sports happens to be an outlet for doing it.

20   I know—and, boy, do I—that it's possible to offend without intending so. But I also know it's possible to be offended when you shouldn't be.

THINKING ABOUT THE TEXT

1. Why does Balzar open with an anecdote about sexual harassment in the workplace? How does it relate to his main focus on team names? How effective is the connection?

2. Although Balzar recognizes that there are more serious problems with organized sports than the problem of team names and nicknames, what makes this problem "a bigger matter" for him? What is his view of the power of words?

3. What is his assessment of the word "Redskins" and his very different sense of "Chiefs" for team names? Does his analysis seem to sufficiently reflect Native American concerns and history? Support your answer with examples.

4. As Balzar is urging readers to "lighten up on enlightenment," where does he seem to be following his own advice? Analyze his tone and meaning when he remarks, "I don't think we'd find ourselves backsliding on social progress if we agreed that part of enlightenment is the ability to relax too" (182).

5. By the end of his essay, is Balzar's thesis clear? Try to state it in your own words and then find support for it in the reading.

WRITING FROM THE TEXT

1. Write an evaluative response (pp. 419–425) of Balzar's thesis and key points. Include choice quotations and relevant experiences of your own to support your thesis.

2. Focus on an experience or several related experiences of your own where words were the source of misunderstandings. Dramatize the scenes, include dialogue, and then analyze why these words had such an effect on the listeners.

3. If your school team, newspaper, club, or other institution has changed its name or any related symbols because of political or social pressure, write an essay analyzing the reasons for this change and your own reaction to it.

CONNECTING WITH OTHER TEXTS

1. Read Ward Churchill's "Crimes Against Humanity" (p. 172) and write an essay analyzing it in light of Balzar's points or analyzing Balzar's essay in light of Churchill's points. Include select quotations from both essays and analyze them fully.

2. Although Balzar recognizes that some language can be offensive, he feels that people frequently over-react and begin purging more terms than needed. Study "Real Men Don't" (p. 71) and write an essay evaluating August's concerns, in light of Balzar's request to "lighten up on enlightenment."

On the Subway
Sharon Olds

A widely anthologized poet and recipient of numerous grants and awards for her poems, Sharon Olds (b. 1942) received a B.A. from Stanford University and a Ph.D. from Columbia University. Having served as director of the creative writing program at New York University, she continues to coordinate their writing program for the disabled at Sigesmund Goldwater Memorial Hospital. Olds was New York State Poet, 1998–2001. Her poetry collections include *Satan Says* (1980), *The Dead and the Living* (1984), *The Father* (1992), *The Wellspring* (1996), and *Blood, Tin, Straw* (1999). Her poems have been translated into Italian, Chinese, French, and Russian. The poem included here is a revised version of the poem published in *The Gold Cell* (1987).

The young man and I face each other.
His feet are huge, in black sneakers
laced with white in a complex pattern like a
set of intentional scars. We are stuck on
5 opposite sides of the car, a couple of
molecules stuck in a rod of light
rapidly moving through darkness. He has
or my white eye imagines he has the
casual cold look of a mugger,
10 alert under hooded lids. He is wearing
red, like the inside of the body

exposed. I am wearing old fur, the
whole skin of an animal taken and
used. I look at his raw face,
15   he looks at my dark coat, and I don't
know if I am in his power—
he could take my coat so easily, my
briefcase, my life—
or if he is in my power, the way I am
20   living off his life, eating the steak
he may not be eating, as if I am taking
the food from his mouth. And he is black
and I am white, and without meaning or
trying to I must profit from his darkness,
25   the way he absorbs the murderous beams of the
nation's heart, as black cotton
absorbs the heat of the sun and holds it. There is
no way to know how easy this
white skin makes my life, this
30   life he could break so easily, the way I
think his back is being broken, the
rod of his soul that at birth was dark and
fluid, rich as the heart of a seedling
ready to thrust up into any available light.

Thinking about the Text

1. If the speaker initially considers this encounter a face-off, in what ways does the boy seem to be intimidating? Analyze the narrator's descriptions of him.

2. Describe the narrator's appearance. Is it consistent with her inner awareness and values? Do you think the boy on the subway would be surprised to know her thoughts?

3. In what way is she in his "power" and he in hers? Does either one of them seem to be choosing to exercise his or her power over the other? Explain the irony here.

4. Cite phrases and images that reveal the narrator's sensitivity. How do these contribute to the tone of the poem?

5. Find images of light versus darkness throughout, and discuss how this image pattern relates to Olds's insights about racial and economic barriers.

6. Does the poem seem hopeful or bleak? Support your interpretation with details from the poem.

WRITING FROM THE TEXT

1. List several insights that can be drawn from this poem. Focus on one of these insights and analyze how the images and tone support it. Cite specific details.

2. Write an essay analyzing the various stereotypes and assumptions implicit in the narrator's descriptions of the boy. Then reverse the point of view and imagine the stereotypes the boy may hold in his perception of the narrator.

3. Olds focuses on a rather commonplace situation and manages to describe it with exceptional sensitivity. Focus on a common encounter of your own and show how it also revealed more complex issues and emotions beneath the surface.

CONNECTING WITH OTHER TEXTS

1. Using specific details from this poem and from "Living in Two Worlds" (p. 144), show how the privileged status of each narrator becomes a source of guilt.

2. Write an essay analyzing how stereotyping is the source of tension in "On the Subway" (p. 184), "Proper Care and Maintenance" (p. 186), and "Black Men and Public Space" (p. 237). You may want to refer to Heilbroner's essay "Don't Let Stereotypes Warp Your Judgments" (p. 469).

 # Proper Care and Maintenance
Susan Straight

Except for the time when she did her M.F.A. work with writer James Baldwin at the University of Massachusetts, Susan Straight (b. 1960) has always lived in Riverside, California, a mile from the hospital where she was born. Straight describes her community as a storytelling one: "Everyone tells stories, almost legends, about people and cars and events, and I've heard them for so many years that I wanted my stories to be on paper instead of only in the air." Straight's determination to write is clearly evident in her novels *Aquaboogie* (1990), which won a Milkweed National Fiction Prize; *I Been in Sorrow's Kitchen and Licked Out All the Pots* (1992); *The Getting Place* (1996); *Highwire Moon* (2001); a children's book, *Bear E. Bear* (1995), as well as numerous short works published in newspapers and magazines. She says, "I write to make myself feel better. When someone I know dies, or goes to prison, or gets addicted to drugs, I know I can't change things, but I can write a story to make things different in my mind. I can control the world on paper. I can stay up all night, after my family goes to sleep, and imagine I'm someone else in a different, safer, better world." True to the values of her community's oral traditions, Susan Straight is an engaging storyteller and speaker on the writing process. The short story presented here first appeared in the *Los Angeles Times Magazine*, in 1991. Darnell, the story's main character, appears again in Straight's novel, *Blacker Than a Thousand Midnights*, which was published in 1994.

1   "See, man, I told you she was gon do it—she pimpin' you, Darnell." Victor shook his head and watched Charolette hang out the window of the El Camino. "She pimpin' you big-time."

2   "Daddy!" she yelled, her round face bobbing furiously above the door. "I want juice! In my *mouth!*"

3   Darnell turned away from Victor and Ronnie and the other men sitting on folding chairs and boxes in the vacant lot. A blackened trash barrel breathed smoke in the early morning cool, and the pepper tree branches dangled around them. "I'm fixin' to go over my dad's," Darnell said. "He told me Sixth Avenue Baptist wants somebody to clean up that lot they got behind the church. I'll be back tomorrow, Victor."

4   He started toward the El Camino, and Victor called out, "Damn, homey, I might be a stockbroker by then." Ronnie and the others laughed.

5   He put Charolette back in her car seat and she said, "*Daddy,* I hungry. Hurry." She watched out the window, saying, "Fire, Daddy," when they circled around the lot to the street.

6   "Yeah, smoke," he said, and she looked triumphant. She was almost two, trying to learn about a hundred words a day. She stuck out her chin and sang to herself now, while he tried not to smile.

7   He hadn't wanted a baby—Brenda had surprised him. When Brenda first brought her home from the hospital and laid her on a quilt in the living room, Charolette had spent hours sleeping on her stomach and Darnell had had all day to stare at her. The government funds had been cut off for seasonal firefighters. He stared at Charolette, but all he could think was that she looked like a horny toad, those rounded-flat lizards that ran past him when he was close to the fire: they'd streak out from the rocks, looking ridiculous. Charolette's belly was distended round and wide, far past her nonexistent butt, and her spindly arms and legs looked useless. He'd sat home watching this baby, impatient with the helpless crying and the way she lay on her back waving her limbs like a turned-over beetle.

8   Now she was old enough to talk smack, and he could jam her right back—she understood. When he pulled into the driveway at his father's

house, she ran inside for his mother's hot biscuits, and then she ran back to him, hollering, "Daddy, blow on it!"

9   "You so bad, blow on it yourself," he said, and she spit rapidly at the steaming biscuit. "Yeah, right," he laughed. "Wet it up."

10   Darnell's mother came to the doorway in her robe. "Brenda restin'?"

11   "Sleepin' 24-7," Darnell said. "All day, except when she at work."

12   "That's how it is your first three months," his mother said, getting that blurry look like every woman who found out Brenda was pregnant again. "You sleep like somebody drop a rock on your chest. I remember."

13   Darnell didn't mind waking up at six, when the curtains were just starting to hold light. Charolette called for him now. If he had a job, he had to start early anyway, before it got too hot. Brenda was a clerk for the County of Rio Seco and didn't have to go to work until nine. So Darnell left her in the warm tangle of sheets and took Charolette to his father's, where the men sat in their trucks drinking coffee before they went out. His father and Roscoe Wiley trimmed trees; Floyd King and his son Nacho hauled trash from construction sites. They all made a big deal of Charolette still in her footed sleeper, stamping from lap to lap and trying to pull dashboard knobs.

14   This morning Roscoe took her into his pickup truck and gave her a smell of his coffee. "Red Man, this girl stubborn as you," he said to Darnell's father.

15   Darnell watched Charolette poke at the glass. "Window dirty," she said.

16   "Least she look a lot better," Floyd said from his cab. "Next one gotta look like Brenda, cause this one look like Darnell spit her out his ownself."

17   Yeah. Brenda hated hearing that, Darnell thought. He remembered when the baby began to stare back at him, to crawl, and then her eyebrows grew in thick-curved like his, her teeth spaced and square like his.

18   His mother came out to the driveway for the newspaper. "Y'all need to look for a bigger place," she said. "A house, for Charolette to play in the yard. And you get a house, we can find a washer so Brenda won't drag that laundry up and down no apartment stairs."

19   "Mr. Nard rentin' out his brother's house on Pablo," Floyd called. "Got three bedrooms, and he want $625 a month."

20   "Yeah, and we can barely pay our $400 now," Darnell said.

21   "I told you get you some yards," his father said. "Steady yards, like I did."

22   "You ain't got no cleanup jobs for me next week?" Darnell said, looking at the thin chain-saw scar on his father's forearm.

23   "Yeah, Sixth Avenue Baptist wants you to do the lot—take two of you, two-day job."

24   "You gon get Victor?" Nacho said.

25   "Yeah." After Charolette, he knew he couldn't go to college for Fire Science, and he'd gotten a warehouse job, but they laid everyone off a few

months later. His father had fixed up the engine on the old El Camino, which had been in the side yard since Roscoe had gotten a new truck. He lent Darnell a mower, blower, weed-whacker and rakes.

26   "Victor a stone alcoholic," Roscoe said. "Livin' at Jackson Park now."

27   Nacho said, "Shoot, he taught me how to draw, back in junior high. The brother was smart, too smart, started talkin' 'bout high school was boring. He just want to hang out, all day."

28   "He hangin' out now," Roscoe said, frowning. "All day."

29   Darnell said. "He just don't like nobody to tell him what to do. He don't like to answer to nobody." He'd always watched Victor, who was five years older than he was; Victor got kicked out of school for spelling out "Superfly" in gold studs down his jeans, for outlining his fly with rhinestones. He'd quit the football team freshman year, refusing to cut off his cornrows.

30   "I'm tellin you, go door-to-door and get you some yards," Darnell's father went on, loud. "Build up a clientele." Sophia and Paula, Darnell's younger sisters, came running out in their nightgowns to see Charolette.

31   "Shoot, every dude with a truck and mower runnin' around calling himself a gardener," Roscoe said. "They want all these new houses gettin' built."

32   "Yeah, you should go see Trent," Nacho said. "He got his own business, landscape design, and he live up there in Grayglen."

33   Floyd laughed. "With the gray men."

34   The houses were laid out in circling streets, and a sea of red-tile roofs was all that showed above miles of sandy block wall. Darnell saw crews of Mexican guys building new walls at one intersection, short Indian-looking men with bowed legs and straw hats. Two white guys with thick, sun-reddened forearms watched.

35   Trent's street was all two-story houses and lush gardens. "A brother livin' up here?" Darnell said to himself. He could tell by the yards most of these people already had gardeners. Trent was in his driveway, loading his truck with black hosing and pipes.

36   "Hey, Darnell," he said, and Darnell was surprised Trent remembered the name. Trent was Victor's age. "What's up?"

37   "Not much," Darnell said. "I heard you were livin' large with your business, and I thought maybe you had too many yards, know somebody who needs a gardener." He watched Trent count sprinkler heads.

38   "Man, I just do the planning and landscaping—I don't cut grass," Trent said, not looking up. "I ain't into maintenance. After the irrigation, I'm gone."

39   "Yeah, Nacho said you went to college for this, huh?" Darnell said, uncomfortable. "I just thought you might have some advice, 'cause I *been* knocked on doors, and that ain't workin'."

40 Trent clicked his spit against his teeth. "I heard you workin' with Victor Small and Ronnie Hunter. But you gotta buy 'em some Olde English 800 to get through the day, huh?" He coiled hosing. "They scare people off."

41 Darnell folded his arms. "Yeah. Depends." *So you think you better, huh, brothaman? Victor and Ronnie love to talk about your ass—grinnin' and skinnin' 'til you drive down the street and shake your head.*

42 "Sorry I can't help you," Trent said, reaching down awkwardly into the truck bed again. "Good luck, bro."

43 "Thanks, *brothaman*," Darnell said. Threading through the streets, he watched for shaggy grass and dandelions. *Had to be a few yards let go in this maze.*

44 At four lawns that looked weeks overgrown, he knocked on doors, his heart beating fast, but no one answered. Another ragged one, and a woman came to the door. He said, "Hi, I'm a gardener and I wondered if you needed your yard done today or on a regular basis." He remembered his father's words, back when Darnell had been small enough to stand on cool porches and listen.

45 "I gave you five dollars yesterday," the woman said impatiently, looking back into her house, and Darnell raised his eyes. She was about forty, her lips more invisible than most white women's—no lipstick, he realized, just when she said, "I can't afford another donation."

46 "I wasn't here yesterday," Darnell said, but she was adding loudly, "I don't need anything done today."

47 "You didn't give me five dollars," he said, finally looking at her eyes, rimmed with green shadow.

48 "Oh, I'm sorry, I—your hat," she said, fingers holding her collar. "A man came by yesterday, he said he was out of work, and I—he had a hat."

49 "Yeah," Darnell said, hard. "Another Raiders fan." He walked back down the bricks, wanting to kick apart the fancy iron mailbox exactly like Trent's.

50 He drove, swerving through the streets until he found the only opening in the block walls. *Where the cops? Can't they see me?* He remembered getting stopped months ago, Victor and Ronnie and him driving around up here looking for yards. The cop said, "You guys have been cruising for a while, knocking on doors. You got a reason?" Victor said, "Mowers in the back, man." He didn't care who he was talking to. "Don't you have a record, didn't you do a few weeks last year?" the cop said to Victor. "What was your first clue, Sherlock?" Victor said. "Was it my big arms?"

51 The tires slipped on loose dirt at the corner. *Yeah, our marketing strategy just ain't gettin' it—door-to-door get us a sentence.* If it was summer, he'd find a fire to make himself feel better, watch the flames shake up brush-covered hills, imagine himself on the line close to the roar and heat.

52   Three new houses were going up, and the bellied, blond construction workers hammering and laying brick looked up at the car. Born that way, he thought, his tongue thick and hot. Come out with hair like that, trucks with toolboxes behind the cab, stomachs already big enough—they get the job just like I can dance. Charolette's car seat rattled empty against his elbow when he scratched the tires on the asphalt, but skidding around a corner didn't make him feel any better. He looked at the crumbs crushed deep into the corduroy chair.

53   He'd used his Clark Kent voice one day on the phone, after he saw an ad for a security guard that read, "Mature white male pref." He'd made the appointment with the cheery secretary just to see if he could, and then he threw a coffee cup against the wall; the clotted breaking sound made him feel better until he heard Charolette's high-pitched screams, like a burning animal caught in dense chaparral. "That's illegal, that ad," Brenda was yelling, and he'd yelled back, "Right, let's call our lawyer immediately, baby, we'll take this all the way to the Supreme Court."

54   He pressed his fingers into the crumbs, feeling cool along his shoulders. I can't pull that act now. Driving down the hill toward the Westside, he thought about going by Jackson Park, hanging out, talking yang about anything, but he slowed at his father's street. "Daddy here!" Charolette screamed. Ain't this crazy? he thought. When he told Victor, "She my buddy now," Victor said, "You weak, nigga—you suppose to let *grown* females whip you."

55   She fell asleep when he drove around the old downtown section, with the big historic houses and huge sloping corner lawns. He and his father had cut some of these, when Darnell was eleven and just learning to mow right.

56   At one old yellow house, ivy hanging over the porch, roses thick, he saw three Mexican guys in the yard. Straightening Charolette's bent, lolling neck, he watched them ripping out a huge circle of ivy in the lawn, talking and chopping with machetes. Their radio blasted Mexican music, horns and swinging voices going so fast Darnell imagined them playing at seventy-eight speed. He saw a shadow at the front screen: a gray-haired lady came out to watch the men, and he pulled away from the curb before she saw him.

57   All weekend, he kept hearing the music; he even turned the radio or TV to Mexican stations. "What are you trippin' about?" Brenda said, folding the laundry that lay in drifts all around the living room. Charolette threaded string into the wrought-iron balcony, the front door open so they could see her.

58   "Nothin'," Darnell said, listening to what he thought was an accordion.

59   "You really miss that firefightin' slave you had, huh?" Victor said when they'd been at the church lot for a few hours. "Crazy nigga loved bein' up there in the mountains with them cowboy white dudes."

60   "No, man," Darnell said. "It wasn't about the other guys. I just liked it up there." They pulled at the skeletal tumbleweeds and burned grass in the hard dirt, gathered bottles and disposable diapers. Darnell saw the rough brush where he'd dug firebreaks, the red-barked manzanita and tiny plants. Now and then he let his vision blur while he tore out weeds, and usually when he raised his head he was surprised to see cars rushing past him. But today he kept seeing the Mexican guys, their hats and laughing and music.

61   After they'd come down the long dirt road from the dump, Darnell gave Victor $50 and kept $75 for himself. He waited in front of Tony's Market, and when Victor came out with the big 40-ounce bottles of Olde English 800, he said, "I can't hang with you guys today; I got somethin' to do."

62   Victor unscrewed the cap. "Take me by Esther's, on your pop's street." He still wore his hair long and cornrowed neatly to his head, the tails stopped just at his neck. He let it go weeks before he could pay Esther to redo it, and today it was rough and clouded between the rows. "You go home to baby-bawlin', man, and I'll be chillin' out, eight-ballin'." He took a big swallow.

63   The next morning his father told him Mrs. Panadoukis, the doctor's wife up in Hillcrest, wanted her whole bank of ice plant cleared. When he got to Jackson Park, Darnell threw the empty car seat in the back, and Victor said, "Nigga, this the last job I want 'til next week. Don't you know black absorbs heat, man?"

64   "Shut up, Victor," Ronnie said. "You know you already broke."

65   "Hey," Victor said, "I ain't *gotta* work every day, like Darnell."

66   The ice plant had died, and the woody, tangled mesh was easy to tear from the dirt, but the piles were heavy. Ronnie and Victor took off their shirts, and Darnell remembered they didn't have anywhere to wash them. Their backs glistened in front of him. Ronnie's radio was far away, the music thumping faintly when they clambered up the steep bank, but at lunch they unwrapped their sandwiches and turned the radio up.

67   "'I don't go nowhere without my jimhat,'" Victor sang along with Digital Underground. Then he said, "Yeah, my man Darnell ain't been usin' no jim-mys—he got another one on the way."

68   Darnell said, "Least I ain't gotta worry about AIDS—you be messin' with them strawberries." He wondered how they'd gotten that name, the desperate, ashy girls who hung out at the park doing anything with anybody for some smoke.

69   "When you need some, man, you don't care," Ronnie said. Darnell heard a scraping step on the cement, and he saw Mrs. Panadoukis, her face frozen, coming around to the back door with her purse. She looked away from them, her lips tight, and fumbled with her keys. They were silent, the music loud.

70   When she'd closed the door, Victor and Ronnie busted up. Darnell saw her held-tight cheeks. He looked at Ronnie's chest, Victor's fresh braids; he remembered the Mexican guys laughing in the ivy. The Mexican guys could be saying anything, talking dirty or yanging about the lady they were working for, but it would be in Spanish and they'd sound happy—their radio was jolly, funny, that bright quick music spangled as mariachi suits. Ronnie's radio—uh-uh. The bass was low, shuffling around her, and the drums slapped her in the face.

71   "You ready?" he said, and they went back up the bank, bending and tearing, Victor making them laugh.

72   "Darnell, you just graduated a few years ago, man, you remember Mr. Rentell, that drivin' teacher? Serious redhead, always tryin' to talk hip. He came by the park the other day, talkin' 'bout, 'Victor, is that you?' He start storyin' 'bout why was I hangin' out, couldn't I do better? I told him, 'Man, I can still drive, don't worry—let me have your car, I'll show you.'" He threw ice plant down the slope to Darnell.

73   They loaded the El Camino in the front yard. Mrs. Panadoukis had paid them, her eyes averted. Darnell thought, Sorry we don't look good. He saw a Baggie on the lawn and bent to pick it up, thinking it had dropped from the car. But someone else had put it on the grass: he saw a green flier inside and a small rock. Looking down the street, he watched a silver Toyota pickup stop for a second at each lawn. A hand threw out Baggies. He saw rakes and shovels against the cab window, mower handles in the bed.

74   "Nguyen's Oriental Gardening Service," the flier read. He spread it on his lap in the car, and Victor said, "Come on, man, it's hot."

75   "Let experienced Oriental Gardeners take care of your lawn and shrubs, we will mow, edge and fertilize for only $60 a month. Weekly." The note had been printed on a computer, and a picture of a bonsai tree was in the corner, with a phone number.

76   Darnell took Victor and Ronnie to the store and then to the park, hearing Mexican music and the voices of the Asian guys he remembered from school. Tim Bui and Don Nguyen—two Vietnamese guys who wanted to be homeboys, hanging out at the picnic tables with Darnell and the brothers. They tried to imitate Darnell's voice, and after a while they could dance better than some of the crew that performed at assemblies. Nguyen—that last name was like Smith in Vietnam, he remembered them explaining. "Like Johnson for niggas," Ronnie had laughed. Alone in the car, he drove to his mother's.

77   Charolette ran out to see him. His father and Roscoe were stacking wood from a pepper tree beside the house. "Y'all finish the doctor's-wife's job?"

78   "Yeah," Darnell said. "Ice plant was dead anyway."

79   "She pay you? She love to talk when she get started," his father said.

80   "She didn't get started with us," Darnell said, slipping the flier into his pocket.

81   "You pay off your crew?" Roscoe said. "You the big boss now—you take your cut?"

82   "What, you think I'm crazy?" All the way home, Charolette put the rock inside the Baggie and took it out. "Little rock?" she said. He looked at the stone—those guys were smart. The flier couldn't blow away, couldn't get wet.

83   He kept thinking of the Vietnamese kids at school, how the teacher had looked at them, but he saw Mexican faces for some reason. When he and Charolette made their weekend shopping trip, he tried not to stare. On the Westside, almost as many Mexican families lived on some streets as black families. He watched the men riding 10-speeds with plastic bags of laundry tied to the handlebars—guys, alone, leaving one to guard clothes in the Laundromat and going in a group to the store. They bought whole chickens, tortillas, chips, fruit, and he watched their faces, knowing that was where he was supposed to look to figure out what he was missing. On the street, he saw a mariachi band walking down the sidewalk with the huge guitars and glittering suits: they went into Our Lady of Guadalupe, where Darnell had gone to Catholic school.

84   On Monday, he drove slowly past the corners where they always gathered, crowds of Mexican men waiting for daywork. And he saw the shortest, Indian-looking guys—their eyes were slanted, their hair thick and straight, their legs bowed into curves.

85   The men shifted and scattered when a construction truck stopped at the curb, crowding around the driver. Darnell watched five guys jump in the back. Some of the disappointed ones stared at him, and he tried to recall what he could of high school Spanish. All that came to his head was *"¿Como se llama?"* and *"Hermano, hermana"*—useless stuff. He licked his lips and leaned.

86   "I need a guy who can speak English," he said, and three came over.

87   "I speak English, bro," a skinny, dark guy said, and Darnell knew he'd been in prison by the teardrops tattooed near his eyes.

88   "I'll give you 10 bucks to help here, man," Darnell said. "I need two dudes who know how to mow lawns, and I want them to look Oriental, you know, like those guys over there." He pointed to the short, slim men.

89   "He wants *los indios*," the guy said, muttering to the men. Several of the Indian men gathered around him, and he brought over four with anxious faces and small, tilted eyes under thick brows. Darnell thought of Charolette's brows suddenly, how delicate they were.

90   "You guys can do gardening?" he asked. They nodded, and he said, "But I have to be able to talk to you—who speaks English, even some?"

91   The youngest one, without a hat, said, "I try speak *pequeño*. My brother not so much." He gestured to the older one next to him, in a baseball cap.

92   "Get in," Darnell said. The two men were so small compared to Victor and Ronnie that air still flowed through to touch his shoulders. "Where you from?"

93   The young one said, "Mexico."

94   "I know—I mean where in Mexico?"

95   "Osaka," he said, and Darnell frowned. Wasn't that a city in Japan?— he'd heard the name. "Write it down, OK?" he said, and the guy wrote *Oaxaca* on the back of the green flier.

96   He watched them work at Mrs. Munson's, where his father had given him the yard. Anyone could mow, and Juan, the younger one, did the front while Jose did the back. Darnell edged and helped them blow the paths clean. It took 25 minutes.

97   "Be back on the corner next Monday," he told them. "I think I got regular work if you want it. Four bucks an hour."

98   Juan said, "All day?"

99   Darnell said, "I hope so. Where you learn English, man?"

100   "I went in college one year," Juan said. "I love English."

101   "Chill out, homey," Darnell smiled. "See you Monday."

102   He wouldn't tell Brenda what he had in mind, and when she said, "You're drivin' me crazy with that little plannin' smile and won't give up no information." Darnell just smiled it again.

103   "I gotta go see Nacho," he said. "Maybe I can make some more money."

104   "The suspense is killing me," she said, rolling her eyes, and he didn't even get angry. He went to Nacho's and said, "You the artist—can you make me a flier, one I can Xerox? I'll show you."

105   He laid out the sheet for Nacho. On it he'd written the message, and Nacho laughed. "You serious, man? You want me to print or script?"

106   "Print," Darnell said. "And put a picture in both corners—those little incense burners like you see in a Japanese garden." He thought for a minute. "Man, I hate to copy, but I bet the pine tree works."

107   He copied 300 of the sheets on light-blue paper, and then he went to the nursery for small, sparkling white rocks in bulk and bought Baggies at the store.

108   He took Charolette with him, long before dawn. She was sleepy for a few minutes, but he whispered to her, and she said, "Dark, Daddy?" He said, "We're cruisin' in the dark, baby. Watch out for trains." He remembered

being angry, in a hurry, stuck behind the long trains that came through the Westside; now he tried to catch them so that she could listen in wonder to the clacking wheels and watch for the engineers.

109   "Choo-choo train!" she yelled.

110   They went to Grayglen first, Darnell driving on the wrong side of the street to drop Baggies on lawns. He pitched two onto Trent's, laughing. Charolette couldn't throw them far enough, and he gave her a pile to wreck so she wouldn't cry. "These dudes ain't even up yet, but they'll go to work soon, and then they'll find this when they get the paper," he told her.

111   "Newspaper?"

112   "You got it." They twisted through all the new streets, then went downtown and dropped more. They ended up in the university neighborhood when the sky turned gray. "We don't want nobody to see us, or we turn into pumpkins," he said, and she remembered Halloween, he could tell, because her face lit up.

113   "Cut pumpkin!" she screamed.

114   "You just like me, don't forget *nothin'*," he said, reaching over to touch her hair. "You're gonna kick some butt in school, girl."

115   His father laughed silly. "'Tuan's Oriental Landscape Maintenance Service,'" he read out loud to Roscoe. "Boy a damn gardener, talkin' 'bout maintenance. 'Expert Asian landscapers will mow, edge, fertilize and maintain your garden with weekly service for only $50 a month. Call now to keep your landscape beautiful.'" His father turned to him. "Who the hell is Tuan?"

116   Darnell said, "Nuh-uh—it's Juan. And Jose. If I get enough calls this week, I'm hirin' two Mexican dudes."

117   Roscoe said, "You know, he ain't crazy. They all want Mexican guys. But I don't know how you gon pull it off when they see your ugly face."

118   "They ain't gotta see me, just send the check here, to your address," Darnell said. "In case we move." His father raised his eyebrows. "And I'ma need to borrow some money, for a new mower. If this works, I'ma have to get a truck."

119   "You got the El Camino," his father said.

120   "Yeah, but I need that for my jobs. I need a used Toyota or Isuzu, for these dudes. Paint the name on the side."

121   The eyebrows went higher. "You serious, huh?"

122   "I want to call Mr. Nard about his house. Serious as a heart attack."

123   He practiced his voice in the bathroom. Brenda was at work. He tried to remember Tim Bui's words, which ones he left out, how he talked. He sat watching Oprah with the sound off, but no one called until the next day, and he was ready. A woman said, "Tuan's Landscape?" and he said, "Yes, ma'am. I can help you."

124   "Are you reliable?"

125   "Yes, ma'am, very reliable. We come every week, and do the best job." He chopped off the words carefully, his heart racing heat all the way to his ears.

126   He told Juan that they would have to comb their hair straight back, and no straw hats. He took them to K mart for white T-shirts, green pants and work boots. "And no talking, if the people are around to watch you," he said. "I don't want them to hear Spanish."

127   When he explained it as best he could, Juan frowned. "But if they say, speak to you? If they want different?"

128   "Just say like this—'Call my boss, he help you.'"

129   Juan looked at the flier closely and smiled. "I am Tuan, eh?"

130   "Maybe, man," Darnell said. "Maybe I am."

131   But he felt strange staying at home, waiting for the calls in the empty, tiny and stifling apartment. Summer—the shimmering bells passed on the sidewalk below, the Mexican popsicle guys with their carts. Darnell went to the bathroom mirror, pulled at his eyes to make them long and narrow. He touched his new haircut, a fade with three lines above each ear. His father hated the razored cuts, said, "What the hell, look like a damn mower got you."

132   He stared at his face. "Homey, don'cha know me?" He'd seen Victor at a stoplight last week, near the park. Victor's eyes were half-slit and hard. "Work been *slow*, huh?"

133   "I been doin' somethin', but I got somethin' for us next week," Darnell had said. He did—his father had told someone Darnell would clean up property for the fire season.

134   He knew Nacho had told Victor about the flier, about Tuan's. He splashed water onto his face. Homey—don'cha know me? His chest was clotted with warmth when he sat on the cold edge of the bathtub. "What you gon do if somebody don't pay?" Roscoe had said.

135   "Go over there and collect."

136   "Who you—Tuan's bodyguard? His butler?" Roscoe laughed.

137   "Shit, whoever I gotta be, long as I get the cash." But he was shaking.

138   "I was just playin'," Roscoe said gently, touching his elbow. "You gon do outside jobs, get a beeper so you don't miss calls. Beepers are cheap."

139   "Yeah, and I'll look like a dope dealer," Darnell had said, turning away. "Ain't that what I'm supposed to look like anyway?"

140   He paced around the living room now, the bells fading, and he turned up the radio to pound the walls.

141   In a few weeks, he had so many yards that his father and Roscoe found a blue Toyota pickup he could buy on time. He took the El Camino to Jackson Park the next day, sweating, thinking of Victor's eyes. He'd rehearsed what he would say. Victor raised his chin half an inch when he saw Darnell. "*Brotha*man," Victor said. "What you need?"

142   "Need you guys for a job," Darnell said.

143   "Homey, don'cha know me? I'm just a nigga with an attitude."

144   "You ready?" Darnell said.

145   Victor smiled. "I heard you was hirin' illegals, man. You don't want no niggas, word is." Ronnie hovered beside him, silent.

146   "If I don't want no niggas, I better kill myself," Darnell said. "I got two Mexican guys doin' yards. Now I can do other jobs all the time. But see, Victor, man, I gotta be sweatin' every day, man, not like you. I can't wait 'til I'm in the mood."

147   "Man, you think you big shit," Victor smiled harder. "At least I ain't no strawberry."

148   Darnell breathed in through his nose. "I ain't pink." He hesitated. He had practiced this, too. "I'm just whipped, by two women. And got another one comin' to further kick my black butt. You always talkin' about 'Niggas ain't meant to be out in the sun, absorbin' that heat.' Proper maintenance keep you from shrinkin' and fadin', man, don't you know?" He waited. "You comin'?"

149   Victor ran his hands over his braids. "I'm thirsty, man."

150   When he got home, the phone rang before he could put Charolette down. He held her giggling under his arm and said, "Tuan's Landscape Maintenance."

151   A man said, "This sounds like a really great deal. I live in the Grayglen area, and your prices are reasonable compared to others."

152   "Yes, we try to make price very cheap." He was out of breath and said, "Please, can you hold, sir?" He put Charolette down. "When you like us to start?"

153   "Well, as soon as possible," the man said. "Can you come Friday?"

154   "Yes, Friday." Everybody wanted a perfect lawn for the weekend. "We come Fridays, and you send a check to Tuan's Oriental Landscape, 2498 Picasso St. Pay by mail once a month."

155   "Picasso Street?" the man said. "Isn't that on the Westside?"

156   "Yes, sir."

157   "I thought you guys were Oriental—I bet you want to get out of a minority area like that. Pretty rough in the black neighborhood."

158   Darnell's face and neck prickled. "Yes, sir, we move soon. Very soon." After he'd hung up, he saw Charolette unfolding the towels Brenda had stacked on the couch. "Daddy talking?" She imitated his clipped voice. "We move soon, sir."

159   "You ain't gotta talk like that," he said roughly. "Leave the towels alone before I get mad." He stared at the laundry, at her round face set hard. "Let's go look at a washing machine for Mama."

160   "Move, Daddy?" she asked again, since it had bothered him when she said it the first time. When he tried to take the towels away, she said angrily,

"*Move,* Daddy!" and shoved him. He pretended to fall over on his back, and then he caught her on his chest to tickle her, so she couldn't get away.

THINKING ABOUT THE TEXT

1. All short stories have conflict; if there is no conflict, there is no story. But some stories do not have an obvious protagonist/antagonist conflict. What are the conflicts in Darnell's life?

2. How does Darnell resolve his problems? How does his creating a steady source of income also embroil him in another conflict?

3. Fiction and film have negatively stereotyped African-American men. Which stereotypes does this short story counter in its portrayal of Darnell?

4. What other cultural stereotypes are understood in this story?

5. The short story has a happy ending and is humorous in tone. How is the humor achieved?

6. What are the serious issues behind this entertaining story?

WRITING FROM THE TEXT

1. Write an analysis of Darnell's character—his values, motivations, and goals—based on inferences you can draw from the text. (See the character analysis section, pp. 484–93.)

2. Write a description of the conflicts in Darnell's life. In what ways is he caught between worlds? How does he resolve his problem?

3. Write a paper that illustrates how stereotyping is the underlying cause of problems for Darnell.

CONNECTING WITH OTHER TEXTS

1. Use this short story and other essays in the text—"Living in Two Worlds" (p. 144) and "Black Men and Public Space" (p. 237)—to write an analysis of some of the problems that African-Americans face.

2. Use the ideas in Robert L. Heilbroner's "Don't Let Stereotypes Warp Your Judgments" (p. 469) to argue that stereotyping is a source of the problems in "Proper Care and Maintenance."

3. Compare the stereotyping of various ethnicities in *Los Vendidos,* the selection that follows, with the stereotypes exposed in "Proper Care and Maintenance." What seems to be the intention of each author?

Los Vendidos[1]
Luis Valdez

Director, actor, and playwright, Luis Valdez (b. 1940) is acclaimed in the worlds of stage and film. The son of migrant farmworkers, Valdez earned his B.A. in English from San Jose State University and worked as a lecturer at the University of California at Berkeley and at Santa Cruz. In 1965 he founded El Teatro Campesino to support the grape boycott and farm-workers' strike. His major plays include *Zoot Suit* (1978), which was made into a film in 1982, and *I Don't Have to Show You No Stinking Badges* (1986). In 1987 he directed *La Bamba*, a film about Chicano pop musician Ritchie Valens, and in 1994 he wrote and directed the television screenplay *The Cisco Kid*. In his theatrical works Valdez created the *acto*—a drama written in both English and Spanish intended to educate and entertain farmworkers as well as urban audiences. *Los Vendidos*, first produced in 1967, is an example of this form.

CHARACTERS

HONEST SANCHO

SECRETARY

FARMWORKER

JOHNNY

REVOLUCIONARIO

MEXICAN AMERICAN

[*Scene: Honest Sancho's Used Mexican Lot and Mexican Curio Shop. Three models are on display in Honest Sancho's shop: to the right, there is a Revolucionario, complete with sombrero, carrilleras,[2] and carabina 30-30. At center, on the floor, there is the Farmworker, under a broad straw sombrero. At stage left is the Pachuco,[3] filero[4] in hand.*]

[*Honest Sancho is moving among his models, dusting them off and preparing for another day of business.*]

SANCHO: Bueno, bueno, mis monos, vamos a ver a quien vendemos ahora, ¿no? [*To audience.*] ¡Quihubo![5] I'm Honest Sancho and this is my shop. Antes fui contratista pero ahora logré tener mi negocito.[6] All I need now is a customer. [*A bell rings offstage.*] Ay, a customer!

SECRETARY: [*entering*] Good morning, I'm Miss Jimenez from—

---

[1]The Sellouts
[2]Cartridge belts.
[3]Chicano youths of the 1940s and 1950s who belonged to street gangs.
[4]Knife (pachuco slang)
[5]Okay, okay, my darlings, let's see which one of you we're going to sell now—right? What's up?
[6]I used to be a labor contractor, but now I have my own little business.

SANCHO: ¡Ah, una chicana! Welcome, welcome Señorita Jiménez.

SECRETARY: [*Anglo pronunciation*] JIM-enez.

SANCHO: ¿Qué?

SECRETARY: My name is Miss JIM-enez. Don't you speak English? What's wrong with you?

SANCHO: Oh, nothing, Señorita *Jim*-enez. I'm here to help you.

SECRETARY: That's better. As I was starting to say, I'm a secretary from the state office building, and we're looking for a Mexican type for the administration.

SANCHO: Well, you come to the right place, lady. This is Honest Sancho's Used Mexican Lot, and we got all types here. Any particular type you want?

SECRETARY: Yes, we were looking for somebody suave—

SANCHO: Suave.

SECRETARY: Debonair.

SANCHO: De buen aire.

SECRETARY: Dark.

SANCHO: Prieto.

SECRETARY: But of course not too dark.

SANCHO: No muy prieto.

SECRETARY: Perhaps, beige.

SANCHO: Beige, just the tone. Así como cafecito con leche, ¿no?[7]

SECRETARY: One more thing. He must be hardworking.

SANCHO: That could only be one model. Step right over here to the center of the shop lady. (*They cross to the Farmworker.*) This is our standard farmworker model. Take special notice of his four-ply Goodyear huaraches, made from the rain tire. This wide-brimmed sombrero is an extra added feature—keeps off the sun, rain, and dust.

SECRETARY: Yes, it does look durable.

SANCHO: And our farmworker model is friendly. Muy amable.[8] Watch. (*Snaps his fingers.*)

FARMWORKER: (*lifts up head*) Buenos días, señorita. (*His head drops.*)

SECRETARY: My, he's friendly.

SANCHO: Didn't I tell you? Loves his patrones![9] But his most attractive feature is that he's hardworking. Let me show you. (*Snaps fingers. Farmworker stands.*)

FARMWORKER: ¡El jale![10] (*He begins to work.*)

---

[7]Somewhat like the color of coffee with milk—right?
[8]Very friendly.
[9]Bosses
[10]Work! (pachuco slang)

SANCHO: As you can see, he is cutting grapes.

SECRETARY: Oh, I wouldn't know.

SANCHO: He also picks cotton. *(Snap. Farmworker begins to pick cotton.)*

SECRETARY: Versatile, isn't he?

SANCHO: He also picks melons. *(Snap. Farmworker picks melons.)* That's his slow speed for late in the season. Here's his fast speed. *(Snap. Farmworker picks faster.)*

SECRETARY: Chihuahua . . . I mean, goodness, he sure is a hard worker.

SANCHO: *(pulls the Farmworker to his feet)* And that isn't the half of it. Do you see these little holes on his arms that appear to be pores? During those hot sluggish days in the field when the vines or the branches get so entangled it's almost impossible to move, these holes emit a certain grease that allows our model to slip and slide right through the crop with no trouble at all.

SECRETARY: Wonderful. But is he economical?

SANCHO: Economical? Señorita, you are looking at the Volkswagen of Mexicans. Pennies a day is all it takes. One plate of beans and tortillas will keep him going all day. That, and chile. Plenty of chile. Chile jalapeños, chile verde, chile colorado. But, of course, if you do give him chile *(Snap. Farmworker turns left face. Snap. Farmworker bends over.),* then you have to change his oil filter once a week.

SECRETARY: What about storage?

SANCHO: No problem. You know the farm labor camps our Honorable Governor Reagan has built out by Parlier or Raisin City? They were designed with our model in mind. Five, six, seven, even ten in one of those shacks will give you no trouble at all. You can also put him in old barns, old cars, riverbanks. You can even leave him out in the field overnight with no worry!

SECRETARY: Remarkable.

SANCHO: And here's an added feature: every year at the end of the season, this model moves on and doesn't return until next spring.

SECRETARY: How about that. But tell me, does he speak English?

SANCHO: Another outstanding feature is that last year this model was programmed to go out on *strike! (Snap.)*

FARMWORKER: ¡HUELGA! ¡HUELGA! Hermanos, sálganse de esos files.[11] *(Snap. He stops.)*

SECRETARY: No! Oh no, we can't strike in the state capital.

SANCHO: Well, he also scabs. *(Snap.)*

---

[11]STRIKE! STRIKE! Get out of those fields, brothers.

FARMWORKER: Me vendo barato, ¿y qué?[12] *(Snap.)*

SECRETARY: That's much better but you didn't answer my question. Does he speak English?

SANCHO: Bueno . . . no, pero[13] he has other—

SECRETARY: No.

SANCHO: Other features.

SECRETARY: *No!* He just won't do!

SANCHO: Okay, okay pues.[14] We have other models.

SECRETARY: I hope so. What we need is something a little more sophisticated.

SANCHO: Sophisti—¿qué?

SECRETARY: An urban model.

SANCHO: Ah, from the city! Step right back. Over here in this corner of the shop is exactly what you're looking for. Introducing our new Johnny Pachuco model! This is our fastback model. Streamlined. Built for speed, low-riding, city life. Take a look at some of these features. Mag shoes, dual exhausts, jet black paint-job, dark-tint windshield, a little poof on top. Let me just turn him on. *(Snap. Johnny walks to stage center with a pachuco bounce.)*

SECRETARY: What was that?

SANCHO: That, señorita, was the Chicano shuffle.

SECRETARY: Okay, what does he do?

SANCHO: Anything and everything necessary for city life. For instance, survival: he knife-fights. *(Snap. Johnny pulls out switchblade and swings at Secretary.)*

[*Secretary screams.*]

sancho: He dances. *(Snap.)*

[*Johnny sings and dances. Sancho snaps his fingers.*]

SANCHO: And here's a feature no city model can be without. He gets arrested, but not without resisting, of course. *(Snap.)*

JOHNNY: I didn't do it! I didn't do it! *(Johnny turns and stands up against an imaginary wall, legs spread out, arms behind his back.)*

SECRETARY: Oh no, we can't have arrests! We must maintain law and order.

SANCHO: But he's bilingual!

SECRETARY: Bilingual?

---

[12]I sell myself cheap—so what?
[13]Well . . . no, but
[14]then

SANCHO: Simón que yes.[15] He speaks English! Johnny, give us some English. *(Snap.)*

JOHNNY: *(comes downstage)* Down with whites! Brown power!

SECRETARY: *(gasps)* Oh! He can't say that!

SANCHO: Well, he learned it in your school.

SECRETARY: I don't care where he learned it.

SANCHO: But he's economical!

SECRETARY: Economical?

SANCHO: Nickels and dimes. You can keep Johnny running on hamburgers, Taco Bell tacos, Lucky Lager beer, Thunderbird wine, yesca—

SECRETARY: ¿Yesca?

SANCHO: Mota.

SECRETARY: ¿Mota?

SANCHO: Leños . . . *Marijuana. (Snap. Johnny inhales on an imaginary joint.)*

SECRETARY: That's against the law!

JOHNNY: *(big smile, holding his breath)* Yeah.

SANCHO: He also snorts coke. *(Snap. Johnny snorts coke. Big smile.)*

JOHNNY: That's too much, ése.[16]

SECRETARY: No, Mr. Sancho, I don't think this—

SANCHO: Wait a minute, he has other qualities I know you'll love. For example, an inferiority complex. *(Snap.)*

JOHNNY: *(to Sancho)* You think you're better than me, huh, ése? *(Swings switchblade.)*

SANCHO: He can also be beaten and he bruises; cut him and he bleeds; kick him and he—*(He beats, bruises, and kicks Johnny.)* Would you like to try it?

SECRETARY: Oh, I couldn't.

SANCHO: Be my guest. He's a great scapegoat.

SECRETARY: No really.

SANCHO: Please.

SECRETARY: Well, all right. Just once. *(She kicks Johnny.)* Oh, he's so soft.

SANCHO: Wasn't that good? Try again.

SECRETARY: *(kicks Johnny)* Oh, he's so wonderful! *(She kicks him again.)*

SANCHO: Okay, that's enough, lady. You ruin the merchandise. Yes, our Johnny Pachuco model can give you many hours of pleasure. Why, one police department just bought twenty of these to train their rookie cops on. And talk about maintenance. Señorita, you are looking at an entirely self-supporting machine. You're never going to find our Johnny Pachuco model on the relief rolls. No, sir, this model knows how to liberate.

---

[15]Yes indeedy. (pachuco slang)

[16]Man (pachuco slang)

SECRETARY: Liberate?

SANCHO: He steals. *(Snap. Johnny rushes the secretary and steals her purse.)*

JOHNNY: ¡Dame esa bolsa, vieja![17] *(He grabs the purse and runs. Snap by Sancho. He stops.)*

[Secretary runs after Johnny and grabs purse away from him, kicking him as she goes.]

SECRETARY: No, no, no! We can't have any more thieves in our state administration. Put him back.

SANCHO: Okay, we still got other models. Come on, Johnny, we'll sell you to some old lady. *(Sancho takes Johnny back to his place.)*

SECRETARY: Mr. Sancho, I don't think you quite understand what we need. What we need is something that will attract the women voters. Something more traditional, more romantic.

SANCHO: Ah, a lover. *(He smiles meaningfully.)* Step right over here, señorita. Introducing our standard Revolucionario and/or Early California Bandit type. As you can see, he is well built, sturdy, durable. This is the International Harvestor of Mexicans.

SECRETARY: What does he do?

SANCHO: You name it, he does it. He rides horses, stays in the mountains, crosses deserts, plains, rivers, leads revolutions, follows revolutions, kills, can be killed, serves as a martyr, hero, movie star—did I say movie star? Did you ever see *Viva Zapata? Viva Villa, Villa Rides, Pancho Villa Returns, Pancho Villa Goes Back, Pancho Villa Meets Abbott and Costello*—

SECRETARY: I've never seen any of those.

SANCHO: Well, he was in all of them. Listen to this. *(Snap.)*

REVOLUCIONARIO: *(scream)* ¡VIVA VILLAAAAA!

SECRETARY: That's awfully loud.

SANCHO: He has a volume control. *(He adjusts volume. Snap.)*

REVOLUCIONARIO: *(mousy voice)* Viva Villa.

SECRETARY: That's better.

SANCHO: And even if you didn't see him in the movies, perhaps you saw him on TV. He makes commercials. *(Snap.)*

REVOLUCIONARIO: Is there a Frito Bandito in your house?

SECRETARY: Oh yes, I've seen that one!

SANCHO: Another feature about this one is that he is economical. He runs on raw horsemeat and tequila!

---

[17]Gimme that purse, lady!

SECRETARY: Isn't that rather savage?

SANCHO: Al contrario,[18] it makes him a lover. *(Snap.)*

REVOLUCIONARIO: *(to Secretary)* ¡Ay, mamasota, cochota, ven pa'cá![19] *(He grabs Secretary and folds her back, Latin-lover style.)*

SANCHO: *(Snap. Revolucionario goes back upright.)* Now wasn't that nice?

SECRETARY: Well, it was rather nice.

SANCHO: And finally, there is one outstanding feature about this model I *know* the ladies are going to love: he's a *genuine* antique! He was made in Mexico in 1910!

SECRETARY: Made in Mexico?

SANCHO: That's right. Once in Tijuana, twice in Guadalajara, three times in Cuernavaca.

SECRETARY: Mr. Sancho, I thought he was an American product.

SANCHO: No, but—

SECRETARY: No, I'm sorry. We can't buy anything but American made products. He just won't do.

SANCHO: But, he's an antique!

SECRETARY: I don't care. You still don't understand what we need. It's true we need Mexican models such as these, but it's more important that he be *American.*

SANCHO: American?

SECRETARY: That's right, and judging from what you've shown me, I don't think you have what we want. Well, my lunch hour's almost over, I better—

SANCHO: Wait a minute! Mexican but American?

SECRETARY: That's correct.

SANCHO: Mexican but . . . *(A sudden flash) American!* Yeah, I think we've got exactly what you want. He just came in today! Give me a minute. *(He exits. Talks from backstage.)* Here he is in the shop. Let me just get some papers off. There. Introducing our new Mexican American! Ta-ra-ra-ra-ra-RA-RAAA!

[*Sancho brings out the Mexican American model, a clean-shaven middle-class type in a business suit, with glasses.*]

SECRETARY: *(impressed)* Where have you been hiding this one?

SANCHO: He just came in this morning. Ain't he a beauty? Feast your eyes on him! Sturdy U.S. Steel frame, streamlined, modern. As a matter of fact, he is built exactly like our Anglo models except that he comes in a variety of darker shades: Naugahyde, leather, or leatherette.

---

[18]On the contrary

[19]Oh mama, you cute thing, come over here!

SECRETARY: Naugahyde.

SANCHO: Well, we'll just write that down. Yes, señorita, this model represents the apex of American engineering! He is bilingual, college-educated, ambitious! Say the word *acculturate* and he accelerates. He is intelligent, well-mannered, clean—did I say clean? *(Snap. Mexican American raises his arm.)* Smell.

SECRETARY: *(smells)* Old Sobaco,[20] my favorite.

SANCHO: *(Snap. Mexican American turns toward Sancho.)* Eric? *(To Secretary)* We call him Eric García. *(To Eric)* I want you to meet Miss *Jim*-enez, Eric.

MEXICAN AMERICAN: Miss *Jim*-enez, I am delighted to make your acquaintance. *(He kisses her hand.)*

SECRETARY: Oh, my, how charming!

SANCHO: Did you feel the suction? He has seven especially engineered suction cups right behind his lips. He's a charmer, all right!

SECRETARY: How about boards—does he function on boards?

SANCHO: You name them, he is on them. Parole boards, draft boards, school boards, taco quality control boards, surfboards, two-by-fours.

SECRETARY: Does he function in politics?

SANCHO: Señorita, you are looking at a political *machine.* Have you ever heard of the OEO, EEOC, COD, War on Poverty? That's our model! Not only that, he makes political speeches.

SECRETARY: May I hear one?

SANCHO: With pleasure. *(Snap.)* Eric, give us a speech

MEXICAN AMERICAN: Mr. Congressman, Mr. Chairman, members of the board, honored guests, ladies and gentlemen. *(Sancho and Secretary applaud.)* Please, please. I come before you as a Mexican American to tell you about the problems of the Mexican. The problems of the Mexican stem from one thing and one thing alone: he's stupid. He's uneducated. He needs to stay in school. He needs to be ambitious, forward-looking, harder-working. He needs to think American, American, American, AMERICAN, AMERICAN, AMERICAN. GOD BLESS AMERICA! GOD BLESS AMERICA! GOD BLESS AMERICA!! *(He goes out of control.)*

[*Sancho snaps frantically and the Mexican American finally slumps forward, bending at the waist.*]

SECRETARY: Oh my, he's patriotic too!

SANCHO: Sí, señorita, he loves his country. Let me just make a little adjustment here. *(Stands Mexican American up.)*

---

[20]Old Armpit

SECRETARY: What about upkeep? Is he economical?

SANCHO: Well, no, I won't lie to you. The Mexican American costs a little bit more, but you get what you pay for. He's worth every extra cent. You can keep him running on dry Martinis and steaks.

SECRETARY: Apple pie?

SANCHO: Only Mom's. Of course, he's also programmed to eat Mexican food at ceremonial functions, but I must warn you: an overdose of beans will plug up his exhaust.

SECRETARY: Fine! There's just one more question: *How much do you want for him?*

SANCHO: Well, I tell you what I'm gonna do. Today and today only, because you've been so sweet, I'm gonna let you steal this model from me! I'm gonna let you drive him off the lot for the simple price of—let's see, taxes and license included—fifteen thousand dollars.

SECRETARY: Fifteen thousand *dollars?* For a *Mexican?*

SANCHO: Mexican? What are you talking, lady? This is a Mexican *American!* We had to melt down two pachucos, a farmworker, and three gabachos[21] to make this model! You want quality, but you gotta pay for it! This is no cheap runabout. He's got class!

SECRETARY: Okay, I'll take him.

SANCHO: You will?

SECRETARY: Here's your money.

SANCHO: You mind if I count it?

SECRETARY: Go right ahead.

SANCHO: Well, you'll get your pink slip in the mail. Oh, do you want me to wrap him up for you? We have a box in the back.

SECRETARY: No, thank you. The Governor is having a luncheon this afternoon, and we need a brown face in the crowd. How do I drive him?

SANCHO: Just snap your fingers. He'll do anything you want.

[*Secretary snaps. Mexican American steps forward.*]

MEXICAN AMERICAN: ¡RAZA QUERIDA, VAMOS LEVANTANDO ARMAS PARA LIBERARNOS DE ESTOS DESGRACIADOS GABACHOS QUE NOS EXPLOTAN! VAMOS—[22]

SECRETARY: What did he say?

SANCHO: Something about lifting arms, killing white people, and so on.

SECRETARY: But he's not supposed to say that!

---

[21]Anglos

[22]Beloved Chicano people, let us take up arms to liberate ourselves from these despicable Anglos that exploit us! Let us—

SANCHO: Look, lady, don't blame me for bugs from the factory. He's your Mexican American, you bought him, now drive him off the lot!

SECRETARY: But he's broken!

SANCHO: Try snapping another finger.

[*Secretary snaps. Mexican American comes to life again.*]

MEXICAN AMERICAN: ¡ESTA GRAN HUMANIDAD HA DICHO BASTA! ¡Y SE HA PUESTO EN MARCHA! ¡BASTA! ¡BASTA! ¡VIVA LA RAZA! ¡VIVA LA CAUSA! ¡VIVA LA HUELGA! ¡VIVAN LOS BROWN BERETS! ¡VIVAN LOS ESTUDIANTES![23] CHICANO POWER!

[*The Mexican American turns toward the Secretary, who gasps and backs up. He keeps turning toward the Pachuco, Farmworker, and Revolucionario, snapping his fingers and turning each of them on, one by one.*]

PACHUCO: *(Snap. To Secretary)* I'm going to get you, baby! Viva la Raza!

FARMWORKER: *(Snap. To Secretary)* ¡Viva la huelga! ¡Viva la huelga! ¡VIVA LA HUELGA!

REVOLUCIONARIO: *(Snap. To Secretary)* ¡Viva la revolucion! ¡VIVA LA REVOLUCION!

[*The three models join together and advance toward the Secretary, who backs up and runs out of the shop screaming. Sancho is at the other end of the shop holding his money in his hand. All freeze. After a few seconds of silence, the Pachuco moves and stretches, shaking his arms and loosening up. The Farmworker and Revolucionario do the same. Sancho stays where he is, frozen to his spot.*]

JOHNNY: Man, that was a long one, ése. *(Others agree with him.)*

FARMWORKER: How did we do?

JOHNNY: Perty good, look all that lana,[24] man! *(He goes over to Sancho and removes the money from his hand. Sancho stays where he is.)*

REVOLUCIONAIRO: En la madre, look at all the money.

JOHNNY: We keep this up, we're going to be rich.

FARMWORKER: They think we're machines.

REVOLUCIONARIO: Burros.

JOHNNY: Puppets.

MEXICAN AMERICAN: The only thing I don't like is, how come I always got to play the Mexican American?

---

[23]This great mass of humanity has said, Enough! And it begins to march! Enough! Enough! Long live the Chicano people! Long La Causa! Long live the strike! Long live the Brown Berets! Long live the students!

[24]Money (colloquial).

JOHNNY: That's what you get for finishing high school.

FARMWORKER: How about our wages, ése?

JOHNNY: Here it comes right now. Three thousand dollars for you, three thousand for you, three thousand for you, and three thousand for me. The rest we put back into the business.

MEXICAN AMERICAN: Too much, man. Hey, where you vatos[25] going tonight?

FARMWORKER: I'm going over to Concha's. There's a party.

JOHNNY: Wait a minute, vatos. What about our salesman? I think he needs an oil job.

REVOLUCIONARIO: Leave him to me.

> [*The Pachuco, Farmworker, and Mexican American exit, talking loudly about their plans for the night. The Revolucionario goes over to Sancho, removes his derby hat and cigar, lifts him up and throws him over his shoulder. Sancho hangs loose, lifeless.*]

REVOLUCIONARIO: *(to audience)* He's the best model we got! ¡Ajua! *(Exit.)*

Thinking about the Text

1. What is Valdez's strategy of setting this play in "Honest Sancho's Used Mexican Lot and Mexican Curio Shop"? How does this setting establish the tone and theme of this play?

2. How does Valdez depict the secretary and how does she see herself? Find specific quotations to support your interpretations.

3. Identify the stereotypes that Valdez uses and analyze his purpose in doing so.

4. What is ironic about "Honest Sancho" and how do you explain the twist at the end? What is Valdez suggesting in this ending?

5. What is the significance of the title, "The Sellouts"? According to Valdez, who are the sellouts and why?

6. Why does Valdez use both English and Spanish in this play? How do you feel about this mixing of languages? If you don't understand Spanish, would you have been able to follow the play without translations in the endnotes? Why?

7. Examine this play as a satire: a literary work that uses humor, ridicule, and exaggeration to expose or criticize certain values, beliefs, myths, practices, or institutions. What are the targets of Valdez's satire and what is he criticizing about each?

---

[25]Guys; dudes (pachuco slang)

WRITING FROM THE TEXT

1. Focusing on the mixture of English and Spanish in *Los Vendidos,* write an essay arguing that the mixing of languages adds to or detracts from an understanding of the play. Include specific quotations from the play to illustrate your claims.

2. In an essay on stereotypes, analyze how Valdez's use of Mexican stereotypes underscores the themes of this play.

3. If you have experienced stereotyping or exploitation because of your culture, write an evaluative response essay relating your experiences to specific conflicts or attitudes in this play.

4. Using materials gathered for exercise 7, page 210, write an analytic essay examining the targets of Valdez's satire. Explain what he is exposing and criticizing throughout this play.

CONNECTING WITH OTHER TEXTS

1. Read "Don't Let Stereotypes Warp Your Judgments" (p. 469) by Robert Heilbroner and write an essay using examples from Valdez's play to support and illustrate Heilbroner's points and cautions.

2. Read "The Myth of the Latin Woman" (p. 223), and write an essay showing how Cofer's experiences reflect those satirized by Luis Valdez. You may include your own observations to create an amusing essay.

3. Focusing on the purposes and strategies involved in satire, write an essay examining the aspects of American society satirized in both "Coke" (p. 287) and *Los Vendidos.* You may want to focus your thesis on common targets of satire.

Chapter 4

Between Perceptions

How we perceive ourselves is intrinsically related to our racial and ethnic roots, as well as to our gender. Our sense of self, however, goes beyond any definition of male or female, race or culture. Self-perception is often conditioned by the roles we assume—as students, workers, family members—but our self-image and how others see us may be distinct from the roles we play. You regard yourself as a college student, but when you are at home you might be the "baby" in the family, or the one diapering the baby. You know that by working extra hours you can earn much-needed overtime pay, but your perception of yourself as an "A" student prompts you to cut back on hours instead. A woman who is physically disabled may not define herself as "handicapped," and a man who qualifies for financial assistance may not see himself as "disadvantaged." Perceiving oneself beyond labels or stereotypes is an essential process, as the readings in this chapter indicate.

Your self-perception is influenced by the images that others form of you. If you feel that you are constantly trying to exist among worlds that perceive you differently, you will relate to the tensions described in the essays by Matthew Soyster and Jennifer Coleman as they fight stereotypes that threaten their self-perceptions. Their essays express the frustrations of productive individuals whose self-acceptance is threatened by the delimiting views of others. Ted Kooser's poem shows how our perceptions of the disabled limit us.

As you may realize, eating disorders often develop from a person's perception of what is attractive or from a need for control. In "Bodily Harm," Pamela Erens chronicles the problems of many women who have eating disorders and who struggle toward self-understanding and acceptance rather than perpetuating destructive behavior. Jenny Jones regrets having breast implants that threaten her health and self-image. Acceptance of oneself is a goal for each of us. As Joan Didion shows in her essay on Georgia O'Keeffe, this artist had a strong enough sense of self to counter traditional perceptions of women and the roles they should play. Neil Steinberg humorously accepts the fact that he's fat even as he regrets the attitudes of some thin people around him. The perceptions of others may prompt Steven Barrie-Anthony to seek remedies for his baldness, but he ultimately recognizes that the costs are too great.

To be perceived as an individual rather than as a racial or ethnic stereotype may be a challenge for you or some of your friends. Fighting stereotypes can be life-threatening, as Brent Staples and Carmen Vazquez reveal in their essays, or irritating, as Judith Ortiz Cofer shows in hers. The poem "Mr. Z" by M. Carl Holman, satirizes people's efforts to deny race and culture in order to create an artificial persona.

Our perception of self is complicated by the multiple roles we play and our disparate self-images based on gender, social class, or ethnicity. Balancing how others see us with who we think we are is the condition of being between perceptions—and the basis of all of the writings in this chapter.

Living Under Circe's Spell

Matthew Soyster

A freelance writer, journalist, and college instructor, Matthew Soyster (b. 1954) earned a B.A. in French and Italian literature from Stanford University and an M.A. in English and Norwegian literature from the University of California at Berkeley. His work has appeared in *Newsweek, Stanford Magazine,* the *San Francisco Examiner,* and numerous other publications. Soyster has been associate editor of *Change Magazine* and a repeated guest on KPFA-FM radio, discussing images of the disabled—"Monster/Victim/Hero"—in Western film literature and popular culture. In 1989 he organized a $10,000 benefit concert for the Multiple Sclerosis Society, and in 1991 he wrote and performed "Shape Shifter," a monologue for the premiere of the Contemporary Dance Company at a Berkeley theater. The following article appeared in *Newsweek* in 1993.

1   "Life is brief, time's a thief." This ribbon of pop lyricism keens from an apartment-house radio into the hot afternoon air. Across the street I am sprawled in the gutter behind my minivan, bits of glass and scrap metal chewing at my knees and elbows, a cut on my hand beginning to well crimson.

2   There has been no assailant, no wound except to my psyche. I'm just a clumsy cripple whose legs buckled before he reached his wheelchair. A moment ago I yanked it from my tailgate, as I've done a thousand times. But when it spun off at a crazy angle I missed the seat and slumped to the ground.

3   Now the spasms start, shooting outward from the small of my back, forcing me prone, grinding my cheek into the asphalt. What will I look like to the first casual passerby before he catches sight of the telltale chair? A wine-soaked rummy? A hit-and-run victim? Maybe an amateur mechanic checking the rear suspension, wrong side up.

4   I'm too young and vital looking to be this helpless. I shrink from the inevitable clucking and concern. Then again, this isn't the best neighborhood. The first person to come along may simply kick me and take my wallet. No wonder I'm ambivalent about rescue, needing but not wanting to be discovered. With detachment I savor the hush of this deserted street, the symphony of birdsong in the treetops.

5   I am trying to remember T. S. Eliot's line about waiting without hope, because hope would be hope for the wrong thing. Instead, that idiot TV commercial for the medical alarm-pager keeps ringing through my brain: "Help me. I've fallen and I can't get up."

6   It was only a matter of time. I've known for months that my hair's-breadth maneuvering would eventually fail me. For years, in fact. When I first learned that I had multiple sclerosis I was a marathon runner and white-water-rafting guide, a cyclist and skier, the quintessential California golden boy. Cardiovascular fitness had long since become our state religion. I lived for and through my legs.

7   But that's only the ad-slick surface of the California dream, the sunshine without the shadow. The town I live in is also the mecca of the disabled, the home of the Independent Living Movement, the place where broken people come to patch together their dignity and their dreams.

8   Yin and yang. In Berkeley, there are wheelchair users on every corner. Propped in sagging hospital-issue chairs. Space-age sports chairs. Motor-driven dreadnoughts. When I could still walk, I crossed the street to avoid them. What an odd tribe they seemed, with their spindly, agitated limbs, always hurtling down the avenue on some manic errand.

9   How could I imagine my own swift decline? A few months or years passed. Soon I was relying on a cane, then crutches, and finally—after many thigh-bruising falls and a numbness so intense it turned my legs to driftwood—a wheelchair. My response to these limitations was compensation and denial. I thought I could become a disabled Olympian: wheelchair racing, tennis, rugby. I thought I could go on as before.

10   Wrong again. To paraphrase Tolstoy, all able-bodied people are alike, but each disabled person is crippled in his own way. MS not only played havoc with my upper-body strength and agility; it clouded my mind and sapped my energy. I could totter a few steps supported at both wrists, but my days in the winter surf, high peaks and desert canyons were over.

11   So what is it like to spend your life forked at the waist, face-level with children? The syndrome has been amply described. People see through me now, or over me. They don't see me at all. Or they fix me with that plangent, aching stare: sympathy.

12   They offer too much assistance, scurrying to open doors, scrambling out of my way with unnecessary apologies, or they leave me no space at all, barking their shins on my foot pedals. My spirit rallies in the face of such humiliations; they have their comic aspect. What disturbs me most is not how others see me, but how I've lost my vision of myself.

13   Growing crippled is a bitch. First your body undergoes a strange enchantment: Circe's spell. Then your identity gives way. You become someone or something other, but for a long time you're not sure what that other is.

14   Along the way, I've had to give up activities and passions that define me, my safe position in society, my very sense of manhood. In our species, the pecking order is distinctly vertical. True for women. Doubly true for men. A man stands tall, stands firm, stands up for things. These are more than metaphors. The very act of sitting implies demotion. Anyone who's witnessed boardroom politics knows this much. Have a seat, barks the boss. It's not an invitation, it's an order.

15   All of this brings me back to the gutter, where I lie listening to birdsong, recognizing but not apologizing for the obstinacy that landed me here. For months my friends and family have watched my legs grow weaker. They've prodded me relentlessly to refit my van with a wheelchair lift in order to avoid just this disaster. But I've refused.

16   Twice a day at least, I've dragged my reluctant legs from beneath the steering column, hauled myself erect beside the driver's seat, inched my way down the roof rail to the rear stowage. And removed the chair by hand, standing.

17   Why have I clung to this ritual, knowing it's dangerous and futile? It's the only task I rise for anymore, in a sitting life. For a moment in the driver's doorway, I'm in control, unreliant on technology or assistance, upright. Or so I've told myself. But that moment is so fragile, the control so illusory.

18   When the time comes to change, I've said, I'll know.

19   Now I know.

20   I feel the lesson, sharp as the rap of a Zen master's stick. Lying in the hot gutter, I take a deep breath and my whole body relaxes. Tuning in to Rod Stewart's tinny wisdom from the window. Listening for a passing car or pedestrian.

21   Waiting.

THINKING ABOUT THE TEXT

1. This essay opens with the writer "sprawled in the gutter" and ends with him still "waiting" for a passing car or pedestrian to help. Analyze the effect of creating such a scene to prompt his discussion and of using the present tense (even though this event happened in the past).

2. Describe, in detail, the writer's life and his attitude about the disabled before he himself became "a clumsy cripple."

3. Soyster explains, "What disturbs me most is not how others see me, but how I've lost my vision of myself" (215). What does he mean by this, and how does his threatened self-image relate to his refusal to refit his van with a wheelchair lift?

4. Throughout this essay Soyster includes a number of *allusions*—indirect references to sources outside the work: pop lyrics, singer Rod Stewart, poet T. S. Eliot, novelist Leo Tolstoy, the myth of Circe, the Zen religion, and yin and yang. Look up these allusions in a dictionary or reader's encyclopedia and explain how each contributes to our understanding of the writer and his perspective.

WRITING FROM THE TEXT

1. Using the information you gathered for exercise 4, write an essay explaining how the allusions in this essay are essential to helping us see the writer as a unique and intriguing individual and not just "a clumsy cripple."

2. Write about an event in your life that caused you to lose a vision of yourself. Dramatize your life before this crisis or event and contrast it with your current life.

CONNECTING WITH OTHER TEXTS

1. Matthew Soyster, S. I. Hayakawa (p. 24), Ted Kooser (p. 217), and Shannon Paaske (p. 522) use different genres (essay, poem, and research paper) to examine the attitudes that many harbor toward the disabled. Using details from these works, write an essay supporting your own thesis about how and why people feel uneasy around the disabled—and what can be done about it.

2. Matthew Soyster, Brent Staples (p. 237), and Jennifer Coleman (p. 243) describe how others have incorrectly stereotyped and humiliated them. Using

details from any of these narratives and from "Don't Let Stereotypes Warp Your Judgment" (p. 469), write an analysis of the causes and effects of such stereotyping on the stereotyped person and the one doing the stereotyping.

3. In an essay show how Matthew Soyster and Frida Kahlo (p. 496) have lively responses to living with physical disabilities. Include observations of people whom you know who also are limited physically.

The Blind Always Come as Such a Surprise
Ted Kooser

Described by a critic as "an authentic poet of the American people," Ted Kooser (b. 1939) is also second vice president of marketing for Lincoln Benefit Insurance Company. Kooser has won national recognition, including the Society for Midlands Authors Prize for the best book of poetry of 1980 (*Sure Signs*). Other publications include *On Common Ground* (1983), *One World at a Time* (1985), *The Blizzard Voices* (1986), and *Weather Central* (1994). His poems often present vivid details and startling images of ordinary life, as does the poem reprinted here from *Sure Signs*. Asked what advice he would give college writers, Kooser repeats E. B. White's suggestion: "Simplify, simplify, simplify."

The blind always come as such a surprise,
suddenly filling an elevator
with a great white porcupine of canes,
or coming down upon us in a noisy crowd
5   like the eye of a hurricane.
The dashboards of cars stopped at crosswalks
and the shoes of commuters on trains
are covered with sentences
struck down in mid-flight by the canes of the blind.
10   Each of them changes our lives,
tapping across the bright circles of our ambitions
like cracks traversing the favorite china.

THINKING ABOUT THE TEXT

1. This poem is written from the point of view of someone who encounters a blind person. What is the poet's predominant point about how people with sight feel when a blind person appears?

2. The poet describes the blind person coming into four public areas. What are these places and what are the specific effects of the blind person's presence?

3. List your responses to the following vivid images and figures of speech by asking yourself what pictures or sounds the poet intends and what many associations you can make with each word. Your analysis of these images will help you understand the specific points that the poet is making beyond his general point.
   - a great white porcupine of canes
   - like the eye of a hurricane
   - The dashboards . . . and the shoes . . . covered with sentences struck down in mid-flight
   - the bright circles of our ambitions
   - like cracks traversing the favorite china

WRITING FROM THE TEXT

1. Write an essay that analyzes the images in this poem and shows how the images contribute to the poet's theme. (See pp. 475–483 for a discussion of how to write poetry analysis.)

2. How do you feel when you meet a disabled person? Do any of Kooser's images reflect some of your responses? In an essay, discuss how you feel and integrate an interpretation of Kooser's images into your discussion.

3. If you are disabled, what is your response to Kooser's poem? Write an essay that describes your feelings about how people respond to you.

CONNECTING WITH OTHER TEXTS

1. In "Living Under Circe's Spell" (p. 213), Matthew Soyster notes that people see through him, over him, or don't see him at all. Write an essay that draws on Soyster's experiences with the disabled before he had multiple sclerosis, and then later as a disabled person, and Ted Kooser's descriptions of people's responses to the blind in this poem. Is the goal of your essay to inspire change in people's attitudes and behavior, or to describe the existing conditions, or do you have yet another goal?

2. Read "The Myth of the Latin Woman" (p. 223) and analyze how Cofer's experiences of being examined as a mythic being rather than a real person are analogous to how we see the blind. Show in your essay what Kooser's poem and Cofer's essay suggest about people's perceptions.

Georgia O'Keeffe
Joan Didion

The subject matter for the writing of novelist, playwright, and essayist Joan Didion (b.1934) is as diverse as her genre. She has examined Haight-Asbury in *SlouchingToward Bethlehem* (1968), hedonist Hollywood in *Play It as It Lays* (1970), social disintegration in *The Book of Common Prayer* (1977), the political impact of Cuban exiles in *Miami* (1987), and American foreign policy in *The Last Thing He Wanted* (1996). As the following essay from *The White Album* (1979), reveals, Didion is also interested in biography.

1   "Where I was born and where and how I have lived is unimportant," Georgia O'Keeffe told us in the book of paintings and words published in her ninetieth year on earth. She seemed to be advising us to forget the beautiful face in the Stieglitz photographs. She appeared to be dismissing the rather condescending romance that had attached to her by then, the romance of extreme good looks and advanced age and deliberate isolation. "It is what I have done with where I have been that should be of interest." I recall an August afternoon in Chicago in 1973 when I took my daughter, then seven, to see what Georgia O'Keeffe had done with where she had been. One of the vast O'Keeffe "Sky Above Clouds" canvases floated over the back stairs in the Chicago Art Institute that day, dominating what seemed to be several stories of empty light, and my daughter looked at it once, ran to the landing, and kept on looking. "Who drew it?" she whispered after a while. I told her. "I need to talk to her," she said finally.

2   My daughter was making, that day in Chicago, an entirely unconscious but quite basic assumption about people and the work they do. She was assuming that the glory she saw in the work reflected a glory in its maker, that the painting was the painter as the poem is the poet, that every choice one made alone—every word chosen or rejected, every brush stroke laid or not laid down—betrayed one's character. *Style is character.* It seemed to me that afternoon that I had rarely seen so instinctive an application of this familiar principle, and I recall being pleased not only that my daughter responded to style as character but that it was Georgia O'Keeffe's particular style to which she responded: this was a hard woman who had imposed her 192 square feet of clouds on Chicago.

3   "Hardness" has not been in our century a quality much admired in women, nor in the past twenty years has it even been in official favor for men. When hardness surfaces in the very old we tend to transform it into "crustiness" or eccentricity, some tonic pepperiness to be indulged at a distance. On the evidence of her work and what she has said about it, Georgia O'Keeffe is neither "crusty" nor eccentric. She is simply hard, a straight shooter, a woman clean of received wisdom and open to what she sees. This is a woman who could early on dismiss

most of her contemporaries as "dreamy," and would later single out one she liked as "a very poor painter." (And then add, apparently by way of softening the judgment: "I guess he wasn't a painter at all. He had no courage and I believe that to create one's own world in any of the arts takes courage.") This is a woman who in 1939 could advise her admirers that they were missing her point, that their appreciation of her famous flowers was merely sentimental. "When I paint a red hill," she observed coolly in the catalogue for an exhibition that year, "you say it is too bad that I don't always paint flowers. A flower touches almost everyone's heart. A red hill doesn't touch everyone's heart." This is a woman who could describe the genesis of one of her most well-known paintings—the "Cow's Skull: Red, White and Blue" owned by the Metropolitan—as an act of quite deliberate and derisive orneriness. "I thought of the city men I had been seeing in the East," she wrote. "They talked so often of writing the Great American Novel—the Great American Play—the Great American Poetry. . . . So as I was painting my cow's head on blue I thought to myself, 'I'll make it an American painting. They will not think it great with the red stripes down the sides—Red, White and Blue—but they will notice it.'"

4   *The city men. The men. They.* The words crop up again and again as this astonishingly aggressive woman tells us what was on her mind when she was making her astonishingly aggressive paintings. It was those city men who stood accused of sentimentalizing her flowers: "I made you take time to look at what I saw and when you took time to really notice my flower you hung all your associations with flowers on my flower and you write about my flower as if I think and see what you think and see—and I don't." *And I don't.* Imagine those words spoken, and the sound you hear is *don't tread on me.* "The men" believed it impossible to paint New York, so Georgia O'Keeffe painted New York. "The men" didn't think much of her bright color, so she made it brighter. The men yearned toward Europe so she went to Texas, and then New Mexico. The men talked about Cézanne, "long involved remarks about the 'plastic quality' of his form and color," and took one another's long involved remarks, in the view of this angelic rattlesnake in their midst, altogether too seriously. "I can paint one of those dismal-colored paintings like the men," the woman who regarded herself always as an outsider remembers thinking one day in 1922, and she did: a painting of a shed "all low-toned and dreary with the tree beside the door." She called this act of rancor "The Shanty" and hung it in her next show. "The men seemed to approve of it," she reported fifty-four years later, her contempt undimmed. "They seemed to think that maybe I was beginning to paint. That was my only low-toned dismal-colored painting."

5   Some women fight and others do not. Like so many successful guerrillas in the war between the sexes, Georgia O'Keeffe seems to have been equipped early with an immutable sense of who she was and a fairly clear understand-

ing that she would be required to prove it. On the surface her upbringing was conventional. She was a child on the Wisconsin prairie who played with china dolls and painted watercolors with cloudy skies because sunlight was too hard to paint and, with her brother and sisters, listened every night to her mother read stories of the Wild West, of Texas, of Kit Carson and Billy the Kid. She told adults that she wanted to be an artist and was embarrassed when they asked what kind of artist she wanted to be: she had no idea "what kind." She had no idea what artists did. She had never seen a picture that interested her, other than a pen-and-ink Maid of Athens in one of her mother's books, some Mother Goose illustrations printed on cloth, a tablet cover that showed a little girl with pink roses, and the painting of Arabs on horseback that hung in her grandmother's parlor. At thirteen, in a Dominican convent, she was mortified when the sister corrected her drawing. At Chatham Episcopal Institute in Virginia she painted lilacs and sneaked time alone to walk out to where she could see the line of the Blue Ridge Mountains on the horizon. At the Art Institute in Chicago she was shocked by the presence of live models and wanted to abandon anatomy lessons. At the Art Students League in New York one of her fellow students advised her that, since he would be a great painter and she would end up teaching painting in a girl's school, any work of hers was less important than modeling for him. Another painted over her work to show her how the Impressionists did trees. She had not before heard how the Impressionists did trees and she did not much care.

6   At twenty-four she left all those opinions behind and went for the first time to live in Texas, where there were no trees to paint and no one to tell her how not to paint them. In Texas there was only the horizon she craved. In Texas she had her sister Claudia with her for a while, and in the late afternoons they would walk away from town and toward the horizon and watch the evening star come out. "That evening star fascinated me," she wrote. "It was in some way very exciting to me. My sister had a gun, and as we walked she would throw bottles into the air and shoot as many as she could before they hit the ground. I had nothing but to walk into nowhere and the wide sunset space with the star. Ten watercolors were made from that star." In a way one's interest is compelled as much by the sister Claudia with the gun as by the painter Georgia with the star, but only the painter left us this shining record. Ten watercolors were made from that star.

THINKING ABOUT THE TEXT

1. Didion opens her essay with a statement from her subject, and an anecdote involving the author's daughter and her response to an O'Keeffe painting. What is Didion's strategy in beginning her essay in this way?

2. The author asserts that "the painting [is] the painter as the poem is the poet." What does Didion mean?

3. Didion infers that Georgia O'Keeffe was "hard" but not "crusty" or "eccentric." What does Didion mean by "hard"? After acknowledging that "hardness" is not a quality admired in women or men of our time, how does Didion nevertheless show that she admires her subject? How does Didion support her inference that O'Keeffe was "a straight-shooter"?

4. How does Didion convince her reader that Georgia O'Keeffe was an aggressive woman who disregarded the conventional thinking of her time period, one of the "successful guerrillas in the war between the sexes"?

WRITING ABOUT THE TEXT

1. Write a short, biographical essay about someone you know, starting with a thesis that focuses on inferences that you can support with specific details you have observed about that person. Review the material and papers on character analysis and the focused biography (pp. 484–505).

2. Start with Didion's statement that "style is character" and write about three or four people you know whose work and other life choices reveal their characters. Use strong, showing details to paint your portraits.

3. How are some people able to deviate from convention in making their life choices? Write an essay that starts with your assertion about the necessary components for approaching life and work unconventionally. You might reread Didion's essay on Georgia O'Keeffe to determine what character traits the artist possessed.

CONNECTING WITH OTHER TEXTS

1. Compare Keith Hamm's revelations about himself in "Dumpster-Diving for Dollars" (p. 319) with the life of Georgia O'Keeffe as Joan Didion describes it. If style is character, as Didion writes, what is revealed about each of these characters in the styles of their lives?

2. If Didion is correct, as the painter is the painting, "the poem is the poet." Read a brief account of Seamus Heaney's life, then write an essay supporting the assertion that the poem "Digging" (p. 43) is autobiographical—that the poem is the poet.

3. Read a full-length biography of Georgia O'Keeffe's life and write an essay based on inferences about her character. Do not write a summary of her life, from birth to death, but rather focus on answering the question: What kind of woman was Georgia O'Keeffe? See pages 493–505 for help in writing this paper.

The Myth of the Latin Woman
Judith Ortiz Cofer

Born in Puerto Rico in 1952, poet, essayist, and novelist Judith Ortiz Cofer has written extensively on being reared with her parents' traditional island culture while growing up in New Jersey. In an interview, Cofer described the contradictions in her cultural identity: "I write in English, yet I write obsessively about my Puerto Rican experience. . . . I am a composite of two worlds." Cofer has published collections of poems, a novel, a story for young adults, and collections of essays. The piece included here is from *The Latin Deli*, published in 1993.

1 On a bus trip to London from Oxford University where I was earning some graduate credits one summer, a young man, obviously fresh from a pub, spotted me and as if struck by inspiration went down on his knees in the aisle. With both hands over his heart, he broke into an Irish tenor's rendition of "Maria" from *West Side Story*. My politely amused fellow passengers gave his lovely voice the round of gentle applause it deserved. Though I was not quite as amused, I managed my version of an English smile: no show of teeth, no extreme contortions of the facial muscles—I was at this time of my life practicing reserve and cool. Oh, that British control, how I coveted it. But "Maria" had followed me to London, reminding me of a prime fact of my life: you can leave the island, master the English language, and travel as far as you can, but if you are a Latina, especially one like me who so obviously belongs to Rita Moreno's gene pool, the island travels with you.

2 This is sometimes a very good thing—it may win you that extra minute of someone's attention. But with some people, the same things can make *you* an island—not a tropical paradise but an Alcatraz, a place nobody wants to visit. As a Puerto Rican girl living in the United States and wanting like most children to "belong," I resented the stereotype that my Hispanic appearance called forth from many people I met.

3 Growing up in a large urban center in New Jersey during the 1960s, I suffered from what I think of as "cultural schizophrenia." Our life was designed by my parents as a microcosm of their *casas* on the island. We spoke in Spanish, ate Puerto Rican food bought at the *bodega,* and practiced strict Catholicism at a church that allotted us a one-hour slot each week for mass, performed in Spanish by a Chinese priest trained as a missionary for Latin America.

4 As a girl I was kept under strict surveillance by my parents, since my virtue and modesty were, by their cultural equation, the same as their honor. As a teenager I was lectured constantly on how to behave as a proper *senorita.* But it was a conflicting message I received, since the Puerto Rican

mothers also encouraged their daughters to look and act like women and to dress in clothes our Anglo friends and their mothers found too "mature" and flashy. The difference was, and is, cultural; yet I often felt humiliated when I appeared at an American friend's party wearing a dress more suitable to a semi-formal than to a playroom birthday celebration. At Puerto Rican festivities, neither the music nor the colors we wore could be too loud.

5   I remember Career Day in our high school, when teachers told us to come dressed as if for a job interview. It quickly became obvious that to the Puerto Rican girls "dressing up" meant wearing their mother's ornate jewelry and clothing, more appropriate (by mainstream standards) for the company Christmas party than as daily office attire. That morning I had agonized in front of my closet, trying to figure out what a "career girl" would wear. I knew how to dress for school (at the Catholic school I attended, we all wore uniforms), I knew how to dress for Sunday mass, and I knew what dresses to wear for parties at my relatives' homes. Though I do not recall the precise details of my Career Day outfit, it must have been a composite of these choices. But I remember a comment my friend (an Italian American) made in later years that coalesced my impressions of the day. She said that at the business school she was attending, the Puerto Rican girls always stood out for wearing "everything at once." She meant, of course, too much jewelry, too many accessories. On that day at school we were simply made the negative models by the nuns, who were themselves not credible fashion experts to any of us. But it was painfully obvious to me that to the others, in their tailored skirts and silk blouses, we must have seemed "hopeless" and "vulgar." Though I now know that most adolescents feel out of step much of the time, I also know that for the Puerto Rican girls of my generation that sense was intensified. The way our teachers and classmates looked at us that day in school was just a taste of the cultural clash that awaited us in the real world, where prospective employers and men on the street would often misinterpret our tight skirts and jingling bracelets as a "come-on."

6   Mixed cultural signals have perpetuated certain stereotypes—for example, that of the Hispanic woman as the "hot tamale" or sexual firebrand. It is a one-dimensional view that the media have found easy to promote. In their special vocabulary, advertisers have designated "sizzling" and "smoldering" as the adjectives of choice for describing not only the foods but also the women of Latin America. From conversations in my house I recall hearing about the harassment that Puerto Rican women endured in factories where the "bossmen" talked to them as if sexual innuendo was all they understood, and worse, often gave them the choice of submitting to their advances or being fired.

7   It is custom, however, not chromosomes, that leads us to choose scarlet over pale pink. As young girls, it was our mothers who influenced our deci-

sions about clothes and colors—mothers who had grown up on a tropical island where the natural environment was a riot of primary colors, where
showing your skin was one way to keep cool as well as to look sexy. Most important of all, on the island, women perhaps felt freer to dress and move
more provocatively since, in most cases, they were protected by the traditions, mores, and laws of a Spanish/Catholic system of morality and
machismo whose main rule was: *You may look at my sister, but if you touch her
I will kill you.* The extended family and church structure could provide a
young woman with a circle of safety in her small pueblo on the island; if a
man "wronged" a girl, everyone would close in to save her family honor.

8   My mother has told me about dressing in her best party clothes on Saturday nights and going to the town's plaza to promenade with her girlfriends
in front of the boys they liked. The males were thus given an opportunity to
admire the women and to express their admiration in the form of *piropos:*
erotically charged street poems they composed on the spot. (I have myself
been subjected to a few *piropos* while visiting the island, and they can be outrageous, although custom dictates that they must never cross into obscenity.)
This ritual, as I understand it, also entails a show of studied indifference on
the woman's part; if she is "decent," she must not acknowledge the man's im-
passioned words. So I do understand how things can be lost in translation.
When a Puerto Rican girl, dressed in her idea of what is attractive, meets a
man from the mainstream culture who has been trained to react to certain
types of clothing as a sexual signal, a clash is likely to take place. I remember the boy who took me to my first formal dance leaning over to plant a
sloppy, over-eager kiss painfully on my mouth; when I didn't respond with
sufficient passion, he remarked resentfully: "I thought you Latin girls were
supposed to mature early," as if I were expected to *ripen* like a fruit or vegetable, not just grow into womanhood like other girls.

9   It is surprising to my professional friends that even today some people,
including those who should know better, still put others "in their place." It
happened to me most recently during a stay at a classy metropolitan hotel
favored by young professional couples for weddings. Late one evening after
the theater, as I walked toward my room with a colleague (a woman with
whom I was coordinating an arts program), a middle-aged man in a tuxedo,
with a young girl in satin and lace on his arm, stepped directly into our path.
With his champagne glass extended toward me, he exclaimed "Evita!"

10   Our way blocked, my companion and I listened as the man half-recited,
half-bellowed "Don't Cry for Me, Argentina." When he finished, the young
girl said: "How about a round of applause for my daddy?" We complied,
hoping this would bring the silly spectacle to a close. I was becoming aware
that our little group was attracting the attention of the other guests.

"Daddy" must have perceived this too, and he once more barred the way as we tried to walk past him. He began to shout-sing a ditty to the tune of "La Bamba"—except the lyrics were about a girl named Maria whose exploits rhymed with her name and gonorrhea. The girl kept saying "Oh, Daddy" and looking at me with pleading eyes. She wanted me to laugh along with the others. My companion and I stood silently waiting for the man to end his offensive song. When he finished, I looked not at him but at his daughter. I advised her calmly never to ask her father what he had done in the army. Then I walked between them and to my room. My friend complimented me on my cool handling of the situation, but I confessed that I had really wanted to push the jerk into the swimming pool. This same man—probably a corporate executive, well-educated, even worldly by most standards—would not have been likely to regale an Anglo woman with a dirty song in public. He might have checked his impulse by assuming that she could be somebody's wife or mother, or at least *somebody* who might take offense. But, to him, I was just an Evita or a Maria: merely a character in his cartoon-populated universe.

11   Another facet of the myth of the Latin woman in the United States is the menial, the domestic—Maria the housemaid or countergirl. It's true that work as domestics, as waitresses, and in factories is all that's available to women with little English and few skills. But the myth of the Hispanic menial—the funny maid, mispronouncing words and cooking up a spicy storm in a shiny California kitchen—has been perpetuated by the media in the same way that "Mammy" from *Gone with the Wind* became America's idea of the black woman for generations. Since I do not wear my diplomas around my neck for all to see, I have on occasion been sent to that "kitchen" where some think I obviously belong.

12   One incident has stayed with me, though I recognize it as a minor offense. My first public poetry reading took place in Miami, at a restaurant where a luncheon was being held before the event. I was nervous and excited as I walked in with notebook in hand. An older woman motioned me to her table, and thinking (foolish me) that she wanted me to autograph a copy of my newly published slender volume of verse, I went over. She ordered a cup of coffee from me, assuming that I was a waitress. (Easy enough to mistake my poems for menus, I suppose.) I know it wasn't an intentional act of cruelty. Yet of all the good things that happened later, I remember that scene most clearly, because it reminded me of what I had to overcome before anyone would take me seriously. In retrospect I understand that my anger gave my reading fire. In fact, I have almost always taken any doubt in my abilities as a challenge, the result most often being the satisfaction of winning a convert, of seeing the cold, appraising eyes warm to my words, the body language change, the smile that indicates I have opened some avenue for com-

munication. So that day as I read, I looked directly at that woman. Her lowered eyes told me she was embarrassed at her faux pas, and when I willed her to look up at me, she graciously allowed me to punish her with my full attention. We shook hands at the end of the reading and I never saw her again. She has probably forgotten the entire incident, but maybe not.

13   Yet I am one of the lucky ones. There are thousands of Latinas without the privilege of an education or the entrees into society that I have. For them life is a constant struggle against the misconceptions perpetuated by the myth of the Latina. My goal is to try to replace the old stereotypes with a much more interesting set of realities. Every time I give a reading, I hope the stories I tell, the dreams and fears I examine in my work, can achieve some universal truth that will get my audience past the particulars of my skin color, my accent, or my clothes.

14   I once wrote a poem in which I called all Latinas "God's brown daughters." This poem is really a prayer of sorts, offered upward, but also, through the human-to-human channel of art, outward. It is a prayer for communication and for respect. In it, Latin women pray "in Spanish to an Anglo God/with a Jewish heritage," and they are "fervently hoping/that if not omnipotent,/at least He be bilingual."

THINKING ABOUT THE TEXT

1. What is the author's strategy in opening her essay with the anecdote about the bus passenger singing to her? What does the author mean when she claims that "you can leave the island" and travel to distant places, "but if you are Latina . . . the island travels with you"? Do you think her awareness reflects the experience of members of other ethnicities as well?

2. Cofer describes the "cultural schizophrenia" of growing up in New Jersey but living in a home that reflected her family's Puerto Rican heritage. In which specific areas did this between-worlds schizophrenia appear?

3. The author is aware that most adolescents feel "out of step much of the time," but how did the codes of her Puerto Rican family intensify the separation she felt from the Anglo culture she lived in?

4. The author writes that "mixed cultural signals have perpetuated certain stereotypes" about the Hispanic woman. What are those stereotypes and how can they be perceived as dangerous as well as irritating? Why are the dress styles and behavior patterns of mothers who grew up on a tropical island not easily transported to a northern, urban society?

5. In addition to being identified with the Maria of *West Side Story* and Evita Peron, the author has also been assumed to be Maria the domestic. In her essay's conclusion, in what specific ways does Cofer use the anecdote about being presumed the waitress?

WRITING FROM THE TEXT

1. Write about a time when you or a friend were stereotyped because of how you looked, perhaps by your "gene pool" that travels with you. Were you amused, irritated, frightened? In your narrative, show how you were treated and how you felt. Review how to write a narrative (p. 409) for help in writing this essay.

2. Describe particular customs that you have observed in your family or the families of friends that seem to keep you or your friends "out of step" in the United States. Is a compromise in style possible or desirable, or is "cultural schizophrenia" inevitable? Perhaps that awareness will be a part of your conclusion.

3. Describe the myths that are attached to particular ethnicities, in a way similar to Cofer's observations of how Latinas are stereotyped as "sexual firebrands" or "domestics." In your analysis, speculate on the origins of the myths connected to certain groups, and in your conclusion speculate on the consequences of such stereotyping.

CONNECTING WITH OTHER TEXTS

1. Cofer's essay and the essays of Yasmine Bahrani (p. 158), Carmen Vazquez (p. 228), and Brent Staples (p. 237) deal with the problems of being perceived as other than one actually is. Write an essay that illustrates how frustrating and potentially dangerous it is to be stereotyped based on appearance. Use the specific experiences of the authors, as well as your own observations, to support your points.

2. Use films such as *Mississippi Massala*, *East Is East*, and *My Big Fat Greek Wedding*, as well as others that you know, to write about the "cultural schizophrenia" described by Judith Ortiz Cofer. Include specific statements from Cofer as well as detailed descriptions and analyses of scenes from the films.

3. In an essay argue that immigrant parents work against their children's assimilation and personal happiness by adhering to values and customs that don't transport to a different country. Use "The Good Daughter" (p. 20) and "The Myth of the Latin Woman" to support your point.

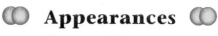

Appearances

Carmen Vazquez

Active in community awareness projects for years, Carmen Vazquez (b. 1949) codirects Promote the Vote, a registration project sponsored by community centers nationwide. She also serves as Director of Public Policy for the Lesbian and Gay Community Services Center in New York City. Her essays and book reviews have appeared in many publications. This essay was first printed in an anthology entitled *Homophobia: How We All Pay the Price* (1992).

1   North of Market Street and east of Twin Peaks, where you can see the white fog mushroom above San Francisco's hills, is a place called the Castro. Gay men, lesbians, and bisexuals stroll leisurely up and down the bustling streets. They jaywalk with abandon. Night and day they fill the cafés and bars, and on weekends they line up for a double feature of vintage classics at their ornate and beloved Castro theater.

2   The 24 bus line brings people into and out of the Castro. People from all walks of life ride the electric-powered coaches. They come from the opulence of San Francisco's Marina and the squalor of Bayview projects. The very gay Castro is in the middle of its route. Every day, boys in pairs or gangs from either end of the city board the bus for a ride through the Castro and a bit of fun. Sometimes their fun is fulfilled with passionately obscene derision: "Fucking cocksucking faggots." "Dyke cunts." "Diseased butt fuckers." Sometimes their fun is brutal.

3   Brian boarded the 24 Divisadero and handed his transfer to the driver one late June night. Epithets were fired at him the moment he turned for a seat. He slid his slight frame into an empty seat next to an old woman with silver blue hair who clutched her handbag and stared straight ahead. Brian stuffed his hands into the pockets of his worn brown bomber jacket and stared with her. He heard the flip of a skateboard in the back. The taunting shouts grew louder. "Faggot!" From the corner of his eye, he saw a beer bottle hurtling past the window and crash on the street. A man in his forties, wearing a Giants baseball cap and warmup jacket, yelled at the driver to stop the bus and get the hoodlums off. The bus driver ignored him and pulled out.

4   Brian dug his hands deeper into his pockets and clenched his jaw. It was just five stops to the top of the hill. When he got up to move toward the exit, the skateboard slammed into his gut and one kick followed another until every boy had got his kick in. Despite the plea of the passengers, the driver never called the police.

5   Brian spent a week in a hospital bed, afraid that he would never walk again. A lawsuit filed by Brian against the city states, "As claimant lay crumpled and bleeding on the floor of the bus, the bus driver tried to force claimant off the bus so that the driver could get off work and go home. Claimant was severely beaten by a gang of young men on the #24 Divisadero Bus who perceived that he was gay."

6   On the south side of Market Street, night brings a chill wind and rough trade. On a brisk November night, men with sculptured torsos and thighs

wrapped in leather walked with precision. The clamor of steel on the heels of their boots echoed in the darkness. Young men and women walked by the men in leather, who smiled in silence. They admired the studded bracelets on Mickey's wrists, the shine of his flowing hair, and the rise of his laughter. They were, each of them, eager to be among the safety of like company where they could dance with abandon to the pulse of hard rock, the hypnotism of disco, or the measured steps of country soul. They looked forward to a few drinks, flirting with strangers, finding Mr. or Ms. Right or, maybe, someone to spend the night with.

7   At the end of the street, a lone black street lamp shone through the mist. The men in leather walked under the light and disappeared into the next street. As they reached the corner, Mickey and his friends could hear the raucous sounds of the Garden spill into the street. They shimmied and rocked down the block and through the doors.

8   The Garden was packed with men and women in sweat-stained shirts. Blue smoke stung the eyes. The sour and sweet smell of beer hung in the air. Strobe lights pulsed over the dancers. Mickey pulled off his wash-faded black denim jacket and wrapped it around his waist. An iridescent blue tank top hung easy on his shoulders. Impatient with the wait for a drink, Mickey steered his girlfriend onto the crowded dance floor.

9   Reeling to the music and immersed in the pleasure of his rhythms, Mickey never saw the ice pick plunge into his neck. It was just a bump with a drunk yelling, "Lame-assed faggot." "Faggot. Faggot. Faggot. Punk faggot." Mickey thought it was a punch to the neck. He ran after the roaring drunk man for seven steps, then lurched and fell on the dance floor, blood gushing everywhere. His girlfriend screamed. The dance floor spun black.

10   Mickey was rushed to San Francisco General Hospital, where thirty-six stitches were used by trauma staff to close the wound on his neck. Doctors said the pick used in the attack against him was millimeters away from his spinal cord. His assailant, charged with attempted murder, pleaded innocent.

11   Mickey and Brian were unfortunate stand-ins for any gay man. Mickey was thin and wiry, a great dancer clad in black denim, earrings dangling from his ear. Brian was slight of build, wore a leather jacket, and boarded a bus in Castro. Dress like a homo, dance like a homo, must be a homo. The homophobic fury directed at lesbians, gay men, and bisexuals in America most often finds its target. Ironclad evidence of sexual orientation, however, is not necessary for someone to qualify as a potential victim of deadly fury. Appearances will do.

12   The incidents described above are based on actual events reported to the San Francisco Police and Community United Against Violence (CUAV), an

agency serving victims of antilesbian and antigay violence where I worked for four years. The names of the victims have been changed. Both men assaulted were straight.

13   Incidents of antilesbian and antigay violence are not uncommon or limited to San Francisco. A *San Francisco Examiner* survey estimates that over one million hate-motivated physical assaults take place each year against lesbians, gays, and bisexuals. The National Gay and Lesbian Task Force conducted a survey in 1984 that found that 94 percent of all lesbians and gay men surveyed reported being physically assaulted, threatened, or harassed in an antigay incident at one time or another. The great majority of these incidents go unreported.

14   To my knowledge, no agency other than CUAV keeps track of incidents of antigay violence involving heterosexuals as victims. An average of 3 percent of the over three hundred victims seen by CUAV each year identify as heterosexuals. This may or may not be an accurate gauge of the actual prevalence of antigay violence directed at heterosexuals. Most law enforcement agencies, including those in San Francisco, have no way of documenting this form of assault other than under a generic "harassment" code. The actual incidence of violence directed at heterosexuals that is motivated by homophobia is probably much higher than CUAV's six to nine victims a year. Despite the official paucity of data, however, it is a fact that incidents of antigay and antilesbian violence in which straight men and women are victimized do occur. Shelters for battered women are filled with stories of lesbian baiting of staff and of women whose husbands and boyfriends repeatedly called them "dykes" or "whores" as they beat them. I have personally experienced verbal abuse while in the company of a straight friend, who was assumed to be my lover.

15   Why does it happen? I have no definitive answers to that question. Understanding homophobic violence is no less complex than understanding racial violence. The institutional and ideological reinforcements of homophobia are myriad and deeply woven into our culture. I offer one perspective that I hope will contribute to a better understanding of how homophobia works and why it threatens all that we value as humane.

16   At the simplest level, looking or behaving like the stereotypical gay man or lesbian is reason enough to provoke a homophobic assault. Beneath the veneer of the effeminate gay male or the butch dyke, however, is a more basic trigger for homophobic violence. I call it *gender betrayal*.

17   The clearest expression I have heard of this sense of gender betrayal comes from Doug Barr, who was acquitted of murder in an incident of gay bashing in San Francisco that resulted in the death of John O'Connell, a gay

man. Barr is currently serving a prison sentence for related assaults on the same night that O'Connell was killed. He was interviewed for a special report on homophobia produced by ABC's *20/20* (10 April 1986). When asked what he and his friends thought of gay men, he said, "We hate homosexuals. They degrade our manhood. We was brought up in a high school where guys are football players, mean and macho. Homosexuals are sissies who wear dresses. I'd rather be seen as a football player."

18 Doug Barr's perspective is one shared by many young men. I have made about three hundred presentations to high school students in San Francisco, to boards of directors and staff of nonprofit organizations, and at conferences and workshops on the topic of homophobia or "being lesbian or gay." Over and over again, I have asked, "Why do gay men and lesbians bother you?" The most popular response to the question is, "Because they act like girls," or, "Because they think they're men." I have even been told, quite explicitly, "I don't care what they do in bed, but they shouldn't act like that."

19 They shouldn't act like that. Women who are not identified by their relationship to a man, who value their female friendships, who like and are knowledgeable about sports, or work as blue-collar laborers and wear what they wish are very likely to be "lesbian baited" at some point in their lives. Men who are not pursuing sexual conquests of women at every available opportunity, who disdain sports, who choose to stay at home and be a househusband, who are employed as hairdressers, designers, or housecleaners, or who dress in any way remotely resembling traditional female attire (an earring will do) are very likely to experience the taunts and sometimes the brutality of "fag bashing."

20 The straitjacket of gender roles suffocates many lesbians, gay men, and bisexuals, forcing them into closets without an exit and threatening our very existence when we tear the closet open. It also, however, threatens all heterosexuals unwilling to be bound by their assigned gender identify. Why, then, does it persist?

21 In *Homophobia: A Weapon of Sexism*, Suzanne Pharr examines homophobia as a phenomenon based in sexism and misogyny and offers a succinct and logical explanation for the violence of homophobia in Western civilization:

> It is not by chance that when children approach puberty and increased sexual awareness they begin to taunt each other by calling these names: "queer," "faggot," "pervert." It is at puberty that the full force of society's pressure to conform to heterosexuality and prepare for marriage is brought to bear. Children know what we have taught them, and we have given clear messages that those who deviate from standard expectations are to be made to get back in line. . . .

To be named as lesbian threatens all women, not just lesbians, with great loss. And any woman who steps out of role risks being called a lesbian. To understand how this is a threat to all women, one must understand that any woman can be called a lesbian and there is no real way she can defend herself: there is no real way to credential one's sexuality. (*The Children's Hour*, a Lillian Hellman play, makes this point when a student asserts two teachers are lesbians and they have no way to disprove it.) She may be married or divorced, have children, dress in the most feminine manner, have sex with men, be celibate—but there are lesbians who do all these things. *Lesbians look like all women and all women look like lesbians.*

I would add that gay men look like all men and all men look like gay men. There is no guaranteed method for identifying sexual orientation. Those small or outrageous deviations we sometimes take from the idealized mystique of "real men" and "real women" place all of us—lesbians, gay men, bisexuals, and heterosexuals alike—at risk of violence, derision, isolation, and hatred.

22   It is a frightening reality. Dorothy Ehrlich, executive director of the Northern California American Civil Liberties Union (ACLU), was the victim of a verbal assault in the Castro several years ago. Dorothy lives with her husband, Gary, and her two children, Jill and Paul, in one of those worn and comfortable Victorian homes that grace so many San Francisco neighborhoods. Their home is several blocks from the Castro, but Dorothy recalls the many times she and Gary could hear, from the safety of their bedroom, shouts of "faggot" and men running in the streets.

23   When Jill was an infant, Gary and Dorothy had occasion to experience for themselves how frightening even the threat of homophobic violence can be. One foggy, chilly night they decided to go for a walk in the Castro. Dorothy is a small woman whom some might call petite; she wore her hair short at the time and delights in the comfort of jeans and oversized wool jackets. Gary is very tall and lean, a bespectacled and bearded cross between a professor and a basketball player who wears jean jackets and tweed jackets with the exact same slouch. On this night they were crossing Castro Street, huddled close together with Jill in Dorothy's arms. As they reached the corner, their backs to the street, they heard a truck rev its engine and roar up Castro, the dreaded "faggot" spewing from young men they could not see in the fog. They looked around them for the intended victims, but there was no one else on the corner with them. They were the target that night: Dorothy and Gary and Jill. They were walking on "gay turf," and it was reason enough to make them a target. "It was so frightening," Dorothy said. "So frightening and unreal."

24   But it is real. The *20/20* report on homophobia ends with the story of Tom and Jan Matarrase, who are married, have a child, and lived in Brooklyn, New York, at the time of their encounter with homophobic violence. On camera, Tom and Jan are walking down a street in Brooklyn lined with brown townhouses and black wrought-iron gates. It is snowing, and, with hands entwined, they walk slowly down the street where they were assaulted. Tom is wearing a khaki trenchcoat, slacks, and loafers. Snowflakes melt into the tight curls on his head. Jan is almost his height, her short bobbed hair moving softly as she walks. She is wearing a black leather jacket, a red scarf, and burnt orange cords. The broadness of her hips and softness of her face belie the tomboy flavor of her carriage and clothes, and it is hard to believe that she was mistaken for a gay man. But she was.

25   They were walking home, holding hands and engrossed with each other. On the other side of the street, Jan saw a group of boys moving toward them. As the gang approached, Jan heard a distinct taunt meant for her and Tom: "Aw, look at the cute gay couple." Tom and Jan quickened their step, but it was too late. Before they could say anything, Tom was being punched in the face and slammed against a car. Jan ran toward Tom and the car, screaming desperately that Tom was her husband. Fists pummeled her face as well. Outnumbered and in fear for their lives, Tom yelled at Jan to please open her jacket and show their assailants that she was a woman. The beating subsided only when Jan was able to show her breasts.

26   For the *20/20* interview, Jan and Tom sat in the warmth of their living room, their infant son in Jan's lap. The interviewer asked them how they felt when people said they looked like a gay couple. "We used to laugh," they said. "But now we realize how heavy the implications are. Now we know what the gay community goes through. We had no idea how widespread it was. It's on every level."

27   Sadly, it *is* on every level. Enforced heterosexism and the pressure to conform to aggressive masculine and passive feminine roles place fag bashers and lesbian baiters in the same psychic prison with their victims, gay or straight. Until all children are free to realize their full potential, until all women and men are free from the stigma, threats, alienation, or violence that come from stepping outside their roles, we are all at risk.

28   The economic and ideological underpinnings of enforced heterosexism and sexism or any other form of systematic oppression are formidable foes and far too complex for the scope of this essay. It is important to remember, however, that bigots are natural allies and that poverty or the fear of it has the power to seduce us all into conformity. In Castro graffiti, *faggot* appears right next to *nigger* and *kike*. Race betrayal or any threat to the sanctimony of light-skinned privilege engenders no less a rage than gender betrayal, most espe-

cially when we have a great stake in the elusive privilege of proper gender roles or the right skin color. *Queer lover* and *fag hag* are cut from the same mold that gave us *nigger lover*, a mold forged by fears of change and a loss of privilege.

29   Unfortunately, our sacrifices to conformity rarely guarantee the privilege or protection we were promised. Lesbians, gay men, and bisexuals who have tried to pass know that. Heterosexuals who have been perceived to be gay know that. Those of us with a vision of tomorrow that goes beyond tolerance to a genuine celebration of humanity's diversity have innumerable fronts to fight on. Homophobia is one of them.

30   But how will this front be won? With a lot of help, and not easily. Challenges to homophobia and the rigidity of gender roles must go beyond the visible lesbian and gay movement. Lesbians, gay men, and bisexuals alone cannot defuse the power of stigmatization and the license it gives to frighten, wound, or kill. Literally millions of us are needed on this front, straight and gay alike. We invite any heterosexual unwilling to live with the damage that "real men" or "real women" messages wreak on them, on their children, and on lesbians, gay men, and bisexuals to join us. We ask that you not let queer jokes go unchallenged at work, at home, in the media, or anywhere. We ask that you foster in your children a genuine respect for themselves and their right to be who and what they wish to be, regardless of their gender. We ask that you embrace your daughter's desire to swing a bat or be a carpenter, that you nurture your son's efforts to express affection and sentiment. We ask that you teach your children how painful and destructive words like *faggot* or *bulldyke* are. We ask that you invite your lesbian, gay, and bisexual friends and relatives into the routine of your lives without demanding silence or discretion from them. We invite you to study our history, read the literature written by our people, patronize our businesses, come into our homes and neighborhoods. We ask that you give us your vote when we need it to protect our privacy or to elect open lesbians, gay men, and bisexuals to office. We ask that you stand with us in public demonstrations to demand our right to live as free people, without fear. We ask that you respect our dignity by acting to end the poison of homophobia.

31   Until individuals are free to choose their roles and be bound only by the limits of their own imagination, *faggot*, *dyke*, and *pervert* will continue to be playground words and adult weapons that hurt and limit far many more people than their intended victims. Whether we like it or not, the romance of virile men and dainty women, of Mother, Father, Dick, Jane, Sally, and Spot is doomed to extinction and dangerous in a world that can no longer meet the expectations conjured by history. There is much to be won and so little to lose in the realization of a world where the dignity of each person is worthy of celebration and protection. The struggle to end homophobia can and must be won, for all our sakes. Personhood is imminent.

THINKING ABOUT THE TEXT

1. Analyze Vazquez's use of narration in her opening paragraphs. Does her description of the Castro district and the Garden prepare us for the violence that follows?

2. Describe the attacks on "Brian" and on "Mickey." Why does Vazquez delay informing readers of their sexual orientation? Does the information make you feel differently about the attacks?

3. Explain what Vazquez means by "gender betrayal." Do you agree that the "straitjacket of gender roles" threatens not only homosexuals but all heterosexuals unwilling to be bound by their "assigned gender identity"? Support your answer.

4. Vazquez refers to Suzanne Pharr's claim that homophobia is "based in sexism and misogyny"—the hatred of women—because any woman can be called a lesbian and "there is no way to credential one's sexuality." Discuss this assertion and Vazquez's application of it to men as well, claiming that "gay men look like all men and all men look like gay men." Illustrate this claim with details from the essay about the two couples who were attacked.

5. Asserting that "challenges to homophobia and the rigidity of gender roles must go beyond the visible lesbian and gay movement," Vazquez outlines a proposal asking all readers for assistance. Specify her requests and her ultimate objective.

WRITING FROM THE TEXT

1. Write an evaluative response of "Appearances," examining Vazquez's thesis, support, and suggestions. See pages 419–425 for help developing this paper and including specific observations from your own experiences and from this essay.

2. In an essay analyze the "mixed methods" (see pp. 401–403) that Vazquez uses to support her thesis. Examine her use of narration, description, definition, comparison-contrast, cause and effect, argument, and analysis. Illustrate the various examples of these methods and her strategy for using each as she does.

CONNECTING WITH OTHER TEXTS

1. Vazquez insists that "bigots are natural allies and that poverty or the fear of it has the power to seduce us all into conformity" (234). Write an analysis of the causes and effects of conformity, using information from "Appearances" and "In Groups We Shrink" (p. 277).

2. Focusing on specific support from "Appearances" and "Black Men and Public Space" (p. 237), write a comparison-contrast essay about homophobic violence and racial violence.

3. Write an analysis of the "straitjacket of gender roles" (p. xxx), using illustrations from "Appearances" and two other essays: "Real Men Don't: Anti-Male Bias in English" (p. 71), "The Second Shift" (p. 84), "Pigskin, Patriarchy, and Pain" (p. 101), "Body of Evidence" (p. 258), or "Bodily Harm" (p. 250).

Black Men and Public Space

Brent Staples

After earning his Ph.D. in psychology from the University of Chicago, Brent Staples (b. 1951) worked at the *Chicago Sun-Times* and wrote for other periodicals. He became an assistant metropolitan editor of the *New York Times* in 1985, and he is presently on that paper's editorial board. In his book *Parallel Time: Growing up in Black and White* (1994), Staples writes about his poor childhood and his present position at the *Times*. Staples says he "despises" the expression "the black experience," and insists that "Black people's lives in this country are too varied to be reduced to a single term." He says that he is writing about "universal themes—family and leaving home and developing your own identity. . . . Being black enriches my experience; it doesn't define me." The essay included here was first published in the September 1986 issue of *Ms.* magazine as one article in a section on men's perspectives.

1   My first victim was a woman—white, well dressed, probably in her early twenties. I came upon her late one evening on a deserted street in Hyde Park, a relatively affluent neighborhood in an otherwise mean, impoverished section of Chicago. As I swung onto the avenue behind her, there seemed to be a discreet, uninflammatory distance between us. Not so. She cast back a worried glance. To her, the youngish black man—a broad six feet two inches with a beard and billowing hair, both hands shoved into the pockets of a bulky military jacket—seemed menacingly close. After a few more quick glimpses, she picked up her pace and was soon running in earnest. Within seconds she disappeared into a cross street.

2   That was more than a decade ago. I was twenty-two years old, a graduate student newly arrived at the University of Chicago. It was in the echo of that terrified woman's footfalls that I first began to know the unwieldy inheritance I'd come into—the ability to alter public space in ugly ways. It was clear that she thought herself the quarry of a mugger, a rapist, or worse. Suffering a

bout of insomnia, however, I was stalking sleep, not defenseless wayfarers. As a softy who is scarcely able to take a knife to a raw chicken—let alone hold it to a person's throat—I was surprised, embarrassed, and dismayed all at once. Her flight made me feel like an accomplice in tyranny. It also made it clear that I was indistinguishable from the muggers who occasionally seeped into the area from the surrounding ghetto. That first encounter, and those that followed, signified that a vast, unnerving gulf lay between nighttime pedestrians—particularly women—and me. And I soon gathered that being perceived as dangerous is a hazard in itself. I only needed to turn a corner into a dicey situation, or crowd some frightened, armed person in a foyer somewhere, or make an errant move after being pulled over by a policeman. Where fear and weapons meet—and they often do in urban America—there is always the possibility of death.

3   In that first year, my first away from my hometown, I was to become thoroughly familiar with the language of fear. At dark, shadowy intersections in Chicago, I could cross in front of a car stopped at a traffic light and elicit the *thunk, thunk, thunk, thunk* of the driver—black, white, male, or female—hammering down the door locks. On less traveled streets after dark, I grew accustomed to but never comfortable with people who crossed to the other side of the street rather than pass me. Then there were the standard unpleasantries with police, doormen, bouncers, cab drivers, and others whose business it is to screen out troublesome individuals *before* there is any nastiness.

4   I moved to New York nearly two years ago and I have remained an avid night walker. In central Manhattan, the near-constant crowd cover minimizes tense one-on-one street encounters. Elsewhere—visiting friends in SoHo, where sidewalks are narrow and tightly spaced buildings shut out the sky—things can get very taut indeed.

5   Black men have a firm place in New York mugging literature. Norman Podhoretz in his famed (or infamous) 1963 essay, "My Negro Problem—And Ours," recalls growing up in terror of black males, they "were tougher than we were, more ruthless," he writes—and as an adult on the Upper West Side of Manhattan, he continues, he cannot constrain his nervousness when he meets black men on certain streets. Similarly, a decade later, the essayist and novelist Edward Hoagland extols a New York where once "Negro bitterness bore down mainly on other Negroes." Where some see mere panhandlers, Hoagland sees "a mugger who is clearly screwing up his nerve to do more than just *ask* for money." But Hoagland has "the New Yorker's quick-hunch posture for broken-field maneuvering," and the bad guy swerves away.

6   I often witness that "hunch posture," from women after dark on the warrenlike streets of Brooklyn where I live. They seem to set their faces on neutral and, with their purse straps strung across their chests bandolier style,

they forge ahead as though bracing themselves against being tackled. I understand, of course, that the danger they perceive is not a hallucination. Women are particularly vulnerable to street violence, and young black males are drastically overrepresented among the perpetrators of that violence. Yet these truths are no solace against the kind of alienation that comes of being ever the suspect, against being set apart, a fearsome entity with whom pedestrians avoid making eye contact.

7   It is not altogether clear to me how I reached the ripe old age of twenty-two without being conscious of the lethality nighttime pedestrians attributed to me. Perhaps it was because in Chester, Pennsylvania, the small, angry industrial town where I came of age in the 1960s, I was scarcely noticeable against a backdrop of gang warfare, street knifings, and murders. I grew up one of the good boys, had perhaps a half-dozen fist fights. In retrospect, my shyness of combat has clear sources.

8   Many things go into the making of a young thug. One of those things is the consummation of the male romance with the power to intimidate. An infant discovers that random flailings send the baby bottle flying out of the crib and crashing to the floor. Delighted, the joyful babe repeats those motions again and again, seeking to duplicate the feat. Just so, I recall the points at which some of my boyhood friends were finally seduced by the perception of themselves as tough guys. When a mark cowered and surrendered his money without resistance, myth and reality merged—and paid off. It is, after all, only manly to embrace the power to frighten and intimidate. We, as men, are not supposed to give an inch of our lane on the highway; we are to seize the fighter's edge in work and in play and even in love; we are to be valiant in the face of hostile forces.

9   Unfortunately, poor and powerless young men seem to take all this nonsense literally. As a boy, I saw countless tough guys locked away; I have since buried several, too. They were babies, really—a teenage cousin, a brother of twenty-two, a childhood friend in his mid-twenties—all gone down in episodes of bravado played out in the streets. I came to doubt the virtues of intimidation early on. I chose, perhaps even unconsciously, to remain a shadow—timid, but a survivor.

10   The fearsomeness mistakenly attributed to me in public places often has a perilous flavor. The most frightening of these confusions occurred in the late 1970s and early 1980s when I worked as a journalist in Chicago. One day, rushing into the office of a magazine I was writing for with a deadline story in hand, I was mistaken for a burglar. The office manager called security and, with an ad hoc posse, pursued me through the labyrinthine halls, nearly to my editor's door. I had no way of proving who I was. I could only move briskly toward the company of someone who knew me.

11   Another time I was on assignment for a local paper and killing time before an interview. I entered a jewelry store on the city's affluent Near North Side. The proprietor excused herself and returned with an enormous red Doberman pinscher straining at the end of a leash. She stood, the dog extended toward me, silent to my questions, her eyes bulging nearly out of her head. I took a cursory look around, nodded, and bade her good night. Relatively speaking, however, I never fared as badly as another black male journalist. He went to nearby Waukegan, Illinois, a couple of summers ago to work on a story about a murderer who was born there. Mistaking the reporter for the killer, police hauled him from his car at gunpoint and but for his press credentials would probably have tried to book him. Such episodes are not uncommon. Black men trade tales like this all the time.

12   In "My Negro Problem—And Ours," Podhoretz writes that the hatred he feels for blacks makes itself known to him through a variety of avenues— one being his discomfort with that "special brand of paranoid touchiness" to which he says blacks are prone. No doubt he is speaking here of black men. In time, I learned to smother the rage I felt at so often being taken for a criminal. Not to do so would surely have led to madness—via that special "paranoid touchiness" that so annoyed Podhoretz at the time he wrote the essay.

13   I began to take precautions to make myself less threatening. I move about with care, particularly late in the evening. I give a wide berth to nervous people on subway platforms during the wee hours, particularly when I have exchanged business clothes for jeans. If I happen to be entering a building behind some people who appear skittish, I may walk by, letting them clear the lobby before I return, so as not to seem to be following them. I have been calm and extremely congenial on those rare occasions when I've been pulled over by the police.

14   And on late-evening constitutionals along streets less traveled by, I employ what has proved to be an excellent tension-reducing measure: I whistle melodies from Beethoven and Vivaldi and the more popular classical composers. Even steely New Yorkers hunching toward nighttime destinations seem to relax, and occasionally they even join in the tune. Virtually everybody seems to sense that a mugger wouldn't be warbling bright, sunny selections from Vivaldi's *Four Seasons*. It is my equivalent of the cowbell that hikers wear when they know they are in bear country.

THINKING ABOUT THE TEXT

1. What is the effect on the reader of Staples's opening paragraph? How does it function to underscore the point of his essay?

2. In what places is Staples's effect on people related to his being black? Where is his maleness and/or stature a threat? Which aspect of his physiology does Staples believe is more threatening?

3. How has Staples adjusted his life to make himself less intimidating?

Writing from the Text

1. Write about a time when you unwittingly threatened someone. Describe the occasion using Staples's essay as a model, so that your reader can see and *hear* (*"thunk, thunk, thunk, thunk"*) the scene.

2. Write an essay in which you describe the problems of being stereotyped as a member of a group that is perceived as threatening. What, if anything, have you done to counter or handle the dangerously charged or uncomfortable environment?

3. Write an essay describing the problem of being intimidated by a group or a member of a group. What have you done to avoid feeling intimidated or threatened?

Connecting with Other Texts

1. Read "Proper Care and Maintenance" (p. 186) and compare Darnell's history, attitudes, and behavior with those of Brent Staples's. Show how the choices they make to adjust to their environments are required for survival.

2. Find periodical articles that feature the stories of African-Americans or Hispanics who have been stereotyped by the police, bouncers, or doormen as muggers, criminals, or gang members. Write an essay that uses the specific examples in the articles for support.

Mr. Z

M. Carl Holman

A poet, professor, and civil rights activist, M. Carl Holman (1919–1988) taught at Clark College in Atlanta, Georgia, from 1949 to 1962. He also worked as an editor on the *Atlanta Inquirer* and was on the U.S. Commission for Civil Rights. He served as president of the National Urban Coalition from 1971 until his death in 1988. Throughout his life, he won numerous awards for public service and for his poetry. The following poem, written in 1967, demonstrates his ability to meld his two passions—poetry and civil rights.

Taught early that his mother's skin was the sign of error,
He dressed and spoke the perfect part of honor;
Won scholarships, attended the best schools.
Disclaimed kinship with jazz and spirituals;
5   Chose prudent, raceless views for each situation.
Or when he could not cleanly skirt dissension.
Faced up to the dilemma, firmly seized
Whatever ground was Anglo-Saxonized.

In diet, too, his practice was exemplary;
10   Of pork in its profane forms he was wary;
Expert in vintage wines, sauces and salads.
His palate shrank from cornbread, yams and collards.

He was as careful whom he chose to kiss;
His bride had somewhere lost her Jewishness.
15   But kept her blue eyes; an Episcopalian
Prelate proclaimed them matched chameleon.
Choosing the right addresses, here, abroad,
They shunned those places where they might be barred;
Even less anxious to be asked to dine
20   Where hosts catered to kosher accent or exotic skin.
And so he climbed, unclogged by ethnic weights,
An airborne plant, flourishing without roots.
Not one false note was struck—until he died;
His subtly grieving widow could have flayed
25   The obit writers, ringing crude changes on a clumsy phrase:
"One of the most distinguished members of his race."

THINKING ABOUT THE TEXT

1. The opening line reveals that Mr. Z was "taught early that his mother's skin was the sign of error," as if it were a mistake, something to correct or avoid. Why does the poet emphasize that he was "taught" this? How can the reader be sure what "his mother's skin" symbolizes? What does he shun?

2. List all the details that support the poet's claim that Mr. Z "dressed and spoke the perfect part of honor." What does "perfect part" imply? What are other words used to show that every decision is calculated?

3. How does Mr. Z's bride seem ideal for him? What is she denying and avoiding? Why are they described as "matched chameleon"? What is telling

about the contrast in the emotion that she exhibits over his death and the emotion that she feels for the "obit writers" who change his obituary?

4. Explain the significance of these lines: "And so he climbed, unclogged by ethnic weights, / An airborne plant, flourishing without roots."

5. How is this poem a satire and what is the poet satirizing?

6. Irony is key to this poem. The poem reads like a list of praises, but what is the attitude of the poet toward Mr. Z? How can the reader be sure? Explain the irony in the last line.

7. What are possible meanings related to the name, "Mr. Z"? How is this name ironic?

WRITING FROM THE TEXT

1. Write an analysis of the use of irony in "Mr. Z." (See poetry analysis, pp. 475–483) Include specific images for support and analyze them fully.

2. Focusing on "Mr. Z," write an essay about any experiences that you or someone close to you has had denying his or her heritage. Were the successes worth the sacrifices? Can you infer Holman's view on this?

CONNECTING WITH OTHER TEXTS

1. Read "The Myth of the Latin Woman" (p. 223) and contrast the author's self-concept and values with those of Mr. Z. In your essay try to account for these differences.

2. Read "Black Men and Public Space" (p. 237) and compare Brent Staple's "solution" to being misperceived by others with the choices that Mr. Z makes. Compare and contrast their motives and their acceptance of their identity.

Discrimination at Large
Jennifer A. Coleman

A graduate of Boston College Law School, Jennifer A. Coleman (b. 1959) is a discrimination and civil rights lawyer in Buffalo, New York. Coleman wrote the essay printed here after seeing the film *Jurassic Park:* "The only bad person in the film is fat, and I'm tired of the stereotyping—which nobody objects to—that makes heavy people objects of ridicule and contempt." In addition to writing legal briefs, pleadings, letters, and a law review article, Coleman teaches constitutional law at Canisius College in Buffalo. The essay that follows first appeared in *Newsweek* in 1993.

1   Fat is the last preserve for unexamined bigotry. Fat people are lampooned without remorse or apology on television, by newspaper columnists, in cartoons, you name it. The overweight are viewed as suffering from moral turpitude and villainy, and since we are at fault for our condition, no tolerance is due. All fat people are "outed" by their appearance.

2   Weight-motivated assaults occur daily and are committed by people who would die before uttering anti-gay slogans or racial epithets. Yet these same people don't hesitate to scream "move your fat ass" when we cross in front of them.

3   Since the time I first ventured out to play with the neighborhood kids, I was told over and over that I was lazy and disgusting. Strangers, adults, classmates offered gratuitous comments with such frequency and urgency that I started to believe them. Much later I needed to prove it wasn't so. I began a regimen of swimming, cycling and jogging that put all but the most compulsive to shame. I ate only cottage cheese, brown rice, fake butter and steamed everything. I really believed I could infiltrate the ranks of the nonfat and thereby establish my worth.

4   I would prove that I was not just a slob, a blimp, a pig. I would finally escape the unsolicited remarks of strangers ranging from the "polite"—"You would really be pretty if you lost weight"—to the hostile ("Lose weight, you fat slob"). Of course, sometimes more subtle commentary sufficed: oinking, mooing, staring, laughing and pointing. Simulating a fog-horn was also popular.

5   My acute exercise phase had many positive points. I was mingling with my obsessively athletic peers. My pulse was as low as anyone's, my cholesterol levels in the basement, my respiration barely detectable. I could swap stats from my last physical with anyone. Except for weight. No matter how hard I tried to run, swim or cycle away from it, my weight found me. Oh sure, I lost weight (never enough) and it inevitably tracked me down and adhered to me more tenaciously than ever. I lived and breathed "Eat to win," "Feel the burn." But in the end I was fit and still fat.

6   I learned that by societal, moral, ethical, soap-operatical, vegetable, political definition, it was impossible to be both fit and fat. Along the way to that knowledge, what I got for my trouble was to be hit with objects from moving cars because I dared to ride my bike in public, and to be mocked by diners at outdoor cafés who trumpeted like a herd of elephants as I jogged by. Incredibly, it was not uncommon for one of them to shout: "Lose some weight, you pig." Go figure.

7   It was confusing for a while. How was it I was still lazy, weak, despised, a slug and a cow if I exercised every waking minute? This confusion persisted

until I finally realized: it didn't matter what I did. I was and always would be the object of sport, derision, antipathy and hostility so long as I stayed in my body. I immediately signed up for a body transplant. I am still waiting for a donor.

8 Until then, I am more settled because I have learned the hard way what thin people have known for years. There simply are some things that fat people must never do. Like: riding a bike ("Hey lady, where's the seat?"), eating in a public place ("No dessert for me, I don't want to look like her"). And the most unforgivable crime: wearing a bathing suit in public ("Whale on the beach!").

9 Things are less confusing now that I know that the nonfat are superior to me, regardless of their personal habits, health, personalities, cholesterol levels or the time they log on the couch. And, as obviously superior to me as they are, it is their destiny to remark on my inferiority regardless of who I'm with, whether they know me, whether it hurts my feelings. I finally understand that the thin have a divine mandate to steal self-esteem from fat people, who have no right to it in the first place.

10 Fat people aren't really jolly. Sometimes we act that way so you will leave us alone. We pay a price for this. But at least we get to hang on to what self-respect we smuggled out of grade school and adolescence.

11 Hating fat people is not inborn; it has to be nurtured and developed. Fortunately, it's taught from the moment most of us are able to walk and speak. We learn it through Saturday-morning cartoons, prime-time TV and movies. Have you ever seen a fat person in a movie who wasn't evil, disgusting, pathetic or lampooned? Santa Claus doesn't count.

12 Kids catch on early to be sensitive to the feelings of gay, black, disabled, elderly and speech-impaired people. At the same time, they learn that fat people are fair game. That we are always available for their personal amusement.

13 The media, legal system, parents, teachers and peers respond to most types of intolerance with outrage and protest. Kids hear that employers can be sued for discriminating, that political careers can be destroyed and baseball owners can lose their teams as a consequence of racism, sexism or almost any other "ism."

14 But the fat kid is taught that she deserves to be mocked. She is not OK. Only if she loses weight will she be OK. Other kids see the response and incorporate the message. Small wonder some (usually girls) get it into their heads that they can never be thin enough.

15 I know a lot about prejudice, even though I am a white, middle-class, professional woman. The worst discrimination I have suffered because of my

gender is nothing compared to what I experience daily because of my weight. I am sick of it. The jokes and attitudes are as wrong and damaging as any racial or ethnic slur. The passive acceptance of this inexcusable behavior is sometimes worse than the initial assault. Some offensive remarks can be excused as the shortcomings of jackasses. But the tacit acceptance of their conduct by mainstream America tells the fat person that the intolerance is understandable and acceptable. Well it isn't.

THINKING ABOUT THE TEXT

1. Jennifer Coleman's focus is evident from the first paragraph of her essay. After you have read the entire essay, what do you assume is her thesis or complete assertion?

2. What is the author's personal history, and how does knowing her background contribute to your understanding of her point?

3. *Are* the jokes and slurs about overweight people "as wrong and damaging as any racial or ethnic slur"?

4. Examine Coleman's word choice in this essay. Which words and expressions specifically contribute to her making her point powerfully?

5. What are *your* feelings as you read the comments that people have made to and about Coleman?

WRITING FROM THE TEXT

1. Write an essay arguing that discrimination against the overweight is "as wrong and damaging as any racial or ethnic slur." You will want to anticipate and counter the objection that people don't *have* to be overweight.

2. Describe the character traits, habits, and values of an overweight person you know. Let the description in your essay *show* what kinds of discrimination and problems your subject has faced.

CONNECTING WITH OTHER TEXTS

1. Body image is a particular preoccupation for many women and, according to Rachel Krell (p. 382), the world associates a thin body with beauty. Write an essay that argues that Jennifer Coleman has virtues that we admire even though she is not thin.

2. Write an essay contrasting the purpose and voice of Jennifer Coleman and Neil Steinberg, in the following essay. You might want to review the comparison/contrast method (p. 439).

3. Use Heilbroner's essay on stereotyping (p. 469) as a definitive starting point for a descriptive essay on the discrimination that overweight people experience. You might contrast specific stereotypical depictions of overweight people in films and on television with an overweight person you know.

O.K., So I'm Fat
Neil Steinberg

A graduate of Northwestern University, Neil Steinberg (b. 1960) has written a column for the *Chicago Sun-Times* for fourteen years. He is the author of *Complete and Utter Failure* and *If at All Possible, Involve a Cow: The Book of College Pranks*. His work has also appeared in *Rolling Stone, Esquire, Sports Illustrated, Eating Well*, and the *National Lampoon*, where he was a contributing editor. The following essay is the chapter "'F' Is For Fat" from Steinberg's book *The Alphabet of Modern Annoyances*. Steinberg says he enjoys "writing about things people have trouble articulating—personal things, but not too personal."

1   Some people are no doubt fat because of glandular disorders or the wrath of an angry God. I am not one of those people. I am fat because I eat a lot.

2   Since fat people are held in such low regard, I should immediately point out that I am not *that* fat. Not fat in the Chinese Buddha, spilling-out-of-the-airplane-seat sense. The neighborhood kids don't skip behind me in the street, banging tin cans together and singing derisive songs.

3   Not yet, anyway.

4   But forget the social stigma of being fat. Ignore the medical peril, the sheer discomfort of dragging all that excess weight around. There is still a final ignominy almost too dire to mention: thin people.

5   All the drawbacks of being overweight could be shucked off—the fat are good at denial—were it not for the standing rebuke and constant insult that thin people offer, sometimes intentionally, sometimes simply by their very existence.

6   "Hey, big guy"—I get that a lot, from overly familiar office mates and, especially, from wiry panhandlers, as if it were a compliment that would inspire me to dig for change. Worse are those bent on my elevation to the sainted ranks of the thin: the sly references to fad diets, the inspirational tales of heroic weight loss. "Can I get you something?" a good friend I was visiting asked. "A Diet Coke, maybe?"

7   Others assume that thinness is forever beyond my grasp. I was once at a dinner party where the hostess was a wisp of a woman with legs like beef

jerky. She prepared some intensely fattening dessert—Bananas Foster, thick slices of ripe bananas awash in butter and sugar and cinnamon and liqueur accompanied by ice cream. The concoction was set before us. I was halfway finished and already thinking about seconds when I noticed that she wasn't eating. I challenged her, nicely. "This is great. Aren't you having any?" She fluttered her eyes and demurred. Oh, no, she said, too sweet, too fattening. And she smiled. A halo didn't form over her head, but it might as well have. The smile said it all—smug superiority, gazing down from on high.

8   I wanted to take my Bananas Foster and grind her face in it. She wasn't having any because it was bad for her. Bad for her, but fine for her piggish guests to ruin themselves on. "Here's some poison I whipped up for you. Bon appetit!"

9   Thanks.

10   That moment of shame and surprise—cheeks packed hamster-full with Bananas Foster while numbly confronting the iron resolve of your moral betters—is the heart of the fat experience. The yin of the primal pleasure of satiation, lips closing happily down on the tip of a thick triangle of stuffed Chicago pizza, balanced against the yang of stunned realization, as the mental fog parts for a moment and you catch sight of yourself in the mirror and see what's really there.

11   Small wonder we get mad at those who keep themselves in check. Envy-stoked anger is natural when dessert suddenly turns into a little lesson about restraint, a lesson I have endured for years but somehow never absorbed or profited by.

12   Surprisingly, I have less trouble with thin people who don't need to think about their weight. Those who are thin despite having eating habits that, if I practiced them, would quickly turn me into one of those elephantine men who periodically turn up on the news, dressed in sheets, removed from their homes through a hole in the wall, quickly weighed on a freight scale for the record, then placed under the personal care of Dick Gregory.

13   My wife's friend Larry, for instance, dresses in those tapered Italian suits and doesn't have enough fat on his body to make a butter pat. He actually keeps big bowls of candy scattered around his house. Not just for show. He'll casually dig his hand up to the wrist into one of the bowls, pull out a fistful of M & Ms and, tilting his head back, funnel them into his mouth.

14   Trim as a pencil. Yet, paradoxically, I find it easy to be around Larry. I'm comfortable, happy, never put off. Maybe it's because those who are effortlessly thin seem to suggest that thinness is a fluke of capricious fate, and thus out of our control. Maybe it's because Larry doesn't exhibit any of the self-control that I, in my greedy-puppy-fat-person way, would egoistically interpret as a reproach.

15   Or maybe it's just because he has all that candy scattered around his house.

THINKING ABOUT THE TEXT

1. Reread the first paragraph and identify the specific ways that Steinberg establishes his stance toward the subject matter, his personal voice, and his purpose in writing the essay.

2. In spite of the humor in this essay, the author *is* making a point. What is it? What is the "final ignominy" that fat people must tolerate?

3. What are people's diverse responses to Steinberg's weight?

4. If Steinberg's tone and purpose were not to amuse, his thesis might be quite different. Create an angry or more intense thesis statement for this essay that Steinberg's specific examples would support.

WRITING FROM THE TEXT

1. In a letter context—perhaps you'll even mail this to a friend—describe four thin and possibly self-righteous people you know. Try to achieve the quality of one of Neil Steinberg's well-crafted images—for example, his description of the hostess "with legs like beef jerky."

2. If you are heavy or overweight, make a list of responses you have heard from friends and strangers about your size. Then write an essay that focuses on the intentional or unintentional comments you have endured. Adopt a voice similar to Steinberg's or one of indignation—as you prefer.

3. If you are weight-conscious or very thin, write an essay that addresses the indifference, gluttony, medical problems, or laziness that you perceive in overweight people. Consider your audience and purpose as you draft your essay.

CONNECTING WITH OTHER TEXTS

1. Compare and contrast the purpose and voice of Jennifer Coleman in "Discrimination at Large" (p. 243) and of Neil Steinberg in "O.K., So I'm Fat." Evaluate the two essays in your conclusion.

2. Matthew Soyster (p. 213), Steven Barrie-Anthony (p. 256), Jennifer Coleman (p. 243), and Neil Steinberg write about their perceptions of their bodies. Write an analysis of your understanding of their attitudes from a thesis that links any three writers and essays. Use details from the three texts to support your analysis.

3. Write a character analysis of Neil Steinberg that draws supporting material from the text. You may stretch your imagination to infer character

traits, but ground your analysis as much as possible in what the author reveals about himself in his essay and biographical material.

4. Read one of Neil Steinberg's books cited in his biographical information (p. 247). Write an analysis of the kinds of humor apparent in his work.

◐◑ **Bodily Harm** ◐◑
Pamela Erens

A 1985 graduate of Yale University, Pamela Erens (b. 1963) has worked as an editor and staff writer for *Connecticut Magazine* and is currently an editor at *Glamour* magazine. Her reviews and articles have appeared in many magazines and newspapers, and she also writes fiction. The essay included here was first published in *Ms.* in 1985, when Erens interned there the summer after her graduation.

1   "Before I'd even heard of bulimia," said Gloria, "I happened to read an article in *People* magazine on Cherry Boone—how she'd used laxatives and vomiting to control her weight. I thought: Wow, what a great idea! I was sure that I would never lose control of my habit."

2   Recent media attention to the binge-purge and self-starvation disorders known as bulimia and anorexia—often detailing gruesome particulars of women's eating behavior—may have exacerbated this serious problem on college campuses. But why would a woman who reads an article on eating disorders want to copy what she reads? Ruth Striegel-Moore, Ph.D., director of Yale University's Eating Disorders Clinic, suggests that eating disorders may be a way to be like other "special" women and at the same time strive to outdo them. "The pursuit of thinness is a way for women to compete with each other, a way that avoids being threatening to men," says Striegel-Moore. Eating disorders as a perverse sort of rivalry? In Carol's freshman year at SUNY-Binghamton, a roommate showed her how to make herself throw up. "Barf buddies" are notorious on many college campuses, especially in sororities and among sports teams. Eating disorders as negative bonding? Even self-help groups on campus can degenerate into the kinds of competitiveness and negative reinforcement that are among the roots of eating disorders in the first place.

3   This is not another article on how women do it. It is an article on how and why some women stopped. The decision to get help is not always an easy one. The shame and secrecy surrounding most eating disorders and the fear or being labeled "sick" may keep a woman from admitting even to herself

that her behavior is hurting her. "We're not weirdos," says Nancy Gengler, a recovered bulimic and number two U.S. squash champion, who asked that I use her real name because "so much of this illness has to do with secrecy and embarrassment." In the first stages of therapy, says Nancy, much of getting better was a result of building up the strength to (literally) "sweat out" the desire to binge and to endure the discomfort of having overeaten rather than throwing up. "I learned to accept such 'failures' and moreover, that they would not make me fat. . . ."

4   Secret shame or college fad, eating disorders among college women are growing at an alarming rate: in a recent study at Wellesley College, more than half the women on campus felt they needed help to correct destructive eating patterns. These included bingeing, chronic dieting, and "aerobic nervosa," the excessive use of exercise to maintain one's body ideal—in most women, invariably five to ten pounds less than whatever she currently weighs.

5   Why now? Wasn't the Women's Movement supposed to free women to be any body size, to explore the full range of creative and emotional possibilities? Instead, women in epidemic numbers are developing symptoms that make them feel hopeless about the future, depleting the energy they have for schoolwork and other activities, and if serious enough, send them right back home or into the infantalizing condition of hospitalization. What has gone wrong?

6   For Brenda, college meant the freedom to question her mother's values about sex. But when she abandoned her mother's guidelines, "I went to the other extreme. I couldn't set limits about sex, food, or anything else." The pressure on college women to appear successful and in control, to know what they want among the myriad new choices they are offered, is severe. So much so that many choose internal havoc over external imperfection. Naomi, a bulimic student at Ohio State University, said she would rather be alcoholic like her father than overweight like her mother because "fat is something you can see."

7   One reason college women hesitate to enter therapy, says Stephen Zimmer, director of the Center for the Study of Anorexia and Bulimia in New York City, is that the eating disorder has become a coping mechanism. It allows the person to function when she feels rotten inside. "In the first session," says Zimmer, "I tell my patients: 'I'm not going to try to take your eating behavior away from you. Until you find something that works better, you get to keep it.' Their relief is immense."

8   Brenda at first did not even tell the counselor whom she was seeing that she was bulimic. She started therapy because of a series of affairs with abu-

sive men. As Brenda developed the sense that she had a right to say no to harmful relationships and to make demands on others, her inability to say no to food also disappeared.

9   However, if a woman is vomiting three times a day, she may be unable to concentrate on long-term therapy. Behavioral therapy, which directly addresses the learned habit of bingeing and purging, is a more immediate alternative. For eight years, Marlene Boskind White, Ph.D., and her husband, William White, Jr., Ph.D., ran weekend workshops for bulimic women at Cornell University, usually as an adjunct to other forms of therapy. The sessions included nutritional counseling, developing techniques of dealing with binge "triggers," feminist consciousness-raising, and examining the hidden "payoffs" that keep a woman from changing her eating behavior. Boskind-White and White report that a follow-up of 300 women they had treated one to three years earlier showed that 70 percent had entirely stopped purging and drastically reduced their bingeing.

10   Group therapy (an increasingly popular resource on college campuses) may be the first time a woman realizes she is not alone with her problem. Rebecca Axelrod, who was bulimic throughout college, and now counsels bulimics herself, found that joining the Cornell workshop and meeting other bulimic women defused many of her fears about herself: "I saw ten other women who were not mentally ill, not unable to function," Axelrod says. She remembers the moment when she understood the meaning of her bingeing and purging. "Saturday afternoon, Marlene took the women off alone, and we discussed the 'superwoman syndrome'—that attempt to be the perfect friend, lover, hostess, student . . . and perfect-looking. And bingeing, I saw, was my form of *defiance*. But if you're living life as the perfect woman, you won't cuss, you won't get drunk or laid or drive too fast. No, in the privacy of your own room you'll eat yourself out of house and home. But how dare you be defiant? And so you punish yourself by throwing it up."

11   But "groups can fall into a cycle I call 'bigger and badder,'" says Axelrod. "It starts when one person comes in and says, 'I feel terrible, I binged yesterday.' Somebody else says: 'Oh, that's okay, so did I.' Then a third person says: 'That's nothing, did you know I. . . .' Pretty soon everyone is lending support to the binge instead of to the woman who needs ways of coping with it."

12   However, Axelrod feels that there is much potential for women to help one another. She encourages bulimics to ask for help from their friends, saying that while she herself was initially frightened that being open about her bulimia would alienate her friends, most were very supportive. "The important thing," says Axelrod, "is to be specific about what you need. Don't say: 'Be there for me.' Tell a friend exactly what she can do: for instance, not to

urge you to go out for pizza if you tell her you're feeling vulnerable. And rely on three friends, not one."

13   One of the most important strategies in treating eating disorders, says Dr. Lee Combrinck-Graham of the newly opened Renfrew Center for anorectics and bulimics in Philadelphia, is breaking old patterns. Renfrew is a residential center that houses patients for between three weeks and two months, a period that can give women with eating disorders a respite from repetitive and destructive habits that are reinforced by the college environment. But Renfrew is not a "retreat"; its residents work hard. They participate in therapy workshops, take seminars in assertiveness-training and women's issues, and even participate in "new attitude" cooking classes. Dr. Combrinck-Graham stresses that therapy itself has often become a "pattern" for women who come to Renfrew. Many of Renfrew's patients, says Dr. Combrinck-Graham, can say exactly what's "wrong" with them and why, yet are still unable to control their eating habits. Renfrew combines a philosophy that recovery is the patient's responsibility—she sets her own goals and contracts for as much supervision as she needs—with innovative art and movement therapy that may bypass some of the rationalizations that block the progress of "talking" therapies.

14   Women who live close to home and whose parents are not separated may want to try family therapy. Family therapy considers the family itself, not the daughter with an eating disorder, to be the "patient." Often, the daughter has taken on the role of diverting attention from unacknowledged conflicts within the family. Family therapists behave somewhat like manic stage managers, interrupting and quizzing various members of a family, orchestrating confrontations in an attempt to expose and demolish old, rigid patterns of relating. Ideally, family therapy benefits all the members of the family. Carol, the student at SUNY-Binghamton, said that family therapy revealed how unhappy her mother was as a homemaker in a traditional Italian family.

15   Situations like Carol's are at the heart of today's epidemic of eating disorders, argues Kim Chernin in her book *The Hungry Self: Women, Eating, and Identity.* Chernin claims that today's college woman is the heir of a particular cultural moment that turns her hunger for identity into an uncontrollable urge for bodily nourishment. Young women of an earlier generation were educated to have children and remain in the home, yet our culture devalued the work they did there. Later, the Women's Movement opened up vast new emotional and career possibilities, and many daughters, on the verge of achieving their mother's suppressed dreams, are struck by panic and guilt.

16   Carol agreed: "I would try to push my mother to take classes, but my father was always against it. I was a good student, but how could I keep on get-

ting smarter than my mother? When I was young, we'd been like one person. I wanted to be a homemaker because she was one. But when I got older, I said to myself: 'This woman has no life. She never leaves the house except to get groceries. And she's miserable.' I wanted to stop growing up, and then she would always be able to lead me and guide me." According to Chernin, an eating disorder may be a way to postpone or put an end to one's development, one's need to choose, the possibility of surpassing one's mother. In a world hostile to the values of closeness and nurturance women learn from and associate with the mother-daughter relationship, an eating disorder can disguise a desire to return to the "nourishment" of that early bond.

17   And why do the daughter's problems focus around food? As Chernin reminds us, originally with her milk, the mother *is* food. Femininity itself has historically been associated with food gathering and preparation. Food—eating it, throwing it up—can become a powerful means of expressing aspects of the mother's life or of traditionally defined femininity that the daughter is trying to ingest or reject. And relationships with other women later in life can replicate this early pattern: food mediates hostility and love.

18   Whatever forms of therapy prove most helpful for women with eating disorders, it is clear that therapy is only half the battle. The Stone Center for Developmental Services and Studies at Wellesley College recognizes the need for early prevention and is preparing a film for adolescents that will feature women and health professionals speaking about the uses and abuses of food in our culture. Janet Surrey, Ph.D., a research associate at the center, stresses the need to educate girls in the 10- to 15-year-old age bracket—66 percent of whom already diet—about the psychological, physical, and reproductive danger of dieting and excessive thinness. Nutritional counseling is another imperative. But to Kim Chernin, our first priority is outreach centers and school programs that will provide developmental counseling and feminist consciousness-raising for this crucial pre–high school group. If women could learn early on to confront their conflicts over their right to development, the use of power, and their place in a still male-dominated world, there might no longer be a need for the "silent language" of eating disorders.

THINKING ABOUT THE TEXT

1. According to Erens, how has popular press coverage of eating disorders exacerbated the problem?

2. What is Erens's purpose in quoting Rebecca Axelrod and others? What do these people and their comments contribute?

3. How can group therapy sessions, frequently joined by people with eating disorders, actually complicate the treatment?

4. What is Kim Chernin's perception of one cause of eating disorders?

5. How effective is Erens's conclusion, a proposal to curtail the number of young women with eating disorders?

WRITING FROM THE TEXT

1. Do you think that women compete with each other by pursuing thinness? Do you think women bond in an effort to achieve thinness? Write an essay in which you describe and analyze the eating patterns of women you know.

2. Argue that the cause of eating disorders is not based in the mother-daughter relationship but in the superthin images in advertising. Cite and *describe* specific examples of advertising to support your view.

CONNECTING WITH OTHER TEXTS

1. Pamela Erens, Jenny Jones (p. 258), Jennifer Coleman (p. 243), and Rachel Krell (p. 382) describe the kinds of harm that can be done to women who try to conform to a standardized concept of beauty. In an analysis essay, examine the problem by connecting the ideas expressed by these three writers.

2. This article, published in 1985, gives a good review of eating problems, but new information may provide increased or different insights. Use Erens's essay as a model but use more current material to analyze the problem of eating disorders.

3. Read Kim Chernin's 1981 study of eating disorders, *The Obsession,* or at least read Chapter 9, where the author argues that males' preference for "little girls" contributes to eating disorders in women. Chernin cites films like *Taxi Driver, Manhattan,* and *The Little Girl Who Lives Down the Lane* as evidence. Argue to support or refute Chernin's point about males' preference for "little girls" with your own evidence.

4. Read the chapter entitled "Hunger" in Naomi Wolf's *The Beauty Myth,* published in 1991. Analyze the support she offers for her thesis: "Women must claim anorexia as political damage done to us by a social order that considers our destruction insignificant because of what we are—less. We should identify it as Jews identify the death camps, as homosexuals identify AIDS, as a disgrace that is not our own, but that of an inhumane social order. . . . To be anorexic or bulimic *is* to be a political prisoner" (208).

Baldness

Steven Barrie-Anthony

Although he is still a student—of religious studies at Occidental College in Los Angeles—Steven Barrie-Anthony (b. 1981) is a well-published writer. He is a coauthor of the chapter "Conversion" in the *Oxford Handbook of New Religions* (2003), has cowritten an article for *The Journal of Terrorism and Political Violence* (2002), and has contributed, to the *Encyclopedia of World Religions*, chapters on "Hinduism" and "Religion in Contemporary India" (2002). On writing, Steven Barrie-Anthony has this advice: "Don't get caught up in what people think. Just get out there and write." The essay that follows, on his incipient baldness, appeared in the *Los Angeles Times* on January 27, 2002.

1 At first I told myself that it couldn't be, it was the way the light hit the cut, maybe my shampoo was too harsh, maybe, oh, I don't know, maybe it's just my notoriously active imagination.

2 Sitting in my dorm room watching "Saturday Night Live," I pointed and told a friend, "It's thinning." He was supposed to say, "Oh, Steven, that's ridiculous," but instead he forgot his lines and just nodded and said, "Yep."

3 But I still didn't believe it. At 20—no, it couldn't be. Maybe at 40 or even 30, little by little so I wouldn't even notice, after I was married and happy and secure and loved.

4 At home for winter break, I stood in front of the bathroom mirror. I turned on all the lights—over the sink, the dome light, in the hall—and then I opened my eyes and looked. There was no way around it. My hairline was receding. Even the hair up on top wasn't as thick as it used to be.

5 I told my mom. Of course she disagreed, but my dad said, "Yeah, I see what you mean."

6 "Look," he said to my mom, "look where his hairline is, and on the top of the head, this used to be a lot fuller, thicker." They got a picture from high school, my senior portrait. Lo and behold, I had more hair back then. Quite a bit.

7 Darn, I thought. This is not what I need now. In the middle of sophomore year, do I really need something to undermine my confidence? Something to make me feel isolated, different?

8 After a while I had to laugh. What the heck—there's nothing to do but grin and bear it. But wait a second, I thought, and made a beeline for the Internet.

9 It turns out that hair loss in men is usually caused by a high level of testosterone, the hormone that basically makes men men, so I guess in a way that's a good thing. I disregarded all the Web sites dedicated to wigs and hairpieces, hair implants and other drastic plastic surgeries. But a few things seemed promising.

10 First, Rogaine, the goop you spread on your scalp twice a day, seems to make a difference for a lot of guys. But you have to do it forever—or you lose

all the hair you would've lost anyway. And being a red-blooded American with a short attention span, I didn't think doing that twice a day for the rest of my life would be doable.

11   There must be a quick fix—this is the 21st century, folks!

12   Finally, I came across what I thought I'd been looking for: Propecia. It's a new drug, a relative of Proscar, which was originally prescribed to treat prostate problems. If taken daily, it apparently grows new hair and prevents continued hair loss in most men. Wow, what a great deal, I thought—until I looked at the possible side effects. Taking Propecia may produce "decreased sexual desire, lowered [sexual] sensitivity, or decreased ejaculate . . ." read the hairloss.org Web site.

13   Hmm, I thought, take that pill and I risk being bald and impotent.

14   Just out of curiosity, I followed the chain of drugs. If I took Propecia to halt hair loss, and Viagra to fix erectile dysfunction, then I'd be as good as new, right? Possibly right—probably wrong.

15   "The most common drug side effects of Viagra are headache, flushing of the face, and upset stomach," reads the mens-sexual-health.org Web site. Others include ". . . temporary changes in color vision . . . eyes being more sensitive to light, or blurred vision." In rare cases, you "may have an erection that lasts many hours."

16   So if I want to be totally intact, I'd have to take: Propecia for hair, Viagra for sexual function, Pepto Bismal for my stomach and Advil or Tylenol for my head. On top of that, I might be flushed, have colored vision and never, *ever*, be able to be confident wearing sweat pants in public. Sound like a good trade for a bit o' thinning up on top?

17   For me right now, a nice hat seems like the better solution.

THINKING ABOUT THE TEXT

1. Reread the author's first paragraph and decide what his strategies are in opening his essay as he has. What are the effects on the reader of this opening paragraph?

2. What assumption does the author make about age and balding? How would his being older make balding easier to accept?

3. What is implied by the author's statement that his mother did not believe he was balding, "of course," but his father agreed that his hairline was receding and the hair thinning. What role playing is suggested?

4. The author discovers, on the Internet, possible pharmaceutical solutions for his balding. What are the possible consequences of taking each of the products? Does the author's reasoned conclusion seem right to you?

5. Beneath the author's humorous tone, his self-awareness and research discoveries embody some serious issues. What are they?

WRITING FROM THE TEXT

1. Focus on a discovery about a change you have observed in your own body or the change in a friend. How do you feel about the changes in your own or your friend's physiological and possibly psychological condition?

2. Argue that the author, like many young people in the United States, is too preoccupied with looks. In your essay, use specific examples of preoccupation with appearance from your own experience and those of your friends. Come to some awareness in the conclusion of your essay.

3. Analyze the tone of Steven Barrie-Anthony's essay. In what specific ways does he use language to create a readable essay? Discuss his writing strategies in an essay of linguistic analysis.

CONNECTING WITH OTHER TEXTS

1. Compare the tone of Neil Steinberg in "O.K., So I'm Fat" (p. 247) with the voice of Steven Barrie-Anthony in "Baldness." Focus your essay on the language used by each writer and your perception of their characters as they are revealed through their voices.

2. In "Bodily Harm" (p. 250), "Body of Evidence" (p. 259), and "Baldness," it is apparent that some individuals will consider taking risks and might suffer serious consequences in order to make themselves look better. Write an essay that explores the motivations, procedures, and consequences of improving looks. Use examples from the essays cited here and some from your own experiences and observations.

3. Find examples of figures from popular culture who are attractive in some way (that you describe and define) but whose external appearance does not conform to the stereotypical concept of beauty that exists in our culture. Focus your essay on some point that can be supported with analysis of your specific examples.

Body of Evidence

Jenny Jones

Talk show host and entertainer Jenny Jones (b. 1946) was born in Israel to parents of Russian and Polish descent. Named Janina Stronski, she grew up in Ontario, Canada, but speaks Polish fluently. Her entertainment career began when she left home at 17 to tour as a drummer in a rock band; soon she was a back-up singer for Wayne Newton and then a lead singer of her own band. Gradually she discovered her comedic talent and eventually was sharing billing with top entertainers. Her nationally syndicated talk show, *The Jenny Jones Show*, first aired in 1991. When her autobiography *Jenny Jones: My Story* was published in 1997, 100 percent of the proceeds went to breast cancer research. The following essay first appeared in *People* magazine in March 1992.

1   Unfortunately, my father was a breast man. My mother and my sister, Elizabeth, were big-breasted, but I was destined to be flat-chested. My father would tell me to rub cold water on my chest in the shower to make my breasts grow. He insisted that I do certain exercises to make my breasts grow. I sent away for that Mark Eden breast developer—that thing with a spring that was in the back of all the magazines in the 1960s. I even had rubber falsies!

2   My parents had immigrated to Canada from Poland after World War II. In Poland they stood in bread lines for food, and when they came to Ontario, where I grew up, they had nothing. My mother was a dressmaker, and they opened a little bridal shop that wound up being a very successful business. My father, who died in 1989, appreciated women and clothing and helped design some of the wedding dresses.

3   After my parents divorced in the late 1950s, my father married Roula Frangos, a dressmaker who worked in his store. I remember one compliment he gave my stepmother some 10 years ago. He said, "The most wonderful thing about my wife here after all these years is she has great boobs."

4   My parents did not know what child psychology was. I guess they thought it was cute to talk about how flat-chested I was. They didn't realize how much damage they were doing. I didn't realize until much later.

5   It didn't help that I went through puberty in the big-breasted Jayne Mansfield era. Later, in my 20s, when I was a backup singer for Wayne Newton, I was always the target of small-breast jokes. People gave me T-shirts with fried eggs. In those days, I couldn't even wear a size 34A bra. I had a closet full of padded bras. Sometimes I would hurt myself pushing up whatever I could possibly get to come up with cleavage.

6   Although I did not date a lot because I was insecure, I did marry at 23. I was married twice. In 1969, when I was engaged to my first husband, Al Gambino, a musician, I would look at sexy nightgowns and lingerie and think that I could never wear them. That marriage was the kind of mistake that people make when they're young. But in my second marriage, to Buz Wilburn, I realized how uncomfortable I still felt about my body. My husband seldom touched my breasts when we were intimate. I could only assume that they were not big enough or attractive enough for him.

7   When that marriage split up in 1980, I was living in Los Angeles, working as an office manager. I thought that only celebrities had breast implants until one day a coworker told me that she had them. She was so excited about hers that she took me into the ladies' room and took off her clothes to show them to me.

8   I went to the Beverly Hills plastic surgeon that she recommended. He wasn't board certified [plastic surgeons need not be board certified to practice], but he was affordable. I asked if there were any dangers. He said that about 10 percent of women who have implants develop hardness but that there was a new silicone implant made by the McGhan Medical Corp. that prevented a lot of that. Besides, he said that if I developed hardness, he would redo my breasts and forgo his fee. It was like buying a car with a one-year guarantee. I said, "How soon can we do it? How much does it cost?" He said, "$1,500."

9   I had a garage sale and sold practically everything I owned to pay for those implants. I sold my sewing machine, books, pots and pans, clothes. There was nothing anyone could have done at that point to talk me out of it. I could not sleep at night. I said, "Please, let the day come."

10   I had my first operation on May 15, 1981. It was outpatient surgery. The first thing I remember was that when I looked down, I could not see my waist anymore. I felt terribly sexy because I still had feeling and sensation in my breast after the first operation. It was such a big change. I think my doctor made my breasts bigger than they should have been for my frame—I'm 5'6" 130 lbs.—and I was actually a little embarrassed. When people did double takes, I didn't know if they were thinking, "Nice body" or "She didn't have those last week!"

11   A week after my surgery, I was still black-and-blue and still had stitches, but I went out to buy a real woman's bra, size 36C. I couldn't wait. I have to admit, though, that it was disconcerting to see men talk to me and look at my chest. That had never happened before.

12   After about six months, my right breast got hard. I knew that was one of the complications, so I wasn't surprised. But there I was with one soft breast and one really hard one. One insensitive male acquaintance told me when I hugged him goodbye, "What do you have, rocks in there?" I was mortified.

13   My implants certainly cut down on my relationships. I was so self-conscious that if I met anyone and wanted to kiss him, I had to tell him I had implants. If anyone felt them, it was embarrassing. But I kept my medical problems secret.

14   It turned out that hardness is very common—and my doctor was wrong when he told me in 1981 that only 10 percent get it. On May 10, 1982, a year

after my first operation, I went back to the surgeon to have my implants replaced. He waived his fee, as he had promised. He used the same kind of implant but made them a little smaller to see if it made a difference.

15   It didn't. Within five months, my new implants started to get hard. In December of 1983, I went back to the doctor. I did not think to get a second opinion. I had heard about other women with hard breasts, so it did not seem that unusual. He gave me general anesthesia and squeezed the implants to break up the capsule that forming around my implants and make my breasts soft again, which was not an unusual practice at the time. [Manufacturers now warn that "excessive manipulation" can lead to ruptures.]

16   It didn't work. I was still in Los Angeles, and by now I was working in comedy clubs. I started reading about a silicone implant with a polyurethane coating that preserved softness. It was called the Meme. I went back to the surgeon and asked for it. I had my third implant operation on Dec. 19, 1983. This operation, like the others, was very painful and left embarrassing scars around both nipples.

17   Worst of all, the problem was not corrected. At one of my checkups, I told the doctor that my implants were getting hard again. He said, "Vogues aren't supposed to do that." I said, "They're not Vogues, they're the Meme." He told me he had put in a Vogue [another polyurethene-coated silicone implant] instead because he thought it would be better for me. This doctor was in a beautiful building in Beverly Hills, highly recommended, and he had never told me that he wasn't putting in the Meme!

18   One day in 1984 I was working with a comic who was a dirt bag. I was standing at the rail watching the other comedians, and he put his hand up my blouse and grabbed my breasts. By this time, all the feeling in my breasts was gone, so I didn't even know it! That was one of my worst moments.

19   On Aug. 13, 1984, my doctor put in the Meme implant, which was later voluntarily recalled by the manufacturer because of possible cancer risks. I went home after the operation, and there was swelling, which did not go down. A week later I had to have surgery to stop internal bleeding.

20   The Meme implants got hard too. But I lived with them from 1984 until 1991. I resigned myself to the fact that my breasts weren't ever going to be soft. It is just something about my body that causes this. Then, as I got into my 40s, gravity began taking its toll. One breast pointed downward a little bit, one pointed up. My cleavage was off. I couldn't wear anything low-cut because my breasts didn't match.

21   In 1985 I met my boyfriend, Denis McCallion. It was so hard to tell Denis about my implants. I must have postponed it for a month. I thought he would never look at me in the same way. I know he liked my shapely figure.

He found me attractive because of what he saw at the beginning. I said, "I've had breast implants, I have had some complications, they don't feel very natural, they don't look particularly attractive." He said, "So what?" Denis urged me to go to some kind of counseling, but I never did because that wouldn't make the implants go away.

22   I did a photo session in 1986 wearing a bustier, and every picture had a ridge line on my right breast. The photographer asked where it came from. I knew that it wasn't noticeable to the eye, but the camera had picked it up. It was embarrassing. I had been told that it was scar tissue, but I later found out that it was silicone in my tissues.

23   Between 1985 and 1991, I went to one doctor after another—all men—asking, "Isn't there something you can do?" They all told me, "Be glad this is all that is wrong with you. Some women's breasts are as hard as cement." What I didn't learn until all the recent publicity about the dangers of breast implants was that some women get collagen diseases, rheumatoid arthritis and other autoimmune disorders.

24   A year ago I went to another doctor who told me about a Misti Gold—a new implant filled with a nonsilicone polymer—that had been successful with people who have a history of hardening. He said, "Your breasts can be 50 percent softer." I said, "That's good enough for me."

25   By now I was commuting from Los Angeles to Las Vegas doing a test run of *The Jenny Jones Show.* Denis tried to talk me out of it, but I had my sixth operation, and my fifth set of implants in Beverly Hills on March 1, 1991. When I went in for a two-week checkup, I had a red splotch on my chest. The doctor said that the old implants had ruptured and the splotch could have been a reaction to the silicone. He couldn't tell me how long ago this had happened. He gave me antibiotics and an antihistamine. It took four weeks to go away.

26   In a couple of months, the Misti Golds hardened too. My breasts were completely numb, and the ridge on the right breast was more prominent. I was giving up. A month ago I went back to the doctor. When I asked him if the silicone ridge was dangerous, he said, "We don't think so." I told him that I really want my implants out. I don't care what my breasts look or feel like. I want them out of my body. I hate them. It was the worst mistake I ever made. The doctor said, "If you have your implants removed, you will be suicidal in two weeks."

27   Even more recently, another surgeon told me, "You can't take out the marble from marbled beef. To get all the silicone out of your body, we would have to take out some of your tissue." It would be reconstruction, and that would create a substantial deformity. My other option would be to have a saline implant, which has a silicone shell. But I don't want silicone in my body. I am in an unfixable situation, and I have no idea what to do.

28   Now both breasts are hard and I have scars. I don't have to wear a bra because my breasts hold themselves up. I wear one at home, though, because I don't want to look at my breasts. I hate my body a thousand times more now than I ever did before. I would sell everything I own to be able to have the body back that I gave up.

29   Denis has been incredibly supportive. If I had had him earlier in my life, I never would have had these implants done. He loves me for what I am. But nothing he can say can make a difference. I still have not told him that I don't have feeling in my breasts, and we have been together for six years. It's as though any kind of sexual activity comes to a complete halt when I am touched above the waist.

30   I am the most unsexy person in the world in my mind. I am proud of my work, but when I get fan letters from men who think I am so sexy, my reaction is, "If they only knew."

31   Now that I'm going public, I feel that a great weight has been lifted from me. I will be able to hug somebody and not wonder if he or she is thinking, "Oh, my God, what are these?" I want to urge other celebrities to come forward. If they'll talk about it, we can start doing some good. My goal is to say to anybody who is considering implants: Don't do it. It's not worth the risk. Learn to love yourself. If I could have learned that, I wouldn't have had to suffer these 11 years of torture.

THINKING ABOUT THE TEXT

1. How did Jones's individual family members contribute to her insecurity about breast size? Jones adds that it didn't help that she "went through puberty in the big-breasted Jayne Mansfield era" (259). Do you think that the particular era conditioned her thinking or does it seem that even to-day big breasts have become synonymous with "sexy"?

2. Although Jones initially felt "sexy" after her implant operation, list all the other consequences—physical, social, emotional, and medical—that be-gan to plague her. What are some additional dangers of breast implants that Jones has discovered from research and from others?

3. After enduring six painful and unsuccessful operations related to her im-plants, Jones reveals this sad irony: "I would sell everything I own to be able to have the body back that I gave up" (263). What are some additional ironies related to breasts that she reveals throughout her essay?

4. Beyond learning of the dangers of breast implants, what else does Jones believe that women who are considering implant surgery need to learn?

WRITING FROM THE TEXT

1. Using information from "Body of Evidence," write an argument to convince women of the potential physical, social, and emotional consequences of getting breast implants.

2. Write an essay contrasting the popular image of Jenny Jones as sexy, witty, and self-assured with the self-portrait that emerges from "Body of Evidence." Use details from the brief biography and the essay itself for both depictions.

3. In an essay, argue that the reader's gender does or does not affect the appreciation of Jones's key experiences and assertions. Can men value this essay as much as females can or is this essay written almost exclusively for women?

4. If you or your family members have ever undergone any elective surgery for cosmetic purposes, write a narrative (see pp. 409–418) or a cause-and-effect analysis (see pp. 434–438) dramatizing the anticipation of the surgery, the actual experience itself, and the outcome.

CONNECTING WITH OTHER TEXTS

1. In "Pigskin, Pain, and Patriarchy" (p. 101), Don Sabo asserts that personal insecurities are often "rooted *outside*, not inside, our skins" (103). Would Jones agree? Using information from both essays, write an analysis of the roots of the pressures and the resulting pains that both men and women endure to attain the "ideal" image.

2. Using details from "Baldness" (p. 256), "Pigskin, Pain, and Patriarchy" (p. 101), "A Work of Artifice" (p. 106), and "Body of Evidence," analyze the health hazards which many people are willing to risk for increased self-confidence and sex appeal.

Chapter 5

Between
Values

This final chapter of readings draws on the other chapters in Part I, because our values are influenced by our age, gender, culture, and self-perceptions. Although our values may have firm roots, they are also constantly evolving as our lives change. In this chapter we examine the contemporary forces that influence our values, and the choices we make as individuals and as citizens. Our current national crisis and our history require that we question authority and our role in response to emergencies. As consumers we also must question how we spend our time and money, and how we use cyberspace and leisure space.

As our nation redefines what it means to be secure, Todd Gitlin demands that we continue in the democratic tradition of questioning authority, and Carol Tavris urges readers to act as individuals rather than succumbing to pressure or lethargy. The ill effects of group pressure are explored by George Orwell and Martin Luther King, Jr., and the effects of commercial pressures are explored by Susan Douglas and Philip Dacey. The prominence of television and film in our lives is pervasive, but not all critics agree about the media's effects on viewers. Robin Swicord argues that the violence on television and in film is responsible for some of the tragedies in our culture, but Howard Rosenberg insists that the media shouldn't be the scapegoat for the traumas in society. Equally diverse in their views are Clifford Stoll and Don Tapscott about the value of computers in education. Our rights and responsibilities as customers are discussed by Jonathan Alter, who protests inefficient telephone routing systems, and Keith David Hamm and David and Arlie Hochschild, who urge us to change our habits as consumers.

◖◗ Patriotism Demands ◖◗ Questioning Authority

Todd Gitlin

Professor of sociology, communication, and journalism, Todd Gitlin (b. 1943) is also an essayist, poet, and novelist. His most popular work reflects his interest in the media, American history, philosophy, and social theory, and his involvement in New Left liberal politics. His titles include *Inside Prime Time* (1983), *The Sixties: Years of Hope, Days of Rage* (1987), *The Twilight of Common Dreams: Why America Is Wracked by Culture Wars* (1995), and *Media Unlimited: How the Torrent of Images and Sounds Overwhelms Our Lives.* The essay included here appeared in the *Los Angeles Times* on November 11, 2001, two months after the terrorist attacks on the World Trade Center Towers and the Pentagon. Some of Gitlin's specific references to the attack and immediate aftermath may seem dated, but his philosophy on questioning authority remains timeless.

1   Years ago, a student of mine at UC Santa Cruz drove a Volkswagen van with a QUESTION AUTHORITY bumper sticker. One day, somebody scratched out the message. Lately, at a time when some people think loyalty must be demonstrated with a shut mouth, I've been thinking of my former student and her anonymous vandal.

2   Whoever felt the need to crush that young woman's audacity was stomping on democractic ideals, failing to understand that questioning is precisely what authority needs. In a democracy, authority needs to convince those it governs. To be convincing, it must be willing and able to defend itself, even—especially—when pointed questions are asked. In his essay "On Liberty," John Stuart Mill wrote that even if one and only one person dissented, the dissent should be heard. First, because the dissenter might just be right. Second, because the authority of the majority opinion—even if close to unanimous—can only be bolstered by having to confront its adversaries. Amid free discussion, arguments only improve. So the expression of rival views is necessary for practical as well as principled reasons.

3   But during the current emergency, a stampede of unthinking censure is muffling the debate we need to have in order to fight the smartest possible campaign against our enemies. Ari Fleischer, the president's press secretary, scolded that Americans should "watch what they say." He was not referring to advance notice of troop movements, which of course no one ought to blurt out. He was referring to a tossed-off remark by talk show host Bill Maher. And Fleischer is not alone in blindly discarding the democratic faith in free discussion. In the *Wall Street Journal* last week, Gregg Easterbrook wrote that, since novelists Barbara Kingsolver and Arundhati Roy have written harshly about the American flag and America's approach to the world, "bookstores may

fairly respond by declining to stock their books." Stocking their books, he suggests, amounts to "promoting" their views.

4   As it happens, I have written passionately against Roy's views in recent weeks, and I vigorously disagree with Kingsolver about the flag. What does their wrong-headedness have to do with their right to be read? As it happens, Easterbrook himself wrote recently in *The New Republic* that American motorists contribute handsomely via oil imports to the Saudi Arabian money gusher that has subsidized Al Qaeda. Should gas-guzzling patrons of Barnes & Noble be catered to if they demand that *his* book be unshelved?

5   A call for the shuttering of minds betrays the opposite of confidence in the American campaign against murderous terrorists. What it betrays is desperation, feebleness of nerve, a pathetic lack of confidence that questions can be answered. If our authorities are already unthinkingly, kneejerkingly disbelieved by too many people around the world, why does it help to ask fewer questions? The quandaries we confront now—and for the foreseeable future—are immensely difficult, surely making the asking of questions a citizen's duty.

6   Yet since Sept. 11 and the decision to go to war in Afghanistan, public officials are taking easy ways out, resorting to platitudes. Democrats and Republicans alike are fearful of vigorous public debate. Faced with a colossal failure of intelligence before Sept. 11, such blank-check confidence in the institutions of national defense is demonstrably foolhardy. Much of the press, particularly television, had deluded itself in recent years that America could afford to ignore international events. Now they are playing catch-up, but timidly. Reporters ask technical military questions that officials properly dance away from, but they shy away from bigger, more important political questions.

7   Now the national self-defense campaign has turned into a war. And war, like it or not, mangles the truth, because propaganda is useful to all parties. The Pentagon can't be expected to change its ways. All the more reason, then, for journalists on other beats to give ample attention to the immense questions before us. One need not make the mistake of thinking that Afghanistan is Vietnam to note that policy unquestioned is policy unbridled.

8   Our questions need to start with one so basic and difficult it needs to be reflected upon calmly, again and again. How is America to live in a world where hundreds of millions of ignorant people, some of whom aim to possess weapons of mass destruction, hate us? From that question will come dozens of others, including:

- What ought to be American policy toward the fundamentalist Islamic regime of Saudi Arabia, which nurtured Bin Laden, the Taliban and the fanatical madrassas of Pakistan? If it is time to stop America's long embrace of the House of Saud, then what? If our need to embrace the Saudi regime in part stems from our dependence on oil, then how can we reduce it?

- What is the danger of famine this winter in Afghanistan? What is the U.N. saying? (Warnings and appeals by Oxfam, the Red Cross and other relief groups have barely registered on the American radar screen.) Who is to be trusted about casualties, famine and other desperate conditions there? The Taliban is trying to manage the news—big surprise. But casualty reports, true or false, are flying around the rest of the world. What is the rest of the world saying? Why are American editors not sifting through these reports, evaluating them as best they can and pulling out the most reliable for Americans?

- Are sanctions against Iraq useful? Are they having the desired effect? How else might we restrain Saddam Hussein's weapons programs and assaults on his own people?

9   The sad truth is that, when deciding what constitutes legitimate controversy, the media take their cues from the two major parties. When the parties agree to keep a question out of play, the news media usually acquiesce, as with the elimination of debate on the president's missile defense system in the wake of Sept. 11. In those days, with huge questions unasked and unanswered, we saw an unseemly haste on both right and left to stake out firm positions on a war without clear aims.

10   In the meantime, those who oppose the current war also evade tough questions. If they oppose the bombing, how do they propose that the nation defend itself? By parachuting subpoenas over Afghan caves? Nothing could be emptier than to say "Bring Bin Laden to justice" when there is no international constabulary, no international army, no international criminal justice system. Today and tomorrow, in the only world we have, how is the government to protect Americans from committed murderers who unrepentantly say they want to kill Americans anywhere and have demonstrated their ability to do so? No American government could deserve respect from its own citizens without a plausible strategy in the here-and-now.

11   Barry Farber, a long-term conservative radio host in New York, had it right. He used to close his show with the words, "Keep asking questions." That was patriotism, not panic.

THINKING ABOUT THE TEXT

1. What is the author's strategy in opening his essay with the anecdote about the bumper sticker? What are the possible reasons someone scratched out

the message on the bumper sticker? How do you interpret the act? How does the author interpret it?

2. What does the author mean when he writes that "questioning is precisely what authority needs"? What are the reasons the author gives for approving the act of questioning?

3. This essay was written shortly after the terrorist attacks that destroyed the World Trade Center towers in New York City and part of the Pentagon in Washington, D.C. The author insists that even in a time of emergency, "unthinking censure" is wrong. How might "muffling debate" work against fighting "the smartest campaign against our enemies"? Should citizens in a democracy ever need to "watch what they say"?

4. Two prominent authors, Arundhati Roy and Barbara Kingsolver, criticized some Americans' response to September 11th and were condemned for it by some speakers and writers. Why does Gitlin think that bookstores' refusal to stock Roy's and Kingsolver's books is a poor decision? What does the author think that the "shuttering of minds" indicates about Americans?

5. What are platitudes and how do they work against "vigorous public debate"? How is the work of journalists especially important in times of war?

6. In spite of the fact that some of the specific questions Gitlin poses will have been answered in some way since this essay was first published, the important questions the author poses remain vital considerations. What are these questions and why are they theoretically and actually still important?

7. The author's conclusion echoes but does not literally return to the image in his opening paragraphs. How do these images reflect the ideas in his essay?

WRITING FROM THE TEXT

1. Write a narrative about a time when you posed questions or opposed an authority figure. What was the situation and what were the consequences of your questioning? Were you right and did you prompt a change in thinking? Or were you wrong? Was the authority's view bolstered by your dissent? Review how to write a narrative (pp. 409–418) for advice on vividly rendering the story you want to tell.

2. Write an analysis of how you, your family, and your friends thought and behaved after the terrorist attacks on September 11, 2001. In what ways do you remember going along with the political and popular consensus of thought during that time? Did your college display American flags? Did you and your friends? Are there ways that you disagreed with the thinking, behavior, or decisions made? Did you then or do you now question the authority that decides American foreign policy?

CONNECTING WITH OTHER TEXTS

1. Do some research in the popular press on one of the questions posed by Todd Gitlin. For example, find out whether Afghanistan experienced famine in the winters following the military engagements there. Were the casualties reported during the war and afterward true or exaggerated? Are sanctions against Iraq useful? How should Americans be protected "from committed murderers"? As Gitlin suggests in his essay, find out about what the rest of the world has reported in its press. Write an essay that uses others' ideas, as well as your own, to answer one of Gitlin's questions. The *World Press Review* will be a useful resource for writing this essay.

2. Read "Shooting an Elephant" (below) with Todd Gitlin's essay in mind. Then write an essay illustrating how questioning authority might have led to a different course of action on Orwell's part.

3. In Carol Tavris's essay "In Groups We Shrink" (p. 277), the author argues that individuals behave responsibly in times of emergency, but when people are in groups, they "shrink." In what ways do her ideas inform Gitlin's essay on patriotism? How do citizens in time of war behave more like a group than like individuals? Integrate the ideas of these authors into your own observations of how Americans behaved after September 11, 2001.

Shooting an Elephant
George Orwell

Renowned writer of prose and fiction, George Orwell (1903–1950) was the pen name of Eric Blair. After graduating from Eton College, Orwell joined the British police in Burma and grew to distrust the methods of the British government there. For years he struggled to support himself with various odd jobs; this experience is described in *Down and Out in Paris and London* (1933). Eventually working as shopkeeper, correspondent, teacher, editor, and radio producer, Orwell tended to empathize with the disenfranchised of society. In *Animal Farm* (1945), Orwell satirizes the Soviet bureaucracy and warns people of the dangers of a totalitarian state. In *1984* (1949), he depicts a rigid government—represented by "Big Brother"—that twists truth and spies on its citizens via two-way television. The following piece is from *Shooting an Elephant and Other Essays* (1950).

1   In Moulmein, in lower Burma, I was hated by large numbers of people—the only time in my life that I have been important enough for this to happen to me. I was sub-divisional police officer of the town, and in an aimless, petty kind of way anti-European feeling was very bitter. No one had the guts to raise a riot, but if a European woman went through the bazaars alone

somebody would probably spit betel juice over her dress. As a police officer I was an obvious target and was baited whenever it seemed safe to do so. When a nimble Burman tripped me up on the football field and the referee (another Burman) looked the other way, the crowd yelled with hideous laughter. This happened more than once. In the end the sneering yellow faces of young men that met me everywhere, the insults hooted after me when I was at a safe distance, got badly on my nerves. The young Buddhist priests were the worst of all. There were several thousands of them in the town and none of them seemed to have anything to do except stand on street corners and jeer at Europeans.

2   All this was perplexing and upsetting. For at that time I had already made up my mind that imperialism was an evil thing and the sooner I chucked up my job and got out of it the better. Theoretically—and secretly, of course—I was all for the Burmese and all against their oppressors, the British. As for the job I was doing, I hated it more bitterly than I can perhaps make clear. In a job like that, you see the dirty work of Empire at close quarters. The wretched prisoners huddling in the stinking cages of the lock-ups, the grey, cowed faces of the long-term convicts, the scarred buttocks of the men who had been flogged with bamboos—all these oppressed me with an intolerable sense of guilt. But I could get nothing into perspective. I was young and ill-educated and I had had to think out my problems in the utter silence that is imposed on every Englishman in the East. I did not even know that the British Empire is dying, still less did I know that it is a great deal better than the younger empires that are going to supplant it. All I knew was that I was stuck between my hatred of the empire I served and my rage against the evil-spirited little beasts who tried to make my job impossible. With one part of my mind I thought of the British as an unbreakable tyranny, as something clamped down, *in saecula saeculorum*, upon the will of prostrate peoples; with another part I thought that the greatest joy in the world would be to drive a bayonet into a Buddhist priest's guts. Feelings like these are the normal by-products of imperialism; ask any Anglo-Indian official, if you can catch him off duty.

3   One day something happened which in a roundabout way was enlightening. It was a tiny incident in itself, but it gave me a better glimpse than I had had before of the real nature of imperialism—the real motive for which despotic governments act. Early one morning the sub-inspector at a police station the other end of the town rang me up on the phone and said that an elephant was ravaging the bazaar. Would I please come and do something about it? I did not know what I could do, but I wanted to see what was happening and I got onto a pony and started out. I took my rifle, an old .44 Winchester and much too small to kill an elephant, but I thought the noise might

be useful *in terrorem*. Various Burmans stopped me on the way and told me about the elephant's doings. It was not, of course, a wild elephant, but a tame one which had gone "must." It had been chained up, as tame elephants always are when their attack of "must" is due, but on the previous night it had broken its chain and escaped. Its mahout, the only person who could manage it when it was in that state, had set out in pursuit, but had taken the wrong direction and was now twelve hours' journey away, and in the morning the elephant had suddenly reappeared in the town. The Burmese population had no weapons and were quite helpless against it. It had already destroyed somebody's bamboo hut, killed a cow and raided some fruit-stalls and devoured the stock; also it had met the municipal rubbish van and, when the driver jumped out and took to his heels, had turned the van over and inflicted violences upon it.

4   The Burmese sub-inspector and some Indian constables were waiting for me in the quarter where the elephant had been seen. It was a very poor quarter, a labyrinth of squalid bamboo huts, thatched with palm-leaf, winding all over a steep hillside. I remember that it was a cloudy, stuffy morning at the beginning of the rains. We began questioning the people as to where the elephant had gone and, as usual, failed to get any definite information. That is invariably the case in the East; a story always sounds clear enough at a distance, but the nearer you get to the scene of events the vaguer it becomes. Some of the people said that the elephant had gone in one direction, some said that he had gone in another, some professed not even to have heard of any elephant. I had almost made up my mind that the whole story was a pack of lies, when we heard yells a little distance away. There was a loud, scandalized cry of "Go away, child! Go away this instant!" and an old woman with a switch in her hand came round the corner of a hut, violently shooing away a crowd of naked children. Some more women followed, clicking their tongues and exclaiming: evidently there was something that the children ought not to have seen. I rounded the hut and saw a man's dead body sprawling in the mud. He was an Indian, a black Dravidian coolie, almost naked, and he could not have been dead many minutes. The people said that the elephant had come suddenly upon him round the corner of the hut, caught him with its trunk, put its foot on his back and ground him into the earth. This was the rainy season and the ground was soft, and his face had scored a trench a foot deep and a couple of yards long. He was lying on his belly with arms crucified and head sharply twisted to one side. His face was coated with mud, the eyes wide open, the teeth bared and grinning with an expression of unendurable agony. (Never tell me, by the way, that the dead look peaceful. Most of the corpses I have seen look devilish.) The friction of the great beast's

foot had stripped the skin from his back as neatly as one skins a rabbit. As soon as I saw the dead man I sent an orderly to a friend's house nearby to borrow an elephant rifle. I had already sent back the pony, not wanting it to go mad with fright and throw me if it smelt the elephant.

5   The orderly came back in a few minutes with a rifle and five cartridges, and meanwhile some Burmans had arrived and told us that the elephant was in the paddy fields below, only a few hundred yards away. As I started forward practically the whole population of the quarter flocked out of the houses and followed me. They had seen the rifle and were all shouting excitedly that I was going to shoot the elephant. They had not shown much interest in the elephant when he was merely ravaging their homes, but it was different now that he was going to be shot. It was a bit of fun to them, as it would be to an English crowd; besides they wanted the meat. It made me vaguely uneasy. I had no intention of shooting the elephant—I had merely sent for the rifle to defend myself if necessary—and it is always unnerving to have a crowd following you. I marched down the hill, looking and feeling a fool, with the rifle over my shoulders and an ever-growing army of people jostling at my heels. At the bottom, when you got away from the huts, there was a metalled road and beyond that a miry waste of paddy fields a thousand yards across, not yet ploughed but soggy from the first rains and dotted with coarse grass. The elephant was standing eight yards from the road, his left side towards us. He took not the slightest notice of the crowd's approach. He was tearing up branches of grass, beating them against his knees to clean them and stuffing them into his mouth.

6   I had halted on the road. As soon as I saw the elephant I knew with perfect certainty that I ought not to shoot him. It is a serious matter to shoot a working elephant—it is comparable to destroying a huge and costly piece of machinery—and obviously one ought not to do it if it can possibly be avoided. And at that distance, peacefully eating, the elephant looked no more dangerous than a cow. I thought then and I think now that his attack of "must" was already passing off; in which case he would merely wander harmlessly about until the mahout came back and caught him. Moreover, I did not in the least want to shoot him. I decided that I would watch him for a little while to make sure that he did not turn savage again, and then go home.

7   But at that moment, I glanced round at the crowd that had followed me. It was an immense crowd, two thousand at the least and growing every minute. It blocked the road for a long distance on either side. I looked at the sea of yellow faces above the garish clothes—faces all happy and excited over this bit of fun, all certain that the elephant was going to be shot. They

were watching me as they would watch a conjurer about to perform a trick. They did not like me, but with the magical rifle in my hands I was momentarily worth watching. And suddenly I realized that I should have to shoot the elephant after all. The people expected it of me and I had got to do it; I could feel their two thousand wills pressing me forward, irresistibly. And it was at this moment, as I stood there with the rifle in my hands, that I first grasped the hollowness, the futility of the white man's dominion in the East. Here was I, the white man with his gun, standing in front of the unarmed native crowd—seemingly the leading actor of the piece; but in reality I was only an absurd puppet pushed to and fro by the will of those yellow faces behind. I perceived in this moment that when the white man turns tyrant it is his own freedoms that he destroys. He becomes a sort of hollow, posing dummy, the conventionalized figure of a sahib. For it is the condition of his rule that he shall spend his life in trying to impress the "natives," and so in every crisis he has got to do what the "natives" expect of him. He wears a mask, and his face grows to fit it. I had got to shoot the elephant. I had committed myself to doing it when I sent for the rifle. A sahib has got to act like a sahib; he has got to appear resolute, to know his own mind and do definite things. To come all that way, rifle in hand, with two thousand people marching at my heels, and then to trail feebly away, having done nothing—no, that was impossible. The crowd would laugh at me. And my whole life, every white man's life in the East, was one long struggle not to be laughed at.

8   But I did not want to shoot the elephant. I watched him beating his bunch of grass against his knees, with that preoccupied grandmotherly air that elephants have. It seemed to me that it would be murder to shoot him. At that age I was not squeamish about killing animals, but I had never shot an elephant and never wanted to. (Somehow it always seems worse to kill a *large* animal.) Besides, there was the beast's owner to be considered. Alive, the elephant was worth at least a hundred pounds; dead, he would only be worth the value of his tusks, five pounds, possibly. But I had to act quickly. I turned to some experienced-looking Burmans who had been there when we arrived, and asked them how the elephant had been behaving. They all said the same thing: he took no notice of you if you left him alone, but he might charge if you went too close to him.

9   It was perfectly clear to me what I ought to do. I ought to walk up to within, say, twenty-five yards of the elephant and test his behavior. If he charged, I could shoot; if he took no notice of me, it would be safe to leave him until the mahout came back. But also I knew that I was going to do no such thing. I was a poor shot with a rifle and the ground was soft mud into which one would sink at every step. If the elephant charged and I missed

him, I should have about as much chance as a toad under a steam-roller. But even then I was not thinking particularly of my own skin, only of the watch-ful yellow faces behind. For at that moment, with the crowd watching me, I was not afraid in the ordinary sense, as I would have been if I had been alone. A white man mustn't be frightened in front of "natives"; and so, in general, he isn't frightened. The sole thought in my mind was that if any-thing went wrong, those two thousand Burmans would see me pursued, caught, trampled on and reduced to a grinning corpse like that Indian up the hill. And if that happened it was quite probable that some of them would laugh. That would never do. There was only one alternative. I shoved the cartridges into the magazine and lay down on the road to get a better aim.

10   The crowd grew very still, and a deep, low, happy sigh, as of people who see the theatre curtain go up at last, breathed from innumerable throats. They were going to have their bit of fun after all. The rifle was a beautiful German thing with cross-hair sights. I did not then know that in shooting an elephant one would shoot to cut an imaginary bar running from ear-hole to ear-hole. I ought, therefore, as the elephant was sideways on, to have aimed straight at his ear-hole; actually I aimed several inches in front of this, think-ing the brain would be further forward.

11   When I pulled the trigger I did not hear the bang or feel the kick—one never does when a shot goes home—but I heard the devilish roar of glee that went up from the crowd. In that instant, in too short a time, one would have thought, even for the bullet to get there, a mysterious, terrible change had come over the elephant. He neither stirred nor fell, but every line of his body had altered. He looked suddenly stricken, shrunken, immensely old, as though the frightful impact of the bullet had paralysed him without knocking him down. At last, after what seemed a long time—it might have been five seconds, I dare say—he sagged flabbily to his knees. His mouth slobbered. An enormous senility seemed to have settled upon him. One could have imagined him thou-sands of years old. I fired again into the same spot. At the second shot he did not collapse but climbed with desperate slowness to his feet and stood weakly upright, with legs sagging and head drooping. I fired a third time. That was the shot that did for him. You could see the agony of it jolt his whole body and knock the last remnant of strength from his legs. But in falling he seemed for a moment to rise, for as his hind legs collapsed beneath him he seemed to tower upward like a huge rock toppling, his trunk reaching skywards like a tree. He trumpeted, for the first and only time. And then down he came, his belly towards me, with a crash that seemed to shake the ground even where I lay.

12   I got up. The Burmans were already racing past me across the mud. It was obvious that the elephant would never rise again, but he was not dead.

He was breathing very rhythmically with long rattling gasps, his great mound of a side painfully rising and falling. His mouth was wide open— I could see far down into caverns of pale pink throat. I waited a long time for him to die, but his breathing did not weaken. Finally I fired my two remaining shots into the spot where I thought his heart must be. The thick blood welled out of him like red velvet, but still he did not die. His body did not even jerk when the shots hit him, the tortured breathing continued without a pause. He was dying, very slowly and in great agony, but in some world remote from me where not even a bullet could damage him further. I felt that I had got to put an end to that dreadful noise. It seemed dreadful to see the great beast lying there, powerless to move and yet powerless to die, and not even to be able to finish him. I sent back for my small rifle and poured shot after shot into his heart and down his throat. They seemed to make no impression. The tortured gasps continued as steadily as the ticking of a clock.

13   In the end I could not stand it any longer and went away. I heard later that it took him half an hour to die. Burmans were bringing dahs and baskets even before I left, and I was told they had stripped his body almost to the bones by the afternoon.

14   Afterwards, of course, there were endless discussions about the shooting of the elephant. The owner was furious, but he was only an Indian and could do nothing. Besides, legally I had done the right thing, for a mad elephant has to be killed, like a mad dog, if its owner fails to control it. Among the Europeans opinion was divided. The older men said I was right, the younger men said it was a damn shame to shoot an elephant for killing a coolie, because an elephant was worth more than any damn Coringhee coolie. And afterwards I was very glad that the coolie had been killed; it put me legally in the right and it gave me a sufficient pretext for shooting the elephant. I often wondered whether any of the others grasped that I had done it solely to avoid looking a fool.

THINKING ABOUT THE TEXT

1. Why was the narrator "hated by large numbers of people" when he lived in Burma? Cite specific examples that reveal how the narrator was truly trapped between worlds.

2. Describe the elephant's destruction and its death. What might the elephant represent here?

3. What do the responses to the shooting of the elephant reveal about the narrator (in his younger days)? About the older Europeans? the younger Europeans? the Burmans?

4. What is significant about the responses to the death of the coolie?

5. What is Orwell suggesting about the effect of imperialism on humanity? Support your response.

6. What are the different insights that can be drawn from this story?

7. Although Orwell's thesis isn't articulated specifically, what do you think it might be?

WRITING FROM THE TEXT

1. Citing specific examples from the text, compare and contrast Orwell as character (in his younger days) with Orwell as interpreter of this incident.

2. Dramatize a time in your life when you felt pressured to do something in order to save face. Parallel Orwell's vivid details. Focus on a strong thesis that shows what you learned from this experience.

CONNECTING WITH OTHER TEXTS

1. Compare Orwell's experience of living between worlds in India with Marcus Mabry's experience of "Living in Two Worlds" (p. 144). In what ways are their experiences similar? Write an essay from a well-formulated thesis.

2. Write an analysis of George Orwell's behavior in a crowd in light of Carol Tavris's explanations from "In Groups We Shrink" (p. 277). Include specific statements from both essays.

3. Read Orwell's autobiographical text, *Down and Out in Paris and London*. Write a character analysis of Eric Blair based on evidence from his texts. Focus on a strong thesis supported by specific character inferences.

In Groups We Shrink
Carol Tavris

After studying sociology and comparative literature at Brandeis University, Carol Tavris (b. 1944) earned her Ph.D. in social psychology at the University of Michigan. Tavris has worked as a freelance writer, taught in UCLA's psychology department, written for *Vogue*, *Harper's*, and *G.Q.*, and served as an editor for *Psychology Today*. She has published extensively in the field of psychology, with emphasis on emotions, anger, sexuality, and gender issues. She has taught at the New School for Social Research in New York City since 1983. Her critically regarded book, *The Mismeasure of Woman*, was published in 1992. The essay printed here appeared in the *Los Angeles Times* in 1991.

1   The ghost of Kitty Genovese would sympathize with Rodney King. Genovese, you may remember, is the symbol of bystander apathy in America. Screaming for help, she was stabbed repeatedly and killed in front of her New York apartment, and not one of the 38 neighbors who heard her, including those who came to their windows to watch, even called for help.

2   One of the things we find appalling in the videotape of King's assault is the image of at least 11 police officers watching four of their colleagues administer the savage beating and doing nothing to intervene. Whatever is the matter with them, we wonder.

3   Something happens to individuals when they collect in a group. They think and act differently than they would on their own. Most people, if they observe some disaster or danger on their own—a woman being stabbed, a pedestrian slammed by a hit-and-run driver—will at least call for help; many will even risk their own safety to intervene. But if they are in a group observing the same danger, they hold back. The reason is not necessarily that they are lazy, cowardly or have 50 other personality deficiencies; it has more to do with the nature of groups than the nature of individuals.

4   In one experiment in behavioral psychology, students were seated in a room, either alone or in groups of three, as a staged emergency occurred: Smoke began pouring through the vents. Students who were on their own usually hesitated a minute, got up, checked the vents and then went out to report what certainly seemed like fire. But the students who were sitting in groups of three did not move. They sat there for six minutes, with smoke so thick they could barely see, rubbing their eyes and coughing.

5   In another experiment, psychologists staged a situation in which people overheard a loud crash, a scream and a woman in pain, moaning that her ankle was broken. Seventy percent of those who were alone when the "accident" occurred went to her aid, compared with only 40 percent of those who heard her in the presence of another person.

6   For victims, obviously, there is no safety in numbers. Why? One reason is that if other people aren't doing anything, the individual assumes that nothing needs to be done. In the smoke-filled room study, the students in groups said they thought that the smoke was caused by "steam pipes," "truth gas" or "leaks in the air conditioning"; not one said what the students on their own did: "I thought it was fire." In the lady-in-distress study, some of those who failed to offer help said, "I didn't want to embarrass her."

7   Often, observers think nothing needs to be done because someone else has already taken care of it, and the more observers there are, the less likely any one person is to call for help. In Albuquerque, New Mexico, 30 people watched for an hour and a half as a building burned to the ground before

they realized that no one had called the fire department. Psychologists call this process "diffusion of responsibility" or "social loafing": The more people in a group, the lazier each individual in it becomes.

8   But there was no mistaking what those officers were doing to Rodney King. There was no way for those observers to discount the severity of the beating King was getting. What kept them silent?

9   One explanation, of course, is that they approved. They may have identified with the abusers, vicariously participating in a beating they rationalized as justified. The widespread racism in the Los Angeles Police Department and the unprovoked abuse of black people is now undeniable. A friend who runs a trucking company told me recently that one of her drivers, a 50-year-old black man, is routinely pulled over by Los Angeles cops for the flimsiest of reasons "and made to lie down on the street like a dog." None of her white drivers has been treated this way.

10   Or the observers may have hated what was happening and been caught in the oldest of human dilemmas: Do the moral thing and be disliked, humiliated, embarrassed and rejected. Our nation, for all its celebration of the Lone Ranger and the independent pioneer, does not really value the individual—at least not when the person is behaving individually and standing up to the group. (We like dissenters, but only when they are dissenting in Russia or China.) Again and again, countless studies have shown that people will go along rather than risk the embarrassment of being disobedient, rude or disloyal.

11   And so the banality of evil is once again confirmed. Most people do not behave badly because they are inherently bad. They behave badly because they aren't paying attention, or they leave it to Harry, or they don't want to rock the boat, or they don't want to embarrass themselves or others if they're wrong.

12   Every time the news reports another story of a group that has behaved mindlessly, violently and stupidly, including the inevitable members who are just "going along," many people shake their heads in shock and anger at the failings of "human nature." But the findings of behavioral research can direct us instead to appreciate the conditions under which individuals in groups will behave morally or not. Once we know the conditions, we can begin to prescribe antidotes. By understanding the impulse to diffuse responsibility, perhaps as individuals we will be more likely to act. By understanding the social pressures that reward groupthink, loyalty and obedience, we can foster those that reward whistle-blowing and moral courage. And, as a society, we can reinforce the belief that they also sin who only stand and watch.

THINKING ABOUT THE TEXT

1. What is Tavris's thesis? How does she support her position?

2. How does the psychologist's term for the behavior Tavris describes explain what actually happens?

3. How does Tavris imagine this condition will right itself?

WRITING FROM THE TEXT

1. Write about an incident that you observed or were a part of that confirms Carol Tavris's point.

2. Write about an incident that you observed or were a part of that shows an exception to Tavris's point.

CONNECTING WITH OTHER TEXTS

1. Read "Discrimination at Large" (p. 243) and argue that people's ridicule of fat people is often part of a group dynamic. Use Tavris's reasoning to show how people in groups sanction such ridicule. As part of your essay, consider Coleman's suggestion that the group can work as a whole to exert pressure on those who discriminate against the fat.

2. Research the Rodney King incident of 1991 to find interviews and court testimony from the police officers involved as participants or observers of the beating. Do their own words and feelings confirm or refute Tavris' thesis?

3. Read "Shooting an Elephant" (p. 270) and write an essay analyzing Orwell's behavior in light of the insights provided by Carol Tavris.

 # Three Ways of Meeting Oppression
Martin Luther King, Jr.

A graduate of Morehouse College, Crozer Theological Seminary, Boston University, and Chicago Theological Seminary, Martin Luther King, Jr. (1929–1968) received numerous awards for his literary work and leadership as well as the Nobel Prize for Peace in 1964. An ordained Baptist minister, King became well known as a national and international spokesperson for Civil Rights after his organization of the successful Montgomery, Alabama bus boycott. In spite of threatening phone calls, being arrested, and having his home bombed, King continued to work with nonviolent resistance and to argue eloquently for racial equality. He was assassinated on April 3, 1968. The following selection is excerpted from *Stride Toward Freedom,* published in 1958.

1   Oppressed people deal with their oppression in three characteristic ways. One way is acquiescence: the oppressed resign themselves to their doom. They tacitly adjust themselves to oppression, and thereby become conditioned to it. In every movement toward freedom some of the oppressed prefer to remain oppressed. Almost 2,800 years ago Moses set out to lead the children of Israel from the slavery of Egypt to the freedom of the promised land. He soon discovered that slaves do not always welcome their deliverers. They become accustomed to being slaves. They would rather bear those ills they have, as Shakespeare pointed out, than flee to others that they know not of. They prefer the "fleshpots of Egypt" to the ordeals of emancipation.

2   There is such a thing as the freedom of exhaustion. Some people are so worn down by the yoke of oppression that they give up. A few years ago in the slum areas of Atlanta, a Negro guitarist used to sing almost daily: "Ben down so long that down don't bother me." This is the type of negative freedom and resignation that often engulfs the life of the oppressed.

3   But this is not the way out. To accept passively an unjust system is to cooperate with that system; thereby the oppressed become as evil as the oppressor. Noncooperation with evil is as much a moral obligation as is cooperation with good. The oppressed must never allow the conscience of the oppressor to slumber. Religion reminds every man that he is his brother's keeper. To accept injustice or segregation passively is to say to the oppressor that his actions are morally right. It is a way of allowing his conscience to fall asleep. At this moment the oppressed fails to be his brother's keeper. So acquiescence—while often the easier way—is not the moral way. It is the way of the coward. The Negro cannot win the respect of his oppressor by acquiescing; he merely increases the oppressor's arrogance and contempt. Acquiescence is interpreted as proof of the Negro's inferiority. The Negro cannot win the respect of the white people of the South or the peoples of the world if he is willing to sell the future of his children for his personal and immediate comfort and safety.

4   A second way that oppressed people sometimes deal with oppression is to resort to physical violence and corroding hatred. Violence often brings about momentary results. Nations have frequently won their independence in battle. But in spite of temporary victories, violence never brings permanent peace. It solves no social problem; it merely creates new and more complicated ones.

5   Violence as a way of achieving racial justice is both impractical and immoral. It is impractical because it is a descending spiral ending in destruction for all. The old law of an eye for an eye leaves everybody blind. It is immoral because it seeks to humiliate the opponent rather than win his understanding; it seeks to annihilate rather than to convert. Violence is immoral because it thrives on hatred rather than love. It destroys a community and

makes brotherhood impossible. It leaves society in monologue rather than dialogue. Violence ends by defeating itself. It creates bitterness in the survivors and brutality in the destroyers. A voice echoes through time saying to every potential Peter, "Put up your sword." History is cluttered with the wreckage of nations that failed to follow this command.

6   If the American Negro and other victims of oppression succumb to the temptation of using violence in the struggle for freedom, future generations will be the recipients of a desolate night of bitterness, and our chief legacy to them will be an endless reign of meaningless chaos. Violence is not the way.

7   The third way open to oppressed people in their quest for freedom is the way of nonviolent resistance. Like the synthesis in Hegelian philosophy, the principle of nonviolent resistance seeks to reconcile the truths of two opposites—acquiescence and violence—while avoiding the extremes and immoralities of both. The nonviolent resister agrees with the person who acquiesces that one should not be physically aggressive toward his opponent but he balances the equation by agreeing with the person of violence that evil must be resisted. He avoids the nonresistance of the former and the violent resistance of the latter. With nonviolent resistance, no individual or group need submit to any wrong, nor need anyone resort to violence in order to right a wrong.

8   It seems to me that this is the method that must guide the actions of the Negro in the present crisis in race relations. Through nonviolent resistance the Negro will be able to rise to the noble height of opposing the unjust system while loving the perpetrators of the system. The Negro must work passionately and unrelentingly for full stature as a citizen, but he must not use inferior methods to gain it. He must never come to terms with falsehood, malice, hate, or destruction.

9   Nonviolent resistance makes it possible for the Negro to remain in the South and struggle for his rights. The Negro's problem will not be solved by running away. He cannot listen to the glib suggestion of those who would urge him to migrate en masse to other sections of the country. By grasping his great opportunity in the South he can make a lasting contribution to the moral strength of the nation and set a sublime example of courage for generations yet unborn.

10   By nonviolent resistance, the Negro can also enlist all men of good will in his struggle for equality. The problem is not a purely racial one, with Negroes set against whites. In the end, it is not a struggle between people at all, but a tension between justice and injustice. Nonviolent resistance is not aimed against oppressors but against oppression. Under its banner consciences, not racial groups, are enlisted.

11   If the Negro is to achieve the goal of integration, he must organize himself into a militant and nonviolent mass movement. All three elements are indispensable. The movement for equality and justice can only be a success if it has both a mass and militant character; the barriers to be overcome require both. Nonviolence is an imperative in order to bring about ultimate community.

THINKING ABOUT THE TEXT

1. What are the three ways that "oppressed people deal with oppression" (281)? Is the first method that King defines actually a way to *"deal"* with oppression?

2. What does King decide about each of the ways he defines and describes? What are the advantages of the method he prefers? Why does he prefer this method?

3. Cite the ways that King establishes that his argument is not only about "the Negro" struggling for rights.

4. King concludes that for "the Negro" to achieve civil rights and integration, "he must organize himself into a militant and nonviolent mass movement" (283). Because King has ruled out violence as a means of meeting oppression, the word *militant* may seem inappropriate. What does the word actually mean?

5. This excerpt from King's writing functions as an essay but lacks an articulated thesis. What do you infer to be the central assertion of this selection?

6. This excerpt is filled with exemplary rhetorical devices. Be prepared to discuss the following in class:

   How does King organize this section of his writing?

   What are King's transitional devices?

   What are the lines that remind the reader that King was a minister who spoke meaningfully and memorably from the pulpit?

   Pronouns are often used as effective connecting devices within paragraphs. (See p. 391 for a discussion of this device.) Examine King's use of the pronoun *it* in paragraph 5.

WRITING FROM THE TEXT

1. King concludes this section of his writing with the awareness that "nonviolence is an imperative in order to bring about ultimate community" (283). Write an essay that describes an "ultimate community" that King would consider acceptable.

2. Write an essay that shows your own experience or observations of specific moments of acquiescence, violence, or nonviolent resistance in response to oppression. Provide details about what worked and what did not work. Does your experience confirm or refute King's position?

CONNECTING WITH OTHER TEXTS

1. Compare and/or contrast King's ideas in this essay published in 1958 with the ideas of a black writer or speaker at the end of the twentieth century. Document the source of the ideas you include for examples in your essay.

2. In an essay, describe how Darnell in "Proper Care and Maintenance" (p. 186) lives in a "community." Integrate King's concepts with your discussion of Darnell's environment.

3. Show how Brent Staples (p. 237) exemplifies, in spite of conflicts, King's mandate. Analyze Staples's responses and methods.

Remote Control: How to Raise a Media Skeptic

Susan Douglas

A professor of media and American studies at Hampshire College in Massachusetts, Susan J. Douglas (b. 1950) is also media critic for the *Progressive* and a contributor to the *Village Voice, Nation, TV Guide, Journal of American History, ART News,* and *In These Times.* Douglas also is the author of *Inventing American Broadcasting, 1899–1922* (1987), *Where the Girls Are: Growing Up Female with the Mass Media* (1994), and *Listening in: Radio and the American Imagination* (1999). In *Where the Girls Are,* Douglas contrasts principles of the women's movement with popular images of women that appear on television, in films, and in the music industry. Douglas is concerned about the images of unattainable beauty popularized in the media, but she also finds positive images for women on television. For example, she believes that *Charlie's Angels* were "strong, intelligent women working together to fight crime." Douglas concludes, however, that "American women today are a bundle of contradictions because much of the media imagery we grew up with was filled with mixed messages about what women should and should not do." The following essay first appeared in the *Utne Reader* in 1997.

1   "Mommy, Mommy, come here now! Hurry, you're gonna miss it. It's Barbie's High-Steppin' Pony, and its legs really move! Hurreeeeey!"

2   "No!" I bark, as I'm wiping the dog barf up from the carpet, stirring the onions again so they don't burn, and slamming the phone down on a caller

from Citibank who wants to know how I'm doin' today. It is 5:56 P.M., and I'm in no mood. "I don't come for commercials, and besides, the horse doesn't really move—they just make it look that way."

3   "Oh yeah?" demands my daughter, sounding like a federal prosecutor. "It can too. It's not like those old ones where you told me they faked it—this one really does move."

4   So now I have to go see and, indeed, the sucker takes batteries, and the stupid horse moves—sort of. "See, Mommy, the commercials don't always lie."

5   Moments like this prompt me to wonder whether I'm a weak-kneed, lazy slug or, dare I say it, a hypocrite. See, I teach media studies, and, even worse, I go around the country lecturing about the importance of media literacy. One of my talking points is how network children's programming is, ideologically, a toxic waste dump. Yet here I am, just like millions of parents during that portion of the day rightly known as hell hour—dinnertime—shoving my kid in front of Nickelodeon so my husband and I can get dinner on the table while we whisper sweet nothings like "It's your turn to take her to Brownies tomorrow" and "Oh, shit, I forgot to tell you that your mother called three days ago with an urgent message."

6   We let her watch Nickelodeon, but I still pop in to ridicule Kool-Aid commercials or to ask her why Clarissa's parents (on *Clarissa Explains It All*) are so dopey. I am trying to have it both ways: to let television distract her, which I desperately need, and to help her see through its lies and banalities. I am very good at rationalizing this approach, but I also think it isn't a bad compromise for overworked parents who believe Barbie is the anti-Christ yet still need to wash out grotty lunch boxes and zap leftovers at the end of the day.

7   It's best to be honest up front: My house is not media proofed. I am not one of those virtuous, haloed parents who has banished the box from the home. I actually believe that there are interesting, fun shows for my daughter to watch on TV. (And I'm not about to give up *ER*.)

8   But I'm also convinced that knowing about television, and growing up with it, provides my daughter with a form of cultural literacy that she will need, that will tie her to her friends and her generation and help her understand her place in the world. So instead of killing my TV, I've tried to show my daughter basic bullshit-detecting techniques. Don't think your choices are either no TV or a zombified kid. Studies show that the simple act of intervening—of talking to your child about what's on television and why it's on there—is one of the most important factors in helping children understand and distance themselves from some of the box's more repugnant imagery.

9   I recommend the quick surgical strike, between throwing the laundry in and picking up the Legos. Watch a few commercials with them and point out

that commercials lie about the toys they show, making them look much better than they are in real life. Count how many male and female characters there are in a particular show or commercial and talk about what we see boys doing and what we see girls doing. Why, you might ask, do we always see girls playing with makeup kits and boys playing with little Johnny Exocet missiles? Real-life dads change diapers, push strollers, and feed kids, but you never see boys doing this with dolls on commercials. Ask where the Asian and African-American kids are. Point out how most of the parents in shows geared to kids are much more stupid than real-life parents. (By the way, children report that TV shows encourage them to talk back to their folks.) Tell them that all those cereals advertised with cartoon characters and rap music (like Cocoa Puffs and Trix) will put giant black holes in their teeth that only a dentist with a drill the size of the space shuttle can fix.

10   One of the best words to use when you're watching TV with your kids is *stupid,* as in "Aren't Barbie's feet—the way she's always forced to walk on her tiptoes—really stupid?" or "Isn't it stupid that Lassie is smarter than the mom on this show?" (My favorite Barbie exercise: Put your kitchen timer on for a minute and make your daughter walk around on her tiptoes just like Barbie: she'll get the point real fast.) *Cool*—a word that never seems to go out of style—is also helpful, as in "Isn't it cool that on *Legends of the Hidden Temple* (a game show on Nickelodeon) the girls are as strong and as fast as the boys?" Pointing out what's good on TV is important too.

11   See, I think complete media-proofing is impossible because the shallow, consumerist, anti-intellectual values of the mass media permeate our culture. And we parents shouldn't beat ourselves up for failing to quarantine our kids. But we can inoculate them—which means exposing them to the virus and showing them how to build up a few antibodies. So don't feel so guilty about letting them watch TV. Instead, have fun teaching them how to talk back to it rather than to you.

THINKING ABOUT THE TEXT

1. What might be Douglas's strategy for opening with a dialogue between herself and her daughter? How would you describe her "voice" throughout? Consider the images of her "wiping the dog barf up," needing to "wash out grotty lunch boxes and zap leftovers at the end of the day," and teaching her daughter "basic bullshit-detecting techniques."

2. List other phrases that reveal the author's sense of humor in this essay. Does her humor seem appropriate for this topic or distracting? Illustrate your response.

3. Rather than "banish the box from the home," how does Douglas try to teach her young daughter to become a more discriminating TV viewer? What are the reasons that she keeps a TV set in her home?

4. Although Douglas admits that we can't "quarantine our kids" from the toxins of television, we can "inoculate them—which means exposing them to the virus and showing them how to build up a few antibodies" (286). Find examples of Douglas's efforts to combine media studies and theories with practical advice for parents.

Writing from the Text

1. Write an essay analyzing Douglas's tone, voice, and use of humor.

2. Write an evaluative response to this essay based on your own experiences teaching children or being taught to be a more discriminating television viewer.

Connecting with Other Texts

1. Read "Dumpster-Diving for Dollars" (p. 319) and compare Hamm's observations about ways to avoid consuming with Douglas's suggestions for rearing a skeptic.

2. Using specific accusations and recommendations from Douglas, Swicord (p. 290), and Rosenberg (p. 297), write your own analysis of the effect of advertising and the television media on young people.

 Coke

Philip Dacey

A part-time college teacher at Southwest State University in Minnesota and a full-time poet, Philip Dacey (b. 1939) is widely published in anthologies and poetry journals. He coedited *Strong Measures: Contemporary American Poetry in Traditional Forms* and is author of *What's Empty Weighs the Most: Twenty-four Sonnets* (1997) and *The Deathbed Playboy* (1998). Dacey has an M.A. in English from Stanford University and a M.F.A. in creative writing from Iowa State University. Dacey's writing and teaching focus totally on poetry now, but he reveals, "For many years I dreamed of writing fiction but came to my senses when I was about fifty" and decided to concentrate on only one genre. The following poem was first published in *Night Shift at the Crucifix Factory* (1991) and later in *Stand Up Poetry: The Anthology* (1994). Dacey has given numerous poetry readings and has recorded "Coke" and other poems set to music by his sons.

I was proud of the Coca-Cola stitched in red
on the pocket of my dad's shirt,
just above his heart.
Coca-Cola was America

5   and my dad drove its truck.

I loved the way the letters curved,
like handwriting, something personal,
a friendly offer of a drink
to a man in need. Bring me your poor,

10   your thirsty.

And on every road I went, faces
under the sign of Coke smiled down
out of billboards at me. We were all
brothers and sisters in the family

15   of man, our bottles to our lips,
tipping our heads back to the sun.

My dad lifted me up when he came home,
his arms strong from stacking
case after case of Coke all day. A couple of

20   cold ones always waited for us in the kitchen.

I believed our President and my dad
were partners. My dad said someday Coke
would be sold in every country in the world,
and when that happened there would be

25   no more wars. "Who can imagine," he asked,
"two people fighting while they swig their Cokes?"
I couldn't. And each night before sleep,
I thanked God for my favorite drink.

When I did, I imagined him tilting the bottle

30   up to his heavenly lips, a little Coke
dribbling down his great white beard.

And sometimes I even thought of his
son on the cross, getting vinegar
but wanting Coke. I knew that if I

35   had been there, I would have handed a Coke
up to him, who would have figured out
how to take it, even though his hands
were nailed down good, because he was God.
And I would have said when he took it,
40   "That's from America, Jesus. I hope
you like it." And then I'd have watched,
amidst the thunder and lightning
on that terrible hill, Jesus' Adam's apple
bob up and down as he drained that bottle
45   in one long divine swallow
like a sweaty player at a sandlot game
between innings, the crucial ninth
coming up next.

And then the dark, sweet flood
50   of American sleep,
sticky and full of tiny bubbles,
would pour over me.

THINKING ABOUT THE TEXT

1. The narrator's opening words, "I was proud . . .", characterize his attitude as a young boy. Find phrases throughout the poem that reveal the numerous sources of his pride.

2. List the various characteristics of Coca-Cola in the poem. What does Coke represent?

3. Is the poet writing this as a young boy or as a man looking back to an earlier time? How can you tell? What was his vision of the world then? Find images to support your view.

4. Characterize the poet's tone. Is he innocent and hopeful? Smiling at his past naïveté? Bitter and disillusioned? Support your interpretation.

5. A number of images are ironic or incongruous—they contradict our expectation of what seems appropriate and, in this poem, contribute to its humor. List the images that seem ironic or comical.

6. What is the poet implying about a young boy's view of the world? What does America stand for here? Why does the narrator end the poem with this image: "the dark, sweet flood / of American sleep, / sticky and full of tiny

bubbles, / would pour over me"? What do these "tiny bubbles" suggest and why does he emphasize that his "American sleep" was "dark" yet "sweet"?

WRITING FROM THE TEXT

1. Write an essay or poem focusing on a key image or symbol from your own childhood and show how your attitude toward this symbol has changed over the years.

2. Read the section on poetry analysis and write an analysis of the product Coke as a critical symbol in this poem. (See exercise 2 above for help in brainstorming this topic.)

3. Write an analysis of what the poet is suggesting about American culture and values. Is he critical or supportive of what America represents? Is this poem to be read as a satire or to be read literally? How can you tell?

4. Compare and contrast the world of the young boy with the world of the adult narrator who seems nostalgic for this earlier time.

CONNECTING WITH OTHER TEXTS

1. Write an essay comparing and contrasting the narrator's attitude toward his dad in "Coke" with the narrator's attitude toward his father and grandfather in "Digging" (p. 42).

2. Write an essay contrasting the views of patriotism reflected by the narrator as a youth and by his father in "Coke" and by Todd Gitlin in "Patriotism Demands Questioning Authority" (p. 266). Analyze the factors that seem responsible for these different perspectives and include specific quotations from each work.

Youth Must Be Served— With Respect

Robin Swicord

Screenwriter of the 1997 NBC production of *Little Women* and the writer of *Shag, The Movie* and *Matilda*, Robin Swicord (b. 1952) earned a B.A. in English and theater from Florida State University. She is the author of two plays: *Last Days at the Dixie Girl Café* and *Criminal Minds*. Swicord is especially concerned about the effects of media on young people; her home is without a television set. Swicord thinks adolescence, when young people go through their first rites of passage, is an extraordinarily special time in life: "We don't have enough reverence for this time period, and most films for teens fail to reflect what it is really like to be a young person." The essay presented here, which first appeared in the *Los Angeles Times* in 1999, elicited numerous responses to the editor and prompted criticism from the author's movie-making associates.

1   "Where were the grownups?" was the refrain heard everywhere after the massacre at Columbine High School. I know where we were: at work, busy as ever, constructing a national culture that treats adolescents with unconcealed contempt.

2   Teenagers are under daily assault, all right—by us, the grown-ups. We design their clothes, manufacture and sell them their guns, produce the music that functions as the soundtrack for their lives, and control every aspect of their sprawling mega-high schools. In a dazzling display of cultural power, we also produce the movies, television shows, advertising and video games that entertain them and shape their minds.

3   We grown-ups in the entertainment industry trumpet our ability to sway young consumers but paradoxically claim that the content of our programs has no other power over the human mind. After the massacre at Littleton, Colorado, that stampeding noise you heard was the sound of entertainment executives retreating from their responsibility—except for ABC Chairman Bob Iger, who had the courage to admit, "When the finger is pointed at them about violence, they say their media has no influence; but they turn around and say just the opposite to advertisers. We should all admit our medium has an influence."

4   What we have as filmmakers and television producers is a great deal more than simple influence: As we enter the twenty-first century, we are the dominant cultural force in this nation. Thirty years ago, our work was considered "pulp fiction." Today, movies and television programs are studied in academia, discussed in the workplace and cited in the Congressional Record. Our influence extends far beyond our borders. A Harvard Medical School study in Fiji found that bulimia and anorexia—previously unknown among Fijians—skyrocketed after the arrival of American television in 1995. When the Sun Vista cruise liner sank near Malaysia earlier this month, 1,000 international passengers kept up their spirits by singing the song from *Titanic*.

5   The films we make shape minds. The movie *Top Gun* has been a phenomenal recruiting device for the Air Force and Navy—not only when it was released 13 years ago but also now, on video. We pride ourselves on being culture makers when we point to *The Shawshank Redemption* and *Schindler's List*, but we won't own up to our influence when it comes to the flood of mindless movies that exploit violence and other bloody spectacle—this in spite of many studies at our nation's top universities that appear to demonstrate a

link between watching violent entertainments and acting aggressively in life. (By the way, why are those ungrateful gun industry people trying to shift the blame to us when we're giving them all that free product placement? Movies are the best thing that ever happened to weapons manufacturers.)

6   Stories change lives and we know it, or we wouldn't be so passionate about writing and producing movies.

7   If the entertainment industry is careless about its influence on young people, it's only because we're embedded in a broader national culture that constantly demonstrates its disrespect toward children and adolescents, in every arena from child care to fashion.

8   Have you taken a young teenager shopping lately? Girls' clothing is available in two styles: "gangsta" or "whore," always with those two distinctive hallmarks of teen clothing—cheap fabric, poor workmanship. If your daughter's taste runs to anything more modest than Ginger Spice's, she might get desperate enough to do as our 12-year-old finally did: Ask for a sewing machine.

9   There's no problem finding "skater" fashions. We grown-ups sell skater clothes, shoes, magazines, skateboards and use skater images to market everything from skin care products to the new animated *Tarzan* movie. What we don't provide is a place to skateboard. All across the nation, we outlaw skaters in virtually every outdoor place where adolescents might be. When skateboarding serves commerce, it's cool. When it serves teens, it's illegal.

10   "Adults should face the fact that they don't like adolescents," says Leon Botstein, president of Bard College, writing for the *New York Times* last month. He argues persuasively that the huge, dysfunctional high schools we've built for our teen children exist largely to warehouse and isolate "the pubescent and hormonally active adolescent" away from the rest of us. How big are those warehouses? In New York and Los Angeles, many schools have enrollments close to 5,000. When Ruth Messinger campaigned against Rudy Giuliani for mayor, she complained about school overcrowding so severe that students were being taught in lavatories. (How much do we hate our kids?)

11   Between 1940 and 1990, the number of elementary and secondary public schools nationwide plummeted 69 percent, despite a 70 percent rise in U.S. population. In 1940, we had 200,000 public schools with about 28 million students; today we have 62,000 public schools, and 50 million school-age kids. To absorb all those adolescent bodies, schools have bulked up into enormous, impersonal office parks, serving students in factory-like shifts. This practice actively works against learning and promotes alienation.

12   "Breaking Ranks," the report by the Carnegie Foundation and the National Association of Secondary School Principals, spells out a hard but obvi-

ous truth: Teenagers learn more in smaller schools, preferably no more than 600 students in a "school unit." The report warns: If schools don't radically change, they "will exert dwindling influence on the ability to deliver learning."

13   What mega-high schools deliver instead is crowd control: security guards and metal detectors, locker searches, drug tests, few civil liberties and a curriculum that feels like a forced march through 50-minute classes covering material of questionable relevance, delivered in bite-sized pieces by overburdened and underpaid (in California, often uncredentialed) teachers—all culminating in standardized exams that help determine a student's future earning power. Are the kids not inspired to work in this environment? Management will fix that with school uniforms and more standardized tests.

14   If this were our life in *our* workplace, we grown-ups would resort to revolution.

15   As a nation, we may hate teens, but we *love* their demographic group. Our 50 million schoolkids spend at least $50 billion each year, and everyone from movie studios to soft drink makers is in a dead heat to separate these children from their money. Why the current glut of youth-oriented TV shows? As a network executive recently explained to *Murphy Brown* creator Diane English, "Kids haven't chosen their toothpaste for life."

16   As advertisers struggle to develop brand loyalty in teens whose adolescent biology hard-wires them for fickle emotions, kids are besieged by adults urgently demanding their consumer attention. My daughters and I curled up to watch the "Daria" special on MTV a couple of Sundays ago and saw "simultaneous commercials": While the audio sold contact-lens cleaner, the visual hawked an unrelated restaurant.

17   Kids can't escape the commercial assault. Check out the new Glencoe/McGraw-Hill textbook *Mathematics: Applications and Connections,* which shoves brand names at young learners.

18   Sample problem: "According to the results of a test conducted by *Zillions* magazine, 12 out of 17 kids prefer Sony PlayStation to Sega Saturn. Suppose there are 3,400 kids in your community. Predict how many will prefer the PlayStation."

19   Movie studios seem no more thoughtful about young people than any other commercial entity.

20   A few years ago, when our daughters were outgrowing *The Little Mermaid,* I spoke to three movie studios about the coming need for "young adult" movies of all kinds—"Y/A" fiction for the screen, rated PG-13. Studios, being unwieldy corporate entities, don't plan for an emerging market so much as react to demand, and their reaction time is gelatinously slow. I received no response to my suggestion, and R-rated *Scream I* and *II* soon filled the breach, followed by a spate of inexpensively produced teen sex comedies, the movie equivalent of the cheapo "gangsta/whore" clothes offered in teen boutiques.

21   Most current teen fare seems relatively harmless, but, as our 10th-grader noted: "They're not *Shakespeare in Love*—we won't be watching them in ten years." These movies may generate short-term box office, but their content rarely answers the real needs of adolescents.

22   Movies and TV give young people a place to rehearse their future autonomy. Teens need to see characters in moral dilemmas, so they can argue the issues. They need historically accurate stories that supplement their understanding of the past; and a dose of fantasy to escape the pressures of their lives, as well as the chance to enter practical worlds as yet closed to them. Above all, young people need to identify with a variety of protagonists, to privately explore different personas and "practice" the big emotions they will feel in real situations.

23   If those are the movies adolescents need, what do they get? Aw, you know what they get. And thanks to video, they get it over and over. Not only are the movies we make imitative of one another, but kids watch the same movies again and again, hit the rewind button to memorize their favorite moments. With DVD, teens can program the player to endlessly repeat the same scene in which the guy's brains fly out as his head comes apart—while they're online or on the phone with peers watching the same scene in their homes.

24   What is the effect of all that repetition? Jacob Riis, the nineteenth-century social reformer, spoke of seeing "a stonecutter hammering away at his rock, perhaps a hundred times without as much as a crack showing in it. Yet at the hundred-and-first blow it will split in two, and I know it was not that blow that did it, but all that had gone before."

25   And our kids really do get hammered—on one side by *The Basketball Diaries* and violent music, on the other by video games. From the Swiss psychologist-philosopher Jean Piaget we know that children learn best through play. When we design "first-person shooter" games such as "Doom" and "Quake," we are providing a form of play in which children learn to kill human targets. How effective is this? The Air Force trains test pilots on video-game-like simulators; the only difference is that in video games the sound effects and graphics are much more real.

26   What adolescents could use from the game industry is a video game that simulates real driving—a driver's education version of "Mavis Beacon," so kids can learn safety before they get behind the wheel. What adolescents get is "Carmageddon," "Interplay Productions," in which virtual motorists rack up points by running down pedestrians, a pursuit the company ad says is "as easy as killing babies with axes."

27   As filmmakers we recoil from the idea of even voluntary censorship in our industry, but I would argue that voluntary censorship is already in place. In a medium shaped by free-market forces, the First Amendment often seems

irrelevant. When producer Julia Chasman and I wanted to film Christine Bell's *The Perez Family,* a studio head told us bluntly, "Who wants to see a movie about a bunch of Cubans?" Here are some things you never or rarely see on film: The main character is a devout Christian (unless they're unhinged, as in *The Apostle*); the female protagonist has more than one lover (James Bond can be promiscuous; Jane Bond, no); tragedies (no dead protagonists, *Titanic* aside); issue-oriented stories ("that's TV"); historical movies, unless they are epics; ambiguous endings; and diseases other than cancer.

28 "Our choices are market-driven!" executives counter. While it's true that what's already popular in the marketplace tends to determine what films are produced (and which movie stars are cast), we do have *some* standards, folks, or Warners and Sony and Paramount et al. would be making lucrative straight-to-video porn. As culture makers, we do feel some responsibility not to exploit the most base human interests.

29 What happened at Columbine provides what educators call "the teachable moment"—an opportunity for us to reexamine what we believe and what kind of cultural contribution we want to make. The entertainment business is jammed with people who are intelligent, well-informed, interesting, moral and politically astute. Why does so little of our work reflect who we are?

30 At any industry screening of a particularly good movie, the most commonly heard phrase is "How did that get made?" Given our power to influence the young people who live inside our culture, what is our responsibility? If we were the sole purveyors of food, would we forgo cancer-fighting Brussels sprouts ("no demand") and sell only chips and candy bars? Or would we feel a civic obligation to provide nourishment as well?

31 If we understood that this is a time of national emergency, we would quickly limit the sheer volume of products that contribute to the culture's atmosphere of violence and incivility. In counterbalance we'd create a wealth of movies and programs that inspire and challenge teens, cause them to think and question, that help to counter the national funk of cynicism, and show human beings solving problems without resorting to violence.

32 It's our responsibility to help reverse the current negative forces—but the good news is that we know we have the power to do so. Stories and images do change lives.

THINKING ABOUT THE TEXT

1. Consider where Robin Swicord's essay was first published to help you determine her intended audience. What is her aim in this essay? What is her claim? What is her strategy in using the statement from ABC Chairman Bob Inger early in her essay?

2. Swicord claims that the film and television industry is "the dominant cultural force in this nation." What does she mean? What evidence does she give to support this claim? Do you agree with her?

3. Swicord claims that the entertainment industry is "careless about its influence on young people," although that industry is only one of many that "demonstrates disrespect toward children and adolescents." What is her diverse support for this assertion? Evaluate her examples.

4. Insisting that "we may hate teens, but we *love* their demographic group," Swicord cynically cites contexts where young adults are valued. Where and why?

5. In analyzing the content of "young adult" movies, Swicord claims that rather than horror movies and sex comedies, teenagers need to prepare for their coming independence. They "need to see characters in moral dilemmas, so they can argue the issues" (294); they need films that are historically accurate and some "fantasy to escape the pressures of their lives." Do you agree that movies and television films for young people should have more profound content?

6. In addition to the television and film industry, Swicord examines the world of video games. What is her view of the electronic game world for young people? Why does she refer to Jean Piaget?

7. Swicord claims that the "entertainment business is jammed with people who are intelligent, well-informed, interesting, moral, and politically astute" (295). And she asks, "Why does so little of our work reflect who we are?" How does her essay answer that question?

8. Swicord concludes her essay by acknowledging that "stories and images do change lives." Reread the last four paragraphs of the essay. What is Swicord's strategy for the conclusion of her essay?

WRITING FROM THE TEXT

1. Write a response to Swicord, or the entire film and movie industry, that draws on Swicord's essay as well as your own experience, to support her claim that American young people are treated with "unconcealed contempt" and that nowhere is this contempt more evident than in the movies made for an adolescent audience.

2. Write an essay arguing that America is a youth-obsessed culture and that families and government are driven by the needs, desires, and even the demands of young people. You might examine how some households are designed to meet the educational and social needs of children.

3. Write an analysis of current television programming and film industry releases that supports or contradicts Swicord's position. Use specific

examples of plots, themes, and even language from the work that you cite as negative or positive media influences.

4. Write an analysis of clothing for young girls that supports or refutes Swicord's claim that it is made of "cheap fabric and poor workmanship" and is available in two styles: "gangsta" or "whore." Instead of writing about clothing for girls, you might consider writing an essay that analyzes the clothing styles and quality available for young men. How will you categorize the styles? Do you feel that contempt is behind the manufacturing of fashions for young people? Let your position show in your essay.

5. Write an essay arguing that the entertainment industry is not responsible for young people's behavior and values. Focus your essay by analyzing the forces that do or should influence youth.

CONNECTING WITH OTHER TEXTS

1. Swicord cites *The Basketball Diaries* as an example of the violent "hammering" that negatively affects young people. In the letters to the newspaper that responded to Swicord's essay, even readers who otherwise supported her views of the industry thought that she was wrong in using *The Basketball Diaries* as an example. Write an analysis of that film that focuses on its positive significance rather than its violence.

2. Howard Rosenberg, a television critic for the *Los Angeles Times*, argues in "Making Media a Familiar Scapegoat" (following) that the television and movie industry is not responsible for the dramatic incidences of adolescent violence that we have seen in the United States. Write an essay that incorporates the ideas of Swicord and Rosenberg to make *your* point.

3. In what ways do Robin Swicord's observations about the entertainment and fashion industries reflect Carol Tavris's idea that "In Groups We Shrink" (p. 277)? Write a paper analyzing how group conformity influences these industries.

Making Media a Familiar Scapegoat

Howard Rosenberg

Renowned television critic Howard Rosenberg (b. 1938) has worked for the *Los Angeles Times* since 1978. He earned a B.A. in history from the University of Oklahoma and an M.A. in political science from the University of Minnesota. In addition to writing for the *Times*, Rosenberg also teaches an ethics of television course and film criticism at two universities in Los Angeles. In 1985 he was awarded a Pulitzer Prize, and he is currently working on a comic mystery novel. The following selection was first published in the April 23, 1999 issue of the *Los Angeles Times* and online at <www.latimes.com>.

1   After presenting Terror in Littleton like a blockbuster ratings-sweeps production, TV has become one of its casualties.

2   That's because some myopic Americans see media as the root of all evil. The mantra: If it's bad, television—or the movies—caused it.

3   This becomes their knee-jerk response to every violent tragedy, the latest being Tuesday's slaughter at Columbine High in Littleton, Colorado, where the body count soared to fifteen, courtesy of two gun-blazing, bomb-lobbing members of the school's Trench Coat Mafia, who capped their efforts by apparently taking their own lives. Now comes the question everyone is asking.

4   What turned Eric Harris and Dylan Klebold—whose class pictures project them as ordinary and benign—into cold-blooded assassins? Although several possible explanations are being floated, one is especially familiar.

5   "We have to look at television, we have to look at cable," Colorado Governor Bill Owens told reporters this week.

6   Of course, blame TV.

7   In a fleeting gesture of benevolence, the Reverend Jerry Falwell acknowledged Wednesday night that Hollywood was not entirely to blame for violence in the United States. Having contributed that, however, no more Mr. Nice Guy.

8   "Certainly the media must take a good part of it [the blame]," Falwell added during a discussion of Littleton on *Hannity & Colmes,* an interview program on the Fox News Channel.

9   "TV and movies have been glorifying violent bloody crime and so forth," Falwell said. "And now it's reached critical mass." Things will get only worse, he predicted, "until we have a spiritual awakening, until we get violence off the screen."

10   In other words, scapegoat time.

11   Falwell passed the anti-TV baton to another easily lathered media watchdog, L. Brent Bozell III, who immediately began frothing over "virtual reality death shows," with opposition from another guest, former talk-show host Richard Bey. The latter's insistence that TV "doesn't make children murderers" was flicked away by Bozell like someone brushing lint from his lapel.

12   As if TV made Harris and Klebold do it, Bozell declared: "Night after night, you are desensitized to very serious issues, and you don't care about life and death, and you blow people away."

13   Bozell bleated out the usual statistics about numerous acts of TV violence seen by the average kid watching entertainment shows, ignoring the point that there are probably ten depictions of goodness on TV for every one of hatred. Thus, if TV is the icon that some insist, it must be making us nicer, right? Or is

hate a more powerful influence than love? In any case, while fishing through his trove of statistics, Bozell omitted those other figures, the latest ones from the FBI showing that violent crime has diminished in the United States.

14 The big screen was the program's next target. Specifically, *The Basketball Diaries,* a 1995 movie in which Leonardo DiCaprio wore a long black coat while blasting away in a classroom with a shotgun.

15 Parents of three high school kids gunned down by a classmate in West Paducah, Kentucky, in 1997 are suing makers of *The Basketball Diaries,* claiming that the movie helped motivate the killer to shoot their children. Just as a paralyzed shooting victim is suing makers of *Natural Born Killers,* insisting that her assailant was influenced by that film.

16 CBS said that plaintiffs in both suits were being interviewed for a segment on Sunday's *60 Minutes,* in which they apparently will issue strong indictments of those movies and other elements of media.

17 The reality is that there are some among us who might receive a message to kill from *Bambi.* And what's to be done about that?

18 There's loose talk now about *The Basketball Diaries* having been a primer in Littleton for Harris and Klebold, who reportedly wore long black coats during their murderous rampage.

19 In that regard, the movie's alleged homicidal influence didn't stop *Hannity & Colmes*—nor newscasts everywhere—from repeatedly showing that scene of DiCaprio blowing away classmates in the movie.

20 Also pondering the villainy of TV vis-à-vis Littleton this week was that buck-skinned smoothie Gerry Spence. Wednesday, on Oprah Winfrey's syndicated talk show, he preached the catchy gospel ("Once we disarm the heart, we don't need to disarm anything else") that he developed the previous night on CNN's *Larry King Live.*

21 After hearing him, disarming Spence's tongue seemed like the best idea of all.

22 The famous defense attorney had TV mostly in mind when mentioning the "seeds of violence that we plant in this country." As evidence that he doesn't watch TV, he cited movie star Arnold Schwarzenegger as one of the "television heroes" serving as role models for kids, asking, "How many does he kill in a night?"

23 Another guest, Maryland Lieutenant Governor Kathleen Kennedy Townsend, pushed hard for child-proofing guns in response to Littleton: "We have safety locks for aspirin, for cars and for lawn mowers. Why do we continue to put guns in a separate category?"

24 King was sympathetic. "It does seem insane, Gerry."

25 Spence wouldn't budge. "Well, I tell ya what I think. She's talking about teaching responsibility to kids, but who's gonna teach responsibility to

the parents? That's where it starts. It starts with television." Going from Schwarzenegger to parents to television seemed quite a leap. But like juries that Spence is famous for charming, King never questioned it.

26   Instead, their selective memories merging, King and Spence talked of the good old days. "You know, when you and I grew up," said Spence, "we had these nice, quiet, soft . . . nobody got . . . we didn't have blood all over. We didn't have people's heads exploding. We didn't see life as valueless. We saw there were the bad guys and the good guys."

27   The talk turned to such super heroes as the Batman of old.

> KING: "Never killed anybody."
>
> SPENCE: "Superman never killed anybody."
>
> KING: "Gene Autry never killed anybody."
>
> SPENCE: "In my time it was Tom Mix and Wild Bill Hickok. They shot somebody, but it was nice and clean, and it was always the bad guy."

28   In other words, violence presented as "nice and clean" passes the test, but the bloody consequences of violence—as reflected in the gore of Littleton—does not?

29   King and Spence appeared to be arguing for depictions of violence to be sanitized and glamorized, exactly what antiviolence advocates for years have been arguing against. Wasn't it Falwell who was objecting to "glorifying violent bloody crime"? Just as critics of *The Basketball Diaries* object to how cool DiCaprio looks when he pulls the trigger.

30   Not that it probably matters. Trench coats don't kill, guns and pipe bombs do.

Thinking about the Text

1. Explain the term "scapegoat" and note all terms that Rosenberg uses in his opening paragraphs to underscore his sense that the media are being unfairly blamed for violence, particularly in the Littleton, Colorado, shootings.

2. What is the effect of including quotations from the Reverend Jerry Falwell, media watchdog L. Brent Bozell III, and defense attorney Gerry Spence? How does Rosenberg reveal his views of their claims?

3. Why does Rosenberg criticize talk show celebrities who express nostalgia for past television shows in which violence was "nice and clean"? What is ironic about their nostalgia?

4. What is Rosenberg's rationale for arguing that films such as *The Basketball Diaries* should not be held responsible for violent actions committed by viewers? Do you agree or disagree, and why?

WRITING FROM THE TEXT

1. Write an essay concurring with or refuting Rosenberg's claim that the television and film media are scapegoats for those seeking an easy solution to violence and for those campaigning to "get violence off the screen" (298).

2. In an essay, analyze Rosenberg's argument strategy: use of reason, evidence, and specific support. Are there any logical fallacies? (See p. 446.) What is Rosenberg's tone throughout and how does his tone and attitude contribute to or detract from his argument?

CONNECTING WITH OTHER TEXTS

1. Read "Youth Must Be Served—With Respect" (p. 291) and list Swicord's charges about violence and the media that oppose Rosenberg's points. Write an essay to convince your reader of *your* view on this debate; use details from both articles.

2. Visit the website for the *Los Angeles Times* (<www.latimes.com>) and read several of the related materials about the shooting at Columbine High School in 1999 (such as "*Times* Stories," "What Happened," or "Government Violence Study"). Select relevant details that you may be able to use in an essay evaluating Rosenberg's position.

3. Rosenberg includes statements from a dialogue between talk show host Larry King and attorney Gerry Spence, both of whom long for the return of shows such as *Batman* and *Superman,* where the violence is "nice and clean." View reruns of these shows or rent the videos and write an essay agreeing or disagreeing with Rosenberg that the violence in these shows is simply "sanitized and glamorized," and therefore equally offensive.

Press 1 to Cut Short Your Life
Jonathan Alter

A graduate of Harvard University, Jonathan Alter (b. 1957) worked as a speechwriter at the White House in 1978 and as a lobbyist for Save the Dunes Council, 1979–1990. In 1980 he began his career with *Newsweek,* working his way up to associate editor and then to his current position as editor. In addition, Alter serves as consultant to the Federal Aviation Administration. He has coauthored *Selecting a President* (1980) and coedited *Inside the System,* Vol. V (1984). The following essay, which appeared in *Newsweek,* May 20, 2002, offers a humorous reaction to high-tech society, blaming "not the software but the soft thinking" that characterizes "corporate America."

1   Some health risks are more immediate than others: Saddam Hussein has weapons of mass destruction, an ice shaft bigger than Manhattan has plummeted into the sea near Antarctica, signaling global warming . . . and *I'm still on hold.* It was only one night last week, but it felt like a year in Jalalabad. Remember the anti-smoking ad that said you lose a minute of life for every minute you smoke? That was a bargain. I figured I was losing a full year of life for every hour of grinding aggravation spent on the phone with that peculiar species known as the customer-service representative.

2   At 2:20 a.m. I finally gave up, unsuccessful in my three-hour effort to restore my Internet service, which had been cut off for unexplained reasons. (No, it wasn't a late bill payment.) The particular company I was having trouble with was Comcast, but its ratings, according to the University of Michigan's American Customer Satisfaction Index, are in the middle of the pack for industry. It could have been practically any company turning a perfectly healthy and even-tempered person into a promising candidate for a coronary.

3   Clearly, if Franz Kafka were alive today he'd be writing about customer service. Just calling directory assistance can set your teeth on edge. In my case, the reps were never rude; they treated me indulgently, as if I were a mental patient who had neglected his medication. But the rules under which they operate are enough to make anyone rage against the machine.

4   I was lucky. At least I talked to actual human beings. *The Wall Street Journal*'s Jane Spencer reported last week that companies are spending billions on automated systems designed to prevent customers from reaching operators. The paper found one man who had to call AT&T WorldNet 15 times and endure 600 minutes on hold just to talk to someone.

5   My own *Groundhog Day* routine involved sitting on hold—often for the length of a sitcom—for "the first available customer representative," who insisted on hearing the details of my situation (which I had already explained several times before), then passed me through two higher levels of supervisor, who said the problem would be taken up by a "provisioning team" at some unspecified future date.

6   Around this time, I heard those fateful taped words ("If you wish to make a call . . .") indicating I had once again been disconnected. Because the reps were not allowed to give me their extensions (for reasons of "efficiency," says a Comcast spokesman), I had to start the whole thing again. As the night wore on and I began tossing around the name of the company's CEO, "Reuben"—or maybe it was "Sue," "Marian" or "Robin"—informed me that my problem was being referred to "escalations." This is apparently their euphemism for: Customer may be armed and dangerous.

7   Of course, if I wanted to pay my tormentors a visit, I would have a hard time finding them. Customer-service reps are everywhere—and nowhere. They have become the disembodied household gods of the age, reminders of our helplessness in the face even of technologies we understand. They don't offend as much as exasperate, as if part of some cosmic conspiracy to see how we will pay in high blood pressure for our amenities.

8   Customers bear a share of the blame because we've become addicted to speed. The modem that once seemed fast now feels interminable. But the real victims of technology are the companies themselves. Bad service in a "service economy" (80 percent of GDP) is a surefire strategy for losing money. Some consultants writing in the *Harvard Business Review* last year (no, not Suzy Wetlaufer) found that more than half of all efforts to improve customer relations fail, mostly because companies see it as an information-technology problem.

9   Wrong. As usual in corporate America, it's not the software but the soft thinking. How often have you heard the recording "We are experiencing a higher-than-usual volume of calls"? And how rarely, asks Charles Fishman in *Fast Company* magazine, have you felt you were "experiencing a higher-than-usual volume of staff"?

10   In a new book, *Once Upon a Town*, Bob Greene writes about a railroad-station canteen in the tiny town of North Platte, Neb., where the locals fed 6 million GIs passing through during World War II. Greene argues that this was "the best America that ever was." Maybe so. Maybe we've lost some old-fashioned American humanity. But I'd argue that the problem is less the people than the roles they're asked to play by corporate America. Can't answer the calls too easily or it might encourage the customer to seek more such human contact. Can't fix the problem without authorization. Can't be accountable.

11   Actually, you could—if you'd just take me off hold.

THINKING ABOUT THE TEXT

1. How does Alter capture reader interest in his opening paragraph? What contributes to his humor and how does he continue amusing readers throughout his essay? Give examples.

2. As Alter recounts his efforts to get his Internet service restored, he not only entertains readers but also educates. What are some of the outside sources that he uses and how does each support his points and portray him as an educated consumer?

3. Alter refers to Austrian writer Franz Kafka (1883–1924), author of "The Metamorphosis" and *The Trial*, who dramatized the absurdities in modern-

day existence. Why does Alter claim that "if Franz Kafka were alive today he'd be writing about customer service"? Which situations in particular might Kafka ridicule?

4. Who does Alter claim are "the real victims" and why? What does Alter feel is ultimately responsible for the inadequacies in customer service?

5. Explain the ironies in Alter's statement that customer-service reps are the "disembodied household gods of the age, reminders of our helplessness in the face even of technologies we understand."

6. Trace how Alter develops the motif of technological frustrations as a health risk. Why is this analogy so effective?

WRITING FROM THE TEXT

1. Focusing on your own frustrating experiences with customer service reps, write an analysis of the causes and effects of each frustration. Use specific references from Alter's essay to support your reasoning.

2. Write an analysis of Alter's techniques to entertain and amuse readers—his use of euphemisms, irony, sarcasm, exaggeration, witty descriptions, and inappropriate responses—while exposing the problems with customer service in corporate America. Evaluate the effectiveness of his humor.

CONNECTING WITH OTHER TEXTS

1. In an essay, use information from Alter's essay and from Stoll's (p. 304) to analyze the limitations of some technological "advancements." Focus your thesis on what you perceive as the main cause of the problems you examine.

2. Using details from Alter's essay, write an essay evaluating the optimistic claims that Tapscott makes in his essay (p. 313) promoting a communications revolution in education today. Include direct quotations from both essays and analyze them fully.

 Makes Learning Fun

Clifford Stoll

An astronomer who is better known for his writings on computer technology, Clifford Stoll (b. 1950) has had the satisfaction of tracking down a computer hacker who constituted a threat to national security, a tale Stoll recounted in *The Cuckoo's Egg: Tracking a*

Spy Through the Maze of Computer Espionage (1989). In spite of his expertise and reliance on computers in his own life, Stoll exposes the harmful effects of computers on children in *Silicon Snake Oil* (1995). In *High-Tech Heretic: Why Computers Don't Belong in the Classroom and Other Reflections by a Computer Contrarian* (1999), Stoll deplores the fact that computers take money away from library books and other educational necessities, even as they take time away from young people's social development. The following excerpt is from *High-Tech Heretic.*

1   Technology promises shortcuts to higher grades and painless learning. Today's edutainment software comes shrink-wrapped in computing's magic mantra: "Makes Learning Fun."

2   You'll hear it from IBM: "The latest Aptivas have a superior selection of top-rated educational software titles like Kid's Room, an Aptiva exclusive that gives your kids a fun place to learn." The fluff goes on about "extreme multimedia delivers full-screen action, blazing graphics and front-row-center-seat sound, resulting in maximum impact in any application."

3   Public schools agree. Here's a press release pushing software developed by the Texas Agricultural Extension Service, and aimed at 4-H clubs: "It may sound fishy, but Texas 4th graders now have the opportunity to go fishing for facts on the computer, improve their academic skills, learn how they can conserve water and maintain its quality in the state's lakes and streams and have fun at the same time."

4   The phrase shows up in promotions for college classes, too: The School of Journalism at University of North Carolina at Chapel Hill teaches a core course in Electronic Information Sources. The class motto: Learning is Fun.

5   An Oregon high school student who's spent plenty of time online wrote: "I mean if I had a choice to learn in a fun matter or a tradtial [sic] book manner I would choice the fun way of learning."

6   Read the promotion for Western Michigan University software to learn about groundwater: It "uses animation, so learning about Calhoun County is more of a video game than a dry lesson or research project . . ."

7   Learn on your own. Blazing graphics and maximum impact. Go fishing for facts. Learning will be more of a video game than a lesson. Technology makes learning fun. Just one problem.

8   It's a lie.

9   Most learning isn't fun. Learning takes work. Discipline. Commitment, from both teacher and student. Responsibility—you have to do your homework. There's no shortcut to a quality education. And the payoff isn't an adrenaline rush, but a deep satisfaction arriving weeks, months, or years later. Equating learning with fun says that if you don't enjoy yourself, you're not learning.

10   What good are glitzy gadgets to a child who can't pay attention in class, won't read more than a paragraph, and is unable to write analytically? If we want our children to read books, why direct them to computer screens, where it's painful to read more than a few pages? If kids watch too much TV, why bring multimedia video systems into schools?

11   These teaching machines direct students away from reading, away from writing, away from scholarship. They dull questioning minds with graphical games where quick answers take the place of understanding, and the trivial is promoted as educational. They substitute quick answers and fast action for reflection and critical thinking. Thinking, after all, involves originality, concentration, and intention.

12   Computing's instant gratification—built into the learning-is-fun mindset—encourages intellectual passivity, driven mainly by conditioned amusement. Fed a diet of interactive insta-grat, students develop a distaste for persistence, trial and error, attentiveness, or patience.

13   This obsession with turning the classroom into a funhouse isn't new. Eighty years ago in *Thirteen Lectures,* Austrian educator Rudolf Steiner wrote, "I've often heard that there must be an education which makes learning a game for children; school must become all joy. The children should laugh all the time and learning will be play. This is the best educational principle to ensure that nothing at all is learned."

14   Yep, kids love computers. Indeed, it's mainly adults who are uncomfortable around keyboards and monitors. But just what do children learn from computers?

15   Turning learning into fun denigrates the most important things we can do in life: to learn and to teach. It cheapens both process and product: Dedicated teachers try to entertain, students expect to learn without working, and scholarship becomes a computer game. When in doubt, turn to the electronic mind-crutch.

16   Is the main problem of today's children that they haven't enough fun? Are kids really deprived of excitement? Are schoolchildren exposed to too few media messages—so that we must bring them the Internet with still more? Must every classroom lesson be sugarcoated by dancing animatrons and singing cartoon characters? Is the job of our schools to provide additional screen time for students who watch three or four hours of television a night?

17   "All schools need high-speed Internet connections and the appropriate computer hardware to deliver the latest educational applications . . . equal resources should be directed to the creation of dynamic, 3-D virtual learning environments," says Linda Hahner, president of Out of the Blue Design Company, who's excited that "Given enough tools, children will be able to build and program their own space missions."

18   Children build their own space missions? I'm impressed when a twelve-year-old carves a balsawood glider.

19   I saw a program for designing Barbie doll clothes . . . it lets kids select styles, colors, and mix outfits. Naturally, it's advertised as a teaching program, though I wonder exactly what it teaches. How to coordinate colors, perhaps, though the kid selects from a most parsimonious palette. You can't mix paints, can't dye cloth, can't stitch things together. At the end of a session, a child has no idea of the tactile difference between calico and corduroy, silk and sailcloth. Can't sew, either.

20   Along with a small group of parents, I visited a kindergarten class near San Francisco. The other visitors were immediately taken by the display of computer graphic printouts hung on the wall . . . clipart, designed by professionals and printed out by the children. The teacher, busy showing several children how to run the computer, didn't notice one frustrated child working at the crafts table.

21   While the visitors chatted about the computers, I watched that six-year-old clumsily fold construction paper into the shape of a house. Struggling with round-nosed scissors, he cut a door, drew windows with a crayon, and pasted the paper onto a base. Near the end of our visit, he completed his project—he called it a firehouse—and proudly showed it to the adults in the room. The teacher gave him a "Go away, I'm busy" nod; none of the other visitors so much as glanced at the boy. You could see his face drop.

22   Well, yes, a six-year-old's crude firehouse hardly compares with a fancy computer printout. But these parents should have recognized the trivial nature of the computer "art."

23   Remember B. F. Skinner? By feeding corn to pigeons whenever they behaved the way he wanted, Skinner showed that he could get animals to learn behavior. In the 1950s, he applied his pigeon experiments to humans, creating a new way for people to learn: programmed instruction.

24   Skinner made machines which would pose questions to students. Correct answers would lead to new topics and further questions; wrong answers caused a review and more questions to answer. It was a primitive form of hypertext—each answer led to another encapsulated lesson. Widely promoted in its day, programmed instruction was supposed to revolutionize education.

25   Skinner's methods fit well with today's computers. Students peck at their keyboards for dollops of sound and animation; administrators get instant reports; parents hear how their kids now enjoy school. This is supposed to make learning fun, not to mention efficient.

26   Aah, efficiency in education! Get the student to correctly answer questions. Minimize costs and wasted time. Augment teachers with mechanical and electronic aids. Sugarcoat lessons with extreme multimedia and blazing

graphics so that student will happily learn on their own, while having fun in the process.

27   But programmed instruction flopped. The machine forced kids to regurgitate whatever answers the programmer wanted. There was no place for innovation, creativity, whimsy, or improvisation. Flashing lights simply couldn't take the place of a live teacher's encouragement. We resent being treated like pigeons.

28   In the wake of Skinner's programmed instruction came even nuttier educational fads—teaching machines, sleep learning, and music-induced hypnotic learning. Anything to make education easy and fun. Despite decades of promotion, they all fizzled.

29   Think Skinner's ideas are dead? Check out the popular children's software program NFL Math. It's designed around professional football and is supposed to teach arithmetic. "Packed with photo-realistic animations," this program "makes hitting a wide receiver with a pass more fun than hitting the books." It promises such "learning skills" as addition, fractions, statistics, and percentages. The kids get to watch short, poorly animated football segments, interrupted by half-baked math questions ("Which is more yards rushed—1,182 or 1,207?"). Result? Your children will "score better grades in math!" Uh, right.

30   The program forces the child to do a math problem in order to be rewarded with two minutes of entertainment. Then the torture begins anew. What a great way to teach hatred of math.

31   NFL Math and its many brethren typically present questions in the format $4 + 3 = ?$ They can accept only the obvious answers. Like Skinner's pigeons, you get rewarded for pressing the right button.

32   A real teacher might well ask, "Seven equals what?" A fascinating question with an infinite number of answers: "Three plus four," "Ten minus three," "Days in a week," "The dwarfs in *Snow White*," "Number of deadly sins," "The Seven Immortals of the Wine Cup," "The Group of Seven revolutionized Canadian painting," "The number of samurai in Kurosawa's best movie," "The German expression *Siebensachen*, which means the baggage you carry on a trip." These answers, incomprehensible to any computer, make perfect sense to a real teacher . . . and open up whole fields for creative discussion. What began as an arithmetic question blossoms into a lesson on language, art, science, history, or culture.

33   New teachers, fresh out of college, seem to be most affected with the connection between gizmos, classrooms, and fun in learning. Ms. Jennifer Donovan, a student teacher from Stetson University, wrote to me, repeating the standard party line: Lessons must be fun in order to compete with television and to motivate students. "In the 1950s, the job market did not call for com-

puter education. But in a changing world, students are hard pressed to find well-paying jobs that do not involve computer technology."

34 These fit together: Jobs go to those who know computers. Computers motivate students. Students won't learn unless it's fun.

35 Well, many subjects aren't fun. I wonder how the fun-to-learn teacher handles the Holocaust, Rape of Nanking, or American slavery. Perhaps her class creates Web sites about these subjects—and the students concentrate on graphic design instead of history. But scholarship isn't about browsing the Internet—it's about understanding events, appreciating history, and interpreting our world.

36 "But you don't understand," say my techie friends. "Computers are wonderful motivators for students. In this age of television, they won't write or do their homework without one."

37 And so we happily provide computers to students and expect them to suddenly become interested in academic topics. We encourage them to play with the machine . . . any scholastic connection is secondary.

38 Kids do seem to be motivated by computers. But doesn't that multimedia machine mainly motivate kids to play with the computer, in the same way that television motivates kids to watch more videos?

39 Motivation—the will to move—comes from yourself. You choose what puts you in motion and causes you to move. Computers cause you to sit in one place and not to move.

40 Don Tapscott, author of *Growing Up Digital*, sees a new kind of young intellectual explorer who will process information and learn differently than those who came before them. "New media tools offer great promise for a new model of learning—one based on discovery and participation," he says. Thanks to cheap computers, we'll see a shift from teaching to "the creation of learning partnerships and learning cultures. The schools can become a place to learn rather than a place to teach."

41 The field of educational technology is filled with such empty clichés. In this dreamworld, empowered students eagerly learn from one another, encouraged by teachers who act more like coaches than instructors. We'll replace the sage on the stage with a guide on the side. Exciting on-line expeditions will replace outmoded chalk-and-talk lectures. Student-centered learning will be tutor-led and context-based rather than rote plug-and-chug. Child-centered classrooms. Blah, blah, blah.

42 Can't blame students for getting sick of teachers lecturing about how the square of the hypotenuse has something to do with the sum of the squares of the legs of a right triangle. We yearn for depth, narrative, passion, involvement. For experience. Along comes the magic machine promising interactive fun. What kid can resist?

43   And I can't blame teachers for getting sick of students sitting there with mouths agape, not listening but not quite sleeping. Perhaps that's why adults figure that making finger motions on a keyboard is an appropriate activity . . . that something must be happening in the kids' brains. In that sense, computers are parent-pleasing devices: machines to give the appearance of learning and the illusion of interactive, instant information.

44   Seems clear that an inspiring teacher doesn't need computers; a mediocre teacher isn't improved by one. I've never met a teacher who feels there's too much classroom time—they always complain that the periods are too short and there's too much material to cover.

45   Teaching, alas, is a low-paid calling. Some teachers attend college and put up with frustrations for a steady pay and eventual retirement. But I'll bet the best teachers are in it for the feedback: the smile on the kid's face and the "Aha" from the chemistry student. These, of course, are the very things that technology removes. The Internet gets the credit and the teacher gets the blame. And that great promised land of low-cost education—distance learning—essentially eliminates interpersonal interaction. Maybe that's why experienced teachers approach computers with hesitation.

46   In *Teachers and Machines*, Larry Cuban points out that teachers are frequently criticized as Luddites resistant to progress. A century of reformers have blamed the slow introduction of teaching devices on reactionary teaching staff. For instance, Charles Hoban, who worked to introduce instructional radio and TV, said, "The current and historical role of the classroom teacher is highly ritualized." Any change in that ritual is "likely to be resisted as an invasion of the sanctuary by the barbarians . . . Any systematic attempt to scientize and rationalize the intuitively determined interaction patterns of the teacher is likely to elicit at least some teacher hostility and resistance."

47   That hostility is well justified. Teachers need only open a closet door to find stacks of obsolete and unused teaching gizmos: filmstrips, instructional television systems, Apple II computers, and any number of educational videotapes. Each promised a revolution in the classroom. None delivered.

48   "Oh, but computers are different from old technologies like radio and television" runs the argument. "Computers are interactive. They're fun!"

49   Well, just why is electronic interactivity good for scholarship? With a computer, you're interacting with something, not someone. Doubtless, even the worst teacher is more versatile and adaptable than the finest computer program. Come to think of it, aren't teachers interactive? It's hard to think of a classroom without interaction.

50   The old saw still rings true: What requires the least effort is least cherished. Yet somehow we expect a simple, easy, fun, digital education to be both lasting and valuable.

51   "But the Internet is important to schools," consultants in computer-aided instruction tell me. "It links students straight to famous scientists. They can chat with researchers at observatories and laboratories. And there's instant homework help available online."

52   Well, no. Famous scientists—and obscure ones, too—don't have time to answer e-mail from distant students. Those academics are taking care of their projects, managing post-docs, teaching classes, and writing grant proposals. Astronomers who enjoy working with kids would far prefer to meet the kids, not answer a slew of messages over the Net. That inquiring mind directed to the Net will likely dead-end in some press release or a mountain of indecipherable jargon.

53   Teachers have the difficult job of not just understanding a body of academic facts—they must understand their students. The teaching method that connects for one child won't work with another. The student who's strong in one area will certainly be weak in another. What seems like a game to someone will feel like work to another. The intention should be enlightenment, not entertainment.

54   Learning isn't about acquiring information, maximizing efficiency, or enjoyment. Learning is about developing human capacity. To turn learning into fun is to denigrate the two most important things we can do as humans: To teach. To learn.

THINKING ABOUT THE TEXT

1. Clifford Stoll begins his essay by quoting enthusiastic language from computer companies and school administrators extolling the use of technology in classrooms. What is Stoll's strategy in opening his essay with so many positive comments that he then deflates with one short sentence expressing his own view: "It's a lie"?

2. When Stoll writes "Most learning isn't fun," what does he mean? Does his essay reflect the voice of a dreary pedant who wants students' knuckles rapped by a yardstick for giving a wrong answer? How can the reader reconcile the tone of the writer who deplores "glitzy gadgets" but recognizes the creativity in the many possible responses to, for example, what the number seven equals?

3. How true is it to your experience that the "payoff" for learning isn't "an adrenaline rush, but a deep satisfaction arriving weeks, months, or years later"? How does the computer's speed work against true learning?

4. Stoll believes that computers "direct students away from reading, away from writing, away from scholarship." What does he mean? Do you agree?

5. The author relates two experiences in watching students work on a computer, designing doll clothes and printing out graphics made on a computer. What is wrong with both of these "educational" experiences, according to Stoll?

6. How relevant to his argument is Stoll's description of the work of B. F. Skinner, the behavioral scientist who fed corn to pigeons? Besides concluding that human beings resent "being treated like pigeons," what else is wrong with Skinner's approach to educating people, according to Stoll?

7. How do you respond to Stoll's assertion that "scholarship isn't about browsing the Internet—it's about understanding events, appreciating history, and interpreting the world"?

8. In addition to writing about the drawbacks for students using computers for learning, Stoll considers the problems for teachers in computer-filled classrooms. Why might teachers rightly be hostile to technology, according to Stoll?

WRITING FROM THE TEXT

1. In an essay, argue that Stoll is right or wrong in asserting that computers "direct students away from reading, away from writing, away from scholarship." Use specific examples of your habits in using computers—to facilitate assignments or perhaps to distract you from accomplishing assigned work.

2. Describe your precollege learning experiences to show that the best of these were or were not connected to computer use. Use Stoll's essay to show your agreement with his points about creativity and interactions with the teacher or to refute his points by illustrating some good learning experiences you have had using a computer.

3. Write an analysis of the methods of your most memorable teacher. Were the instructor's methods interactive, creative, personal and motivating— a "sage on the stage"—or did other qualities make this professional an important part of your learning experience? Use strong, descriptive details in your essay.

CONNECTING WITH OTHER TEXTS

1. Read the excerpt from Don Tapscott's book *Growing Up Digital* (p. 313) and decide which of the authors makes the stronger point about the use of computers in education. Make your claim and then use the material from both essays to support your point.

2. Stoll describes schools with closets of "obsolete and unused teaching gizmos," one reason teachers are hostile about additional equipment coming

to their campus in the form of computers. Gain permission from the administrator of a school close to your college and interview teachers there to ascertain whether they do have closets of obsolete "gizmos." How do the teachers feel about the computers installed in their classrooms?

3. Compare the role of the teacher as described in Clifford Stoll's essay and the essay by Don Tapscott (below). How does each perceive the instructor's position in the classroom? Write an essay to compare and/or contrast the authors' perceptions. Review how to organize a comparison/contrast essay (p. 439) for help in organizing your work.

From Learning as Torture to Learning as Fun

Don Tapscott

An expert on the application of technology in business, Don Tapscott (b. 1947) cofounded Digital 4Sight, a company that researches and designs new business models for Global 2000 organizations. He earned a B.S. and B.A. in psychology and statistics from Trent University and an M. Ed. in Research Methodology and an honorary doctor of laws from the University of Alberta. He has authored or coauthored seven books, including *Digital Capital: Harnessing the Power of Business Webs* (2000), *The Digital Economy: Promise and Peril in the Age of Networked Intelligence* (1996), and *Paradigm Shift: The New Promise of Information Technology* (1992). The following essay is an excerpt from *Growing Up Digital: The Rise of the New Generation* (1998), which, as Tapscott explains in the initial pages, was written on the Internet: "The research team collaborated with several hundred children and adults located on six continents. The analysis, drafting, and editing were conducted by a core team in five locations using a shared digital workspace, electronic mail, and computer conferencing. The main reference source was the Web." Tapscott welcomes your views and related experiences at <http://www.growingupdigital.com>, where you can find additional information and links to related topics.

1   Maybe torture is an exaggeration, but for many kids class is not exactly the highlight of their day. Some educators have decried the fact that a generation schooled on *Sesame Street* expects to be entertained at school—to enjoy the learning experience. These educators argue that the learning and entertainment should be clearly separated. As Neil Postman says, ". . . *Sesame Street* does not encourage children to love school or anything about school. It teaches them to love television."

2   But doesn't that say more about today's schools—which are not exactly exciting places for many students—than it does about the integration of

learning and entertainment? I'm convinced that one of the design goals of the New School should be to make learning fun! Learning math should be an enjoyable, challenging, and yes, entertaining activity just like learning a video game is. And it can be! Besides, *Sesame Street* let the entertainment horse out of the barn. So did video games, the Web, FreeZone, MaMaMedia, and a thousand others.

3   It is said, however, that if learning is fun it can't be challenging. Wrong! Try getting through the seven levels of Crash Bandicoot or FIFA soccer on your kids' video game if you think entertainment and challenge are opposites. The challenge provides much of the entertainment value and vice versa.

4   Why shouldn't learning be entertaining? *Webster's Ninth College Dictionary* gives the third and fourth definitions of the verb "to entertain" as "to keep, hold, or maintain in the mind," and "to receive and take into consideration." In other words, entertainment has always been a profound part of the learning process and teachers have, throughout history, been asked to convince their students to entertain ideas. From this perspective, the best teachers were entertainers. Using the new media, the teacher becomes the entertainer and in doing so builds enjoyment, motivation, and responsibility for learning.

5   Learning is becoming a social activity facilitated by a new generation of educators.

6   The topic is saltwater fish. The teacher divides the grade 6 class into teams, asking each to prepare a presentation on a fish of its choice covering the topics of history, breathing, propulsion, reproduction, diet, predators, and "cool facts." The students have access to the Web and are allowed to use any resources they want. Questions should be addressed to others in their team or to the others in the class, not the teacher.

7   Two weeks later, Melissa's group is up first. The students in the group have created a shark project home page with hot links for each of the topics. The presentation is projected onto a screen at the front of the class as the girls talk. They have video clips of different types of sharks and also a clip of Jacques Cousteau discussing the shark as an endangered species. They then go live to Aquarius—an underwater Web site located off the Florida keys. The class can ask questions of the Aquarius staff, but most inquires are directed at the project team. One of the big discussions is about the dangers posed to humans by sharks versus the dangers to sharks posed by humans.

8   The class decides to hold an online forum on this and invite kids from their sister classes in other countries to participate. The team invites the classes to browse through its project at any time, from any location, as the

site will be "up" for the rest of the school year. In fact, the team decides to maintain the site, adding new links and fresh information throughout the year. It becomes a living project. Other learners from other countries find the shark homepage helpful in their projects and build links to it. The team has to resource the information, tools, and materials it needs.

9   The teacher acts as a resource and consultant to the teams. He is also a youth worker—as one of the students was having considerable problems at home and was not motivated to participate in a team. Although the teacher can't solve such problems, he takes them into account and also refers the student to the guidance counselor. The teacher also facilitates the learning process, among other things participating as a technical consultant on the new media. He learns much from Melissa's group, which actually knows more about sharks than he does (his background is art and literature, not science). The teacher doesn't compete with Jacques Cousteau, but rather is supported by him.

10   This scenario is not science fiction. It is currently occurring in advanced schools in several countries. The teacher is not an instructional transmitter. He is a facilitator to social learning whereby learners construct their own knowledge. The students will remember what they learned about sharks as the topic now interests them. More importantly, they have acquired collaborative, research, analytical, presentation, and resourcing skills. With the assistance of a teacher, they are constructing knowledge and their world.

11   Needless to say, a whole generation of teachers needs to learn new tools, new approaches, and new skills. This will be a challenge—not just because of resistance to change by some teachers, but also because of the current atmosphere of cutbacks, low teacher morale, lack of time due to the pressures of increased workloads, and reduced retraining budgets. . . .

12   What is the new teacher like?

13   Small miracles have been occurring over the last three years at William Lyon Mackenzie Collegiate in North York, Ontario. The Emerging Technologies program mixes grades 10 to 12 to work on projects involving teams and the new media. The students learn by discovery. Through teams they source answers to their questions and resources to conduct their projects—from other students, outside parties, and the Net. The learning model is one of student-centered discovery enabled by emerging technologies.

14   When the program began, teacher Richard Ford told the students on their first day of class that their first project was for each to design their own Web page and present it to the group by Friday. When he asked how many knew how to design a Web page, 6 of the 32 kids in the class indicated they had some experience. Richard then suggested to the class that they should remember those faces, "because they are your mentors."

15   The students learn to cooperate, work in teams, solve problems, and take responsibility for their own learning—by doing. If there's something they don't understand, they must ask everyone else in the class before they can ask the teacher. Right after the first class, one girl asks, "What's a Web page?" Richard shrugs and says, "I don't know." Within a few days the kids have gotten the message. "And who's the last person you ask for help?" says Richard. Everyone replies in unison, "You are."

16   The model is that everyone relies on everyone else, sharing their expertise. Richard told them that if everyone didn't present their Web page on Friday, then everyone would get a zero. On the second day of class some of the kids were going around asking others if they needed help. However, when the learners have exhausted all routes and cannot find a solution to something, they can approach the teacher (called the facilitator). He then will work with them as a team member to find a solution or a resource which can help them.

17   In this class, there were only 15 computers for 30 kids—so they had to share the technology. The class was also very diverse, with children from Korea, India, Pakistan, Sri Lanka, Switzerland, Ukraine, and Russia. There were 15 different languages spoken in the class, with several of the learners having poor English skills.

18   Several kids were petrified to give presentations, but they got a lot of support from the class. One boy who spoke almost no English had to be coaxed by the others to stand up in front of the class. He mustered up the courage to approach the front of the room, then, turning stood there and said, "My Web page. . . . First time. . . . Graphics. . . . See link. Thank you." All the other kids applauded. "It was a very emotional moment for everyone," says Richard. "Everyone knew what an accomplishment it was for this boy to speak in front of everyone else in another language, presenting his first Web page." Afterward, outside the classroom, he approached Richard and said to him, smiling broadly, "I am proud."

19   For Richard, "There is something that happens when you decide for yourself that you're going to learn something and do something. This is much more powerful than when someone else says you have to do this."

20   "The kids not only learned about the new media and developed language and presentation skills, they learned about how to interact with clients and meet deadlines and, most importantly, they learned about how to share expertise and how to source it as well," says project coordinator Vicki Saunders. "The kids work 10 times longer because they are so excited about their projects."

21   After the first week the learners launched into Web design for real clients. One group built the software for the Canadian Broadcasting Corporation movie Web site. Another did the design for a New York-based artist named Carter Kustera—who came into the class for a week to work with them. IBM

hired the group to do a CD-ROM about a conference called "Minds Meeting Media," where 1,900 kids came together in Toronto to present their projects to other kids from across the city. Kids from grade 2 to 13 presented their animation and multimedia projects and all this was captured on a CD.

22   For their midterm "exam," the students had to create a three-page Web site or a three-minute video. They were placed in groups of four, selected intentionally to help them overcome their obstacles to development. For example, all the "blockers" were put in one group. The project had to have a purpose. The students also had to discuss their own individual contributions and to assign marks to each other. The kids really had to wake up and work hard. A lot of buttons were pushed.

23   According to Vicki, "Richard is able to find the hook that turns kids on."

24   Richard has a radical view of the role of the teacher. "I don't teach. If I teach, who knows what they will learn. Teaching's out. I tell kids that there are no limits. You can create whatever you want to create. If it's impossible, it will just take a bit longer. My main function is to get kids excited, to consider things that they haven't done before. I'm working to create citizens in a global society."

25   He also deemphasizes his role as a judge. "We're trying to create a stage for them to present their ideas and their work to others. If a student hands something in to a teacher, she doesn't necessarily learn. The intention of the work becomes to satisfy the teacher's vision. We're not expanding the student's vision.

26   "For example, I whisper to a student who is doing a project on his home country, 'What about if you were to present this project on the Web?' The student realizes people will read it and see it. They might e-mail him back. They might set up a newsgroup. Maybe someone from their home town might join the conference. He may be able to share his ideas with others around the world."

27   Richard acts as a facilitator to set a hook. "If they grab hold, they're off on a voyage of discovery. We both discover. I learn through each of them— I learn about how people carry each other from village to village when he puts a photo on the Web. I learn about his culture when people begin to communicate with him from the other side of the globe.

28   "Everything you do affects others. We're asking kids to create their place in this global society. Whatever you want is possible. There are no limits. You create who you are in your space."

29   Student Aziz Hurzook took Richard literally. Aziz is a real innovator. He learned how to use a music synthesizer for his project and then created an audio CD. For his presentation he told the class to listen to campus radio at midnight. The radio station played the world premier of his music. He later

set up a booth advertising Web development services at a conference on the new media. The experience was very positive. People were buzzing all around his booth and he realized there was a big opportunity here: Aziz created a company called "Caught in the Web" and took on his first client. The company had $1.5 million in revenue last year.

30   Says Richard: "If they can't create their own network, then they'll have to go to an authority figure. But if they stop and think about it, they are the authority! They are in charge of their own learning. Only they can decide to do something. And if they choose to do it, there is nobody on this earth who can stop them. Not only will they do something far more creative than you can imagine, they will probably break new ground while doing so."

THINKING ABOUT THE TEXT

1. Although Tapscott admits that "learning as torture" may be an exaggeration, what might be his reason for opening with this simile and how does it contrast with his view of learning?

2. Specify the key features of the learning "teams" that Tapscott describes.

3. What does Tapscott mean when he claims that "in advanced schools . . . the teacher is not an instructional transmitter. He is a facilitator to social learning whereby learners construct their own knowledge"? Do you see any problems with this concept?

4. What are the most important aspects of Richard's new type of teaching? Evaluate its strengths and flaws.

WRITING FROM THE TEXT

1. Using details from this essay, write a paper defining the ideal teacher, according to Tapscott. Include specific examples from his essay and analyze each.

2. In an essay, compare and contrast your favorite class in high school with the example that Tapscott provides of Richard's teaching. Your thesis should assert your view of these classes.

3. Write an evaluative response of Tapscott's thesis and of the key components of these "advanced classes" and teachers that he describes.

CONNECTING WITH OTHER TEXTS

1. Read "Makes Learning Fun" (p. 304) and write an essay contrasting Stoll's views with Tapscott's. Your thesis should clarify which view seems more reasonable and compelling to you.

2. Reflect on Alter's essay (p. 301) about his frustrations with technology and with service reps, and write a paper analyzing Tapscott's optimistic view of technology and service to students in light of Alter's frustrations.

 # Dumpster-Diving for Dollars
Keith David Hamm

Freelance writer Keith David Hamm (b. 1971) was an environmental studies major with an emphasis in marine biology when he took a journalism course and discovered the pleasure of writing. His first job, at the Santa Barbara *Independent,* was as a science writer. He is a contributing writer to that newspaper, the *Santa Barbara Magazine,* the *Los Angeles New Times,* and the *Los Angeles Times.* Hamm is currently writing a book on skateboarding. The premier printed issue of the online magazine *Friction* (July 2002) contained a longer version of the essay printed below. The author no longer dumpster-dives, but he does pick up useful discards because "there is too much stuff floating around the planet."

1   I was in my first year at UC Santa Barbara, living in Isla Vista, an enchanting college slum cradled by the Santa Ynez Mountains and the blue Pacific and overflowing with students. I noticed that quite a few of my neighbors had folks who were footing the bills, from tuition and books to room and board, this largess topped off with a fat wad of "play money." As a result, they managed to waft through college with an insouciance toward life's luxuries. And when they moved out of their apartments at the end of the school year, much got dumped. This was fine by me. One man's trash, as they say, is another man's treasure.

2   A few enterprising friends and I labeled the first week of summer "dumpster-diving season," and when it arrived, we creatively capitalized on the discards. My short list of dumpster-dredged treasures: a fully operational, top-of-the-line microwave; Mr. Coffee makers and unopened bags and tins of French roast; an internal-frame Kelty backpack with a collapsible fishing pole stashed in a side pocket; a paper bag filled with more than 15,000 pennies; sports balls, rackets, clubs, bats and mitts; Levi Strauss denim jackets in need of nothing more than a warm-water wash; cast-iron skillets and chef knives; and, like plucking bills from a money tree, science textbooks in good condition, each of which fetched a buy-back price topping $20. I also collected abandoned beach cruisers, rebuilt them— with salvaged parts and cans of spray paint—and sold them to incoming freshmen in the fall.

3   On our own beach cruisers, equipped with roomy "grocery-getter" baskets, we rode the streets of Isla Vista, digging through every promising dumpster and curbside trash can, probing with our makeshift digging tools (broomsticks, hoes, bent curtain rods) to unearth our finds. We knew it was illegal; once the students had thrown their discards into the dumpster, it became the property of MarBorg Industries, Isla Vista's trash collector. But if a dumpster proved to be a virtual breadbasket of discarded things of value, we would climb inside and root deeply in its far corners, carefully avoiding broken glass and rotting food. Rummaging of this sort typically drew long stares from the students as they emerged from their apartments with armloads of perfectly usable, valuable items—toaster ovens, brass candlesticks, framed photos—they could no longer be bothered with. They often looked at us with a mix of pity and condescension, and probably thought us desperate and crazy. But to me, it was they who were the spectacle, perfect examples of America's addiction to indifferent consumption.

4   In addition to bagging obvious goods, my friend S.P. ripped Marlboro Dollars and Camel Bucks from empty cigarette packs. I think he eventually cashed them in for a Windbreaker, or maybe a pool cue. He also provisioned his bathroom, laundry room and kitchen with half-full bottles of shampoo, boxes and bottles of detergent, unused Brillo pads, dishwashing soap, bath mats, dish towels, cutting boards and anything else to complement the converted garage he called home. Another friend, Rudy, lifted unopened 10-pound bags of jasmine rice and Costco-sized containers of Ortega chili beans and peanut butter—chunky if he was lucky—from the refuse. Each summer he fed himself safely and somewhat healthfully on salvaged foodstuffs, perfectly edible post-consumer waste.

5   Discovering the internal-frame backpack was quite the score, of course, and I kept it—the winter after graduation I stuffed it with essentials and shouldered it across Costa Rica for two months. But I was really dumpster-diving for the monetary payoff. Indeed, we kept hardly anything for ourselves. Rather, we scavenged until the pile outside S.P.'s garage became a bit unwieldy, then we tossed it all into the back of his '59 Chevy Apache, hauled it to the swap meet at the crack of dawn on a Sunday and sold it all. We haggled good prices for high-end items (spotless microwaves, upright Hoover vacuums, CD boomboxes, 50-foot garden hoses) and parted with low-end junk (Steve Miller cassette tapes, Christmas ornaments, three-ring notebooks, beat-up pots and pans) for a quarter or 50 cents a pop. Typically, before noon, each of us had pocketed more than $100. With our pockets stuffed with wads of five and ones and bulging with quarters, dimes and nickels, we traditionally drove straight to Lupita's restaurant in Isla Vista and purchased several ice-cold pitchers of Mexican beer and broad plates of chicken enchi-

ladas. Sometimes, though we knew it was a rather inconsiderate move, we paid the entire lunch tab with loose change.

6   I scavenged to stay out of debt, to keep my wallet above the poverty line as I burned through the early '90s sitting through class and studying during the day and stealing from my sleep five or six nights a week to flip fish at a seafood restaurant. Being a "poor, starving student," I soon discovered, came at a hefty price. Fortunately, my fish-grilling gig cut me a steady paycheck, one meal per shift, and some tips. But it was scarcely enough to break even. Out of financial necessity, I maintained a low overhead. I rarely ate out. I opted for incredibly cheap but hardly protective car insurance. I drove less. When I needed new clothes, I brought old clothes from thrift stores, swap meets and yard sales. And I scavenged.

7   Plus, scavenging was kind of fascinating, in a grubby sort of way. Not something to write home about (although I did once, instilling in my mother the fear that her youngest son would accidentally step on a discarded hypodermic needle and wind up dying from a dumpster-diving mishap). Surprisingly, I learned quite a bit about myself and the world I'm from during those early Saturday and Sunday mornings, as the tattered summer fog hung in the streets and the community slept off the hangovers of a week's worth of year-end partying. And I made a few new friends, some of whom were strapped students like myself, others who were the hard-working husbands and fathers of struggling families who had recently arrived in the United States.

8   Another thing that kept me preoccupied with the waste stream was budding, burning idealism. (You know what college can do to a young mind.) I was a student of the nation's oldest environmental studies program. And although I spent most of my time avoiding the 18-year-old born-again-hippie environmentalists—you know, the ones who bemoan animal cruelty and meat-eating but bedeck themselves in leather—I did learn a thing or two about humankind's habits of consumption and disposal. Basically, we buy too much that we think we need but don't, then when we no longer need said stuff—and fail to find an incentive to recycle it all—we dump most of it into a huge, growing hole in the ground somewhere out of sight and out of mind. I didn't want to be part of that problem. Scavenging was my way to subvert the system.

9   These days, a decade later, I can no longer count myself among the ranks of the true scavengers, but I rarely walk past a dumpster without giving what's inside at least a quick scan. I am still driven, however—by financial necessity, by the intrigue of the hunt, by the style and quality of things made long ago—to discover the practical (or just plain cool) treasures buried at most swap meets, yard sales and thrift stores. And I remain slightly dismayed and amused by the consumption that still fills all those Isla Vista dumpsters.

THINKING ABOUT THE TEXT

1. What is Hamm's strategy in beginning his essay describing the setting of the college he attended and his student neighbors?

2. What treasures did Hamm find trashed in the dumpsters the first week after classes adjourned for summer? What do the objects reveal about the student body of his school? What kind of looks did people give the author when they saw him diving in dumpsters?

3. What did Hamm and his friends do with the objects they found? How do you feel about his entrepreneurial spirit? How do you feel about his friends' use of found food and toiletries?

4. In addition to the practical reason the author scavenged—"to keep [his] wallet above the poverty line"—what are his professed philosophies favoring dumpster-diving? A decade after his student scavenging days, how does the author show his values have not changed?

5. The author gives indications of his and his friends' values. What telling details are embedded in Hamm's narrative?

WRITING FROM THE TEXT

1. "One man's trash, as they say, is another man's treasure." With Hamm's statement as your thesis, illustrate with specific, vivid examples from your own observations and experiences. You may want to change the gender in Hamm's assertion.

2. The author describes the students at his university as "perfect examples of America's addiction to indifferent consumption." Write an analysis of the buying habits of your family and friends. Do their patterns reflect or deny Hamm's perception of American buying habits?

3. The author describes how he managed to stay out of debt and how his habits, in addition to dumpster-diving, kept him enrolled in school and paying his rent. What are your schemes for surviving the costs of tuition, room, and board? Do you also have ways "to subvert the system"? Describe your methods so that your reader will gain some ideas and also be entertained by your essay.

CONNECTING WITH OTHER TEXTS

1. In "Hooray for the Red, White, Blue, and Green" (p. 323), the Hochschilds review America's war-time history of making do with less. Connect their ideas to those in Hamm's work to show how Americans might consume less.

2. Would Adair Lara's friends described in "Who's Cheap?" (p. 94) think Keith Hamm a good date? Do you? Support your focus with specific details from both essays as well as expression of your own values and observations.

3. Compare the character traits of Keith David Hamm with those of Darnell in "Proper Care and Maintenance" (p. 186). Find three or four traits for comparison in an essay analyzing the two men.

Hooray for Red, White, Blue, and Green

David Hochschild and Arlie Hochschild

Cofounder of Vote Solar Initiative, David Hochschild (b. 1971) is committed to trying to get more cities to pass solar energy bonds similar to the one recently passed in San Francisco. With a B.A. in English literature from Swarthmore and an M.A. in public policy from Harvard, David Hochschild provided the impetus and information for this collaborative essay with his mother, Arlie, who is a sociologist and also writer. For David, writing is a critical tool to advance important work. He notes that there is plenty of information available about solar energy but that "there needs to be more clear thinking and effective writing to help people process that information." He invites readers to check out the Website, http://www.Votesolar.org.

Author and professor of sociology at UC Berkeley, Arlie Hochschild (b. 1940) has published works that have attracted mainstream audiences as well as earned acclaim from professionals in her field. Her publications include *The Unexpected Community: Portrait of an Old Age Subculture* (1978), *The Managed Heart: Commercialization of Human Feeling* (1983), *The Second Shift: Working Parents and the Revolution at Home* (1989), and *The Time Bind: When Work Becomes Home and Home Becomes Work* (1997). Both Arlie and David have installed solar panels in their homes to generate all the electricity they use. The following essay first appeared in the *Los Angeles Times* on January 11, 2001.

1   In 1942, in the aftermath of Pearl Harbor, Americans began to understand that in order to win the war and to live again in a world at peace, they would have to make great personal sacrifices on the "home front." America began producing tanks and planes, and reduced or stopped producing many household items such as toasters and waffle irons made with materials needed for the war.

2   The government was specific in what it asked citizens to give up, and it spelled out what their altruism would mean to the war effort. In his book *Don't You Know There's a War On?* Richard R. Lingeman describes the kinds of

trade-offs put before the American public. "If every family in America would forgo buying one [tin] can a week, this would save 2,500 tons of tin and 190,000 tons of steel—the equivalent of 5,000 tanks or 38 Liberty ships. Thirty thousand razor blades contained enough steel to make fifty 30-caliber machine guns." Bernard Baruch, appointed by President Franklin D. Roosevelt to get Americans to conserve essential resources, rationed gas and lowered speed limits to 35 miles per hour on national highways.

3   People didn't just do without; they did things differently. Victory gardens—20,000,000 of them in parks, vacant plots and backyards—produced 40% of all the vegetables grown in the country. People also changed their tastes. Because rubber was scarce, companies stopped making women's rubber girdles, and fashion designers created new dress styles in response. In essence, during World War II, Americans saved, substituted, recycled and proudly did with less. They invented the idea of "green"—before they had the term—and put it together with red, white and blue.

4   The Sept. 11 attacks have launched us into a very different kind of war. And it may be time now to take a leaf from our history and respond in the same spirit. Many Americans would like to help out—if they only knew how.

5   They also need to know why. The main reason is this: we're in a war started by Osama bin Laden but linked—profoundly and more lastingly— to oil. Since the 1970s both our consumption of oil and our dependence on foreign oil have risen. Today, more than half of the oil consumed in the United States comes from overseas, much of it from the Persian Gulf. We consume 25% of the oil produced in the world each year, yet have only 2% of the world's known reserves. This oil dependency enmeshes us with repressive regimes and countries locked in struggles between harsh oligarchies and fundamentalist rebels. Our involvement with such a regime in Iran ended disastrously, and a similar story may lie ahead in Saudi Arabia.

6   Indeed, our oil dependence may lead us to more unwanted conflicts in Central Asia. The next big source of oil is Central Asia, where the regimes are, if anything, harsher, and where our presence may create even more unrest. U.S. oil companies are already there, cutting deals and planning pipelines—aligning us with unsavory regimes in ways that make ordinary people hate us. In the end, our entanglements may make costly military interventions inevitable. In 1998, Dick Cheney, then CEO of Halliburton Co.— which during his watch landed $2.3 billion in U.S. government contracts or taxpayer-guaranteed loans to drill oil—said, "I can't think of a time when we've had a region emerge as suddenly to become as strategically significant as the Caspian." The major way to get Caspian oil and gas out to where it can be loaded on ocean-going tankers is through Afghanistan.

7   So, while many factors led up to Sept. 11, oil is one of them. And if oil remains our primary energy source of choice, we can look forward to future hot spots in Uzbekistan, Tajikistan, Kazakhstan and Turkmenistan.

8   A shift toward renewable energy and conservation can also help reduce our vulnerability to terrorist attacks. Thank God, people are saying, that the hijacked planes didn't hit one of America's 109 nuclear power plants. But next time they could. Oil pipelines can be sabotaged and tankers sunk as well.

9   Given all this, perhaps the most meaningful and lasting contribution Americans can make to the antiterrorism efforts is to break the oil habit. We cannot drill our way to an oil-based energy independence even if we try. All the oil in the Arctic National Wildlife Refuge would only yield enough to supply the nation for six months. Holland, Denmark and Norway have all set themselves the goal of achieving energy independence based on renewable energy, and we could do the same. We could declare it our "home front."

10   It will be a tough job. We will have to break some habits, but we won't have to change our values. Americans already believe in conservation, in green technology and in living within the globe's means. According to a recent ABC poll, 78% of Americans would like to see more energy conservation. Some 80% support more solar and wind power. We believe in conservation and renewable energy; we just don't yet act on our beliefs.

11   In a similar way 40 years ago, most Americans believed smoking led to cancer, emphysema and heart disease. Still, many of us kept smoking in restaurants, airplanes, workplaces and homes. In the last 40 years, Americans have cut their tobacco consumption in half, and lung cancer, heart disease and emphysema death rates have plummeted. It wasn't easy. It took education, legislation and litigation. We went up against a big industry. But we did it—and are doing it still.

12   In the same spirit, we can "green" our way to energy independence—by conserving energy and by generating the energy we need from renewable sources such as solar and wind power. The Bush administration will not lead on this; both President Bush and Vice President Cheney have made huge fortunes in oil. National Security Advisor Condoleezza Rice not only served on Chevron's board of directors; in 1993 the company actually named an oil tanker after her.

13   But one of the beauties of patriotic action on the home front is that we don't need to wait for leadership from on high: We can all lead. We can commit to personal acts of conservation like replacing gas-guzzling cars with fuel-efficent ones, taking public transportation or insulating our houses.

14   Legislators can travel by public transportation. Movie stars can dismount at premieres from hybrid cars. Enlightened corporate CEOs can erect wind

turbines on company property—with flags on top. School boards can order solar panels for school roofs and link environmental curricula to them.

15   State and local governments can pass new laws. In 2002, San Francisco voters approved a $100-million revenue bond—the largest municipal energy bond measure in the country—to purchase solar panels and wind turbines to be placed on city property. Ultimately, the expenditures will be entirely offset by energy savings. Since 1980, the cost of solar energy has decreased by 71% and the cost of wind energy by 89%. The more the people move to solar and wind power, the greater the economies of scale, and the less it will cost.

16   In recent weeks, Americans have contributed hundreds of millions of dollars to the victims of Sept. 11 and lined up for hours to donate blood. We're a good people. By using our most precious resources—our can-do spirits, our good will—we can achieve energy independence through clean and renewable energy. The seeds of today's victory gardens are already in our hands, but this time the "gardens" may be on our roofs.

THINKING ABOUT THE TEXT

1. In an essay about the aftermath of the September 11th attacks, why do the authors begin with an account of the aftermath of Pearl Harbor?

2. During World War II, what were some of the "great personal sacrifices" that Americans were willing to make, not only in terms of consumption but also concerning lifestyle? What do the writers mean when they claim that Americans during that era "invented the idea of 'green'—before they had the term— and put it together with red, white, and blue"?

3. What do the writers feel is an underlying cause of the war in Afghanistan? Explain.

4. How do the authors contend that "we can 'green' our way to energy independence"? Why do they believe that President Bush and Vice President Cheney will not lead in this struggle? What can all citizens as well as state and local governments do to "green" America?

5. Explain why the authors refer to the antismoking efforts during the last forty years and to the generous donations and volunteer efforts made to aid victims? What do the writers mean when they conclude, "The seeds of today's victory gardens are already in our hands, but this time the 'gardens' may be on our roofs"?

WRITING FROM THE TEXT

1. Write an evaluative response essay analyzing the authors' thesis and key points. Include relevant supporting quotations from the essay and details

from your own observations and experience. See pp. 419-425 for help organizing this essay.

2. In a persuasive essay, use details from the Hochschilds' essay to convince your fellow students what they can do as individuals as well as a community to help conserve energy and to generate energy from renewable sources.

CONNECTING WITH OTHER TEXTS

1. Read "Patriotism Demands Questioning Authority" (p. 266) and review the Hochschilds' essay. Then write a paper explaining what *you* believe is a truly "patriotic" response in the aftermath of an attack like September 11th. Use details from both essays, but feel free to agree or disagree with the authors on particular points.

2. Using ideas from the Hochschilds' essay and from "Dumpster-Diving for Dollars" (p. 319), write an essay to convince readers of the importance of conserving and recycling. Use ideas from both essays and offer suggestions and solutions of your own.

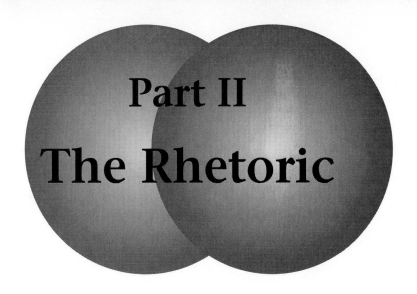

Part II
The Rhetoric

Part II—the rhetoric—is designed for you to use as an easy and constant reference, not only in class with your instructor but also at home when you are on your own. The instruction is deliberately focused and practical. We are convinced that you will only learn to write better by actually writing, and our prewriting exercises prompt you to do just that. We guide you through the entire process, from discovering a topic and writing a draft to supporting a thesis and revising the essay.

Throughout this rhetoric, you will gain skills to craft the varied types of papers that you will need to write. We provide instruction, examples, and discussions of particular methods for developing essays, and we show you how to draft these essays, too. We offer opportunities for you to practice active reading, note taking, incorporating quotations, and interviewing—all important skills to help you write successful papers. We show how important it is to consider audience and style. In addition to the many shorter assignments, we provide instruction for all stages of a longer research paper, with guides to the most current Modern Language Association (MLA) and American Psychological Association (APA) documentation forms. We have provided a brief glossary of terms related to the computer and have included examples of how to document electronic sources.

Chapter 6

Getting Started . . . Now!

Before you become anxious about your next writing assignment or bored from merely *reading* about writing, we would like to introduce you to Anne Lamott—a writer who understands anxiety and is never boring. Lamott's advice should help you keep the stress where it belongs—in the writing, not on you, the writer. She urges writers to bite off just a bit of the assignment at a time, keeping it manageable and appetizing. As you read her essay, highlight key points and vivid wordings. What do you like about her voice, tone, and attitude? What keeps you reading? What does she have to share? The following essay is from *Bird by Bird: Some Instructions on Writing and Life* (1994).

Short Assignments

Anne Lamott

1   The first useful concept is the idea of short assignments. Often when you sit down to write, what you have in mind is an autobiographical novel about your childhood, or a play about the immigrant experience, or a history of—oh, say—women. But this is like trying to scale a glacier. It's hard to get your footing, and your fingertips get all red and frozen and torn up. Then your mental illnesses arrive at the desk like your sickest, most secretive relatives. And they pull up chairs in a semicircle around the computer, and they try to

be quiet but you know they are there with their weird coppery breath, leering at you behind your back.

2   What I do at this point, as the panic mounts and the jungle drums begin beating and I realize that the well has run dry and that my future is behind me and I'm going to have to get a job only I'm completely unemployable, is to stop. First I try to breathe, because I'm either sitting there panting like a lapdog or I'm unintentionally making slow asthmatic death rattles. So I just sit there for a minute, breathing slowly, quietly. I let my mind wander. After a moment I may notice that I'm trying to decide whether or not I am too old for orthodontia and whether right now would be a good time to make a few calls, and then I start to think about learning to use makeup and how maybe I could find some boyfriend who is not a total and complete fixer-upper and then my life would be totally great and I'd be happy all the time, and then I think about all the people I should have called back before I sat down to work, and how I should probably at least check in with my agent and tell him this great idea I have and see if he thinks it's a good idea, and see if *he* thinks I need orthodontia—if that is what he is actually thinking whenever we have lunch together. Then I think about someone I'm really annoyed with, or some financial problem that is driving me crazy, and decide that I must resolve this before I get down to today's work. So I become a dog with a chew toy, worrying it for a while, wrestling it to the ground, flinging it over my shoulder, chasing it, licking it, chewing it, flinging it back over my shoulder. I stop just short of actually barking. But all of this only takes somewhere between one and two minutes, so I haven't actually wasted that much time. Still, it leaves me winded. I go back to trying to breathe, slowly and calmly, and I finally notice the one-inch picture frame that I put on my desk to remind me of short assignments.

3   It reminds me that all I have to do is to write down as much as I can see through a one-inch picture frame. This is all I have to bite off for the time being. All I am going to do right now, for example, is write that one paragraph that sets the story in my hometown, in the late fifties, when the trains were still running. I am going to paint a picture of it, in words, on my word processor. Or all I am going to do is to describe the main character the very first time we meet her, when she first walks out the front door and onto the porch. I am not even going to describe the expression on her face when she first notices the blind dog sitting behind the wheel of her car—just what I can see through the one-inch picture frame, just one paragraph describing this woman, in the town where I grew up, the first time we encounter her.

4   E. L. Doctorow once said that "writing a novel is like driving a car at night. You can see only as far as your headlights, but you can make the

whole trip that way." You don't have to see where you're going, you don't have to see your destination or everything you will pass along the way. You just have to see two or three feet ahead of you. This is right up there with the best advice about writing, or life, I have ever heard.

5   So after I've completely exhausted myself thinking about the people I most resent in the world, and my more arresting financial problems, and, of course, the orthodontia, I remember to pick up the one-inch picture frame and to figure out a one-inch piece of my story to tell, one small scene, one memory, one exchange. I also remember a story that I know I've told elsewhere but that over and over helps me to get a grip; thirty years ago my older brother, who was ten years old at the time, was trying to get a report on birds written that he'd had three months to write, which was due the next day. We were out at our family cabin in Bolinas, and he was at the kitchen table close to tears, surrounded by binder paper and pencils and unopened books on birds, immobilized by the hugeness of the task ahead. Then my father sat down beside him, put his arm around my brother's shoulder, and said, "Bird by bird, buddy. Just take it bird by bird."

6   I tell this story again because it usually makes a dent in the tremendous sense of being overwhelmed that my students experience. Sometimes it actually gives them hope, and hope, as Chesterton said, is the power of being cheerful in circumstances that we know to be desperate. Writing can be a pretty desperate endeavor, because it is about some of our deepest needs: our need to be visible, to be heard, our need to make sense of our lives, to wake up and grow and belong. It is no wonder if we sometimes tend to take ourselves perhaps a bit too seriously. So here is another story I tell often.

7   In the Bill Murray movie *Stripes,* in which he joins the army, there is a scene that takes place the first night of boot camp, where Murray's platoon is assembled in the barracks. They are supposed to be getting to know their sergeant, played by Warren Oates, and one another. So each man takes a few moments to say a few things about who he is and where he is from. Finally it is the turn of this incredibly intense, angry guy named Francis. "My name is Francis," he says. "No one calls me Francis—anyone here calls me Francis and I'll kill them. And another thing. I don't like to be touched. Anyone here ever tries to touch me, I'll kill them," at which point Warren Oates jumps in and says, "Hey—lighten up, Francis."

8   This is not a bad line to have taped to the wall of your office.

9   Say to yourself in the kindest possible way, Look, honey, all we're going to do for now is to write a description of the river at sunrise, or the young child swimming in the pool at the club, or the first time the man sees the woman he will marry. That is all we are going to do for now. We are just going to take this bird by bird. But we are going to finish this *one* short assignment.

Analyzing Lamott's Purpose

Because Lamott's style is so witty and casual, it is easy to overlook all she has to say about writing. Yet despite her relaxed manner, her writing is focused and unified around her purpose for writing and her central points. After we read an essay, and before we write one, it helps to clarify the aim and the claim.

What's the Aim? . . . What's the Claim?

Anne Lamott's *aim* (or purpose) seems clear—to help writers avoid becoming overwhelmed by the writing task or assignment. She provides suggestions, personal anecdotes, and encouragement, all chosen to propel the writer to start and to finish one short assignment.

Anne Lamott's *claim* (or point) is that even large projects and tasks may get started sooner and be done better if we tackle them step by step or "bird by bird" rather than feeling paralyzed by the task at hand.

Analyzing Lamott's Strategy

From the beginning, Lamott speaks in her own voice and shares her real experiences: she wonders if she could "find some boyfriend who is not a total and complete fixer-upper," she tries to decide if she is "too old for orthodontia," and she fears that she has run out of writing ideas and is "completely unemployable." These are all problems that we can identify with. Her strategy is to use a voice that sounds authentic—the voice of a friend sharing anxieties, not a professional writer offering advice from on high. Further, to engage us, she amuses us with fresh and zany images. She refers to those "mental illnesses"—an overstated image of insecurities—that arrive at your desk like "your sickest, most secretive relatives" who inhibit your writing as they "form a semicircle around the computer," condemning, criticizing, and censoring your efforts. And she depicts herself as a "dog with a chew toy" as she wrestles with the problems that keep her from getting down to work. Who hasn't had these same experiences, such as putting off an assignment or fearing the censure of a peer reader or instructor? Thus, Lamott's strategy of personal stories and self-deprecation make her credible and compelling.

Part of her strategy also involves the use of effective language. The absence of clichés and stale language create our perception of her as a lively, spirited individual, without pretension or airs. In fact, her diction (word choice) is far from pretentious. She admits to having financial problems that are "driving me crazy" and to worrying about daily concerns that "leave me winded." Because her strategy is to make her advice accessible to the reader, she uses words that would not be appropriate in all types of assignments. Like the film character in *Stripes* who advises his fellow platoon member to "lighten up," she tries to relax her reader. "Say to yourself in the kindest possible way, Look, honey. . . ."

"Lighten up" may be just the advice you need to get started on a class assignment so that you don't start to censor yourself before you can get your ideas down on the page. In the following section, we will demonstrate prewriting techniques that may help you warm up to your writing assignments.

Prewriting as Discovery

It seems paradoxical to suggest that you will discover what you want to write by writing. But students frequently tell us—and our own writing habits confirm—that the very act of working with words, ideas, or feelings on a page or computer screen helps writers learn what they want to express about a topic.

Sometimes a spirited exchange with a classmate or roommate will help you "get going" on a writing topic because you start to reconsider and refine your ideas as you discuss them, and you start to care whether your ideas have been communicated or accepted. Actually, the best thing you can do when you are assigned a writing task is immediately to jot down any responses and ideas. Consider this initial, quick writing as a conversation with yourself, because that is what it is.

To help you get moving, here are some prewriting exercises that come from the reading and writing topics in this book. Try these different methods; you may find a few that help you get beyond the blank page or screen.

Freewriting

As the term implies, *freewriting* involves jotting down uncensored thoughts as quickly as you can. Don't concern yourself with form or correctness. Write whatever comes into your mind without rejecting ideas that may seem silly or irrelevant. In freewriting, one thought might trigger a more intriguing or significant one, so anything that comes into your head may be valuable. Here is one student's freewriting response to the topic of stereotyping:

```
    Stereotyping? I don't think I stereotype--maybe I do. But I
sure have had it done to me. When people see my tatoo they seem
to think I'm in Hell's Angels or a skinhead. Talk about prejudge-
ments! It's as if the snake coiling up my arm is going to get
them, the way they look at it and pull back from me. I remember
once, in a campground in Alaska, a bunch of us campers were
stranded when the road washed out. As food and supplies dwindled,
people started borrowing from each other. In the john one morning
I asked this guy if I could borrow a razor blade and he jumped
back. Not till he looked away from my arm and into my eyes did he
relax. He gave me a blade, we talked, later shared some campfires
together....I could write about that experience, a good story.
```

```
I wonder if people with tatooes have always been connected with

trouble--pirates maybe, sailors, bikers and gang members today

anyhow. It could be interesting to find out if the negative

stereotypes about tatooes have always been there even though

I just read they estimate about 20 million people have tatts now.

That's some research I could get into.
```

Pete's response to the topic of stereotyping starts with his personal feeling that the subject doesn't really relate to him. But then he thinks about the fact that he has been stereotyped by others. As he considers how people react to his tattoo, he recalls an incident he thinks he could write as a narrative. As he thinks more about the nature of tattoos, he finds an aspect of stereotyping that concerns him and that he might like to research. If he had not written down his feelings about stereotyping, he might have settled for a more predictable response to the assignment.

Notice that Pete's freewriting starts with a question that he asks himself about the topic—a perfect way to get himself warmed up and moving. He's not worried about checking his spelling. He can consult a dictionary when he is drafting his paper to learn that *tattoos* and *prejudgments* are the correct spellings. Pete also uses language in his prewriting that might not be appropriate in his essays: "guy," "bunch," "john," "anyhow," and "get into." Most important is that Pete got started on his assignment and explored his own unique thoughts and feelings. He found a personal experience he might relate and discovered research that he would like to do.

PRACTICING FREEWRITING

To help you see how freewriting can lead to discovery, write for fifteen minutes, without stopping, on one of the following topics. Do not worry about form and do not censor any idea, fact, picture, or feeling that comes to you. Freewrite about the following:

1. One of your parents or one of your children

2. A time spent with a grandparent

3. A family occasion when you learned something

4. Your response to "Are Families Dangerous" (p. 11)

5. "I had internalized the not-so-subtle message that once you reach your magical eighteenth birthday, you should be completely self-reliant" (p. 9). With this quotation at the top of your page, respond fully.

Your freewriting may be written on a sheet of paper, composed at a computer, or jotted down in your journal.

Journal Writing

Journal writing may be looked upon as a conversation with yourself, as a way to warm up before writing a paper or to discover your ideas; in fact, many professional writers rely on journals to store ideas for future stories, articles, editorials, and poems.

Your professor may ask you to keep a journal while you are in a composition course. Nearly all of the "Thinking about the Text" questions and many of the "Writing from the Text" assignments in Part I make ideal topics for a journal. Using your journal to write responses to assigned readings will provide many benefits:

- You will be better prepared for class discussions.
- You will retain more material from the readings.
- You will gain more writing practice.

For your journal entries, you can use a notebook of any size, but many students prefer to compose directly on the computer and find that they write considerably more than they would in longhand.

Using a Journal for Active Reading

One type of assigned active reading is a *dialectical journal.* In this kind of journal you write down specific phrases or meaningful lines from your readings and then record your thoughts about these phrases; in effect, you have a conversation with your reading material. Include specific details that you want to interpret or analyze. Record your responses to those lines and phrases; those responses may be valuable if you later decide to write a paper on the topic.

Imagine Pete, the student who did freewriting about stereotypes, responding specifically to the essay "Don't Let Stereotypes Warp Your Judgments" (p. 469). His journal response to the essay might look like this:

```
"Are criminals more likely to be dark than blond?" That's a
provocative question the author asks. It makes me think about all
the bad guys in movies. Aren't they always dark? You never see
Robert Redford playing a villain--or do you? I think some of our
stereotyping comes from film, which is Heilbroner's point when he
writes about "type-casts." Maybe only bad films use "types." I like
what the author says about stereotypes making us "mentally lazy."
I can see what he means when he says there are two people hurt in
stereotyping--the person who is unjustly lumped into some category
```

<u>and</u> the person who is "impoverished" by his laziness. Heilbroner says that a person can't "see the world in his own absolutely unique, inimitable and independent fashion." That makes sense about being independent. But I wonder what "inimitable" means?

Notice that Pete begins his journal entry with a question from the essay itself; he also might have started with his own question about the work. Pete jots down ideas that come to him as he responds to the reading. Note that he puts quotation marks around any words, phrases, or sentences from the text; in case he uses these later, Pete wants to remember that the ideas and language belong to the author of the essay.

In addition to moving Pete into his assigned topic, his journal writing lets him record his responses to parts of Heilbroner's essay. He is practicing finding the essence of the essay, as well as parts that he might want to quote in his own work. Further, if Pete reads "Proper Care and Maintenance" (p. 186) and "Black Men and Public Space" (p. 237), he will have relevant material in his journal that he can connect to these other readings, either for his own interest or for other writing assignments.

 ### PRACTICING JOURNAL WRITING

Respond to any of the following quoted lines by conversing with yourself in an uncensored dialogue:

1. Meghan Daum p. 112: "I wanted my ego not merely massaged but kneaded. I wanted unfettered affection, soul-mating, true romance."

2. Don Sabo, p. 102: "Winning at sport meant winning friends and carving a place for myself within the male pecking order."

3. Ellen Goodman, p. 4: "We don't have to achieve to be accepted by our families. We just have to be."

Clustering

Clustering is a more visual grouping of ideas on a page. Many students use clustering for in-class writing assignments, including essay exams, where the object is not to discover a topic but to organize information that they already have.

A student named Rachel started with the assigned question of how she was "between worlds" and used that as a center or starting point for her personal inquiry into areas where she felt "betweenness."

She wrote the assignment as a question in the middle of the page, then she drew lines from the topics to several subtopics, which she placed in boxes. As you can see in the illustration, her subtopics are based on the chapter titles in Part I of this book. She placed "perceptions" and "genders" in the same box because, for her, these areas were closely related. Next to each subtopic, she then wrote down a brief phrase or reference to experiences and concerns that related to it. By clustering her responses, Rachel discovered topics that were important to her.

She was also able to group related issues—an immediate advantage of clustering. You may want to read the paper (p. 382) that came from this prewriting discovery work. But first look at Rachel's clustering exercise, which is reproduced below.

◐ PRACTICING CLUSTERING

1. Center "self and family" in a box on a page. As you cluster, consider how you are "a part of" your family and how you are "apart from" your family.

2. Center "incidents that united my family" in a box on a page. Draw lines to other boxes that will include specific outings, celebrations, crises, customs, and events that have united your family. Don't forget the surprising or unlikely incidents that no one expected would draw you together.

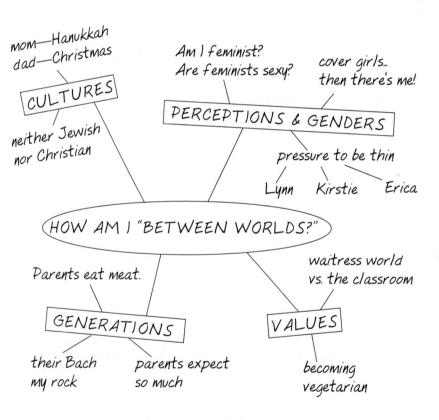

Clustering may help you in the process of discovering topics that interest you as well as finding relationships between ideas that you have written on your page.

Listing

Listing is a way of making a quick inventory of thoughts, ideas, feelings, or facts about a topic. The object is to list everything, again without censoring any notion that comes to you. In addition to clustering her "between-worlds" experiences, Rachel listed her ideas after she discovered a topic for her paper. (You can see her list on p. 357.)

If you are answering a specific question or know what your topic is, you can also use listing to collect from your reading the data that will be useful in your paper. Listing will help you see ways to group and to arrange the material that you have found.

For example, a student who is assigned a character analysis based on a particular reading may list details from the text that indicate the character's traits. In order to write a character analysis of Connie, the central character in the short story "Where Are You Going, Where Have You Been?" (p. 126), student Marianela Enriquez wrote the list shown on page 484. Notice how Marianela's list helps her find important details and then organize those details for her essay.

⚌ PRACTICING LISTING

1. Write a list of options or advantages your parents or grandparents had that you feel you do not have. List options or advantages you have that they did not.

2. List the tensions among the different generations in your family.

3. List the customs, habits, and values in your family that have been transferred among generations.

4. List the behavior traits of Marcus in "Peaches" (p. 147).

Active Reading

Active reading can help you focus on, retain, and perceive the organization scheme of a work you are reading (p. 339). Active reading is also an appropriate prewriting strategy when you are asked to write a specific response to something that you have read, or when you know that your own experience and knowledge provide insufficient information for a meaningful essay.

Active reading involves reading with a pen in your hand. As you read your own text or the photocopied pages of a library book, do the following:

- *Underline* the thesis (if it is explicitly stated), key points or topic sentence, and supporting details.
- *Mark* meaningful or quotable language.
- *Place checkmarks and asterisks* next to important lines.
- *Jot* brief summary or commentary notes in the margins. Infer the thesis and write it in the margin if it is not explicitly stated.
- *Circle* unfamiliar words and references to look up later.
- *Ask* questions as you read.
- *Seek* answers to those questions.
- *Question* the writer's assumptions and assertions as well as your own.

Reading actively will allow you to examine and challenge the ideas of an author. It will also help you find important lines more easily so that you don't have to reread the entire work each time that you refer to it during class discussions or in your essays. Don't underline or highlight *everything*, however, or you will defeat your purpose of finding just the important points.

Rachel, the student who used clustering to discover her concern about the pressure among her friends to be thin, decided to do some reading about eating disorders. The excerpt presented here from "Bodily Harm" (p. 250) illustrates her active reading.

check specific definitions

Recent media attention to the binge-purge and self-starvation disorders known as <u>bulimia</u> and <u>anorexia</u>—often detailing gruesome particulars of women's eating behaviors—may have exacerbated this serious problem on college campuses. But why would a woman who reads an article on eating disorders want to copy what she reads? Ruth Striegel-Moore, Ph.D., director of Yale University's Eating Disorders Clinic, suggests that <u>eating disorders</u> may be a way to be like other "special" women and at the same time strive to outdo them. "The pursuit of thinness is a way for women to compete with each other, a way that <u>avoids being threatening to men</u>," says Striegel-Moore. Eating disorders as a <u>perverse sort of rivalry?</u> In Carol's freshman year at SUNY-Binghamton, a roommate showed her how to make herself throw up. (Barf buddies) are notorious on many college campuses, especially in sororities and among sports teams. Eating disorders as <u>negative bonding?</u> Even self-help groups on campus can degenerate into the kinds of competitiveness and negative reinforcement that are among the roots of eating disorders in the first place.

Media may exacerbate the problem

"special" = how to be unique?

general term

thinness as competition— without threatening men.

Self-help groups as negative reinforcement

How ironic!

This is <u>not</u> another <u>article on how women do it</u>. It is an article on <u>how and why some women stopped</u>. The decision to get help is not always an easy one. The shame and secrecy surrounding most eating dis-

Key focus:

orders and the fear of being labeled "<u>sick</u>" may keep a woman from admitting even to herself that her behavior is hurting her. "We're not weirdos," says Nancy Gengler, a recovered bulimic and number two U.S. squash champion, who asked that I use her real name because "so much of this illness has to do with <u>secrecy and embarrassment</u>." In the first stages of therapy, says Nancy, <u>much of getting better was a result of building up the strength to (literally) "sweat out" the desire to binge and to <u>endure the discomfort of having overeaten</u> rather than throwing up. "I learned to accept such 'failures' and moreover, <u>that they would not make me fat."

labeled "sick"

secrecy is part of the problem

Need to accept our "failures"

Writing notes in the margins helped Rachel to stay involved as she read and to remember details from the essay.

 ### Practicing Active Reading

1. Practice the steps listed on page 340 and actively read the next work that you have been assigned in this course. Do you feel better prepared for class discussion? Did you find the central point or thesis of the essay as a result of your active reading? Was the author's organization scheme apparent to you?

2. Actively read "My Deep, Dark Secret?" (p. 8), "The Only Child" (p. 31), or "The Good Daughter" (p. 20). After you have actively read one of these essays, join a small group of other students who have read the same essay. Compare your active-reading notes with those of others in your group.

Group Brainstorming— Collaborative Learning

Writing doesn't have to be an isolated, lonely activity. In fact, much professional writing is a collaborative effort in which writers work together or consult editors. Corporations, educational institutions, and governmental organizations hold regular "brainstorming" sessions so that everyone can offer ideas, consider options, and exchange opinions. Reporters often work together on a story, business experts pool ideas to draft a proposal, and lawyers work as a team on a brief. Many of your textbooks—including this one—are the result of extensive collaboration.

Your college writing classes may offer you opportunities to work together in small groups, brainstorm for topics or supporting details, and critique and edit your classmates' writing. These small groups can stimulate new thoughts, multiple perspectives, and critical questions. Small-group discussion should prompt you to consider the ideas of others and help alleviate the fear that you have nothing to say.

In the classroom, groups of four or five work well, with each person recording the group's comments and key ideas for an assigned question. Students in the group can alternate explaining each response, so that the burden of reporting the discussion does not fall on any one group member. Your instructor, however, may ask that someone from each group serve as "group secretary," recording responses and then reading them. Either way, the goal is to generate as many different responses as possible to a given topic or question. As in all of the prewriting activities, no idea or comment should be censored.

Let's assume you have been assigned a paper about growing up with or without siblings. Each group can take a different aspect of this topic:

- The advantages of growing up with siblings
- The advantages of growing up as an only child
- The ways that only children find "substitutes" for siblings
- The reasons for sibling rivalry and competition, and the solutions to these problems
- The unexpected bonds that develop between siblings
- The reasons that sibling friendships fail

After ten to fifteen minutes of discussion, each group shares its key points with the class. After each group's report, all students should be invited to add comments or insights on that topic.

Group brainstorming is an ideal way to discuss reading assignments, and most of the "Thinking about the Text" questions in Part I are designed for collaborative work. Next you will find brainstorming exercises for both general topics and specific readings.

PRACTICING BRAINSTORMING IN SMALL GROUPS

1. Brainstorm about the forces threatening the family unit today, and consider ways of preventing or solving particular conflicts. (All groups can work on this topic because the responses will vary.)

2. Discuss the extent to which grandparents are or are not valued by families. Support the discussion with your own experience.

3. Discuss the various types of families currently portrayed on television. Topics:
   - Analyze the impact of the media on the family.
   - Compare sitcoms with family dramas or PBS specials on the family.
   - Contrast portraits of more conventional families with those of less conventional ones.
   - Suggest programs that could help or support the family.
   - Evaluate programs for their level of violence.

4. Read "Living in Two Worlds" (p. 144) and "The Only Child" (p. 31) and discuss specific ways that family members develop different values and habits. You may add your own experiences to this discussion.

5. Read "The Good Daughter" (p. 20) and discuss children's rights and parents' responsibilities.

Why Brainstorm?

Brainstorming lets you see the perspectives of others and consider their views in relation to your own—an awareness you will need when you are writing for an audience other than yourself. Collaborative work gets you away from the isolation of your own desk or computer screen and into a social context.

Incubation

After you have tried one or more of the prewriting strategies to get started on an assignment, allow yourself an incubation period—time to think about your topic before you begin to draft the paper. Students often comment on experiencing flashes of insight about their papers while in the shower, falling asleep, or doing some physical activity.

You, too, will find that your brain will continue to "work" on your paper if you are preoccupied with it when you are away from it, and thus it is a good idea to leave time for incubation at each point in the writing process. For example, if you do some prewriting on your paper when it is first assigned, your early thoughts and ideas may develop during incubation. Later, you may also be able to refine the purpose of your essay, which in turn will help you hone your topic, improve the support of your main points, discover connections among ideas in your paper, and recall words that will sharpen your meaning.

Considering Audience

Identifying Your Audience

All writing is intended for readers—that is, for an audience. But who *is* the audience?

In some situations, you can easily define the audience: for example, your reader may be a friend or family member who will receive your letter. You are surely aware that your writing tone—the voice that you use that affects your word choice and emphasis—will differ if you are writing to your lover, brother, elderly aunt, or mother. However, you may be less able to define the audience for other writing situations.

In general, you should not assume that your only reader is your composition instructor, for that conclusion will prompt you to write for a very small audience. Furthermore, your English teacher may be your easiest audience, because he or she is *required* to read what you have written, comment on your thinking and writing skills, and then perhaps place a grade on your work.

Academic Audiences.   Academic readers (your instructors and classmates) will expect a certain depth of response, even in a short paper. The reader will expect to learn specific facts, find actual examples, discover important insights, or see particular relationships that she or he was not aware of prior to reading your paper.

An academic audience will also expect you to have worked with integrity if you incorporate the ideas, facts, or words of another writer. (See the discussions of plagiarism on p. 368 and on p. 516.) An academic audience will expect you to make some point and to support that point logically, with sufficient details (of description, fact, or example) to be convincing.

Academic readers will expect your material to be presented in an orderly way. Finally, they will expect the language of your work to be appropriate: standard English and well-chosen words, edited to remove errors in grammar, spelling, and mechanics.

Nonacademic Audiences.   For writing outside the classroom—for example, a letter to a newspaper, a report for your boss, or an analysis for a community project—you must engage an audience that is not required to read your writing. What are the expectations of this audience? For the most part, nonacademic audiences also expect good organization, no errors or plagiarism, and logically supported points.

In addition, you may need to convince nonacademic readers that your subject and the way you have treated it are worth their time. You may have to establish the value of your subject and the quality of your writing in the first few sentences. Developing an engaging style will help keep your reader interested.

Voice.   Most instructors will tell you to "write in your own voice." This means that they want you to write using the vocabulary, sentence structure, and style that you use for communicating as an adult. You do not want to use pretentious words or artificial language, nor do you want to use diction that is more appropriate for talking with a friend.

Stance and Tone.   To engage your audience quickly, you may want to assume a stance and tone that is positive for all readers, even those who are disinterested or hostile to the topic you are writing about. You may want to anticipate possible objections, doubts, or lack of interest by writing in a tone that does not put off any reader. Consider these two opening sentences:

> Only someone ignorant of contract law will find ambiguity in the handling of surrogate parenting disputes.

> Surrogate parenting disputes may occur because the parties involved have unrealistic expectations about surrogate parenting agreements and because the legal world has not yet found a clear way to judge these cases of ethical dilemma.

The tone of the first sentence is bold, the assertion straightforward. Some readers will be put off by the claim that "only someone ignorant of contract law will find ambiguity" because some of the audience may be ignorant of contract law, and the "will" suggests no room for consideration. The use of "ignorant" will be offensive to some readers and perhaps compelling to others. Some readers may continue to read in spite of the brash voice, or even because of it. But others may conclude that the tone is too hostile to tolerate, and those readers will stop reading.

In contrast, the tone of the second sentence is cautious ("may occur") and contemplative: perhaps "unrealistic expectations" are a reason, or perhaps "the legal world" is unable to rule clearly. By suggesting that there is room for discussion, the writer may win the reader who is interested in an unbiased exploration of surrogate parenting disputes. The writer of the second sentence has tried to create a reasonable and informing relationship between writer and reader, one that should attract readers.

You will need to choose the tone that you want to use for your particular writing assignment. The subject matter of your work and the audience for whom you are writing will help you determine whether a neutral tone will keep your audience engaged.

Style. *Style* is conscious use of language, and good style will help ensure the attention of an audience. Style includes the following elements:

- Word choice—precisely chosen words, wordplay, and level of diction (formal, conversational, or slang); see also pages 611–614
- Sentence structure—length, types, and variety
- Voice—real, rather than artificial or pretentious
- Tone—your attitude and relationship with the reader

Consider the opening line from an article in the *Harvard Health Letter*. The topic is controversial, and the reader may have opinions about the subject. Notice that the style of the author, Ruth Papazian, is apparent to the reader in her first sentence.

A Hot Issue

In January 1992, when Florida shoppers bought strawberries that had been treated with gamma rays, food irradiation moved from the realm of theory to America's kitchen tables.

First, the author uses wit and wordplay in her title. There's nothing wrong with evoking a chuckle from a reader, even when the subject matter is serious or scientific. Further, the writer creates an immediate and natural bond with any reader who has bought strawberries; that reader would wonder, "Hey! Do my strawberries get zapped?" The writer secures that bond by further noting that the issue moved from "theory"—which some readers may not care about—to "America's kitchen tables." Notice that the writer does not write "dining room tables." This writing is clearly directed toward general readers, all of whom eat, and the kitchen image evokes a folksiness that engages the audience.

In the rest of the article, the author uses sentences that further win the reader. For example, after establishing the topic, she writes in her seventh paragraph, "Since a caveperson first tossed a chunk of mastodon onto glowing embers, humans have been cooking with infrared radiation." Notice the gender-neutral *caveperson* instead of the sexist term *caveman,* and notice the diction of *chunk,* the humorous specificity of *mastodon,* and the effective imagery of *glowing embers.* Who wouldn't want to read this entire essay? (It's in the August 1992 issue, if you're intrigued by the topic or want to see more of this author's style.)

Academic readers who are required to read your writing may not insist on lively style, wit, or exquisite word choice. And they may tolerate a brash tone or hostile stance. Nevertheless, engaging the audience is as applicable to writing done for academics as it is to the writing done for nonacademics.

 PRACTICING STYLE

1. Write two letters—one to your best friend, and one to your parents or children—describing a party that you recently attended. (Your letters probably will vary in vocabulary, kinds of details, sentence structure, and tone.)

2. Write two memos—one to a coworker who is a friend, and one to your boss—arguing for a particular change at work.

Analyzing Audience Awareness

We can profit from the study of techniques that writers use to hold their particular audience. The following essay by William F. Harrison has been published in a number of places, including the *Los Angeles Times* on July 7, 1996. Harrison is an obstetrician and gynecologist who practices in Fayetteville, Arkansas. A smoker of twenty years, Harrison saw the effects of cigarette addiction on his own body. For ten years he tried to stop smoking and, because he limited himself to a single cigarette a day, he thought he was not harming himself. Nevertheless, he had chronic bronchitis and laryngitis. After consulting with pulmonologists and pathologists, he learned that even one cigarette a day harms the body irreparably. He knew that he needed to stop entirely, and he did. He also knew that he needed to convince his patients to stop smoking. This essay reports the results of Harrison's research. Does the writer convince his reader?

EXAMPLE: CONVINCING AN AUDIENCE

Why Stop Smoking?
Let's Get Clinical
William F. Harrison

1   Most of us in medicine now accept that tobacco is associated with major health consequences and constitutes the No. 1 health problem in this country.

2   What smokers have not yet come to terms with is that if they continue smoking, the probability of developing one or more of the major complications of smoking is 100 percent. It absolutely will happen. They will develop chronic bronchitis, laryngitis, pharyngitis, sinusitis and some degree of emphysema. It is also highly probable that they will develop serious disease in the arteries of all vital organs, including the brain and heart, markedly increasing their risk of heart attack and stroke. If they continue, they increase the probability of developing cancer of the lips, gums, tongue, pharynx, larynx, trachea, bronchi and lungs, of the bladder, cervix, gallbladder and other organs. Smoking contributes to rapid aging of the skin and connective tissues—women and men who smoke usually have the skin age of a person ten to twenty years older than one who doesn't smoke, given the same degree of exposure to the sun.

3   About 415,000 people die prematurely each year in the United States as a result of smoking—the equivalent of eighteen 747s crashing every week with no survivors. Many of these victims die after long and excruciating illnesses, burdens to themselves, their families and society. The cost of this misery is incalculable, but we do know that the tobacco industry grosses about $50 billion a year from the agonies it inflicts.

4   How does all this damage come about?

5   In normal lungs, the trachea and bronchi—the large and small tubes leading to the alveoli (the tiny sacs that do the actual work of the lungs)—are lined with a film of tissue that is one cell layer thick. The surface of these cells is covered with tiny, finger-like structures called cilia. These cilia beat constantly in a waving motion, which moves small particles and toxic substances out of the lung and into the back of the throat where they are swallowed. In a smoker or someone like a coal miner, who constantly breathes in large amounts of toxic substances, many of the cilia soon disappear. If exposure continues, some ciliated cells die and are replaced by squamous cells, the same type that form the skin. Without the cleansing function of the ciliated cells, toxic materials and particles are breathed further into the lungs, staying longer in contact with all the tissue. Each group of ciliated cells killed and

replaced by squamous cells decreases by a certain fraction the lungs' ability to cleanse themselves. As this occurs, the amount of damage done by each cigarette increases to a greater and greater degree. By the time one has been a pack-a-day smoker for ten years or so, extensive damage has already been done. By twenty years, much of the damage is irreversible and progresses more rapidly. After ten years of smoking, each cigarette may do as much damage to the body as three or more packs did when a smoker first started.

6   The longer one smokes, the harder it gets to quit. Smoking is one of the most addictive of human habits, perhaps as addicting as crack cocaine or heroin. One has to quit every day, and there are no magic pills or crutches that make stopping easy. It is tough to do. Only those who keep trying ever quit. And even those who have smoked for only a short time or a few cigarettes a day will probably find it difficult to stop. But the sooner a smoker makes this self-commitment, the more probable it is that he or she will quit before having done major damage to the body.

Analyzing the Essay

Clearly, William Harrison's purpose in writing is to convince readers who are smokers to stop smoking. His obligation as a writer is to produce plenty of research to answer the question: "Why Stop Smoking?" His intention also may be to prevent people from starting and to arm nonsmokers with specific evidence to help persuade a family member or a friend who smokes to stop.

His opening engages the reader because he is straightforward in his presentation of facts. Harrison specifically cites those diseases that all smokers definitely will get and those diseases that smokers probably will get. No organ of the body remains untouched, and Harrison might have written just that statement. But by actually citing the organs, the reader is almost overwhelmed by the catalog of specific details. In addition, to catch the interest of the person indifferent to health, Harrison appeals to the reader's vanity by stating that smokers' skin is aged ten to twenty years beyond that of nonsmokers.

When Harrison provides the number of smokers who die prematurely—415,000 per year—he also gives a disturbing equivalent for this figure: "eighteen 747s crashing every week with no survivors." The writer's purpose here is to shock us. We may be complacent about the number of smokers who die each year, but we all know the effect of a newspaper headline announcing the crash of a single plane. Imagine reading that eighteen planes crashed each week all year! Cleverly, Harrison admits he doesn't know the cost of the "excruciating illnesses"—and the misery—that precede death from smoking-related diseases. But he knows and gives the profits of the tobacco industry—"$50 billion a year."

Harrison might have generalized what happens to the lungs when people smoke, but instead he credits his readers' intelligence by providing a highly specific and scientific account of how the cilia cells that normally cleanse the lungs disappear. In fact his word choice is that the "ciliated cells die," a far more emphatic way to show that toxic material is no longer filtered out. By showing the human body as a mechanical organism, he convinces the reader that the smoker's body has no more chance to continue running well than a car would if it were deprived of oil or gasoline.

To drive home his point about the toxicity of smoking, Harrison equates the smoker with "a coal miner"; both breathe in "large amounts of toxic substances." He notes that after ten years of smoking the lungs are so vulnerable that "each cigarette may do as much damage to the body as three or more packs did when a smoker first started." He uses this startling research to convince both the smoker who planned to stop after a few years and the smoker of ten years who cuts down to an occasional cigarette, that profound harm is done to the body regardless of the smoker's intention.

Harrison's conclusion has to do with nicotine addiction, and he compares the addiction to quitting cocaine or heroin. In his frightening comparison, he provides any young person considering smoking ample reason not to start, and he gives any person who loves a smoker the impetus to seek professional help to rid the smoker of this powerful and deadly addiction.

Finally, Harrison's title is an effective play on words. He's relying on the reader to hear "Let's Get Physical," a lyric from a popular song, in "Let's Get Clinical." His essay provides vivid clinical evidence of the physical damage the smoker will do to his body, information as far from a popular tune as it can be.

 ## PRACTICING AUDIENCE AWARENESS

1. Write a letter to your college president or dean of student affairs to convince the administrator that your college needs more stringently enforced "no smoking" zones.

2. Write a letter to a friend who smokes to convince that person to stop. Use the data in Harrison's essay for your letter.

A Final Word about Audience

Good style—achieved with deliberately chosen vocabulary, sentence structure, and tone—can engage your reader immediately. Providing solid support will sustain that reader. With a realistic understanding of your audience in mind, you are ready to begin organizing and drafting your essay.

Chapter 7

Organizing
and Drafting an Essay

From Prewriting to Purpose

The prewriting exercises presented in the previous chapter should have helped you discover focus points and different ways that you might respond to your writing assignment. You were also given some ideas about considering the audience for your writing, to help you select an appropriate stance and tone. The stance or position that you take will be influenced by your aim in writing and the assignment you have been given.

Purpose in Writing

Clearly your purpose or aim in writing is to satisfy your instructor's assignment—and to get a good grade on your paper! Your primary purpose—assigned by your instructor or discovered on your own—may be to (1) express, (2) inform, (3) analyze, or (4) persuade. For example, if your instructor assigns an evaluative, analytic, or persuasive essay, your aim has been delineated for you. But if you have been given a more open-ended assignment—to write on a topic or respond to readings—you will need to discover your aim for yourself.

What's Your Aim?

Throughout Part I, we asked you to consider the writer's aim in writing because even when writers address the same topic, their essays will be quite different if their purposes vary. Let's examine the essays of two writers who explore what it means to be heavy in a culture that reveres thinness: Jennifer

Coleman's "Discrimination at Large" (p. 243) and Neil Steinberg's "O.K., So I'm Fat" (p. 247). We think that you will agree that these authors have distinctly different aims.

In "Discrimination at Large," Jennifer Coleman asserts that discrimination against heavy people, in jokes and attitudes, is as "damaging as any racial or ethnic slur" (p. 246). In this essay, her purpose is to persuade the reader that attitudes and actions against "fat people" need to be changed so that ridicule is not tolerated. She argues that people who would not tolerate jibes about someone's race, culture, disability, or sexual orientation do mock fat people.

Coleman expresses her feelings about being harassed for simply ordering food at a restaurant or appearing on a beach, but her main purpose extends beyond expressing herself. She wants to persuade her reader that discrimination because of weight is as unfair and unacceptable as discrimination because of race and ethnicity. As in any argument, she must present evidence of how she has been harassed. She does this by reporting hostile attacks like "Move your fat ass" and unsolicited comments like "You would really be pretty if you lost weight."

Her aim, to persuade her reader, also requires her to anticipate an opponent who might argue that this harassment is not the same as racial and ethnic slurs because weight, unlike race or ethnicity, can be controlled. The average reader might contend that she should diet and exercise. Coleman anticipates this objection by delineating the details of her acute exercise and dietary phase. She reveals that her pulse, cholesterol level, and respiration were excellent; she was fit but still fat. Finally, she exposes the poor reasoning of those who want her to exercise but still attack her for riding a bike ("Hey lady, where's the seat") or denigrate her by trumpeting like elephants while she is jogging. While she exercises, she has heard people shout, "Lose some weight, you pig." She demands that her reader "go figure," emphasizing how irrational some people are, perhaps even some readers. We think that her primary goal is achieved—to persuade readers that such harassment should not be tolerated or perpetuated by anyone who is sensitive and reasonable.

In "O.K., So I'm Fat," Neil Steinberg does not have the same goal in writing. What is his aim? We see this as an expressive essay because Steinberg is revealing how he feels about the "smug superiority" of some thin people, but he probably does not aim to change people's opinions or behavior. He is expressing himself and entertaining us rather than arguing a point. He acknowledges that there is "a social stigma" in being fat as well as "medical peril" and some discomfort in "dragging all that excess weight around." But what he wants to express is that the "ignominy" for fat people is "thin people." He cites as evidence "overly familiar office mates" and "wiry panhandlers" who address him as "big guy," and those who slyly refer to fad diets or offer him a Diet Coke, hoping to elevate him to the "sainted ranks of the thin." He cites the "wisp of a woman" hostess with "legs like beef jerky" who prepared "an intensely fattening dessert—Bananas Foster, thick slices of ripe bananas awash in butter and sugar and cinnamon and liqueur accompanied by ice cream" but who didn't have any herself. He notes the smug superiority in her refusal as she "gazes down" on him. Steinberg also mentions that he is not bothered by thin people who don't need to watch what they eat; he is "comfortable, happy, never put off" by them. Clearly, Steinberg's purpose is to express his perceptions about the superior attitude of thin people—not to change his readers' opinions or behavior. Steinberg makes it clear that thin people's attitude toward the obese is not, dare we say, a weighty subject. In both Coleman's and Steinberg's essays, each writer's purpose or aim is evident from the first few words of the essay and from the implied or explicit thesis or central claim of the essay.

What's Your Claim?

Every essay requires a thesis—a claim that establishes a writer's purpose. This assertion clarifies the focus of the essay for both the writer and the reader. Throughout your writing, it will help to hear your reader asking, "What's your aim? What's your claim?"—two questions that will ensure that you are staying focused. Remember also that your claim or thesis may change a number of times as you draft and revise your paper.

In "Discrimination at Large," Jennifer Coleman's aim is to convince readers that discrimination because of weight is unjust and cannot be tolerated. Her claim or thesis is explicitly stated at the end of her essay. In "O.K., So I'm Fat," Neil Steinberg's aim is to express his annoyance and his claim is that some thin people have superior attitudes that make him feel uncomfortable. He is not trying to persuade or reform his readers, but he still needs a focus or implied claim.

Developing a Thesis

A thesis is an assertion about a limited subject that will be supported, proved, or described by the writer of the essay. Often, but not always, the view of the writer shows in the language of the thesis. Sometimes the writer constructs a thesis to forecast the plan or organization of the paper. The thesis should always reflect the aim or intention of the paper.

Let's imagine that Pete is deciding from his prewriting experiences (pp. 334–335) how to respond to his assignment on stereotyping. His particular interest has to do with his tattoo and how he is stereotyped because of it, an awareness he gained in freewriting. Pete realized that he had a good focus for a story he could narrate. He also discovered that he was interested in doing some reading about the history of tattoos to learn whether they were always regarded negatively.

If Pete's assignment had been to write about a personal experience involving stereotyping, he probably would have written about the incident in the

Alaskan campground. Had his purpose been to define stereotyping, show its consequences, and persuade his reader that it is wrong, Pete might have recalled his dialectical journal prewriting (pp. 336–337) on the essay "Don't Let Stereotypes Warp Your Judgments" (p. 469), and he would have developed his paper in a different way. Pete may have used any of the following for a working thesis, depending on his purpose in writing the paper:

- An experience in Alaska showed me how uncomfortable stereotyping can be for the person stereotyped.
- Stereotyping, or prejudgments based on "standardized pictures" in our heads, can create unnecessary anxiety and deprive us of worthwhile experiences.
- Because tattoos have been worn by the lower classes and fringe members of various cultures throughout history, there has been prejudice against them.
- Because prominent citizens of the world have started to wear tattoos, earlier prejudice against tattoos has diminished.

Each of these assertions requires Pete to develop his paper in a slightly different way. The first thesis can be supported with his own experience. The second statement requires using some definitive and appropriately documented material from Heilbroner's essay on stereotyping, as well as personal experience. The third and fourth thesis statements will require Pete to research material in order to support his claims. Like Pete, your personal interests, as well as the aim of the assignment itself, will help you decide on a suitable thesis.

Recognizing a Thesis

If a thesis is a complete sentence that makes an assertion about a limited subject, which of the following are supportable thesis statements? Which are not? Which statements forecast a plan or direction for the paper?

1. Sexism in college courses.

2. Sexist language in college textbooks can be eliminated with the right attitude and language awareness.

3. I think the school's cafeteria should post a nutritional analysis of every meal it offers.

4. When grandparents live with two younger generations, everyone learns flexibility and new reasons to laugh.

5. Should Americans buy only American-made products?

6. Siblings can remind us of our family's history and values and can provide physical and emotional support as we age.

The first example may be a suitable subject or topic for an essay, but it is not a thesis. As the absence of a verb indicates, the example lacks an assertion that makes a claim about sexism. The second example does make a claim about sexist language and is a reasonable thesis. It has a limited subject (sexist language in college textbooks), and it forecasts that "attitude" and "language awareness" will be the subtopics discussed to support the thesis. Example 3 on page 353 contains a clear assertion, but "I think" is unnecessary. The thesis should directly express this conviction: The school's cafeteria should post a nutritional analysis of every meal it offers. The fourth example is an effective thesis that forecasts two benefits of generations living together. A question like that in the fifth example may be a good way to engage a reader in an introduction, but it is not an assertion, so it is not a suitable thesis. The question encourages an unfocused, disorganized response. Contrast the direction implicit in the statements of examples 2, 4, or 6 with this question, and you will see why it is not effective. The sixth example is a very explicit thesis statement. It cites exactly the areas of support that will come in the paper: the "family's history and values" and "physical and emotional support." Writers who work from a strong thesis will know where they are going, and so will their readers.

Changing the Thesis

A thesis statement can undergo many changes in the course of drafting and rewriting a paper. All writers have had the experience of finishing a draft only to discover that their feelings about the subject have changed. In order to reflect that new awareness in the paper, the writer will want to return to the thesis, revise it, and then reshape the points in the paper so they will adequately support the new assertion. Writers will find that it is perhaps best to consider any thesis as only a working thesis until they are about to edit their final draft. (See Rachel's work on developing a thesis, pp. 357–362.)

The "Missing" Thesis

Some writers do not explicitly state their thesis, and some instructors do not demand one. Sometimes the overt assertion may spoil the sense of discovery that the writer intends for the reader. But even if a thesis is implied rather than stated, in a well-structured essay you should be able to articulate the writer's fundamental assertion.

Positioning the Thesis

For many writers, and for many essays, placing the thesis at the conclusion of the introduction makes sense. The thesis follows logically from the introductory materials used to engage the audience, and the plan or direction of the paper is set forth so that the reader knows not only what is coming but in what order the support will be presented. This forecasting also helps the writer of the essay to stay organized and on target.

Essays that are tightly written, with very well-organized support, may conclude with the thesis to bring an inevitable (if not predictable) sense of closure. The reader will perceive where the writer is headed, so the assertion at the end of the paper will not come as a surprise.

Many writing instructors, tired of wondering and writing "Where is all of this going?" in the margins of student papers, will require that you place your thesis within the first few paragraphs of your essay. These instructors favor the clearly stated thesis that forecasts the subtopics and their order of presentation. In any case, a strong focus—whether stated in a thesis or implied—contributes to good writing, and you will want to perfect your ability to focus your work.

The more essays you read, the more you will recognize how a thesis statement sounds. Take, for example, the thesis of Robin Swicord's "Youth Must Be Served—With Respect" (p. 290): "If the entertainment industry is careless about its influence on young people, it's only because we're embedded in a broader national culture that constantly demonstrates its disrespect toward children and adolescents, in every arena from child care to fashion" (292). The subject of her essay is the entertainment industry's effect on young people. The author wants to show that this industry and others disrespect young people. The author asserts her point in a statement, a thesis, that forecasts those areas that she will examine—education and child care—two places she insists our culture shows its disrespect for young people.

Although reading other writers' thesis statements will help you understand the mechanics of thesis writing, you need to practice writing your own assertions for your own papers. You also need to have readers critique the thesis statements that you have written.

PRACTICING THESIS WRITING

1. Return to one of your prewriting exercises or freewrite for fifteen minutes on the subject of a parent's ability or inability to be open to new and possibly controversial ideas. Then reread what you have written. Find an aspect of that material that interests you. Limit your focus and write two or three different thesis statements that you can support with the ideas in your freewriting. Type or write these assertions neatly on a sheet of paper and make three copies prior to your next class session.

2. Work in groups of four students to comment on each other's assertions. Let each student in the group make comments about one thesis statement before you go on to look at each person's second assertion. Determine which statements are true assertions that can be supported. Then predict the type of support that is necessary (narrative of personal experience, definition, or examples from research material) for each thesis.

Critical Thinking and the "So What?" Response

After you have a tentative assertion around which to direct your support, ask yourself, "So what?" A sure way to realize that your assumed assertion isn't headed anywhere meaningful is to discover yourself shrugging indifferently at your own claim. And as you jot down answers to this question, you will start to see what you are actually claiming. For example, imagine what would happen if you started with this assertion:

> **Thesis:** Many people in the world are victims of stereotyping.

"So what?"

Some people have preconceived ideas about others.

"So what?"

It's unfair. People see them as types, not individuals.

"So what?"

These prejudgments limit the people who are stereotyped *and* the people doing the stereotyping.

As you continue to answer the "So what?" questions, you may discover a way to state your assertion that makes your reader more eager to read your paper. Compare the following assertion with the first one. In what way is it better?

> **Thesis:** Prejudgments limit the lives of the stereotyped individual and the person doing the stereotyping.

Notice how this statement conforms to the requirements of a thesis. It is a complete sentence, not a question or a phrase, and it articulates a definite opinion or assertion. Unlike the first attempt at a thesis, this statement establishes a definite focus on prejudgments (they "limit . . . lives"), and it suggests an order for the analysis ("the stereotyped individual" and "the person doing the stereotyping").

By asking yourself "So what?" *throughout* your writing, you will not only sharpen your thesis but also help yourself discover points and insights worth sharing with readers. If you continue to ask this question, you will prompt yourself to think more critically about each claim as you make it. You also will ensure that you are writing from a worthwhile assertion and that you are explaining your points to your reader.

Supporting a Thesis

Drafting

No one writer drafts the same way; in fact, there are as many methods (and "nonmethods") for drafting as there are writers. But there are countless strategies and approaches that help writers organize, develop, and support their ideas and assertions.

On the following pages, we will trace how one student, Rachel, drafted her paper. Look back to pages 337 to 338 to see Rachel's clustering exercise where she discovered a topic related to living "between worlds." From this initial prewriting, she perceived that recurrent topics of interest were related to food: her vegetarianism, her friends' preoccupation with slimness, her awareness that her body does not fit the cover-girl mold, and even her job as a waitress.

Developing Support

Reviewing all of these food-related topics, Rachel realized she was most interested in her friends' eating problems. She started by actively reading "Bodily Harm" (p. 250). You can read an excerpt from this prewriting exercise on pages 358–359. This active reading helped stimulate Rachel's thinking and helped her understand her friends' experiences.

Listing

After her prewriting activities, Rachel started to list more specific ideas and experiences that related to eating disorders:

- My friend, Lynn, hospitalized for anorexia, nearly died.
- Another friend, Kirstie, was proud she could vomit automatically every time she ate.
- My friend, Erica, in a treatment program, was shocked by the number of women over thirty still plagued by eating disorders.
- Binge-and-purge syndrome needs to be explained.
- Ads depict tall models in size 3 bikinis.
- "Bodily Harm" examines psychological motives, "barf buddies," and "aerobic nervosa."
- Jane Fonda, once bulimic, hooked so many on her "Work Out" videos.
- Princess Di—bulimic and suicidal—the myth collapses.
- Kate Moss and Calista Flockhart are skinny superstars.
- My own insecurity involves my weight.
- My cousin spent weeks in a hospital program for anorexics.
- Weight loss—the ultimate "control" mechanism?
- Women's movement trying to free women from such images.
- Young women torn between being feminist or sexy—why either/or?
- Sexy women are always pictured as thin.
- Women competing without threatening men.

Working Thesis

From this list, Rachel linked certain topics: friends' experiences, celebrities with serious eating disorders, advertising images of women, psychological motives, the women's movement, and dieting as a control mechanism. These groupings helped her draft a working thesis so she could start planning her paper.

Working Thesis: Many women suffer from eating disorders.

Using this preliminary thesis as a guide, Rachel started to write.

First Draft

In this day and age many women suffer from eating disorders. Influenced by television commercials and movies, most women have been conditioned to believe they must be thin to be beautiful. Who wouldn't want to hear friends whisper, "What a body! She really knows how to stay in shape!" or "Don't you hate someone who looks that good?" Either way, the sense of envy is clear. A thin girl has something that others don't--and this gives her power and control. She can make herself in the image of the cover girls. "The pursuit of thinness is a way for women to compete with each other, a way that avoids being threatening to men" (Erens 250).

Unfortunately, this competition keeps women from seeking or obtaining the help they might otherwise get from close friends. Many bulimics keep their secret as guarded as they can. For example, my friend Kirstie did this. She waited for years before she told friends (and later, her family) that she was bulimic. At first, only her "barf buddy" (from Erens?) knew.

Kirstie seemed to have a good life with her family and friends. But years later, she revealed to me that her greatest pride was when she discovered that she was now vomiting automatically after eating, without needing to use a finger or spoon.

Erica was another friend who needed help. In fact, her situation was so bad that she needed to go into a hospital. And my friend Lynn would have died had she not entered the hospital when

she did. She had to drop out of Berkeley immediately and get prolonged therapy for herself and her family. As Erens notes, "Family
therapy considers the family itself, not the daughter with the
eating disorder, to be the 'patient.' Often the daughter has taken
on the role of diverting attention from unacknowledged conflicts
within the family."

One problem Lynn had was conforming to her parents' expectations. Lynn decided to major in art even though her parents wanted
her to get a degree in computer science so she would have a job
when she graduated. There was so much stress in that house every
time Lynn enrolled in another art class. Maybe she felt that
the only thing she could control in her life was how thin she
could get.

The message to be thin comes from popular role models. In the
80s, actress Jane Fonda sold many on the value of her "Work Out"
and helped spawn "aerobic nervosa" (Erens 251). Many women who
admire her shape may not know that Fonda was once bulimic. And no
one watching the televised spectacle of Prince Charles and
Princess Diana's wedding could have predicted that years later
biographers would be discussing "Di's bulimia."

Not just the supermodels like Kate Moss, or the popular television stars like Calista Flockhart who played successful lawyer
Ally McBeal, but most popular personalities seem incredibly thin
today. It seems that many women--celebrities, models, and my
friends--have not escaped this curse.

Evaluating the First Draft

As Rachel was writing this draft she found herself crossing out occasional
words and adding phrases, but her main concern was getting her ideas down
on the page. She remembered relevant ideas from some assigned readings in
Between Worlds, and she put some of the quoted material in her draft. She didn't
worry about the form of her quotes, but she was careful to copy the page
numbers correctly so she wouldn't have to waste time searching for them
later. Once she had written this rough draft, she reread it with a pen in hand,

spotting weak areas and making quick notes to herself. Her critique of her first draft follows.

cliche?   *dull*

(In this day and age) many women suffer from eating disorders. Influenced by television commercials and movies, most women have been conditioned to believe they must be thin to be beautiful. Who wouldn't want to hear friends whisper, "What a body! She really knows how to stay in shape!" or "Don't you hate someone who looks that good?" Either way, the sense of envy is clear. A thin girl has something that others don't--and this gives her power and control. She can make herself in the image of cover girls. "The pursuit of thinness is a way for women to compete with each other, a way that avoids being threatening to men" (Erens 250).

maybe save…

put thesis here?

Unfortunately, this competition keeps women from seeking or obtaining the help they might otherwise get from close friends. Many bulimics keep their secret as guarded as they can. For example, my friend Kirstie did this. She waited for years before she told friends (and later, her family) that she was bulimic. At first, only her "barf buddy" (from Erens) knew.

page?

Kirstie seemed to have a good life with her family and friends. But years later, she revealed to me that her greatest pride was when she discovered that she was now vomiting auto-> matically after eating, without needing to use a finger or spoon.

illustrate

develop

too gross? or OK?

better link here?

Erica was another friend who needed help. In fact, her situation was so bad that she needed to go into a hospital. And my friend Lynn would have died had she not entered the hospital when she did. She had to drop out of Berkeley immediately and get prolonged therapy for herself and her family. As Erens notes, "Family therapy considers the family itself, not the daughter with the eating disorder, to be the 'patient.' Often the daughter has taken on the role of diverting attention from unacknowledged conflicts within the family."

develop

discuss & link better to next ¶

One problem Lynn had was conforming to her parents' expectations. Lynn decided to major in art even though her parents wanted
her to get a degree in computer science so she would have a job when
she graduated. There was so much stress in that house every time
Lynn enrolled in another art class. Maybe she felt that the only
thing she could control in her life was how thin she could get. *link?*

The message to be thin comes from popular role models.
Actress Jane Fonda has sold many on the value of her "Work Out"
and has helped spawn "aerobic nervosa" (Erens 251). Many women
who admire her shape may not know that Fonda was once bulimic.   *Put earlier*
And no one watching the televised spectacle of Prince Charles
and Princess Diana's wedding could have predicted that years
later biographers would be discussing "Di's bulimia."

Not just the supermodels like Kate Moss, or the popular television stars like Calista Flockhart who played successful lawyer
Ally McBeal, but most popular personalities seem incredibly thin
today. It seems that many women--celebrities, models, and my
friends--have not escaped this curse.   *OK for thesis?*

Revising the Thesis: What's Your Aim? What's Your Claim?

Writing the draft helped Rachel realize the link between her friends' experiences and the influence of the media. Once she had a more defined aim—to
criticize the media's influence on women's self-perceptions—she needed to revise her claim to reflect this criticism. Her claim is expressed in her new working thesis.

> **New Working Thesis:** Magazine ads and commercials influence how women see
> themselves and how they behave.

Rachel felt that her material—both her personal experiences and readings—would support her new thesis. She also realized that this thesis helped
her link the influence of the media on women's actions and behavior. Rachel
showed her thesis to her instructor, who suggested she apply the "So what?"
response to this assertion:

> Ads and commercials influence women's self-perceptions.
>
> "So what?"

Women try to look like the skinny models.

"So what?"

It's dangerous! Women are starving themselves.

"So what?"

The media has to change—they are responsible for programming women this way.

After thinking about this conversation with herself, Rachel now had a stronger claim and she revised her working thesis again:

> **Revised Working Thesis:** The media must be forced to stop programming young women to believe skeletal models are the ideal.

Rachel's revised thesis more accurately reflected her claim that the media must change what they are doing to women, and her reference to the "skeletal models" would permit her to discuss her friends' experiences.

Writing an Outline

Organizing to Highlight Key Points

Excellent ideas and interesting information can get lost or buried in a paper that is not carefully arranged and organized. If you arrange your thesis to reflect your organization scheme, you can more easily draft your essay.

Notice how Rachel's thesis forecasts her essay's key points:

> The media must be forced to stop programming young women to believe skeletal models are the ideal.

Rachel's thesis suggests that she will first look at how the media is "programming" women, and then she will show how specific women become "skeletal" victims of the advertising that they see. Further, her assertion that the media "must be forced to stop" this practice invites her to propose a solution. Although Rachel devised a general scheme for organizing her paper, she knew she needed a more detailed outline.

To Outline or Not to Outline

By helping you arrange your materials effectively, an outline can save you time and frustration. Just as most drivers need a map to direct them through unfamiliar territory, most writers need outlines in order to draft their papers.

However, you probably have had the experience of being in a car without a map, when someone could intuit the right direction and get you where you needed to be. Some writers have that intuition and therefore find detailed outlines unnecessary. But these writers will still craft a strong thesis and rely on their intrinsic sense of organization to guide them as they write.

Most of us have also been in cars with drivers who were convinced they could manage without a map, but couldn't. Such indirection or "backtracking" in papers prompts instructors to note in the margins: "Order?" "Repetitious," "Organization needs work," "Relevant?" "Transition needed," or "Where is this going?" If you see these indicators on your papers, you know your sense of direction is failing you. Outline before you write! Unless your instructor requires a particular outline form, your outline may be an informal "map" of key points and ideas in whatever order seems both logical and effective.

Ordering Ideas

You have a number of options for effective organization, and your purpose in writing will help you determine your arrangement. For example, Rachel's purpose was to convince readers that the media must stop promoting thinness as an ideal. Because this was the most important part of her argument, she saved it until the end, building support for it as she wrote. Rachel thus chose an emphatic arrangement scheme.

In an *emphatic* or *dramatic organization,* you arrange your material so that the most important, significant, worthy, or interesting material (for which you generally have the most information) is at the end of the paper. This is the principle that guides Ellen Goodman in her essay, "When a Woman Says No" (p. 124). Goodman presents summaries of three court cases involving charges of rape. She deliberately orders the three cases so that the most controversial one—involving the woman's prior sexual conduct—is last. The virtue of this type of organization is that it permits the writer to end in a dramatic way, using the most vital material or emphatic support for a concluding impression.

Some papers, however, invite a *spatial arrangement.* Often used in description, this kind of arrangement permits you to present your points in a systematic movement through space. In "The Only Child" (p. 31), John Leonard deliberately moves from external descriptions of his brother's shabby boarding house to internal descriptions of his filthy room. From these physical descriptions, he then moves further inward to an analysis of his brother's psychological condition.

In order to narrate a series of events, a chronological ordering may be useful. Kim Edwards's essay, "In Rooms of Women" (p. 161), chronicles a two-year period in her life when she discovers the importance of body freedom and its relationship to clothing. A *chronological arrangement* is useful to tell a story, give historical detail, or contrast past and present.

An Informal Outline

Because Rachel found it was difficult to focus her initial draft and order her supporting details, she decided to write an informal outline: a list of points, written in a logical order, that she planned to cover in her essay. She knew this outline would simply be a personal guide to help her include all relevant materials, so she didn't spend hours on the outline or concern herself with its wording.

Rachel wrote her working thesis first and then listed her key points in the order she planned to cover them. She planned to focus on the stories of three friends, and she had to decide how to order their stories. The chronology of these friendships seemed less relevant than the differences in their problems and treatment programs. She decided to begin with Kirstie, who received out-patient treatment but continued to deny her problem. She ended with Lynn, who had the most extreme eating disorder—she came close to death—and the most dramatic recovery. Lynn's experience provided the most emphatic evidence for Rachel's essay, so Rachel knew that she wanted to end her examples with Lynn's experience. Rachel also knew that she would add other points or perhaps modify this order as she wrote the paper, but at least she would have a map to head her in the right direction.

> **Thesis:** The media must be forced to stop programming young women to believe skeletal models are the ideal.

INTRODUCTION

> —Typical ad described: model in bikini
>
> —Models as unhealthy and obsessed with being thin
>
> —The horror: skinny models seem "right"
>
> —Thesis

ANOREXIA AND BULIMIA AS EPIDEMICS

> —Jane Fonda and her "Work Out"
>
> —Princess Di, reputed bulimic
>
> —Kate Moss and Calista Flockhart perpetuate the skinny image
>
> —Women competing with each other (use Erens)

MY FRIEND KIRSTIE, BULIMIC

> —Kept this secret; only her "barf buddy" and I knew
>
> —Obsessed with food
>
> —Outpatient counseling didn't really work
>
> —I didn't know how to help her

MY FRIEND ERICA, ANOREXIC

> —Enrolled in in-hospital program
>
> —Shocked by number of older women in program
>
> —Received nutritional and emotional help

MY FRIEND LYNN, ANOREXIC, ALMOST DIED

> —Dropped out of Berkeley, enrolled in hospital
>
> —Family received treatment too (use Erens)
>
> —These friends felt programmed by the media to be thin
>
> —Diet industry undermines women's control

CONCLUSION

> —A time for shock *and* action
>
> —Refuse to support products that promote these images

In an informal outline like this, the ideas that you loosely group as "information blocks" may become paragraphs. In some cases, your grouping or block may end up being split into two or more paragraphs. This outline includes supporting details, but the topic sentences are not written out; therefore the outline is still rather sketchy. In Rachel's case, she didn't feel she needed more elaboration because she had already done some prewriting and initial drafting.

Writing a Paragraph

Focusing the Paragraph

Once you have done some prewriting and have written a working thesis, you are ready to draft your essay. Your thesis has made an assertion you need to support, and the body of your essay consists of paragraphs that build this support. Each of those paragraphs may include a *topic sentence*—a sentence that expresses the central idea of that paragraph. The topic sentences emerge naturally from the groupings discovered in prewriting and from the subtopics of the outline.

Not all paragraphs in an essay will have a topic sentence, but all paragraphs must have a focus. The value of a topic sentence is analogous to the value of a thesis: both keep the writer and reader on track. Again, like the thesis, the topic sentence should be deliberately placed to help the reader understand the focus of the paragraph.

Let's look at some short paragraphs that lack topic sentences.

 ### PRACTICING TOPIC SENTENCES

Practice writing your own topic sentence (the central idea) for each of the following paragraphs:

1. Registration lines extend beyond the walls of the gymnasium. Because the health service requires proof of insurance, students wait in long lines to argue for exemptions. The financial aid office assigns appointment times,

but invariably lines form there, too. At the bookstore, students wait 20 minutes at a register, and I need to have my out-of-state check verified in a separate line. Even before classes begin, I'm exhausted.

2. A great amount of corn is used as feed for cattle, poultry, and hogs. Corn is also distilled into ethanol—a fuel for cars and a component in bourbon. Corn is made into a sweetener used in snacks and soft drinks and a thickener for foods and industrial products. A small amount of corn is consumed at dining tables in kernel or processed form.

Although each paragraph is clearly focused, both would profit from an explicit assertion. Compare your topic sentences with your classmates' assertions before reading the following possibilities. Although topic sentences may be placed anywhere in the paragraph, the topic sentences here seem to be most effective as the first or last sentence in these paragraphs. Here are some possibilities for the first example:

- Going back to school means getting in lines.
- Lines are an inevitability at my college.
- Lines are the worst aspect of returning to school.

Here are some possibilities for the second example:

- Corn is used for extraordinarily diverse purposes.
- Humans, animals, and machines profit from products made of corn.
- Corn is a remarkably useful grain.

In addition to evaluating your classmates' topic sentences, it may be worthwhile to evaluate the relative strengths of the sentences above. Which are stronger, and why?

Analyzing an Effective Paragraph

In the following paragraph, notice how Rachel includes very good supporting details but lacks a topic sentence that expresses the central idea of the paragraph:

During Kirstie's senior year in high school, she was dating a college guy, was enrolled in college prep classes, jogged religiously every morning and every evening, and loved to ski with her family and beat her brothers down the slope. She seemed to crave the compliments she received from her brothers and their friends because of her good looks, and she received plenty! But years later, she revealed to me that her greatest pride at that

```
time was when she discovered that she could vomit automatically
after eating, without needing to use a finger or spoon.
```

Rachel realized that she had not articulated the focus of her paragraph. She went back to clarify her point—that "Kirstie had it all." But Rachel also realized that her perception of her friend was an illusion. Rachel brought the two ideas together to form a topic sentence:

```
Few of us ever suspected that Kirstie was in trouble because
she seemed to have it all.
```

Rachel asserts that Kirstie "seemed to have it all" but was really "in trouble." First Rachel shows specific examples of Kirstie's seemingly happy life: "dating a college guy," being in "college prep classes," jogging "religiously," and skiing with her family. Then Rachel supports the fact that Kirstie was really a troubled young woman.

It is important that you use very specific examples to support your topic sentence. It would not have been enough for Rachel to claim that Kirstie had "everything" without showing specifically what that meant. She doesn't just mention that Kirstie had a boyfriend, but that he was a "college guy." Kirstie doesn't simply have a close family; they go skiing together, and she spends time with her brothers' friends. Rachel's support is vivid, visual, and specific. Her shocking last sentence is graphic and unforgettable because it is so detailed in its description.

Unifying the Paragraph

This last sentence also contributes to paragraph coherence and unity. Rachel's opening sentence suggests Kirstie was in trouble, even though she did not appear to be. Subtle references to this trouble appear in the paragraph: Kirstie seems obsessed with exercise, and she craves compliments. Finally, after enumerating Kirstie's apparent successes—what she *should* be proud of—Rachel stuns the reader with the irony of Kirstie's "greatest pride," her ability to vomit automatically. Thus the concept of pride unites the paragraph. The key word in the topic sentence, "seemed," predicts the illusions that permeate and unite the paragraph. (For more on paragraph unity and coherence, see pp. 387–390.)

Developing a Paragraph

When you have a topic sentence or controlling idea for a paragraph, it is essential to support it with examples and any necessary explanation. Try to anticipate questions or objections your reader may have; you can use the "So what?" response here to make sure the significance of your idea is clear. Support for your topic sentences can be drawn from your own ideas, experiences, and observations, as well as from your readings.

Using Sources for Support
Giving Credit and Avoiding Plagiarism

Although in a formal research paper you may be required (or prefer) to use notecards or photocopies for recording data, for a short paper with a single source, you might choose to work directly from the margin notes you made during your active reading. No matter how you have recorded your supporting material, you must give the exact source and page number for borrowed ideas and for quoted material. In addition, you need to put quotation marks around the quoted words. By including the author's name and a page number after every idea or quotation that she used, Rachel avoided *plagiarism*—using other writers' words or ideas without giving them credit.

Even if she *paraphrased the material*—put the ideas in her own words— Rachel knew she had to give the author credit for the idea or concept. Had she neglected to do this, she would have inadvertently plagiarized those ideas. (For more discussion of inadvertent plagiarism, see p. 516.)

Rachel's instructor required her to use the documentation form recommended by the Modern Language Association (MLA). Therefore she gave credit by either citing the author's name before the material and then giving the source's page number in parentheses afterward or by including both the author and page citations in parentheses immediately following the quotation. For example, Rachel wrote that Jane Fonda helped spawn "aerobic nervosa" (Erens 251). Two popularly used documentation forms (MLA and APA) are described in detail with examples in Chapter 11.

Remember, giving credit means the following:

- Using quotation marks around borrowed words or phrases
- Acknowledging the source and page number of any borrowed words or paraphrased ideas immediately afterward
- Including the complete source—author, title, and publishing information—in the list of works at the end of the paper.

Incorporating Quoted Material

Quoted material may support your ideas and may be a vital component of your paper. If the original material is particularly well written or precise, or if the material is bold or controversial, it makes sense to quote the author's words so you can examine them in detail.

All quoted material needs to be introduced in some way. It is a mistake to think that quoted material can stand on its own, no matter how incisive it is. Often, in fact, it is vital to introduce and also to comment on the quoted material. Let's look at an example from Rachel's paper:

```
Lynn's family became involved in her therapy, too. Erens
emphasizes the importance of the family in any treatment plan:
"Often, the daughter has taken on the role of diverting atten-
tion from unacknowledged conflicts within the family" (253). In
therapy, Lynn and her family gradually learned that her parents'
"unacknowledged conflicts" over Lynn's choice of art as a major
instead of computer science contributed to Lynn's stress. Therapy
involved acknowledging these internalized conflicts as well as
seeing a relationship between her eating disorder and that stress.
```

In this passage, Rachel uses Lynn's experience to lead into the quoted material. The quote provides an explanation of family dynamics that reflects Lynn's situation. Rather than letting the quotation stand by itself, Rachel *uses* it by discussing the connection between the quoted material and her friend's specific experience. In order to understand how Rachel has incorporated quoted material in her essay, let's look at a strategy we call "the sandwich."

The Sandwich as a Development Technique

If you have had instructors comment that your papers need more development, or you have trouble meeting the required length for an assignment, or you find that you are merely "padding" your paper with strings of quotations, you will discover that the "sandwich" strategy is a solution to your problem. Even if your papers seem to satisfy the page requirement but you are earning B's instead of A's on your papers, the problem may be that you have not critically thought about and *used* your supporting material. Because effective supporting material is often quoted from sources, you need to incorporate direct quotations effectively. The "sandwich" technique will help you write better-developed and more convincing papers.

Just as bread holds the contents of a sandwich together, a writer needs to use the introduction to the quotation and the discussion about it to hold the quoted material together.

It may help to visualize the "sandwich":

- **The lead-in or introduction**—the top slice of bread—appeals to the reader and helps by identifying the author or speaker and any necessary background or credentials. The introduction should provide enough of a context or an awareness of the plot for the quoted material to make sense and should anticipate and identify any pronouns used within the quotation. The lead-in may also emphasize the focus point that you intend to support with the quoted material. The introduction needs to be informative without duplicating the material in the quotation.

- **The direct quotation**—the "meat" of the sandwich—comes next.
- **The analysis or commentary**—that essential bottom slice of bread—provides those necessary lines of clarification, interpretation, analysis, or discussion after the quotation. You need to explain or define the author's terms or discuss the significance of the quotation to the work as a whole. Most importantly, your analysis demonstrates the necessity of that quoted material for the point you are making.

In the previous example from Rachel's paper, Rachel introduces the quotation by identifying the author's last name so that she needs to give only the page number in parentheses after the quote. In her lead-in, Rachel also anticipates Erens's focus point about "the importance of the family in any treatment plan" without repeating Erens's exact words. Her analytic comment after the quotation is a good example of how to use the author's words. When Rachel returns to Erens's observation about the family's "unacknowledged conflicts," she works with the quotation and underscores Erens's meaning.

 PRACTICING THE "SANDWICH"

The following passage appears in Brent Staples's essay "Black Men and Public Space" (p. 237):

> I often witness that "hunch posture," from women after dark on the warrenlike streets of Brooklyn where I live. They seem to set their faces on neutral and, with their purse straps strung across their chests bandolier style, they forge ahead as though bracing themselves against being tackled.

Because the passage that begins "They seem to set their faces on neutral . . ." has such memorable language to describe the women that Staples sees walking at night, students often choose to incorporate his description. Try writing a lead-in and then your analysis of that one line.

LEAD-IN:

_____

_____

_____

_____

_____

"They seem to set their faces on neutral and, with their purse straps strung across their chests bandolier style, they forge ahead as though bracing themselves against being tackled" (238).

ANALYSIS:

_____

_____

_____

_____

_____

_____

You might want to compare your sandwich with a classmate's. See if you both managed to avoid the following problems in your lead-in. Can you identify the reasons that these lead-ins are weak?

1. _Brent Staples says,_ "They seem to set their faces on neutral and, with their purse straps strung across their chests bandolier style, they forge ahead as though bracing themselves against being tackled" (237).

2. _In paragraph six, Brent Staples quotes,_ "They seem to set their faces on neutral and, with their purse straps strung across their chests bandolier style, they forge ahead as though bracing themselves against being tackled" (237).

3. _Brent Staples feels like a criminal:_ "They seem to set their faces on neutral and, with their purse straps strung across their chests bandolier style, they forge ahead as though bracing themselves against being tackled" (237).

4. _Recent statistics show that urban violence is epidemic:_ "They seem to set their faces on neutral and, with their purse straps strung across their chests bandolier style, they forge ahead as though bracing themselves against being tackled" (237).

5. _Staples' essay shows that women who walk at night_ "They seem to set their faces on neutral and, with their purse straps strung across their chests bandolier style, they forge ahead as though bracing themselves against being tackled" (237).

Explanation of the Errors:

1. This lead-in effectively identifies the author, but it doesn't give a context for the quotation that follows. The reader cannot know who "they" are. (See pronoun reference, p. 567, for an explanation of this error.) Further,

the writer needs to prepare the reader for what is important in the quotation so that it makes sense to the reader.

2. This lead-in also identifies the author, but there is nothing gained by starting with the paragraph number and, in fact, this pointless information is distracting. Furthermore, the writer does not prepare the reader for this quotation. It is also not accurate to write that "Brent Staples quotes" because Staples is not quoting anyone; he is the writer who is being quoted.

3. The writer seems to understand the discomfort that Brent Staples feels—"like a criminal"—but he has not shown how this feeling is a consequence of the women's posture. Moreover, there is no referent for "they."

4. This lead-in doesn't accurately anticipate the quotation. It may be true that "urban violence is epidemic," but this lead-in does not prepare the reader for the description of the women's posture.

5. This lead-in is effective because it identifies, before the reader is confused, that "they" are the "women who walk at night." However, the writer has a grammar error in the double subject—"women" and "they"—which prompts the reader to stumble between the lead-in and the quotation. The writer could easily correct this by starting the quotation with "seem" to avoid the double subject and moving smoothly from lead-in to quotation: Staples's essay shows that women who walk at night "seem to set their faces on neutral. . . ."

Here is one example of an effective sandwich—good lead-in *and* analysis—using the quotation from Brent Staples:

> **In "Black Men and Public Space," Brent Staples describes the posture of women who walk at night:** "They seem to set their faces on neutral and, with their purse straps strung across their chests bandolier style, they forge ahead as though bracing themselves against being tackled" (237). **Staples suggests that these women need to play multiple roles. They must appear to be indifferent to their environment and not make eye contact as they "set their faces on neutral." Further they become soldiers with bandoliers and defensive football players guarding themselves against being attacked.**

Analyzing the Example. Notice that the lead-in identifies the title and author so that only a page reference will be necessary in the parenthetical citation. Further, the referent for the pronoun "they," which begins the quotation, is clarified in the lead-in—"women who walk at night."

Students often neglect the analysis portion of the sandwich, assuming that the quotation is self-explanatory. However, the only way to convince your reader of your interpretation of the quoted material is to analyze it—to work with it.

Notice that the analysis is quite complete. The first statement—"These women need to play multiple roles"—is a general assertion drawn from the specific images of women as soldiers with their bandoliers and as football players guarding "against being tackled." Because the women are on the defensive, the student explains that they don't make eye contact and they "appear to be indifferent" as they "set their faces on neutral." The student has analyzed the word choice and imagery so that he can convince the reader of his interpretation of Staples's description.

Paraphrasing

Paraphrasing a writer's ideas makes that information available to the reader in a condensed form. Sometimes you will want to put into your own words the essence of an entire piece that you have read; other times you will want to paraphrase just one section of the work. If the author's idea is useful but the material is wordy, filled with jargon, or contains information you do not need, you will want to paraphrase rather than quote the text.

Illustrating Paraphrasing

Here we will examine how to paraphrase one section of given works. Assume that you have been asked to write an essay in which you respond to Anna Quindlen's "Uncle Sam and Aunt Samantha" (p. 98). Part of your argument may include using the statistical information about women who have served in the military.

Original from "Uncle Sam and Aunt Samantha"

Women have indeed served in combat positions, in the Balkans and the Middle East. More than 40,000 managed to serve in the Persian Gulf without destroying unit cohesion or failing because of upper-body strength. Some are even now taking out targets in Afghanistan from fighter jets, and apparently without any male soldier's falling prey to some predicted excess of chivalry or lust.

Paraphrase

It is important to recall that 40,000 American women have already served in battles in the Balkans, Persian Gulf, and Afghanistan without disrupting morale, failing their responsibilities because of lack of strength, or inciting inappropriate behavior in the men (Quindlen 99).

The important parts of Quindlen's argument are retained: that women have already served in combat without weakening the military.

Practice paraphrasing the following paragraph before you read the paraphrase that follows it.

Original from "Why Stop Smoking? Let's Get Clinical" (p. 346)

In normal lungs, the trachea and bronchi—the large and small tubes leading to the alveoli (the tiny sacs that do the actual work of the lungs)—are lined with a film of tissue that is one cell layer thick. The surface of these cells is covered with tiny, finger-like structures called cilia. These cilia beat constantly in a waving motion, which moves small particles and toxic substances out of the lung and into the back of the throat where they are swallowed. In a smoker or someone like a coal miner, who constantly breathes in large amounts of toxic substances, many of the cilia soon disappear. If exposure continues, some ciliated cells die and are replaced by squamous cells, the same type that form the skin. Without the cleansing function of the ciliated cells, toxic materials and particles are breathed into the lungs, staying longer in contact with all the tissue. Each group of ciliated cells killed and replaced by squamous cells decreases by a certain fraction the lungs' ability to cleanse themselves. As this occurs, the amount of damage done by each cigarette increases to a greater and greater degree.

Paraphrase

Healthy lungs contain tiny sacs that are lined with cilia, hair-like fingers that move poisons out of the lungs. In coal miners or smokers, these cilia are destroyed and are replaced by cells that can't do the cleansing so the toxics touch more tissue longer. With the cleansing cells gone, the damage continues to increase each time smoke is inhaled (Harrison 347).

Combining Paraphrase and Quotation

Most often, the material you use to support your points will be a blend of paraphrase and direct quotation. You can capture the essence of an author's idea by paraphrasing it, but there will be well-crafted phrases and key ideas that need to be quoted to convey the flavor of the original work. When you combine paraphrase and direct quotation, you still need to be careful to give credit for both.

Original from "The Second Shift" (p. 84)

The exodus of women from the home to the workplace has not been accompanied by a new view of marriage and work that would make this transition smooth. Most workplaces have remained inflexible in the face of the changing needs of workers with families, and most men have yet to really adapt to the changes in women. I call the strain caused by the disparity between the change in women and the absence of change elsewhere the "stalled revolution."

Paraphrase with Quotation

In "The Second Shift," Arlie Hochschild observes that in spite of the number of women who are now employed outside of the home, neither employers nor mates have responded to the special needs of working women with families. This lack of response creates a tension that Hochschild terms the "stalled revolution" (85).

If you are paraphrasing an expert, you will gain credibility by introducing the title and author of the work prior to your paraphrase as illustrated here. Because a key term, the "stalled revolution," is used in the paraphrase, the quotation marks need to be retained and the entire reference cited.

 ## PRACTICING COMBINING PARAPHRASE AND QUOTATION

Practice incorporating choice quotations into your paraphrased versions of the following passages. In your lead-in, you may want to include the author's name and the source of the material. Compare your paraphrases with those written by your classmates. The page numbers given are from the essays as they appear in this textbook.

1. From "Press 1 to Cut Short Your Life" (p. 301): "Clearly, if Franz Kafka were alive today he'd be writing about customer service. Just calling directory assistance can set your teeth on edge. In my case, the reps were never rude; they treated me indulgently, as if I were a mental patient who had neglected his medication. But the rules under which they operate are enough to make anyone rage against the machine."

2. From "Why Stop Smoking? Let's Get Clinical" (p. 346): "By the time one has been a pack-a-day smoker for ten years or so, extensive damage has already been done. By twenty years, much of the damage is irreversible and progresses more rapidly. After ten years of smoking, each cigarette may do as much damage to the body as three or more packs did when a smoker first started."

3. From "Makes Learning Fun" (p. 306): "Computing's instant gratification—built into the learning-is-fun mind-set—encourages intellectual passivity, driven mainly by conditioned amusement. Fed a diet of interactive insta-grat, students develop a distaste for persistence, trial and error, attentiveness, or patience."

As you work on refining your incorporation of paraphrased and quoted material, you also will be revising your essay. Rewriting is such a critical activity in preparing an essay that we have devoted the entire next chapter to various aspects of revision.

Chapter 8

Revising an Essay

Rewriting and Rewriting

It is essential that you give yourself ample time to reconsider your rough draft in its entirety and revise it before handing it in as your final paper. Usually this revision involves sharpening the thesis, reorganizing ideas, developing sketchy points, adding new material for support, removing irrelevant material, improving transitions between ideas, strengthening the introduction and conclusion, and editing for word choice, mechanics, and spelling.

Thinking Critically for an Audience

Every phase of the writing process involves thinking critically—reasoning, analyzing, and assessing—so that your points are clear and understandable to your audience. The act of revision calls on these same skills.

As you begin to organize your prewriting notes into a coherent essay, ask yourself: Can a reader follow my logic? Do the examples support my main point? What, if any, examples should I cut? Your decision to remove irrelevant details reflects your awareness that irrelevant points not only weaken your support but also confuse your readers.

The need for clarity and precision continues throughout drafting and revision. As you revise, continue to question whether the depth of your analysis and support for your assertions are sufficient. You will need to reconsider your focus, the logic of your organization, and the strength of your conclusion. As you edit, scrutinize your word choice, sentence structure, grammar, and mechanics so that surface flaws do not frustrate your reader.

Thinking critically requires you to recognize that your audience does not necessarily share your views. Thus the writing process forces you to challenge your own assertions and consider your readers' perspectives. Although it may appear that these stages of writing a paper involve a step-by-step process, all of these writing activities occur concurrently.

You may revise while you are drafting your paper, and possibly edit from the early drafts until the moment you hand the paper to your instructor. As noted in the previous chapter, Rachel started revising her draft as soon as she had a printout from her computer. Thinking critically about her aim in writing this essay—to persuade readers of the media's role in fostering eating disorders—Rachel made substantial changes as she revised her rough draft.

Revising a Rough Draft

Working from her own evaluation of her rough draft (see pp. 358–359), Rachel rewrote her draft and, as required by the assignment, showed it to her instructor for comments. Rachel's paper had started out very rough, as most first drafts do, but she continued to develop her ideas and rearrange them. She felt that her second draft was stronger than the first but still could be improved. Her instructor helped her by identifying weak areas and suggesting improvements.

EXAMPLE: DRAFT WITH INSTRUCTOR'S COMMENTS

Eating Disorders and the Media 〉 *more striking or suggestive title*

Bare, (with the exception of a bikini,) *except for?* the deep-tanned model poses at a beach. She is surrounded by five adoring guys. She is sipping a frothy soda and inviting all of us *Tighten—avoid repeating "she is"* to do the same . . . if we want to get the guys . . . if we want to be the envy of our friends. She is thin but tall. *How thin? How tall?* Viewers don't notice the bony ribs, (how hungry she is,) and *not//* all the "diet pills" she popped to stay that thin. A picture doesn't reveal the vomit on her breath or the *very graphic* spearmint gum used to mask it. In fact, our magazines and T.V. commercials present us with these ads until such *stronger verb?* girls don't seem skinny any more--they seem right. *✓ clear point*

It doesn't seem to matter that, for some years now, the media has been reporting the epidemic among college *diction (old-fashioned?)* *briefly distinguish* "coeds" of eating disorders, anorexia and bulimia. It doesn't seem to matter that the Women's Movement has tried to free women from being so caught up on the way they

look. Despite the varied opportunities now available to
women, many women say they would rather lose pounds than
achieve academic or career goals. In the early years of
aerobics, actress Jane Fonda has sold many on the value of
her "Work Out" and has helped spawn "aerobic nervosa" *What is?*
(Erens 251). Many women who admire Jane Fonda's shape may
not know that Fonda was once a bulimic. And no one watching the televised spectacle of Prince Charles and Princess
Diana's wedding could have predicted that years later, biographers would be discussing "Di's bulimia." > *transition?*

Who wouldn't want to hear friends whisper, "What a
body! She really knows how to stay in shape!" or "Don't you *necessary?*
hate someone who looks that good?" Either way, the sense of
specify what is wrong with this admiration and affirmation is clear. A thin girl has something that others don't—and this gives her power and con-
trol. She can make herself in the image of the cover girls.
In "Bodily Harm," the author quotes Ruth Striegel: "The *You need Erens's name here or in your ( ) at end of this line.*
pursuit of thinness is a way for women to compete with each
other, a way that avoids being threatening to men" (250).

Unfortunately, this competition keeps women from seeking or obtaining the help they might otherwise get from
close friends. Many bulimics keep their secret as guarded as
their mothers might have kept their sex life. My friend
Kirstie did this. She waited for years before she told her *tighten*
friends (and later, her family) that she was bulimic. At
awk split of subj/verb first, only her "barf buddy" (Erens 250)—a cousin who had
initially introduced her to this "great diet plan"—knew.
Gradually, their friendship revolved exclusively around this
dark secret and was eroded by their unacknowledged rivalry.

Few of us ever suspected Kirstie was in trouble: she *develop*
seemed to have it all. But years later, she revealed to me *illustrate*
that her greatest pride at that time was when she discovered that she was now vomiting automatically after eating,
without needing to use a finger or spoon.

Even when Kirstie received out-patient counseling and
her family thought she was "cured," she wasn't.↓ *How could you tell?* For her it
was either fasting or bingeing——there was no in-between.
As her friend, I often felt trapped between either respecting her confidence or letting some adult know so she
might get the help she needed. While encouraging her to
find other interests and to be open with her therapist, I
felt quite helpless. I didn't want to betray her confidence and tell her parents, but I worried that my silence
was betraying our friendship.) *transition?*

According to another friend, many young women continue
to have obsessions with food for years afterwards. My friend
Erica was shocked by the number of women over ~~who were~~
thirty in her hospital treatment program for anorexics. She
Ref?   admitted that (this) is what made her decide she needed help
while she was still in college. Unlike Kirstie, Erica
decided she needed an in-hospital treatment program that
cut her off from her old habits and helped her deal with
her emotions and learn better nutritional habits. Erica
managed to enter the program as soon as her finals were
good   over and therefore she didn't jeopardize her schooling.
transition   But some don't have that choice. My friend Lynn would
have died had she not entered the hospital when she did. She
had to drop out of Berkeley immediately and get prolonged
therapy before she could be released to her parents and begin her recovery. Her family became involved in her therapy,
too. As Erens notes, "Family therapy considers the family
itself, not the daughter with the eating disorder, to be the
'patient.' Often, the daughter has taken on the role of diverting attention from unacknowledged conflicts within the
family" (253). In therapy, Lynn and her family gradually
learned that her parents' "unacknowledged conflicts" over
tighten this   her mother's return to work and over Lynn's choice of art
discussion?   instead of computer science as a major contributed to Lynn's

stress. Therapy involved acknowledging these internalized conflicts as well as examining the pressure to be thin.

In addition to absorbing family conflicts, each of these friends felt that they were programmed by advertisers to accept and seek a lean look as the ideal. Fashion magazines often use underweight preteen models who are made up and dressed to seem older than they are. This makes women with real hips and breasts feel overweight. In fact, the fashion world does not seem to view large bodies, strength, or maturity as attractive features for women.

effective link between personal experience & reading

It is ironic that this should happen at a time when women have more freedom to control their lives and their bodies. Unfortunately, women still spend much of their earnings on the cosmetic and diet industries. Our generation has witnessed the weight of fashion models drop way down and the number of eating disorders go way up.

develop or combine these short paragraphs

It is time to let ourselves become shocked again. And then we need to move beyond shock and take action. Those who make the images will only change when those of us who support them stop buying products and tuning in on shows that continue to impose "bodily harm" on us. *Return to your opening image, if you can, and sharpen your thesis. Don't forget "Works Cited."*

Revising Can Make the Difference

Every paper can benefit from careful revision and editing, but many students do not have their instructors' comments on their drafts to use as they revise. Occasionally students can find trained tutors at the college writing center, for example, or peers who will offer feedback and suggestions. These students' comments may not be as thorough as those Rachel received, but they can help the writer see the essay from another perspective.

Some instructors may spend time helping students work in small groups as "peer editors" who critique each other's papers. A good peer editor need not excel at grammar nor be an excellent writer. An effective editor needs to be a careful *reader*, one who is sensitive to the writer's main point and supporting details.

A Checklist for Revising and Editing Papers

Whether you are revising your own essay or commenting on a classmate's, the following checklist should help:

- *Purpose:* Is the purpose of the essay apparent? Are the expectations of the audience met?
- *Focus:* Is the thesis clear? Provocative? Convincing?
- *Support:* Are all points illustrated and supported?
- *Organization:* Is the order logical? Are the transitions smooth?
- *Paragraphs:* Is each paragraph well focused? Well developed?
- *Sentences:* Are all sentences coherent? Are the sentences varied?
- *Wording:* Any unnecessary/confusing words?
- *Introduction:* Is it captivating? Developed? Does it set the right tone?
- *Conclusion:* Is there a sense of resolution? Does it return to the thesis?
- *Style:* Is the diction consistent with the purpose of the essay? Does the essay flow? Any stumbling blocks?
- *Mechanics:* Correct punctuation? Grammar? Spelling?

If you are editing a classmate's essay, you do not have to be able to correct the errors. A peer editor needs only to point out areas that seem flawed or confusing; it is then the writer's responsibility to use a handbook (like the one in this book) and correct the errors.

After studying the instructor's comments and corrections, Rachel continued modifying her draft. She rewrote certain phrases and paragraphs a number of times, shifted words and sentences, and found ways to "tighten" her prose by eliminating unnecessary words. Most of all, she tried to replace sluggish words with more precise and specific details. Notice below how her title gained more punch and how the opening is tighter and less repetitive. She also took the time to develop certain thoughts and paragraphs and to clarify her points. The following version is her final essay.

STUDENT EXAMPLE: FINAL ESSAY

Krell 1

Rachel Krell

Professor Ansite

English 1A

October 7, 2001

Dieting Daze: No In-Between

Bare, except for a bikini, the deep-tanned model poses at a beach surrounded by five adoring and adorable guys. She is sipping a frothy diet drink and inviting us to do the same, if we want to get the guys and be the envy of our friends. She stands 5'10" and wears

---

Krell 2

a size 3. Viewers don't notice the bony ribs, the hunger pangs, and the "diet pills" she popped to stay that thin. A picture doesn't reveal the vomit on her breath or the spearmint gum used to mask it. In fact, our magazines and TV commercials bombard us with these ads until such girls don't seem skinny any more---they seem right.

It doesn't seem to matter that, for years now, the media has been reporting the epidemic among college women of eating disorders, anorexia (self-starvation) and bulimia (binge and purge). It doesn't seem to matter that the women's movement has tried to free women from bondage to their bodies. Despite the varied opportunities now available to women, many women say they would rather lose pounds than achieve academic or career goals. In the early years of aerobics, actress Jane Fonda sold many on the value of her "Work Out" and helped spawn "aerobic nervosa"---the excessive use of exercise to maintain an ideal weight (Erens 251). Many women who admired Jane Fonda's shape may not know that Fonda was once bulimic. And no one watching the televised spectacle of Prince Charles and Princess Diana's wedding could have predicted that years later, biographers would be discussing "Di's bulimia." Current super models such as Kate Moss and popular television stars like Calista Flockhart who played lawyer Ally McBeal, perpetuate the concept that to be successful, one must be thin.

Such celebrities, and those females in the ads, are held up as models for all of us to mirror. A thin girl has something that others don't---and this gives her power and control. She can make her body resemble a cover girl's. In "Bodily Harm," Pamela Erens quotes Ruth Striegel, Ph.D., director of Yale University's Eating Disorders Clinic: "The pursuit of thinness is a way for women to compete with each other, a way that avoids being threatening to men" (250). But this competition threatens and endangers the women's well-being because it keeps women from seeking the help they might otherwise get from close friends.

In fact, many bulimics keep their secret as guarded as their mothers might have kept their sex life. My friend Kirstie waited for years before she told friends (and later, her family) that she was bulimic. At first the only one who knew about her bulimia was her cousin who had initially introduced her to "this great diet plan." This cousin became Kirstie's "barf buddy" (Erens 250). Gradually, their friendship revolved exclusively around this dark secret and was eroded by their unacknowledged rivalry.

Few of us ever suspected Kirstie was in trouble, because she seemed to have it all. During her senior year in high school, she was dating a college guy, was enrolled in college prep classes, jogged religiously every morning and every evening, and loved to ski with her family and beat her brothers down the slope. She seemed to crave the compliments she received from her brothers and their friends because of her good looks—and she received plenty! But years later, she revealed to me that her greatest pride at that time was when she discovered she could vomit automatically after eating, without needing to use a finger or spoon.

Even when Kirstie received out-patient counseling and her family thought she was "cured," she would still binge and purge at will. Every conversation with Kirstie inevitably returned to the subject of food—fasting or bingeing—there was no in-between. As her close friend, I often felt helpless, trapped between either respecting her confidence and keeping her dark secret or letting an adult know and perhaps getting her more help. I didn't want to betray her confidence and tell her parents, but I worried that my silence was betraying our friendship. Even though we each went to different colleges and gradually lost touch, I find myself wondering if Kirstie ever got the help she needed.

According to another friend, even mature women continue to
have obsessions with food. My friend Erica was shocked by the
number of women over thirty in her hospital treatment program
for anorexics. She admitted that seeing these older women is what
convinced her she needed help while she was still in college.
Unlike Kirstie, Erica decided she needed an in-hospital treatment
program that cut her off from her old habits and helped her deal
with her emotions and learn better nutritional habits. Erica managed to enter the program as soon as her finals were over, and
therefore she didn't jeopardize her schooling.

But some don't have that choice. My friend Lynn would have
died had she not entered the hospital when she did. She had to
drop out of Berkeley immediately and get prolonged therapy before
she could be released to her parents and begin her recovery.
Lynn's family became involved in her therapy, too. Erens emphasizes the importance of the family in any treatment plan: "Often,
the daughter has taken on the role of diverting attention from
unacknowledged conflicts within the family" (253). In therapy
Lynn and her family gradually learned that her parents' "unacknowledged conflicts" over Lynn's choice of art as a major instead of computer science contributed to her stress. Therapy involved acknowledging these internalized conflicts as well as
seeing a relationship between her eating disorder and that
stress.

In addition to absorbing family conflicts, each of these
friends felt that she was programmed by advertisers to accept
a lean look as the ideal. Fashion magazines often use underweight, preteen models who are made up and dressed to seem
older than they are. This makes women with normal hips and
breasts feel overweight. In fact, the fashion world does not

Krell 4

seem to view large bodies, strength, or maturity as attractive features for women.

It is ironic that this should happen at a time when women have more freedom to control their lives and their bodies. Unfortunately, women still spend much of their earnings on cosmetic and diet products. Our generation has witnessed the weight of fashion models decline and the number of eating disorders increase while women often feel powerless. Stripped of control, many women feel compelled to diet constantly; images of emaciated models that were once so shocking have now become commonplace.

It is time to let ourselves become shocked again—shocked by an epidemic that is destroying women's lives. And then we need to move beyond shock and take action. Insisting that our television sponsors, magazines, and video artists stop perpetrating such deadly images of women is something we can all do. A letter from one viewer carries clout because stations often assume that each letter represents many who didn't take the time to write. Ten letters from ten viewers wield even more power. It is time to protest the images of bikini-clad models parading before us and demand images that reflect the emotional and intellectual scope and diversity among women in our society. With some of our best and brightest dying among us, there is no in-between position any more. Those who make the images will only change when those of us who support them stop buying products and stop tuning in on programs that continue to impose "bodily harm" on us.

Work Cited

Erens, Pamela. "Bodily Harm." Between Worlds: A Reader, Rhetoric, and Handbook. Ed. Susan Bachmann and Melinda Barth. 4th ed. New York: Longman, 2004. 250-254.

Rewriting for Coherence

As you may have noticed, Rachel devoted considerable attention to the way she linked information and ideas within and between her paragraphs. The goal, of course, is to ensure that all parts of the paper cohere (that is, that they hold together).

To sustain your readers' interest and ensure their comprehension of your work, you will want to examine the drafts of your essays to see if your ideas hold together. Each idea should follow logically from the one before, and all of your points must support your focus. That logical connection must be clear to the reader—not just to you, the writer of the essay, who may gloss over a link that is not obvious. All readers value clear connections between phrases, sentences, and paragraphs.

A Paragraph That Lacks Coherence

If writing is carefully organized, the reader will not stumble over irrelevant chunks of material or hesitate at unbridged gaps. Let's examine an incoherent paragraph:

```
    Students who commute to campus suffer indignities that
dorm students can't imagine. Parking is expensive and lots are
jammed. It is embarrassing to walk into class late. Often it
takes over a half hour to find a spot. Commuters feel cut off
from students who can return to the dorm to eat or rest. Commu-
ters seldom have a telephone number to get missed lecture notes.
Study groups readily form in dorms. Dorm students have a sense
of independence and freedom. Commuters need to conform to old
family rules and schedules, to say nothing of the need to baby-
sit or cook for younger siblings and drive grandparents to the
bank.
```

Although this paragraph has a clear focus and the ideas are all relevant, its coherence needs to be improved. You may sense that the information is out of order, the logic of the writer is not always obvious to the reader, sentences do not flow together, words are repeated, and emphasis is lost.

In the pages that follow, you will learn how to correct paragraphs like this and to avoid these problems in your own writing. You will also have the opportunity to correct this paragraph.

Using Transitions

Even when material is carefully organized, well-chosen transition words and devices will help you connect sentences and paragraphs and will help your points cohere. You are familiar with most of these words and expressions. But if you have been trying for more than five minutes to find a specific word to connect two ideas or sentences in your essay, the following list of transition terms will at one time or another enable you to gain unity in your essay.

Transition Terms

- *Time relationship:* first, second, before, then, next, meantime, meanwhile, finally, at last, eventually, later, afterward, frequently, often, occasionally, during, now, subsequently, concurrently

- *Spatial relationship:* above, below, inside, outside, across, along, in front of, behind, beyond, there, here, in the distance, alongside, near, next to, close to, adjacent, within

- *Contrast:* in contrast, on the contrary, on the other hand, still, however, yet, but, nevertheless, despite, even so, even though, whereas

- *Comparison:* similarly, in the same way

- *Examples or illustrations:* for example, for instance, to illustrate, to show, in particular, specifically, that is, in addition, moreover

- *Causes or effects:* as a result, accordingly, therefore, then, because, so, thus, consequently, hence, since

- *Conclusions or summaries:* in conclusion, finally, in summary, evidently, clearly, of course, to sum up, therefore

Noticing Transitions

If you are writing a narrative, some part of your essay—if not the entire work—probably will be arranged chronologically. See if you can spot the *time signals* in the following excerpt from Judith Ortiz Cofer's "The Myth of the Latin Woman" and underline them.

> It is surprising to my professional friends that even today some people, including those who should know better, still put others "in their place." It happened to me most recently during a stay at a classy metropolitan hotel favored by young professional couples for weddings. Late one evening after the theater, as I walked toward my room with a colleague (a woman with whom I was coordinating an arts program), a middle-aged man in a tuxedo, with a young girl in satin and lace on his arm, stepped directly into our path. With his champagne glass extended toward me, he exclaimed "Evita!" (225).

Can you see how "even today," "still," "most recently," "late one evening," and "as I walked" are transitions used to help the reader connect the actions in the narrative?

With three or four of your classmates, read the next paragraph of this essay (which starts on p. 223) and underline the transition words that have to do with the essay's chronological connections.

Chronological concepts may also be important for gaining transition and coherence in non-narrative essays. Look at this paragraph from "Discrimination at Large" (p. 243) to see if you can identify the time concept around which this paragraph is structured.

> Since the time I first ventured out to play with the neighborhood kids, I was told over and over that I was lazy and disgusting. Strangers, adults, classmates offered gratuitous comments with such frequency and urgency that I started to believe them. Much later I needed to prove it wasn't so. I began a regimen of swimming, cycling, and jogging that put all but the most compulsive to shame. I ate only cottage cheese, brown rice, fake butter, and steamed everything. I really believed I could infiltrate the ranks of the nonfat and thereby establish my worth.

You may rightly perceive that "since the time I first," "I began," and "much later" are the three terms that denote the passage of time within this paragraph. But you may also note that the writer uses the past tense, as if what Jennifer Coleman "really believed" at one time is different from what she believes now. The chronological ordering of the essay emphasizes this fact. Read the rest of the essay to observe how Coleman uses these time-relationship transitions—"along the way," "for awhile," "still," "until," "until then," and "now" and "finally"—to emphasize the history that led to her change in self-perception.

Essays that include description often require terms that connect sentences or paragraphs in a *spatial relationship*. Notice the spatial concepts that connect the descriptions in this paragraph from "The Only Child" (the complete essay starts on p. 31).

> The room is a slum, and it stinks. It is wall-to-wall beer cans, hundreds of them, under a film of ash. He lights cigarettes and leaves them burning on the windowsill or the edge of the dresser or the lip of the sink, while he thinks of something else—Gupta sculpture, maybe, or the Sephiroth Tree of the Kabbalah. The sink is filthy, and so is the toilet. Holes have been burnt in the sheet on the bed, where he sits. He likes to crush the beer cans after he has emptied them, then toss them aside.

Do you see this paragraph, as we do, as a movement from the periphery to the interior? We sense that the author moves from broad description—

"wall-to-wall beer cans" around the room—to smaller, interior descriptions—
"holes [that] have been burnt in the sheet on the bed, where he sits." The out-
side-to-inside movement of this description parallels the author's description
of elements outside of his brother (in his room) to his observation of what is
closer and more central to him (his thoughts, his talk, his gestures). The
arrangement also complements the author's argument that his brother's life
and mind were destroyed by drugs—the external environment destroying the
interior.

The use of the transition words will seem contrived if you rely on them too
often in any one essay, or if you use the same ones in every essay you write.
You also have other, more subtle ways to gain connections between sentences
and paragraphs in your essays.

Key Word Repetition

In some cases you will want to repeat a word that emphasizes an important
point that you are making. Such repetition will reinforce the focus of your
paragraph and essay.

In another paragraph from "The Only Child," the author emphasizes his
disdain for his brother's living conditions by repeating his brother's explanation. Can you hear the irony or sarcasm in the author's repetition?

> He tells me that he is making a statement, that this room is a statement,
> that the landlord will understand the meaning of his statement. In a
> week or so, according to the pattern, they will evict him, and someone
> will find him another room, which he will turn into another statement,
> with the help of the welfare checks he receives on account of his dis-
> ability, which is the static in his head.

Notice that the repetition of "statement" is very deliberate and strategic,
rather than boring for the reader, because it emphasizes the nonreasoning to
which the brother's mind has been reduced.

Synonyms or Key Word Substitutions

You can connect the ideas or concepts within a paragraph and throughout
your essay by skillfully using synonyms or key word substitutions—words that
have the same or similar meanings—to emphasize your focus. Notice how
Jennifer Coleman in "Discrimination at Large" (p. 243) piles word substitutions into her sentences to simulate for her reader the effect of being assaulted, as fat people are, by denigrating words:

> It was confusing for awhile. How was it I was still lazy, weak, despised,
> a slug, and a cow if I exercised every waking minute? This confusion
> persisted until I finally realized: it didn't matter what I did. I was and

always would be the object of sport, derision, antipathy and hostility so long as I stayed in my body. I immediately signed up for a body transplant. I am still waiting for a donor.

How many substitutions for "lazy" did you find? How many implied substitutions for "contempt"? Coleman cites many specific terms for how she has been perceived and treated to make clear to the reader that these attacks come under many names, but the intention to denigrate is always the same.

Pronouns

Pronouns, words substituting for nouns that clearly precede or follow them, can effectively connect parts of a paragraph. By prompting the reader to mentally supply the missing noun or see the relationship the pronouns imply, the writer also has a way to engage the reader. To emphasize the contrast between people who are fat and those who are not, Coleman uses pronoun substitutions to unite her paragraphs:

> Things are less confusing now that I know that the nonfat are superior to me regardless of their personal habits, health, personalities, cholesterol levels, or the time they log on the couch. And, as obviously superior to me as they are, it is their destiny to remark on my inferiority regardless of who I'm with, whether they know me, whether it hurts my feelings. I finally understand that the thin have a divine mandate to steal self-esteem from fat people, who have no right to it in the first place.
>
> Fat people aren't really jolly. Sometimes we act that way so you will leave us alone. We pay a price for this. But at least we get to hang on to what self-respect we smuggled out of grade school and adolescence.

In the first paragraph, *I* and *me* contrast with *they* and *their* to emphasize the separation between the author and the "nonfat" and "superior" other people. In the second paragraph the author unites herself with "fat people," repeatedly saying "we" to emphasize their unity. Coleman's entire essay coheres because she skillfully employs numerous unifying devices within and between her paragraphs. Read the essay in its entirety (p. 243) to see how key word repetition, synonyms, and transitions between sentences and paragraphs create coherence within an essay.

Transitions Between Paragraphs

Key word repetition is also an important way to achieve the important goal of *connection between paragraphs*. While your reader may be able to follow your movement and sustain your ideas within a paragraph, coherence within your essay as a whole requires transition sentences and, in longer essays, entire paragraphs of transitions.

One device that works well is to offer a specific example to illustrate a general point that concludes the previous paragraph and use it toward the beginning of the new paragraph. Notice the following excerpts from Shannon Paaske's research paper, which begins on page 522. What moves the reader between paragraphs?

> According to Jan Gavlin, director of assistive technology at the National Rehabilitation Hospital in Washington, "If you can move one muscle in your body, wiggle a pinkie or twitch an eyebrow, we can design a switch to allow you to operate in your environment" (qtd. in Blackman 71).
>
> An example of one such device is the Eyegaze Response Interface Computer Aid (ERICA), developed by biomedical engineer Thomas Hutchinson at the University of Virginia. . . .

By giving a specific example of "assistive technology" introduced in theory in the previous paragraph, the author is able to connect the two paragraphs.

In another section of her research paper, Shannon uses a question to help her reader move from one paragraph to another:

> Rebecca Acuirre, 16, who has cerebral palsy, says that she recently asked a stranger what time it was and he kept walking as though he didn't hear her. "Some people are prejudiced and ignore us. That makes me angry," she says.
>
> How can these prejudices be abolished? "We need more exposure," says DeVries.

The repetition of the word "prejudice" helps these paragraphs cohere. The question engages the reader because most of us feel obliged to think about answers to questions. And this rhetorical question does not merely repeat the word. Instead, it moves the reader beyond the previous aspect of prejudice to the solution Paaske will discuss in the next section.

Although all paragraphs in your essay should hold together, the device of repeating key words should not be overused or strained. You may irritate your readers if they perceive your technique as a formula. For example, let's imagine you have written a paragraph that ended with the sentence "These are rationalizations, not reasons." Avoid merely repeating the exact phrasing, like "Although these are rationalizations, not reasons," at the start of your next paragraph. Instead, you might want to begin with something like this: "Such rationalizations are understandable if one considers the. . . ." With conscious practice of the technique, you'll improve your skills.

Avoiding Gaps

Transition terms and devices will help you achieve coherence in your work, but they can't fill in for gaps in logic—sentences or paragraphs that just don't go together, or that are out of order. You can't expect your readers to move from one point to another if you have failed to put your reasoning into words. For example, in the incoherent paragraph on page 387, the writer places the following two sentences together:

```
    Parking is expensive and lots are jammed. It is embarrassing
to walk into class late.
```

In the writer's mind, there is a logical connection between these two thoughts. That link is not at all apparent to readers, and a transition term like *and* or *therefore* will not bridge that gap. The writer must write something to express the connection between the two sentences so there is no gap and no need for the readers to invent their own bridge. The writer needs to explain the relationship between "jammed" and "expensive" parking lots and the embarrassment of "walking into class late." You can work on this skill in the next exercise.

  PRACTICING COHERENCE

In small groups, return to the incoherent paragraph on page 387 and discuss its problems. As a group, rewrite the paragraph so that all information is included, but also so that the ideas are logically linked. As you fill in the gaps in logic, practice using the transition terms and devices that will ensure coherence in this paragraph. Here is one solution to improve the coherence of the paragraph.

> Students who commute to campus suffer indignities that dorm students can't imagine. Even before commuting students get to classes they have a problem. Parking on campus is expensive and hard to find because the lots are jammed. Often it takes over half an hour to find a spot. By then class has started, and it is embarrassing to walk into class late. Commuters also feel cut off from those students who can return to the dorm to eat or rest. And while study groups readily form in dorms, commuting students seldom have even a telephone number to get missed lecture notes. Dorm students have a sense of independence and freedom from their families, but commuters need to

conform to old family rules and schedules. Often the indignities of living at home include doing those tasks the students did through high school, like baby sitting or cooking for younger siblings, or driving grandparents to the bank.

Writing Introductions

Introductions and Audience

Typically, a strong introduction "hooks" the reader and then expands on the hook while building to the thesis statement, which often concludes the introduction. The introduction to an essay—the aim—has two obligations: (1) to attract the reader to the subject of the essay and (2) to establish for the reader the particular purpose and focus of the writer—the claim. The focus of the writer—the claim he or she is making about a limited subject—is contained in the thesis statement. The thesis statement does not have to be at the end of the introduction, but that is often a natural place for it because both the writer and reader are then immediately aware of the key assertion that will be supported in the essay. The concept of the thesis is discussed in more detail on page 352.

If you have not discovered in your prewriting activities a useful way to lead to your thesis, you may find the ideas below helpful. Some subjects will seem best introduced by one type of introduction rather than another, and it's a good idea to keep your audience in mind as you draft possible "hooks" to your topic

Types of Introductions

You may find that if you deliberately vary your introductions, perhaps trying each of the methods suggested here, you will not be intimidated by that blank sheet of paper or empty computer screen each time you start to write.

Direct Quotation. An essay that begins with the words of another person, especially a well-known person, should help convince your reader that you are a prepared writer who has researched the views of others on the subject and found relevance in their words. For example, when we were preparing Part I of this book, we discovered that Ellen Goodman had incorporated into her essay a particularly compelling comment by André Malraux, which we decided to use in our chapter introduction. André Malraux—a French novelist, political activist, and art critic—is not a noted authority on the sociology or psychology of family life. Nevertheless, his mildly philosophical statements about the family interested us, and we found his thoughts relevant for our introduction. Notice how we use Malraux's words throughout our introduction.

In the essay that we used to demonstrate active reading (p. 3), author Ellen Goodman quotes André Malraux that "without a family" the individual "alone in the world, trembles with the cold" (qtd. in Goodman 4). The family often nurtures its members and tolerates differences and failings that friends and lovers cannot accept. But as you may realize from your own experiences and observations, people also tremble with fear or anxiety even within the family unit. The writers in this chapter show the family as a source of both nurturing and anxiety.

Description.   An introduction using description—whether it is a vivid picture of nature or of a person—can appeal to the imagination and the senses simultaneously. The power of the opening can be enhanced if the writer also postpones specific identification of the subject, place, or person until the reader is engaged. In the following paragraph from "The Only Child" (p. 31), notice that John Leonard does not reveal his subject. In fact, the reader does not know that he or she is reading about Leonard's brother until the last line of the essay.

> He is big. He always has been, over six feet, with that slump of the shoulders and tuck in the neck big men in this country often affect, as if to apologize for being above the democratic norm in size. (In high school and at college he played varsity basketball. In high school he was senior class president.) And he looks healthy enough, blue-eyed behind his beard, like a trapper or a mountain man, acquainted with silences. He also grins a lot.

Question.   The psychology behind asking a reader a question probably lies in the fact that most of us feel obliged to at least *consider* answering a writer who has asked us something. If we don't have an immediate answer, we consider the subject and then continue with the reading—exactly what the writer wants us to do. But readers may find questions irritating if they seem silly or contrived, like "What is capital punishment?" Notice your own interest as you read the questions in the introduction to Robert Heilbroner's essay "Don't Let Stereotypes Warp Your Judgments" (p. 469).

> Is a girl called Gloria apt to be better-looking than one called Bertha? Are criminals more likely to be dark than blond? Can you tell a good deal about someone's personality from hearing his voice briefly over the phone? Can a person's nationality be pretty accurately guessed from his photograph? Does the fact that someone wears glasses imply that he is intelligent?

Anecdote or Illustration.   Just as listeners look up attentively when a speaker begins a speech with a story, all readers are engaged by an anecdote. If the story opens dramatically, the involvement of the reader is assured. In the following example, from Brent Staples's essay "Black Men and Public

Space" (p. 237), the author initially misleads the reader into thinking the writer has malicious intentions—exactly the misconception that is the subject matter of his essay.

> My first victim was a woman—white, well dressed, probably in her early twenties. I came upon her late one evening on a deserted street in Hyde Park, a relatively affluent neighborhood in an otherwise mean, impoverished section of Chicago. As I swung onto the avenue behind her, there seemed to be a discreet, uninflammatory distance between us. Not so. She cast back a worried glance. To her, the youngish black man—a broad six feet two inches with a beard and billowing hair, both hands shoved into the pockets of a bulky military jacket—seemed menacingly close. After a few more quick glimpses, she picked up her pace and was soon running in earnest. Within seconds she disappeared into a cross street.

Definition.   Often the definition of a term is a necessary element of an essay, and a definition may interest the reader in the subject (if the writer does not resort to that boring and cliché opener, "According to the dictionary . . ."). Sometimes the term may be unfamiliar, but often the term might be well known but the meanings may vary according to each reader. Recognizing these multiple meanings in "O.K., So I'm Fat" (p. 247), Neil Steinberg clarifies *his* definition of "fat" by using humor and by negation—explaining what "fat" does not mean:

> Some people are no doubt fat because of glandular disorders or the wrath of an angry God. I am not one of those people. I am fat because I eat a lot. Since fat people are held in such low regard, I should immediately point out that I am not that fat. Not fat in the Chinese Buddha, spilling-out-of-the-airplane-seat sense. The neighborhood kids don't skip behind me in the street, banging tin cans together and singing derisive songs. Not yet, anyway.

Deliberate Contradiction.   Sometimes a writer may start a paper with a view or statement that will be contradicted or contrasted with the subject matter of the essay. In his essay "Makes Learning Fun," Clifford Stoll does just that in an introduction that starts:

> Technology promises shortcuts to higher grades and painless learning. Today's edutainment software comes shrink-wrapped in computing's magic mantra: "Makes Learning Fun." . . . Just one problem. It's a lie. (304)

Statistic or Startling Fact or Idea.   An essay that starts with a dramatic statistic or idea engages the reader at once. Notice how the following introduction from William F. Harrison's "Why Stop Smoking? Let's Get Clinical" (p. 346) uses statistics to engage (or frighten) the reader:

> Most of us in medicine now accept that tobacco is associated with major health consequences and constitutes the No. 1 health problem in this country.
> What smokers have not yet come to terms with is that if they continue smoking, the probability of developing one or more of the major complications of smoking is 100 percent. It absolutely will happen. They will develop chronic bronchitis, laryngitis, pharyngitis, sinusitis and some degree of emphysema.

Mixture of Methods. Many well-crafted introductions will combine the approaches described above. For example, the introductory paragraph of "In Rooms of Women" (p. 161) employs narration, a statistic, description, illustration, and ironic contradiction to attract the reader to the subject of being an outsider in Malaysia.

> When I lived on the East Coast of Malaysia, I used to do aerobics over a Chinese grocery store. I went there almost every afternoon, climbed up a tunnel of concrete stairs to a narrow room infused with the perfume of hair gel and perspiration, cosmetics and worn shoes. In Malaysia, where more than half the female population drifts through the tropical days beneath layers of concealing polyester, this room was an unusual domain of women. We were relaxed here, exposed in our leotards and shorts, our determination as strong as the situation was ironic. For an hour each day we stretched and ran and sweated, devoting ourselves entirely to the care of bodies which, in the outside world, we were encouraged to hide.

Writing Conclusions

The conclusion of an essay should give the reader a feeling of completion or satisfaction. Ideally, the conclusion will fit like the lid on a box. You might return to your introduction and thesis, select key images or phrases that you used, and reflect them in your conclusion. This return to the start of the paper assures your reader that all aspects of your assertion have been met in the essay. Furthermore, the purpose of your paper—to express, inform, analyze, or persuade—should be consistent with the tone and stance of your conclusion. If your aim has been to persuade your reader, your conclusion will need to be more forceful than if you only had intended to inform your reader. An effective conclusion is one that echoes the tone of the introduction without merely repeating the exact words of the thesis (a type of conclusion that is contrived and dull). Although your ending may be weakened by "tacking on" a new topic or concept without sufficient explanation and development, you may want to suggest that there is some broader issue to think about, or some additional goal that might be achieved if the situation you have discussed were satisfied.

For his conclusion to the essay "Don't Let Stereotypes Warp Your Judgments" (p. 469), Robert Heilbroner returns to the images of the pictures in our mind, the ideas stirred by the questions he had asked earlier in his introduction:

> Most of the time, when we type-cast the world, we are not in fact generalizing about people at all. We are only revealing the embarrassing facts about the pictures that hang in the gallery of stereotypes in our own heads.

Another effective conclusion appears in Marcus Mabry's "Living in Two Worlds" (p. 144). Mabry refers to his opening line describing the sign that proclaims "We built a proud new feeling." Throughout his essay, he contrasts the "two universes" of his home and school environments. Now in his conclusion, he creates the phrase that will also be the title of his essay:

> Somewhere in the midst of all that misery, my family has built, within me, "a proud feeling." As I travel between the two worlds, it becomes harder to remember just how proud I should be—not just because of where I have come from and where I am going, but because of where they are. The fact that they survive in the world in which they live is something to be very proud of, indeed. It inspires within me a sense of tenacity and accomplishment that I hope every college graduate will someday possess.

Mabry's conclusion also reflects his broader thoughts about pride, not only about his pride in where he is headed but also his pride in his family's ability to survive. He brings his reader a sense of hope and inspiration and gives his essay closure.

The student papers in this book also show effective techniques in their conclusions. Rachel, who wrote the paper on eating disorders (pp. 382–386), was advised by her instructor to strengthen the conclusion of her rough draft (pp. 378–381) by returning to the images and key words of her introduction. Rachel did this in her final paper. She was also able to echo the title of a source that she used in her essay. The following part of her conclusion mirrors her introduction:

```
It is time to protest the images of bikini-clad models parading
before us and demand images that reflect the emotional and intellec-
tual scope and diversity among women in our society. With some of
```

our best and brightest dying among us, there is no in-between position any more. Those who make the images will only change when those
of us who support them stop buying products and stop tuning in on
programs that continue to impose "bodily harm" on us.

Shannon Paaske also returned to her introduction to conclude her research paper on the disabled, "From Access to Acceptance: Enabling America's Largest Minority." Her thesis and conclusion are printed here, but you
can read her entire essay on pages 522–540.

Thesis

Although combinations of technological advances, equality-
promoting legislation, and increasing media exposure have worked
as a collective force in bringing about improvements in the lives
of the people who make up what is sometimes termed "America's
largest minority" (Davidson 61), ignorance and prejudice continue
to plague the disabled.

Conclusion

The legislation and technology that were developed at the
end of the twentieth century will continue to make new worlds
accessible to the disabled. Ideally, these developments will
permit the disabled to be viewed in terms of their capabilities
rather than their disabilities. In that climate, the disabled can
gain acceptance in the worlds to which they have access. With the
steps being taken by government, science, and the media, individuals alone are needed to make the dream of acceptance a reality
for the disabled.

Notice that the title of Shannon's essay also is echoed in her conclusion.

Final Tips for Writing Conclusions

To draft a good conclusion, try the following:

- Return to your thesis and restate it in different words. Incorporate that re-
  statement into your conclusion.

- Examine your introduction and try to incorporate the key words, images, description, anecdote, or response to the question into your conclusion.
- Consider your reader: Have you brought a sense of significant closure to your topic?

You have been considering your reader and the aim of your paper throughout as you have rewritten your rough drafts, verified the logic of your organization, strengthened the introduction and conclusion, and edited for surface errors. These essential revision strategies can help you with any paper that you write.

Chapter 9

Methods for Developing Essays

Your instructor may ask you to write a paper using a particular method of development for presenting your support, such as a narrative or a comparison/contrast study. If your instructor doesn't assign a particular type of paper, then your purpose for writing will influence the methods of development you choose to achieve your goal. To help you better understand how these types of support differ from one another, we have identified the following models for discussion: summary, narration, evaluative response, definition, cause and effect, comparison-contrast, argument, and analysis (see Chapter 10). By examining these methods in isolation, we do not mean to suggest that all paper topics will fit precisely into one of these categories. Nothing could be further from our experience as students, teachers, and writers.

You may recall that Rachel's essay "Dieting Daze" (p. 382) incorporates narrative, definition, description, and comparison-contrast in a problem analysis paper that argues for a change. These multiple approaches are ideal complements, and together they helped Rachel meet her goal. Her purpose was to convince her reader that advertisers need to be more responsible for the body images they promulgate.

Combining Multiple Methods

Because you may be asked to develop a paper with a single and particular strategy, we have included in this chapter models of the methods most often assigned. But because we believe that most essays are developed with combined methods, we will start our discussion with John Balzar's "Lighten Up on Enlightenment" (p. 181), an essay that combines multiple strategies.

After reading it, you will see the kinds of support the author used: narration, definition, cause and effect, comparison-contrast, and analysis. All of these techniques enable him to argue his point and defend his thesis—that we should reconsider our notion that all Native American team names are offensive. Let's now look at each method in more detail.

Analyzing Mixed Methods

Narration.   To engage his reader, Balzar opens his essay with a firsthand experience about his employers' program to reduce harassment in the workplace. Balzar realizes that readers enjoy personal stories, especially about a topic that has been in the news. When expressed with vivid details, such anecdotes capture attention and support an argument. His narrative is also engaging because he uses humor, recalling the time he and an editor facetiously called each other "sweetie" and "honey" in response to the new anti-harassment policy.

Cause and Effect.   Balzar notes that the anti-harassment policy was effective because "vulnerable employees felt slightly more secure, having right officially on their side," but acknowledges that the policy caused the workplace to become "drearier." The effect was that workers felt reluctant to say anything that might be misconstrued as intimate or offensive; "suspicions were heightened and distance was widened" among employees.

In another section of his essay, Balzar again employs cause and effect by acknowledging that "oppression has been diminished and awareness heightened by those who police our language." The effect is that "ours is a better society for the way we speak of each other now." However, Balzar cautions that a further consequence is that our society is "wound very tight on these matters," and "we are in danger of draining away not just bigotry and offensiveness in our language but things worth celebrating." It is vital for his thesis that Balzar show how policies governing word choice have had negative effects.

Definition.   In moving from harassment in the workplace to his argument that using Native American sport team names has been deemed harassment, Balzar realizes he must define harassment. He does, but it is not a dictionary definition: "Harassment is anything that anyone says it is. That is, if you feel harassed, you are." By using his own definition of harassment, he underscores what is ultimately his point—that interpretations of harassment are indeed personal.

Comparison-Contrast.   Balzar agrees that the word "Redskins" is a pejorative term and that "surrendering the word would be a victory for our ideals." But Balzar then contrasts that word with "Chiefs," which he argues "has far more going for it than against it" because the word suggests "strength, unity, leadership, perhaps even integrity." Ultimately, Balzar is comparing the loss of levity in offices with the potential loss of cheers in stadiums. By comparing the two consequences, he compels the reader to question the renaming of sports teams.

Analysis.   Throughout Balzar's essay, he analyzes the use and misuse of language. He even quotes the French writer Antoine de Saint-Exupéry, who wrote, "Words are the source of misunderstandings." But Balzar argues that "fortunately, they are also the source of understanding." Ultimately, Balzar's analysis of current policy on word choice prompts readers to "lighten up on enlightenment."

Why This Analysis?

The purpose of this analysis of "Lighten Up on Enlightenment" is to encourage you to recognize the multiple modes and devices that professional writers use to engage and persuade their readers. Employing these devices will improve your writing. By practicing the single-development assignments given in the "Writing from the Text" topics and described in Part I, you will learn to employ multiple methods confidently to write an engaging and convincing paper. Let's now look at each strategy in more detail.

Summary

Summarizing is an important skill that demonstrates your ability to understand both the content of the reading and the way the material is arranged. A summary demonstrates your ability to read, comprehend, and write. Summaries of assigned readings in any class can become particularly useful personal learning tools, serving as study guides for examinations. But you may be asked in some classes—from undergraduate through graduate studies—to submit summaries to show that you have read and understood journal articles, essays, or books. Your purpose in writing a summary is to give your audience a condensed but complete view of the original work. In a sense, you are saving your reader the time and effort of reading the original—if your summary is accurate!

Organizing and Developing a Summary

The following steps can be used to summarize assignments in any class—from psychology, education, and philosophy, to political science and English. These same steps may also be the first you take if you are asked to summarize an essay and then evaluate it, an assignment frequently given in college courses.

1. Read the work actively, marking directly on the copy (if possible) the obvious divisions or sections within the text. Underline the thesis, if one is explicitly stated, as well as any key points or examples you see as you read.

2. Reread the text. On a separate sheet of paper, write a few sentences of summary (combining paraphrased and quoted material) for each section of the work that you have marked in the margins of the original.

3. Write the author's thesis or what you infer to be the central assertion of the entire essay. You may write a general thesis or one that forecasts the points the writer will use to support the assertion.

4. Write a draft that starts with the thesis, even if the writer delayed the central assertion of the work. Continue the draft with the sentence summaries that you wrote for each of the sections of the text. Use the full name of the author of the work once, then use only his or her last name in other places in your summary. It is important to use the writer's name so that your reader is reminded who had the ideas in the original text.

5. Reread your draft to be sure of the following:
   - Your thesis reflects the author's *full* point.
   - Each section of your summary has its own assertion (or topic sentence) and sufficient support from the original.

- Your summary parallels the original in tone and order.
- Your summary is both objective and complete. *Objective* means that none of your feelings about the text are reflected in statements or tone. *Complete* means that you have not left out any sections of the original.

6. Reread your summary to be certain that you use quotation marks around any key words or phrases that you have taken from the text. Most of the summary should be in your own words, but a particularly memorable phrase or expression will resist paraphrasing. You will want to include this memorable language in your summary within quotation marks. Check for spelling, mechanical errors, and sentence correctness. Insert necessary transition words and phrases prior to your final writing.

7. Unlike an essay that you have written, a summary of someone else's work does not need a conclusion. End your summary with the author's final point.

STUDENT EXAMPLE: A SUMMARY

The following is an example of one student's summary of the essay by Martin Luther King, Jr., that appears on page 280.

Thomas 1

Chris Thomas

English 1A

Professor Blake

February 3, 2002

A Summary of "Three Ways of Meeting Oppression"

In an excerpt from his book <u>Stride Toward Freedom</u>, Dr. Martin Luther King, Jr., shows that oppressed people deal with their oppression in three characteristic ways: with acquiescence, violence, or nonviolent resistance. King shows that only a mass movement committed to nonviolent resistance will bring a permanent peace and unite all people.

Although acquiescence--passive acceptance of an unjust system-- is the easiest method of dealing with injustice, King insists that it is both morally wrong and the way of the coward. To acquiesce

---

to unfair treatment is to passively condone the behavior of one's oppressors. King says, "Noncooperation with evil is as much a moral obligation as is cooperation with good. The oppressed must never allow the conscience of the oppressor to slumber" (281). King maintains that respect for Negroes and their children will never be won if they do not actively stand against the system.

However, King contends that violence is no solution because it never concerns itself with changing the belief system of oppressors. "In spite of temporary victories, violence never brings permanent peace" (281). Thus King insists that violence is impractical as well as immoral: "The old law of an eye for an eye leaves everybody blind" (281). King states that bitterness and corruption become the legacy of this destructive method that "annihilates" rather than "converts." Thus violence destroys any possibility of brotherhood.

King's principle of nonviolent resistance is his answer to how one must deal with oppression. It is confrontational without resorting to physical aggression. Nonviolent resistance avoids "the extremes and immoralities" of the other two methods while integrating the positive aspects of each. The nonviolent resister, like the person who acquiesces, agrees that violence is wrong, but like the violent resister, he believes that "evil must be resisted" (282). King insists that this is the method that oppressed people must use to oppose oppression. It allows neither cowardice nor hatred. "Through nonviolent resistance the Negro will be able to rise to the noble height of opposing the unjust system while loving the perpetrators of the system" (282).

King states that by using nonviolent resistance, the American Negro and other oppressed people can "enlist all men of good

Thomas 3

will in [the] struggle for equality" (282). He maintains that the struggle is not between people or races but is "a tension between justice and injustice" (282). Only a mass movement of nonviolent resistance will unite people in a community.

Work Cited

King, Martin Luther, Jr. "Three Ways of Meeting Oppression." Between Worlds: A Reader, Rhetoric, and Handbook. Ed. Susan Bachmann and Melinda Barth. 4th ed. New York: Longman, 2004. 280–283.

Analyzing the Writer's Strategy

Chris begins his summary of the excerpt by identifying its source and the author's complete name. Although King does not state his thesis explicitly, Chris infers it from King's writing and then states it in the first paragraph. Chris's thesis and paragraphs reflect the three main points of King's essay, so Chris has organized his summary to parallel the original. This is a tremendous help to his readers, who immediately gain an overview of the entire work. The quoted material that he chose from King's essay reflects what Chris found most significant in language and specificity to support King's points. Although a different summary writer might choose other quotations to define and illustrate those points, the points and thesis would be nearly the same in each summary.

Summary as Part of a Larger Assignment

Chris's assignment was to write a complete and objective summary of another writer's work. Other assignments might require a response or evaluation of the content in addition to the summary. A character analysis might have an introduction that summarizes the plot of the story in a few sentences. An even more abbreviated use of summary occurs when writers incorporate direct quotation into their essays and need to briefly summarize the context as they introduce the quotation. An argument essay might progress from a short summary of an experiment or survey. Even poetry analysis, which must go beyond summary to be effective, will, nevertheless, employ limited summary of plot or context. The act of summarizing will help you see what you do and do not understand about a reading. Your effective summary then can convince your reader that you comprehend the original well enough to incorporate it into your own points.

Final Tips for a Summary

- Begin with a statement of the author's complete thesis; include the author's full name.
- Focus each paragraph of your summary to reflect the sections of the original.
- Parallel the original in tone and order.
- Summarize all parts of the essay and be objective.
- Paraphrase most of the essay but incorporate memorable language in quotation marks.
- End with the author's final point; no conclusion is necessary in your summary.

Narration

Everyone loves a good story, and most people enjoy telling one. This process of narration—telling a single story or several related ones—is often associated with myths, fairy tales, short stories, and novels, but writers of all types of essays use narrative strategies. The purpose of narration is to use first-hand experiences to engage or entertain, inform, or persuade an audience.

When to Use Narration

Narration can be used to argue a point, define a concept, or reveal a truth. Writers in all disciplines have discovered the power of the narrative. Journalists, historians, sociologists, and essayists often "hook" their readers by opening with a personal anecdote or a human interest story to capture the reader and illustrate points. In fact, many writers use narration to persuade their audiences about a course of action. For example, George Orwell's famous narrative "Shooting an Elephant" (p. 270) is a compelling indictment of imperialism.

Personal narratives can be powerful if they focus on a provocative insight and if the details are carefully selected and shaped. Therefore narratives are more than mere diary entries because certain details may be omitted while others may be altered. Narratives may help the writer better understand the significance of an experience, and they help readers "see for themselves." Typically narratives require no library research (our lives are rich with resources for this type of essay), but often writers may choose to supplement personal narration with research and outside sources to move beyond their own experience.

Organizing and Developing a Narrative

Narratives often focus on an incident involving a conflict, whether it is between opposing people, values, or perceptions. This incident is then dramatized so the reader can picture what happened and can hear what was said. Such incidents often involve some aspect of change—a contrast between "before" and "after"—even though the change may be internal (a change in awareness) rather than external or physical.

Narratives do not have to feature life-shattering incidents or have a somber tone. In fact, some superb narratives may be humorous and may have a witty or ironic outcome. Many of the best narratives often involve profound changes that are not always obvious to others. In the essay "In Rooms of Women" (p. 161), Kim Edwards tells stories from her teaching experiences on the east coast of Malaysia, concluding with a beautiful narrative of her epiphany in a hot spring in Japan where she discovers an acceptance of women's bodies that was lacking in Malaysia. Although her conclusion involves little action, it is memorable, reflecting those quiet moments in our lives that, when rendered skillfully, make compelling narratives.

Brainstorming for a Subject

Writers usually need to dig deep to find those buried experiences that have changed their attitudes and views. To help generate ideas, you will find specific narrative assignments at the end of many essays, poems, and stories in the "Writing from the Text" sections in Part I. If your assignment is more general—to write about any significant moment or change in your life—it will help to consider these questions.

- What are my most vivid memories of
  Kindergarten? First grade? Second? Third? Fourth? Fifth?
  Middle school? High school? College?
  Team sports?
  Learning to laugh at myself?
  Overcoming a challenge?
  Dealing with failure or illness?
  Living in another culture?
  Staying with friends or relatives?
  Getting a job or working?
  Making a costly mistake?

- When did I first
  Try too hard to impress others?
  Feel ashamed (or proud) of myself?
  Stand up to my parents?
  Realize teachers make mistakes?
  Give in to peer pressure?
  Pressure another to go against authority?
  Wish I had different parents?
  Wish someone would disappear from my life?
  Want to change who I am?

- How did one incident show me
  What living between two worlds really means?
  How foolish we can be?
  How it feels to be alone?
  Why conformity isn't always best?

How stereotyping has affected me?

How different I am from my sister/brother/friend?

Why we have a certain law?

How it feels to live with a physical disability?

How little I know myself?

Additional Prewriting

If you prefer a visual strategy, you might try clustering or mapping your ideas. One method is to write your topic—for example, "significant changes"—in a circle in the center of your page and then draw spokes outward from it. At the end of each spoke, write down a specific incident that triggered important changes in your life. Write the incident in a box and then use more spokes, radiating from the box, to specify all the changes that resulted. (For an illustration of clustering, see pp. 337–338.)

After you have brainstormed about all possible changes, choose the incident that seems most vivid and worth narrating. Then use another sheet of paper and write about a specific change in a circle at the center and write down all the details that relate to it. After you have recorded all relevant details, you are ready to focus these thoughts and draft your paper.

From Brainstorming to Drafting a Paper

In a narrative essay, the thesis is not always articulated in the essay itself because it can ruin the sense of surprise or discovery often associated with narratives. In fact, an explicit thesis can slow the momentum of the story or spoil the ending. Whether it is articulated or implied, however, a thesis is still essential in order to keep the writer focused and to ensure that the story has a point or insight to share.

Beginning with a Working Thesis.   For example, in the student essay that follows, Rebekah Hall-Nakanuma focuses on a time when her sister's illness prompted her own discoveries about family and self. When she began writing about her sister's unexpected illness, Rebekah probably did not begin with a thesis because the insight, focus, or assertion is seldom clear at first. Rebekah had only a topic, her sister's hospitalization. But after she clustered or listed some details, she probably wrote a *working* thesis—a preliminary assertion that could be changed and refined as the narrative took shape.

> **Working Thesis:** My sister's hospitalization took us all by surprise.

Discovering the Real Thesis.   Most writers aren't lucky enough to identify a thesis immediately. Often, particularly in a narrative, it takes considerable writing before the best thesis is discovered. Therefore writers typically continue sharpening their thesis throughout the writing process as they, too, discover the point of their story. As Rebekah narrated this experience, it developed as a genuine "between worlds" experience.

Discovered Thesis: The pressure to be perfect can ultimately cause family members to bury or deny very real fears and needs.

Once the thesis becomes clear to the writer, the rough draft needs to be revised so that all the details relate to this new thesis. Notice, however, that the thesis statement does not need to be specified in the actual essay.

The following essay written by student Rebekah Hall-Naganuma describes a family's discovery that "crept in through the cracks" when least expected.

STUDENT EXAMPLE: A NARRATIVE

Hall-Naganuma 1

Rebekah Hall-Naganuma

Professor Anderson

English 1A

January 20, 2002

Through the Cracks

It was late at night as I listened to my father's low rumble, his face buried in the phone receiver that was nearly resting on his chest. I sat on the edge of the coffee table, straining to understand the words he used. Dad was not easily disturbed. He took the unexpected in stride, so his now hushed tone scared me. I looked around, trying to clarify the moment. Craig's ears were plugged with headphones; his thoughts seemed inside the computer directly in front of him. Mom moved about the kitchen, her lips spread in the thin line that told me she was troubled. Normally voluble, her silence was foreboding.

Finally, Dad ended the conversation. I leaned forward, reaching for some kind of explanation. I watched his face, hoping for a revelation. His face was pale and closed. He didn't return my look but stood up and walked into the kitchen. I followed and stared at Mom's straightened back.

"Heather is in the hospital," Dad said, his voice raspy, as he told us about my older sister. I noticed his Adam's apple dip and heard him swallow. Mom turned around, her posture unnatural. She tilted her head in question. Dad continued, "She had a blackout and checked herself into the hospital. They're running some tests." He watched my mother's face as if to relay a secret message. She didn't get the message.

"What do you mean by 'blackout?'" she asked, with a look of confusion on her face.

"She ended up in Houston somehow and then couldn't remember how she got there." Dad began to sound matter-of-fact, as if this were second-hand local news.

We didn't say anything. I could imagine all sorts of scenarios--disease, drugs, brain tumor. I did not want to believe any of these. Mom began to bustle around the tidy kitchen, smiling and singing. Her cheerfulness, her way of pretending that everything was under control, irritated me.

But she had taught us well. We all had an uncanny ability to hide our flaws. Our unconscious goal was to be perfect. We were perfectionists stranded in the never-ending desert of dysfunctionalism. Owning up to the defects in our family would mean giving up on our ideals. It would mean sacrificing the commendation of others. People would always comment on how close we all were and how happy we always looked together. We had developed our skills well in fabricating happiness.

The next day one result was in; it turned out that Heather would be in a psychiatric ward for awhile. Her doctor didn't know for how long. "Craig . . . Rebekah . . . I don't want you talking about your sister's condition with anyone. I think this should stay in the family," Dad cautioned, after sitting us down one day. His eyes were serious, and his hands were folded in front of him, almost as if he were praying.

Mom had decided to fly to Texas, where Heather lived with her husband and children. She was going there, "to straighten things out," she said, as if it were merely a miscommunication that needed clarification. They had both told the church, where dad pastored, that Heather needed help with her kids. I wanted to laugh aloud at them; at the same time, I wanted to pound my fists against them.

My parents had a way of being silent when matters required questions, confessions, and tears. I tried to understand it-- they came from the era of church picnics, nice homes and nice cars. They dreamed of a nice family that would fit into their plans. They had us instead: Heather with her drug problems, Duane with his alcoholism, Kim with her bartending career, and me with my loud music and cigarettes. Craig was really the only one who went along with their scheme. My mother's camaraderie with him had always angered me as though he proved her point of motherhood.

The front that they kept up was like water just beginning to boil, but I knew it would someday. My dad had been the counselor and the mentor to the lost and the troubled; he had kept our image pure. We weren't allowed to listen to rock music at home, yet somehow mental illness had crept in through the cracks in our family. We could see the signs beneath the surface and behind closed doors.

Heather's problems set free a flood of dark emotion in our family. We had to admit that no matter how hard we tried, sadness and tragedy could not be avoided. It could not be covered up. Heather's honesty began to open up the doors that we had never

been allowed to walk through. We gradually discovered our own
humanity through the questions prompted by Heather's illness.
The pictures of blood and gore that Heather drew in art therapy,
the shock treatment, the crazy hairstyles that Heather flaunted
at 35 years of age gave us a glimpse outside the wonderland of
daisies and rainbows. And it let out the dogs that had been howl-
ing inside of me.

I hadn't been able to sleep well for weeks. I started having
the most frightening nightmares. Images were in my subconscious
that I never would have guessed were there: people attacking me,
wars raging, fires out of control. Then the panic attacks began--
the sleepless nights, the senseless roaming with friends at night.
I needed someone to explain it all to me. I searched for someone
to tell me what to do. Dad was never good at opening up his mind
to these things. I knew what his answer would be: "It's because
you're listening to that rock music" or "because you are so rebellious." And somehow, no matter how much I disliked my mother's in-
cessant optimism, I had become like her. I could not explain my
problems to anyone; I could not show my sorrows. Maybe that is
part of the reason why I decided to tell Mom about my anxiety.

Her response surprised me. We were talking on the phone, and
I started telling her about the nightmares and the craziness of
my life. "Rebekah," she said slowly. "The time that I have been
spending here with Heather has helped me to understand some
things." She paused as if she were lifting a veil and not sure
what she would find underneath. "I always thought that simply being a kind person would make everything okay. I thought I could
be a good mother by just being thoughtful."

And she told me how, in this latest phase of her life, she
had learned that people deserved more than just an occasional

"please" and "thank you." People were filled with anger, sorrow, frustration, silliness, hate, exhaustion, deceit, and fear. And all of those emotions did not make a person weak, wrong, or mistaken. Those emotions made a person human. The anger turned the forgiveness into a beautiful act of love. The sorrow made the laughter more joyous. All of those years she had thought that her duty as a mother was to protect us from our dark sides, to wash away our tears with cake or promises or smiles. But instead of just letting us cry, she had made us stop.

After Heather's breakdown, we all began to talk--and cry--more and to heal. It wasn't painless or automatic. But we found ways to express fears, and to listen, and to kid each other rather than to hold feelings in and stay silent. I could feel us turning onto a new road, one that would be bumpier and more cracked, but where the scenery would be fresh and often exhilarating at times.

Analyzing the Writer's Strategy

When writers narrate a story, they try to recreate scenes—to show rather than tell—so that the reader can experience the moment as they did. Rather than simply telling us what they felt, they try to *show* us. For example, in the student model, Rebekah could have simply told us of her sister's "blackout" and subsequent hospitalization. Instead, she lets us observe and hear as her father discloses this unexpected news to her and her family:

I watched his face, hoping for a revelation. His face was pale and closed. He didn't return my look but stood up and walked into the kitchen. I followed and stared at Mom's straightened back.

"Heather is in the hospital," Dad said, his voice raspy, as he told us about my older sister. I noticed his Adam's apple dip and heard him swallow. Mom turned around, her posture unnatural. She tilted her head in question. Dad continued, "She had a blackout and checked herself into the hospital. They're running some

tests." He watched my mother's face as if to relay a secret message. She didn't get the message.

"What do you mean by 'blackout?'" she asked, with a look of
confusion on her face.

Such a scene draws the reader in because each of us can sense the confusion and concern that the family members feel. The writer doesn't need to write, "My entire family was worried" because she has *shown* this more vividly than any claim she could make. Rebekah's use of dialogue, action, and vivid details (her father's "pale and closed" face and "raspy voice," her mother's "straightened back" and "unnatural" posture) makes us sense their anxiety.

Selecting Telling Details.   The key to describing scenes and characters is to make sure each detail is revealing. It is not important to know the narrator's hair color or height, so such details would not be relevant or "telling." But the fact that she listens to rock music even though it wasn't allowed at home reveals that she is not willing to conform totally to the family's standards and rules. Such details help us to understand better the narrator's character as well as the dynamics within her family.

Similarly, the setting can be revealing. Although the time of day is not always important in a story, here it seems fitting that it is "late at night" when the father hears that Cheryl has been hospitalized and that it is during the night that the narrator roams senselessly with friends and also is awakened by panic attacks and nightmares. All of these nighttime activities underscore the inability to avoid or deny the darker reality of their lives.

 ## PRACTICING WRITING ESSAYS WITH NARRATION

Many of the topics in the "Writing from the Text" sections in Part I invite you to relate your own experience to the particular readings and to respond with a narrative. Here are some additional assignments:

1. Write an essay describing one home or school experience that taught you an unexpected lesson. Show us the incident as it happened, and describe what you learned and why it was unexpected.

2. Write an essay focusing on a time when you bullied or were bullied by someone else. Let us see what happened and what you discovered about yourself and others.

3. Write about a time when one of your peers, parents, or children embarrassed you. Was the situation funny or painful, or a little of both? Recreate the moment of embarrassment so that your reader sees and hears what happened.

4. Write about an incident when you felt that your cultural or family background was incorrectly prejudged. Describe what happened so that your reader can understand the event and your response to it. Did you make any discoveries as a result of this experience?

5. Write about an event that revealed that something you once believed or thought was important had lost its validity or importance. Dramatize the revelation as vividly as you can.

Final Tips for a Narrative

- Focus on a provocative insight so that your story reflects some real thought.
- Continue sharpening your thesis as your narrative develops. Remember, the thesis does not need to be explicitly stated in the essay.
- Dramatize a scene or two, using action and dialogue. Don't just tell the reader; show the scene.
- Include telling details that reveal relevant character traits. Have your characters interact with each other.
- Rewrite sentences and revise paragraphs to eliminate wordiness and generalizations.
- Study other narratives in the text, looking for techniques and strategies. Experiment!

Evaluative Response

Each day when you appraise or assess the value or quality of something—a movie, editorial, song lyric, college course—you are evaluating it. Informally, a friend may ask how you liked a particular film, and you will offer your evaluation, without defining your criteria. Sometimes, however, you need to give a written evaluation. You may be asked to fill out an evaluation form on a course you are taking or on the instructor. You may be asked to write a movie or book review for a newspaper or a course. In some cases, you will need to evaluate something using specific criteria—established by you or someone else. In most cases, you will support your evaluation with examples from a text—a film, an essay, a book, or an editorial. The purpose of an evaluative response essay is to give your judgment of a work based on both your experience and a careful reading of the text.

When to Write an Evaluative Response Essay

Throughout your college writing, you will be asked to respond to assigned readings and texts. You will be expected to summarize passages, analyze key points, incorporate direct quotations, and evaluate assertions and evidence. In English classes, such an assignment may involve your relating your own observations or experiences to the readings.

Organizing and Developing an Evaluative Response Essay

To write an evaluative response essay, you need to present the author's thesis and key points, and then respond to them in terms of your own views, experiences, and judgments. Your essay must show that you have read the text closely, and it should include quotations from the text and a discussion of each quotation. Overall, your essay should both analyze and evaluate the text: What are the author's central points? Do you agree or disagree with them?

You may find that you agree with some of the author's points but not with others, and you will need to explain and support your stance on each. Most importantly, your thesis should articulate your main focus as well as your view of the author's key claims. For example, in the student essay that follows, Marin Kheng briefly summarizes Ellen Goodman's position in "Thanksgiving" (p. 3) but shows how she disagrees with it:

```
While Goodman's essay is a suitable guide to how a family
should function, it is essentially an idealistic portrayal of the
family, and thus it ignores the harsher realities that are present
in many American households.
```

Marin's essay will be a treatment of "the harsher realities" that she has observed in families she knows. She includes meaningful passages from the original text and uses her own observations to counter them. For example, Marin writes: "Goodman assures us that 'while the world may abandon us, the family promises . . . to protect us'" (423). She then uses this quotation as a departure point to describe a contrasting case of her friend Brahim whose family deserted him. In your own essays, you will want to show how the original concurs—or doesn't concur—with your own experiences or observations. Whether you agree or disagree with the author, you will be evaluating the original and supporting your stance.

In any case, you will want to make sure that you have sufficiently understood and represented the text. It is not enough in an evaluative essay to simply give the title and author and then progress with your own story. Instead, you want to *use* the material that you have read. You might think of your response essay as a kind of conversation with the writer: you will be listening to, reflecting on, and evaluating the writer's many points and then inserting your own examples that parallel, extend, or counter the author's perspective.

Student Example: An Evaluative Response Essay

To satisfy an assignment for her composition class, Marin Kheng was asked to respond to and evaluate one of the essays in *Between Worlds*. She chose Ellen Goodman's "Thanksgiving" (p. 3) because she found that her observations of friends' experiences countered the world that Goodman describes, and Marin thought that this contrast would create a compelling essay.

Kheng 1

Marin Kheng

Professor Breckheimer

English 1A

March 11, 2002

Thanksgiving Beyond the Cleaver Family

The boy sits alone in the darkness of the family room, his eyes wide and yearning, hungry for the images that flash across his TV set. A family--mothers, fathers, siblings, uncles, aunts, cousins, grandparents--all sit down at the dining table to share their Thanksgiving dinner and a part of their lives. They are

smiling, talking, laughing, at times bickering, as cranberry
sauce and slices of turkey meat are passed around from person
to person. The images play across the boy's face, inviting him
to join in the warmth and the camaraderie before cruelly slipping
away from his grasp and back into the dark black haven of the TV
screen. The commercial has ended, and the boy is left alone in
his family room with his 2-for-3-dollars TV dinner before him
and the muffled sounds of screaming adult voices seeping through
from his parents' bedroom. This is his Thanksgiving.

This is not, however, the Thanksgiving depicted in Ellen
Goodman's essay, "Thanksgiving" (3). According to Goodman, Thanksgiving is a time for individuals in all parts of the United States
to reconvene with their families in remembrance of and appreciation
for the warmth, love, and support that the family structure provides. Goodman also contends that Americans are constantly struggling between the freedom and loneliness that the world of the individual brings and the selflessness and support that the world of
the family brings. They cannot deny themselves either world because
both the family and the individual are intrinsically connected
and dependent upon each other. While Goodman's essay is a suitable
guide to how a family should function, it is essentially an idealistic portrayal of the family, and thus it ignores the harsher
realities that are present in many American households. The truth
is that for many Americans like the boy, the workings of the ideal
family described in Goodman's essay are in sharp contrast with what
actually goes on in their own families.

Goodman believes that a contradiction exists in being
"raised in families . . . to be individuals" (4) because individualism must arise from a structure promoting togetherness. For my
friend Nicole, there is no dilemma in being an individual within

Kheng 3

a family because there is no threat of the loss of individualism in her family. With a father who spends the little spare time he has at the neighborhood bar and a negligent mother who constantly eats to escape her marital problems, Nicole has had to be independent for most of her life, doing for herself the things most children have taken for granted. She has had to work parttime jobs to pay for basic expenses such as food and clothing, walk down to the free clinic by herself when she is ill, and spend family-oriented holidays by herself or with friends. For Nicole there will not be "a ritual of belonging" around a dining table (4). To Nicole, the idea of togetherness and unity do not align themselves with family. Instead, the only words that correspond with family are independence, maturity, and adult responsibilities forced onto a girl far from grown up.

Other families, like that of my cousin Jana's do not force their children to raise themselves, but instead require them to earn the privilege of being accepted by the family. Contrary to Goodman's assertion that "we don't have to achieve to be accepted by our families. We just have to be" (4), Jana has to be everything that her parents desire in order to be given praise and affection, and more importantly to Jana, to stop the criticism inflicted on her by her parents. The pressure is increased when her older sister Heny, who at 21 is getting her Ph.D. in chemistry at Harvard University, comes to visit. This demand for perfection placed on Jana has led her to become an AP student with a 4.2 GPA, co-captain of the varsity swimming team and a star tennis player, president of various campus clubs, treasurer for her student council, an intern at a prestigious law firm, and a manic-depressive neurotic. In September, two weeks after the start of her senior year, she suffered a nervous breakdown and attempted suicide. When she survived, her parents stood beside her hospital bed and told her, "We are very disappointed in you. Heny would never have done something like this." While Goodman asserts that the family is "not the place where people ruthlessly compete with each other," Jana's parents clearly cultivate sibling rivalry and don't seem to understand that the family is "not for the survival of the fittest but for the weakest" (5). Although Jana's parents have given her every material comfort a teen could desire, the demands they make in return for these comforts threaten her physical, mental, and emotional well-being. But they have never given her the one thing she needs most, which ironically no amount of money could ever buy. They have never given her their acceptance.

Complete abandonment, however, is perhaps the worst thing parents can do to one of their own. Goodman assures us that "while the world may abandon us, the family promises . . . to protect us" (5). In the case of my friend Brahim, his family left one day and never came back. A straight-A student who grew up in a neighborhood infamous for its drugs and its hookers, he had been the filial son, patiently dragging his drunken brother up the stairs to their motel room, selling cheap marijuana to pay the rent when his father had spent a month's wages on a night at the Bicycle Club Casino, and assuring his teachers his black eye and the welts on his arm were caused in a fist fight with another boy when, in fact, they were caused by his own mother. Yet, despite all his efforts at holding his family together, he was abandoned in the end. At 13, he was homeless on the streets of North Hollywood with pocket change and a trash bag full of clothes. The ideal of a family that supports and protects its members and measures "their common legacy . . . the children" (4) means nothing to him because he realized at that young age the ridiculousness and cruelty of this ideal.

Kheng 5

If Nicole, Jana, Brahim, the boy eating his TV dinner alone, or any of the countless number of Americans with dysfunctional families were to read "Thanksgiving," they would not be able to understand the ideals of family that Goodman espouses or the people she gathers around her dining table. It is not that they do not know what a family should be like, or that they do not want a family, but for them Goodman's family belongs in another world, a world that no amount of wishing and desiring could ever realize. Their eyes will linger at Andre Malraux's statement that "Without a family, man, alone in the world, trembles with the cold" (4). Some may become angry, some may snort in lonely contempt, or some may simply be perplexed, because the sad irony in their reality is that although they have families, they, too, are trembling alone in the cold.

Work Cited

Goodman, Ellen. "Thanksgiving." <u>Between Worlds: A Reader,</u>
    <u>Rhetoric, and Handbook.</u> Ed. Susan Bachmann and Melinda
    Barth. 4th ed. New York: Longman, 2004. 3–5.

Analyzing the Writer's Strategy

Marin's purpose is to show that while Goodman's essay is a suitable guide to how a family should function, it is an idealistic portrayal of the family, and thus ignores the harsher realities of many American households. In her opening, her strategy is to use narration to dramatize an anonymous character who could be anyone her reader might know.

Marin's thesis is clear. She states that "the truth is that for many Americans like the boy, the workings of the ideal family described in Goodman's essay are in sharp contrast with what actually goes on in their own families." She builds her support by incorporating direct quotations, and she contrasts these with her own experiences. For example, Marin writes: "Goodman assures us that "while the world may abandon us, the family promises . . . to protect us." She then shows how her friend Brahim's family deserted, rather than protected, him. In Marin's conclusion, she returns to the notion that "Goodman's family belongs in another world that no amount of wishing and desiring could ever bring" to the friends she describes.

In your own evaluative essays, you will assess the original in light of your own views and experiences. You may find that you agree with some points that the author makes but not with all of them. Regardless of your stance, you will need to examine specific quotations from the original work.

⬤⬤ Practicing Writing an Evaluative Response Essay

1. Write an evaluative response to "Makes Learning Fun" (p. 304) that takes a stand on the use of computers in education. After fully explaining Stoll's position, use examples from your own academic experience to support or oppose his thesis and key points.

2. Use either "The Second Shift" (p. 84) or "Let 'em Eat Leftovers" (p. 91) to evaluate and respond to how domestic responsibilities were or are handled in your own household.

3. Evaluate and respond to the ideas in "The Good Daughter" (p. 20) in terms of your parents' expectations and your responses to them.

4. Respond to and evaluate any of the essays in *Between Worlds*, perhaps one that has not been discussed in class.

Final Tips for an Evaluative Response

• Read carefully the essay you intend to evaluate, underlining or recording in a journal any language that you find interesting.

• Determine whether you agree with or oppose the author's main point and shape this view into your thesis.

• Find good material in the text, especially choice language, as well as examples from your own experience to support your position.

• Reread the original essay after you have written your evaluative response to see if there is additional material you should pull into your paper.

Definition

Whether your entire essay is a definition or you have incorporated a definition into your essay to clarify a term or concept for your reader, explaining what a term means is an integral part of writing. Knowing your intended audience and purpose in writing will help you determine which words you need to define.

When to Use Definition

In a paper for a psychology class, for example, you would not need to define terms generally used in that field. But when you write for a general reader and use language unfamiliar to most people—a technical or foreign term, or a word peculiar to an academic discipline—you will need to define the term so your reader can understand it. Even if you are using a familiar word, you need to explain its meaning if you or an author you are quoting use it in a unique way.

Sometimes a brief definition is all that you need. In that case, a few words of clarification, or even a synonym, may be incorporated into your text quite easily:

> *Los Vendidos,* or "The Sellouts," is the Spanish-language title of Luis Valdez's play.

> Achondroplasia—a type of dwarfism—may affect overall bone structure and cause arms and legs to be disproportionately smaller than the rest of the body.

> Eating disorders include "bingeing, chronic dieting, and 'aerobic nervosa,' the excessive use of exercise to remain one's body ideal" (Erens 251).

As these examples show, incorporating definition into your text is unobtrusive and superior to writing a separate sentence to define the term.

However, formal definition may be required for some writing situations. In that case, you will need to follow the dictionary model of establishing the term in a class and then distinguishing the term from its class by citing its difference, or *differentia:*

> Haiku is a form of poetry composed of seventeen syllables in a 5–7–5 pattern of three lines.

> A paring chisel is a woodworking tool with a knife-sharp edge, pushed by hand and used to finish a rough cut of wood.

Organizing and Developing a Definition Essay

When an assignment calls for an extended definition of a concept or term, the following methods may be used alone or in combination:

- *Dictionary definition:* Including a formal definition of a word from a dictionary before developing your point. Even common words may require you to take this route so that you and your reader have the same sphere of reference.

- *Expert's definition:* Presenting an expert's definition of a term to show that you have sound support for your understanding of a word.

- *Comparison-contrast:* Contrasting your definition of a word with the way it is typically used or with the actual dictionary definition of the term. If the term is unfamiliar, you might show how it is similar to another concept.

- *Description:* Defining a term by describing its characteristics: size, shape, texture, color, noise, and other telling traits.

- *Exemplification:* Giving examples and illustrations of a concept to enable your reader to understand it better. Because such examples are rather specific, they should only help supplement a definition rather than be used by themselves.

- *Negation:* Explaining what something is NOT in order to help limit the definition and eliminate misconceptions.

The Purpose of Defining

You may be asked to write a "definition essay"—a paper that develops with the primary intention of increasing the reader's understanding of a term—in a psychology, sociology, history, philosophy, or English course. Usually, however, your goal will be something else. You may be attempting to convince your reader to consider the explained term in a positive light, or to compare it—even to prefer it—to something else. Sometimes the persuasive aspect of the essay relies on the reader's understanding the definition of a word, as occurs in the next essay.

EXAMPLE: AN ESSAY BASED ON DEFINITION

The following essay was written by Andrew Vachss (pronounced "Vax"), an attorney who has 30 years experience exclusively protecting young people. He has been a federal investigator in sexually transmitted diseases, a social services caseworker, and director of a maximum-security prison for "aggressive-violent" youth. More information about Mr. Vachss and his work is available at vachss.com. Throughout this essay, Vachss relies on definition to build his argument.

The Difference Between
"Sick" and "Evil"
Andrew Vachss

1   The shock waves caused by the recent exposures of so-called "pedophile priests" have reverberated throughout America. But beneath our anger and revulsion, a fundamental question pulsates: Are those who abuse positions of trust to prey upon children—a category certainly not limited to those in religious orders—sick . . . Or are they evil?

2   We need the answer to that fundamental question. Because, without the truth, we cannot act. And until we act, nothing will change.

3   My job is protecting children. It has taken me from big cities to rural outposts, from ghettos to penthouses and from courtrooms to genocidal battlefields. But whatever the venue, the truth remains constant: Some humans intentionally hurt children. They commit unspeakable acts—for their pleasure, their profit, or both.

4   Many people who hear of my cases against humans who rape, torture and package children for sale or rent immediately respond with, "That's sick!" Crimes against children seem so grotesquely abnormal that the most obvious explanation is that the perpetrator must be mentally ill—helpless in the grip of a force beyond his or her control.

5   But that very natural reaction has, inadvertently, created a special category of "blameless predator." That confusion of "sick" with "sickening" is the single greatest barrier to our primary biological and ethical mandate: the protection of our children.

6   The difference between sick and evil cannot be dismissed with facile eye-of-the-beholder rhetoric. There are specific criteria we can employ to give us the answers in every case, every time.

7   Some of those answers are self-evident and beyond dispute: A mother who puts her baby in the oven because she hears voices commanding her to bake the devil out of the child's spirit is sick; and a mother who sells or rents her baby to child pornographers is evil. But most cases of children sexual abuse—especially those whose "nonviolent" perpetrators come from within the child's circle of trust—seem, on their surface, to be far more complex.

8   That complexity is an illusion. The trust is as simple as it is terrifying:

9   Sickness is a condition.

10   Evil is a behavior.

11   Evil is always a matter of choice. Evil is not thought; it is conduct. And that conduct is always volitional.

12   And just as evil is always a choice, sickness is always the absence of choice. Sickness happens. Evil is inflicted.

13   Until we perceive the difference clearly, we will continue to give aid and comfort to our most pernicious enemies. We, as a society, decide whether something is sick or evil. Either decision confers an obligation upon us. Sickness should be treated. Evil must be fought.

14   If a person has desires or fantasies about sexually exploiting children, that individual may be sick. (Indeed, if such desires are disturbing, as opposed to gratifying to the individual, there may even be a "cure.") But if the individual chooses to act upon those feelings, that conduct is evil. People are not what they think; they are what they do.

15   Our society distrusts the term "evil." It has an almost biblical ring to it—something we believe in (or not) but never actually understand. We prefer scientific-sounding terms, such as "sociopath." But sociopathy is not a mental condition; it is a specified cluster of behaviors. The diagnosis is only made from actual criminal conduct.

16   No reputable psychiatrist claims to be able to cure a sociopath—or, for that matter, a predatory pedophile. Even the most optimistic professionals do not aim to change such a person's thoughts and feelings. What they hope is that the predator can learn self-control, leading to a change in behavior.

17   Such hopes ignore the inescapable fact that the overwhelming majority of those who prey upon children don't want to change their behavior—they want only to minimize the consequences of being caught at it.

18   In the animal kingdom, there is a food chain—predators and prey. But among humans, there is no such natural order. Among our species, predators select themselves for that role.

19   Psychology has given us many insights of great value. But it also has clouded our vision with euphemisms. To say a person suffers from the "disease" of pedophilia is to absolve the predator of responsibility for his behavior.

20   Imagine if an attorney, defending someone accused of committing a dozen holdups, told the jury his poor client was suffering from "armed-robberia." That jury would decide that the only crazy person in this courtroom was the lawyer.

21   When a perpetrator claims to be sick, the *timing* of that claim is critical to discovering the truth. Predatory pedophiles carefully insinuate themselves into positions of trust. They select their prey and approach cautiously. Gradually, sometimes over a period of years, they gain greater control over their victims. Eventually, they leave dozens of permanently damaged children in their wake.

22   But only when they are caught do predatory pedophiles declare themselves to be sick. And the higher the victim count, the sicker (and therefore less responsible) they claim to be.

23   In too many cases, a veil of secrecy and protection then descends. The predator's own organization appoints itself judge and jury. The perpetrator is deemed sick and sent off for in-house "treatment." The truth is never made public. And when some secret tribunal decides that a cure has been achieved, the perpetrator's rights and privileges are restored, and he or she is given a new assignment.

24   In fact, such privileged predators actually are assisted. They enter new communities with the blessing of their own organization, their history and propensities kept secret. As a direct result, unsuspecting parents entrust their children to them. Inevitably, the predator eventually resumes his or her conduct and preys upon children again. And when that conduct comes to light, the claim of "sickness" re-emerges as well.

25   Too often, our society contorts itself to excuse such predators. We are so eager to call those who sexually abuse children "sick," so quick to understand their demons. Why? Because sickness not only offers the possibility of finding a cure but also assures us that the predator didn't really mean it. After all, it is human nature to try to understand inhuman conduct.

26   Conversely, the concept of evil terrifies us. The idea that some humans *choose* to prey upon our children is frightening, and their demonstrated skill at camouflage only heightens this fear.

27   For some, the question, "Does evil exist?" is philosophical. But for those who have confronted or been victimized by predatory pedophiles, there is no question at all. We are what we do.

28   Just as conduct is a choice, so is our present helplessness. We may be powerless to change the arrogance of those who believe they alone should have the authority to decide whether predatory pedophiles are "sick" or when they are "cured." But, as with the perpetrators themselves, we do have the power to change their behavior.

29   In every state, laws designate certain professions that regularly come into contact with children—such as teachers, doctors, social workers and day-care employees—as "mandated reporters." Such personnel are required to report reasonable suspicion of child abuse when it comes to their attention. Failure to do so is a crime.

30   Until now, we have exempted religious organizations from mandated-reporter laws. Recent events have proved the catastrophic consequences of this exemption. We must demand—now—that our legislators close this pathway to evil.

31   A predatory pedophile who is recycled into an unsuspecting community enters it cloaked with a protection no other sex offender enjoys. If members

of religious orders were mandated reporters, we would not have to rely on their good-faith belief that a predator is cured. We could make our own informed decisions on this most vital issue.

32   Modifying the law in this way would not interfere with priest-penitent privileges: When child victims or their parents disclose abuse, they are not confessing, they are crying for help. Neither confidentiality nor religious freedom would in any way be compromised by mandatory reporting.

33   Changing the laws so that religious orders join the ranks of mandated reporters is the right thing to do. And the time is right now.

Analyzing the Writer's Strategy

The purpose of this essay is to convince the reader that there is a difference between "evil" and "sick," and that unless we understand this critical distinction, we will continue to protect criminals, even priests, who deserve to be punished. Further, Vachss argues that priests should not be exempt from the "mandated reporter" laws that apply to all other professionals who work with children.

- *Comparison-contrast:* Vachss devotes much of his essay to defining "evil" as a behavior and contrasting it with "sick," which he sees as a condition. He insists that "evil is always a matter of choice. Evil is not thought; it is conduct. And that conduct is always volitional." He stresses that "evil is inflicted." In contrast, he claims that "sickness is always the absence of choice. Sickness happens. " The author must convince the reader of the clear distinction between these terms in order to reach his goal: the punishment of individuals who commit evil acts. Indeed, Vachss continues contrasting these terms as he argues, "Sickness should be treated. Evil must be fought."

- *Negation:* The author recognizes that our immediate response to horrific behavior against children is to exclaim, "That's sick." However, he points out that what we really mean is that the repulsive behavior is "sickening." We must not conflate these two terms. We are so appalled by crimes against children that we assume the perpetrator is mentally ill. If we see the predators of children as "sick" or mentally ill, we think of them as "blameless" and feel an obligation to treat and cure them. Vachss warns that we should not use the word "sick" to describe the criminal when we really mean that his or her behavior is "sickening." Throughout his essay, Vachss negates the use of the word "sick" to describe "evil" behavior.

- *Connotation:* Vachss anticipates the reader's possible aversion to the word "evil." He writes, "Our society distrusts the term 'evil.' It has an almost biblical ring to it." In an essay that relies on definition, it is important that the writer acknowledges the connotation or associations that readers have with particular words. Vachss notes that readers may reject the term "evil" because of their subjective associations with this word. He further recognizes that people prefer "scientific-sounding terms, such as 'sociopath.'" However, he rejects that term because it connotes mental illness; he stresses that "sociopathy is not a mental condition" but a "cluster of behaviors" that are criminal.

- *Euphemism:* Our language is filled with euphemisms—inoffensive terms that often obscure what we really mean (p. 612). Vachss observes that the field of psychology has provided us with useful insights but also has "clouded our vision with euphemisms." If we think of pedophilia as a "disease," we "absolve the predator of responsibility for his behavior." This euphemism destroys our correct perception of the pedophile as a criminal who needs to be punished.

- *Exemplification:* Vachss expands his definition of "sick" and "evil" by including examples of each. He illustrates "sick" by describing a mother who hears voices mandating her to put her baby in the oven. He exemplifies "evil" as the mother who sells or rents her baby to child pornographers.

- *Definition:* Vachss cites the laws that designate that people who work with children—teachers, doctors, social workers and day-care employees—are "mandated reporters." He must define this legal term because his readers will not be familiar with it and yet the concept is critical to his argument. The author's goal is to convince his reader that religious institutions, thus far exempt from "mandated-reporter laws," should be legally required to report suspected child abusers, even fellow clergy.

In this argument essay, Andrew Vachss uses these different methods of definition to persuade his readers of his thesis: "Changing the laws so that religious orders join the ranks of mandated reporters is the right thing to do."

 ## Practicing Writing Definition Essays

1. In your college papers, you will frequently use short definitions to clarify terms. In small groups, armed with dictionaries, practice writing one-sentence definitions of the following terms:

   a. schizophrenia

   b. satire

   c. Marxist

   d. interface

   e. Cubist

   f. picaresque

2. Although you will use definition most often as a component of your papers, it is useful to practice writing short definition essays. In small groups, collaborate with your classmates to write a short essay that defines one of the following:

    a. power

    b. "between worlds"

    c. artifice

    d. witty

    e. unconditional love

    f. disabled

3. Read a current newspaper or magazine article that reports a repugnant crime. Using the definitions Vachss gives in his essay, determine whether the perpetrator is "sick" or "evil."

Final Tips for a Definition Essay

*   Is your purpose for defining to inform? To analyze? To persuade?

*   Identify the needs of your audience; determine the terms that your readers cannot be expected to know or may misunderstand.

*   Decide if your definition will be a part of your essay or comprise the entire piece.

*   Whenever possible, incorporate into your text the necessary clarification of a term. Avoid writing a separate sentence to define the term.

*   For a formal definition, first establish the term in a class and then distinguish it from this class by citing its difference.

*   Remember that definitions can also be developed by comparing and contrasting that word with other terms, by describing the characteristics of a term, by presenting examples, and by illustrating what the term is not.

Cause and Effect

Throughout your life you have been made aware of the consequences of your behavior: not getting your allowance because you didn't keep your room clean; winning a class election because you ran a vigorous campaign; getting a C on an exam because you didn't review all of the material. In all of these cases, a particular behavior seems to *cause* or result in a certain *effect.* In the case of the denied allowance, for example, your parents may have identified the cause: not keeping your room clean.

Causes are not always so easy to identify, however, for there may be a number of indirect causes of an action or inaction. For example, you may have won an election because of your reputation as a leader, your popularity, your opponent's inadequacies, your vigorous campaign, or even a cause that you may not have known about or been able to control. Effects usually are more evident: homeless families, few jobs for college graduates, small businesses failing, and houses remaining on the market for years are all obvious effects of a recession. What has caused the recession typically is more difficult to discern, but good critical thinking involves speculating about possible causes and their effects.

When to Use Cause-and-Effect Development

Cause-and-effect development can be used in diverse writing situations. For example, you would use this strategy to trace the reasons for a historical event, such as the causes and results of the American entry into World War II. You perceive cause-and-effect relationships when you analyze and write about broad social problems (like runaway teens) or more personal concerns (such as why you and your siblings are risk takers). All of these thinking and writing tasks invite you to examine the apparent effects and to question what has caused them. This questioning inevitably involves speculation about causes rather than absolute answers, but this speculation can lead to fruitful analysis and provocative papers.

Organizing and Developing a Cause-and-Effect Essay

To get started, you may want to brainstorm freely and let all of your hunches emerge. In fact, a lively prewriting session is the key to a lively cause-and-effect paper. To produce a paper that goes beyond predictable or obvious discussion, take time to think about diverse causes for an effect you have observed and to contemplate the most dramatic effects of causes that you perceive.

You may find that you want to focus more on the causes or on the effects rather than trying to spend equal time on both. The wording of your thesis will be critical to forecast your emphasis and clarify your stance to your reader. For example, the following essay focuses entirely on the effects of the writer's experience as a soldier in an unpopular war. Notice how he analyzes his feelings of shame, anger, envy, and pain—all effects of a single cause, serving in the Marines during the Vietnam War.

EXAMPLE: A CAUSE-AND-EFFECT ESSAY

Robert McKelvey's goal in "I Confess Some Envy" is to present an analysis of a social issue. McKelvey, a Bronze Star recipient for his service in Vietnam and now a child psychiatrist and professor at Baylor University, analyzes the causes of the envy he felt while watching the Desert Storm troops receive public acclaim. He cites the reasons that his generation of soldiers failed to gain support and the effects of this failure on him and his peers. This essay first appeared in the *Los Angeles Times* on June 16, 1991, shortly after the return of American troops from the Persian Gulf.

I Confess Some Envy
Robert McKelvey

1   Every year on the Marine Corps' birthday, the commandant sends a message to all Marine units worldwide commemorating the event. On November 10, 1969, I was stationed with the 11th Marine Regiment northwest of Da Nang in Vietnam. It was my task to read the commandant's message to the Marines of our unit.

2   One sentence, in particular, caught my attention: "Here's to our wives and loved ones supporting us at home." Ironically, that week my wife had joined tens of thousands of others marching on the nation's capital to protest U.S. involvement in Vietnam.

3   It was a divisive, unhappy time. Few people believed the war could be won or that we had any right to interfere in Vietnam's internal affairs. However, for those of us "in country," there was a more pressing issue. Our lives were on the line. Even though our family and friends meant us no harm by protesting our efforts, and probably believed they were speeding our return, their actions had a demoralizing effect.

4   Couldn't they at least wait until we were safely home before expressing their distaste for what we were doing? But by then, the military had become

scapegoats for the nation's loathing of its war, a war where draft dodgers were cast as heroes and soldiers as villains.

5   Watching the Desert Storm victory parades on television, I was struck by the contrast between this grand and glorious homecoming and the sad, silent and shameful return of so many of us 20-odd years ago. Disembarking from a troop ship in Long Beach, my contingent of Marines was greeted at the pier by a general and a brass band. There were no family, friends, well-wishers, representatives of the Veterans of Foreign Wars, or children waving American flags.

6   We were bused to Camp Pendleton, quickly processed and sent our separate ways. After a two-week wait for my orders to be cut, during which time I spent most days at the San Diego Zoo, I was discharged from active duty. I packed up and flew home to begin premedical studies.

7   As the plane landed in Detroit, the on-board classical music channel happened to be playing Charles Ives's "America." The piece's ironic, teasing variations on the theme, "My Country 'Tis of Thee," seemed a fitting end to my military service.

8   My wife met me at the airport and drove me directly to Ann Arbor for a job interview. We were candidates for a job as house parents for the Religious Society of Friends (Quakers) International Co-op. Face to face with these sincere, fervent pacifists, I felt almost ashamed of the uniform I was still wearing with its ribbons and insignia.

9   I recalled stories of comrades who had been spat upon in airports and called "baby killers." The Friends, however, were exceptionally gentle and kind. They, at least, seemed able to see beyond the symbols of the war they hated to the individual human being beneath the paraphernalia. Much to my surprise, we got the job.

10   I took off my uniform that day, put it away and tried to resume the camouflage of student life. I seldom spoke of my service in Vietnam. It was somehow not a topic for polite conversation, and when it did come up the discussion seemed always to become angry and polarized.

11   Like many other Vietnam veterans, I began to feel as if I had done something terribly wrong in serving my country in Vietnam, and that I had better try to hush it up. I joined no veterans' organizations and, on those rare times when I encountered men who had served with me in Vietnam, I felt embarrassed and eager to get away. We never made plans to get together and reminisce. The past was buried deep within us, and that is where we wanted it to stay.

12   The feelings aroused in me by the sight of our victorious troops marching across the television screen are mixed and unsettling. There is pride, of course, at their stunning achievement. Certainly they deserve their victory parade. But there is also envy. Were we so much different from them?

13   Soldiers do not choose the wars they fight. Theirs happened to be short and sweet, ours long and bitter. Yet we were all young men and women doing what our country had asked us. Seeing my fellow Vietnam veterans marching with the Desert Storm troops, watching them try, at last, to be recognized and applauded for their now-distant sacrifices, is poignant and sad.

14   We have come out of hiding in recent years as the war's pain has receded. It has become almost fashionable to be a veteran and sport one's jungle fatigues. Still, a sense of hurt lingers and, with it, a touch of anger. Anger that the country we loved, and continue to love, could use us, abuse us, discard and then try to forget us, as if we were the authors of her misery rather than her loyal sons and daughters. It was our curious, sad fate to be blamed for the war we had not chosen to fight, when in reality we were among its victims.

Analyzing the Writer's Strategy

McKelvey's purpose is to express his pain and sorrow as he reviews his history as a veteran of the Vietnam War. He analyzes the causes of his personal frustrations and the effects of American response to that war in contrast to the response to the Persian Gulf War twenty years later.

McKelvey's strategy is to dramatize moments in his personal history and to lead his reader to discover the irony implicit in these events. For example, while he was reading to his unit the commandant's message applauding the support of "wives and loved ones" at home, his own wife had joined a massive demonstration in Washington protesting U.S. involvement in Vietnam. McKelvey contrasts the "grand and glorious homecoming" of the Desert Storm Troops with his own "sad, silent and shameful return." He shows himself "almost ashamed" of his uniform with its ribbons and insignia when he applied to be a house parent for the Quakers. He notes that "soldiers do not choose the wars they fight," and yet the Desert Storm troops were celebrated as heroes while he and his fellow vets from Vietnam were called "baby killers" and spat upon when they returned.

Through irony, McKelvey helps his reader understand the effects of the anti-Vietnam War sentiment on one individual who articulates for many suffering but silent soldiers, also the "victims" of that war. He avoids using the terms "cause" and "effect" or the predictable "cause and effect" paragraph structure, favoring instead subtle juxtaposition of causes and their profound effects.

 PRACTICING WRITING ESSAYS ABOUT CAUSES AND EFFECTS

Write an essay that focuses on the causes and/or effects of one of the following:

1. Your having revealed an important truth about yourself to a member of your family

2. A friend or family member abusing alcohol or using drugs

3. Your family getting together for a holiday occasion

4. Being misjudged by someone's first impressions of you as described in "Appearances" (p. 228)

5. Your sense of being caught living between two worlds, as Marcus Mabry (p. 144), Kim Edwards (p. 161), and Judith Ortiz Cofer (223) describe

6. Your discovery that you are unwillingly intimidating others, as Brent Staples describes (p. 237)

7. Your feeling of being manipulated by the media's depiction of ideal female body shapes as discussed by Rachel Krell (p. 382) and Jenny Jones (p. 258)

Final Tips for Cause and Effect Development

- Brainstorm energetically to come up with every possible cause and/or effect for your particular topic.

- Review your list of causes and effects to determine whether each point is reasonable and supportable. Eliminate any that are illogical or for which you lack data. Do research if additional evidence is needed.

- Apply the "So what?" standard (see pp. 356 and 361–362). Will this cause or effect analysis make worthwhile reading?

- Group ideas that belong together and order your evidence to conclude with your most emphatic and well-developed support.

- Develop your explanations fully so that your reader doesn't need to guess your assumptions.

Comparison and Contrast

Whether you are examining your own experiences or responding to texts, you will inevitably rely on comparison and contrast thinking. To realize how two people, places, works of art, films, economic plans, laboratory procedures, or aspects of literature—or anything else—may be alike or different is to perceive important distinctions between them.

While we may start an analysis process believing that two subjects are remarkably different (how they *contrast*), after thoughtful scrutiny we may see that there are important similarities between them. Conversely, although we may have detected clear similarities in two subjects (how they *compare*), the complete analysis may reveal surprising differences. Therefore, while comparison implies similarity and contrast implies difference, these two thinking processes work together to enhance perception.

When to Use Comparison-Contrast Development

Subtle comparison-contrast cues are embedded in writing assignments, both in-class exams and out-of-class papers. For example, an economics instructor may ask for a study of prewar and postwar inflation; a philosophy instructor may ask for examples showing how one philosophical system departs from another; a psychology instructor may require an explanation of how two different psychologists interpret dreams; or a literature instructor may assign an analysis of how a character changes within a certain novel.

The prevalence of such assignments in all disciplines underscores the importance of comparison and contrast in many experiences and learning situations. Assignments that ask writers to explain the unfamiliar, evaluate certain choices, analyze how someone or something has changed, establish distinction, discover similarities, and propose a compromise all require some degree of comparison and contrast.

For example, a writer may initially believe that women and men have quite different complaints about their lives. Women feel that they need to be attractive; they feel limited in their choice of career and restricted by the career heights and pay they may attain; and they feel obligated to be domestic (good mothers, cooks, and housekeepers). Men feel they need to be successful at work to be attractive to women; they feel burdened to select high-status, high-paying jobs regardless of their real interests; and they must work continuously. Many feel precluded from domestic life—cut off from their children and home life.

At first, the complaints of each gender appear to be quite different. But the writer examining these complaints may perceive that they have something in common: that women *and* men suffer from "an invisible curriculum," a series of social expectations that deprive human beings of choice. A thesis for this study might look like this:

> **Thesis:** Although women and men seem to have different problems, both genders feel hampered by an "invisible curriculum" that affects their self-esteem and limits their choices at work and in their families.

Organizing and Developing a Comparison-Contrast Essay

There are two basic methods for organizing data to compare or contrast. In the **block** method, the writer would organize the material for a study of conflicts affecting gender like this:

BLOCK 1. WOMEN

1. Need to feel attractive to be successful
2. Feel limited in workplace choices, level, pay
3. Feel obligated to be mothers, domestic successes

BLOCK 2. MEN

1. Need to feel successful at work to feel attractive
2. Feel burdened to achieve high position, work continuously
3. Feel cut off from children and domestic choices

In the **point-by-point** method, the writer would organize the material like this:

POINT 1. FACTORS THAT GOVERN SELF-ESTEEM

a. Women need to feel attractive
b. Men need to feel successful at work

POINT 2. RELATIONSHIP TO WORK

a. Women feel restricted in choice, level, pay
b. Men feel burdened to achieve high position, work continuously

Which Method to Use: Block or Point by Point?

Although the block method may seem easier, it tends to allow the writer to ramble vaguely about each subject without concentrating on specific points of comparison or contrast. The resulting essay may resemble two separate discussions that could be cut apart with scissors. The advantage of the point-by-point method is that it keeps the writer focused on the relationship between both works and on the similarities or differences between them. Writers are less likely to digress and wander off-topic in a point-by-point arrangement and they are more likely to emphasize the points that they are making. Moreover, the summary statement that appears at the end of each paragraph in point-by-point organization tends to unify the essay more emphatically than the summary statement at the end of each block.

EXAMPLE: A COMPARISON-CONTRAST ESSAY

Writers do not always announce their intention to compare and contrast in their thesis, even though comparison and contrast elements predominate in the development of their thinking and writing. The following essay, published in the *Los Angeles Times* on June 16, 1999, was written by Alex Garcia, a staff photographer who lived in Cuba for several months. Although Garcia does not articulate his contrast plan in a thesis, from the first sentence of his essay he makes clear his intention to contrast the worlds of the United States and Cuba.

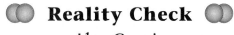

Reality Check

Alex Garcia

1   It appears Uncle Sam and El Comandante, while not quite seeing eye to eye, are exchanging curious glances. On baseball fields, in concert halls and in schoolyards, the citizens of Cuba and the United States have recently been getting a glimpse of cultures that have been closed to one another for four decades. The United States says it hopes these exchanges will make it easier to export cultural values to Fidel Castro's Cuba. But it's worth underscoring that such exchanges go both ways.

2   I recently spent several months in Havana and the Cuban countryside as part of a language and cultural program hosted by San Francisco–based Global Exchange, one of the few organizations in the United States that legally sponsors trips to the island. As someone of Cuban origin, I stepped into such waters cautiously.

3   I have a cousin now living in the United States who risked his life swimming to the naval base at Guantánamo Bay to escape what he considers a prison. I also have a cousin who became president of his neighborhood block committee in Havana out of loyalty to what he believes is a worker's paradise. Both have made tremendous sacrifices to stay true to the values they

hold dear. That I would find some of my values in conflict with those I found in Cuba came as no surprise. But I was uncomfortable with how even my most basic assumptions would be challenged.

4   For example, as one of our core values, U.S. citizens presume the inherent goodness of individualism, of being ruggedly independent, John Wayne-style. So it came as a surprise when one of my tutors said, "I would never want to think of myself as independent." "Me neither," another said coldly.

5   Come again? As a program participant, I was paired with University of Havana students who served as language tutors and cultural assistants. We had been talking about their future hopes, and I had asked what they were going to do once they were independent.

6   "Being independent means being selfish, cold, unwilling to help other people," my tutor told me. After years of struggling to be independent myself, I was at first uneasy with that idea. But I recalled the communal spirit of the many Cubans I met: the ubiquitous hitchhikers getting free rides from passing motorists; neighbors borrowing the car and the telephone as if they were family; hotel workers trading shifts and bicycles in a spirit of *compañerismo,* or camaraderie.

7   And there was the pedestrian who jumped into my cab to mooch a ride, defending his appropriation of my fare by saying to the driver, "Hey we're Cuban, aren't we?" I can't imagine hitchhiking in downtown Los Angeles, or even calling my neighbor "cousin," much less sharing with him a roll of toilet paper—a commodity rationed in Cuba. The U.S. model encourages people to value individual effort over shared sacrifice. But to many Cubans, it can seem a lonely path to take.

8   Expressing the values I believe the United States stands for was not simple either, in large part because Cuban television shows the flip side of them, through news and entertainment. For instance, if I cite civil liberties, the state-run television network Cubavision will air a Hollywood movie about the Ku Klux Klan, hate crimes or out-of-control gangbangers in Los Angeles. If I advocate multi-party democracy, a Cubavision documentary will point to a two-party system in the United States tainted by special-interest money and embarrassed by a 30% voter turnout. If I stress the benefits of upward mobility, the government-controlled national newspaper *Granma* will remark that the majority of people who are born in poverty in the United States die in poverty.

9   Fair or not, the contrarian views fostered in the Cuban media take away the shine with which we like to present ourselves.

10   Wastefulness isn't exactly one of my core values, but it certainly revealed itself as a personal trait while I was in Cuba. Given the choice between buying a new backpack, or repairing an old one by hand—sewing it with used dental

floss—which do you think I chose? Or using my family's old kerosene lantern during blackouts versus pulling out my fancy flashlight that, oops, used expensive and rare batteries? Or tossing plastic bottles without considering their secondary storage value? I guess seeing thousands of commercials by age 10 has pushed me to think: "Where can I go to get or buy what I need?"

11   By contrast, most Cubans first ask, "What do I already have that I could use?" Some even bragged about such *resolver,* or resourcefulness. My relatives, not terribly amused with my lack of *resolver,* were quite patient. Their frugality is probably borne of necessity rather than virtue, but my lack of it was embarrassing to me. Perhaps I've been too busy shopping for values instead of cultivating them.

12   More embarrassing was a discussion about personal hygiene and what it seems to say about one's priorities. I was blindsided when asked, "Why do you all have the habit of showering in the morning before work instead of after work? You mean to tell me you come home to be with your family or friends, and you don't shower then? You go to bed with your wife after a full day of sweat? Eeeeeyyyyewww!"

13   It was surprising for me, as an American photojournalist, to see how images in our media that seem clear-cut can have quite another meaning for a Cuban. In Havana, I met a Cuban photographer working for an international news agency who showed me a picture he'd taken that day. It was of Castro, excitedly raising his fists in the air as he stood behind a lectern. "Ha? Ha? Isn't that great?" the photographer said proudly. "This will show the exiles in Miami that Fidel is still going strong!" I looked at him, incredulous. From a certain U.S. perspective, the gray-haired leader waving his fists appeared as the stereotypical crazed pariah.

14   Becoming aware of our own preconceptions or biases, and accepting them, may well be the ultimate value of any culture exchange. Staging a sing-along, a ballgame or other cultural encounter might have great symbolic value and surface appeal. But if the two nations are to make a genuine connection and resolve the decades' old conflict, we need to look deeper and not get lost on an island of assumptions.

Analyzing the Writer's Strategy

Garcia's stance is established in his first sentence, when he shows his footing in two worlds, the United States and Cuba. He creates the image of "Uncle Sam and El Comandante . . . not quite seeing eye to eye . . . exchanging curious glances" to establish the *differences* in the two cultures he observed during his stay in Cuba. Using these informal nicknames, he establishes a lighthearted tone that softens the negative aspects of American values as viewed through the eyes of his Cuban hosts.

Garcia notes that while the goal of the language and cultural program is that it "will make it easier to export cultural values to Fidel Castro's Cuba," ironically he returned questioning his own values. Irony abounds in his family background and in the discoveries he makes. He has family on both sides of the political spectrum: one cousin escaped Cuba, calling it "a prison," and another cousin serves as a leader in Cuba, believing it to be "a worker's paradise." Therefore, Garcia expected to find some of his values in conflict with those he found in Cuba, but he did not expect to have his "most basic assumptions" challenged. Rather than promoting American values to the Cubans, Garcia came to question them.

Garcia's sense of irony comes through in his examples of American life that don't make sense to Cubans: that American individualism is won at the expense of greater good for the group, that American civil liberties allow the existence of racist groups such as the Ku Klux Klan, that Americans enjoy the right to vote but turn out in embarrassingly low numbers, that America is praised as the land of opportunity yet most of its citizens who are born poor also die poor. As he says, "The contrarian views fostered in the Cuban media take away the shine with which we like to present ourselves."

After exposing the ironies of public and political life, Garcia moves to personal observations on his wastefulness, indifference to environmental protection, and consumerism, and he concludes that perhaps he has been "too busy shopping for values instead of cultivating them." His carefully worked out irony and well-chosen words earn him the empathy rather than the antagonism of his American readers.

To illustrate how far apart cultural perceptions can be, Garcia juxtaposes two responses to the same photo of Castro, with his fists raised. The Cuban's view is that the photo shows Fidel is "still going strong," but the American is more likely to see the gray-haired leader as "the stereotypical crazed pariah." Garcia concludes his essay by admitting that the highest value of a cultural exchange program might be that we become "aware of our own preconceptions or biases." By acknowledging that his stay in Cuba forced him to confront his own assumptions, he creates the same opportunity for his reader. He finally hopes that both nations will "make a genuine connection" and "not get lost on an island of assumptions," a final well-crafted allusion to the isolation of cultural boundaries.

 ## Practicing Writing Essays That Use Comparison and Contrast

Select one topic to write an essay that uses comparison or contrast.

1. A family member's response to an important decision; how you expected that person to respond

2. A perception of a family member that you held in your youth; a view of that person that you have today

3. Your understanding or interpretation of a particular movie, song, or event; a friend's view of the same thing

4. Your concept of ideal employment; a job you have held or hold now

5. The role of computers in education as described in "Makes Learning Fun" (p. 304) and "From Learning as Torture to Learning as Fun" (p. 313)

6. The authors' attitudes about being fat in "Discrimination at Large" (p. 243) and in "O.K., So I'm Fat" (p. 247)

7. The father-child relationship in "Peaches" (p. 147) and in "Proper Care and Maintenance" (p. 186)

Final Tips for Comparison and Contrast

- Make sure that your thesis includes both subjects that are being compared and contrasted, and that the wording is specific. Avoid a thesis that simply claims they are both alike and different.

- Consider using the point-by-point method of comparison-contrast for a more emphatic delivery of information.

- Continue interrelating the two subjects so that you never make a point about one without showing how it relates to the other.

- Search for subtle links and distinctions as well as for the obvious ones. Then analyze the reasons for those differences.

Argument

Convincing others that your beliefs and perspectives are worth understanding, and perhaps even supporting, can be a definite challenge. Sometimes you may have to counter both preconceptions and convictions in order to get readers to modify their beliefs or change their behavior. In fact, persuasion is a part of many writing situations, and to convince a reader that a certain assertion or opinion is supportable is the heart of argument.

Arguments and Proposals

A distinction can be made between two types of writing that attempt to convince readers to reconsider their views and beliefs:

An *argument* employs logic to reason a point and get the reader to think.

A *proposal* employs logic to influence others and get the reader to think and act.

Although these types of writing often overlap, some assignments seem to fit more in one category than the other. If you are asked to analyze an essay and argue for or against the writer's views, your essay will involve *argumentation*. You will be expected to focus on a thesis that can provoke the reader's thoughts and to use supporting evidence that is logically presented and carefully analyzed.

If you are asked to offer a solution to a problem or to persuade others to modify or change their behavior, your essay will need to include a *proposal* in addition to argumentation. You will be expected to focus on a thesis that provokes a response. Therefore you will also need to suggest a reasonable plan of action or activities for your reader.

When to Use Argument

Argument strategies may be used in all types of essays. Whenever you are attempting to convince a reader that one course of action is superior to another (comparison-contrast), that a particular behavior caused a certain consequence (cause and effect), or that one interpretation of a reading has validity (analysis), you will need to employ argument strategies. Because you are attempting to convince readers of a view that may be different from their own, it often helps to begin by illustrating what is wrong with the current thinking or practice on this issue.

For example, if a writer is arguing that female students in the early grades need greater encouragement to succeed in math and science classes, then it would make sense to establish the need first. The introduction and part of the body of the essay might demonstrate how females are discouraged from pursuing math and science majors and how few women today excel in these fields, even though studies indicate females are no less capable of succeeding in science and math than males are.

Audience and Argument

It is critical to identify one's *audience* and to find an approach that would best appeal to them. Identification of the audience may include asking these questions:

- Is the reader aware that the problem exists?
- Will the reader find the problem sufficiently important?
- Is the reader affected by the problem?
- Do any readers have special interests or biases that will cause them to resist the information? The argument? The essay?

If the writer can determine whether the audience is likely to be sympathetic, neutral, or hostile, the approach can then be designed with this in mind.

Organizing and Developing an Argument

An outline can be critical for keeping the argument focused and organized. Often this involves an informal list of points, written in a logical order, that the writer plans to cover. The outline may also help an instructor follow the argument and detect any flaws or gaps before the essay is actually written. In such cases, a more formal outline may be required. (For an illustration of an informal outline for an argument, see pp. 363–365.)

Avoiding Logical Fallacies

If the thinking and analysis in an argument are not logical and have no basis or foundation in reason, a *logical fallacy* will result, discrediting the argument and eroding the reader's trust. Let's look at some of the most common types:

- *Name-calling, personal attacks, illogical claims:* Whether intentional or not, these slurs are often associated with advertisers and politicians, whose careers may depend on their power to manipulate and mislead the public. Calling someone a "liberal" or a "redneck" is intended to get the audience to respond emotionally to a prejudice rather than to think rationally about an issue. Often these attacks are designed to divert attention from the issue to the opponent's personal traits or associates, with the aim of casting doubt on his or her character or expertise.

- *Circular argument:* Does not prove anything because it simply restates the assertion. ("Instructors who teach writing are better teachers because good instructors teach writing.")

- *Either/or argument:* Sets up a false black-and-white dilemma, assuming that a particular viewpoint or course of action can have only two diametrically opposed outcomes. ("College professors either require writing assignments or they are poor teachers.")

- *Hasty generalization:* Consists of drawing a broad conclusion from a few unrepresentative generalizations ("Math teachers use Scantron tests; math teachers don't teach students to think critically.")

- *False analogy:* Compares two things that aren't really comparable and therefore results in a false conclusion. ("If developmental math classes can be taught effectively in a large lecture hall, developmental English classes can be, too.")

- *Bandwagon appeal:* Suggests that "everyone is doing this—why don't you?" This pressures the reader to conform whether or not the view or action seems logical or right. ("All good teachers are dividing students into small-group workshops in their classes today.")

These are only some of the many logical fallacies that can weaken an argument. Instead of relying on illogical attacks and charges, writers must seek logical support for their positions and seek legitimate flaws in their opponent's argument.

Conceding and Refuting

Rather than twisting facts or attacking an opponent, it is best to anticipate objections and refute them, logically and directly, before the reader can utter "But . . .". Overlooking or ignoring potential holes in an argument can render it vulnerable to attack. Your argument will not necessarily be weakened if you recognize what may appear to be a weakness in your plan—provided you can refute it and show that it doesn't really undermine your argument.

Another effective strategy is to acknowledge conflicting viewpoints and perhaps even admit they have merit, but then show how your solution or viewpoint is still superior. Such a strategy suggests that you are informed, open-minded, and reasonable—qualities that will make the reader more receptive to your argument.

Arguments and proposals written by students can be more than mere classroom exercises. They can be sent to newspapers, television stations, corporations, and government boards. Several of the argument assignments in the "Writing from the Text" and "Connecting with Other Texts" sections in Part I involve college-related issues and may be appropriate for the editorial or opinion page of your campus or local newspaper.

Evaluating an Argument

As you read an argument, consider these questions to evaluate its effectiveness:

- Who is the targeted audience, and how does the writer appeal to this audience?
- What is the problem? What is the thesis?
- What are the supporting points?
- What are the strengths of the argument?
- Does the writer anticipate and refute objections?
- What are the weaknesses? Are there any logical fallacies?
- How does the ending bring satisfying closure to the essay?

EXAMPLE: AN ARGUMENT ESSAY

The following argument was written by Joe Goodwin, who was in high school when he published this essay in the "Campus Correspondence" section of the *Los Angeles Times* on August 9, 1992. Goodwin responds to the controversy surrounding a policy mandating community service for junior high through high school students in Maryland schools. In 1997, Maryland made it a graduation requirement that students need to complete seventy-five hours of community service. The numbers in the margin of this essay correspond to the numbers of the explanatory notes on the facing page.

My Favorite School Class: Involuntary Servitude

1 2   Like most teen-agers, I hate to be told what to do. I chafe
at curfews, refuse to patronize restaurants that tell me what to
wear, and complain daily about the braces my parents and dentist
want me to have. Yet, I look forward to the "forced opportunity"
3   for community service my high school requires. While criticism
4   mounts against Maryland's action in becoming the first state to
mandate students to perform 75 hours of community service over
seven years, it is well to look at the experience of local school
districts that have instituted similar programs.

For five years, every student at the Concord-Carlisle Re-
gional High School in Massachusetts has been required to perform
5a   40 hours of community service in order to graduate. Conventional
wisdom would have us believe that this would be an especially
burdensome task, perhaps an impossible one, for students who
hold outside paying jobs. But the graduation requirement may be
satisfied within the school by working as teacher's aides, library assistants, or tutors. Outside school, the requirement may
be met by working at hospitals, nursing homes, senior citizens'
centers, soup kitchens, or for the town's park service or recre-
ational department.

5b   To be sure, it would be wonderful if students volunteered
such service. But the great benefit of the mandated program is
the responsibility it places on the school to work with community leaders to locate the places where students can best make
a solid contribution. It is unrealistic to expect students to
roam from place to place in search of service opportunities.
Once the arrangements for those opportunities are made, the student needs only to decide which kind of service best fits his or
her personality.

5c   Those who oppose the community-service mandate fear it will
interfere with the regular school curriculum. But what more

Explanatory Notes for the Argument Essay

The numbers on these explanatory notes correspond to the numbers in the margin of the argument essay.

1. *Audience:* Goodwin's targeted audience is students, who might resist community service or their parents, who might not want the school day lengthened with extra work, or taxpayers or school boards, who might be voting on whether to institute the compulsory service requirement in their communities.

2. *Appeal:* Goodwin appeals to his audience by identifying himself as a typical teenager who "hate[s] to be told what to do." He creates an image of himself as a teen who resents curfews, dress codes, and wearing braces.

3. *Thesis:* Goodwin's thesis is that in spite of his resistance to being told what to do, he sees a program of mandatory community service as a valuable "forced opportunity" for students.

4. *Problem:* Goodwin identifies the problem as those who resist mandatory community service.

5. *Objections/Refutations:* Goodwin anticipates objections and refutes them:

   a. Doing community service is a burden for students who hold outside paying jobs. (Students can choose to work on campus or off.)

   b. Students should volunteer for such service. (He concedes that they should volunteer but believes that it is unrealistic to expect students to search for such opportunities on their own.)

   c. Community service will interfere with regular curriculum. (He believes that community service is as important as any class and that it teaches students to apply what they are learning in the classroom.)

6 important class can a student take than one that teaches values and responsibility? Clearly it is better to be helping the elderly and homeless rather than listening to long lectures about their plight.

5d Some say that schools should not be in the business of fostering civic concerns among its youth. But what more important role can a school play than in shaping values--respect for the elderly, patience for those younger, compassion for those less fortunate--among its young? These and related values used to be taught in the home. Now, they must be learned elsewhere, since we live in a world in which many families have two parents working long hours every day and many more have just a single parent.

7

8 Sociologists and journalists decry the decline of American society and the disintegration of the American family. Yet, when those who find pleasure in lecturing about this decline are faced with a solution that would help strengthen society, they fall back on the past. It is this negative attitude toward change that has caused the country to reach the point of such neglect.

9 Today, the passion and commitment that marked my parents' generation--the 1960s--is gone, replaced by an ominous silence. I listen to my parents talk of their experiences with the civil-rights movement, the sit-ins, the war on poverty, and I am impatient for the time when my own generation is similarly involved in the great public events of our day. Although 40 hours of community service is not very much, it is a beginning.

My interest in community service was heightened last spring. While on a class trip to the Science Museum in Boston, a group of students in my 8th-grade class were involved in an altercation with another group of students from a largely black school in Roxbury, a neighborhood near downtown. Taunts were exchanged, a fight broke out. It was unsettling.

Explanatory Notes *(continued)*

    d. Schools should not be in the business of fostering civic concerns among students. (He argues that schools must help shape values, especially since many children do not get such training at home.)

        Logical Fallacy: Goodwin's point about values is a good one, but he has a logical fallacy: *hasty generalization.* He claims that values "used to be taught in the home" and that homes with two parents working or with single parents are not teaching values. These are assumptions Goodwin can't support. He could have written "now values *may* need to be learned elsewhere" because *some* working or single parents *aren't always* available to teach values or reinforce the ones they have taught.

6. *Support:* Goodwin supports his argument by insisting that it is better to be working directly with the elderly rather than reading about or hearing lectures about their "plight."

7. *Support:* Goodwin supports his argument by asserting that the school should do what many homes are not doing—teaching and reinforcing the values "of respect for the elderly, patience for those younger, compassion for those less fortunate."

8. *Clarification:* Goodwin clarifies the problem: weak values contribute to the "decline of American society" and "the disintegration of the American family" and yet many people resist a program that could strengthen values.

9. *Support:* Goodwin supports his argument by arguing that the "passion and commitment" of his parents' generation, sadly lacking in youth today, might be reinvigorated by community service.

10   The following week, teachers from both schools arranged a daylong meeting of a representative sampling of students at each school. The discussion that resulted was an extraordinary experience. As I listened to black students describe their stereotypes of whites in the suburbs, as I heard one black girl say she cried herself to sleep the night of the fight in fear and frustration that racial relations would never improve, I realized how far America was from the ideals of equality and justice. If community service could help to bridge the gap between ideal and reality, I will feel happy indeed.

Explanatory Notes *(continued)*

10. *Logical fallacy:* Goodwin attempts to support his argument with a personal anecdote about a class trip to an inner-city museum. In his mind, his discovery on the trip supports the need for community service programs. However, his reasoning is not clear to the reader. Goodwin makes a leap that the reader can't comprehend. Goodwin may have meant that "community service could move students into worlds they don't routinely inhabit and could bridge communication gaps." If he had articulated the connection between the racial tension on the class trip and community service, he would have had a stronger conclusion to his argument.

Throughout his essay, Goodwin's tone is restrained and reasonable. His writing reflects a healthy balance between idealism (free choice) and realism (mandatory service). He might have been tempted to resort to name-calling or offensive attacks, but instead he relies on examples and explanation to support his case.

 ### PRACTICING WRITING ARGUMENT ESSAYS

Write an essay to convince your reader of one of the following assertions:

1. All college students, regardless of age, ethnicity, or status, are (or are not) caught "between worlds."

2. Graffiti taggers should (or should not) be prosecuted for leaving their marks around the community.

3. Year-round school is (or is not) a viable solution to overcrowding.

4. The lyrics in contemporary music reflect (or incite) societal tension.

5. Ward Churchill (p. 172) is correct (or incorrect) in saying that using Native American names for sport teams denigrates Native Americans.

6. Football should or should not be played in high school (p. 101).

7. The burka does or does not limit the world's perception of the woman who wears it (p. 168).

8. Rita should (or should not) continue her relationship with Marc (p. 147).

9. Internet dating is or is not a reliable way to meet a mate (p. 108).

Final Tips for Argument

- Recognize your purpose (argument or proposal).
- Identify your readers, consider their perspective, and prepare your appeal. Avoid insulting or attacking them.
- Word your thesis carefully to provoke thought or action.
- Outline your argument so it is focused and organized.
- Support all claims with convincing evidence and reasoned analysis.
- Anticipate objections and differing viewpoints, and show why your argument is stronger even if the others have some merit.
- Guard against logical fallacies; they weaken any argument.
- Make sure your conclusion brings satisfying closure to your argument. Avoid tacking on any new points.

Writing an Essay Exam

An in-class essay exam requires you to retrieve information that you know, to present it in an orderly way, and to develop your ideas in enough depth to convince your instructor that you understand the material. To prepare for an in-class essay, you should review reading material and class notes and anticipate possible test questions. Use the key words that follow to formulate possible questions that might be on the test. By anticipating the test questions, you will have reviewed the materials and, if you're lucky, one of your questions may appear on the exam. Here is a six-step strategy that will help you present information on the test itself.

A Six-Step Strategy

1. Read the question more than once.

2. Determine what the question specifically requires you to do. Have you been asked to *define, list, summarize, compare or contrast, explain,* or *analyze?* See the list on pages 458–459 for definitions of words that are commonly used on essay exams.

3. Briefly outline the material that will satisfy the question you were asked. Do not spend much time on this step; the outline can be brief, with only key words or phrases to remind you of material that you need to include.

4. Write a thesis that will focus your answer and possibly forecast the areas you will develop in your response to the question.

5. Write the essay.

6. Reread your answer to correct errors in spelling and grammar. Use a dictionary if you are permitted to bring one to the exam. Do *not* plan to rewrite; you will seldom have sufficient time. If you recall material that would improve your essay, indicate that you have an insertion and write the added material on another sheet of paper.

It is most important that you understand exactly what the question requires you to do. For example, if the test question asks you to *list* the chemical elements commonly called salts, you are to enumerate—present in a list or outline form—the specific chemical elements called salts. An essay is not required, would be inappropriate, and might cost you points. If the question asks you to *compare and contrast* two subjects, and you only show how the subjects contrast, you have missed part of the question—how the subjects compare. The chart that follows here will help you understand what is expected on exams. The first example in parentheses provides a typical exam topic from a college course; the second example is drawn from readings in this textbook.

Key Words Used on Exams

Word	Meaning and Examples
analyze	Break into elements or parts and examine ("Analyze the job of the Attorney General of the United States," or "Analyze the drawbacks of families in 'Are Families Dangerous?'").
compare	Look for and bring out points of similarity, qualities that resemble each other ("Compare the legislative branches of the state and national governments" or "Compare how Hochschild and McGrady perceive the job of the stay-at-home partner").
contrast	Stress the dissimilarities, differences ("Contrast the characteristics of an Impressionist portrait with a Cubist portrait" or "Contrast the parenting styles of Ace and Darnell").
define	Give the meaning of a word or concept ("Define the term *archetype*" or "Define the multiple meanings of the word *artifice* in 'A Work of Artifice'").
describe	Give an account, word picture, or narration ("Describe the Aztec civilization at Teotihuacan," or "Describe the characteristics of a child born with Down Syndrome").
discuss	Examine, consider from different points of view ("Discuss the use of pesticides in controlling mosquitoes" or "Discuss the problems inherent in playing high school football according to Don Sabo").
explain	Make clear, interpret, tell the meaning of, tell how ("Explain how humans can, at times, trigger a rainstorm" or "Explain the distinction that Vachss makes between 'sick' and 'evil'").
illustrate	Clarify with examples or analogies; exemplify ("Illustrate how current rap lyrics reflect inner city tensions" or "Illustrate how youth is disrespected in our culture according to Robin Swicord").
justify	Show good reason for, give evidence to support your position ("Justify the American bombing of Afghanistan" or "Justify changing sport team names that refer to Native Americans").
relate	Show correlation, how things are connected ("Relate an early childhood education program to elementary school academic success" or "Relate the pressures within a group to how people respond in an emergency").

summarize   Give the main points or facts in condensed form, omitting details ("Summarize the myth of Oedipus" or "Summarize 'Where Are You Going, Where Have You Been?'").

trace   In narrative form, describe the progress, development, or history of events ("Trace the opening of the American West through the development of wagon-train trails" or "Trace the steps to prepare a Web page").

If you understand the meaning of words used in exams, you will not lose points or time by pursuing a direction that will fail to give you full credit for the information that you know.

An Outline for an In-Class Essay

Any of the practice assignments on page 456 could be used for in-class essay exams. First we present an informal outline that would lead to a focused in-class essay. We have included more details than you would need to jot down in your brief in-class outline. Your outline should only take a few minutes to write so that you have plenty of time to develop the actual essay.

Try outlining answers to the practice assignments to improve your skills and to review the essays that you have read. For an in-class assignment, your outline should be brief and should include key ideas and phrases, not necessarily complete sentences.

Assignment: Define and discuss the three types of anti-male usage in the English language in Eugene R. August's essay (p. 71).

Outline:
Introduction: The English language has been scrutinized for its depiction of language that exploits and demeans females, but studies that show anti-male bias has been neglected. There are three types of anti-male language in English that need to be recognized and abolished.

1. Type 1: Gender-exclusive language omits males from certain kinds of considerations
   - excludes males as parents: mothering becomes a synonym for parenting—"Choosy Moms choose Jif"
   - excludes males as victim: newspapers report the deaths of many innocent women and children

2. Type 2: Gender-restrictive language attempts to limit males to an accepted gender role:
   - being a man—"real men don't" syndrome
   - girls may be tomboys but boys are ridiculed for being sissies, cowards
   - being "all boy" carries penalties—less lovable and more demanding
   - homophobic terms: fairy, queer, pansy

- military terms: draft dodger, traitor, slacker
- failures with women: jerk, louse, heel, creep

3. Type 3: Negative stereotyping
   - male as criminal—linked to crime, evil, and guilt
   - rape always implies males
   - spouse abuse typically implies males
   - vices like drinking associated with men: drunkard, boozer, bum
   - "sexist" is always associated with males
   - patriarchal society is often blamed: male-dominated

<u>Conclusion</u>: Women and men of good will must recognize and condemn anti-male bias in language to destroy the "myth of the monstrous male"

The body of the essay consists of a *definition* and specific examples of each type of anti-male language bias in English; an introduction and conclusion complete the requirements of a full essay. Each of the numbered points would be treated as separate paragraphs, with the key ideas developed in the *discussion* of August's essay. The introduction includes an overview and general statements about language bias and the next three numbered points each comprise a body paragraph. The conclusion repeats the author's point that anti-male language bias must be eliminated.

PRACTICING OUTLINING FOR AN IN-CLASS ESSAY

1. Illustrate the ways Judith Ortiz Cofer is stereotyped in "The Myth of the Latin Woman" (p. 223).

2. Compare and contrast the values of Cubans and Americans as explored in Alex Garcia's "Reality Check" (p. 441).

3. Using Martin Luther King's essay "Three Ways of Meeting Oppression" (p. 280), discuss how people meet oppression and explain why King favors one response over the others.

Chapter 10

Analysis

Analysis of a Process, Problem, or Subject

All essays involve analysis. Whether the method of development is comparison-contrast, cause and effect, or any other strategy, all college writing requires analysis—a close examination of the parts in order to better understand the whole. The "parts" may include a scrutiny of a particular author's key points, supporting examples, word choice, and organizational strategy. The purpose of any analysis is not merely to take the process, problem, or subject apart, but to see the value of the individual parts and to appreciate their interaction in creating the whole.

When to Use Analysis

Written analysis is assigned in every academic discipline. Whether you are writing a lab report on the dissection of a frog in biology, interpreting a painting in art history, examining a short story in English, reviewing curriculum in education, exploring a management problem in business, or studying a discrimination problem in law, you will be expected to write analytical papers.

These papers will be specifically targeted to the subject you are studying, but three basic types of analytical assignments predominate: analysis of (1) a process, (2) a problem, or (3) a subject. Sometimes these distinctions blur, depending on the writer's purpose and audience. All papers involve breaking the whole into parts and examining the parts to show a reader their importance to the whole.

Analysis of a Process

A paper that examines a process explains how to do something or how the process itself is done. Examples might include performing a swimming pool rescue, getting a classmate to ask you out, cooking in a wok, paying car insurance while earning minimum wage, or getting a roommate's friend to move out.

Brainstorming for a Topic

If a topic has not been assigned, brainstorm for possibilities. Consider what you know how to do that others don't or what you would like to learn in order to explain that process to a reader. Don't overlook the unusual: how to get your parents to start a compost pile or how to get your roommate to shower daily. Remember that a process analysis paper doesn't need to be dull or tedious. It can in fact be quite lively if you use ingenuity and a little prewriting energy.

Organizing and Developing a Process Analysis

If you are writing a paper that tells your reader how to do something, or one that describes how something happens, these tips will help:

1. Determine whether or not the chronology is important. For some processes the sequence of the steps is critical (performing a swimming pool rescue), while for others it isn't as important (getting a classmate to ask you out).

2. If the chronology is important, list the steps and reexamine your list to make sure any reader can follow the logic of your arrangement.

3. Write each step completely, including all of the necessary information and removing confusing or irrelevant details. Imagine yourself in your readers' position, trying to follow your instructions for something they have never done.

4. Write a thesis that clearly asserts your point:

   Thesis: Creating bonsai arrangements is satisfying and lucrative.

   Thesis: Following the proper sequence of steps will facilitate a swimming pool rescue.

5. Draft your essay by linking each step with appropriate transitions to move your reader smoothly through this process.

6. Rewrite and edit your essay so that the language is vivid and the directions are precise.

PRACTICING PROCESS ANALYSIS IN SMALL GROUPS

In small groups, write down the steps explaining how to do the following:

1. Find summer employment

2. Balance a diet to achieve good nutrition

3. Prepare a three-year-old for a romp in the snow

4. Stay awake in a dull lecture

5. Convince an unwilling landlord to make a repair

6. Use library computers to find a book or an article on immigrants seeking political asylum

Spend time reaching accord within your group to ensure that all steps follow logically and that no necessary steps are left out. Aim for clarity and precision; remove words that obscure your directions. Any one of these analyses could be drafted into a collaborative paper.

Sections throughout this book explain various processes—for example, how to conduct an interview; how to cluster, list, and read actively; how to incorporate quoted material. These sections may be useful to you as models of process analysis, and they also underscore how important process is to both teaching and learning.

EXAMPLE: A PROCESS ANALYSIS ESSAY

In the following essay, Walter Gajewski, Webmaster for Academic Computing Services at California State University, Long Beach, describes the process of creating a Web page. In addition to reading the essay presented here, you can visit the author's website at <http://www.csulb.edu/~gajewski/> and read the essay while you link onto the various sites he mentions. The author has set up this site so you can send him a question or feedback by email.

Oh, What a Web We Weave
Walter Gajewski

1   You don't have to surf the World Wide Web for too long before realizing that communicating with the entire world is no longer an activity limited to multimillion-dollar corporations. A college freshman wanting to connect with people who enjoy music can list the CDs in his music collection and contact the same readers that CDNOW <http://www.cdnow.com>

and Amazon.com <http://www.amazon.com> can reach. A school news-paper could never afford to print enough copies to compete with the printed version of the *New York Times*. However, by using the school's computer net-work, a university editor can place copies of her publication on cyberspace doormats around the world and offer all the news that the *New York Times* electronic edition <http://www.nytimes.com/ee> does not see fit to print.

2   World Wide Web technology is not only ubiquitous and inexpensive, but it gets easier to use all the time. This makes it possible for computer neo-phytes to present their work in the same "marketplace" that the professional webmasters use. For years I have helped faculty at my university publish web pages, and the remark I hear most is, "Creating a web page is so much easier than I ever imagined!"

3   It is possible to lay out and publish a web page with Netscape Composer, a software application included with the free Netscape Web Browser. To install Netscape on your own computer, go out to the Netscape web site <http://home.netscape.com> and click on "Downloads". From the downloads page you can either install Netscape directly to your personal computer or have Netscape mail you their free CD-ROM. Once Netscape is installed on your computer, you're ready to create your first web page.

4   However, before you start authoring your online masterpiece, you will have to apply for a campus web account. Your school's web administrator will issue you a user name and password. She can also provide three vital pieces of additional information:

1. Your new web address
2. The name of the campus ftp (file transfer protocol) server
3. The name of the directory into which you will place your web files

5   Once you have all the necessary information, connect to the Internet and launch Netscape by double-clicking on the Netscape icon on your computer desktop. If Netscape presents you with a checkbox, click on "Start Netscape 7.0" and Netscape will continue to launch. Once the program is up and run-ning, go to the top menu and click on "File", select "New", and then "Com-poser Page" from the drop-down menu. The Composer window will open up, as shown opposite.

6   First, you'll create the heading that reads "Welcome to my page". Before you start typing, notice the menu choice that reads "Body Text" located near the top of the Composer window. With your mouse, click the down arrow im-mediately to the right of "Body Text" to reveal alternatives. Select "Heading 1." This sets the font to a size appropriate for the heading of your web page. Now you can type the words "Welcome to my page."

7   Next you will create a clickable "link" that takes your readers to a different web site. Hit the "Enter" key twice to move down the page two lines. Type
the words "Many fine textbooks are published by Allyn & Bacon/Longman."
While holding down your mouse button, drag across the name of the publisher to highlight the words "Allyn & Bacon/Longman." While these words
are highlighted, click on "Link" located on the menu bar at the top right corner of the Composer window. The "Link Properties" dialog box will appear.
In the space labeled "Link Location", type the web address for the book publisher's web site <http://www.ablongman.com>. Click on "OK".

8   Now that you have a basic web page, you can save your work in preparation for presentation over the World Wide Web. Click on "File" from the top
menu and then select "Save As . . ." to open the "Page Title" dialog box. Type
your name in the space provided and then click on "OK". A "Save As . . ." dialog box will appear. Type "index.html" in the space provided for file name.
Take note of the folder to which this file is being saved and then click on the
"Save" button.

9   You are now ready to publish your web page for the world to see. Move a
copy of your page to your school's World Wide Web server. Click on the "publish" button located on the Netscape Composer menu bar. A "Publish Page"
dialog box with two tabs will appear. If the "Publish" tab is not already
selected, click on it. Type your name in the space provided for "Page Title".
You should type "index.html" into the space provided for "Filename". In the
space labeled "Site subdirectory for this page", type in the directory name
provided by your campus web administrator.

10   Now you can select the "Settings" tab by clicking on it to reveal spaces for
typing additional information. For "Site Name" type "My home page". The
"Publishing address" should be the name of the ftp (file transfer protocol)
server provided by your campus web administrator (e.g., ftp://ftp.csulb.edu).

The HTTP address of your home page was also provided by your web administrator (e.g., http://www.csulb.edu/~gajewski). After inserting your user name and password, click on the "Publish" button at the bottom of the Dialog box.

11   A new Dialog box appears and declares "Publishing", followed by the name you entered as your page title. After about half a minute, you will see "Publishing Complete" and then the "Publishing" box will disappear. You can now use any web browser to go out to the World Wide Web and view your new home page. Find it by using the address supplied by the campus web administrator.

12   Congratulations! You now have as many potential readers as the *New York Times* Electronic Edition.

Analyzing the Writer's Strategy

Although Gajewski is writing the steps of a technical process—creating a Web page—his title is drawn from a familiar literary image from Sir Walter Scott. Gajewski also shows how every student—not just powerful companies—can communicate to a worldwide audience. He dispels any doubts his reader might have about developing his own Web page by quoting the people he helps: "Creating a Web page is so much easier than I ever imagined."

Recognizing that his audience may not have a technical vocabulary, Gajewski defines terms and explains what the reader needs to do before he launches into the step-by-step process. His strategy is to move his reader systematically through each step needed to create the page, anticipating what will appear on the screen so that the reader will not be surprised by any commands or find headings that are unexpected. He concludes his essay by informing readers that they have the potential audience of the *New York Times*—a return to an introductory image that helps frame his essay.

 ### PRACTICING WRITING A PROCESS ANALYSIS ESSAY

Select and describe a process that you know well from the following list:

1. How social cliques form

2. How a camera or videocamera works

3. How a college orients its freshmen

4. How glaciers form

5. How Olympic teams are created

6. How a batik is made

7. How pool, backgammon, or your favorite game or sport is played

8. How a musical piece is practiced for performance

Write your description as precisely as you can so that a reader can learn the process. Does your interest in the topic show in your description?

Final Tips for a Process Analysis Essay

- Review the order of the steps you have written to determine that your reader can follow your instructions or description.
- Examine the details you have given to remove any confusing instructions or irrelevant details.
- Put yourself in your reader's position to see if you have defined necessary terms and provided necessary details.
- Reread your work to see if appropriate transitions link the steps or the parts of your analysis.

Analysis of a Problem

Another kind of analysis paper describes a problem; it may or may not offer a solution. The writer may trace the history of the problem, but chronology is not as vital to this type of analysis as it is in a step-by-step process analysis. What is critical is that the writer establishes the problem, examines its parts, and shows how the parts are related to the problem as a whole.

When to Use Problem Analysis

More than any other single type of writing, problem analysis appears in every academic field and profession. Our daily newspapers and monthly news magazines as well as the readings in this textbook all feature essays analyzing a variety of problems: drug abuse, irresponsible parenting, stereotyping, isolation of the disabled, group conformity, and racial, ethnic, and gender discrimination. In spite of the wide range of issues, writers of problem analysis share similar strategies when they examine an issue.

Organizing and Developing a Problem Analysis Essay

Engaging your readers is critical in problem analysis. Why should your readers care about stereotypes, ethnic bias, the rights of the disabled, or any other subject that doesn't directly relate to them? It is your job to create reader interest, and you can do this in a number of ways. Sometimes startling statistics or a bold anecdote will jar complacent readers out of apathy. Sometimes posing a direct question to readers prompts them to consider their responses and become involved in the topic—at least enough to read the work. After you have engaged your readers, decide how much background information they require in order to understand the problem. For example, if you are writing an analysis of changing interest rates, you will include less background material if you are writing the paper for your business class than for your English class.

Then, as in all analysis papers, you will need to choose which parts of the problem you want to examine. You must describe the problem so that any reader can understand it. This might include a discussion of the severity of the problem, the numbers affected by it, which population is most affected, and the consequences if this problem is uncorrected. A detailed study of each aspect of the problem and how it relates to the other parts will constitute the body of your paper. If it is relevant to your analysis, you might speculate about the barriers to solving this problem (such as cost, social bias, frustration with earlier failures, indifference, or denial).

It is important that this analysis has a focus and a clear point or assertion. For example, if you are concerned about the fact that Americans are on the job more than workers in other countries, it is not enough merely to identify the number of hours that American employees work each week. Nor is it enough to show that they work more hours per week and more weeks per year than their European counterparts, or that they are not routinely given flexible work schedules so they can coordinate their family's needs with their work responsibilities. All of these important facts could support a point, but the point must be made.

You will need to clarify, in the form of a thesis or assertion, why the analysis of these facts is important: that American workers are overworked, that Americans have insufficient leisure time, that American children grow up deprived of their parents, or any other point that you deem significant as a result of your analysis. But without a point, you have no paper.

Once you have determined your assertion, you are ready to outline, draft, and revise your paper. Specific suggestions about outlining, drafting, and revising can be found in the student example of a problem analysis on eating disorders (pp. 382–386).

Example: A Problem Analysis Essay

The following analysis was written by a Harvard-educated economist, Robert L. Heilbroner, who has written extensively on economics and business. This essay, originally published in *Reader's Digest*, contains a unique perception of a common problem.

Don't Let Stereotypes Warp Your Judgments

Robert L. Heilbroner

1   Is a girl called Gloria apt to be better-looking than one called Bertha? Are criminals more likely to be dark than blond? Can you tell a good deal about someone's personality from hearing his voice briefly over the phone? Can a person's nationality be pretty accurately guessed from his photograph? Does the fact that someone wears glasses imply that he is intelligent?

2   The answer to all these questions is obviously, "No."

3   Yet, from all the evidence at hand, most of us believe these things. Ask any college boy if he'd rather take his chances with a Gloria or a Bertha, or ask a college girl if she'd rather blind-date a Richard or a Cuthbert. In fact, you don't have to ask: college students in questionnaires have revealed that names conjure up the same images in their minds as they do in yours—and for as little reason.

4   Look into the favorite suspects of persons who report "suspicious characters" and you will find a large percentage of them to be "swarthy" or "dark and foreign-looking"—despite the testimony of criminologists that criminals do not tend to be dark, foreign, or "wild-eyed." Delve into the main asset of a telephone stock swindler and you will find it to be a marvelously confidence-inspiring telephone "personality." And whereas we all think we know what an Italian or a Swede looks like, it is the sad fact that when a group of Nebraska students sought to match faces and nationalities of fifteen European countries, they were scored wrong in 93 percent of their identifications. Finally, for all the fact that horn-rimmed glasses have now become the standard television sign of an "intellectual," optometrists know that the main thing that distinguishes people with glasses is just bad eyes.

5   Stereotypes are a kind of gossip about the world, a gossip that makes us prejudge people before we ever lay eyes on them. Hence it is not surprising that stereotypes have something to do with the dark world of prejudice. Explore most prejudices (note that the word means prejudgment) and you will find a cruel stereotype at the core of each one.

6   For it is the extraordinary fact that once we have typecast the world, we tend to see people in terms of our standardized pictures. In another demonstration of the power of stereotypes to affect our vision, a number of Columbia and Barnard students were shown thirty photographs of pretty but unidentified girls, and asked to rate each in terms of "general liking," "intelligence," "beauty," and so on. Two months later, the same group were shown

the same photographs, this time with fictitious Irish, Italian, Jewish, and "American" names attached to the pictures. Right away the ratings changed. Faces which were now seen as representing a national group went down in looks and still farther down in likability, while the "American" girls suddenly looked decidedly prettier and nicer.

7   Why is it that we stereotype the world in such irrational and harmful fashion? In part, we begin to type-cast people in our childhood years. Early in life, as every parent whose child has watched a TV Western knows, we learn to spot the Good Guys from the Bad Guys. Some years ago, a social psychologist showed very clearly how powerful these stereotypes of childhood vision are. He secretly asked the most popular youngsters in an elementary school to make errors in their morning gym exercises. Afterwards, he asked the class if anyone had noticed any mistakes during gym period. Oh, yes, said the children. But it was the unpopular members of the class—the "bad guys"—they remembered as being out of step.

8   We not only grow up with standardized pictures forming inside of us, but as grown-ups we are constantly having them thrust upon us. Some of them, like the half-joking, half-serious stereotypes of mothers-in-law, or country yokels, or psychiatrists, are dinned into us by the stock jokes we hear and repeat. In fact, without such stereotypes, there would be a lot fewer jokes. Still other stereotypes are perpetuated by the advertisements we read, the movies we see, the books we read.

9   And finally, we tend to stereotype because it helps us make sense out of a highly confusing world, a world which William James once described as "one great, blooming, buzzing confusion." It is a curious fact that if we don't know what we're looking at, we are often quite literally unable to see what we're looking at. People who recover their sight after a lifetime of blindness actually cannot at first tell a triangle from a square. A visitor to a factory sees only noisy chaos where the superintendent sees a perfectly synchronized flow of work. As Walter Lippmann has said, "For the most part we do not first see, and then define; we define first, and then we see."

10   Stereotypes are one way in which we "define" the world in order to see it. They classify the infinite variety of human beings into a convenient handful of "types" toward whom we learn to act in stereotyped fashion. Life would be a wearing process if we had to start from scratch with each and every human contact. Stereotypes economize on our mental effort by covering up the blooming, buzzing confusion with big recognizable cut-outs. They save us the "trouble" of finding out what the world is like—they give it its accustomed look.

11   Thus the trouble is that stereotypes make us mentally lazy. As S. I. Hayakawa, the authority on semantics, has written: "The danger of stereo-

types lies not in their existence, but in the fact that they become for all people some of the time, and for some people all the time, substitutes for observation." Worse yet, stereotypes get in the way of our judgment, even when we do observe the world. Someone who has formed rigid preconceptions of all Latins as "excitable," or all teenagers as "wild," doesn't alter his point of view when he meets a calm and deliberate Genoese, or a serious-minded high school student. He brushes them aside as "exceptions that prove the rule." And, of course, if he meets someone true to type, he stands triumphantly vindicated. "They're all like that," he proclaims, having encountered an excited Latin, an ill-behaved adolescent.

12   Hence, quite aside from the injustice which stereotypes do to others, they impoverish ourselves. A person who lumps the world into simple categories, who type-casts all labor leaders as "racketeers," all businessmen as "reactionaries," all Harvard men as "snobs," and all Frenchmen as "sexy," is in danger of becoming a stereotype himself. He loses his capacity to be himself—which is to say, to see the world in his own absolutely unique, inimitable and independent fashion.

13   Instead, he votes for the man who fits his standardized picture of what a candidate "should" look like or sound like, buys the goods that someone in his "situation" in life "should" own, lives the life that others define for him. The mark of the stereotyped person is that he never surprises us, that we do indeed have him "typed." And no one fits this straitjacket so perfectly as someone whose opinions about other people are fixed and inflexible.

14   Impoverishing as they are, stereotypes are not easy to get rid of. The world we type-cast may be no better than a Grade B movie, but at least we know what to expect of our stock characters. When we let them act for themselves in the strangely unpredictable way that people do act, who knows but that many of our fondest convictions will be proved wrong?

15   Nor do we suddenly drop our standardized pictures for a blinding vision of the Truth. Sharp swings of ideas about people often just substitute one stereotype for another. The true process of change is a slow one that adds bits and pieces of reality to the pictures in our heads, until gradually they take on some of the blurriness of life itself. Little by little, we learn not that Jews and Negroes and Catholics and Puerto Ricans are "just like everybody else"—for that, too, is a stereotype—but that each and every one of them is unique, special, different and individual. Often we do not even know that we have let a stereotype lapse until we hear someone saying, "all so-and-so's are like such-and-such," and we hear ourselves saying, "Well-maybe."

16   Can we speed the process along? Of course we can.

17   First, we can become aware of the standardized pictures in our heads, in other people's heads, in the world around us.

18   Second, we can become suspicious of all judgments that we allow exceptions to "prove." There is no more chastening thought than that in the vast
intellectual adventure of science, it takes but one tiny exception to topple a
whole edifice of ideas.

19   Third, we can learn to be chary of generalizations about people. As
F. Scott Fitzgerald once wrote: "Begin with an individual, and before you
know it you have created a type; begin with a type, and you find you have
created—nothing."

20   Most of the time, when we type-cast the world, we are not in fact general-
izing about people at all. We are only revealing the embarrassing facts about
the pictures that hang in the gallery of stereotypes in our own heads.

Analyzing the Writer's Strategy

Heilbroner's immediate goal is to convince his readers that they stereotype, even though they may think that they do not. Throughout his essay,
Heilbroner's tone is light and not accusatory because most people intellectu-
ally know that stereotyping is unfair—and would even deny that they do it.
His strategy is to engage his readers by asking an entire paragraph of carefully chosen questions that he knows everybody answers in the same predictable way—evidence of the pervasiveness of stereotyping. Using statistical
evidence from tests that have been given to college students (seemingly people of above average intelligence), Heilbroner then shows that all people
"typecast the world." The author incorporates quoted statements about
stereotyping from famous thinkers and philosophers to illustrate his own
views.

Ultimately Heilbroner's strategy is to convince his readers that stereotyping "impoverishes" the person who does the stereotyping because it makes
that person "mentally lazy." He can accomplish this only by giving many specific examples of how people substitute stereotypes for true observation. His
strategy is further to convince his readers that a slow process of conscious
awareness can reduce the tendency to stereotype.

 ### PRACTICING WRITING A PROBLEM ANALYSIS ESSAY

Problem analysis assignments appear after many of the readings in this text.
In addition to those that reflect the theme of being "between worlds," you
might write an analysis of any of these problems:

1. Limited inexpensive housing available for college students

2. Policies at work or school that seem poorly conceived

3. A family's inability to communicate

4. Athletes' use of drugs

5. Unnecessary packaging of everyday products

6. Overdrinking and overeating in our society

Final Tips for a Problem Analysis Essay

- Engage your readers to convince them of the importance of the problem.
- Provide sufficient background information for your intended audience.
- Make sure that your thesis expresses why your analysis of the problem is important.
- Reread and revise to ascertain that you have adequately discussed the parts of the problem that require analysis, and that you have related those parts to the problem as a whole.

Analysis of a Subject

Another type of analysis paper examines a subject—a painting, short story, or budget—or a particular aspect of the subject—the composition of a painting, a character in a short story, or an entertainment allowance in a budget. These papers, like problem and process analysis, involve breaking the subject into parts and closely examining its parts to show the reader their importance to the subject as a whole.

Brainstorming for a Topic

If a topic has not been assigned, brainstorm to find a subject that interests you or for which you have some information, but don't select a subject that is too familiar. The purpose of any writing assignment is discovery, and nothing will help you understand a subject better than careful analysis.

When to Use Subject Analysis

Instructors expect analysis when their assignments and exam questions contain words like *explain, interpret, describe, explore why, show how, explicate, discuss, relate,* or *trace.* If you have been asked to examine an art object, interpret a poem, explore the ramifications of affirmative action in college admissions, or describe a community's recycling plan, you are required to examine the parts—or a part that has been assigned—and show how that part or those parts relate to the whole.

Organizing and Developing a Subject Analysis

Examine carefully the subject that you have selected or that has been assigned. Question the significance of the work, responding to it freshly. Determine for yourself why the subject is worth the time that you will devote to examining it.

If you have not been assigned a particular part to analyze, make a list of as many aspects or parts of the subject as you can. Then consider which parts are most significant and which you can most productively examine. In some cases, the success of your paper and how you will be evaluated will be determined by your ability to limit your selection to particularly provocative or relevant aspects. Ultimately, your job will be to show the significance of the parts or a particular part in relation to the entire work.

As introductory material, before you begin your analysis of the parts, describe the whole subject *briefly*. Remember that description is not the same thing as analysis, but realize also that your reader can't care about the parts without knowing something about the whole. Depending on the subject of your analysis, this introductory description might involve a historical context, an overall physical description, or a summary.

Write your minute description and detailed perception of the parts that you perceive to be the most significant for an understanding of the work. As you write an analysis of each part, keep your eye on the whole. You will need to return to your subject repeatedly to be sure that you are seeing or reading it thoroughly and carefully. You will not be able to write an analysis of a painting quickly glimpsed or a poem read only once.

Focus your paper with an assertion that shows your perception of the parts in relation to the subject that you are analyzing. Expressing your perception in the form of a thesis will keep both you and your reader on target.

Essay Assignments for Subject Analysis

Practice writing an analysis of one of the following subjects:

1. A favorite painting or a photo from a magazine

2. The lyrics to a piece of music

3. A controversial campus policy

4. The setting or music in a particular film

5. Mrs. Ardavi in "Your Place Is Empty" (p. 45)

6. Rita or Marc in "Peaches" (p. 147)

7. The images in "The Blind Always Come as Such a Surprise" (p. 217)

8. The grandfather in "Blue Spruce" (p.17)

Poetry and Character Analysis

What Is Poetry Analysis?

When you are asked to write an essay about a poem, you will be expected to analyze it—that is, to study its parts and explain how they relate to the whole. This examination involves a closer scrutiny than an overview or summary. In a summary, you tell what the poem is about or what happens in the poem. In an analysis, you explain how certain elements function in the poem and why the poem is written as it is. Although summary cannot take the place of analysis, you might need to summarize as a part of analysis. But poetry analysis requires a close look at the elements—key words, images, and figures of speech—of the poem.

An exploration of *key words* is a productive way to analyze a poem. Even though you may feel you know what a word means, the poet may be using a less-known meaning of the word. Since most of us don't know the origin or obscure meanings of a word, a dictionary is indispensable when reading a poem. In addition to the *denotation,* or dictionary definition of a word, you may be aware of the *connotation* or emotional association that the word conveys, and the poet may be counting on your feelings about the word. Knowing the connotations, unusual definitions, or multiple meanings of a word is critical to understanding the poem.

For example, in Marge Piercy's "A Work of Artifice" (p. 106), the first connotation—or association you may make with the word "artifice"—is its connection with the word "artificial." Confirm your hunch by checking a dictionary where you see that the word "artifice" comes from Latin words that mean "to make art." In fact, the poem does feature a gardener creating a bonsai tree, a work of art. You will also want to know the multiple denotations of the word "artifice" because they will help you understand the poem. Indeed, another meaning of the word "artifice" is a clever trick or strategem, and Piercy also shows that trickery and manipulation are related to the poem's theme. There are additional meanings of the word "artifice," and each contributes to an understanding of the poem. Because words are the most basic element of any poem, the dictionary is a useful first step in analyzing poetry and helping you understand the other elements. Your knowledge of the multiple meanings of words can provide the focus for your analytic essay.

All poems consist of *images*—words that stir the senses: sight, sound, smell, touch, and taste. Because images are such vital elements of a poem, a productive analysis of a poem often involves examining particular images or patterns of images that seem to work together. In "On the Subway" (p. 184), Sharon Olds describes the passengers as "molecules stuck in a rod of light / rapidly moving through darkness." Olds creates an image—in this case, a visual one—of passengers who seem insignificant, as tiny as molecules. These passengers are "stuck" on the subway car, which resembles a rod of light moving through the dark underground tunnels. The poet creates a visual picture of the entire subway world, and a close analysis of the imagery will help us understand that the poem is partially about being "stuck" and in the dark.

Images used suggestively rather than literally are called *figures of speech*, and a study of these figures can enhance your discussion of imagery. There are many kinds of figures of speech, but the most common are metaphor, simile, and personification. A *metaphor* is an implied comparison between two unlike things. Poets aren't the only ones who use metaphors; you probably use them daily without realizing it. For example, when you say, "My boyfriend is a gem," you are comparing him to something that is valuable, dazzling, impressive, and maybe even sparkling! In Sharon Olds's image, the poet implies a comparison between the subway car and a "rod of light." Part of your job in analyzing "On the Subway" would be to discuss the many comparisons between a subway car and a rod of light.

A *simile* is an explicit comparison using the words "like" or "as." In another poem, "Digging" (p. 42), the narrator claims that he holds his pen between his finger and thumb and the fit is "snug as a gun." If you were focusing on the figures of speech in "Digging," you would want to analyze Seamus Heaney's comparison between the fit of a pen and the fit of a gun. You might also want to look at Heaney's use of *personification*—giving human characteristics to an inanimate object, animal, or abstraction—in the line "the squat pen rests." Heaney is creating the image of a pen that, like a human being, "rests," or lies tranquil.

You may hear people refer to a *symbol* or to *symbolism* when they are discussing poetry and, for that reason, we will define and discuss the terms here. A symbol is something concrete used to represent or suggest something more abstract. For example, in Sharon Olds's poem "On the Subway," the narrator is carrying a briefcase—an object that suggests she has a professional life. Her perception of how her life contrasts with the life of the boy sitting across from her encourages us to view her briefcase as a symbol. The briefcase does not just represent a job or profession. The briefcase suggests many abstractions: her social class, her affluence, her dignity, her power and perhaps her control over her life. Like a stone tossed into water, a symbol sends out ripples of reverberating suggestions that contribute to our expanding notions of what the poet intends.

How to Actively Read a Poem

When you are assigned a poem to read, you need to read it through without worrying about what you don't understand. In a second or third reading, read the poem aloud, so that your ear catches connections that the poet intends. Then, just as you have been reading the essays in this book—actively—with a pen in hand, read the poem again and circle unfamiliar words, underline key words or lines, mark important ideas, and jot down comments in the margin. This is the time to use the dictionary to look up not only the words that may be new to you but words that may be used by the poet differently than you would expect. You need to write down, on the page with the poem or on a separate paper, the multiple meanings of each word as well as relevant origins of the word.

As you read, mark the examples of simile, metaphor, and personification, as well as images that relate to each other by similarity or contrast. Ask questions as you read: why does the poet use a particular word or how do two images relate? Your responses to these questions provide notes that will help you choose the focus for your analysis.

Here is an example of active reading that a student, Jennifer Tabaldo, did to prepare for class discussion of Seamus Heaney's "Digging" (p. 42).

Active Reading of a Poem

Digging   by Seamus Heaney

short & thick — Between my finger and my thumb   *speaker holding pen*
position of a digger The (squat) pen rests; snug as a gun. —— *surprising simile →aggressive*

Under my window, a clean rasping sound
When the spade sinks into gravelly ground:
5   My father, digging. I look down

Till his straining rump among the flowerbeds
Bends low, comes up twenty years away
Stooping in rhythm through potato (drills)   *strange word*
Where he was digging.

10   The coarse boot nested on the lug, the shaft⟩ *father holding spade*
Against the inside knee was levered firmly.
He rooted out tall tops, buried the bright edge deep
To scatter new potatoes that we picked
Loving their cool hardness in our hands.

15   By God, the old man could handle a spade.   *Proud of father!*
Just like his old man.

My grandfather cut more turf in a day   *Proud of grandfather!*
Than any other man on Toner's bog.
Once I carried him milk in a bottle
20   Corked sloppily with paper. He straightened up
To drink it, then fell to right away   *grandfather*
Nicking and slicing neatly, heaving sods   *holding spade*
Over his shoulder, going down and down
For the good turf. Digging.

harsh 25   The cold smell of potato mould, the squelch and slap
images: Of soggy peat, the curt cuts of an edge   *?*
smell,   Through living roots awaken in my head.
sound,   But I've no spade to follow men like them.
touch

repeats opening   Between my finger and my thumb
30   The squat pen rests.   →*no gun simile*
I'll dig with it.   →*metaphor?*

Active Reading Discussed

You will notice that Jennifer circled key words, perhaps words she needed to look up because she didn't know the meanings or thought the word might have an unusual meaning. She also blocked off words that repeated and underlined similes and metaphors. She noted images and apparently discovered a pattern: narrator, father, and grandfather are all holding tools, whether spade or pen. She also marked images of harsh smells, sounds, and textures and commented on the narrator's "proud" tone as he praises his father's and grandfather's skills. Her active reading not only prepared her for class discussion but also for the essay that she was later assigned.

Although Jennifer and her classmates went through the poem line by line, questioning meanings and making observations about Heaney's word choices and imagery, Jennifer's instructor had warned the students that a written line-by-line explication could easily slip into mere summary. Therefore, the instructor required that the students write an analysis that stems from a thesis. In a thesis-driven analysis, the writer controls the organization of ideas rather than just following the lines of the poem.

The instructor also reminded students of the value of using the "sandwich" when incorporating quoted lines from the poem. (You may want to review this technique on pp. 369–370.) You will notice in Jennifer's paper, which follows, how skillfully she introduces the line she is quoting and how deliberately she explains and analyzes the words and images in each line that she includes. Notice that poetry lines are documented by line number in parentheses and that a break between two lines of a poem is indicated by a slash with a space on each side. (See p. 608 for discussion of the slash.)

When Jennifer refers to the "narrator" of the poem, she means the speaker or "I" of the poem. In poetry analysis it is important not to assume that the poet and speaker in a poem are always the same person. Although in this particular poem, Seamus Heaney may seem to be the speaker because he is a writer, Jennifer avoids an unprovable assumption by using the word "narrator" or "speaker."

Jennifer used her active reading notes and ideas from class discussion to prepare the following analysis. Notice that she found the focus for her paper in the image patterns that she highlighted when she actively read the poem.

STUDENT EXAMPLE: POETRY ANALYSIS

Tabaldo 1

Jennifer Tabaldo

Professor Waterworth

English 1A

3 May 2002

Digging Deep

Often a person is caught between his family's expectations for him and his own life choices. For some, this struggle results in frustration, rebellion, or a fear of inadequacy--of not measuring up to the family's standards. The fear of breaking tradition is the narrator's concern in Seamus Heaney's poem "Digging" (42). He reviews and comes to terms with his family's history as he discovers an acceptance of his own chosen career. In the poem, this acceptance is revealed in the images depicting the relationship between the family members and their tools.

The narrator's ambivalence toward his choice of writing as his life's labor becomes apparent in central images early in the poem. Although he depicts himself as a writer, a key simile reveals his discomfort in his relationship with his pen: "Between my finger and my thumb / The squat pen rests; snug as a gun" (1-2). Clearly, a writer's most valuable relationship should be that which exists between his pen and himself. The fit of the pen is so natural that it simply "rests" comfortably in his fingers. The pen's existence is so vital to him that his grasp is "snug," an image of him protecting the pen. The pen is warm and cozy in his grasp, but then the narrator shocks the reader with an unexpected simile: "snug as a gun" (2). Heaney's comparison between the pen and gun suggests the tension that the writer feels harboring a potentially powerful weapon or tool. The narrator seems insecure in his choice of writing as a career, and perhaps uses the gun simile defensively or rebelliously to protect himself from family criticism.

The narrator views his choice to become a writer as a choice not to become an actual digger and not to follow in his father's footsteps. His father was a potato farmer and spent a lifetime perfecting the art of digging. The son recalls his father at work, "the coarse boot nestled on the lug, the shaft / Against the inside knee was levered firmly" (10-11). These images of strength and skill illustrate the father's ease and comfort with his tool. The "coarse boot" is designed for heavy, fast, and rugged work and is "nestled on the lug" as if the two objects, the boot and lug, were meant to fit together, snugly and comfort- ably. The shaft is "nestled" securely against the father's inside knee in a position that would exact the most efficient digging "rhythm." The son respects the competence and confidence that his father exhibits with his shovel.

This respect is apparent as he exclaims in awe, "By God, the old man could handle a spade. / Just like his old man" (15-16). It is obvious that the narrator's pride extends to his grandfa- ther who "cut more turf in a day / Than any other man on Toner's bog" (17-18). The narrator's image shows the grandfather's effi-

Tabaldo 3

ciency and power "nicking and slicing neatly, heaving sods / Over
his shoulder, going down and down / For the good turf" (22-24).
Like the speaker's father, the grandfather developed an easy rhythm,
"nicking and slicing neatly." His digging probably required even
more physical energy than his son used in potato farming because
"heaving sods / Over his shoulder" must have been back-breaking
work.

   Although the narrator admires his father and grandfather, he
is also ambivalent, as we observe in the harsh images that attack
our nose and ears: "the cold smell of potato mould, the squelch
and slap / Of soggy peat" (25-26). Finally, it is the "curt cuts
/ Through living roots" that prompt the narrator to admit: "I've
no spade to follow men like them" (28). Feeling apart from
"them," he is unable to sever "living roots" as the men in his
family do. But he is acutely aware of the patriarchal lineage
that has existed in his family. He may sense his inability to
excel at hard work as his father and grandfather did, and he sees
that his failure to accept their physical, manly labor departs
from the linear pattern and family tradition.

   But he also must sense that the image of "going down and down
for the good turf" is like the writer's search through layers of
meaning to discover the truth. His forefathers' act of digging into
the ground can be compared to the narrator's use of the pen to dig.
Ultimately, the narrator must realize he can dig through many layers of experiences and family history--the living roots--to unearth
the thoughts and feelings that he can put into words. He discovers
that "digging" is a metaphor for his life's work, and we realize
that he has found a common ground between the generations.

   The narrator's epiphany is that he has carried on his family's tradition but with a different tool. Comfortable with this

Tabaldo 4

decision, he drops the opening simile that the pen is "snug as
a gun"; it now simply "rests." The narrator hopes to attain, in
his writing, the excellence that the grandfather achieved digging
peat and that the father had digging potatoes. Ultimately, the
narrator invites readers to experience the same epiphany: to
discover that they, too, can admire their family's excellence
and yet select their own life's work without conforming to
family patterns and expectations.

Work Cited

Heaney, Seamus. "Digging." <u>Between Worlds: A Reader, Rhetoric,</u>
     <u>and</u> <u>Handbook.</u> Ed. Susan Bachmann and Melinda Barth. 4th ed.
     New York: Longman, 2004. 42-44.

Analyzing the Writer's Strategy

Jennifer's introduction opens with a few lines to capture audience interest in
her topic—family expectations and children's fear of inadequacy—before she
mentions the title and author of the poem she is analyzing. Then she builds a
bridge to the thesis that she derived from her active reading notes. Her thesis
sets up the organization for her paper because it requires that she examine
"the relationship between family members and their tools." Thus she orga-
nizes her paper around a discussion of those images that show each family
member—narrator, father, and grandfather—in relationship to tools.

The discussion of those images is the heart of her analysis. She not only
incorporates the line smoothly but also works with the language of the image.
You may be surprised that her entire second paragraph is devoted exclusively
to a discussion of the first two lines of the poem. Jennifer never expects the
quoted line to stand on its own without her analyzing it. She also is careful to
make sure that her interpretations of certain lines make sense in the context
of the poem as a whole. Often there is intentional ambiguity in a poem and it
is worthwhile to address it. For example, Jennifer speculates about the gun
simile. She conjectures that "perhaps" the narrator "uses the gun simile defensively or rebelliously to protect himself from family criticism." Another
reader of the poem might infer a different meaning in this simile. If you aren't

sure about the poet's intention, you can soften your assertion with "perhaps" or "probably."

In her conclusion, Jennifer avoids repeating her exact words but returns to her opening ideas about family patterns and expectations. She refers to an "epiphany"—a moment of sudden insight or profound revelation—a word that undoubtedly came from class discussion. Her entire paper, from the thesis on, anticipates the narrator's new awareness, even though she uses the term "epiphany" only in her conclusion.

 ### PRACTICING WRITING POETRY ANALYSIS

In small groups select one of the following poems and write a list of images that would be interesting to analyze: "Blue Spruce" (p. 17), "A Work of Artifice" (p. 106), "On the Subway" (p. 184), "The Blind Always Come as Such a Surprise" (p. 217), or "Coke" (p. 287). Group the images that belong together, arrange the images in an order that makes sense, and write an assertion—a thesis—that would be workable for an analysis of the poem.

Final Tips for Poetry Analysis

- Actively read the poem several times, marking key words, images, figures of speech, and your impressions.

- Note repetitions and image patterns that might help you find a focus for your analysis.

- Decide which elements provide the most productive approach to the poem and formulate a thesis based on that decision.

- Analyze the quoted words or lines you have chosen to support your thesis. Remember to use the "sandwich."

- In your introduction, engage your audience and then briefly prepare your reader for your thesis. Briefly summarize the poem so that your reader has some context for your study.

- In the conclusion, return to your opening idea and thesis without repeating yourself.

What Is Character Analysis?

Character Analysis: Short Story

Because narratives, short stories, novels, and biographies are often read in freshman composition classes, we include here a character analysis to demonstrate the process of analyzing a subject—a fictitious character or an actual person. Whether you are examining a subject from life or print, you will want to observe and record telling details—those that reveal something significant about the person. As you study a character, you will accumulate lots of facts, some that you will discard as irrelevant and others that you will decide are indicative of the person's character. From these facts you will be able to make assumptions about your subject's personality and character. In fact, the heart of your analysis will depend on inference—that is, a hypothesis that you formulate about character based on the facts that you have observed.

Prewriting for a Text-based Character Study

As you actively read the narrative or short story, list specific examples of speech, behavior, and thought that reveal the character. Mix facts and your responses or inferences about them as you go along. Simply write your list; you will sort, eliminate, and reword examples later.

Listing Information from a Short Story

If you are taking notes from a short story for a character analysis, you need to record telling descriptions, behaviors, and speech that will help you determine what kind of person that character is. It helps to list all revealing observations in the left-hand column and leave room between observations so you can group similar details. As you list and group related ideas, jot down in the right-hand column an inference about that character. An inference is a hypothesis or supposition about a character that you will later prove or refute from the data collected. Here is a list of observations and inferences about Connie in Joyce Carol Oates's short story, "Where Are You Going, Where Have You Been?" (p. 126):

Observations about Connie	Inferences about Connie
"quick nervous giggling habit"	self-conscious
cranes neck to glance into mirrors	vain
ignores a boy from the high school	callous
leaves her friend to go off with Eddie	callous, self-absorbed

Observations about Connie	Inferences about Connie
checks "other people's faces to make sure her own was all right"	self-conscious, insecure
"she knew she was pretty and that was everything"	self-assured, superficial
thought her mother preferred her to June because Connie was prettier	self-assured, superficial
checks her hair and worries about how bad she looks when a strange car pulls in driveway	insecure, self-conscious
"wished her mother were dead and she herself were dead and it were all over"	depressed
"everything about her had two sides to it, one for home and one for anywhere that was not home" jersey her walk lipstick laughter	two-sided, sneaky? rebellious?
says she is going to the movies but goes to drive-in restaurant	deceitful
avoids conversation with family about "movie" and "Pettinger girl"	sneaky, evasive
doesn't go to family barbecue—rolls her eyes at mother	indifferent, evasive, rebellious?
goes to Eddie's car	likes being with boys
"her mind slipped over into thoughts of the boy she had been with the night before"	daydreamer, romantic
daydreams about the boys she hangs out with, "how sweet it always was . . . the way it was in movies and promised in songs"	romanticizes about love, naive
"her eyes wander over the windshields and faces all around her"	always on lookout for cute guys
"smirked and let her hair fall loose over one shoulder"	flirtatious
couldn't decide if Arnold Friend is attractive or a jerk	naive

Observations about Connie	Inferences about Connie
doesn't realize at first that Friend is so much older	naive
flattered by Friend's interest in her	naive

amazed by all Friend knows about her
    her name
    friends' names
    description of June
    family at barbecue
    fat woman at barbecue
    neighbor with chickens
	naive, vulnerable

appalled by Friend's graphic talk of sex	intimidated, innocent
cries out for mother	childlike, needy
can't phone police	inexperienced, terrified, paralyzed
realizes she will never see mother or sleep in her bed again	childlike

Arranging and Thesis Construction

Consider how you will arrange your character traits and the specific examples that support the traits. What do you want to emphasize in your analysis? Consider ending your character analysis with the trait that you find more significant or most indicative of character. By using your most emphatic point in the terminal spot in your paper, you will have a natural conclusion—one that gets at both the heart of your subject and the theme of the short story.

Perhaps the place to start is with the most obvious feature of the subject for analysis because it will take less effort to convince your audience of your perception if your reader shares your perception. In the case of Connie, the writer might address her preoccupation with her looks or her apparent self-assuredness. The writer might also want to look at her flawed family relationships or her boy-craziness. Depending on how you perceive Connie, you may want to order the inferences in your thesis to reflect the reasons for her behavior. Your final character inference should lead naturally to the conclusion of your paper, and you will want to keep this in mind as you order the inferences in your thesis.

Determining a Thesis. You need to have a thesis for your character study, whether or not you include it in your paper. You can determine one by using the character traits that you perceived during grouping. Remember that your thesis expresses a view about a limited subject, such as Connie's character. If you have many observations on your prewriting list, you know you have good support ready.

Possible Thesis Statements. Here are some possibilities for thesis statements for the character analysis of Connie. Remember, each writer's perceptions and preferences will determine the thesis and the order in which the information will be presented.

1. Although Connie appears to be a self-assured teenager, she is actually an insecure, sexually innocent, two-sided girl whose inexperience does not prepare her for the encounter with Arnold Friend.

2. Connie seeks male attention, hangs out with older kids, and affects a sexy exterior, but she is no match for someone with criminal intentions.

3. Connie's life is filled with paradoxes: she is a gregarious girl without a true friend; she lives in a traditional family but has no real bonds with family members; she craves the attention of boys but does not know how to protect herself. Ultimately, these paradoxes render her vulnerable to an attack by someone like Arnold Friend.

4. Because Connie's home life is deficient, Connie develops survival mechanisms. She daydreams, evades interaction with her family, and deceives her family and friends—behavior that could not help her withstand Arnold Friend.

5. Connie projects a brazen, rebellious exterior that masks the naive, insecure girl within.

STUDENT EXAMPLE: CHARACTER ANALYSIS ESSAY

As you read the following character analysis by student writer **Marianela Enriquez**, notice that in addition to an examination of the separate qualities of Connie's character, Marianela returns to the essence of the entire work to bring closure to her study.

Enriquez 1

Marianela Enriquez

Professor Hackner

English 1A

April 16, 2002

Who Were You, Connie, and Why Did You Go?

　　Readers of "Where Are You Going, Where Have You Been?"

(126) may be tempted to condemn the protagonist, Connie, as a

---

Enriquez 2

self-absorbed and superficial 15-year-old and to reduce the story to a simple warning against risky behavior. But it would be a mistake to do so. Throughout the work, author Joyce Carol Oates takes great care to illustrate situations and describe feelings and a personality all survivors of teenage angst have experienced and can recognize. In this way, her chilling short story about a rapist and his teenage victim becomes much more than a tale of fear. It becomes a tragedy of a teenage girl struggling with adolescence on her own and dealing with all the insecurities of her age. Although Connie appears to be a self-assured teenager, she is actually an insecure, sexually innocent, two-sided, and naive girl whose inexperience cannot prepare her for the encounter with Arnold Friend.

Connie herself is pretty, with long, dark blonde hair and brown eyes, and like most girls her age, she is preoccupied with her looks. But even in realizing that this is a typical teenage trait, one can see that Connie's preoccupation is a sign of her insecurity. She has habits of always looking at herself in mirrors and "checking other people's faces to make sure her own was all right," two practices that reveal her insecurity and contradict the self-assuredness of her belief that "she was pretty and that was everything" (127). Even when a "car she didn't know" pulls into her driveway, Connie's first concern is to check her hair and wonder "how bad she looked" (131). She feels that her physical attractiveness is at the root of everything. She reasons that the tension existing between herself and her mother is because her mother is jealous that her own looks are gone. But, in spite of that thinking, she also reasons that her mother preferred her to her sister June because Connie is the prettier of the two. Connie's beauty seems to be the only asset recognized by

other people, so in her insecurity, Connie clings to people's
compliments. When seen in this light, one can start to understand
Connie not as a conceited person, but as a confused girl who
attempts to work the one good quality she thinks she has.

Because Connie believes that beauty is everything, she naturally moves toward people who will appreciate her beauty--boys.
Whether she is at the shopping plaza or a drive-in restaurant
"where older kids hung out" (128), Connie always has her eye out
for someone to fulfill her dreams of romance. While she does enter cars with boys she barely knows, there is no evidence that
Connie actually has intercourse with any of them. According to
Connie, her experiences are always sweet, "not the way someone
like [her sister] June would suppose but sweet, gentle, the way
it was in movies and promised in songs" (130). Connie doesn't
have one special boyfriend about whom she dreams. In fact, "all
the boys fell back and dissolved into a face that was not even
a face, but an idea, a feeling" of romance. Even Arnold Friend
recognizes Connie as sexually innocent when he claims he will
be her "lover" but adds, "You don't know what that is, but you
will" (136). Her shock at his graphic language and her insistence
that "people don't talk like that" (136) confirm her innocence
as well.

Perhaps the greatest key to understanding Connie's character
is to understand her duality. Oates specifies that "everything
about her had two sides to it, one for home and one for anywhere
that was not home" (128). Connie is full of contrasts: "She wore
a pullover jersey blouse that looked one way when she was at home
and another when she was away from home" (128). In addition to
rearranging her clothing to look older, she changes her walk
"that could be childlike and bobbing" when she is at home or

"languid" when she is out. "Her mouth that is pale and smirking most of the time, but bright and pink on evenings out" suggests that Connie is rebelling against her parents' make-up rules, and deliberately making herself look older when she leaves her house. Connie's laughter "was cynical and drawling at home," probably in response to family jokes, but is "high pitched and nervous anywhere else" (128). This duality includes deceit. For example, while her family thinks that she and a friend are going to the movies, they often "went across the highway, ducking fast across the busy road" (128). And when her mother bluntly asks, "What's this about the Pettinger girl?" Connie dismisses the question, refusing to let her mother into her world. Whether consciously or unconsciously, Connie builds walls around herself and doesn't talk to anyone with any sort of depth. She can't relate to her older sister, June, who is praised by their mother, and her father ignores the family to "read the newspaper at supper" (127). The indifference of her family is damaging to Connie who is, in actuality, a lonely girl desperate for some kind of positive attention.

Her desire for attention and her teenage naivete makes her the perfect victim for Arnold Friend. It is ironic that Connie's killer should be the only one in the story who has any kind of understanding into her character. Apparently, the man has been watching Connie for some time and knows of her love for music, of her innocent encounters with boys, and of her family situation so that he can intimidate Connie with what he knows or can guess. Friend is able to create an image of himself that Connie finds appealing. She is interested that they are listening to the same radio station, and she finds his car impressive. She "liked the way he was dressed, which was the way all of them dressed" (132) and at first she is so blinded by the familiarity of his looks that she can't tell if "she liked him or if he was just a jerk" (131). Because of her naivete, Connie at first doesn't notice that Arnold and his friend are much older than the boys Connie knows. Because Connie craves attention, she is easily flattered by Arnold Friend even though her intuition tells her that something is wrong with these two older men.

Taking advantage of Connie's insecurity and naivete, Friend manipulates her responses and plays upon her existing insecurities. Armed with facts about Connie's life, Friend plays upon the rivalry between June and Connie by calling her sister "fat" and a "poor, sad bitch" (136), and he plays on Connie's feelings of abandonment, created by her father's disinterest, by repeating that her father isn't coming back for her. Arnold lets her know that locking the door will not keep him out. Connie's vulnerability is evident in the story's most disturbing scene when Connie tries to telephone the police. Arnold's abuse puts Connie in such a hysterical state that she botches her one chance to escape. Oates's description of "her breath jerking back and forth in her lungs as if it were something Arnold Friend were stabbing her with again and again" (139) is powerful with its sexual implications, and we realize that Connie is raped emotionally before she is physically raped. He let her know that she is hopelessly trapped.

Connie becomes paralyzed by the knowledge that she is alone and vulnerable and that if she doesn't go along with Friend, her family will be murdered. She must feel guilty remembering "how she sucked in her breath just at the moment she passed him" and "how she must have looked at him" at the restaurant (133). In the end, Connie breaks and resigns herself to a sure death. No longer the teenager, Connie is a little girl who can only think, "I'm not going to see my mother again . . . I'm not going to sleep in my bed again" (140).

In creating a character so recognizable in her insecurities, duality, and naivete, Joyce Carol Oates also creates a character we can pity. Oates creates a sense that the difference in where Connie is going and where we may have gone at the tender age of 15 may not be so much the result of differences in action but the result of differences in fate. This awareness completely destroys the security that comes with thinking that through the avoidance of certain behaviors, we can prevent negative outcomes, and this realization heightens the horror of Connie's story. We are forced to reckon with the uncontrollable nature of chance, a chance that doesn't shrink away from giving a 15 year old innocent girl a Friend who may take her life.

Work Cited

Oates, Joyce Carol. "Where Are You Going, Where Have You Been?"
    Between Worlds: A Reader, Rhetoric, and Handbook. Ed. Susan
    Bachmann and Melinda Barth. 4th ed. New York: Longman, 2004.
    126-141.

Analyzing the Writer's Strategy

Marienela begins her analysis by acknowledging that some readers will find Connie merely a "self-absorbed and superficial" teenager and will "reduce the story to a simple warning against risky behavior," but Marienela cautions that "it would be a mistake to do so." In fact, she defends Connie to the point of saying that Connie is not to be blamed for what happens to her, and throughout her analysis of Connie's character, Marienela illustrates the forces that contribute to Connie's personality, values, and vulnerability. Marienela supports her inferences about Connie's character with well-integrated and analyzed quoted material from the story, recognizing the importance of including and interpreting many specific illustrations to prove her claims about Connie.

PRACTICING WRITING A CHARACTER ANALYSIS

In small groups, select one of the following individuals and write a list of character traits: Darnell from "Proper Care and Maintenance" (p. 186), Mrs. Ardavi from "Your Place is Empty" (p. 45), Rita or Marcus in "Peaches" (p. 147), or Ace from "Ace in the Hole" (p. 34). Group the details that belong together, arrange the details, and write an assertion—a thesis—that would be workable for a character analysis.

Character Analysis: Biography

Reading a good biography—the study of a person's life—can be a great pleasure. We learn something intimate, entertaining, and instructive about the subject of the book and the time period in which the person lived. Even readers who would not elect to read a history book discover that a biography vicariously connects them to a culture and time they may not know and permits them to glimpse choices the subject of the biography made that perhaps even influenced that epoch.

Joan Didion, in her essay on Georgia O'Keeffe (pp. 219–221), informs a reader who may know only O'Keeffe's paintings that the artist was "a hard woman," perhaps a woman who painted with "derisive orneriness." Didion's reader learns that when the men in her time period deemed New York too "impossible" to render on canvas, O'Keeffe painted images of the city. When the critics found the painter's work too bright, she created even brighter work. Readers who study Georgia O'Keeffe's life, even in Didion's short essay, learn something about personal conviction and about a period of time not their own—discoveries that can be both informative and inspirational. In addition, a longer character analysis written from reading a full-length biography can be a rewarding research project.

Gathering Information from a Book: Inference Cards

If you are taking notes for a paper based on a biographical study and are using a full-length book, keep separate index cards for each character trait that you observe while you are reading. For example, if you find that your subject was "strong-willed," even in childhood, you would head an index card with that inference. As you read the book, every time you see that trait reflected in an action of your subject or a comment made by someone about the character, simply record the page number. When you infer another trait, perhaps "maternal" or "ambitious," start new cards and continue to record page numbers. When you have completed a 300- or 400-page biography, you may have twenty or thirty "inference cards," each with a different trait at the top and each with many recorded page numbers. It may seem time-consuming and even awkward to stop reading to record a page number on an existing card or to start a new card with an inferred trait, but you will not need to reread the full-length book in order to write a good paper if you keep track of traits from the beginning of your reading. You will be actively reading and inferring traits, focusing your reading from the start.

Grouping Cards

After you have finished reading the biography and writing inference cards, group the cards that seem to belong together. For example, if you have cards with "strong-willed," "determined," and "obsessed," you should be able to combine those cards for one section of your subject analysis. The number of page references that you have noted on the cards will help you decide if the trait that you observed is supportable.

A Working Thesis

Write a working thesis featuring those traits that seem to have sufficient support, based on the pages you have recorded on the index cards. You wouldn't want a thesis that features each trait that you have observed, so you'll need to be selective, even if you have grouped two or three different cards that will work together to form one section of your paper. Georgina Montoya, whose analysis of Frida Kahlo appears on pp. 496–503, had inference cards indicating that Kahlo was "rebellious," "charismatic," "had a sense of humor," and was "flamboyant." She ultimately selected "flamboyant" and "charismatic" for her thesis, but she returned to the other words as she drafted her paper and included examples from each of the cards.

Decide which traits and terms most fairly and completely represent your subject. Write a thesis based on those traits, knowing that you may decide to change the thesis or rearrange it as you draft your paper.

Arranging the Support

Decide what you want to emphasize about your subject: if the traits that you have observed are both negative and positive, determine which predominate. Arrange the traits in your thesis to project the organization of your paper. Do you want your paper to conclude with surprising information about your subject—inferences that you have discovered in reading the full study of your subject's life—or would you rather have your reader be comforted with a conclusion of familiar material about the subject of your paper? Do you want to emphasize the negative by concluding with those traits, or do you want to show that in spite of problems, your character triumphed?

Georgina had to decide whether she wanted to conclude her analysis of Frida Kahlo with the observation that she "suffered" throughout her life, and especially at the end of her life, or to avoid a chronological arrangement and emphasize that in spite of the suffering, Kahlo was regarded as "charismatic" and "flamboyant." Georgina decided that she wanted to conclude her analysis with the positive information about her subject's life and character, so she placed those details at the end of her analysis.

From Inference Cards to Drafted Paper

After you have arranged the inference cards in an order that makes sense for your thesis, return to the note cards and look up the page numbers that support each trait. You will want to select examples of behavior, anecdotes, statements from people about your subject, and statements from your subject that most vividly show your subject's personality and character. Your goal is to render a lively portrait of your subject. Remember that you can "tell" your reader many times that your subject was "charismatic," but one "showing" illustration or revealing anecdote will do more to create a vivid image in your reader's mind.

As you use the material from the page numbers on your cards, combine paraphrased and quoted material. Use your own words to narrate an example most of the time, but where there is vivid description by the author of your biography, or quoted material from someone about your subject, use direct quotation, too. In Georgina's paper, she uses Frida Kahlo's own voice to help her reader hear the kind of person she was. In a letter Kahlo wrote to her boyfriend Alejandro, she revealed that she was so hurt by the accident that when the doctors and nurses moved her, she would "cry quarts of tears" (Herrera 53). She also admitted that her foot "also hurts a lot since as you must realize it is very smashed" (53). By letting her subject speak in her own voice, Georgina captures the tone of a young girl who is in pain but still young and full of hyperbole, crying "quarts of tears" because her foot was "very smashed."

Be certain as you draft that you note the page number where you derived both the paraphrased and quoted material that supports your inferred trait. Compose directly on the computer, if you can, but if you write longhand, write on only one side of the lined paper so that if you later want to cut the draft up to rearrange sections, you will be able to do so. If you compose directly on the computer, you will be able to cut and paste to rearrange sections of your draft. Develop each section of the paper before you go on to another trait.

Transitions Between Sections

When you have finished drafting each section of the paper, look for ways to create transitions between the sections of analysis. You may decide to rearrange some of your support so that the illustration or quotation that concludes one section can be used as a bridge to the next trait or section of analysis. Georgina finished one section of her analysis of Kahlo's generosity with this sentence:

> Frida was not only generous with her money, but she shared her spirit with people and they were happy to be around her.

The next section of Georgina's paper is focused on other ways Frida "cared for others." The new section begins with this sentence:

> In addition to being caring and cheerful, Frida Kahlo was a good listener and her friends valued this quality.

As you connect the parts of your paper, check to see that you are returning to the focus of each section with key word repetition or synonyms, perhaps alternative words that were on your inference cards. See pp. 388–390 for help on transitions.

Writing the Introduction

After you have drafted each section of the paper to support a particular trait, write an introduction to your paper, perhaps by reexamining any circled page numbers on your inference cards that indicate a lively anecdote about your subject that could be used to precede your thesis. Georgina was impressed by the color plates of Frida Kahlo's paintings that are included in Hayden Herrera's biography, and she decided that a description of one painting that illustrates the two sides of Frida would be a vivid opening to her analysis of Kahlo's duality. But as you read Georgina Montoya's "Mirror Image," notice how the author avoids the trap of writing an art analysis paper that would be more appropriate for another assignment. Notice, too, how the paper is structured to support the thesis based on inferred character traits and that it is not a mere summary of the book.

STUDENT EXAMPLE: BIOGRAPHY ESSAY

```
                                                          Montoya 1

Georgina I. Montoya

English 1A 6261

Professor Barth

June 5, 2003
                         Mirror Image
     It is almost six feet square, an oil-on-canvas painting of

two women sitting on a bench, side by side, holding hands. The

viewer will see that the women in the painting have the same

face--the face of Frida Kahlo. The Frida on the right is wearing
```

Montoya 2

a Tehuana skirt and blouse, symbolizing the Mexican Indian side of her heritage, and she is holding a small portrait of her husband as he looked as a child. The Frida on the viewer's left is wearing a white Victorian dress, symbolizing the subject's European heritage. There is a long, blood-red vein that connects to the small portrait, travels up Frida's arm and through both of the Fridas' exposed hearts. The vein ends with the cut of surgical scissors which Frida is holding, and the dripping blood creates two puddles on the Victorian Frida's lap. The Tehuana Frida's heart is full, suggesting that she is loved. The Victorian Frida has a broken heart because she feels her husband, Diego Rivera, no longer loves her.

Frida Kahlo painted The Two Fridas in 1939, during her divorce from Diego Rivera (Herrera 277), and it depicts the duality the subject felt most of her life. Frida Kahlo is known to the world as a talented, respected, strong woman who suffered throughout her life. The other side of Frida Kahlo that the public might not know is that she was also a caring friend to many people and, in spite of her suffering, was a flamboyant and charismatic personality.

Frida Kahlo was an extremely talented artist. She not only painted with great detail, but she poured her soul into her artwork. Frida painted her first self-portrait for her boyfriend Alejandro Gomez Arias, to reconcile a spat, and she named her portrait "Your Botticeli [sic]" (Herrera 61). According to Hayden Herrera, she used her portrait as a vehicle to express her thoughts, something she did throughout her life. Her ability to intensely reveal her feelings in her artwork was one reason she was a highly regarded artist even during her lifetime.

Many of Frida Kahlo's paintings reveal her suffering after a bus accident that almost claimed her life. Referring to Kahlo's paintings, Herrera writes, "Her face is always a mask; her body is often naked and wounded, like her feelings . . . the girl whose ambition was to study medicine turned to painting as a form of psychological surgery" (74). Even though Frida's first plan was to become a doctor, her talent was obviously in painting, an awareness she and her family gained when her father gave her art materials to amuse her as she recovered from the accident. During her lifetime, Kahlo painted over 140 paintings (Milner 6), most of them self-expressive.

Frida Kahlo had many art exhibits during her life and her first show in New York City, in 1938, was attended by many famous artists and collectors, including Ben Shahn, Alfred Stieglitz, Lewis Mumford and Nelson and John Rockefeller (229). Her first solo exhibit in Mexico City, in Lola Alvarez Bravo's gallery in 1953, was a dramatic triumph with crowds of a hundred people pushing to enter the exhibit opening day (Herrera 407). Calls from outside Mexico indicated Frida was developing an international reputation, a fact that amazed the artist (Herrera 409).

Frida Kahlo was respected not only for her paintings but also for her character. Diego Rivera had established himself as a great muralist even before Frida began to paint, but he still valued her opinions when it came to his work and depended on them through the years (Herrera 105). The French painter Andre Breton "was entranced" by Frida and he admired her work so much that he organized an exhibition for her in Paris (227-28). Another one of Frida's admirers was Pablo Picasso. During the Paris exhibition, Picasso "sang praises" to her and was "under her spell" (Herrera 251). Picasso was so fond of Frida that "as a token of his affection for her, [he] gave Frida a pair of earrings in the form of tiny tortoise-shell hands with gold cuffs" (251). Even

prominent artists like Breton and Picasso held Frida Kahlo in
high esteem.

Frida taught art at La Esmeralda, the Ministry of Public
Education's School of Painting and Sculpture, and she left a
great impression on some of her students. One, Fanny Rabel,
describes Kahlo: "Frida's great teaching was to see through
artist's eyes, to open our eyes to see the world, to see Mexico . . .
she was instinctive, spontaneous. She would become happy in front
of any beautiful thing" (qtd. in Herrera 331-32). Frida's students were enthusiastic about art and respected her way of teaching. Four students developed such a close relationship with Frida
that they called themselves "Los Fridos," and maintained that
title with pride even after their teacher's death (343).

Frida earned respect in part because she was a strong woman
who overcame everything that life threw at her. At the age of
six, polio left Frida with a deformed leg. But she was determined
not to let this deformity show, so she played many sports and
became a champion swimmer. "When she walked, she made little
jumps so that she seemed to float like a bird in flight" (Aurora
Reyes qtd. in Herrara 16). Because of her movements and poise,
people noticed her grace and not her crippled leg.

The bus accident that occurred when she was 18 completely
changed her life. As Frida described it, "The crash bounced us
forward and a handrail pierced me the way a sword pierces a bull"
(qtd. in Herrera 48). Because of this accident, she had over
thirty surgeries during her lifetime and the injuries to her body
are quite possibly the reason she was not able to bear children.
After the accident she wrote to Alejandro: "It hurts more than you
can imagine, at every jerk they give me I cry quarts of tears . . .
my foot also hurts a lot since as you must realize it is very

smashed" (qtd. in Herrera 53). Yet after her rehabilitation, she moved with grace, even when her body was in great pain.

Quite possibly greater than Frida Kahlo's physical pain was the emotional pain that she had to endure. The greatest love of her life was Diego Rivera, and although he helped her through her surgeries and recovery, he was the one who cause her emotional torment. Frida realized this when she said, "I suffered two grave accidents in my life, one in which a streetcar knocked me down . . . The other accident is Diego" (qtd. in Herrera 107). Despite the fact that Frida loved Diego, she knew that marrying him would be as much a tragedy as her bus accident. For example, even though Frida wanted to have children, "Diego was very cruel to [her] about having a child" (Wolfe qtd. in Herrera 147). Rivera insisted that they shouldn't have children because of Frida's health, but Diego really didn't want any children.

Diego also caused Frida pain by having numerous affairs during their marriage, including one with Frida's sister Christina. When this happened, Frida felt "murdered by life" (181) and expressed in a letter to her doctor, "I have suffered so much in these months that it is going to be difficult for me to feel completely well soon" (qtd. in Herrera 183-84). Christina was not only Frida's sister but her best friend. Although the affair caused her months of torment, Frida was a caring person and eventually forgave both her sister and Diego.

Frida gave of herself in the form of love and material things. She gave her niece and nephew presents and paid for dance and music lessons. She was attentive to Diego's needs, bringing delicious lunches up to the scaffold when he was working on his murals. A shopkeeper recalls that "Fridita" did not like to see her toothless, so Frida provided her with new gold teeth (Herrera

Character Analysis: Biography **501**

306). And her students recalled that on field trips, Kahlo would
have the bus stop in front of a snack bar and cry out, "Mucha-
chos, to the pulqueria!" and Frida would pick up the bill for
everyone in the place (Herrera 332). Frida was not only generous
with her money, but she shared her spirit with people and they
were happy to be around her.

   In addition to being caring and cheerful, Frida Kahlo was a
good listener and her friends valued this quality. Elena Vasquez
Gomez said, "We healthy people who went to visit her [after her
surgeries] came away comforted, morally fortified. We all needed
her" (qtd. in Herrera 390). When Frida was sick, her friends
would visit her to get her mind off her pain, but instead Frida
would say, "Tell me things. Tell me about your childhood" (390).
Frida would listen to them and would entertain her visitors. "She
did not concentrate on herself"; others came first (Rabel qtd.
in Herrera 390). Because of Frida's exceptional qualities, she
had a loyal following.

   Frida Kahlo enjoyed being the center of attention and
achieved this with her unique style. She dressed flamboyantly
and enjoyed costumes. Talking about her style, Frida said,
"In [one] period I dressed like a boy with shaved hair, pants,
boots, and a leather jacket . . . but when I went to see Diego
I put on a Tehuana costume" (qtd. in Herrera 109). Neither her
boyish nor colorful costumes were characteristic of the dress
of Mexican girls her age. Once, when Frida attended a concert
in the Palace of Fine Arts, she turned out to be the main
attraction: "Everyone stared at Frida, who wore her Tehuana
dress and all of Diego's gold jewelry, and clanked like a knight
in armor" (Amaya qtd. in Herrera 275). She even covered her
teeth with "gold caps with rose diamonds in front so that her

smile really sparkled" (275). Undoubtedly, Frida Kahlo's distinct style of dress was unique.

Frida's sense of humor was also extraordinary. Even as a child at home, she teased her German father by calling him "Herr Kahlo" (13), a reference to Hitler he did not like. Frida's sense of humor became more daring when she was attending the National Preparatory and she and her friends, "The Cachuchas," threw a six-inch firecracker into a large assembly hall while a professor was giving a lecture. The loud explosion broke glass that hailed down on the professor (Herrera 28). Frida loved shocking everyone with her humor and once, during an interview while she was lying in bed, she put the long stick of a candy she was sucking under the blankets to simulate a phallus in erection (Bloch qtd. in Herrara 163). She kept a straight face throughout the interview and was thrilled to observe the reporter's embarrassment. Frida was able to entertain herself even when she was in the hospital, and "clung to her sense of the ridiculous" (388). One time she made a stage from the contraptions that elevated her right leg and she had a puppet show with her feet. She enjoyed the fact that the bone bank sent a bone labeled "Francisco Villa" and Frida exclaimed, "With my new bone I feel like shooting my way out of this hospital and starting my own revolution!" (qtd. in Herrera 388), a reference to Poncho Villa. With such humor, Frida had the talent, vibrancy and charisma to win her audience.

There is no question that Frida Kahlo had two sides to her. The public Frida was gay and strong with accentuated qualities of vivaciousness, generosity and wit (Herrera 76). The other side of Frida could be seen in her portraits, "in images of herself foot-less, headless, cracked open, bleeding" (347). Frida Kahlo was an extraordinary woman who not only overcame unimaginable physical

Montoya 8

pain and emotional suffering, but who exceeded the norm and developed into one of the most influential artists of all times. Her cremation ceremony might symbolize her extraordinary life. "Mourners were stunned to see her corpse appear to sit up in reaction to the intense heat. [Frida] Kahlo seemed to be confronting them as her hair blazed in a halo around her head . . . It was, as she would probably have seen it, her final work of art" (Howell 234).

Works Cited

Herrera, Hayden. FRIDA: A Biography of Frida Kahlo. New York: Harper, 1983.

Howell, Georgina. "Frida Kahlo." Harper's Bazaar Nov. 2001: 234. MasterFilePremier. EBSCO Publishing. El Camino Coll. Lib., Torrance. 18 Mar. 2002 <http://search.epnet.com/login.asp>.

Milner, Frank. Frida Kahlo. London: PRC, 1995.

Analyzing the Writer's Strategy

The purpose of a character analysis of a once-living person is not entirely different from a character analysis of a fictitious character. The goal is to create a vivid portrait of the subject by focusing on inferred traits that can be supported with text. The analysis must be focused around a thesis based on inferences about the person so that the paper does not become a birth-to-death summary of the subject's life, or a mere review of the book read about the subject.

Writing the Thesis

There is plenty of creative opportunity for the writer to decide which character traits may best represent the subject's life. Most of us are complex personalities, and our lives are filled with moments of strength and weakness, failure and triumph. Georgina was most interested in the struggles that Frida Kahlo overcame, and how her life developed after a nearly fatal accident left her crippled but alive. Georgina knew that Kahlo was famous for paintings and her tempestuous relationship with the famous artist Diego Rivera. However, in her reading of Hayden Herrera's fine biography, Georgina discovered traits about Frida Kahlo that most people wouldn't know, and she wanted to make those traits known to the reader of her paper. Her thesis focuses on the inferences Georgina thought most fully represent Kahlo and traits she could support from her reading:

> Frida Kahlo is known to the world as a talented, respected, strong woman who suffered throughout her life. The other side of Frida Kahlo that the public might not know is that she was also a caring friend to many people and, in spite of her suffering, was a flamboyant and charismatic personality (497).

Georgina arranged the points of her thesis so that she could meet her reader's expectation of what a biography on Frida Kahlo would include—that she was "talented" and "strong." But then she shifts her analysis to reflect the person behind the public icon, to show that Kahlo was "a caring friend" and "a charismatic personality."

Selecting Support to "Show" not "Tell"

Georgina uses statements from other people as well as Kahlo herself to support the points in her paper and to create a vivid portrait of her subject. In order to show that Kahlo wanted people to overlook the polio that left her with a deformed leg, Georgina uses a friend's description of Kahlo's lively and confident movement: "When she walked, she made little jumps so that she seemed to float like a bird in flight" (499). After giving the quoted statement, Georgina drives home the point that she wants her reader to see: "Because of her movements and poise, people noticed her grace and not her crippled leg" (499).

To show that Kahlo dressed flamboyantly, Georgina uses Kahlo's own description of herself that is recorded in the biography: "I dressed like a boy with shaved hair, pants, boots, and a leather jacket . . . but when I went to see Diego I put on a Tehuana costume" (501). And Georgina employs the description of one of Kahlo's friends who described how Kahlo appeared at a concert in the Palace of Fine Arts in Mexico City: "She wore her Tehuana dress and all of Diego's gold jewelry, and clanked like a knight in armor" (501). Georgina concludes that revealing anecdote with the detail that Frida even "covered her teeth with gold caps with rose diamonds in front so that her smile really sparkled.'" Georgina emphasizes the point that she is making in this section of her paper with a concluding statement: "Undoubtedly, Frida Kahlo's distinct style of dress was unique." Throughout her analysis, Georgina selects memorable descriptions and anecdotes to show her subject, reveal Kahlo's character, and promote the reader's interest.

Introductions and Conclusions

All introductions need to "hook" the audience, so a captivating opening paragraph is essential. The focused biography, then, should not begin with the birth and death dates and places of the subject because nothing is more certain to put the reader to sleep. Strive for an anecdote or description of your subject that will interest your reader. Georgina opens her paper with a description of one of Frida Kahlo's paintings, a description that will lead to her thesis that Kahlo's life mirrored some of the dualities apparent in the painting. Georgina's introductory description creates a natural bridge to her thesis.

Georgina used the Internet to see if there was additional information about Frida Kahlo that wasn't in the biography she read. This search isn't usually necessary if the biography is a good one, but Georgina discovered a description not included in Herrera's book and one that she could use to conclude her analysis—the shocking image of Frida Kahlo's cremation. Georgina found a way to draw the parts of her paper together to leave her reader with an image of Kahlo's "final work of art" that is unforgettable.

Final Tips for Writing a Focused Biography

- Select a good biography to read, one that has documented sources. When in doubt, get advice from your school librarian or your instructor.
- Write a thesis based on character inference, using traits you can support.
- Arrange the traits in the thesis thoughtfully to reflect your full perception of the subject.
- Use anecdotes about the character, comments quoted from your subject and comments made about the subject to support your thesis and to *show* your subject.
- Use a variety of transitional devices between sections of your paper in order to gain unity, coherence, and emphasis.
- Write an enticing introduction to your analysis and conclude meaningfully, perhaps with some insight about your perception of the person's life.
- Use in-text parenthetical references to document the source of ideas, facts, and quotations.
- Title your work to engage your reader.

Chapter 11

Writing the
Research Paper

The research paper—routinely assigned by most freshman composition instructors and universally dreaded by freshman composition students—has a worse reputation than it deserves. Like most tasks that at first seem overwhelming, the research paper needs time and organization. The steps suggested here, and the model of a student paper in this section, should help you handle such an assignment.

Planning the Research Paper

Even if you had outstanding luck in high school and welded a research paper together in an amazing overnight session, your college professor probably won't look upon the results of such marathon events favorably, and you may find your course grade threatened. Instead, admit to yourself that the research paper requires your attention through a number of steps, all of which you can handle.

In addition, the paper encourages you to experience the pleasure of discovering new interests and information. If your instructor allows you to choose your topic, take advantage of this opportunity to pursue one that intrigues you, one that is worth the time and energy that you will devote to the investigation. Enjoy the discovery!

New Tools, New Choices

Computers can make the process of discovering an intriguing topic more fun than ever. All libraries now have computers that not only can direct you to books but also provide you with immediate feedback about the status of the book—whether it is in the library or when it should be returned. You can also request that the book be held for you or sent from another library. Periodical searches are equally easy and, in some cases, you can print out the full text of an article or an abstract—a brief summary—that will help you determine whether you want to find the original full text.

On the Internet, you can type in one or two key words for your initial search, and the titles that appear may lead you to discover topics that you did not even realize existed. You are no longer restricted to your own library's collection but now can "roam the stacks" of the best libraries worldwide.

Time Schedule for the Research Paper

If your instructor does not assign due dates for the various stages of the paper, try dividing the time between the assigned date and the due date into four approximately equal parts. For example, if you have two months for the preparation of a paper, each stage will have two weeks. If you have one month, you can give each stage a week of your time.

STAGE 1—DISCOVERING TOPIC AND MATERIALS

- Determine the topic that interests you and satisfies the paper assignment. Allow a few days for this, but do not let yourself postpone that first decision for longer than a few days.
- Go to the library and begin your search for materials. Use the computers and meet the reference room librarian—the researcher's best friend. Ask the librarian if your topic has additional subject headings that you should be aware of so that you can do a complete search while you are in the library.
- Make bibliography note cards for each source. (See the model note cards on p. 515–516.)

STAGE 2—TAKING NOTES

- Read and take notes on the material that you find. If you take notes in the library on material that you do not intend to photocopy and take home with you, write direct quotations and paraphrase these later, when you know how much material you want to use. If you are printing from electronic sources, be selective or you will be hauling home piles of paper. Read widely; print rarely!
- Keep accurate records of titles, authors, page and volume numbers, and record completely and accurately all Web addresses so that you do not need to return to the sources to find information for necessary documentation. (This step will be discussed more completely on p. 515–516.) As you take notes, think about how you might focus your paper.

STAGE 3—DRAFTING AND REVISING

- Determine a working thesis and write an outline for the paper.

- Use the computer to draft your paper. The extra time you spend preparing your paper on a disk will be doubly compensated in revision speed and quality. Remember to click on "save" often. Be sure to save your work not only on your hard drive but also on a back-up disk.

- Meet with your instructor or writing center staff for feedback before you continue.

- Revise your manuscript, strengthening the thesis, improving the arrangement, using more emphatic support, improving word choice and transitions, and clarifying any writing that your reader found ambiguous or weak.

STAGE 4—EDITING AND PROOFREADING

- Examine your paper for coherence and unity. Read for effective transitions between paragraphs and within long paragraphs (see pp. 388–394). Edit carefully. Don't rely on spell-check or grammar-check. Proofread for typical "computer errors." Make sure that you have used quotation marks at the beginning and the ending of all quotations and that you have parenthetical citations for all ideas and quotations you have incorporated (see pp. 368 and 516–517).

- Print out the revised copy of your paper, the works-cited page, and, if your instructor has asked for one, a cover sheet that includes the title (in standard font), your name, section, professor's name, and date. (See the MLA model on pp. 521–541.)

If you divide the research paper assignment into parts, you will not be overwhelmed by the task. You may also realize that you need longer to draft your paper but less time for revision because the computer has expedited this process.

Gathering Library Material

Getting Started

Shannon Paaske's instructor required a research paper that was more developed, and used more sources, than the shorter documented papers that had been assigned earlier in her composition course. In addition to the length and source requirements, Shannon's assignment was to respond more fully to one of the subjects included in Part I of *Between Worlds*. Shannon decided that she wanted to learn more about the world of the disabled.

Her initial response to the research paper may have been posed in the form of questions: What are the problems the disabled have in attending classes? In working? In their social lives? There appears to be interesting technology for the disabled on my campus; what is available to help the disabled? What kind of legislation exists to help the disabled? How do the disabled feel about their conditions? Are the attitudes of Soyster characteristic of the disabled? Has he written any other articles?

With these questions in mind, Shannon went to her college library.

Meeting the Librarian

The reference librarian can show you how to use the computers, CD-ROM sources, the Internet, and indexed guides for book and periodical searches. The librarian also can show you how to find books in the stacks and how to find and use the microfilm machines. All libraries have trained assistants whose job it is to teach you how to find the microfilm reels and how to thread the film into the machine. You should never feel embarrassed to ask for help and instruction. Even professors who have used microfilm numerous times will ask for help when they haven't used the machines for a semester or two. Most schools have short courses or workshops to orient students to the Internet.

Finding Information

Each library has its own computer system with particular options for searching (such as "keyword" or "browse"). Ask the librarian to recommend a method for searching for books and periodicals. If you cannot locate articles under a particular topic, ask the reference librarian for the Library of Congress Subject Headings which may provide an alternative term. Many students leave libraries empty-handed or with few sources because they have not used the correct search method or because they have not entered all the appropriate headings.

Using Electronic Sources

Electronic sources offer you several advantages: (1) You can locate materials that are in your local libraries and in libraries thousands of miles from your campus; (2) you can read materials on the Internet that may not yet be available in print because they were posted as recently as the day of your search; (3) you can also tap into the knowledge of other researchers by logging into certain computer services, such as Usenet News, to post questions that readers around the world may help you answer; (4) you can subscribe to a *listserv*, a mailing service that will email you up-to-date articles on specialized topics; and (5) using certain services, you can obtain maps, pictures, and graphics that will enhance your paper.

If your topic requires up-to-date information (news events, current legislation, technological or medical data, or recent statistics), you will want to consult periodicals or the Internet. If your writing calls for historical overview (of legislative changes, economic patterns, fashion trends, or art or political movements), you may want the depth and perspective that books provide. In addition to periodicals, books, and Internet materials, don't neglect videos, films, CD-ROMs, and interviews as potential sources of information.

Your library has information on just about every topic, so if you are not finding what you need, realize that you may be using an incorrect heading or misspelling a term. Computers are helpful, but it often takes a human being— a librarian—to show you how to access that help.

Using the Internet

If you are new to the Internet and intend to use it to gather information for your research paper, some general advice may help. The Internet is a vast information network, and to use it successfully, you must find the right "search terms." Although you won't necessarily want to restrict your search terms in your initial information-gathering phase, eventually you will want to refine your search or you will be overwhelmed with more sources than you can handle.

When Shannon Paaske updated the research paper that we published in the first edition of this textbook, she knew that the Internet would provide her with current and useful material. She entered the keyword "disability," and then refined her search by adding "AND" and the terms "assistive and technology," to locate Web sites about the current technology designed to assist the disabled. Many Web sites have links to other sites, so she could click on terms like "data," or "history of," or "products" to find new information for her paper.

Before starting a Web search, define your research goal and then list on paper the terms associated with that topic. You should enter those terms in the search box of a *search engine*—an Internet tool such as Goggle, Ask Jeeves, or Yahoo, designed to comb through Web pages and look for matches. As you explore each term one at a time, you may sense that your terms are too general. You can then join the key terms with common words like "and," "or," "but not," so that the selections more closely reflect your interest and the number is not unmanageable. If your term is too general, you will have either thousands of "hits" or none—and you will most likely be overwhelmed or discouraged. Because every search engine has its own system, be sure to click on the "help" icon of the particular search engine to learn the best search strategies.

Keeping Track of Internet Sources

To decide what to print, quickly read the material on the screen and print only those pages that you sense will be useful. If you want to return to a Web page, you can add a "bookmark" to mark it. Avoid bookmarking too many sites— a mistake similar to highlighting an entire page rather than selective passages of a textbook.

Keep track of all information and addresses of sites that you use, including the author of the Web page, if there is one, so that you have complete information to provide on your list of works cited. Because the reader of your paper may wish to learn more about a particular aspect of your topic, your Web addresses must be accurate.

The Abuse of Electronic Sources

It may seem a researcher's dream to discover 3,000 hits on a topic with a print button handy and a fresh supply of paper in the printer. However, our own quick searches of Internet materials have produced mixed results. We found some articles that were well written and prepared with exemplary support. We also found too many trivial, unsigned, poorly written pieces—work that no serious college student should consider using. We thus have serious reservations about students who rely exclusively on the Internet, and we would undoubtedly fail papers that were last-minute patch jobs of poorly reasoned Web material.

Evaluating Online Sources

Just as student researchers have always needed to consider the quality of their sources, you too will need to evaluate what you have read and printed from the Internet. Students working from books have the clear advantage of knowing that an editorial staff has evaluated the text and verified the data in it. However, no such safeguards exist on the Internet where literally *anybody* can publish *anything*. So while your job as a student researcher may be lightened in the discovery phase, your job in evaluating material from the Net is more challenging. Let's look at a process for evaluating Web sources that we derived from criteria distributed on the Internet by Susan E. Beck, Instruction Coordinator, New Mexico State University Library. (You can visit this site at <http://lib.nmsu.edu/staff/susabeck/evalcrit.html>.) Use the following questions to evaluate the accuracy, authority, objectivity, currency, and coverage of the material that you find on the Web.

EVALUATION CRITERIA FOR WEB SOURCES

I. Accuracy
   - Is the information reliable and error-free?
   - Is there an editor or someone who verifies the information?

   Rationale
   - Anyone can publish anything on the Web.
   - Unlike traditional print resources, Web resources rarely have editors or fact-checkers.
   - Currently, no Web standards exist to ensure accuracy.

II. Authority

- Is there an author? Is the page signed?
- Is the author qualified? An expert?
- Who is the sponsor?
- Is the sponsor of the page reputable? How reputable?
- Is there a link to information about the author or the sponsor?
- If the page includes neither a signature nor a sponsor, is there any other way to determine its origin?

  Look for a header or footer showing affiliation.

  Look at the URL: <http://www.fbi.gov>

  Look at the domain to determine if the site is an educational institution (.edu), commercial enterprise (.com), nonprofit organization (.org), government institution (.gov) or computer network (.net)

  Is there an editor or someone who verifies the information?

Rationale

- Again, anyone can publish anything on the Web.
- It is often difficult to determine a Web page's authorship.
- Even if a page is signed, qualifications aren't usually given.
- Sponsorship isn't usually indicated.

III. Objectivity

- Does the information show a minimum of bias?
- Is the page designed to sway opinion?
- Is there any advertising on the page?

Rationale

- Frequently the goals of the sponsors/authors aren't clearly stated.
- Often the Web serves as a soapbox for opinions and propaganda.

IV. Currency

- Is the page dated?
- If so, when was the last update?
- How current are the links? Have some expired or moved?

Rationale

- Publication or revision dates not always provided.
- If a date is provided, it may have various meanings:

  It may indicate when the material was first written.

  It may indicate when the material was first placed on the Web.

  It may indicate when the material was last revised.

V. Coverage
- What topics are covered?
- What does this page offer that is not found elsewhere?
- What is its intrinsic value?
- How in-depth is the material?

Rationale
- Web coverage often differs from print coverage.
- Frequently, it's difficult to determine the extent of coverage.
- Sometimes Web information is just-for-fun or outright silliness.

Think critically about material that you find on the Web and balance it with material from library shelves.

Using Traditional Methods

The traditional librarian-and-book search sometimes can be faster and more productive than computers. Many superb materials are not available on a computer attached to a printer but are in conventional bound books on library shelves. So don't settle for fast-food takeout when there is an entire banquet in the library.

Computer-Related Terms

The following list of terms is not comprehensive, but it will help you understand some of the vocabulary associated with computers.

angle brackets < >: The symbols indicating that all of the characters within the brackets must be treated as a single unit, with no spaces between parts. Used to distinguish Web site locations and email addresses. Omit angle brackets when you are typing within an address box.

Boolean search: A search using a connective like "AND," "OR," or "NOT" that limits or expands a Web search. For example, when you are searching for information on "disabilities," you can qualify your search by adding "AND 'education'" or "NOT 'technology.'"

browser: A World Wide Web program for searching the Internet. Browsers typically display formatted pages, graphics, and links to other Web pages. Popular graphic browsers include Internet Explorer, Netscape, and Mozilla; a commonly used, text-only browser is Lynx. To use a browser, you either need to know the address of the Web page that you want to view or need to click on a link that takes you to a specific page. In contrast, a "search engine" provides you with lists of Web page addresses based on the topics or keywords you designated.

CD-ROM (Compact Disk Read-Only Memory): A disk that stores text, data, graphics, and sound.

database: A collection of data, such as bibliographies, abstracts (summaries), full texts, and spreadsheets that are stored electronically.

disk, floppy disk: A portable storage medium, typically 3½ inches in diameter, used to save files and to move and retrieve information from computer to computer.

electronic mail (email): A system for sending and receiving individual or organizational messages over the computer.

FAQ (Frequently Asked Questions; rhymes with "back"): Common questions with answers posted at a Usenet news site or an online journal or report.

FTP (file transfer protocol): A set of commands used to transfer files between computers on the Internet.

hardware: The actual machinery such as the computer, printer, keyboard, monitor, mouse, modem, and disk drive.

homepage: Typically, the first page you see when you access a Web site. Individuals as well as organizations can have their own homepage.

hypertext: Computerized documents that contain built-in special phrases that link to other documents, pictures, or sounds. These links are usually designated by being underlined or color-coded; clicking on a link (with a computer's mouse) causes the computer to access this new material.

Internet: A global "network of computer networks" connecting universities, libraries, government offices, and corporations. Initially most users were educators, writers, scientists and researchers, but now people use the Internet to bank, shop, chat with strangers or celebrities, play games, or catch up on news events. The Internet has an electronic mail system that lets users exchange E-mail with other subscribers.

Internet service providers: Companies such as Netcom, AT&T Worldnet, and Earthlink that provide fee-based access to the Internet. Providers such as America Online offer online services in addition to access to the Internet.

listserv: A mailing list that directs information to email subscribers interested in particular topics. People who subscribe to special listservs want to interact with others and stay up-to-date in specialized fields.

modem: A device that converts material from a computer into tones that can be sent through telephone lines. Similarly, material from another computer can be converted into tones and received into a computer through a modem.

publication medium: Any type of information source, such as a book, magazine, newspaper, film, videotape, CD-ROM, World Wide Web, and diskette.

search engine: Indexed programs that help you find subjects on the Web. Popular search engines include Google, Ask Jeeves, Yahoo!, Lycos, and Alta Vista, but there are many more. The search engine scours Web sites for a particular word or phrase. The search can be broad, like "oil spill," in which case thousands of hits may appear, or the search can be narrowed, like "oil spill AND cleanup," in which case the number of hits will be fewer.

software: The programs that direct the operation of a computer or that process electronic data such as word processing programs, databases, and games.

Usenet News: An Internet service that can be compared to a global bulletin board system. It includes postings and responses to the postings—all organized by topic.

URL (Uniform Resource Locator): The address of a site on the Internet such as a World Wide Web page. You should be aware that occasionally a Web site will cease to exist or may have a new address.

Wilson Line: An electronic index service (with some full-text sources available). Sources include the *Reader's Guide to Periodical Literature* (an index of articles published in popular magazines such as *Time* and *Newsweek*), the *Humanities Index* (an index of articles published in scholarly journals in literature, history, and the arts), and the *Social Sciences Abstracts Index* (summaries of research on social issues).

World Wide Web (also called Web, WWW, or W3): An Internet service that provides global access to information in the form of texts, pictures, movies, and sounds. As a hypertext-based system, the Web allows the user to move from document to document by clicking on a link that is underlined or color-coded.

Sample Bibliography Cards

Whether your information comes from the Internet or printed materials, your instructor may require you to record the sources on index cards. If your library provides you with a printed list of the bibliographic information of books and periodicals that you are using for your essay, you may decide to use those sheets, arranging them in alphabetical order by author's last name when you write your works-cited page.

Here are sample bibliography cards for the note-taking phase:

For a book

P5	Mairs, Nancy.
508	"On Being a Cripple" from
P56	<u>With Wings: An Anthology of Literature</u>
W58	<u>by and about Women with Disabilities.</u>
1987	Ed. Marsha Saxon and Florence Howe. New York.
	Feminist Press, 1987. 118–27.

For a periodical

> *Rab, Victoria Y. and Geraldine Youcha "Body." Omni*
> *June 1990: 22+.*

Make certain, even from the first note-taking session, that you have correctly recorded all of the information that you will need for your works-cited page.

Plagiarism

Whether you use note cards or photocopied pages from a book, you must record all of the necessary information so you can give credit and avoid plagiarism—using someone else's ideas or language as your own. Whether this is done accidentally or deliberately, it is a serious offense that schools may punish with expulsion. If you are desperate to complete an assigned paper, using somebody else's work, including work published on the Internet, may seem like a good idea to you. *Don't do it.* Failing a course or risking expulsion from school is not worth it. Realize that you are capable of doing the work that you have been assigned and that accomplishing this task with integrity will strengthen your skills and confidence as a writer.

Plagiarism most often occurs inadvertently—often because of sloppy note taking, poor record keeping, or even ignorance. You can avoid this problem by assiduously recording, from your earliest notes on, the source of every idea—even in summary or paraphrased form—and of every key word or phrase of another writer that you are using. Furthermore, if you change or omit anything in the text that you are quoting, you need to use brackets (see p. 607–608) and ellipses (see pp. 605–606) to signify to your reader that you have made a change. It is important that you use quotation marks as soon as you begin using the author's words. Finally, you need to completely and accurately cite the source of material that you have used. Failure to adhere to these conventions may result in a charge of plagiarism, however inadvertent it may be. Examples of inadvertent plagiarism are shown below, so that you can avoid this error in your own work.

Inadvertent Plagiarism.   Plagiarism occurs if a quotation is not used or documented correctly. In the following excerpt, read the original, from Marcus Mabry's "Living in Two Worlds" (p. 144) and the incorrect uses of the quotation.

Original

Most students who travel between the universes of poverty and afflu-ence during breaks experience similar conditions, as well as the guilt, the helplessness and, sometimes, the embarrassment associated with them. Our friends are willing to listen, but most of them are unable to imagine the pain of the impoverished lives that we see every six months. Each time I return home I feel further away from the realities of poverty in America and more ashamed that they are allowed to per-sist. What frightens me most is not that the American socioeconomic system permits poverty to continue, but that by participating in that system I share some of the blame.

 ### PRACTICE FINDING THE ERRORS

Identify the incorrect uses of the material in each of these examples:

1. Marcus Mabry talks about the student who travels between the universes of poverty and affluence during school breaks.

2. Mabry is frightened by the fact that "the American socioeconomic system permits poverty to continue" and that "by participating in that system" he shares some of the blame (145).

3. One student who was studying at Stanford describes the guilt, helpless-ness and the embarrassment that he and other students feel when they move between their school lives and their home lives when they return home for vacation.

4. Mabry is concerned not that "the American socioeconomic system per-mits poverty to continue, but that by participating in that system he shares some of the blame" (145).

Explanation of errors

1. In his mistaken notion that he has "only paraphrased," this writer has failed to place quotation marks around Mabry's words ("who travel be-tween the universes of poverty and affluence"). Additionally, the student has not documented with parenthetical information the source of the ma-terial that he has taken from Marcus Mabry. Even if the student were to use only the image of the "universes of poverty and affluence," the image is Mabry's and must be documented.

2. This writer has misrepresented Mabry. The original expresses the idea that it is *not* America's "socioeconomic system" that frightens him but his fear that "by participating in that system" he "shares some of the blame."

The writer has written a combination of paraphrase and quotation that does not correctly express Mabry's point.

3. The writer here has attempted a paraphrase of Mabry's words that stays too close to the original in repeating "guilt," "helplessness," and "embarrassment," without using quotation marks and which fails, in any case, to attribute and document the source of the idea.

4. This writer has made a change in Mabry's quoted material in order to merge his or her text smoothly with Mabry's words. But the writer has failed to use brackets to inform the reader that there is a change in the quoted material. This is how the quotation should look: "'The American socioeconomic system permits poverty to continue, but that by participating in that [he shares] some of the blame.'"

If you carefully copy material from another source, double-check your paraphrases, and inspect your quoted material and compare it with the original to verify that you have been accurate in your sense as well as in the use of quotation marks, brackets, and parentheses, you will avoid the inadvertent plagiarism that threatens your integrity as a writer and flaws the writing that you produce.

Sample Note Cards

Your instructor may require that you prepare note cards from the materials you have gathered for your research paper. These cards may contain direct quotations, paraphrased material, a combination of paraphrase and quotation, or summary. With the goal in mind of paraphrasing and quoting carefully those relevant sections of her collected texts, Shannon began making note cards for her paper.

Original text

People without the use of their arms or legs can now rely on computerized 'sip and puff' machines. With light puffs into a plastic straw, users can switch on the TV and change its channels, telephone a friend and play computer games. (Blackman 70)

Direct quotation

> Blackman 70
> "People without the use of their arms or legs can now rely on computerized 'sip and puff' machines. With light puffs into a plastic straw, users can switch on the TV and change its channels, telephone a friend and play computer games."

Paraphrased note card

> Blackman 70
>   With new developments in technology, quadriplegics can use
>   the phone, operate the television and even play games on the
>   computer by blowing into a straw.

Combination of quotation and paraphrase

> Blackman 70
>   Other developments include "computerized 'sip and puff' machines"
>   which enable persons "without the use of their arms or legs" to
>   change television channels, talk on the phone, and "play computer
>   games" by inhaling or exhaling into a straw.

Developing a Working Thesis

While Shannon read from her collection of materials and took notes, she began to focus on her subject in a sharper way. She realized that there were a number of ways to approach the subject of the disabled, but that she was especially interested in three: (1) technology that equips the disabled to leave home and enter the outside world, (2) the media's recent interest in depicting the disabled, and (3) the attitudes of the nondisabled person toward the disabled. Her working thesis looked something like this:

> Technology and the media have improved life for the disabled, but they still suffer social isolation and indignities.

Shannon talked with her instructor about her working thesis and the rough outline of the three parts that she planned to write. (For a discussion of outlining and for illustrations, see pp. 362–365.) After discussing her plan and what she had found in her research, Shannon and her instructor concluded that she did not have enough information about the social isolation of the disabled, and that her own casual observations would be insufficient for a well-developed research paper. The instructor suggested that Shannon approach the special resources center on the campus to arrange interviews with disabled students who would be willing to talk about their social situations. Furthermore, both the instructor and Shannon concluded that they knew very little about legislation that gave rights to the disabled, and both realized that any reader would want to know something about this legislation.

Gathering Additional Information: The Interview

Before she started the first draft of her paper, Shannon returned to the library to collect information on the legislation that guarantees the disabled access and ensures their rights. In the process, she discovered some old laws that were so ridiculous that they could provide a dramatic introduction for her paper.

Shannon also contacted the director of her campus special resources center, who gave her names and telephone numbers of students who volunteered to talk with her. These face-to-face interviews proved to be a valuable resource in her paper. Shannon was able to describe the experiences of real individuals and to catch their actual voices in print.

Preparing for the Interview

In order to "catch" the voices of your interviewees, you need to do some prior work. First, as you draft your questions, think through exactly what information you want to gain from the interview. Start with an "icebreaker" question or two to put your interviewees at ease. If you suspect they may be guarded or unwilling to reveal the information you need—particularly for an argument essay, where they may represent the opposing position—you should order your questions so that the milder ones come first. Once the interviewees are engaged in conversation, it will be easier to get them to answer more hard-hitting questions.

Conducting the Interview

Although you have prepared questions and ordered them, you may find that the answers cause you to skip to another question or to think up a question on the spot. Your ability to respond with follow-up questions and encouragement ("Why do you think that happened?" "How did you respond?") may determine the depth of the interview. Such follow-up questions may prompt the interviewees to move from predictable responses to those that are fresh and candid.

As you take notes, concentrate on getting down key phrases and controversial claims. Shannon recorded this from one of her interviewees: "Some people are prejudiced and ignore us. That makes me angry." Shannon put quotation marks around exact words so she could remember which words were her subject's and which she added or paraphrased. As you interview your subjects, don't hesitate to ask them to clarify points or expand on ideas so you can get the necessary information.

Some interviewers use portable tape recorders as a backup to capture precise words, but make sure you ask permission to do so. Tape recorders haven't replaced notebooks and relying on tape recorders can be disastrous if the machine is malfunctioning or the tape turns out to be inaudible. Even if the tape is clear, it is tedious to sit through an hour or two of taped conversation in order to transcribe the key quotations. Before you leave, remember to ask about additional sources or reference materials (reading materials, brochures, and names of other specialists). Also, check the spelling of each interviewee's name.

Because these people are giving you some valuable time for the interview, it is essential that you offer to meet where and when it is convenient for *them.* Arrive on time, don't overstay your welcome, and prepare your questions before the meeting. Remember to be exceptionally courteous and to show appreciation for their time and help.

Writing up the Interview

Immediately after the interview, write out or type up the questions and answers while the session is still fresh in your mind. If you discover you have missed any important material or may have misunderstood a point, call back your interviewee immediately for a clarification.

When you integrate the interviewees' comments into your paper, be careful to quote exactly and to represent the context of the statement accurately. Misusing quotations or distorting their intended meaning destroys your integrity as a writer. Shannon found that her conversations with the disabled provided insights that her readings could not. The strength of her argument, however, could not rely only on interviews and personal experiences. She used nine printed sources, and three electronic sources to develop her argument.

SAMPLE STUDENT PAPER

You may be interested to know that our former student, Shannon Paaske, who wrote the research paper that we published in the first edition of *Between Worlds,* has finished her undergraduate work and is now a first-grade teacher in Los Angeles. It is probably every student's nightmare that a former teacher would track her down, but we did. Shannon agreed to update her paper using more current material, including the Internet. The numbers in the margin of the manuscript correspond to the numbers of the explanations on the facing page. These explanations will guide you through both rhetorical and mechanical considerations for your own paper.

1

2 3

4

5

6

7

8

Shannon Paaske

Professor Bachmann

English 1A

3 May 1999

From Access to Acceptance:

Enabling America's Largest Minority

In the early 1900s, a Chicago city ordinance stated that no "unsightly, deformed or maimed person can appear on the public thoroughfares" (Davidson 62). A court case in Wisconsin in 1919 upheld the expulsion from school of a twelve-year-old boy with cerebral palsy because his teachers and fellow students regarded him as "depressing and nauseating" (62). In contrast to these unjust laws of the first half of the twentieth century, the second half drafted legislation and designed equipment to improve life for the disabled. In 1990, the Americans with Disabilities Act was passed by Congress. This enormous piece of legislation, among other things, requires both public buildings and private businesses to provide architectural access for disabled persons and it prohibits discrimination against them in the workplace. Helping to remove even more barriers, the Assistive Technology Act was signed into law eight years later. This act promotes the use of technological devices designed to help disabled persons lead independent lives. A customized, computerized van allows a man paralyzed from the chest down to operate a motor vehicle by himself. And near the end of the twentieth century, major network television shows such as Life Goes On, L.A. Law, and Star Trek: The Next Generation regularly featured people with all types of disabilities.

Clearly, America's institutions have come a long way in acknowledging the 43 million people in this country with disabilities (Blackman 70). Although combinations of technological

Explanatory Notes for the Research Paper

The numbers on these explanatory notes correspond to the numbers in the margin of the research paper.

1. *Securing the paper.* When your paper is finished, staple the pages in the upper left-hand corner. Don't use a folder or plastic binder.
2. *Form.* Type your last name and the page number, as Shannon does, in the upper right-hand corner of each page, one-half inch from the top. All other margins will be one inch.

3. *Heading.* Begin your heading one inch from the top of the first page and flush with the left margin. Include your full name, instructor's name, the course number, and the date, double-spacing between lines. Double space again and center the title, and then double space between title and first line of the paper.

4. *Title.* Your title should engage your reader and establish an expectation for what the paper is about. It should please your reader's ears and eyes. If your reader stumbles while reading your title, it needs more work. Shannon's focus is unmistakable: the disabled person's wish for "access" and "acceptance." Do not underline or put quotation marks around your title.

5. *Citations.* Shannon's opening sentence includes a quotation, so she must document the source and page number in parentheses. The second time that Shannon quotes material from Davidson's article, she needs only the page number because Davidson's name has just been given.

6. *Introduction.* Shannon's introduction is a dramatic, abbreviated history of the legislation, equipment changes, and social responses to the disabled in this century. She quotes the exact language of the ordinances because the wording jolts the reader.

7. *Statistic.* Shannon notes that there are "43 million" disabled people in the United States and cites Blackman and the page where she located this figure.

8. *Thesis.* Shannon's thesis which begins with "although" forecasts her intention: to look at the technical and legislative changes, and increased media exposure, as improvements for the disabled. She will also examine the problems that plague the disabled and prevent their full "acceptance."

advances, equality-promoting legislation, and increasing media exposure have worked as a collective force in bringing about improvements in the lives of the people who make up what is sometimes termed "America's largest minority" (Davidson 61), ignorance and prejudice continue to plague the disabled.

Technological developments, almost exclusively computer-oriented, have revolutionized the world of the disabled person. Citizens who were once confined to home, forbidden to travel by air, and unable to attend classes or hold jobs have been liberated by recent inventions that encourage independence as well as allow for enriching life experiences. Just how extensive is the new technology? According to Jan Gavlin, director of assistive technology at the National Rehabilitation Hospital in Washington, "If you can move one muscle in your body, wiggle a pinkie or twitch an eyebrow, we can design a switch to allow you to operate in your environment" (qtd. in Blackman 71).

An example of one such device is the Eyegaze Response Interface Computer Aid (ERICA), developed by biomedical engineer Thomas Hutchinson at the University of Virginia. This eye-controlled computer empowers severely disabled yet bright people with the ability to learn and communicate. Ten years ago these people would have been misdiagnosed as mentally retarded by traditional tests that are unable to correctly measure their intelligence. Originally designed for children who previously might have been misdiagnosed, ERICA and other systems like it instead "create pathways for kids to express themselves and for teachers to engage their minds" (Rab and Youcha 22).

This technology also allows severely disabled adults to pursue careers, as in the case of Brian Dickinson. "Mr. Dickinson has amyotrophic lateral sclerosis [better known as Lou Gehrig's

Explanatory Notes *(continued)*

9. *Uncommon knowledge quoted.* It is not common knowledge that the disabled are "America's largest minority," so Shannon documents the source of this statement.

10. *Summarized material.* Noting past limitations, Shannon summarizes the technological developments that now "enable" the disabled.

11. *Quotation within the article.* Shannon credits a knowledgeable source, Jan Gavlin, as he is quoted in Blackman's article. Because she has wisely used Gavlin's name in her lead, Shannon needs only to cite that he is "quoted" in Blackman and give the page number. If she had not used Gavlin's name in her lead, her parenthetical reference would be: (Gavlin qtd. in Blackman 71).

12. *Two-author citation.* The parenthetical reference from an article written by two authors contains the last name of each author, connected with "and," and the page number of the article.

13. *Altering a quotation.* Shannon adds a clarification to her quoted material using brackets so that the reader knows that she has altered the quotation. A quotation should not be altered unless it is essential for clarity and then the alteration should not change the meaning of the original text.

disease], which has stripped him of the power to speak, swallow, move his legs or arms, wiggle his fingers or turn his head" (Felton 1). With the help of an Eyegaze system, Dickinson continues writing his column for <u>The Providence Journal-Bulletin</u> in Rhode Island. He selects certain functions on his computer screen simply by looking at the appropriate keys.

14   Other developments include computerized "sip and puff" machines which enable people without the use of their arms or legs to change television channels, talk on the phone, and play computer games simply by inhaling or exhaling into a plastic straw (Blackman 70). A system called DragonDictate is a computer program that prints dictation onto a monitor when the user speaks into a microphone (70). This type of program is especially useful to people who are unable to type because of poor muscle control (a characteristic of cerebral palsy) or who have various types of paralysis. The system even comes with a spell-check mode that responds to the incorrect word with an "oops."

    Modern wheelchair designs also reflect the recent advancements that permit the disabled to leave home and enter the world. Robert Cushmac, 16, who was paralyzed from the neck down in a car accident when he was 10, gets from class to class at his Virginia high school, where he is an honors student, in a wheelchair activated by a chin-controlled joystick (Blackman 71). The Hi-Rider is a "standing wheelchair" that was designed by Tom Houston who is paralyzed from the waist down. His design makes it possible for him to perform tasks previously impossible, such as reaching an object on an overhead shelf, or greeting someone face to face (Blackman 70).

15   As these examples show, the continuous headway being made in adaptive technology has considerably altered the way of life for

Explanatory Notes *(continued)*

14. *Paraphrased material.* Even though Shannon describes in her own words how the "sip and puff" machine is used, she must document the source of her information. If Shannon had felt there would be any confusion in her reader's mind about the source of her information, she would have repeated Blackman's name as she does in the next paragraph.

15. *Transition.* Shannon moves from her review of the technological advancements designed to enhance the lives of the disabled to a review of legislation that has given them rights. Notice that her transition establishes that the technological advancements would not have occurred without the legislative changes. This is a more critically perceptive transition, showing a cause and effect relationship, than one that suggests merely "another change for the disabled is in the area of legislation."

many disabled people. However, it is highly unlikely that much of this progress could have been accomplished without the help of a sympathetic political climate. Federal Disability Laws passed by Congress since 1968 addressed the environmental needs of the disabled and particularly focused on independent living as a goal. This goal expressed the desire of people with disabilities to view themselves and be viewed "no longer as passive victims deserving of charitable intervention but as self-directed individuals seeking to remove environmental barriers that preclude their full participation in society" (DeJong and Lifchez 45).

16

Laws such as the Architectural Barriers Act of 1968 required structures built with federal funds or leased by the federal government to be made accessible, and the Urban Mass Transportation Act and Federal Aid Highway Act of 1970 and 1973 worked to make transportation a reality for the disabled (DeJong and Lifchez 42). Later laws were created to achieve the attitudinal changes implicit in the objectives of the independent living movement. One law is The Rehabilitation Act of 1973, which prohibits discrimination against disabled people in programs, services, and benefits that are federally funded. The Rehabilitation Comprehensive Services and Developmental Disability Amendments of 1978 established independent living as a priority for state vocational programs and provided federal funding for independent living centers (DeJong and Lifchez 42). The Social Security Disability Amendments of 1980 gave disabled people more incentives to work by letting them deduct independent-living expenses from their taxes (42). The Americans with Disabilities Act, signed in 1990, reinforced the legislation that was not earlier implemented.

More recently, the Assistive Technology Act of 1998 ensures funding for statewide programs to promote the use of technological

Explanatory Notes *(continued)*

16. *Paraphrased and quoted material.* Shannon summarizes the various laws and acts and documents her source of information, the *Scientific American* article written by the two authors noted in her parenthetical references throughout this portion of her text. Her review of this legislation is historical, and it is chronologically arranged.

17 devices that improve the functional capabilities of disabled persons ("The ATA"). Because of the important role that such devices play to increase the independence of individuals with disabilities, the impact of this legislation is major. The speed and extent to which this impact can be felt is heavily influenced by the advent of the Internet. Through Websites such as ABLEDATA, ATA (Alliance for Technology Access) and RESNA (Rehabilitation Engineering and Assistive Technology Society of North America) users can look up specific information on assistive technology devices, get help with problems or questions, and even make personal con-

18 nections in chat rooms (ABLEDATA).

19 It is undeniable that new legislation, together with the flourishing of adaptive technology and Internet-based sources of support, have created greater awareness of the disabled in our communities. The increasing number of disabled characters in movies and television reflects that awareness. Deaf actress Marlee Matlin, for example, enjoyed success starring in the Academy

20 award-winning Children of a Lesser God in 1986, and later in the television series Reasonable Doubts. In assessing Matlin's charac-

21 ter in Reasonable Doubts, Ben Mattlin (no relation), a writer with a muscular dystrophy-related disease, says he "can't say enough good things about working a highly visible disability into a major character" (Mattlin 8). Ben Mattlin also finds it significant that this character is portrayed as both intelligent and sexy. In addi-

22 tion, on ABC's Life Goes On, Christopher Burke, an actor who has Down's Syndrome, played Corky, a "competent, high-functioning integral part of his family" (Mattlin 8). Because Matlin and Burke are disabled actors who portray disabled characters--in contrast to the many able-bodied actors who play disabled roles--they have helped mark a path of new acceptance for the disabled.

Explanatory Notes *(continued)*

17. *Documenting electronic sources.* Shannon used the Internet to find the most recent legislation affecting the disabled. Because there was no author, she credits the abbreviated *title* of the site in her parenthetical citation. "The ATA" is an abbreviation for "The Assistive Technology Act," found in the Works Cited section with the Web address so that the reader also can locate the information.

18. *Another electronic source.* Here again Shannon does not have an author so she uses the title of the site in her parenthetical reference.

19. *Conclusion to one section and transition to the next.* Shannon concludes her review of the legislation with a statement that the provisions of the most recent act for which she has information have not yet been fully implemented. She believes the impact will be "undeniable" when the act is fully in effect.

20. *New focus point.* Again, Shannon relates the next section of her paper to the previous sections by asserting that technology and legislation have made the disabled visible citizens in our communities. The media have reflected this visibility by increasing the number of disabled employed in film, television, and advertising.

21. *Parenthetical explanation.* Shannon makes a point of noting that the media critic, Ben Mattlin, is no relation to Marlee Matlin. She is then free to use Mattlin's name in parenthetical documentation without concern that her reader will be confused .

22. *Summary and direct quotation.* In a combination of summarized information and direct quotation, Shannon uses Ben Mattlin's article about the depictions of disabled actors in various media. She was tempted to use Mattlin's critical comments about the "distorted images" of the disabled in particular films, but she realized that this digression would change the balance and focus of her paper. From Mattlin's article, she used only what was relevant to her essay—brief references to actual programs and actors, and the appreciation of a disabled writer for positive portrayals of the disabled in film.

In addition, retail stores that employ the disabled to model
in their advertising create new public acceptance of the disabled.
In 1991, retail store Kids R Us hired disabled children from hospital pediatric wards to work as professional models for their
catalogues and circulars. Some of the store's executives got the
idea while watching these kids play. Vice President Ernie Speranza
reasoned, "They think of themselves as average kids, so we decided
we should too" (Speranza qtd. in Yorks 1). Kids R Us was not the
first retail store to make this move, and since 1990, Target and
Nordstrom's--representing both ends of the economic spectrum--
have hired disabled people of all ages as models in an effort
to better represent the diversity of its clientele (Yorks 1).

Also helping to bring more exposure through the media is
a television newsmagazine, a series of programs created by the
mother of an autistic child who wanted to create a television
show devoted to disabled people. This series provides "profiles
of courage and accomplishment and informs viewers of a wide range
of issues and opportunities to enhance quality of life through
greater self-sufficiency" (Disabilities and Possibilities). Winner of many awards, including an Emmy, this program has aired on
PBS stations throughout North America and aims to unify abled and
disabled people.

The arts community appears to be responding with greater
awareness as well. In 1999, a five-day festival in Los Angeles
celebrating "the arts, disability, and culture" hosted more than
eight international dance companies featuring disabled performers
(Haskins 108). Although efforts such as these indicate that the
media have "started to get a broader perspective on real life"
(Olson), people with disabilities have yet to enjoy full acceptance by American society. Nancy Mairs, a woman with multiple

Explanatory Notes *(continued)*

23. *Quotation within the article.* The vice president of a retail store is quoted within an article that Shannon read about the use of the disabled as models in advertising. She quotes him in her text and notes his name and the page of the quotation in her parenthetical reference.

24. *Quotation from an interview.* Because there are no page numbers associated with interviews, only the last name of the subject interviewed is enclosed in the parentheses. Shannon uses Steve Olson's comment about the value of images of the disabled in advertising as a transition to the final section of her paper. This section focuses on the feelings the disabled have about nondisabled people's perceptions of them. Shannon gained these insights in interviews as well as readings.

25. *Paraphrased and summarized material.* An experience noted by an author in her essay is summarized and paraphrased by Shannon, and the source of the material is documented.

Paaske 7

sclerosis who balances a college teaching and lecturing career with the demands of a marriage and motherhood, finds that while her family and the people she works with have accepted her disability, she still has had to endure an end-of-the-semester evaluation by a student who was perturbed by her disability (122).

While no longer blatantly discriminated against, the disabled often continue to suffer the burden of social bias. Even those remarkable individuals who are able to triumph over physical barriers have trouble surmounting social barriers. Post-polio actor Henry Holden relates his own experience with social discrimination:

> A guy with paralyzed legs is not supposed to be able to sell insurance, but I did very well at it in New Jersey before I became an actor. A guy with paralyzed legs is not supposed to climb mountains, but I made the trek up the cliff at Masada in Israel at four o'clock in the morning. A guy with paralyzed legs is not supposed to ride horses, but I rode in an exhibition in Madison Square Garden. Yet I am not generally accepted by nondisabled people in social situations. The attitude in the country is that, if you have a disability, you should stay home. (Holden qtd. in Davidson 63)

Susan Rodde, who has cerebral palsy, confirms that in most social situations, "we, the physically challenged, have to be the icebreakers." At parties and social gatherings, the disabled person is often isolated or ignored. Having used a wheelchair since a surfing accident, Berkeley student Steve Olson confirms this experience: "Sometimes I meet people at parties who feel uncomfortable about [my disability]. I talk and tell jokes to break the ice, and soon no one realizes there's a disabled person--

Explanatory Notes *(continued)*

26. *Long quotations.* Because the experience of the actor Henry Holden is especially revealing, Shannon decided to include the long quotation in her paper. Because the quotation is longer than four typed lines, it cannot be incorporated within the manuscript. Instead, the longer quotation is set off from the rest of the paper with double-spacing at the top and bottom of the quotation, and it is indented ten spaces or one inch from the left margin. The quotation itself is double-spaced, and the final period precedes the parenthetical information. If the first line of the quoted passage begins a new paragraph, it is indented 15 spaces.

27. *Brackets.* Shannon has enclosed in brackets a change that she has made in material from an interview. It is possible that her subject used a pronoun that would have been ambiguous to the reader; Shannon substituted the noun and placed the clarifying term in brackets. The reader understands that the brackets are used to clarify or change tense or other language forms to permit easy reading of the quoted material as it is integrated with the writer's text. No changes may be made and put into brackets that would alter the meaning of the material quoted. (See p. 607–608 for more information about brackets.)

me--sitting in the room with them." Unfortunately, the "ice" does need to be broken because many people feel uncomfortable around disabled or disfigured people, and so far, the responsibility of making social contact lies with the disabled person.

28   But many of the disabled report that fully abled people have a hard time "respecting the fact that we're the same as they are," says Diane DeVries, who was born with no legs and only par-tial arms. Perhaps because of ignorance or fear, our disabilities
29 "remind people of their own vulnerabilities" (DeVries). As Nancy Mairs says, "Society is no readier to accept crippledness than to
30 accept death, war, sex, sweat, or wrinkles" (119). Because they may feel vulnerable, able-bodied people tend not to form close relationships with disabled people, and some even refuse casual contact. Rebecca Acuirre, 16, who has cerebral palsy, says that she recently asked a stranger what time it was and he kept walk-ing as though he didn't hear her. "Some people are prejudiced and ignore us. That makes me angry," she says.

       How can these prejudices be abolished? "We need more expo-sure," says DeVries. Acuirre concurs, saying the media should do more to educate the public. On a personal level, Bill Davidson, in "Our Largest Minority, Americans with Handicaps," recommends
31 the nondisabled public "help reverse centuries of discrimina-tion" by getting to know disabled people "at work, in the mar-ketplace, at school" and by making "contact that is real--not just casual" (63). Able-bodied people can help overcome their own preconceived notions and realize that if disabled people seem bitter, "it's not because of their disability ... but because of society's attitude toward them." Prejudices can be stopped before they start by encouraging children "not to shun and fear" the disabled (63).

Explanatory Notes *(continued)*

28. *Incorporating short quotations.* Shannon incorporates into her text the specific quoted material from her reading and interviews. When the subject of an interview is named in the text, there is no need for additional documentation.

29. *Interview subject quoted.* Because Shannon does not reuse Diane DeVries's name in her text, she documents the source of the quotation by using DeVries's last name in parentheses.

30. *Documentation from a book.* Nancy Mairs's name is used in Shannon's text, so only the page number of the book is cited in parentheses.

31. *Incorporating summary and quotations.* Shannon introduces the author and title of the article in her text. This attribution within her text facilitates Shannon's documentation; she needs to note only the page number within the parentheses. Her citations document the specific quoted material as well as the paraphrased content of Davidson's article.

Paaske 9

The legislation and technology that were developed at the end of the twentieth century will continue to make new worlds accessible to the disabled. Ideally, these developments will permit the disabled to be viewed in terms of their capabilities rather than their disabilities. In that climate, the disabled can gain acceptance in the worlds to which they have access. With the steps being taken by government, science, and the media, individuals alone are needed to make the dream of acceptance a reality for the disabled.

32

Explanatory Notes *(continued)*

32. *Conclusion.* In her conclusion, Shannon reviews the relationship between the points she has made in her paper. She concludes by asserting that the advancements for the disabled lie in the hands of individuals, not only institutions. She uses the language of her title to bring a more dramatic closure to her analysis.

Works Cited

ABLEDATA. The National Institute on Disability and Rehabilitation Research. U.S. Department of Education. 11 Apr. 1999 <http://www.abledata.com>.

Acuirre, Rebecca. Personal interview. 23 Sept. 1992.

"The Assistive Technology Act of 1998." RESNA. 11 Apr. 1999 <http://www.resna.org/ata/>.

Blackman, Ann. "Machines That Work Miracles." Time 18 Feb. 1991: 70-71.

Davidson, Bill. "Our Largest Minority: Americans with Handicaps." McCall's Sept. 1987: 61-68.

Dejong, Gerben, and Raymond Lifchez. "Physical Disability and Public Policy." Scientific American June 1983: 40-49.

DeVries, Diane. Telephone interview. 22 Sept. 1992.

Disabilities and Possibilities Television Newsmagazine. 10 April 1999 <http://www.disabilities-tv.com/>.

Felton, Bruce. "Technologies That Enabled the Disabled: High-tech or Low, Devices Enrich Work." New York Times 14 Sept. 1997, late ed.: Sec 3, 1+.

Haskins, Ann. "Dance Listings." LA Weekly. 28 May 1999: 108.

Paaske 10

Mairs, Nancy. "On Being a Cripple." With Wings: An Anthology of Literature by and about Women with Disabilities. Ed. Marsha Saxon and Florence Howe. New York: Feminist Press, 1987. 118-27.

Mattlin, Ben. "Beyond Reasonable Doubts: The Media and People with Disabilities." Television and Families 13.3 (1991): 4-8.

Olson, Steve. Telephone interview. 18 Sept. 1992.

Rab, Victoria Y., and Geraldine Youcha. "Body." Omni June 1990: 22+.

Rodde, Susan. Telephone interview. 20 Sept. 1992.

Yorks, Cindy LaFavre. "Challenging Images." Los Angeles Times. 22 Nov. 1991: E1-2.

Explanatory Notes *(continued)*

33. *The form for the list of sources used in the text.* The Works Cited page should always begin on a new numbered page at the end of the paper. The head is centered on the line, one inch from the top of the page. The first cited work is typed two lines beneath the heading. The entire list is double-spaced. The list is alphabetically arranged by the author or speaker's last name or by the first word in the title of an unsigned article. The entry begins at the left margin. If it is longer than one line, its second line begins five spaces indented from the left margin. (More complete information on MLA form begins on p. 542.)

34. Entry for an electronic source.

35. Entry for a personal interview. The date of the interview is noted.

36. Entry for an electronic source.

37. Entry for a signed article in a weekly periodical.

38. Entry for a signed article in a monthly periodical.

39. Entry for a magazine article written by two authors.

40. Entry for a telephone interview. The date of the interview is noted.

41. Entry for an electronic source.

42. Entry for a signed daily newspaper article. Notice the plus sign (1) after page 1 to indicate that after the first page the article continues on nonconsecutive pages.

43. Entry for a signed column in a weekly newspaper.

44. Entry for a chapter within an anthology with two editors. Notice that the name of the author of the chapter Shannon used is listed first.

45. Entry for a signed article in a periodical with volume and number.

46. Entry for a telephone interview.

47. Entry for two authors of an article within a monthly periodical. Notice that the article started on page 22 but did not appear on continuous pages. The "1" symbol indicates that the pages were not consecutive.

48. Entry for a telephone interview.

49. Entry for a signed article in a daily newspaper. Notice the "E" prior to the page number to indicate the section of the newspaper in which the article appeared.

Documenting the Research Paper: MLA Style

Whenever you use the words, information, or ideas of another writer—even if in your own words you summarize or paraphrase—you must credit the source. The following forms show you exactly how to provide the necessary information for documenting your sources according to the Modern Language Association (MLA) style guide. You can check the MLA Website <http://www.mla.org/> for additional documentation information and updating. The sixth edition (2003) of the *MLA Handbook for Writers of Research Papers* is the source for this section, and it is certainly the form that your college English instructors will want you to use.

Writing Parenthetical Citations

Your in-text citation should give just enough information so that your reader can find the origin of your material on the works-cited page (your bibliography) at the end of your paper. Here are sample parenthetical citations to illustrate MLA format:

Author Not Named in the Text. When you haven't included the author's name in your text, you must note in parentheses the author's last name and the page or pages of your source.

> "The first steps toward the mechanical measurement of time, the beginnings of the modern clock in Europe, came not from farmers or shepherds, nor from merchants or craftsmen, but from religious persons anxious to perform promptly and regularly their duties to God" (Boorstin 36).

Author Named in the Text. It is often advantageous to introduce your paraphrased or quoted material by noting the author's name within your text, especially if your author is an authority on the subject. If you do include the author's name in the text, your parenthetical citation will be brief and less intrusive, containing only the page number by itself.

> According to Daniel Boorstin, the senior historian of the Smithsonian Institute, "the first steps toward the mechanical measurement of time, the beginnings of the modern clock in Europe, came not from farmers or shepherds, nor from merchants or craftsmen, but from religious persons anxious to perform promptly and regularly their duties to God" (36).

Two Books by the Same Author.   If your paper contains two different works by the same author, each parenthetical reference should give an abbreviated form of the title, with the page number, so that your reader will know which work you are citing in each section of your paper.

Ben Mattlin deplores the pity for the disabled that Jerry
Lewis's yearly telethon evokes ("Open Letter" 6). Mattlin also exposes the hypocrisy in depicting the disabled as superheroes. His
point is that "courage and determination are often necessary when
living with a disability. But there's nothing special in that, because there's no choice. Flattering appraisals sound patronizing"
("Beyond Reasonable Doubts" 5).

A Work with Two or Three Authors.   If the work was written by two or three authors, use each of their names in your text or in the parenthetical citations.

In their study of John Irving's The World According to Garp,
Janice Doane and Devon Hodges analyze the author's attitude toward
female authority: "Even novels that contain sympathetic female
characters, as Irving's novel does, may still be oppressive to
women" (11).

Critics have charged that John Irving's The World According
to Garp doesn't really support female authority: "Even novels that
contain sympathetic female characters, as Irving's does, may still
be oppressive to women" (Doane and Hodges 11).

A Work with More Than Three Authors.   If your source was written by more than three authors, you may use only the first author's last name, followed by "et al." and the page number in parentheses or you may list all of the authors' last names in the text or with the page number in parentheses.

In Women's Ways of Knowing: The Development of Self, Voice,
and Mind, the authors note that there are many women who "believed
they were stupid and helpless. They had grown up either in actual
physical danger or in such intimidating circumstances that they
feared being wrong, revealing their ignorance, being laughed at"
(Belenky et al. 57).

In Women's Ways of Knowing: The Development of Self, Voice,
and Mind, the authors note that there are many women who "believed

they were stupid and helpless. They had grown up either in actual physical danger or in such intimidating circumstances that they feared being wrong, revealing their ignorance, being laughed at" (Belenky, Clinchy, Goldberger, and Tarule 57).

In Women's Ways of Knowing: The Development of Self, Voice, and Mind, Belenky, Clinchy, Goldberger, and Tarule note that there are many women who "believed they were stupid and helpless. They had grown up either in actual physical danger or in such intimidating circumstances that they feared being wrong, revealing their ignorance, being laughed at" (57).

Author's Name Not Given.   If the author is anonymous, use the complete title in your text or an abbreviated form of the title with the page number in the parentheses.

The obituary for Allan Bloom in Newsweek describes him as the man who "ignited a national debate on higher education" and "defended the classics of Western Culture and excoriated what he saw as the intellectual and moral relativism of the modern academy" ("Transition" 73).

Corporate Author or Government Publication.   Either name the corporate author in your text or include an abbreviated form in the parentheses. If the name is long, try to work it into your text to avoid an intrusive citation.

Southern California Edison, in a reminder to customers to "Conserve and Recycle," gives the shocking statistic that "every hour, Americans go through 2.5 million plastic bottles, only a small percentage of which are now recycled" (Customer Update 4).

Literature: Novel, Play, Poem.   Because works appear in various editions, it is best to give the chapter number or part in addition to the page number to help your reader find the reference you are citing.

Novel

In the novel Invisible Man, Ralph Ellison uses a grotesque comparison to describe eyes: "A pair of eyes peered down through lenses as thick as the bottom of a Coca-Cola bottle, eyes protruding, luminous and veined, like an old biology specimen preserved in alcohol" (230; ch. 11).

Play

The parenthetical citation includes just the arabic numbers for the act, scene, and lines. These numbers are separated by periods: (4.3.89-90).

```
     In William Shakespeare's Othello, Emilia sounds like a twen-
tieth-century feminist when she claims that "it is their husbands'
faults" if their wives have affairs (4.3.89-90).
```

Poem

The parenthetical citation includes the line or lines of the poem cited: (13-14).

```
     Poet Robert Hass, in "Misery and Splendor," describes the
frustration of lovers longing to be completely united: "They are
trying to become one creature, / and something will not have it"
(13-14).
```

Indirect Source.   When you use the words of a writer who is quoted in another author's work, begin the citation with the abbreviation "qtd. in" and both writers' last names if you have not used them in your text.

```
     Women and men both cite increased "freedom" as a benefit of
divorce. But Riessman discovered that women meant that they
"gained independence and autonomy" while men meant that they felt
"less confined," "less claustrophobic," and had "fewer responsi-
bilities" (Kohler Riessman qtd. in Tanner 40-41).
```

More Than One Work.   If you want to show that two works are the sources of your information, separate the references with a semicolon.

```
     Two recent writers concerned with men's issues observe that
many women have options to work full time or part time, stay at
home, or combine staying at home with a career. On the other hand,
men need to stay in the corporate world and provide for the family
full time (Allis 81; Farrell 90).
```

Online Sources

Online Source—Author Given

When you incorporate online sources, use the same form as you would for a book or periodical: Give the author's name in parentheses followed by the page number if the entry is longer than one page. If it is one page or less, give only the author's name.

```
     "Making Media a Familiar Scapegoat" concludes with the claim:
"Trench coats don't kill, guns and pipe bombs do" (Rosenberg 3-4).
```

If the Internet material uses paragraph numbers rather than page numbers, give the relevant number or numbers preceded by the abbreviation *par.* or *pars.*

> In the study "National and Colonial Education in Shake-speare's The Tempest," Prospero's character is not limited to that of a dramatist: "Throughout the play Prospero teaches all the characters, and the teacher role could be seen to fit him better than even the customary playwright" (Carey-Webb par. 11).

If the material is not on numbered pages or lacks numbered paragraphs, identify by screen number, followed by the number of the screen or screens, in parentheses.

Online Source—Author Unknown

Often no author is given for material available on the Internet. In such cases, use the same form you would for an unsigned article in a periodical or reference book: an abbreviated form of the title (first significant word or two).

> An advancement such as the Eyegaze System "enables people with severe motor disabilities to do many things with their eyes that they would otherwise do with their hands" ("Unique Products").

If no author or title is available, use the name of the Website.

> Through the Internet, the disabled can look up specific information on assistive technology devices, get help with problems or questions, and even make personal connections in chat rooms (ABLEDATA).

Preparing the Works-Cited Page

Whenever you note in parentheses that you have used someone else's material, you will need to explain that source completely in the works-cited list (the bibliography) at the end of your research paper. The Works Cited always begins on a new and numbered page at the end of the paper. The entries are arranged alphabetically, according to authors' last names. If there are no authors named, then the works are listed according to title. If the title begins with "A" or "The," keep the article in the title but alphabetize according to the second word.

All sources—whether book or journal article—are arranged together on one list. Do not have a list of books and then a list of periodical titles. Do not number the entries. Double space between all lines, both within an entry and between entries. Each entry starts at the left-hand margin and extends to the right-hand margin. If additional lines are needed for an entry, indent 5 spaces or one-half inch. To see how the Works Cited page should look, turn to the student research paper on page 540.

Because the complete source is listed only in the works cited, it is essential that each entry conform exactly to standard form so that the reader can easily locate your source. Most of the forms that you will need are illustrated here.

Elements of a Citation

1. 2.

Fiedler, Leslie. <u>Freaks: Myths and Images of the Secret Self</u>.

6.{ New York: Simon, 1978.

3. 4. 5.

1. Use the author's full name—last name first—followed by a comma and then the first name and any middle name or initial. Omit any titles (Dr., Ph.D., Rev.). End with a period and one space.

2. Print the book's full title including any subtitles. Underline the title and capitalize the first and last words as well as all important words. If there is a subtitle, separate the main title and the subtitle with a colon and one space. Place a period after the title and leave one space.

3. Type the publication information beginning with the city of publication, followed by a colon and one space.

4. Print the name of the publisher, followed by a comma. Shorten the name by removing "and Co." or "Inc." Abbreviate multiple names to include only the first name. (The "Simon" in the example refers to Simon and Schuster.) If you are citing a university press, abbreviate as "UP." See the Boardman citation below.

5. Include the date of publication and end with a period.

6. Any line after the first line is double-spaced and indented one-half inch (or five spaces if you are using a typewriter).

Sample MLA Entries

BOOKS

One Author

Fiedler, Leslie. <u>Freaks: Myths and the Images of the Secret Self</u>.
    New York: Simon, 1978.

Two or Three Authors

Doane, Janice, and Devon Hodges. <u>Nostalgia and Sexual Difference:</u>
    <u>The Resistance to Contemporary Feminism</u>. New York: Methuen,
    1987.

Notice that any authors' names after the first author are written with the first name before the last name.

More Than Three Authors or Editors

Boardman, John, et al., eds. <u>The Oxford History of the Classical</u>

<u>World</u>. New York: Oxford UP, 1986.

or

Boardman, John, Jasper Griffin, and Oswyn Murray, eds. <u>The Oxford</u>

<u>History of the Classical World</u>. New York: Oxford UP, 1986.

With more than three authors, you have the choice of shortening the entry to provide only the first author's name, followed by the Latin abbreviation "et al." (which means "and others"), or you may provide all of the names. Notice that Oxford University Press is abbreviated "Oxford UP."

Author with an Editor or Editors

Shakespeare, William. <u>King Lear</u>. Ed. Barbara A. Mowat and Paul

Werstine. New York: Washington Square, 1993.

Cite the name of the author first and then, after the title of the work, give the editor's name or names, preceded by "Ed."—an abbreviation for "edited by."

Book with an Editor and No Author Cited

Webb, Charles H., ed. <u>Stand Up Poetry: The Anthology</u>. Long Beach:

UP California State U, 1994.

If the book does not have an author, cite the editor's name, followed by "ed."

Selection from an Anthology or Collection

Mabry, Marcus. "Living in Two Worlds." <u>Between Worlds: A Reader,</u>

<u>Rhetoric, and Handbook</u>. Ed. Susan Bachmann and Melinda Barth.

4th ed. New York: Longman, 2004. 144–146.

Mairs, Nancy. "On Being a Cripple." <u>With Wings: An Anthology of</u>

<u>Literature by and about Women with Disabilities</u>. Ed. Marsha

Saxton and Florence Howe. New York: Feminist P at City U NY,

1987. 118–27.

Olds, Sharon. "True Love." <u>The Wellspring</u>. New York: Knopf, 1996.

88.

Give the author and title of the selection, using quotation marks around the title. Then give the title of the anthology, underlined. If the anthology has an editor, note the name or names after the "Ed." Give the page numbers for the entire selection as shown.

Two or More Selections from the Same Anthology

Bachmann, Susan, and Melinda Barth, eds. <u>Between Worlds: A Reader,</u>

    <u>Rhetoric, and Handbook</u>. 4th ed. New York: Longman, 2004.

Holman, M. Carl. "Mr. Z." Bachmann 241-242.

Staples, Brent. "Black Men and Public Space." Bachmann

    237-240.

To avoid repetition, give the full citation for the book once, under the editor's last name. Then list all articles under the individual authors' names, followed by the title of their work. After each title, put the editor's name as a cross-reference to the complete citation.

Two or More Books by the Same Author(s)

Lamott, Anne. <u>All New People</u>. New York: Doubleday, 1991.

---. <u>Bird by Bird: Some Instruction on Writing and Life</u>. New York:

    Doubleday, 1994.

Give the author's name for the first entry only. After that, type three hyphens in place of the name, followed by a period and one space and then the next title. The three hyphens always stand for exactly the same name as in the preceding entry. The titles of the author's works should be listed alphabetically.

Corporate Author

National Council of Teachers of English. <u>Guidelines for Nonsexist</u>

    <u>Use of Language in NCTE Publications</u>. Urbana, Illinois:

    NCTE, 1975.

Use the name of the institution or corporation as the author even if it is also the name of the publisher. Abbreviate the institution's name if it is repeated: NCTE.

Author Not Named

<u>Webster's College Dictionary</u>. New York: Random House, 1995.

If a book has no author noted on the title page, begin the entry with the title and alphabetize according to the first word other than "a," "an," or "the."

Other Than First Edition

    If you are citing an edition other than the first, place the edition number between the title and the publication information.

Republication

Melville, Herman. <u>Billy Budd, Sailor (An Inside Narrative)</u>. 1924.

    Chicago: U Chicago P, 1962.

If you are citing a work that has been published by different publishers, place the original date of publication (but not the place or publisher's name) after the title. Then provide the complete information for the source you are using.

Book Title Within the Title

Gilbert, Stuart. <u>James Joyce's</u> Ulysses. New York: Vintage,

    1955.

If the title of the work that you are using contains another book title, do not underline or place the original book title in quotation marks.

Story or Poem Title Within the Title

Cisneros, Sandra. <u>"Woman Hollering Creek" and Other Stories</u>. New

    York: Random House, 1991.

If the title of the work that you are using contains a title that is normally enclosed in quotation marks (a short story or poem), keep the quotation marks and underline the entire title, extending the underlining to include the final period and the opening or closing quotation mark: <u>Dare to Eat a Peach: A Study of "The Love Song of J. Alfred Prufrock."</u>

Multivolume Work

Raine, Kathleen. <u>Blake and Tradition</u>. 2 vols. Princeton: Princeton

    UP, 1968.

If you have used two or more volumes of a multivolume work, state the total number of volumes in the work. Place this information ("2 vols.") between the title and publishing information.

Malone, Dumas. <u>The Sage of Monticello</u>. Boston: Little, Brown,

    1981. Vol. 6 of <u>Jefferson and His Time</u>. 6 vols. 1943–1981.

If you are using only one volume of a multivolume work, give the title of that volume after the author's name and then give the publishing information. After the publishing date, note the volume number, the title of the book, and the number of volumes in the collection. If the volumes were published over a period of years, indicate the dates.

Translation

Marquez, Gabriel García. <u>Love in the Time of Cholera</u>. Trans. Edith

    Grossman. New York: Penguin, 1988.

When citing a work that has been translated, give the author's name first. After the title, give the translator's name, preceded by "Trans."

Introduction, Preface, Foreword, or Afterword

Grumbach, Doris. Foreword. <u>Aquaboogie</u>. By Susan Straight. Min-
neapolis: Milkweed, 1990.

If you are citing material from an introduction, preface, foreword, or afterword written by someone other than the author of the book, give the name of the writer and designate the section she or he wrote. Notice also that "Foreword" is without underlining or quotation marks. After the title of the work, "By" precedes the author's name.

If the author of the introduction or preface is the same as the author of the book, give only the last name after the title:

Conrad, Joseph. Author's Note. <u>Youth: A Narrative; and Two Other</u>
<u>Stories</u>. By Conrad. New York: Heinemann, 1917. 3-5.

Article in an Encyclopedia or Other Reference Books

Benet, William Rose. "Courtly Love." <u>The Reader's Encyclopedia</u>.
1987 ed.

"Hodgkin's Disease." <u>The New Columbia Encyclopedia</u>. 4th ed.
1975.

If there is an author of the edition or article, alphabetize by last name. Otherwise, alphabetize in the works-cited page by the title of the entry.

PERIODICALS: JOURNALS, MAGAZINES, AND NEWSPAPERS

Journal with Continuous Pagination

Cooper, Mary H. "Setting Environmental Priorities." <u>Congressional</u>
<u>Quarterly Researcher</u> 9.19 (21 May 1999): 425-28.

Fowler, Rowena. "Moments and Metamorphoses: Virginia Woolf's
Greece." <u>Comparative Literature</u> 51.3 (1999): 217-42.

Journals sometimes paginate consecutively throughout a year. Each issue, after the first one, continues numbering from where the previous issue ended. After the title, give the volume number followed by a period and the issue number, if there is one. (See the first example, "Cooper".) Conclude with the publication date in parentheses, followed by a colon and the page numbers.

Journal That Paginates Each Issue Separately

Anderson, Maxwell L. "Museums of the Future: The Impact of Technology on Museum Practices." <u>Daedalus</u> 128.3 (1999): 129-62.

```
Heilbrun, Carolyn. "Contemporary Memoirs." The American Scholar
     68.3 (1999): 35-42.
```

If the journal numbers each issue separately, give the volume number, a period, and the issue number (as in "68.3" above) after the title of the journal.

Monthly or Bimonthly Periodical

```
Schulhofer, Stephen. "Unwanted Sex." Atlantic Monthly Oct. 1998:
     55-66.
```

Notice that in a monthly or bimonthly periodical, the month of publication is abbreviated (except for May, June, and July), and no volume or issue numbers are given.

Weekly or Biweekly Periodical

```
Anderson, Jan Lee. "The Power of García Marquez." New Yorker 27
     Sept. 1999: 56-71.
```

Daily Newspaper, Signed Article

```
Yee, Amy. "Please Leave Your Stereotypes at the Door." Christian
     Science Monitor 7 July 1999: 15.
```

Daily Newspaper, Unsigned Article or Editorial

```
"Jerusalem and Disney." Jerusalem Post 24 Sept. 1999: A26.
```

If the newspaper is divided into numbered or lettered sections, give the section designation before the page number, as in "A26". If the article continues on a nonconsecutive page, write only the first page number followed immediately (no space) by a 1 and a period.

```
Rosenbaum, David E. "Budgetary Posturing." New York Times.
     2 Mar. 1995, late ed.: A1.
```

If the newspaper has editions (late ed., natl ed.) include this item after the date and before the colon.

Titled Review

```
Friedman, Jane. "An Artist Who Promotes Glass Consciousness."
     Washington Post. 26 Sept. 1999 G1+.
```

The page number "G1+" in the citation indicates that the article starts on page G1 but does not continue on consecutive pages.

Untitled Review

```
Shore, Paul. Rev. of Backlash: The Undeclared War Against American
     Women, by Susan Faludi. The Humanist Sept.-Oct. 1992: 47-48.
```

OTHER SOURCES

Interview

```
Cuff, Ross. Personal Interview. 12 Feb. 2000.
Daigh, Sarah. Telephone interview. 18 Mar. 2000.
```

Film or Videotape

```
In the Line of Fire. Dir. Wolfgang Petersen. Perf. Clint Eastwood,
     John Malkovich, Rene Russo, and Dylan McDermott. Columbia,
     1993.
```

If you want to refer to a particular individual involved with the film, cite that person's name first:

```
Malkovich, John, actor. In the Line of Fire. Dir. Wolfgang Pe-
     tersen. Perf. Clint Eastwood, Rene Russo, and Dylan McDer-
     mott. Columbia, 1993.
```

Television or Radio Program

```
"Inspector Morse: Cherubim and Seraphim." 2 episodes. Mystery. Perf.
     John Thaw, Kevin Whateley. PBS. WNET, New York. 2 Mar. 1995.
```

As in a film citation, if you wish to refer to a particular person in the program, cite that name first, followed by the rest of the listing. The episode is put in quotation marks; the program name is underlined. A series name (if any) is neither put in quotation marks nor underlined. Except for the comma between the local station and the city, a period follows every item. Narrators, directors, adapters, or performers can be listed if relevant.

ELECTRONIC SOURCES

To cite an electronic source, you will include the standard elements of a typical citation as well as additional information specifically for electronic sources. Characteristic citations are illustrated here.

An Article in an Online Periodical

A typical entry for an article from a periodical will include the following:

1. Author (if given)
2. Title of the article (in quotation marks)
3. Title of the journal or newspaper (underlined or in italics)
4. Publication information: volume number, issue number or other identifying number

5. Year only, of original publication (in parentheses); complete date of original publication (no parentheses)

6. Number of pages (if more than one); or paragraphs (if numbered); or number of screen(s); or n. pag. (to indicate "no pagination")

7. Date of access. Because electronic material is often changed or updated, you need to give the date when you obtained your information.

8. Electronic address in angle brackets (< >). There are no spaces between the letters and symbols in the address. If your address fills more than one line, break the address only after a forward slash. Your citation will end with a final period, but this period is *not* part of the electronic address.

If some of the information is not available, cite what is available.

Ventura, Michael. "Shattered Illusions: Los Angeles Preparing for
the Unknown." <u>Los Angeles Times</u>. 22 Jan. 1995, home ed.: M1.
14 Aug. 1996. <http://www.latimes.com/HOME/RESEARCH/>.

Markels, Alex. "MCI Unit Finds Culture Shock After Relocating to
Colorado." <u>Wall Street Journal Interactive Edition</u>. 25 June
1996. 7 pp. 8 June 1996. Available <http://www.wsj.com/>.

Because the pages of the online article were numbered and a total number of pages given, the documentation includes "7 pp." The article was accessed on June 28, three days after it was put online. The mailing address is given in this citation.

An Article from a Subscription Service

College libraries subscribe to different services. When you access material from one of the services, include the name and publisher of the database and the subscribing institution and the city where it is located in addition to the basic Web information.

Tyrell, R Emmett Jr. "The Worst Book of the Year." <u>American Spec-</u>
<u>tator</u> May 1997:18. <u>MasterFilePremier</u>. EBSCO Publishing.
El Camino Coll. Lib., Torrance. 14 Apr. 2000 <http://
search.epnet.com/login.asp>.

"Gabriel (Jose) Garcia Marquez." <u>Contemporary Authors</u>. 13 Feb.
2001. 32 pars. <u>Gale Literary Databases</u>. Gale Group.
El Camino Coll. Lib., Torrance. 11 Oct. 2001. <http://
infotrac.galenet.com/servlet/GLD?loclD=cclc_el>.

An Article in a Scholarly Journal

Carey-Webb, Allen. "National and Colonial Education in

    Shakespeare's The Tempest." Early Modern Literary Studies 5.1

    (1999): 39 pars. 5 Sept. 1999 <http://purl.oclc.org/emls/

    05-1/cwebtemp.html>.

A Scholarly Project or Information Database

A characteristic entry for an online project or database will include the
following:

1. Title of the project or database underlined

2. Name of the editor of the project or database if given

3. Electronic publication information, including version number if given,
   date of electronic publication or of the latest update, and name of any
   sponsoring institution or organization

4. Date of access and network address

The Walt Whitman Hypertext Archive. Eds. Kenneth M. Price and Ed

    Folsom. 16 Mar. 1998. College of William and Mary. 3 Apr.

    1998 <http://jefferson.village.virginia.edu/whitman/>.

An Online Book Available Independently

A characteristic entry for a complete online book consists of the following
items:

1. Author's name if given; if an editor, compiler, translator is identified, cite
   that person's name followed by the appropriate abbreviation (ed., comp.,
   trans.).

2. Title of the work underlined

3. Name of the editor, compiler, or translator if relevant

4. Publication information, including facts about the original print version
   if they are given in the source

5. Date of access and network address

If you cannot find some of the information, cite what is available.

Austen, Jane. Pride and Prejudice. Ed. Henry Churchyard. 1996. 5

    Sept. 1999 <http://www.pemberley.com/janeinfo/pridprej.html>.

A Professional or Personal Site

A typical entry for a professional or personal site will include the following:

1. The name of the person who created the site, if given and relevant

2. Title of the site underlined (If no title, give a description such as *Home page,* which is neither underlined nor in quotation marks.)

3. Name of any institution or organization

4. Date of access

5. Network address

```
Gajewski, Walter. "Oh, What a Web We Weave." California State U,
      Long Beach. 25 Feb 2003 <http://www.csulb.edu/~gajewski/web/>.
Perry, Stephen. Poems. 5 Sept. 1999 <http://www.bunnyape.com>.
```

An Online Government Publication

For a typical government publication, use the following entry as a model:

```
United States. CIA Publications and Handbooks. 1995 World Fact-book.
      Washington, D.C.: Central Intelligence Agency (1995). 3 Jan.
      1996. <http://www.odci.gov/cia/publications/95fact/index.html>.
```

If no author is given, as in a government publication, cite the institution or publishing agency.

Electronic Conference

```
Sagady, Alexander. "Mich 'Hands on' Family Law Workshop."
      4 June 1996. Newsgroup alt.dad's-rights. Usenet. 15 July
      1996. <asagady@sojournl.sojourn.com>.
```

For electronic conferences, include the name of the computer network and any headings (as in "Newsgroup alt.dad's-rights"). Note that the posting date and the access date here are different.

Electronic Source Not in Print

```
Nowviskie, Bethany. "John Keats: A Hypermedia Guide." Wake Forest
      U. 26 Feb 2003. <http://www.wfu.edu/~nowvibp4/keats.htm>.
```

A CD-ROM

Many journals, magazines, newspapers, and periodically published reference works are published both in print and on CD-ROM. A characteristic entry will include the following:

1. Author's name if given

2. Publication information for the printed source, including title and date of print publication

3. Title of database, underlined

4. Publication medium (CD-ROM)

5. Name of vendor if relevant

6. Electronic publication date

If some of this information is incomplete, include what you do have.

```
Nehemiah, Marcia. "Nicholas Negroponte." Digit. Issue #8.

     CD-ROM. PC Carullo. pp. 55-60.

The Oxford English Dictionary. 2nd ed. CD-ROM. New York:

     Oxford UP, 1992.
```

If you are using only a part of the work, state which part. If the part is a book-length work, underline the title. If you are using a shorter part, such as an article, essay, poem, or short story, enclose the title in quotation marks.

```
"Artifice." The Oxford English Dictionary. 2nd ed. CD-ROM. New

     York: Oxford UP, 1992.
```

Documenting the Research Paper: APA Style

Although most English instructors will require MLA form for documenting sources, instructors from other disciplines may prefer American Psychological Association (APA) form. Check with your instructors to see which of the two forms they prefer. *These two styles are very different;* don't *confuse them.*

Writing Parenthetical Citations

The differences between MLA and APA forms are that in APA parenthetical citations, the date of publication and sometimes the page number of the source are included. The punctuation is also different.

According to APA form, if the sentence preceding quoted material includes the author's name, the date of publication will follow in parentheses. Then, at the end of the quotation, include the page number in parentheses.

```
     In Ben Mattlin's recent study (1991) of the media and people

with disabilities, he approves Christopher Burke's role as a "com-

petent, high-functioning, integral part of his family" (p. 8).
```

Notice that the date of the study is included within the introduction to the quotation, and then the page number is abbreviated as "p." within the final parentheses.

If you do not use the author's name when you introduce the quoted material, place the author's name, the date, and the page number in parentheses at the end of the quoted material. Use commas between the items in the parentheses.

```
    One critic approves Christopher Burke's role as a "competent,

high-functioning, integral part of his family" (Mattlin, 1991,

p. 8).
```

If you paraphrase the material rather than quoting it specifically, include the author's last name and the date of publication either in your text or in the parentheses at the end of the summarized material. Do not include the page number.

```
According to Ben Mattlin (1991), disabled actors are playing im-

portant roles in television dramas.
```

```
One writer who has examined the media's treatment of the disabled

reports some positive changes in television (Mattlin, 1991).
```

To cite an Internet document in the body of a paper, provide the name of the author, followed by the date. If no author is given, begin with the name of the document. If you use a direct quotation, provide the page number or paragraph number in the parenthesis, after the date: (Markels, 1996, p. 6) or (Markels, 1996, para. 4).

Specific Examples of APA Form

Here are specific examples of common situations you may need to document in APA form.

A Work with Two Authors.   If your material was written by two authors, name both in the introduction to the material or in the final parentheses each time you cite the work. In the parentheses, use "&" rather than "and."

```
    DeJong and Lifchez (1983) examine state and federal funding

for vocational programs and independent living centers provided

for disabled citizens.
```

```
    Two writers have reported on The Rehabilitation Comprehen-

sive Services and Developmental Disability Amendments (DeJong &

Lifchez, 1983).
```

Author's Name Not Given.   If the author of the material that you are using is not given, either use the complete title in your introduction to the material or use the first few words of the title in the parenthetical citation with the date.

    Retired Supreme Court Justice Thurgood Marshall graduated
first in his class at Howard Law School and then sued the University of Maryland Law School, which had rejected him because he
was black ("Milestones," 1993).

    An obituary from "Milestones" (1993) noted that Thurgood
Marshall graduated first in his class at Howard Law School and
then sued the University of Maryland Law School, which had rejected him because he was black.

Corporate Author.   If you are using a work with a corporate or group author
that is particularly long, write out the full name the first time you use it, followed
by an abbreviation in brackets. In later citations, use just the abbreviation.

    The American Philosophical Association has prepared "Guide-
lines for Non-Sexist Use of Language" because philosophers are
"attuned to the emotive force of words and to the ways in which
language influences thought and behavior" (American Philosophical
Association [APA], 1978).

Indirect Source.   If you use work that is cited in another source, you need to
acknowledge that you did not use the original source.

    Actor Henry Holden relates his own experience with social dis-
crimination by noting that he is "not generally accepted by nondisabled people in social situations" (cited in Davidson, 1987).

Preparing the References Page

In APA form, the alphabetical listing of works used in the manuscript is entitled "References." (In MLA form, this listing is entitled "Works Cited.") Here
are some general guidelines for the references page.

- Double-space the entries. The first line should be flush with the left margin, and all subsequent lines should be indented five spaces or ½ inch
  from the left margin.

- Alphabetize the list by the last name of the author or editor. If the work is
  anonymous, alphabetize by the first word of the title, excluding "a," "an,"
  or "the."

- All authors' names should be listed last name first, with the parts of
  names separated with commas. Do not use "et al." unless there are six or
  more authors. Use initials for first and middle names. Use an ampersand
  ("&") rather than the word "and."

- In contrast to the way titles normally appear, APA style limits capitalizations of book titles and of articles to the first word of the title and subtitle as well as to all proper nouns. However, all the main words of the titles of journals or magazines are capitalized as they normally appear.
- Italicize the titles of books, journals, and any volume numbers. Do not underline or use quotations marks around the titles of articles.
- Give the full names of publishers, excluding "Inc." and "Co."
- Use the abbreviation "p." or "pp." before page numbers in books, magazines, and newspapers, but not for scholarly journals. For inclusive page numbers, include all figures (365–370, not 365–70).

Sample APA Entries

BOOKS

One Author

Fiedler, L. (1978). *Freaks: Myths and images of the secret self.*
New York: Simon & Schuster.

Two or More Authors

Doane, J., & Hodges, D. (1987). *Nostalgia and sexual difference:*
The resistance to contemporary feminism. New York: Methuen.

Editor

Allen, D. M. (Ed.). (1960). *The new American poetry.* New York:
Grove Press.

Translator

Ibsen, H. (1965). *A doll's house and other plays.* (P. Watts,
Trans.). New York: Penguin Books.

Author Not Named

The Oxford dictionary of quotations. (1964). New York: Oxford
University Press.

Later Edition

Fowler, R. H., & Aaron, J. E (1992). *The Little, Brown handbook.*
(5th ed.). New York: HarperCollins.

Multivolume Work

Raine, K. (1968). *Blake and tradition* (Vol. 2). Princeton:
Princeton University Press.

Malone, D. (1943-1981). *Jefferson and his time* (Vols. 1-6).
Boston: Little, Brown.

Work in an Anthology

Mairs, N. On being a cripple. (1987). In M. Saxton & F. Howe
(Eds.), With wings: An anthology of literature by and about
women with disabilities (pp. 118-127). New York: Feminist
Press at City University of New York.

Two or More Books by the Same Author

Olsen, T. (1979). *Silences*. New York: Dell Publishing.

Olsen, T. (1985). *Tell me a riddle*. New York: Dell Publishing.

PERIODICALS: JOURNALS, MAGAZINES, AND NEWSPAPERS

Journal with Continuous Pagination

Culp, M. B. (1983). Religion in the poetry of Langston Hughes.
Phylon, *48*, 240-245.

Journal That Paginates Each Issue Separately

Hardwick, J. (1992). Widowhood and patriarchy in seventeenth-
century France. *Journal of Social History,* 26(1), 133-148.

Article in a Magazine

Mazzatenta, O. L. (1992, August). A Chinese emperor's army for
eternity. *National Geographic*, pp. 114-130.

Article in a Daily Newspaper, Signed

Soto, O. R. (1992, January 28). Putting the tag on graffiti-
smearers. *Press Telegram*, sec. B, p. 3.

Article in a Daily Newspaper, Unsigned or Editorial

Back to Future. (1992, May 3). *Los Angeles Times*, p. M-4.

Titled Review

Ansa, T. M. (1992, July 5). Taboo territory [Review of *Possessing
the secret of joy]. Los Angeles Times Book Review*,
pp. 4, 8.

Motion Picture (note: the final period is deleted).

Petersen, W. (Director). (1993). In the line of fire [Motion
picture]. United States: Columbia

Personal Interview

Interviews that you conduct yourself are not listed in APA references. Instead, use an in-text parenthetical citation. If the subject's name is in your text, use this form: "(personal communication, Feb. 12, 2003)." If the subject's name is not in your text, use this form: "(S. Daigh, personal communication, Mar. 18, 2003)."

Electronic Sources

The documentation form for electronic sources is still in flux, but the goal is to provide your reader with sufficient information to locate the material you have found. A typical citation will include the conventional APA form for the source, whether it is an article or book, the page numbers if provided, followed by the address (URL). In APA style, writers may divide a URL only after a slash or before a period. There is no end period after a URL (so readers will not think the period is part of the URL). If the online publication exactly duplicates the print version, simply add the description [Electronic version] after the title of the article. If you have reason to believe the text has been changed or updated since the original was published, add the date you retrieved the item and the URL.

Book in Print and Online

Austen, J. (1813). *Pride and prejudice* [Electronic version].

    http:// uts.cc.utexas.edu/~churchh/pridprej.html

Article in Print and Online

Markels, A. (1996). MCI unit finds culture shock after relocating

    to Colorado. *The Wall Street Journal Interactive Edition*.

    7 pp. Retrieved January 23, 2002, from http://www.wsj.com/

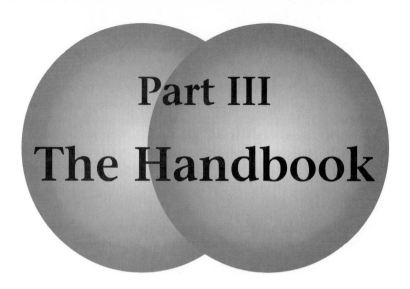

Part III

The Handbook

Part III—the handbook—is designed to help you use words and control sentences in order to write convincing, error-free papers. It will help you in drafting and revising your essays as well as in understanding the comments that your instructors write in the margins of your papers.

We do not believe that you need an extensive background in grammar in order to write clearly and well. But we are convinced that control of grammar and punctuation will give you power over both your ideas *and* your readers.

You may feel discouraged by the numerous mistakes on your papers and by the prevalence of circled words and marginal notes from your instructor. However, if you and your classmates were to examine all of your papers, you would discover that you do not make a great number of *different* errors so much as you repeat the same kind of error many times. For that reason, we have isolated those recurrent errors for discussion and correction.

This handbook begins with a deliberately succinct chapter entitled "Understanding How Sentences Work." We try to meet your needs in this chapter without telling you more than you ever wanted (or needed) to know about the elements of a sentence. Chapter 13 precisely identifies and describes the recurrent errors—the "terrible ten"—that typically appear in student papers. Chapter 14 discusses punctuation and will help you eliminate guesswork and punctuate accurately. Chapter 15 focuses on faulty word choice and will show you how well-chosen words can strengthen your essays. To determine quickly whether your word choice is sound, you can use the alphabetical list of troublesome words in Chapter 16.

As you are revising your drafts, you can use this handbook whenever you feel uncertain about your grammar or mechanics. When a paper is returned, you can use it as a guide to error correction by matching your instructor's marginal notes with the symbols used in this book. Ultimately, this handbook is designed to empower you without overwhelming you.

Editing Symbols

The following annotations may be used by your instructor to indicate errors in your paper. These symbols also appear on the inside back cover of this book.

agr	agreement (subject/verb, pronoun)	pp. 583–585
awk	awkward	p. 591
≡	cap or capitalize	
/	no capital (use lower case)	
cliché	overused expression	p. 611
◌	close up space	
coh	coherence	pp. 387–394
cs	comma splice	p. 577
?	confusing, unclear	
ℒ	delete	
d or dic	diction or inappropriate word choice	pp. 612–614
dbl neg	double negative	p. 619
✓	excellent point or wording	
frag	fragment	pp. 575–577
fs	fused sentence	pp. 577–580
∧	insert (such as a missing word or punctuation)	
∧,	insert comma	pp. 593–596
mm	misplaced modifier	pp. 590–591
mixed	mixed construction	pp. 588–589
¶	new paragraph	pp. 391–393
no ¶	no paragraph	pp. 391–393
//	(faulty) parallelism	pp. 591–592
P	(faulty) punctuation	pp. 593–610
"?"	quotation marks needed?	pp. 516–518; 602–605

ref	(pronoun) reference	pp. 580–582
red	redundant	p. 613
ros or r-o	run-on sentence	pp. 577–580
shift	shift in person, number, or verb tense	pp. 585–588
#	space needed	
sp	spelling error	
sv agr	subject-verb agreement	pp. 583–585
trans	transition needed	pp. 387–394
∿	transpose (reverse letters or words)	
vb	verb form incorrect	pp. 568–569; 586–587
wd ch	word choice	pp. 611–614
wdy	wordy	p. 613
ww	wrong word	pp. 612–614

Chapter 12

Understanding How Sentences Work

Understanding how sentences work will give you the vocabulary you need to discuss your writing and to correct errors that have been noted in your papers. Such knowledge will also increase your power and versatility as a writer. By eliminating some of the guesswork that can hamper student writers, this handbook can help give you the tools and confidence to write with conviction.

As you probably know, every sentence must contain a **subject** and a **verb.** This basic unit is called a **clause.** (For more on clauses, see pp. 572–573.) In key examples throughout this section, we have often underlined the subject once and the verb twice to help you identify them quickly.

Subjects

A **subject** is who or what a clause is about.

    At Berkeley, Ryan plays on a basketball team with his roommates.

    [Subjects may precede verbs.]

    There are several guitars in Adam's room.

    [Subjects may follow verbs.]

Noun as Subject

The subject of the clause may be a **noun** or a **pronoun.** A **noun** can be a

- *Person:* athlete, Whitney Houston, veterinarian

- *Place:* Lake Erie, bike path, the Acropolis
- *Thing:* computer, hammock, Harley-Davidson
- *Quality/idea/activity:* wit, peace, dancing

Pronoun as Subject

A **pronoun** takes the place of a noun and can also function as the subject of a clause. Pronouns can be

- *Personal:* I, you, he, she, it, we, they

  `They reviewed their lecture notes.`

- *Indefinite:* all, any, anybody, anything, each, either, everybody, everyone, neither, nobody, none, no one, nothing, one, some, somebody, someone, something

  `Everybody needs to recycle.`

- *Demonstrative:* that, this, such, these, those

  `Those are the sale items.`

- *Relative:* who, whom, whoever, whomever, whose, which, whichever, that, what

  `The order that is ready is the deluxe pizza.`

  [In this example, that is the subject of the dependent or relative clause. The subject of the independent clause is order.] (For more about clauses, see pp. xxx–xxx.)

- *Interrogative:* who, whom, whoever, whomever, whose, which, that, what

  `Who recommended this awful film?`

Compound Subject

Subjects may be **compound,** as in these sentences:

`Julie and Joe restore old automobiles.`

`Books and papers collected on his desk.`

`Here are questions and assignments for each reading.`

`The dietician and nurses gave the patients new menus.`

Objects

Direct Object

Not all nouns function as the subject of a clause. A noun that receives the action of the verb is called a **direct object.** In the sentence "Julie and Joe restore old automobiles," the noun *automobiles* answers the question, "What do Julie and Joe restore?" *Automobiles* is thus the direct object of the verb *restore.*

Indirect Object

A noun that identifies to or for whom or what the action of the verb is performed is the **indirect object.** In the sentence "The dietician and nurses gave the patients new menus," the noun *patients* answers the question, "To whom were the menus given?"

Object of the Preposition

A noun that follows a preposition (see list on p. 570) is called the **object of the preposition.** In the sentence "Books and papers collected on his desk," the noun *desk* is the object of the preposition *on.*

Objects may provide important information in a sentence, but they are not necessary in order to have a clause. *Verbs,* however, are essential.

Verbs

A **verb** is what the subject does, is, has, or has done to it. The verb may be more than one word (*may be coming*). The verb also changes form to agree with the subject (*he drives; they drive*) and to indicate time (*he drove, he has driven*). Regular verbs form their past tense by adding *-ed,* but there are a number of irregular forms like *drive* that have special forms.

Action Verbs

An **action verb** specifies what the subject does, has, or has done to it. The action does not have to be physical in any sense: *meditate* is an action verb. Other action verbs include *dance, think, laugh, provoke, erupt,* and *suggest:*

    Every Christmas Eve Janine and Tim entertain their relatives
    with holiday tunes.

    Dr. Sanders wrote an insightful study of Oates's work.

State-of-Being Verbs

A **state-of-being** or **linking verb** specifies what the subject is. State-of-being verbs include the following: *is, are, was, were, am, feel, seem, be, being, been,* *do, does, did, have, has, had.* These can be main verbs or helping verbs. For more on helping verbs, see the following section.

```
Evan is interested in architecture and engineering.
```

[*is* as main verb]

```
Dylan is teaching history at North High.
```

[*is* as a helping verb]

Note: Words ending in *-ing* need a helping verb in order to function as the main verb of a sentence. The *-ing* form of the verb can also function as a noun: *Playing is a form of learning for small children.* Here *playing* is the subject, and *learning* is the object of the preposition *of.* Thus, just because there is an *-ing* word in a word group, there is not necessarily a verb.

Helping Verbs

The **helping verb** is always used with a main verb. Helping verbs include *can, will, shall, should, could, would, may, might,* and *must.*

```
The designated driver will get everyone home safely.

Some of the Friedmanns could have camped with the VanValkenburgh

family at Yosemite.
```

Adjectives and Adverbs

Many sentences contain modifying words that describe the nouns and verbs. **Adjectives** modify nouns (*corroded pipes, hectic schedule*) and pronouns (*the curious one*). **Adverbs** modify verbs (*cautiously responded*), adjectives (*truly generous*), adverbs (*very slowly*), and word groups (*Eventually, he entered the room.*) Adverbs answer the questions *how? when? where?* and *why?* They often end in *-ly,* but not always.

The following sentence contains both adjectives and adverbs. Can you identify each?

```
According to Barbara Ehrenreich, angry young men often will

vent their frustrations on vulnerable, weaker beings--typically

children or women.
```

The adjectives *angry* and *young* modify the noun *men;* the adjectives *vulnerable* and *weaker* modify the noun *beings.* The adverbs *often* and *typically* modify the verb *will vent.*

Adjectives and adverbs can provide valuable details, but they can be overused. Being descriptive doesn't require a string of adjectives and adverbs. Often a strong verb gives a more precise picture in fewer words:

```
The drunken man walked unsteadily and unevenly from the bar.

The drunken man staggered from the bar.
```

The verb *staggered* is vivid and precise. The pile-up of adverbs in the first sentence is wordy and imprecise. Such tightening often improves writing and saves space for more necessary depth and development.

Phrases

A **phrase** is a group of words, typically without the subject and verb of the sentence. Just as clauses do not necessarily have objects, adjectives, and adverbs, clauses also do not necessarily have any phrases. While phrases may provide additional information, they seldom contain the subject and verb in the sentence. Therefore, if you are checking to see that you have a subject and verb, in order to avoid fragments, you can eliminate phrases from your search. There are many types of phrases, but here we discuss two of the most common.

Prepositional Phrases

A **prepositional phrase** always starts with a **preposition**—a word that shows relationships in time and space—and ends with the **object** of the preposition. The most common prepositions are listed here.

about	beside	from	outside	under
above	besides	in	over	underneath
across	between	inside	past	unlike
after	beyond	into	plus	until
against	but	like	regarding	unto
along	by	near	respecting	up
among	concerning	next	round	upon
around	considering	of	since	with
as	despite	off	than	without
at	down	on	through	out
before	during	onto	till	
behind	except	opposite	to	
below	for	out	toward	

Some prepositions are more than one word long: *along with, as well as, in addition to, next to,* and *up to* are some examples.

The object of the preposition is always a noun or pronoun:

<u>Elaine</u> <u>assists</u> the dean **of Fine Arts with registration problems.**

During the summer <u>Becky</u> and Joey <u>work</u> **at Niagara Produce.**

For two weeks in January, <u>Anne</u> <u>vacations</u> **with her daughter's**
family in Long Beach.

[In the last sentence, "for two weeks," "in January," "with her daughter's family," and
"in Long Beach" are all prepositional phrases. Note how much easier it is to locate
the subject and verb when the prepositional phrases are eliminated.]

Verbal Phrases

Verbal phrases resemble verbs, but they do not function as the main verb of the
clause. Verbal phrases may serve as subjects, objects, adjectives, and adverbs.
Two main types of verbal phrases are **infinitive phrases** and **-ing phrases.**

Infinitive Phrases.   If the verb is preceded by *to* (*to ski*), the verb is in the
infinitive form. It helps to recognize infinitives because they cannot be the
main verbs.

Most <u>professors</u> <u>like</u> **to challenge** students.

To think <u>is</u> **to question.**

[Infinitives can function as subjects.]

-ing Phrases.   A word ending in *-ing* may look like a verb, but it needs a helping verb or a main verb elsewhere in the sentence. Notice how *working* serves
a different function in each of the following sentences (only in the first sentence is it part of the main verb):

<u>Rise Daniels</u> **is working** as an art instructor.

Working as an art instructor <u>requires</u> overtime hours.

[When *-ing* words function as subjects, they are called **gerunds.**]

The **working** <u>artist</u> <u>exhibited</u> her paintings.

[When *-ing* words function as adjectives, they are called **participles.**]

Words and phrases ending in *-ing* can often lead writers to believe they
have a complete sentence—that is, at least one independent clause—when
they may have only a fragment. For example, "In the evening after arriving
home from work" is not an independent clause; it simply consists of three
phrases.

One way to determine if there is an independent clause, and therefore a sentence, is to draw a line through each phrase:

~~In the evening~~ ~~after arriving home~~ ~~from work~~, <u>Bill</u> <u>retreats</u> ~~to his studio~~ ~~for hours~~ ~~to play piano~~ and ~~to compose new songs~~.

Now that you can recognize the most important parts of a sentence, you can better understand how clauses work and how they can be combined.

Clauses

A **clause** is a group of words with a subject and main verb. There are two basic types of clauses: (1) independent and (2) dependent.

Independent Clauses

The **independent (or main) clause** has a subject and main verb and can stand alone:

<u>Dottie</u> <u>is receiving</u> mail from fans each day.

<u>Alyssa</u> <u>loves</u> singing with Robert and Susie.

The <u>poet</u> <u>invited</u> Gigi and Keith backstage.

Dependent Clauses

The **dependent (or subordinate) clause** has a subject and main verb but cannot stand alone. Dependent clauses begin with one of these subordinating conjunctions:

after	if, even if	what, whatever
although	in order that	when, whenever
as, as if	since	whether
because	that, so that	which, whichever
before	unless	while
how	until	who, whom, whose

Whenever a clause begins with one of these words (unless it is a question), it is a dependent clause. If we take an independent clause such as

<u>We</u> <u>jogged</u>

and put one of the subordinating conjunctions in front of it, the independent clause becomes dependent (and therefore a fragment):

```
After we jogged

Because we jogged
```

To make a complete sentence, we need to add an independent clause (or delete the subordinating conjunction):

```
After we jogged, we went for a swim.

Because we jogged, we justified eating brownies.
```

Every sentence must have at least one independent clause in it.

Sentence Variation

If you know how to control and combine clauses, you can vary your sentences for greater emphasis, more clarity, and less monotony. The four basic sentence types are illustrated here.

Simple Sentences

Simple sentences contain **one independent clause:**

```
Professor Hodges's students submitted fine critical analyses of
the textbook.

Despite his busy schedule, Walter spent hours with his sons
each night.
```

Compound Sentences

Compound sentences contain **two independent clauses.** There are only two ways to punctuate a compound sentence:

1. A **comma** followed by a coordinating conjunction (*and, but, for, or, nor, yet, so*):

```
We arrived at the cabin, so they left.
```

2. A **semicolon** by itself (or it may be followed by a word like *nevertheless* or *however*):

```
We arrived; they left.

We arrived; therefore, they left.
```

Notice that the writer's decision to use a coordinate conjunction or a semicolon is not arbitrary. If the writer wishes to clarify or emphasize the relationship between the two clauses, he or she will use a coordinate conjunction (such as *so*) or a conjunctive adverb (such as *therefore*). If the writer prefers not to define the relationship between the clauses, then the semicolon by itself is more appropriate.

Complex Sentences

Complex sentences contain **one independent clause and one or more dependent clauses.** The following dependent clauses are underscored with a broken underline.

> When the dependent clause comes first in the sentence, a comma
>
> is necessary.

> A comma isn't necessary when the dependent clause comes at the
>
> end.

Compound-Complex Sentences

Compound-complex sentences contain **two or more independent clauses and one or more dependent clauses.** The dependent clause or clauses may be at the beginning, at the end, or between the independent clauses. Here one dependent clause begins the sentence, and another ends the sentence:

> Although Jane was a senior citizen, she swam competitively, and
>
> we were all impressed that she won so many medals.

In the following sentence, the dependent clause is between the two independent clauses:

> At work Tammy cares for an elderly man who requires constant
>
> help, so she enjoys returning home each night to play with
>
> Jamie, Paul, and Duane.

 PRACTICING SENTENCE VARIATION

Using details from the last essay that you discussed in class, write your own sentences to illustrate each sentence type: simple, compound, complex, and compound-complex. Then underline all <u>subjects once</u> and all <u>verbs twice</u> to make sure you have the necessary clauses. Manipulating these sentence types will help you vary your sentences and combine your ideas more smoothly.

Chapter 13

Understanding Common Errors

In this chapter, we examine the ten errors that appear most frequently in student papers: fragments, run-on or fused sentences, comma splice, pronoun reference agreement, verb-noun agreement, shifts in number or person, shifts in verb tense, shifts in voice, mixed sentences, misplaced (and dangling) modifiers, and faulty parallelism. These errors may be noted in the margins of your papers with the symbols that appear on pages 564 and 565 as well as on the inside back cover.

Fragments

Although sentence fragments are used frequently in fiction and advertising copy to simulate spoken English, the sentence fragment is considered nonstandard in formal writing. Fragments may confuse the reader, and they will make your writing seem choppy and your ideas disconnected.

A **fragment** is a group of words that, for some reason, **cannot stand alone** as a complete sentence. The reason may be any one of the following: *frag*

1. The word group may lack a subject.

   ```
   While the students prepared their finals, they sunbathed at the
   same time. Became involved in discussions that distracted them
   from their studies.
   ```
   frag

   [Add a subject.]

While the students prepared their finals, they sunbathed at
the same time. Soon <u>they</u> <u>became involved</u> in discussions that
distracted them from their studies.

2. **The word group may lack a complete verb.**

frag

Arriving before the concert began, we enjoyed the excitement in
the air. The <u>band</u> tuning up before their opening song.

[Add a helping verb.]

Arriving before the concert began, we enjoyed the excitement in
the air. The <u>band</u> <u>was tuning</u> up before their opening song.

3. **The word group may lack both a subject and a verb.**

frag

I value my piano teacher. A bright and patient woman. She encourages perfection even while she tolerates my mistakes.

[Attach the phrase *a bright and patient woman* to the independent clause before or
after it.]

I value my piano teacher, a bright and patient woman. She encourages perfection even while she tolerates my mistakes.

or

I value my piano teacher. A bright and patient woman, she encourages perfection even while she tolerates my mistakes.

4. **The word group may contain both a subject and a verb but be simply a
   dependent clause.**

Native American music and dances are national treasures.

frag

Which is why our dance company performs them regularly.

[Avoid starting any sentence with *which* unless you are asking a question.]

Native American music and dances are national treasures.
<u>This</u> <u>is</u> why our dance company performs them regularly.

or

Because Native American music and dances are national treasures, our dance company performs them regularly.

Another example of such a fragment is the following:

Although rap music has been criticized for its violence and

frag

harsh language. Rap really reflects the tension in the cities
rather than causes it.

```
Although rap music has been criticized for its violence and

harsh language, rap really reflects the tension in the cities

rather than causes it.
```

As noted earlier, writers may deliberately use a fragment for emphasis or to mimic conversation, but these uses are always controlled and planned. Otherwise, fragments make an essay confusing or choppy. Sometimes the simplest solution is to connect the fragment to an independent clause that is either right before or after it.

Run-on or Fused Sentences

Run-on or **fused sentences,** or sentences flawed with a **comma splice,** occur when a writer perceives that the thoughts in two complete sentences are related but fails to join the thoughts appropriately. Sometimes the writer makes the mistake of inserting a comma between the independent clauses, creating a comma splice. No punctuation at all between the independent clauses creates a run-on or fused sentence. Both errors occur because the writer sees a relationship between sentences and isn't sure what to do to show the relationship.   *coh*

The "sentence" that follows is one anyone might say, and a writer might be tempted to write:

```
It snowed for days the skiers were ecstatic.
```
coh

The writer has clearly perceived a relationship between the joy of the skiers and the weather conditions. But the word group is incorrectly punctuated and is a run-on or fused sentence.

Comma Splice

The writer may decide to "correct" the error by inserting a comma between the two independent clauses:

```
It snowed for days, the skiers were ecstatic.
```
CS

The comma is inadequate punctuation, however, for separating the independent clauses. That "correction" results in the sentence fault called a **comma splice,** which is noted as "**CS**" in the margin of a paper.

Correcting Run-on Sentences

The following methods illustrate alternatives for correcting run-on sentences. Notice that the five choices are all grammatically correct, but each places different emphasis on the two clauses and may change the meaning of the sentence.

1. Separate each independent clause with a period.

```
It snowed for days. The skiers were ecstatic.
```

2. Use a comma plus a coordinating conjunction (*and, but, for, or, nor, yet, so*) between the independent clauses.

```
It snowed for days, and the skiers were ecstatic.
```

or

```
It snowed for days, yet the skiers were ecstatic.
```

or

```
It snowed for days, so the skiers were ecstatic.
```

3. Use a semicolon between the independent clauses.

```
It snowed for days; the skiers were ecstatic.
```

4. Change one independent clause into a dependent clause.

```
Because it snowed for days, the skiers were ecstatic.
```

or

```
The skiers were ecstatic because it snowed for days.
```

Notice that when the dependent clause begins the sentence, a comma separates it from the main clause. Conversely, when the independent clause begins the sentence, there is no comma before the dependent clause that concludes the sentence. See page 572 for a list of words that begin dependent clauses.

5. Use a semicolon after the first independent clause, and then a conjunctive adverb (see below) followed by a comma:

```
It snowed for days; consequently, the skiers were ecstatic.
```

or

```
It snowed for days; nevertheless, the skiers were ecstatic.
```

Conjunctive Adverbs

Conjunctive adverbs include *accordingly, also, anyway, besides, certainly, consequently, conversely, finally, furthermore, hence, however, incidentally, indeed, instead, likewise, meanwhile, moreover, nevertheless, next, nonetheless, otherwise, similarly, specifically, still, subsequently, then, therefore,* and *thus.*

Style and Meaning

Grammatical correction of a run-on sentence is not the only concern of the writer. Style emphasis and meaning also should be considered when you are deciding which conjunction to use. Notice the difference in emphasis in the following examples:

```
It snowed for days. The skiers were ecstatic.
```

```
Because it snowed for days, the skiers were ecstatic.
```

In the first example, the writer asks the reader to infer the relationship between the skiers' being "ecstatic" and the fact that "it snowed for days." In the second example, the cause-and-effect relationship is defined clearly. Take the following simple sentences, also fused, and notice what happens to the meaning, emphasis, or relationship between the independent clauses when different corrections are employed:

```
Renée pitched the team won.
```

1. ```
Renée pitched. The team won.
```

The writer has not defined a relationship between the facts stated in the two sentences.

2. ```
Renée pitched, and the team won.
```

A mild relationship is suggested by connecting the two events with *and*.

```
Renée pitched, so the team won.
```

The relationship between the team's victory and the person who pitched is defined in this construction using *so*.

```
Renée pitched, yet the team won.
```

The use of *yet*, which signals something contrary to expectation, changes the relationship between the independent clauses in this example. The word *yet* tells the reader that in spite of the fact that Renée pitched, the team won.

3. ```
Renée pitched; the team won.
```

The semicolon does not define the relationship between the two independent clauses although a subtle relationship *is* suggested by the writer's using a semicolon instead of a period. The semicolon is a compromise punctuation symbol. It is stronger than a comma, but it is not as complete a stop as a period.

4. ```
Whenever Renée pitched, the team won.
```

```
The team won because Renée pitched.
```

```
Although Renée pitched, the team won.
```

```
The team won unless Renée pitched.
```

The dependent clause, whether it begins or ends the sentence, defines the exact relationship between the two clauses in the sentence. Clearly, the subordinate conjunction chosen has everything to do with the meaning of the sentence.

5. Renée pitched; therefore, the team won.

Renée pitched; nevertheless, the team won.

Again, the conjunctive adverb defines the precise relationship between the two clauses of the sentence. For the purpose of connecting two short independent clauses, most writers would find the combination of semicolon and conjunctive adverb and comma too cumbersome. A coordinating conjunction with a comma would probably be a better method of linking the two clauses.

Pronoun Reference Agreement

Pronouns are words that **take the place of nouns.** In most cases, pronouns are an advantage to the writer because they permit reference to nouns named without the writer having to repeat the noun or finding a clear substitute (or synonym) for it. Ambiguity, vagueness, or confusion can result, however, if the *ref* writer has not used pronouns responsibly. The margin symbol "**ref**" indicates a problem with the pronoun reference.

The following chart shows the forms that personal pronouns take.

Singular

Subjective	Possessive	Objective
I	my, mine	me
You	your, yours	you
He	his	him
She	her, hers	her
It	its	it

Plural

We	our, ours	us
You	your, yours	you
They	their, theirs	them

Indefinite pronouns include *all, any, anybody, anything, each, either, everybody, everyone, everything, neither, nobody, none, no one, nothing, one, some, somebody, someone,* and *something.*

Pronoun problems occur when the reader does not know what noun is referred to by the noun substitute, the pronoun.

1. Sometimes the pronoun used could refer to either of two nouns:

ref   When Karen told Pat the news, she burst into tears.

She can refer to either Karen or Pat. The ambiguity must be resolved for the reader:

```
Pat burst into tears when Karen told her the news.
```

or

```
Karen burst into tears when she told Pat the news.
```

2. Sometimes the subject is implied by the writer but is not stated in the sentence. The pronoun does not clearly refer to any given noun, and confusion results for the reader:

```
For years, Pete carried rocks from the quarry, and it strained
his back.
```
ref

It cannot refer to the plural *rocks,* and the singular noun *quarry* didn't "strain his back." The writer probably means "this work" or "the constant hauling of heavy rocks." The writer needs to make that clarification in the sentence:

```
For years, Pete carried rocks from the quarry, and this work
strained his back.
```

3. Indefinite pronouns can also pose a problem for writer and reader if the singular form of the indefinite pronoun is inconsistent with the meaning of the sentence or the gender of the pronoun is assumed by the writer to be a generic *he.* Generally, a singular pronoun should be used with an indefinite pronoun:

```
Each boy on the football team has his own locker.

Anybody who has her doubts about the safety of breast implants
should read Jenny Jones's essay "Body of Evidence" on
pages 258-263.
```

In the examples above, the gender of the possessive pronoun is clear from the context of the sentence. However, if you are not sure of the gender or number (singular or plural) of your subject, reword your sentence so that the subject pronoun is plural. For example:

```
Everybody running for class office should report to his
counselor.
```
ref

Everybody is a singular pronoun and requires a singular possessive pronoun: *his* or *her. Their* is plural and can't be used in this sentence. But should the writer assume the generic *his?* A reader might object that the implication of the sentence is that only males may run for class office. A similar misunderstanding would occur if the writer opted for *her* as the singular possessive pronoun. If this were a single-sentence statement, as in a school bulletin, the writer might choose *his or her* for a correct and clear mandate. But the repetitive use of *his or her* (or his/her) can be a burden in a lengthy manuscript.

Learn to find alternatives. A plural noun and plural possessive pronoun will take care of the problem:

```
All of the candidates for class office should report to their
counselors.
```

You may also want to see the discussion of sexist language (pp. 613–614) in Chapter 15.

Pronoun Case

In addition to problems with pronoun referents, writers often have trouble deciding when to use the subjective case pronouns and when to use the objective case pronouns (see chart in the previous section, Pronoun Referent Agreement, p. 580).

Subjective pronouns are used for the subject of the sentence or clause:

```
We listen to hiphop music.

Because Dr. Connor is so supportive, he brought the team home
for a barbecue.
```

Subjective pronouns are also used when the pronoun follows a linking verb:

```
It is I who volunteered.

It was they who chose that route.
```

Objective pronouns are used for any objects:

Direct object:

```
The Cuseos invited us to visit Chili and Willy.
```

Indirect object:

```
Tony's band gave him a standing ovation.
```

Object of the preposition:

```
Aaron enjoyed performing on stage for them.
```

Pronoun pairs such as "you and I" and "you and me" tend to confuse writers, but the same principles apply. Determine whether the pronoun is serving as a subject or object and then choose the correct form (see chart, p. 580). Often it is easier to make this determination if you eliminate the first noun or name in the pair:

Subject:

```
Garrick and (I? me?) went to the concert together.
```

Eliminate "Garrick": **I** went. So choose: Garrick and **I** went to the concert together.

Direct Object:

```
Josh drove Mike and (I? me?) to the surfing competition.
```

Eliminate "Mike": Josh drove me. So choose: Josh drove Mike and **me** to the surfing competition.

Indirect Object:

```
David showed Julia and (we? us?) his new stallion.
```

Eliminate "Julia": David showed **us.** So choose: David showed Julia and **us** his new stallion.

Object of a preposition:

```
Tiana flew to Paris with her roommate and (he? him?)
```

Eliminate "her roommate": Tiana flew to Paris with **him.** So choose: Tiana flew to Paris with her roommate and **him.**

Subject-Verb Agreement

The margin note "**agr**" means that there is an agreement problem; the subject *agr* and the verb do not agree in number. Both subject and verb should be singular or both should be plural. Speakers who are comfortable with standard English usually will not have trouble selecting the correct verb form for the subject of sentences. But some sentences, especially those that have groups of words separating the subject and verb, may offer a temporary problem for any writer. Some conditions to be aware of are listed here.

1. A prepositional phrase does not influence the verb of the sentence:

   ```
   The birds in the nest need food from the mother bird.
   ```

   ```
   Our first five days of vacation are going to be in New Orleans.
   ```

   ```
   Her secretary, in addition to her staff, prefers the new computer.
   ```

   Notice that by removing the prepositional phrases from your consideration, you will use the correct verb form for the subject of the sentence.

2. Subjects connected by *and* usually have a plural verb:

   `Alfredo's academic load and work time keep him busy.`

   Some exceptions:

   a. When the compound subject (nouns connected by *and*) is regarded as a unit, the subject is regarded as singular and has a singular verb:

      `Peanut butter and jelly remains Dalton's favorite lunch.`

   b. If the double nouns refer to the same person or thing, the verb is singular:

      `Danika's home and studio is 215 Thompson Street.`

   c. When *each* or *every* precedes the multiple nouns, use a singular verb:

      `Each instructor, student, and staff member prefers the new insurance plan.`

   d. When nouns are connected by *or* or *nor,* the verb agrees with the noun closer to it:

      `Your student ID or room key guarantees the loan of a beach chair.`

      `Your student ID or room keys guarantee the loan of a beach chair.`

      `Neither the police officer nor his cadets were attending the lecture.`

      `Either Arthur or Michael plays the solo tonight.`

3. Most indefinite pronouns have a singular verb, even if the pronoun seems to convey a plural sense. Indefinite pronouns include *anybody, anyone, each, either, everybody, everyone, everything, neither, none, no one, someone,* and *something.* Notice how each indefinite pronoun is used in the following sentences:

   `Each of the band members has two free tickets.`

   `Everybody endures the stress of two finals a day.`

   `Everyone on the school board votes at each meeting.`

   All, any, or *some,* however, may be singular or plural depending on what the pronoun refers to:

```
All of the pizza is gone.

All of the books are shelved.
```

4. Collective nouns (like *band, family, committee, class, jury,* and *audience*) require a singular verb unless the meaning of the noun is plural, or individuality is to be emphasized:

```
The jury presents its decision today.

The jury are undecided about a verdict.
```

5. Even when the subject follows the verb, the verb must be in the correct form:

```
There remains too little time to organize the campaign.
```

6. Titles require singular verbs:

```
Roots is the book we will read next.

Jacoby and Associates is the law firm on the corner.

Mysteries is the section of the library Carlos prefers.
```

7. Nouns describing academic disciplines—like *economics, statistics,* or *physics*—and diseases that end in an *s*—like *mumps* and *measles*—and *news*—are treated as singular nouns:

```
Physics challenges Maria, but she does well in the course.

Measles usually attacks only the children who have not been
inoculated.
```

Shifts

The margin note "**shift**" marks an inconsistency in the text in person, number, *shift* or verb tense.

Shifts in Person and Number

Shifts in person and number sometimes occur because you are not certain from what point of view to write or because you move from one perspective to another without being conscious of the change. You may begin with the idea of addressing a general audience—"someone"—and then decide to address the reader as "you." Or you may begin with a singular reader in mind and switch to a plural sense of "all readers." If you start to write from one perspective and switch to another, a distracting shift occurs:

```
If someone in the group writes a paper, they may present it.        shift
```

Corrections:

If a <u>person</u> writes a paper, <u>he or she</u> may present it.

or, better:

If <u>people</u> write papers, <u>they</u> may present them.

shift

<u>The vegetarian</u> learns to prepare interesting and nutritious meals with vegetables and grains, but then <u>you</u> have to assure <u>your</u> friends that <u>you're</u> getting enough protein.

Corrections:

If <u>you</u> are a vegetarian, <u>you</u> learn to prepare interesting and nutritious meals with vegetables and grains, but then <u>you</u> have to assure your friends that <u>you're</u> getting enough protein.

or, better:

<u>Vegetarians</u> learn to prepare interesting and nutritious meals with vegetables and grains, but then <u>they</u> have to assure <u>their</u> friends that <u>they</u> are getting enough protein.

Shifts in Verb Tense

Shifts in verb tense will confuse a reader about when the action takes place. You have probably heard oral storytellers shift from one tense to another. Eventually you may have figured out the course of the narration, perhaps by asking the speaker to clarify the time of the action. But a shift in tense is particularly distracting in writing because you can't ask a writer for a clarification of the text. Notice how the verb tense in the following example shifts from the past to the present:

shift

Shortly after we <u>arrived</u> at the picnic site, it <u>started</u> to rain. So we <u>pack</u> up the bread, salami, and fruit and <u>rush</u> to the cars.

Correction for verb tense consistency:

Shortly after we <u>arrived</u> at the picnic site, it <u>started</u> to rain. So we <u>packed</u> up the bread, salami, and fruit and <u>rushed</u> to the cars.

Use the present tense throughout to write a summary or a description of a literary work:

Daisy Miller first <u>meets</u> Winterbourne in Geneva, and she later <u>met</u> him in Rome where she <u>is dating</u> the charming Giovanelli.   *shift* Winterbourne <u>was</u> furious that Daisy <u>doesn't</u> <u>realize</u> that Giovanelli <u>wasn't</u> a "real" gentleman.

Correction for verb tense consistency:

Daisy Miller first <u>meets</u> Winterbourne in Geneva, and she later <u>meets</u> him in Rome where she <u>is dating</u> the charming Giovanelli. Winterbourne <u>is</u> furious that Daisy <u>doesn't</u> <u>realize</u> that Giovanelli <u>isn't</u> a "real" gentleman.

Shifts in Voice

Just as a shift in number or tense can be distracting, a shift from the active to the passive voice can confuse or distract your reader. Use the voice consistently.

When the subject of a sentence does the action, the sentence is in the **active voice:**

<u>Lester</u> <u>brought</u> the tossed salad.

When the subject *receives* the action, the verb is in the **passive voice.** Notice that the passive voice is less effective than the active voice because it is less direct:

The tossed salad <u>was brought</u> by Lester.

When the active and passive voice are combined, the sentence is inconsistent in voice and would be marked with a "shift" in the margin of the paper:

<u>Lester</u> <u>brought</u> the tossed salad, and the soft <u>drinks</u> <u>were</u>   *shift* <u>brought</u> by Mike.

Correction:

<u>Lester</u> <u>brought</u> the tossed salad, and <u>Mike</u> <u>brought</u> the soft drinks.

In some cases, the passive voice is necessary because what might be the subject of the sentence is unknown or unimportant:

The <u>car</u> <u>was hijacked</u> last week.

Because the hijacker is apparently unknown, the sentence is in the passive voice, with the action being done to the car, the subject of the sentence.

```
NASA was granted additional funds to complete the study for the

space station.
```

The name of the agency that granted NASA the funds for the study may be unimportant to the writer of this sentence; the important point is that NASA has the funds for the project.

Passive voice constructions may create suspicion that the writer is deliberately hiding information:

```
The city council was voted unlimited travel funds.
```

Clearly, the city resident who reads that sentence in the local paper would want to know *who* did the voting, and why the newspaper failed to name the subject of the verb *voted*. Use the active voice whenever you know and wish to identify the "doer" of a particular act.

Mixed Sentences

mixed The margin note "**mixed**" indicates a mixed construction involving sentence parts that don't go together. The sentence may start with one subject and shift to another, or the verb may not fit the true subject of the sentence. The sentence also may begin with one grammatical construction and end with another. The problem, then, is a misfit in grammar or in logic, so the sentence is confusing to the reader:

mixed
```
Although he is active in the men's movement doesn't mean he is

a misogynist.
```

In this sentence the writer tries to make the dependent clause *Although he is active in the men's movement* the subject of the sentence. The writer probably intends *he* to be the subject of the sentence; rewriting the sentence to show this *and* selecting a correct verb for the subject will eliminate the confusion:

```
Although he is active in the men's movement, he is not a misog-

ynist.
```

Confused Sentence Parts

Each of the mixed sentences above contains a confusion between sentence parts. In some cases, the writer has started with one subject in mind and has ended the sentence with a different or implied subject. In other cases, the grammatical form of the first part of the sentence is inconsistent with the end of the sentence. Most often the revision involves correct identification of the true subject of the sentence and then the selection of an appropriate verb.

Among those women suffering with eating disorders, they are not *mixed* always bulimic.

Not all women with eating disorders are bulimic.

By prewriting, outlining, drafting, and revising is how he *mixed* wrote good papers.

He wrote good papers by prewriting, outlining, drafting, and revising his work.

The subject of ecology involves controversy. *mixed*

Ecology involves controversy.

Faulty Verb Choice

In some sentences with mixed meaning, the fault occurs because the subject is said to do or to be something that is illogical.

A realization between the academic senate and the dean would be *mixed* the ideal policy on plagiarism.

The sentence says that "a realization" would be "the ideal policy," which is not exactly what the writer means. Correction of the faulty use of the verb *would be* will clarify the sentence.

Ideally, a policy on plagiarism would be decided between the academic senate and the dean.

or

Ideally, the academic senate and the dean would realize the necessity for a policy on plagiarism.

In speech, *is when* and *is where* are common constructions for defining words, but these are mixed constructions and should be corrected in writing.

Acquiescence is when you give in to your oppressor. *mixed*

Acquiescence means giving in to an oppressor.

A final exam is where you show comprehensive knowledge. *mixed*

On a final exam you show comprehensive knowledge.

Misplaced (and Dangling) Modifiers

MM The margin note "**mm**" indicates a misplaced modifier. A **modifier** is a word, phrase, or clause used to describe another word in the sentence. The modifier should be as close to that word as possible, or the meaning can be confusing or unintentionally humorous.

MM   `Attacking our canary, I caught the cat.`

Written this way, *attacking the canary* appears to describe *I* rather than *cat.* Such a misplaced modifier can be easily corrected by rearranging the phrase so it describes *cat:*

    `I caught the cat attacking our canary.`

Sometimes there may not be a word for the modifier to describe. In these cases, the sentence needs to be rewritten:

MM   `At the age of 12, my family hiked into the Grand Canyon.`

Here the writer probably does not mean that his or her family was 12 years old, but this sentence does not contain a word for the opening phrase to describe. Therefore, *at the age of 12* is called a **dangling modifier**—a modifier that fails to refer logically to any word in the sentence. Dangling modifiers can be corrected by the following methods:

1. Keeping the modifier as it is and adding a word for the modifier to describe.

    `At the age of 12, I hiked into the Grand Canyon with my family.`

2. Turning the modifier into a dependent clause so that the meaning is clear.

    `When I was 12, my family hiked into the Grand Canyon.`

Often the modifier is not simply "dangling" but is oddly placed in the sentence so that the meaning is absurd:

MM   `You will value the difficult classes you took semesters`
    `from now.`

    `Semesters from now, you will value the difficult classes`
    `you took.`

MM   `Yuko's blind date was described as a six-foot-tall musician`
    `with a long ponytail weighing only 160 pounds.`

    `Yuko's blind date was described as a 160-pound, six-foot-tall`
    `musician with a long ponytail.`

Misplaced words can turn even the most serious dissertation into a comedy of errors! Occasionally an instructor may simply write "awk" (awkward) or "confusing" or "reword" in the margins when the error is actually a misplaced modifier. Becoming aware of the importance of the *placement* of each word or phrase in a sentence can help you detect and prevent such comical and confusing meanings before you type your final draft.

Faulty Parallelism

To achieve clarity, emphasis, and harmony in writing, use **parallel construction** for parts of sentences that you repeat. The "parts" may be single words, phrases, or clauses. Therefore, when you write any kind of list, put the items in similar grammatical form (all *-ing* words, all infinitives, and so on). Instead of writing "He likes hiking and to ski," you should write "He likes hiking and skiing" or "He likes to hike and to ski."

If faulty parallelism is noted in the margin of your paper, you have not **//** kept the parts of your sentence in the same grammatical form.

Single Words

//

The movie entertained and was enlightening.

The movie was **entertaining** and **enlightening.**

Phrases

Karen enjoys telling complicated jokes, performing the latest   **//** dances, and exotic food.

Karen enjoys **telling complicated jokes, performing the latest dances,** and **eating exotic food.**

Dependent Clauses

Professor Jaffe reminded the students that papers must be sub-   **//** mitted on time and to prepare reading assignments before class.

Professor Jaffe reminded the students **that papers must be submitted on time** and **that reading assignments must be prepared before class.**

Independent Clauses

//   "I came, I did some learning, and I triumphed," announced the jubilant graduate.

      "**I came, I learned,** and **I triumphed,**" announced the jubilant graduate.

You can also achieve greater clarity, emphasis, and balance by using parallel constructions with correlative conjunctions (paired terms such as *not only . . . but also; either . . . or;* and *neither . . . nor*):

//   We discovered fast walking is good for health and also for friendship.

      We discovered that fast walking is good **not only for health but also for friendship.**

//   Fran doesn't work as a waitress any longer, and neither does Donna.

      Neither Fran nor Donna works as a waitress any longer.

Chapter 14

Understanding Punctuation

A **"P"** in the margin of an essay indicates some sort of error in punctuation. This chapter covers all punctuation symbols. Because the comma is the most frequently used of them, most errors occur in comma use. Commas usually function to separate elements within a sentence, but they also have standard uses in dates, addresses, and in multiple-digit numbers. Below are models of the standard uses of the comma, with brief explanations to help you avoid comma errors.

 P

The Comma

1. Use a comma before a coordinating conjunction joining independent clauses. (Coordinating conjunctions are *and, but, for, or, nor, yet,* and *so.* See also pp. 573–574.)

   ```
   The school board has slashed the budget, so activity fees will
   increase this year.
   ```

   ```
   Many men want to take paternity leave when their babies are
   born, but most companies are not prepared for the requests.
   ```

   Short independent clauses may not need a comma with the conjunction, but if there is any doubt about the need or clarity, use a comma.

   ```
   He arrived so I left.
   ```

   ```
   He arrived, so I left.
   ```

2. Use a comma to separate introductory elements from the rest of the sentence:

   ```
   To register for classes, bring your advisor's signature card.
   ```

   ```
   If elementary schools continue to close, increased bus service
   will be necessary.
   ```

   ```
   Exhilarated, the climber reached the summit.
   ```

   ```
   By the next century, most college graduates will be in service-
   related careers.
   ```

3. Use a comma to separate items in a series.

   ```
   The campus bookstore has been criticized for selling sexist mag-
   azines, cigarettes, and greeting cards of questionable taste.
   ```

   ```
   Triathlons require quick running, swimming, and cycling.
   ```

   ```
   The requirements for ownership of the condominium include a
   bank-approved loan, a satisfactory security rating, and a will-
   ingness to comply with the homeowners' rules and procedures.
   ```

4. Use a comma between coordinate adjectives—adjectives that modify the same word equally—if there is not a conjunction.

   ```
   The shady, blooming, fragrant garden welcomed the walkers.
   ```

   ```
   A shady and fragrant garden welcomed the walkers.
   ```

   If the first adjective modifies the second adjective, do not use a comma.

   ```
   That mansion's most interesting feature is a white oak staircase.
   ```

   ```
   Professor Pierce's exams require complicated mathematical
   computations.
   ```

5. Use commas to set off nonrestrictive word groups. Nonrestrictive elements describe nouns or pronouns by giving extra or nonessential information. The nonrestrictive element could be removed from the sentence without sacrificing the meaning of the sentence.

   ```
   Walden Pond, which is located outside of Concord, was the site
   of Thoreau's one-room shelter and bean field.
   ```

   ```
   Amy Tan's first novel, The Joy Luck Club, was written in a few
   months.
   ```

   ```
   The Rolls Royce, its silver hood ornament gleaming in the sun,
   was completely out of gas.
   ```

6. Do *not* use commas with restrictive word groups. Restrictive elements limit the meaning of words or provide vital (or restricting) information.

   ```
   The entrees on the left side of the menu are suitable for din-
   ers who prefer low-cholesterol diets.
   ```

   The sentence gives the information that only the entrees on the left side of the menu are low in cholesterol. Presumably, the other items on the menu are not especially suited for clients who prefer low cholesterol.

   ```
   Our son who lives in Texas teaches anthropology.
   ```

   For a family with sons residing in different states, the restrictive clause is essential and commas should not be used.

   ```
   Customers using credit cards collect free airline mileage.
   ```

   Again, the lack of commas shows that the information is restrictive. Only those customers who use credit cards will collect airline mileage; customers who pay by check or cash do not.

7. Use commas to separate transitional or parenthetical expressions, conjunctive adverbs, contrasting elements, and most phrases from the main part of the sentence.

   ```
   Silk, for example, can be washed by hand.

   Joseph Heller, as the story goes, wanted to call his novel
   Catch-18 instead of Catch-22.

   A medium avocado contains 324 calories; therefore, it is not an
   ideal fruit for people watching their weight.

   Darren, unlike his brother Stephen, can be reasonable.

   Her medical studies completed, Nancy started a practice in Fresno.
   ```

8. Use commas to set off expressions and questions of direct address, the words *yes* or *no*, and interjections.

   ```
   Sorry, Professor Bender, only two of those books are in the stacks.

   You will complete the immigration papers, won't you?

   Yes, most readers prefer the new MLA documentation form.

   Oh, I can't decide if we really need an attorney.
   ```

9. Use commas for dates, addresses, and titles.

   ```
   James Joyce was born on February 2, 1882, which was St. Brid-
   get's Day and Groundhog Day, too.
   ```

> The special delivery letter was sent to 10350 Dover Street, Westminster, Colorado.
>
> Will Wood, PhD, begins his law practice at Duke University.

10. Use commas to set off direct quotations.

> As Richard Ellmann notes, "Stephen Dedalus said the family was a net which he would fly past."
>
> "I too believe in Taos, without having seen it. I also believe in Indians. But they must do <u>half</u> the believing: in me as well as in the sun," wrote D. H. Lawrence to Mabel Luhan.

11. Do *not* use a comma to separate a verb from its subject or object. The following examples all show **incorrect** uses of the comma:

⟋ Fast walking around a track, can be painless but effective exercise.

⟋ Christine explained to Larry, that practicing law has precedence over going to films.

12. Do *not* use a comma between compound elements if the word groups are not independent clauses. The following examples show **incorrect** uses of the comma:

⟋ Louise can prepare a multi-course meal, and weed her garden on the same day.

⟋ Sara understands that the conference is in June, and that she will need to grade finals while she is attending it.

13. A comma should not be used to separate an adjective from the noun that follows it. The following examples are **incorrect** uses of the comma:

⟋ It was a sunny, warm, and windless, day.

⟋ A massive, polished, ornately carved, buffet stood in the dining room.

The Apostrophe

An **apostrophe** is used most frequently to form **contractions** and **possessives**.

Contractions

When two words are merged into one, the apostrophe takes the place of any missing letters:

```
does not           doesn't

it is              it's

should have        should've

I would            I'd
```

Contractions tend to make writing seem more conversational and informal; therefore, they are often avoided in formal writing and in research papers. Remember that the apostrophe takes the place of the missing letter and does not ever belong in the break between the two words:

```
couldn't [not could'nt]
```

Other instances where apostrophes indicate a missing letter or letters are commonly found in informal writing and speech, particularly in dialogues from narratives and fiction:

```
around             'round

until              'til

1950s              '50s

playing            playin'
```

Again, such forms are typically reserved for writing that is intended to sound conversational.

Possessives

Possessive nouns indicate belonging or ownership and are typically placed immediately before whatever is owned. Rather than write "the trumpet of Jason" or "the office of his doctor," we eliminate the *of* and move the owner in front of the possession:

```
Jason's trumpet

his doctor's office
```

Sometimes such ownership is loosely implied:

```
tonight's party

Thursday's test

one day's sick leave

two weeks' vacation
```

But, in a sense, the party really does "belong" to tonight (not tomorrow) and the test "belongs" to Thursday (not Friday). Similarly, the sick leave is "of one day" and the vacation is "of two weeks." Clearly, the possessive form here makes the writing smoother and less wordy.

To indicate possession, obey the following guidelines:

1. Add -'s if the possessive noun does not end in s (whether it is singular or plural):

   ```
   Sarah's acting

   Ben's collections

   the men's movement

   the children's enthusiasm
   ```

2. Add an apostrophe at the end of the word if the plural possessive noun ends in an s (including proper names):

   ```
   those actors' salaries

   five students' projects

   two months' salary

   the Knights' generosity

   the Walshes' Super Bowl party
   ```

3. If a singular proper name ends in s, add an ' and a second s.

   ```
   James's routine

   Oates's story
   ```

Joint Possession.   When two or more people possess the same thing, show joint possession by using -'s (or -s') with the last noun only:

```
We relaxed at Jule and Marsha's home in Colorado Springs.

Nate and Jess's help was appreciated.
```

Individual Possession.   When two or more people possess distinct things, show individual possession by using -'s (or -s') with both nouns:

```
Andy's and Beth's summer projects aren't completed yet.

Luis's and Charles's questions were both fascinating.
```

Compound Nouns.   If a noun is compound, use -'s (or -s') with the last component of that noun term:

```
My brother-in-law's woodworking is very professional.

Barbara and Joe took their sisters-in-laws' advice.
```

Indefinite Pronouns.   Indefinite pronouns are those that refer to no specific person or thing: *everyone, anyone, no one,* and *something.* These pronouns also need an apostrophe to indicate possession:

```
We asked everybody's opinion of the film.

Is someone's safety in jeopardy?
```

Possessive Pronouns. Possessive pronouns are already possessive and need no apostrophes:

my, mine	its
you, yours	our, ours
her, hers	their, theirs
his	whose

```
Whose car should we drive?

I would prefer to ride in yours rather than theirs.
```

Plurals of Letters. Use -'s to pluralize the letters of the alphabet:

```
He earned three B's this term.

She has two t's in her last name.
```

Plurals of Numbers and Abbreviations. The apostrophe should *not* be used for plurals of numbers or abbreviations:

```
They all marched in twos.

By the end of the 1990s, community recycling was widespread.

Many students like to purchase used CDs at their local music stores.

All candidates must have earned their BAs.
```

Some reminders:

1. Make sure a noun is possessive (and not merely plural) before you use an apostrophe. The noun *passengers* does not "own" anything in the following sentence; therefore it is a simple plural.
   ```
                passengers
   The passenger's were not allowed to smoke.
   ```

2. Possessive pronouns need no apostrophes.
   ```
                       its
   The crowd expressed it's pleasure.
                       hers
   That responsibility is her's.
   ```

3. Many instructors prefer that their students not use contractions in formal writing and research papers.

The Period, Question Mark, and Exclamation Point

The most obvious use of the period is to mark the end of a sentence—unless the sentence is a direct question or needs an exclamation point:

```
Do you remember learning punctuation symbols in elementary
school?

Yes, and it all seemed so easy then!
```

Because the exclamation point is used for strong commands and emphatic statements, it should not be overused. Furthermore, an exclamation mark is never used with a period, a comma, or another exclamation point.

Don't use a question mark for an indirect or implied question:

```
I wonder if I ever had trouble with punctuation in elementary
school.
```

Use the period for abbreviations:

```
Mr. / Mrs. / Ms.    Dr. / Rev. / Capt.    i.e / e.g. / etc.

BC / AD          am / pm          BS / MA / PhD
```

Notice that no period is used with postal abbreviations:

```
CA   NY   TX   IL
```

Do not use periods with acronyms (words that are made from the first letters of many words and are pronounced as words):

```
NATO    UNICEF
```

Usually no period is used in abbreviations of the names of organizations or schools:

```
NBC    NATO    UN    NBA    NYU
```

The Semicolon

The semicolon is most often used to connect two independent clauses:

```
Students with an advisor's signature card register in their
division office; students without a signature must register
in the gym.
```

Notice that the semicolon is used in place of a period to show that the two independent ideas—clauses that could stand alone as separate sentences—are *related*. The semicolon suggests the relationship without defining it.

The semicolon is also used after an independent clause and before some transitional phrases (like *on the other hand* or *in contrast*) and after conjunctive adverbs (such as *therefore, however,* and *furthermore;* see the complete list on p. 578).

```
Newcomers to the United States often enjoy material advantages

that they lacked in their native lands; on the other hand,

they often feel spiritually deprived in their new country.

Professor Smiley will accept late papers; however, he reduces

the grade for each day the paper is late.
```

The semicolon is used for separating items in a list if the punctuation within the list includes commas. Notice Naomi Wolf's use of the semicolon in this example from *The Beauty Myth:*

```
In 1984, in the United States, "male lawyers aged 25-34

earn $27,563, but female lawyers the same age, $20,573;

retail salesmen earn $13,002 to retail saleswomen's $7,479;

male bus drivers make $15,611 and female bus drivers $9,903;

female hairdressers earn $7,603 less than male hairdressers"

(49).
```

The Colon

A colon is used to introduce and call attention to a statement, to introduce a list, to introduce a quotation if the quotation is at the end of a sentence, in bibliographic forms, in reporting time, for separating main titles from subtitles, and in distinguishing chapters from verses in the Bible. A colon is usually preceded by a main clause (a word group containing a subject and verb). The main clause does not need to be followed by a complete clause, but if it is a complete clause, capitalize the first word.

```
The candidates need to realize that women form a significant

majority in this country: six million more potential votes.

The application form requires the following: a final transcript,

a housing request, a medical report, and the first tuition check.

Women do not expect promotions or high salaries: "Women are

often unsure of their intrinsic worth in the marketplace"

(Sidel qtd. in Wolf 49).

New York: Longman

Between Worlds: A Reader, Rhetoric, and Handbook

The train departs at 5:30 in the morning.
```

In some cases, a colon should not be used. For example, do *not* place a colon between a subject and a verb, between a verb and its complements, or between a preposition and its object:

P   The animals in that section of the zoo include: panthers, leop-
     ards, lions, and tigers.

P   The courses he needs to take are: biology, chemistry, physics,
     and calculus.

P   Don't put luggage on: the bed, the desk, or the reading chair.

The Dash

The dash (which is sometimes created by typing two hyphens with no spaces around or between them) is used sparingly for dramatic emphasis, to call attention to material the dash sets off. Sometimes the dash is used in places where a colon could also be used, but the dash is considered more informal. Because the dash indicates a sudden shift in thought and is used for dramatic emphasis, it should not be overused. In formal writing a comma, colon, or period may be more appropriate punctuation symbols.

    We all believe that environmental protection is an obligation

    of our era--but we still use toxic cleaners in our homes.

Here the dash is used to emphasize the contrast between what "we all believe" and what we do. A comma could also be used in this sentence.

    Both successful women and less-successful women have the same

    goal--to "marry up"--so men still have a constant psychological

    need to be successful at work.

The dash is used here to set off the definitive information, the "same goal" the writer believes women have. A comma could have been used, but the dash achieves more emphasis.

The dash may also be used in the same manner as the colon to announce a dramatic point:

    The candidates need to realize that women form a significant

    majority in this country--six million more potential votes.

Quotation Marks

Quotation marks are used to enclose direct quotations, some titles, and occasionally words defined or used in a special way. Quotation marks are used in pairs.

A *direct quotation* states in exact words what someone has said or written. It is enclosed with quotation marks.

```
Brigid Brophy insists, "If modern civilisation has invented
methods of education which make it possible for men to feed ba-
bies and for women to think logically, we are betraying civili-
sation itself if we do not set both sexes free to make a free
choice."
```

Notice that Brophy's spelling of *civilisation* is British, and that the writer quoting her is not permitted to change her spelling without indicating the change in brackets: "civili[z]ation." See more on brackets on pages 607–608.

An *indirect quotation* notes what has been said in a paraphrased or indirect way. No quotation marks are needed:

```
Brigid Brophy believes that men and women should be free to make
the choices that education and technology have made possible.
```

A *quotation within a quotation* requires the use of standard quotation marks around the outside quotation and single quotation marks around the interior quotation:

```
According to Naomi Wolf, "Every generation since about 1830 has
had to fight its version of the beauty myth. 'It is very little
to me' said the suffragist Lucy Stone in 1855, 'to have the
right to vote, to own property, etcetera, if I may not keep my
body, and its uses, in my absolute right.'"
```

Commas and periods are placed inside quotation marks:

```
Brigid Brophy thinks that both genders should be "free to make
a free choice."
```

```
If we do not let men and women make choices, "we are betraying
civilisation itself," believes Brigid Brophy.
```

Semicolons and colons are placed outside quotation marks:

```
Brophy says we are all "free to make a free choice"; in fact,
we let convention limit our awareness of choice.
```

```
Brophy says we are all "free to make a free choice": about our
educations, our careers, our domesticity.
```

Question marks go inside quotation marks if they are part of the quotation but belong outside of quotation marks if the quoted statement is being used as a question by the writer quoting the material:

```
The professor asked, "Who agrees with Brigid Brophy's thesis?"
```

```
Does Brophy think we "should be free to make a free choice"?
```

If you are quoting a conversation, begin a new paragraph for each speaker. Notice the punctuation of the quoted conversation in this excerpt from Rebekah Hall-Naganuma's narrative, which begins on page 412.

```
"What do you mean by 'blackout?'" she asked, with a look of
confusion on her face.
```

```
"She ended up in Houston somehow and then couldn't remember
how she got there."
```

If you are quoting poetry, integrate into your own text quoted single lines of poetry. Two or three lines of poetry may be brought into your text and enclosed in quotation marks, or they may be set off from your text, without quotation marks but indented ten spaces from the left margin:

```
The gardener in Marge Piercy's poem "A Work of Artifice"
"croons" to the plant as he "whittles" it into his desired
shape. He says:

    It is your nature

    To be small and cozy

    domestic and weak;
```

or

```
The gardener in Marge Piercy's poem "A Work of Artifice"
"croons" to the plant as he "whittles" it into his desired
shape. He says, "It is your nature / To be small and cozy / do-
mestic and weak."
```

The slash (/) is used when poetry lines are incorporated into a text to indicate the end of a poetry line. (The use of the slash is described further on p. 608.) Set off poetry quotations of more than three lines and prose quotations of more than four lines.

Titles of short stories, songs, essays, poems, articles, parts of books, and the titles of episodes on television and radio are enclosed in quotation marks:

```
"Ace in the Hole"
```

```
"Chicago"
```

```
"Don't Let Stereotypes Warp Your Judgments"
```

```
"A Work of Artifice"

"Tracks" in Aquaboogie
```

In special instances, quotation marks can be used to enclose words that are defined or used in a special way:

```
The "artifice" is not so much the "skill or ingenuity" used

to shape women but the "trickery or craft" that keeps them

dependent.
```

Do not use quotation marks around a word that you feel self-conscious about using. Instead, change the word:

```
The morning meeting is held to give the staff the "rundown" on

the advertising goals for the day.

The morning meeting is held to explain that day's advertising

goals to the staff.
```

The Ellipsis

The ellipsis, a set of three spaced periods (. . .), informs the reader that something has been left out of a quotation. For example, a writer quoting material from Naomi Wolf's book *The Beauty Myth* might decide to leave out some material unnecessary to the text he or she is writing. Here Wolf writes about the phenomenon of eating disorders in countries other than the United States:

```
It is spreading to other industrialized nations: The United

Kingdom now has 3.5 million anorexics or bulimics (95 percent

of them female), with 6,000 new cases yearly (183).
```

Here the passage is revised using an ellipsis:

```
It is spreading to other industrialized nations: The United

Kingdom now has 3.5 million anorexics or bulimics . . . with

6,000 new cases yearly (183).
```

The decision to remove material and use the ellipsis must be governed by the writer's intent. But the ellipsis may not be used to remove anything that would change the meaning of the section that the writer is quoting. The fact that 95 percent of the cases of eating disorders in the United Kingdom involve women may not be relevant to the writer of the revised text, so the ellipsis is used as a convenient tool to shorten the quoted material and keep the emphasis where the writer wants it. The missing words in this case do not change the meaning of the original.

If you remove material from the quoted material at the end of the sentence, use a period before the three periods of the ellipsis. Notice this example of quoted material from H. Patricia Hynes's 1990 edition of *EarthRight:*

```
The United States creates about 450,000 tons of residential and
commercial solid waste every day. By the year 2000, this amount
is expected to reach 530,000 tons per day.... The Environmen-
tal Protection Agency estimates that in the next five to ten
years more than twenty-seven states and half of the country's
cities will run out of landfill space. (47)
```

If a parenthetical reference follows an ellipsis at the end of a sentence, use three spaced periods and then place the period to conclude the sentence after the final parenthesis:

```
As Lisa Appignanesi records in her biography Simone de
Beauvoir, Beauvoir believed that "the genuinely moral person
can never have an easy conscience ..." (79).
```

To avoid using the ellipsis too often, integrate carefully selected parts of quoted material into your text:

```
As Carol Tavris notes, people respond "in shock and anger at
the failings of 'human nature.'"
```

By paraphrasing part of the quotation and integrating the author's text with your own, you can avoid both using lengthy quotations *and* overusing the ellipsis.

Parentheses

Use parentheses to separate a digression or aside from the main sentence:

```
Their house number (usually painted on the curb) was on the
mail box.
```

```
Because an increasing number of women (and men) are suffering
from eating disorders, we must address the problem at our next
NOW conference.
```

Rules govern the use of punctuation within and outside of parentheses. If a sentence requires a comma in addition to parentheses, use the comma after the second or closing parenthesis:

```
During the Civil War (1861-65), African Americans were trained
for active duty and fought in segregated units.
```

If the information within the parentheses is a complete sentence, the final punctuation is enclosed within the parentheses:

```
More information on gardens that require little water appears

throughout the book. (See the chapters on cactus and native

plants, especially.)
```

Parentheses also are used in documentation to enclose the source of paraphrased or quoted information. In these cases, the terminal punctuation appears outside the parentheses:

```
As Virginia Woolf says in Orlando, "Clothes have . . . more impor-

tant offices than merely to keep us warm. They change our view of

the world and the world's view of us" (187).
```

(For a more complete discussion of how parentheses are used in MLA documentation, see p. 542 , and for their use in APA documentation, see p. 557.)

Brackets

Use brackets to enclose words or phrases that you have added to a quotation, to show any changes that you have made in quoted material, or to record your own comments about quoted material:

```
Today, more attention is being paid "to the relationship

between eating disorders [anorexia and bulimia] and the

compulsive eating of many women."
```

In the preceding example, the writer has clarified a point for the reader by defining within the quotation types of eating disorders. The brackets indicate that the words are not part of the original quotation.

```
The Duke of Ferrara, in Robert Browning's poem "My Last

Duchess," is disturbed that the Duchess "ranked [his] gift

of a nine-hundred-years-old name / With anybody's gift."
```

In this example, the writer changed the original –"ranked my gift of a nine-hundred-years-old name"– to fit into a text. To show the change from *my* to *his*, the writer placed brackets around the change. The diagonal line (or slash) between "name" and "With" indicates the end of the line in the poem.

```
The "Poison Pen Letters" greeting card says, "Everything

has it's [sic] price . . . but I didn't know you came

so cheap!"
```

The brackets are used to enclose *sic,* a Latin word meaning "in this manner." The *[sic]* used after *it's* in the above example indicates that the error of not using *its* is in the original, and is not an error made by the person quoting the original.

The Slash

The slash may be used sparingly to show options, like pass/fail or Dean/Department Head. Notice that there is no space between the words and the slash when the slash is used to show options.

The slash is also used to define the end of a line of poetry if the line is incorporated into a text. For example, notice how the writer incorporates into a poetry explication some words from Stephen Perry's poem "Blue Spruce":

```
The speaker in the poem reveals that his "grandfather had an

affair / with the girl who did their nails" (19-20).
```

The slash indicates where the line ends in the original work (which appears on p. 17). Notice that a space appears on either side of the slash when it is used to indicate the end of a line of poetry.

In bulletins, reports, and some business correspondence, the slash is used in the form *he/she,* as in this sentence:

```
The person who lost a ring in the library may claim it after

he/she describes it to campus police.
```

In formal writing, you should avoid the form *he/she* by writing *he or she,* as in this sentence:

```
The student who aspires to a law degree may attain it if he or

she is willing to work hard.
```

Both *he/she* and *he or she* can be avoided by rewriting the sentence:

```
The person who lost a ring in the library may claim it by de-

scribing it to campus police.
```

```
The student who aspires to a law degree may attain it by work-

ing hard.
```

The Hyphen

The hyphen is used to divide a word or to form a compound word. To divide a word that will not fit on the typed or written line, separate the part of the word that will fit on the line with a hyphen at a syllable break, then conclude the word on the next line. The break must occur only between syllables and should not leave fewer than two letters at the end of the line or fewer than three letters at the beginning of the next line. The hyphen appears at the end of the first line, *not* at the beginning of the next line. If you are using a computer, the word processing program automatically moves the full word to the next line (unless directed to hyphenate words).

Notice how each error is corrected:

```
Of all of the applicants for the job, she was the best te-      𝒫

acher for the class.
```

```
Of all of the applicants for the job, she was the best

teacher for the class.
```

If you choose to hyphenate, a word can be broken between syllables if the break will leave at least two letters at the end of the line and three or more letters at the beginning of the next line. Because the syllables of *teach-* and *-er* will not fit that rule, the entire word must be moved to the next line.

```
After his paper was completed, the frustrated student fo-      𝒫

und another critical article.
```

```
After his paper was completed, the frustrated student

found another critical article.
```

[A one-syllable word cannot be broken, so *found* must be moved to the next line.]

```
Since the 1993 Presidential inauguration, interest in the po-   𝒫

-etry of Maya Angelou has increased.
```

```
Since the 1993 Presidential inauguration, interest in the

poetry of Maya Angelou has increased.
```

[The hyphen is used *only* at the end of the first line.]

Divide compound words only where the hyphen already exists:

```
He gave the family heirloom to his sis-                         𝒫

ter-in-law.
```

```
He gave the family heirloom to his sister-

in-law.
```

p   `Histories of popular music describe the heart-throb-`

`bing gestures of Elvis Presley.`

`Histories of popular music describe the heart-`

`throbbing gestures of Elvis Presley.`

Hyphens are also used to form compound words that modify a noun:

`The grade-conscious students knew the best sequence for the`

`courses.`

`The award-winning play went on to Broadway.`

If the modifiers follow the noun, the hyphens are usually left out.

`The students are grade conscious.`

`The play was award winning and went on to Broadway.`

Hyphens are used in spelled-out fractions and compound whole numbers from twenty-one to ninety-nine:

`Over one-half of the voters will stay home election day.`

`Everyone hates that old school bus song, "Ninety-Nine Bottles`

`of Beer on the Wall."`

Hyphens are used to attach some prefixes and suffixes. Usually, prefixes are attached to a word without a hyphen: *preconceived, disinterested, unhappy.* But prefixes such as *ex-, self-,* and *all-,* prefixes that precede a capitalized word, or prefixes that are a capitalized letter usually require a hyphen; for example, *self-supporting, ex-champion, anti-European,* and *U-boat.* Sometimes, to prevent confusion, a hyphen is necessary to separate a prefix ending in a vowel and a main word that starts with a vowel; for example, *de-escalate, re-invent,* and *pre-advise.*

Chapter 15

Understanding Faulty Word Choice

P oor word choice will weaken writing, and instructors will note these *wd ch* errors in the margins of your papers. (Specific examples are cited in the alphabetically arranged list of commonly confused words in Chapter 16.) The types of word choice problems are defined and illustrated here.

Clichés

Clichés, or overused words or expressions, should be avoided. Predictable language is stale, and expressions that were once novel and even colorful inevitably lose their descriptive quality through overuse. Like a faded carpet, clichés no longer add color to the space they occupy. If you can complete the following expressions automatically, you know that you have examples of a cliché:

```
The bread was hard as a _____.

We searched all day, but it was like looking for a needle

_____.
```

Good writing is clear, fresh, and vivid:

```
The bread was as hard as aged camel dung and about as tasty.

We searched all day, but it was like looking for a button in

my mother's tool drawer.
```

Slang, Jargon, and Colloquial Words

Some of our most vivid language is considered **slang** (highly informal, often coined words used in speaking) or **jargon** (the special vocabulary of people who have the same job, interest, or way of life). In fact, in conversation, if pretentious language were substituted for some of the commonly used **colloquial** words—*intoxicated* for *drunk* or *children* for *kids*—our conversations would sound stuffy or silly. Slang is often vigorous and colorful, but it is nonstandard and therefore unacceptable in most formal writing. And the jargon that is acceptable in conversation or memos at work may be unintelligible to the general reader. If you think your "funky," "laid-back," or "awesome" word choice is going to influence negatively your reader's feelings about your integrity as a writer, elevate your language and remove the inappropriate word.

Archaic Words, Euphemisms, and Pretentious Words

Some words that appear in literature, especially poetry, may not be appropriate for expository writing:

wd ch   Marcus Mabry was amongst the minority students accepted

at Stanford.

Marcus Mabry was among the minority students accepted

at Stanford.

The word *amongst,* used in poetry, sounds inflated in expository texts.

Writers sometimes use **euphemisms**—substitutes for words perceived as offensive—to limit emotional impact. For example, a war report might describe the results of a bombing mission as "collateral casualties" rather than "civilians killed." A *Newsweek* article states that "the collateral damage of the drug war has been immense"—a euphemism avoiding the recognition that it is human beings who are being incarcerated and homes which are being destroyed in overly aggressive police actions.

Euphemisms are often deliberately used to mask a harsher reality. At best, they are often imprecise, as in this sentence: "We lost our grandmother last week." The reader might wonder if she is still wandering in the parking lot of the local mall. To avoid this confusion and to communicate accurately, use direct and precise language: "Our grandmother died last week."

Pretentious language is used by writers who believe it will make their work appear more refined or elegant. Avoid words like *facilitate* or *utilize* when *help* and *use* are adequate. Some pretentious words have persisted and reached cliché status: *viable* and *parameters,* for example.

Writers who are insecure about their writing may be tempted to overuse a thesaurus or pad their papers with contrived and inflated diction. Readers can usually detect this as a desperate attempt to pump up flat or shallow ideas. Instead of developing their thinking and analysis, pretentious writers try to bluff it. Typically, the end result is wordy, confused, stuffy prose rather than writing that is concise, accurate and honest. Here are some examples, from student essays, of contrived or inflated diction:

Inflated and wordy diction:

```
The imagery that Baldwin employs engulfs the situation to a
reality status.
```

Precise:

```
Baldwin's imagery makes the scene realistic.
```

Inflated and wordy diction:

```
The story commences with the creation of an atmosphere that
posited the couple's affluency.
```

Precise:

```
The setting suggests the couple is wealthy.
```

Redundancies

The legal profession has contributed some double-talk, such as *aid and abet*, to our language, and some other redundancies have persisted even though they are bulky or inane: *each and every, revert back, end result, temporary respite*, or *true fact*. You can see that *each* and *every* mean the same thing, so the words should not be used together. To revert means "to go back." And what is a fact if it isn't true? If you regard these redundancies as you would clichés—language that is predictable and imprecise—you will eliminate them from your writing.

Sexist Language

Language that demeans women or men is **sexist.** Most writers would know not to use *chick, broad, stud,* or *hunk* in their work, but more subtle and insidious sexist language also needs to be avoided. If you exclude or offend a portion of your audience, you will lose your reader—even if the rest of your essay is strong—as in the following examples:

```
Every professor uses his wisdom to remain objective.

Each nurse is required to store her lunch in a locker.
```

```
A clever lawyer parks his car in the free lot.

The competent PTA president uses her gavel rarely.
```

Even a superficial look at job and lifestyle choices in the last decades would confirm the necessity of unbiased language in print. Nurses and lawyers are both female and male; nowhere is it prescribed that only women will be PTA presidents. Consider the following solutions illustrated below for freeing the above sentences of sexist language:

```
A professor uses wisdom to remain objective.

Professors use their wisdom to remain objective.

Nurses are required to store their lunches in lockers.

Each nurse is required to store his or her lunch in a locker.

Clever lawyers park their cars in the free lot.
```

Avoid the *his/her* construction in formal writing and the *his or her* pattern. You can eliminate both of these bulky and awkward constructions by using the article instead of a possessive pronoun, or by using a plural noun as the subject:

```
The competent PTA president uses the gavel rarely.

Competent PTA presidents use their gavels rarely.
```

Do not assume any job is gender specific. *Fireman* should be *firefighter*, *clergyman* should be *minister* or *member of the clergy*, and *mailman* should be *letter carrier* or *mail carrier*. Do not add *lady* to job titles; "She is a lady doctor" is as inane as "He is a male artist."

You can further free your writing from sexism by eliminating the generic use of *man* in examples like the following:

wd ch
```
Mankind is more aware of stereotypes than it was a decade ago.

Humanity is more aware of stereotypes than it was a decade ago.

People are more aware of stereotypes than they were a decade
ago.
```

Chapter 16

Understanding Commonly Confused Words

O ur language contains a number of words that are often confused or misused by many writers, not just college students. Some words on this list are nonstandard—that is, they are not considered acceptable for written work (for example, *should of* instead of *should have*). The list also contains many homonyms—words that sound alike but have different meanings (for example, *there/their/they're*). When you are deciding on the words you will include in your writing, your audience and your intention will govern your choice. But when you have an error noted in the margin of one of your papers, look here for an explanation that will help you revise the language you used.

Your instructor may use any one of the symbols listed on the inside of the back cover to denote your error.

Commonly Confused Words

a, an Use *a* before words beginning with consonant sounds, including those spelled with an initial pronounced *h* (*a* horse) and those spelled with vowels that are sounded as consonants (*a* one-hour final, *a* university). Use *an* before words beginning with vowel sounds, including those spelled with an initial *h* (*an* igloo, *an* hour).

a/an, the *A* and *an* are indefinite articles and are used before nouns that are nonspecific or general (*a* game, *an* acrobat). *The* is a definite article and used before nouns that refer to something specific (*the* game, *the* acrobat).

<u>An</u> avid sports fan, Bill watches <u>a</u> televised football game
every weekend.

His favorite team is <u>the</u> Miami Dolphins although his friend always cheers for <u>the</u> Buffalo Bills.

accept, except   *Accept* is a verb meaning "to receive." *Except* is a preposition
meaning "excluding" or "but."

I <u>accept</u> your plan to tour all of New York City <u>except</u> for Central Park.

advice, advise   *Advice* is the noun meaning "recommendation about what to
do." *Advise* is the verb meaning "to give opinion or counsel."

I <u>advise</u> you to follow your counselor's <u>advice</u>.

affect, effect   *Affect* is usually a verb meaning "to influence." *Effect* is a noun
meaning "result." In psychology, *affect* is used as a noun meaning "a feeling or emotion." *Effect* can be used as a verb meaning "to implement, or
to bring about."

The eyedrops do not <u>affect</u> his driving.

Candles create a romantic <u>effect</u> in the dining room.

An examination of <u>affect</u> is critical in understanding personality.

Congress must <u>effect</u> a change in the tax laws.

aisle, isle   *Aisle* means a walkway between sections of seats, shelves, or
counters. *Isle* means an island.

Deborah and Jeff decided it was time to amble down the <u>aisle</u>
together.

The pet food <u>aisle</u> of the supermarket seems to expand each
year.

Melanie and Bill were dreaming about snorkeling near some faraway <u>isle</u> in the Pacific.

all ready, already   *All ready* means "completely prepared." *Already* means
"by now" or "before now."

We were <u>all ready</u> for the trip, but the bus had <u>already</u> left.

all right   *All right* is typically spelled as two words. (*Alright* appears in some
dictionaries, but most readers still consider it a misspelling.)

all together, altogether   *All together* means "in a common location," "in unison," or "as a group." *Altogether* means "completely" or "entirely."

We are <u>altogether</u> certain that caging the rabbits <u>all together</u>
is a mistake.

allude/elude   *Allude* means "to refer to"; *elude* means "to escape."

Mimi <u>alluded</u> to the time when Katie studied in France and managed to <u>elude</u> tedious professors.

allusion, illusion   An *allusion* is an "indirect reference"; an *illusion* is "a de-
ceptive appearance" or "a fantasy that may be confused with reality."

Joyce's use of mythological <u>allusions</u> gives the <u>illusion</u> that
she is a classicist.

a lot   *A lot* is always two words, never *alot*.

altar, alter   The noun *altar* means "an elevated place or structure where
religious rites are performed." *Alter* is a verb that means "to change or
modify."

She needed to <u>alter</u> her schedule to allow time to decorate the
church <u>altar</u> with fresh daisies for the wedding.

among, between   Use *between* when referring to two; use *among* for three or
more.

<u>Between</u> you and me, Alex is <u>among</u> the most creative students in
our program.

amount, number   *Amount* refers to a quantity of something that cannot be
counted. *Number* refers to items that can be counted.

The <u>amount</u> of flour used depends on the <u>number</u> of cookies you
want to bake.

anxious   *Anxious* means "apprehensive" or "worried." Often it is confused
with the word *eager,* which means "anticipating" or "looking forward to."

Yumiko was <u>anxious</u> about her performance review because she was
<u>eager</u> to be promoted.

a while, awhile   *A while* is an article and a noun; *awhile* is an adverb.

We spoke for <u>a while</u> and then parted.

Wait <u>awhile</u> before you swim.

basically   This word is greatly overused and often unnecessary:

Avoid: Tia and Delaiah are, basically, ideal daughters-in-law.

Better: Tia and Delaiah are ideal daughters-in-law.

being as, being that   These terms should not be used for *because* or *since.*

```
Because Quarterback Drew Bledsoe is so popular with fans, the
games in Buffalo are always sold out.
```

```
Since he signed with the Lakers, Shaq has been a top scorer for
the team.
```

beside, besides   *Beside* is a preposition meaning "next to." *Besides* is a preposition meaning "except," as well as an adverb meaning "in addition to."

```
The secretary sat beside his dean.
```

```
Everyone besides the team rides the school bus to each game.
```

```
Your expertise is needed; besides, you know how to have fun!
```

brake, break   *Brake* means to slow or stop a vehicle or the device used to stop a vehicle. *Break* means to smash, shatter, become separated, interrupt, or halt.

```
If that driver doesn't brake soon, he will break the bikes that
are in the driveway.
```

can, may   *Can* means "is able to." *May* indicates permission.

```
You can talk on the telephone for three hours, but you may not
in my house!
```

capital, capitol   *Capital* refers to the city and is the word to describe an uppercase letter. *Capitol* indicates the building where government meets.

```
The capital is the destination for the class trip, but a visit to
the capitol is impossible because the ceiling is under repair.
```

censor, censure   *Censor* functions as a verb (meaning "to suppress or remove objectionable material") and as a noun (the person who suppresses the objectionable material). *Censure* is a verb meaning "to criticize severely."

```
The librarian refused to work with citizens who censor the
classics.
```

```
The censor of a few decades ago considered The Adventures of
Huckleberry Finn subversive.
```

```
The city council needs to censure neon signs in "Old Town."
```

cite, site, sight   *Cite* means "to quote by way of example, authority, or proof." *Site* is "the location of." *Sight* is a "spectacle or view."

```
The tourist sights were on the site of an ancient village cited
in the guidebook.
```

complement, compliment *Complement* means "to complete" or "something that completes or supplements another." *Compliment* is a noun or verb that means "to praise."

```
His sensitivity complements her assertiveness.
```

```
Most people see through false compliments.
```

conscience, conscious *Conscience* is a noun referring to one's sense of right and wrong. *Conscious* is an adjective that means "alert to" or "aware of."

```
The jury member was conscious of his nagging conscience.
```

could of, should of, would of These are incorrect forms for *could have, should have,* and *would have. Of* is a preposition, not a part of a verb.

```
The trainer should have exercised his horse today.
```

discreet/discrete *Discreet* means "tactful" or "diplomatic"; *discrete* means "separate" or distinct.

```
Dean Lew is always discreet about students' comments on evalua-
tion forms.
```

```
Bobbi's and Charlotte's duties are discrete from each other.
```

double negative Double negatives to emphasize negativity are nonstandard in English.

```
I didn't see anything [not nothing].
```

```
The child could hardly control [not couldn't hardly control] his
tears.
```

due to *Due to* is acceptable following a linking verb but is considered less acceptable at the beginning of a sentence.

```
Most minor injuries during earthquakes are due to panic.
```

```
Because of [not due to] rain, the beach party was canceled.
```

due to the fact that Use *because* to avoid wordiness.

each *Each* is singular. (See also pp. 580–581.)

effect See **affect.**

e.g. This is a Latin abbreviation meaning "for example." It is sometimes confused with *i.e.,* which means "that is." Neither of these abbreviations should be used in the text of a manuscript, but they can be used in parenthetical expressions.

either   *Either* is singular. (See also pp. 580–581.)

> Jim and Marti offered to tow the van; <u>either</u> is willing to
> drive to Coalinga.

elicit, illicit   *Elicit* is a verb meaning "to evoke." *Illicit* is an adjective meaning "illegal or unlawful."

> The attorney was unable to <u>elicit</u> any information from her
> client about <u>illicit</u> drug sales in the neighborhood.

emigrate from, immigrate to   *Emigrate* means "to leave a country or region to settle elsewhere." *Immigrate* means "to enter another country and live there."

> When Pano <u>emigrated</u> from Turkey, he missed living near the sea.

> After the Revolution, many Cubans <u>immigrated</u> to the United
> States.

eminent, imminent   *Eminent* means "celebrated" or "exalted." *Imminent* means "about to happen."

> The <u>eminent</u> seismologist predicted that an earthquake was
> <u>imminent</u>.

especially, specially   *Especially* means "particularly" or "more than other things." *Specially* means "for a specific reason."

> Ryder <u>especially</u> values working on cabinets. He's known for
> <u>specially</u> ordered fine pieces of exotic woods.

etc.   Avoid ending a list with the abbreviation *etc.* Writers often overuse it to suggest they have more information than they do. The Latin expression is *et cetera,* which means "and others" or "and other things." The expression is best avoided in your essays because it is vague. It is also often misspelled as "ect."

everybody, everyone   *Everybody* and *everyone* are singular. (See also pp. 580–581.)

except   See **accept.**

farther, further   *Farther* refers to distance. *Further* implies quantity or degree. *Further* is now widely accepted for both meanings.

> Janae swam <u>farther</u> than everyone in her water fitness class.

> Jerry is <u>further</u> along on his computer project than he
> expected.

fewer, less *Fewer* refers to items that can be counted. *Less* refers to measurable amounts.

```
Nate has fewer expenses and therefore needs less spending money
working for the national parks.
```

firstly *Firstly* is pretentious. Use *first.*

fun *Fun* is colloquial when used as an adjective and should be avoided.

```
Jess enjoyed the amusing [not fun] movie.
```

further See **farther.**

good, well *Good* is an adjective; *well* is usually an adverb.

```
Good work is almost always well rewarded.
```

hanged, hung *Hanged* refers to people. *Hung* refers to pictures and things that can be suspended.

```
The criminal hanged himself in his prison cell.
```

```
The Walshes hung Debbie's recent paintings in the living room.
```

he, he/she, his/her The writer should no longer assume that *he* is an acceptable pronoun for all nouns. Furthermore, *he/she* or *his/her* are awkward. To avoid this construction, use the plural or a specific noun instead of the pronoun. (See also pp. 613–614.)

Instead of: `When a student works in a small group, he/she par-`
`ticipates more.`

Write: `When students work in small groups, they participate more.`

hisself *Hisself* is nonstandard. Use *himself.*

hung See **hanged.**

i.e. This Latin abbreviation for *id est* should be replaced by the English *that is.*

illusion See **allusion.**

imminent See **eminent.**

imply, infer *Imply* means "to state indirectly or to suggest." *Infer* means "to come to a conclusion based on the evidence given."

```
By covering his ears, he implied that he no longer wanted to
listen.
```

```
We can infer that the Duke of Ferrara is an arrogant man be-
cause he refused to "stoop" to speak to his wife.
```

irregardless   *Irregardless* is nonstandard. Use *regardless.*

its, it's   *Its* is the possessive form. *It's* is the contraction for *it is* or *it has.* (See also p. 580.)

```
It's too bad that Dick and Jean's cat has injured its tail.
```

```
It's been a bad day for the Jacobys' cat.
```

later, latter   *Later* refers to time. *Latter* refers to the second of two things named.

```
Initially many southern European immigrants came to this
country, but later the immigration policy restricted the
numbers.
```

```
Both Diego Rivera and his wife Frida Kahlo painted, but the
latter has gained more public recognition in the last few
years.
```

lay, lie   *Lay* means "to place or put" and requires an object. (The past tense is *laid.*) *Lie* means "to rest or recline." (The past tense of *lie* is *lay,* and so the two words are sometimes confused.)

```
Lay the piano music on the bench where Mrs. Main laid it yes-
terday.
```

```
Twinkle will lie down exactly where she lay yesterday.
```

lead, led   The present tense of the verb is *lead* and the past tense is *led.* However, *lead* is also used as a noun, meaning a gray metal, and confusion results because it is pronounced the same as "led."

```
Barbara will lead the tour to Istanbul, and then it will be led
by Lexa.
```

```
Usually plumbers replace lead pipes with copper.
```

less   See **fewer.**

lie   See **lay.**

loose, lose   *Loose* is an adjective meaning "unrestrained or unfastened." *Lose* is a verb meaning "to misplace" or "to be defeated."

```
If his bathing suit is too loose, Lester will lose it in the
next wave.
```

lots, lots of   Avoid these constructions in formal writing. Elevate the diction to *many* or *much.*

mankind   Avoid this term, as its sexism offends many readers. Use *humans, humanity,* or *humankind* instead.

```
It was one small step for the man who walked on the moon, but

it was a giant step for humanity.
```

maybe, may be   *Maybe* is an adverb meaning "perhaps." *May be* is a verb.

```
Maybe Vince will open his own restaurant in Oregon, and Sherry

may be ready to train their employees again.
```

may of, might of   These are nonstandard forms of *may have* and *might have.*

media, medium   *Media* is the plural of *medium.*

```
Picasso created ceramics and sculptures in clay, wood, and

wire, but paint is the medium for which he is best known. Per-

haps the media should review his other art forms.
```

myself   *Myself* is a reflexive or intensive pronoun and, like the other *-self* pronouns, should not be used in place of personal pronouns.

```
I drove myself to the hospital because no one else was home.
```

```
"I can do it myself!" the toddler protested.
```

```
Juan ladled the chili for his father and me [not myself].
```

neither   *Neither* is singular. (See also p. 580.)

```
Neither of us is available to babysit for the Trosts tonight.
```

nohow   *Nohow* is nonstandard for *in any way.*

none   *None* can be singular or plural depending on meaning.

```
None of the alternatives seem reasonable.
```

```
None of the football players is injured.
```

nowheres   *Nowheres* is nonstandard for *nowhere.*

number   See **amount.**

of   *Of* is a preposition. It should not be used in place of *have* in constructions like *should have* or *would have.*

off of   *Of* is not necessary with *off.* Use *off* alone or use *from.*

```
The marbles rolled off the table and continued rolling around

Monahan's room.
```

O.K., OK, okay   All three forms are acceptable, but in formal writing these expressions are inappropriate.

on account of   A wordy way to write *because*.

owing to the fact that   A wordy way to write *because*.

passed, past   *Passed* is the past tense of the verb that means having gone by, having completed a test or course, having transferred a ball or puck to a teammate. *Past* is not a verb. Rather, it is used as a noun, adjective, adverb, or preposition and means a time gone by or having elapsed in time. If you remember to use the form "passed" when you need a verb, you will be correct.

> VERB: Julia <u>passed</u> Debra in the hall and told her that Miori had <u>passed</u> the test.

> VERB: The Maguires <u>passed</u> around reviews of the film <u>In the Line of Fire</u>.

> VERB: During the game Tyler <u>passed</u> the ball to David.

> VERB: Jane and Pete <u>passed</u> their summer days at the cabin.

> NOUN: In the <u>past</u>, Julia and Debra met to discuss the student's progress.

> ADJECTIVE: The Maguires have collected <u>past</u> reviews of <u>In the Line of Fire</u>.

> ADVERB: Tyler liked to run <u>past</u> the pier during his morning runs.

> PREPOSITION: It was <u>past</u> noon when Jane and Pete arrived at their cabin.

plus   *Plus* is not appropriately used as a conjunction to join independent clauses. Use a standard coordinating or adverbial conjunction such "moreover" or "in addition."

> We celebrated the Fourth of July with hot dogs, corn on the cob, potato salad, and watermelon; in addition, [not *plus*] we enjoyed the firework display at Zaca Lake.

precede, proceed   The verb *precede* means "come before" (note the prefix *pre-*). The verb *proceed* means "go forward" or "move on."

> Spanish 4 <u>precedes</u> Spanish 5, "Literature of Mexico."

> To <u>proceed</u> without a contract would be foolish.

prejudice, prejudiced   *Prejudice* is a noun; *prejudiced* is an adjective. Do not leave out the *-d* from the adjective.

```
Prejudice that starts in childhood is difficult to obliterate,

and he was distinctly prejudiced against working mothers.
```

principal, principle   *Principal* is a noun for the "chief official" or, in finance, the "capital sum." As an adjective, principal means "major" or "most important." *Principle* is a noun meaning "a law or truth, rule, or axiom."

```
The school's principal uses various principles for deciding the

graduation speakers; the principal factor seems to be related

to academics.
```

proceed, precede   See **precede.**

raise, rise   *Raise* is a verb meaning "to move or cause to move up," and it takes an object. *Rise* is a verb meaning "to go up," and it does not take a direct object.

```
The farmers who raise cows are concerned about the disease.
```

```
They rise early to attend to the livestock.
```

reason is because   In speech, this expression is common. In formal writing, it is not appropriate. A clause using *that* is the preferred form:

```
The reason the Arnolds drove their trailer was that [not

because] they could transport dune buggies for the Dennis

family, too.
```

reason why   The expression *reason why* is redundant. *Reason* is sufficient.

```
The reason [not reason why] Jorge attends law school at night is

not obvious to anyone but his family.
```

rise, raise   See **raise, rise.**

should of   *Should of* is nonstandard; use *should have.*

```
He should have [not should of] known not to build a campfire

on that windy hill.
```

since   *Since* is sometimes used to mean *because,* but it is best to use it only as a conjunction in constructions having to do with time.

```
Andy has been waiting since January for his tax forms.
```

```
Since [or because?] you left, I've been dating others.
```

sit, set   *Sit* means "to rest the weight of the body" as on a chair. *Set* means "to place."

> Dorothy wants you to <u>sit</u> on the black leather sofa.
>
> Tom would rather you not <u>set</u> stoneware dishes on his cherry-wood table.

site, cite, sight   See **cite, site, sight.**

somebody, someone   *Somebody* and *someone* are singular. (See also p. 580.)

sometime, some time, sometimes   *Sometime* is an adverb meaning "at an indefinite time." *Some time* is the adjective *some* modifying the noun *time*. *Sometimes* means "now and then."

> <u>Sometime</u> we should get together and play tennis.
>
> Raul devoted <u>some time</u> to perfecting his pronunciation.
>
> <u>Sometimes</u> Ken discards every yolk from the eggs as he prepares his omelette.

stationary/stationery   *Stationary* is an adjective meaning "immovable, fixed in place." *Stationery* (with an "e" just as in "letter") is a noun meaning "writing material."

> Despite the brisk wind, the sign remained <u>stationary</u>.
>
> Leslie wrote the letter on <u>stationery</u> from the cruise ship.

supposed to, used to   Don't neglect to use the *-d* ending on these often used and often misspelled words!

> He is <u>supposed to</u> [not *suppose to*] bring the wine for the dinner.
>
> Ariane became <u>used to</u> [not *use to*] Dee's indifferent housekeeping.

than, then   *Than* is used in comparisons. *Then* is an adverb denoting time.

> There are many more calories in avocados <u>than</u> in apples.
>
> First Sylvia Plath attended the school, and <u>then</u> she taught there.

their, there, they're   *Their* is a possessive pronoun. *There* is an adverb denoting place. *They're* is a contraction meaning *they are*.

> <u>Their</u> plans for hang gliding <u>there</u> in the park are apt to be postponed because <u>they're</u> not ready to pass the safety test.

then, than   See **than, then.**

there is, there are   The verb following the expletive "there" is singular or plural according to the number of the subject that follows the verb. (See also pp. 566 and 581.)

`There is` a dictionary on the table. `There are` books and keys on the table.

this here, these here, that there, them there Nonstandard for *this, these, that,* or *those.*

till, until, 'til *Till* and *until* have the same meaning and both have standard uses. *'Til* is an informal contraction of *until.*

thru *Thru* is a nonstandard spelling of *through* that should be avoided in all formal writing.

thusly Use *thus,* which is less pretentious.

to, too, two *To* is a preposition meaning "toward" and is part of the infinitive form of the verb (for example, to *run*). *Too* is an adverb meaning "overly." *Two* is a number.

`Two` trips `to` the market in one day are not `too` many for a fine cook like Mike.

toward, towards Either form is acceptable, but *toward* is preferred.

try and *Try and* is nonstandard; *try to* is preferred.

`Try to` [not *try and*] meet Mohammed before he locks up his bike.

unique *Unique* means "distinctively characteristic." It is an absolute adjective that should not be modified by "most" or "very."

A tuxedo shirt and jacket, bow tie, and Bermuda shorts create a `unique` [not *most unique*] style for a hot-weather prom.

until See **till, until, 'til.**

usage The noun *use* should be used whenever possible. *Usage* refers only to convention, as in *language usage.*

The `use` [not *usage*] of computers has facilitated essay writing, but papers with correct `usage` have not increased.

used to See **supposed to, used to.**

weather, whether *Weather* refers to the atmospheric conditions. *Whether* can be used interchangeably with *if.*

Gail wasn't certain `whether` the stormy `weather` would keep John and Mark from jogging to Niagara Falls.

well See **good, well.**

which, in which Writers occasionally use *in which* in places where *which* is sufficient. Read work carefully to eliminate the unnecessary preposition.

Salma grabbed the gray cape, `which` [not *in which*] had been left on the sofa.

which, who   *Which* is used for things, not for people. Use *who* for people.

> Martin Luther King, the American <u>who</u> defined civil disobedience
> for his generation, was a theologian as well as a political
> figure. His letter from Birmingham, <u>which</u> he wrote in jail,
> defines his position.

while   Do not use *while* to mean *although* if there is a chance of confusion for the reader. Like *since, while* should be reserved for time sense. Unless the point is to show that the actions occur at the same time, *although* is the better word.

> Nick begins cooking dinner <u>while</u> Chris drives home from Richmond.
>
> <u>Although</u> [not *while*] Elizabeth continues to invest their savings,
> Bill never resists a rug sale.

who's, whose   *Who's* is the contraction for *who is* or *who has. Whose* is a possessive pronoun.

> <u>Who's</u> going to stay at the Sea Bird Motel in Wildwood?
>
> <u>Who's</u> been having dinner with the Grebners every Sunday?
>
> Mike asked Lucy <u>whose</u> design she preferred.

would of   *would of* is nonstandard for the complete verb *would have.*

> <u>Los Vendidos</u> <u>would have</u> [not *would of*] been a perfect theater
> experience for Cinco de Mayo.

you   The indefinite use of *you,* or even its use to mean "you the reader," can be incongruous or offensive and can be avoided:

> A decade ago, the fit hiker [rather than *you*] could camp on the
> beach with the seals at Pt. Sal, but now even the poor trail
> has eroded.
>
> It is common practice in some African tribes for prepubescent
> females [rather than *you*] to be scarified.

your, you're   *Your* is a possessive pronoun. *You're* is the contraction of *you are.*

> <u>Your</u> savings will disappear if <u>you're</u> not careful.

Acknowledgments

Laila Al-Marayati and Semeen Issa, "Muslim Women: An Identity Reduced to a Burka" from *Los Angeles Times* (January 20, 2002). Reprinted by permission.

Jonathan Alter, "Press 1 to Cut Short Your Life" from *Newsweek* (May 20, 2002). Copyright © 2002 Newsweek, Inc. All rights reserved. Reprinted by permission.

Eugene R. August, "Real Men Don't: Anti-Male Bias in English" from *The University of Dayton Review*, 18 (Winter/Spring, 1986–87). Reprinted by permission of Eugene R. August.

Yasmine Bahrani, "Why Does My Race Matter?" from *Los Angeles Times* (February 1, 1998). Reprinted by permission of the author.

Jack M. Balkin, "Diversity Offers Everyone a Stake" from *Los Angeles Times* (May 17, 2002). Reprinted by permission of the author.

John Balzar, "Lighten Up on Enlightenment" from *Los Angeles Times* (June 2, 2002). Copyright © 2002 Los Angeles Times. Reprinted by permission.

Steven Barrie-Anthony, "Baldness Remedies." First appeared in *Los Angeles Times* (January 27, 2002). Reprinted by permission of the author.

Ward Churchill, "Crimes Against Humanity" from *Z Magazine* (1993). Reprinted by permission of the author.

Judith Ortiz Cofer, "The Myth of the Latin Woman" from *The Latin Deli: Prose and Poetry* by Judith Ortiz Cofer. Copyright © 1993 by Judith Ortiz Cofer. Reprinted by permission of The University of Georgia Press.

Jennifer A. Coleman, "Discrimination at Large" from *Newsweek* (August 2, 1993). Reprinted by permission of the author.

Philip Dacey, "Coke" from *Night Shift at the Crucifix Factory* (Iowa City: University of Iowa Press, 1991). Copyright © 1991 by Philip Dacey. Reprinted by permission of the author.

Meghan Daum, "On the Fringes of the Physical World" from *My Misspent Youth* (Open City Books, 2001). First published in *The New Yorker*. Reprinted by permission of the author.

"Georgia O'Keeffe" from *The White Album* by Joan Didion. Copyright © 1979 by Joan Didion. Reprinted by permission of Farrar, Straus and Giroux, LLC.

Susan Douglas, "Remote Control: How to Raise a Media Skeptic" from *The Utne Reader* (January/February 1997). Reprinted by permission of the author.

Kim Edwards, "In Rooms of Women." Originally published as a longer essay in the *Michigan Quarterly*. Reprinted by permission of the author.

Barbara Ehrenreich, "Oh, Those Family Values" from *Time* (July 18, 1994). Copyright © 1994 Time Inc. Reprinted by permission.

Marianela Enriquez, "Who Were You, Connie, and Why Did You Go?" (student essay). Reprinted by permission of the author.

Pamela Erens, "Bodily Harm" from *Ms.* Magazine (October 1985). Reprinted by permission of the author.

"Oh What a Web We Weave" by Walter Gajewski, Webmaster for Academic Computing Services at California State University, Long Beach. Reprinted by permission of the author.

Alex Garcia, "Reality Check" from *Los Angeles Times* (June 16, 1999). Copyright © 1999 Alex Garcia. Reprinted by permission of the author.

Todd Gitlin, "Patriotism Demands Questioning Authority" from *Los Angeles Times* (November 11, 2001). Reprinted by permission of the author.

Ellen Goodman, "Thanksgiving" and "When a Woman Says No." Both articles first published in *The Boston Globe*. Copyright © 1996 The Washington Post Writers Group. Reprinted with permission.

Joe Goodwin, "My Favorite School Class: Involuntary Servitude" (student essay). Reprinted by permission of the author.

Rebekah Hall-Naganuma, "Through the Cracks" (student essay). Reprinted by permission of the author.

Keith David Hamm, "Dumpster-Diving for Dollars." Essay originally appeared in *Friction*

Magazine (July 2002). Reprinted by permission of the author.

S. I. Hayakawa, "Our Son Mark" from *Through the Communications Barrier* (New York: Harper & Row, 1979).

"Digging" from *Opened Ground: Selected Poems 1966–1987* by Seamus Heaney. Copyright © 1998 by Seamus Heaney. Reprinted by permission of Farrar, Straus and Giroux, LLC and Faber and Faber Ltd.

Robert L. Heilbroner, "Don't Let Stereotypes Warp Your Judgments" from *Think Magazine* (June 1961). Reprinted by permission of the author.

Arlie Hochschild, "The Second Shift" from *The Second Shift: Working Parents and the Revolution at Home* (Viking, 1989). Reprinted by permission of the author.

David Hochschild and Arlie Hochschild, "Hooray for the Red, White, Blue, and Green" from *Los Angeles Times* (January 11, 2001). Reprinted by permission of Arlie Hochschild.

M. Carl Holman, "Mr. Z." Copyright 1967. Reprinted by permission of The Estate of M. Carl Holman, Mariella A. Holman.

Caroline Hwang, "The Good Daughter" from *Newsweek* (September 21, 1998). Reprinted with the permission of the author.

Susan Jacoby, "Common Decency" from *The New York Times Magazine* (May 19, 1991). Copyright © 1991 by The New York Times Co. Reprinted with permission.

Jenny Jones, "Body of Evidence" as told to Giovanna Breu/*People Weekly* (March 1992). Copyright ©1992 Time Inc. All rights reserved. Reprinted by permission.

Marin Kheng, "Thanksgiving Beyond the Cleaver Family" (student essay). Reprinted by permission of the author.

Martin Luther King, Jr., "Three Ways of Meeting Oppression" from *Stride Toward Freedom* (New York: Harper & Row, 1958). Copyright © 1958 by Martin Luther King, Jr.; copyright © renewed 1986 by Coretta Scott King. Reprinted by arrangement with the Estate of Martin Luther King, Jr., c/o Writers House as agent for the proprietor, New York, NY.

Ted Kooser, "The Blind Always Come as Such a Surprise" from *Heartland II: Poets of the Midwest*, edited by Lucien Stryk. Copyright © 1975 by

Northern Illinois University Press. Used by permission of the publisher.

Adair Lara, "Who's Cheap?" from *San Francisco Chronicle*. Reprinted with the permission of the author and publisher.

John Leonard, "The Only Child" from *Private Lives in the Imperial City* (New York: Alfred A. Knopf, 1979). Copyright © 1979 by John Leonard. Reprinted by permission of the author.

"Living in Two Worlds" by Marcus Mabry. Originally printed in *Newsweek On Campus,* 1988. Reprinted with the permission of the author.

Eric Marcus, "Ignorance Is Not Bliss" from *Newsweek* (July 5, 1993). Copyright © 1993 Newsweek, Inc. All rights reserved. Reprinted by permission.

Michael McGrady, "Let 'em Eat Leftovers" from *Newsweek* (1976). Reprinted by permission of Sterling Lord Literistic, Inc. Copyright © 1976 by Michael McGrady.

"Peaches" from *Moustapha's Eclipse* by Reginald McKnight, © 1988. Reprinted by permission of the University of Pittsburgh Press.

Georgina I. Montoya, "Mirror Image" (student essay). Reprinted by permission of the author.

Hadley Moore, "My Deep, Dark Secret?" from *Newsweek* (January 14, 2002). All rights reserved. Reprinted by permission.

Joyce Carol Oates, "Where Are You Going, Where Have You Been?" from *The Wheel of Love and Other Stories*. Copyright © 1970 by Ontario Review Inc. Reprinted by permission of John Hawkins & Associates, Inc.

"On the Subway" from *The Gold Cell* by Sharon Olds. Copyright © 1987 by Sharon Olds. Used by permission of Alfred A. Knopf, a division of Random House, Inc.

"Shooting an Elephant" from *Shooting an Elephant and Other Essays* by George Orwell. Copyright 1936 by George Orwell and Copyright 1950 by Sonia Brownell Orwell and renewed 1978 by Sonia Pitt-Rivers. Reprinted by permission of Harcourt, Inc. and by permission of Bill Hamilton (A. M. Heath & Co. Ltd.) as the literary Executor of the Estate of Late Sonia Brownell Orwell and Secker & Warburg Ltd.

Shannon Paaske, "From Access to Acceptance: Enabling America's Largest Minority" (student essay).

Reprinted by permission of the author.

Stephen Perry, "Blue Spruce" from *The New Yorker* (January 28, 1991). Reprinted by permission of the author.

"A Work of Artifice" from *Circles on the Water* by Marge Piercy. Copyright © 1982 by Marge Piercy. Used by permission of Alfred A. Knopf, a division of Random House, Inc.

Anna Quindlen, "Uncle Sam and Aunt Samantha" from *Newsweek* (November 5, 2001). Reprinted by permission of International Creative Management, Inc. Copyright © 2001 by Anna Quindlen. First appeared in *Newsweek* Magazine.

Howard Rosenberg, "Making Media a Familiar Scapegoat" from *Los Angeles Times* (April 23, 1999). Copyright © 1999 Los Angeles Times. Reprinted by permission.

Don Sabo, "Pigskin, Patriarchy, and Pain" from *Winning Isn't Everything: Men and Sport* (The Crossing Press, 1994). Reprinted by permission of the author.

Matthew Soyster, "Living Under Circe's Spell" from *Newsweek* (October 11, 1993). All rights reserved. Reprinted by permission.

Brent Staples, "Just Walk On By: Black Men in Public Space" from *Ms.* Magazine (September 1986). Copyright © 1986 by Brent Staples. Reprinted by permission of the author.

Neil Steinberg, "O.K., So I'm Fat" from *The New York Times Magazine* (September 8, 1996). Copyright © 1996 by Neil Steinberg. Reprinted with the permission of the author.

From *High Tech Heretic* by Clifford Stoll. Copyright © 1999 by Clifford Stoll. Used by permission of Doubleday, a division of Random House, Inc.

Susan Straight, "Proper Care and Maintenance" from *Los Angeles Times Magazine* (June 30, 1991). Copyright © by Susan Straight. Reprinted with the permission of The Richard Parks Agency.

Robin Swicord, "Youth Must Be Served—With Respect" from *Los Angeles Times* (May 30, 1999). Copyright © 1999 by Robin Swicord. Reprinted by permission of the author.

Jennifer Tabaldo, "Digging Deep" (student essay). Reprinted by permission of the author.

Don Tapscott, *Growing Up Digital: The Rise of the Net Generation* (McGraw-Hill, 1998), pp. 147–149, 154–157. Reprinted with the permission of The McGraw-Hill Companies.

Carol Tavris, "In Groups We Shrink from Loner's Heroics." Copyright © 1991 by Carol Tavris. Originally appeared in the *Los Angeles Times*. Reprinted by permission of Lescher & Lescher, Ltd. All rights reserved.

Chris Thomas, "A Summary of 'Three Ways of Meeting Oppression'" (student essay). Reprinted by permission of the author.

Jill Tweedie, "The Future of Love" from *In the Name of Love* (I.B. Taurus, 2000). Reprinted by permission of I.B. Taurus & Co. Ltd.

Anne Tyler, "Your Place Is Empty" from *The New Yorker* (November 22, 1976). Reprinted by permission of Russell & Volkening as agents for the author. Copyright © 1976 by Anne Tyler.

John Updike, "Ace in the Hole" from *The Same Door*. Originally published in *The New Yorker*. Copyright © 1955 by John Updike. Reprinted with the permission of Alfred A. Knopf, a division of Random House, Inc.

Andrew Vachss, "The Difference Between 'Sick' and 'Evil.'" First appeared in *Parade* Magazine (July 14, 2002). Reprinted with the permission of *Parade*, copyright © 2002, and Andrew Vachss.

Luis Valdez, *Los Vendidos*. Copyright © 1967 by Luis Valdez. Reprinted by permission of Arte Publico Press.

"Appearances" by Carmen Vasquez from *Homophobia* by Warren J. Blumenfeld. Copyright ©1992 by Warren J. Blumenfeld. Reprinted by permission of Beacon Press, Boston.

Author Index

Note: Boldface indicates location of reading.

Subject and Title Index

Note: Boldface indicates location of reading.

633